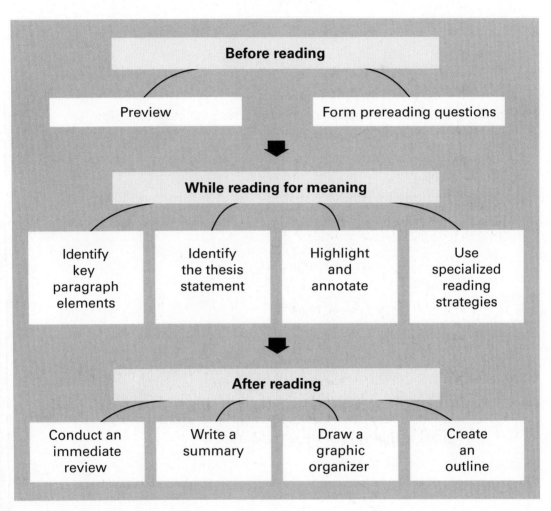

Strategies for Active Reading
(see Chapter 2, p. 24)

Before reading

Preview → Form prereading questions

While reading for meaning

Identify key paragraph elements → Identify the thesis statement → Highlight and annotate → Use specific reading strategies

After reading

Conduct an immediate review → Write a summary → Draw a graphic organizer → Create an outline

Strategies for Active Reading
(see Chapter 2, p. 24)

REFLECTIONS

Patterns for Reading and Writing

REFLECTIONS

Patterns for Reading and Writing

SECOND EDITION

Kathleen T. McWhorter

Niagara County Community College

 bedford/st.martin's
Macmillan Learning

Boston | New York

For Bedford/St. Martin's

Vice President, Editorial, Macmillan Learning Humanities: Edwin Hill
Editorial Director, English: Karen S. Henry
Senior Publisher for Composition, Business and Technical Writing, Developmental Writing: Leasa Burton
Executive Editor for Development: Karita dos Santos
Developmental Editor: Michelle McSweeney
Production Editor: Louis C. Bruno Jr.
Media Producer: Rand Thomas
Publishing Services Manager: Andrea Cava
Production Supervisor: Robert Cherry
Marketing Manager: Joy Fisher Williams
Project Management: Lifland et al., Bookmakers
Photo Editor: Martha Friedman
Photo Researcher: Richard Fox
Permissions Editor: Margaret Gorenstein
Senior Art Director: Anna Palchik
Text Design: Claire Seng-Niemoeller
Cover Design: John Callahan
Cover Photo: AGF/Getty Images
Composition: Jouve
Printing and Binding: RR Donnelley and Sons

Manufactured in the United States of America.

1   0   9   8   7   6
f   e   d   c   b   a

For information, write: Bedford/St. Martin's, 75 Arlington Street, Boston, MA 02116
(617-399-4000)

ISBN 978-1-319-04346-9 (Student Edition)
ISBN 978-1-319-04439-8 (Instructor's Edition)
ISBN 978-1-319-07045-8 (Loose-leaf Edition)

Acknowledgments

Text acknowledgments and copyrights appear at the back of the book on pages 717–19, which constitute an extension of the copyright page. Art acknowledgments and copyrights appear on the same page as the art selections they cover.

Preface

The goal of *Reflections* is to offer students an integrated approach to reading and writing through scaffolded instruction that guides them through comprehension, analysis, evaluation, and written response — skills that they need to be successful in college.

The title, *Reflections*, emphasizes that reading and writing are mirror images of each other and share the same end result — communication. Readers consider what the writer says and means, and writers are concerned with how to express their ideas clearly and effectively so as to be understood by their readers. Because reading and writing work together and reflect each other, it makes sense that they be taught together. The awareness of connections between reading and writing is important for all college students, perhaps most of all for those who have struggled with reading and writing.

The book and its chapters have a unique structure based on a key principle of learning theory — scaffolding. Scaffolding enables students to build on previous learning and uses gradual, small-step learning. Students initially receive extensive direct support and guidance. These cues gradually diminish, and students are able to draw on what they have learned to perform increasingly difficult or complex tasks with less and less guidance.

In this book, reading and writing skills build on one another, and students progress from basic to more complex skills. Chapters in Part 1, "Skills for Success in Reading and Writing," cover all the basic skills. Within each chapter in Part 2, "Readings for Writers," readings and their apparatus increase in difficulty, shifting from an emphasis on understanding to an emphasis on analysis and evaluation. Writing tasks progress from paragraph to essay and move from personal response to more objective interpretation and finally to research.

In each Part 2 chapter, the introductory portions and first essays offer abundant instructional support, including visual aids such as annotations and graphic organizers, to help students develop strategies and build confidence. Later parts of the chapter offer less instructional support, encouraging students to rely on the skills and strategies they have learned to approach reading and writing tasks.

The following features make *Reflections* exceptionally useful for both readers and writers.

New to This Edition

GRAMMAR HANDBOOK

Reflections now includes an all-new Part 4, "Handbook: Writing Problems and How to Correct Them," which provides students with practical and comprehensive help with basic grammar, sentence problems, punctuation, and mechanics.

- The handbook reviews **parts of speech** and **sentence structures** and shows students how to deal with common problem areas such as **pronouns, fragments, commas,** and **subject-verb agreement.**

- **Exercises, some with answers,** provide practice to help students master grammatical skills.

- Intuitive graphics, such as **easy-to-follow revision flowcharts** and **hand-edited sentences** that show an error and its correction at a glance, help visual learners grasp grammatical concepts.

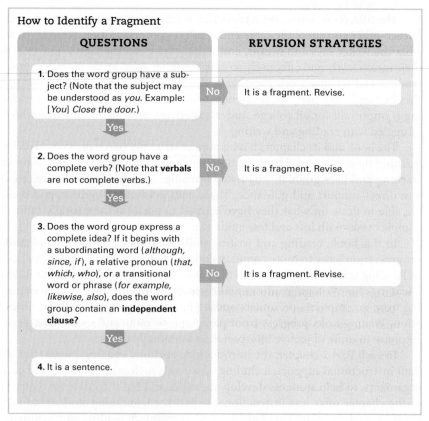

Revision flow chart from Part 4.

- **Links to *LaunchPad Solo for Readers and Writers*** extend the grammar instruction and practice exercises beyond the printed page. Interactive videos, adaptive quizzes, study pages, and more boost students' ability to improve their writing skills at their own pace.

STRONGER READING AND WRITING COVERAGE

Building on the success of the first edition, *Reflections* has been revised to provide stronger, more integrated reading and writing advice.

- **Students start reading sooner in all chapters of the book.** All Part 2 chapters now open with a model professional essay that is referred to throughout the chapter to demonstrate and teach the characteristics of the chapter's mode. Chapter 1 also includes a new reading up front about taking notes by hand.
- **Newly designed Reading|Writing boxes** with a side-by-side format better showcase readers' and writers' perspectives on important literacy issues such as thesis statements, evidence, bias, and tone.

Reading 🕮 Writing Thesis Statements and Generalizations in an Illustration Essay	
The Reader's Perspective	**The Writer's Perspective**
When reading an illustration essay, identify the thesis or generalization and observe how it is supported and explained through examples.	When writing an illustration essay, focus on composing a clear and effective statement of your thesis or the generalization you're making. Highlight the thesis/generalization and refer back to it often as you revise, checking to make sure that each example in your essay supports it.

Example of Reading|Writing box from Chapter 12.

- **Each Part 2 chapter now concludes with a summary Reading|Writing box** specific to that chapter's mode. These boxes provide a helpful review and reference for students working through both reading and writing assignments in each of the rhetorical patterns.
- **Newly designed chapter openers include a list of objectives and a new "Reflect on a Visual Text" feature** that provides step-by-step guidance for writing about the chapter's opening visual. Drawing on metacognition and visual learning, the new Reflect feature jump-starts the writing process and serves as a useful in-class activity.

NEW READINGS

To maximize student engagement, the collection of readings in *Reflections* has been updated to include more of the contemporary topics about which students will want to read.

- **Of the 40 readings by professional authors, 16 are new** to this edition, addressing current and compelling issues such as terrorism, raising the minimum wage, and paying off student loan debt.
- **Half of the 8 textbook excerpts are also new,** and these readings cover disciplines such as psychology, health, and information technology. Each textbook reading is accompanied by discipline-specific questions students are likely to see in a college-level course.
- **Student essays throughout the book — 3 out of 10 of them new —** model the types of writing students are expected to master.

EXPANDED AND UPDATED RESEARCH COVERAGE

In a newly expanded Part 3, "Student Research Guide," *Reflections* provides students with specialized support for approaching research projects.

- **An up-to-date chapter on finding and using sources** helps students search for and evaluate sources, incorporate quotations, and avoid plagiarism.
- **A new chapter dedicated to documenting sources now includes both MLA and APA style,** with samples of student writing in each.
- **Updated MLA coverage** conforms to new documentation guidelines released by MLA in 2016.

Features

INTEGRATION OF READING AND WRITING

While many readers include writing coverage and many composition texts include readings as models, *Reflections* is the first modes reader to truly integrate reading and writing.

- **Part 1 chapters place equal emphasis on the processes of reading and writing,** with a special focus on the connections between them. For example, Chapters 2 and 3 introduce the processes of understanding, analyzing, and evaluating texts both for reading others' work and for revising one's own work.
- **Reading|Writing Perspectives boxes integrate reading and writing skills** by showing how readers and writers approach the same element of writing. They are marked with this icon: ⬤. (See the "New to This Edition" section on page ix for more on this feature.)

Reading ⬤ Writing   Paragraph Elements

Paragraph Element	The Reader's Perspective	The Writer's Perspective
Topic	Identifying the topic of each paragraph enables you to build a mental framework for the reading. As you read, your knowledge of the topic increases.	Developing a clear topic for each paragraph is often the key to writing an effective essay. (See pp. 82–85 for help with choosing and narrowing a topic.)
Main Idea / Topic Sentence	To understand a paragraph, look for a topic sentence and the paragraph's main idea. Many exams test your understanding of main ideas.	Use a topic sentence to state a paragraph's most important point for the reader — that is, its main idea. (See pp. 110–14 for help with writing topic sentences.)
Supporting Details	Supporting details clarify, explain, and provide additional details about the main idea. If the main idea is abstract or difficult to understand, supporting details may help you make connections and increase your comprehension.	Use supporting details to strengthen your case and to provide specific support for your topic sentence. If you do not provide interesting, relevant supporting details, you will not be able to convince your readers that your ideas or conclusions are valid. (See pp. 114–19 for help with including support.)
Transitions	Transitions are signals to readers; they help you follow the writer's train of thought or hint that a line of thought is about to change.	Transitions help to connect your ideas. They also prevent your essay from sounding choppy or disconnected. (See pp. 120–22 for help with writing transitions.)

Example of Reading|Writing feature from Chapter 2.

- **In Part 2, the rhetorical patterns are taught from the points of view of both readers and writers.** Each chapter starts with a discussion of characteristics of the pattern from both perspectives, followed by a section on reading and writing essays in that pattern.

- **The Writing Your Own Essay section** in each Part 2 chapter reactivates the comprehension, analysis, and evaluation skills practiced earlier in the chapter (and in the book), starting with an annotated, color-coded model student essay.

- **The Readings for Practice, Ideas for Writing section** in each Part 2 chapter includes apparatus that focuses students equally on working with the readings and writing about them or about related topics.

SCAFFOLDING OF SKILLS

From its general organization through its detailed content, *Reflections* is designed to scaffold students' skill development in reading and writing. Moreover, ample opportunities for active participation and practice—before, during, and after reading—enable students to solidify their acquisition of reading and writing skills.

- **Models in Part 1 chapters help students develop the reading and writing skills they need to work through the assignments in the Part 2 chapters.** In addition to seeing model essays analyzed, students work through model summaries, annotations, analyses, and evaluations. They also follow a student writer from prewriting through revision (on pages marked with a beige-tipped edge) and are prompted to work through the stages of writing their own essay, using the "Essay in Progress" exercises.

Revised Draft

A Trend Taken Too Far: The Reality of Real TV

Do you remember life before the reality TV craze? Before reality TV, television viewers seemed interested only in situational comedies and serial dramas. Characters were played by professional actors, and the shows were written by professional writers. Except for a few early reality-type shows, such as *Cops* and *Candid Camera*, this simple formula was what network television offered. Then came MTV's

Deleted: One look at a *TV Guide* today shows an overload of reality-based programming, even with the guaranteed failure of most of these shows.

Deleted: there was mostly

Abundant models in Part 1 guide students in the fundamentals.

- **The readings in each Part 2 chapter generally progress in difficulty,** so that students' work with shorter, more accessible readings scaffolds their work with longer, more difficult texts. The final selection in Chapters 10–17 is a textbook reading that combines patterns.

- **Questions following reading selections move from understanding through analysis to evaluation;** in addition, as readings become more difficult, the balance of questions shifts. For example, understanding vocabulary in context is especially emphasized in questions following early readings in chapters, whereas more analytical and evaluative questions follow later readings.

📊 Understanding the Reading

📊 Analyzing the Reading

📊 Evaluating the Reading

Questions following readings lead students through understanding, analysis, and evaluation.

- **Writing tasks progress from paragraph to essay and move from personal response to more objective interpretation and finally to research.** Questions are clearly labeled, focusing students on the skills they are practicing.

EMPHASIS ON VISUAL LITERACY AND VISUAL LEARNING

Because students tend to be visual learners, and because they are expected to both interpret visuals they read and select or create visuals to include in their writing, this book emphasizes visual literacy.

- **Chapters 2 and 3 feature instruction on reading and interpreting graphics.** Students learn strategies for understanding, interpreting, and evaluating graphics and images.

- **Color-coded graphic organizers provide students with a tool both for analyzing readings and for planning and revising their own essays.** Used extensively throughout the chapters, these color-coded visual representations of content and structure help students to see at a glance how essays are structured and to work out and assess a structure for their own essays.

Figure 3.1   Sample Advertisement: World Wildlife Fund

There are as few as 3,200 tigers left in the wild.
Don't wait until they're gone.

Protect the future of nature.

World Wildlife Fund 2010 PSA "Don't wait until they're gone." Deforestation image: © Alain Compost/WWF; Tiger image: Frédy Mercay.

Visual from Part 1

Figure 12.2   Graphic Organizer for "Snoopers at Work"

Title	Snoopers at Work
Introduction	**Background:** Example of changing-room surveillance; reference to book *The Right to Privacy*
	Thesis: Technology, employer paranoia, and commercial greed have resulted in increasing invasions of privacy for many Americans.
Body paragraphs	**Example 1:** Medical-record surveillance
	Example 2: Phone and computer surveillance
	Example 3: Video surveillance
	Example 4: Drug-use entrapment
	Detail: Personal anecdote about a friend who experienced entrapment
	Example 5: TAD rules
	Example 6: "Active badge" tracking
Conclusion	Humorous approval of surveillance of restaurant employees washing hands after using lavatory

Each chapter in Part 2 includes one or more graphic organizers showing students how to analyze an essay. Students are also prompted to use graphic organizers while working with essays they're reading and writing.

- **Revision flowcharts** for the patterns in Part 2 provide students with a visual guide for improving their own essays.

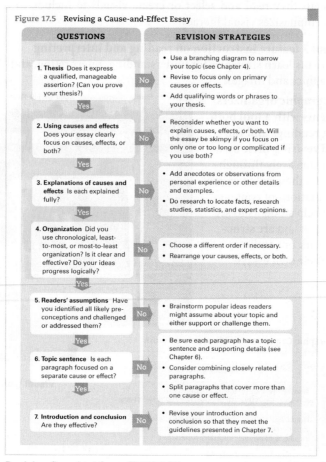

Revision flowchart from Chapter 17.

- **Annotated professional and student essays use consistent color coding to highlight different elements.** This use of color supports students in analyzing the essays.
- **Photographs serve as prompts for writing.** Every chapter in the book opens with a new "Reflect on a Visual Text" feature, a photo followed by a series of steps prompting students to think and write about a photograph. (See more about this new feature on page ix.)
- **Readings frequently include visuals for students to analyze,** reflecting the importance of visuals in college reading and other reading today. In addition, **the design of the readings reflects their appearance in their original context** — whether it be a newspaper, a magazine, a textbook, a

trade book, or a Web site — to aid students' comprehension, analysis, and evaluation.

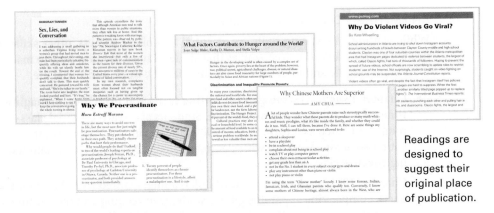

Readings are designed to suggest their original place of publication.

AN EMPHASIS ON CRITICAL THINKING

Critical thinking skills are essential for readers and writers, both in college and in the workplace. These skills are emphasized through the following features.

- **Chapter 3 focuses on strategies for critical reading and thinking.** Topics include examining an author's purpose, style, and intended audience; grasping nuances of words; distinguishing between fact and opinion; analyzing tone; looking for omissions; and making inferences. Students learn to read texts critically by identifying bias, evaluating the source, assessing the reliability of supporting information, recognizing assumptions, and judging relevancy and sufficiency of evidence.

- **Each chapter in Part 2 offers instruction on analyzing and evaluating the rhetorical pattern taught in the chapter.** Analysis in Action and Evaluation in Action exercises provide examples of student thinking and writing and give students the opportunity to practice these important skills.

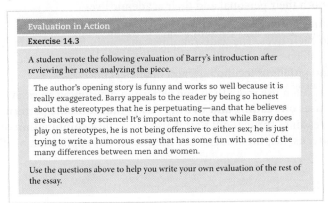

Evaluation in Action exercise from Chapter 14.

- **The apparatus for each reading guides students to think critically** about the focus, content, purpose, and effectiveness of each reading.

AN EMPHASIS ON STUDENT SUCCESS

While reading and writing skills are essential for college success, other skills are needed as well. *Reflections* recognizes that students need to know how to manage their academic life and integrate it with their family, work, and social life.

- **Chapter 1 suggests strategies for setting goals and priorities, managing time, and avoiding procrastination.** Students also learn essential classroom skills such as creating a positive academic image, communicating with instructors, working with classmates, using electronic tools, and taking effective class notes.
- **Chapters 10–17 each contain a textbook reading, marked with this icon:** 📖. The accompanying apparatus guides students in reading and responding to textbooks, in using skills such as annotating and highlighting, and in predicting essay-exam questions and writing their answers.

ENGAGING AND ACCESSIBLE READINGS
AND A STRATEGIC USE OF RHETORICAL PATTERNS

Because students who enjoy what they are reading will approach assignments with interest and enthusiasm, the forty-eight professional readings and ten student essays were carefully chosen to engage students and to provide strong rhetorical models. The rhetorical patterns provide students with a structure and template within which to organize and connect ideas, both when reading and when writing.

- **The readings include a mix of reliable, class-tested essays** by well-known writers like Brent Staples, Deborah Tannen, Dave Barry, and Amy Tan, **and they come from a wide range of sources,** including newspapers, popular magazines, Web sites, and textbooks, representing the diverse texts students encounter in both their personal and their academic lives.
- **Topics help students connect reading with issues relevant to college success and to their lives.** The wide-ranging topics include health, stress management, interpersonal relationships, race relations, consequences of war, virtues and pitfalls of technology, and financial concerns.
- Because writers often use more than one pattern in developing an essay, **Chapter 9 focuses on reading and writing essays that combine patterns.** The textbook readings throughout Part 2 also illustrate a **combination of rhetorical patterns**, helping students see the day-to-day application of all the patterns.

Acknowledgments

A number of instructors and students from across the country have helped me develop *Reflections*. I would like to express my gratitude to the following instructors, who provided detailed, valuable comments and suggestions about the manuscript and choice of reading selections: Gail Bradstreet (Cincinnati State Technical and Community College); Kelley Evans (Brunswick Community College); Tammy Forbes (Patrick Henry Community College); Ellen Gallimore (Forsyth Technical Community College); Anne Helms (Alamance Community College); Caroline Helsabeck (Forsyth Technical Community College); Kathryn Lane (Northwestern Oklahoma State University); Rachel Lintula (University of Minnesota Duluth); Kim Meeks (Oconee Fall Line Technical College); Adam Oldaker (Illinois Valley Community College); Nancy Shaffer (University of Texas at El Paso); Carrie Thompson (Palm Beach State College); Vanessa Uriegas (Southwest Texas Junior College); Michelle Van de Sande (Arapahoe Community College); and Samantha Veneruso (Montgomery College).

Many people at Bedford/St. Martin's contributed to the creation and development of *Reflections*. Each person with whom I worked demonstrates high standards and expertise in the field of college writing. I thank my developmental editor, Michelle McSweeney, for her exceptional help planning and composing the book, and Sally Lifland for her careful and judicious copyediting of my final draft. I thank Caroline Thompson, who managed the editorial process; Cara Kaufman, who commissioned and synthesized reviews and performed numerous other essential tasks; Lou Bruno, who conscientiously and capably guided the text through the production process; and Vivian Garcia, who provided invaluable advice and guidance on the market and other big-picture issues. I also thank Leasa Burton, Karen Henry, and Edwin Hill, who have always supported and encouraged my work.

Last, but in no way least, I thank the many students who have inspired me to create a book that directly addresses their needs and learning characteristics. They have shown me how they think and learn, and as a result I have discovered effective teaching strategies that can help all students learn to read and write. My students have made the most significant contribution to this book; they are the reason I enjoy both teaching and writing.

Kathleen McWhorter

Get the Most out of Your Course with Reflections

Bedford/St. Martin's offers resources and format choices that help you and your students get even more out of your book and your course. To learn more about or to order any of the following products, contact your Bedford/St. Martin's sales representative, e-mail sales support (sales_support@bfwpub.com), or visit the Web site at macmillanlearning.com.

E-BOOK OPTIONS

Reflections is available as a value-priced e-book. For details, visit macmillanlearning.com/ebooks.

SELECT VALUE PACKAGES

Add value to your text by packaging one of the following resources with *Reflections*. To learn more about package options for any of the following products, contact your Bedford/St. Martin's sales representative or visit **macmillanlearning .com**.

LaunchPad Solo *LaunchPad Solo for Readers and Writers* allows students to work on whatever they need help with the most. At home or in class, students learn at their own pace, with instruction tailored to each student's unique needs. *LaunchPad Solo for Readers and Writers* features

- **Pre-built units that support a learning arc** Each easy-to-assign unit is composed of a pre-test check, multimedia instruction and assessment, and a post-test that assesses what students have learned about critical reading, writing process, using sources, grammar, style, mechanics, and help for multilingual writers.

- **Diagnostics that help establish a baseline** Two comprehensive tests for grammar and two for reading allow instructors to assign diagnostics in a pre/post format and serve to help students and instructors identify areas of strength and areas for improvement. Through a reports screen, instructors can preview questions and view results by skill, roster, or individual student.

- **A video introduction to many topics** Introductions offer an overview of the unit's topic, and many include a brief, accessible video to illustrate the concepts at hand.

- **Adaptive quizzing for targeted learning** Most units include Learning-Curve, game-like adaptive quizzing that focuses on the areas in which each student needs the most help.

- **Twenty-five reading selections, with quizzes** Assign a range of classic and contemporary essays, each of which includes a label indicating Lexile level to help you scaffold instruction in critical reading.

- **The ability to monitor student progress** Use our Gradebook to see which students are on track and which need additional help with specific topics.

LaunchPad Solo for Readers and Writers can be **packaged at a significant discount**. Order ISBN 978-1-319-10377-4 to ensure your students can take full advantage. Visit macmillanlearning.com/readwrite for more information.

Writer's Help 2.0 Writer's Help 2.0 is a powerful online writing resource
macmillan learning that helps students find answers whether they are searching for writing advice on their own or as part of an assignment.

- **Smart search** Built on research with more than 1,600 student writers, the smart search in Writer's Help 2.0 provides reliable results even when students use novice terms, such as *flow* and *unstuck*.

- **Trusted content from our best-selling handbooks** Choose *Writer's Help 2.0, Hacker Version* or *Writer's Help 2.0, Lunsford Version* to ensure that students have clear advice and examples for all of their writing questions.

- **Adaptive exercises that engage students** Writer's Help 2.0 includes LearningCurve, game-like online quizzing that adapts to what students already know and helps them focus on what they need to learn.

Student access can be packaged with *Reflections* at a significant discount. To ensure that your students have easy access to online writing support, contact your sales representative for a package ISBN. Students who rent a book or buy a used book can purchase access to Writer's Help 2.0 at macmillanlearning.com /writershelp2.

Instructors may request free access by registering as an instructor at macmillanlearning.com/writershelp2.

LearningCurve *LearningCurve for Readers and Writers*, Bedford/
macmillan learning St. Martin's adaptive quizzing program, quickly learns what students already know and helps them practice what they don't yet understand. Game-like quizzing motivates students to engage with their course, and reporting tools help teachers discern their students' needs. *LearningCurve for Readers and Writers* can be packaged with *Reflections* at a significant discount. An activation code is required. To order *LearningCurve* packaged with the print book, contact your sales representative for a package ISBN. For details, visit learningcurveworks.com.

The Bedford/St. Martin's ESL Workbook includes a broad range of exercises covering grammar issues for multilingual students of varying language skills and backgrounds. Answers are at the back. To order the ESL Workbook packaged with the print book, contact your sales representative for a package ISBN.

Bedford/St. Martin's Planner includes everything that students need to plan and use their time effectively, with advice on preparing schedules and to-do lists plus blank schedules and calendars (monthly and weekly). The planner fits easily into a backpack or purse, so students can take it anywhere. To order the Planner packaged with the print book, contact your sales representative for a package ISBN.

INSTRUCTOR RESOURCES

macmillanlearning.com
You have a lot to do in your course. Bedford/St. Martin's wants to make it easy for you to find the support you need — and to get to it quickly.

The *Instructor's Edition of Reflections* includes all material from the Instructor's Manual (see below) bound into the back of the student edition. To order the Instructor's Edition, contact your Macmillan sales representative or use ISBN 978-1-319-04439-8.

The *Instructor's Manual for Reflections* is available as a PDF that can be downloaded from the Bedford/St. Martin's online catalog at the URL above. Visit the Instructor Resources tab for *Reflections*. Prepared with assistance from Mark Gallaher, the Instructor's Manual provides new and seasoned instructors alike with the support they need for teaching writing. Unit 1 includes sample syllabi along with chapters on teaching with *Reflections* and helping underprepared students in the first-year writing classroom. Unit 2 includes teaching tips for each chapter in *Reflections*, including a brief overview of each of the readings in the book and sample answers to questions.

The **Macmillan English Community** is now Bedford/St. Martin's home for professional resources, featuring Bedford *Bits*, our popular blog site offering new ideas for your course. Connect and converse with a growing team of Bedford authors and top scholars who blog on *Bits*, including Andrea Lunsford, Nancy Sommers, Susan Bernstein, and Elizabeth Wardle.

In addition, you'll find an expanding collection of additional resources that support your teaching.

- Find redesign resources ranging from webinars and PowerPoints to state correlations and Lexile levels.
- Sign up for webinars.
- Download resources from our professional resource series that support your teaching.
- Start a discussion or ask a question.
- Follow your favorite members.
- Review projects in the pipeline.

Visit **community.macmillan.com** to join the conversation with your fellow teachers.

Teaching with *LaunchPad Solo for Readers and Writers*

Pairing Reflections *with* LaunchPad Solo for Readers and Writers *helps students succeed at their own pace.*

You can use *LaunchPad Solo for Readers and Writers* to integrate skills-based practice into your teaching with *Reflections,* allowing you to more efficiently track students' progress with reading, writing, and grammar skills in an active learning arc that complements the book. To package *LaunchPad Solo for Readers and Writers* with *Reflections* at a significant discount, use ISBN 978-1-319-10377-4.

Assigning a project for which students will need to develop a strong thesis?

Start with the unit on thesis statements in *LaunchPad Solo for Readers and Writers* **to assess what students know.** Before turning to Chapter 5: Developing and Supporting a Thesis in *Reflections,* have students complete the **pre-test** to get perspective on what they already know. With this insight, you can meet them where they are.

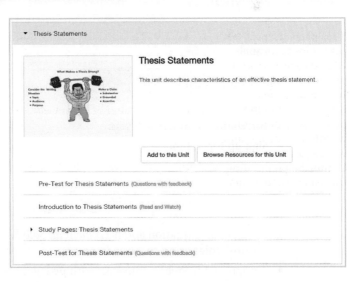

Then, from *Reflections*, assign appropriate exercises based on the results of the pre-test. For example, if the pre-test shows that many students cannot identify strong thesis statements, you might choose to spend considerable class time on Exercise 5.1, which asks students to discuss and revise thesis statements in small groups.

In the writing lab or at home, students can learn to think like a writer using LearningCurve, game-like adaptive quizzing that helps students practice the decision-making approach they'll need to apply to their own writing. Students who struggle with the material are guided back to the unit's study pages and videos, which explain concepts simply.

If assigned, the post-test asks students to apply what they've learned in the skill unit to different writing situations. You can use results from the post-test to determine whether some students will require more help as they begin building theses for their projects.

Exercise 5.1

Working in a group of two or three students, discuss what is wrong with each of the following thesis statements. Then revise each thesis to make it more effective.

1. In this paper, I will discuss the causes of asthma, which include exposure to smoke, chemicals, and allergic reactions.
2. Jogging is an enjoyable aerobic sport.
3. The crime rate is decreasing in American cities.
4. Living in an apartment has many advantages.
5. Children's toys can be dangerous, instructional, or creative.

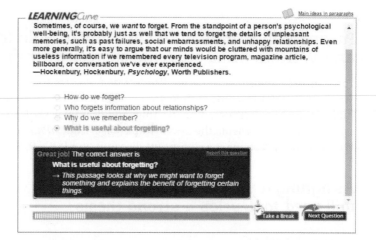

- For more information about *LaunchPad Solo for Readers and Writers,* visit **macmillanlearning.com/readwrite**.
- To sign up for WebEx trainings with pedagogical specialists and access round-the-clock tech support, visit **macmillanlearning.com/support**.

Contents

Part 1	Skills for Success in Reading and Writing	1

1 Succeeding in College   3

Robinson Meyer, To Remember a Lecture Better, Take Notes by Hand   4

"Normally she used her laptop to take notes, but, without it, she'd have to rely on a more traditional approach. So she put pen to paper—and found something surprising."

Strategies for College Success   6

Manage Your Time 7 • Organize a Reading, Writing, and Study Area 9 • Develop Concentration Skills 9 • Manage Stress 10

Classroom Skills   12

Polish Your Academic Image 12 • Demonstrate Academic Integrity 14 • Communicate with Your Instructors 14 • Use Electronic Tools Effectively 14 • Listen Carefully and Critically 15 • Ask and Answer Questions 16 • Work with Classmates 16 • Take Effective Notes in Class 17 • Manage Online Course Work 19

2 Active Reading   21

Strategies for Active Reading   22

Before Reading: Previewing and Forming Prereading Questions   24

Morgan Lowrie, Comparing Online and Traditional Education   25

"I will be forever grateful for the existence of online learning, as it gave me the opportunity to take my dream job without having to sacrifice my education."

Preview 28 • Form Prereading Questions 28

Writing Your Own Description Essay   239

Madeleine Massey, Small Town New Orleans

"This little community celebration lacks the exotic atmosphere that is rumored to captivate the 'real' Mardi Gras partiers, but it carries a more subdued and old-fashioned charm that appeals to a slightly more conservative southern community."

Readings for Practice, Ideas for Writing   248

Richard Selzer, The Discus Thrower   248

"I spy on my patients. Ought not a doctor to observe his patients by any means and from any stance, that he might more fully assemble evidence? So I stand in the doorways of hospital rooms and gaze."

Jordan Kisner, Rain Is Sizzling Bacon, Cars Are Lions Roaring: The Art of Sound in Movies   253

"The two cars rest smoking and crumpled in the middle of a suburban intersection. . . . There is the sound of engines hissing and crackling . . . ; there is a mostly unnoticeable rustle of leaves in the trees; . . . there is the sound of a car rolling through an intersection a block or two over, off camera; a dog barks somewhere far away."

Veronica Chambers, The Secret Latina   260

"Having dark skin and growing up in Brooklyn in the 1970s meant I was Black, period. You could meet me and not know I was of Latin heritage."

COMBINING THE PATTERNS | TEXTBOOK EXCERPT: FILM STUDIES

Louis Giannetti, Costumes   265

"In the most sensitive films and plays, costumes and makeup aren't merely frills added to enhance an illusion, but aspects of character and theme."

18   Argumentation: Supporting a Claim   544

Thematic Contents

RELATIONSHIPS

SCIENCE AND MEDICINE

TECHNOLOGY

Part 1

Skills for Success in Reading and Writing

1

Succeeding in College

In this chapter, you will learn to

- Develop strategies for college success, such as time management tactics, study and concentration skills, and stress-management techniques.

- Develop classroom skills expected of college students, including the ability to communicate, collaborate, and take notes effectively.

Rido/Shutterstock

Reflect on a Visual Text

This photograph shows successful students engaged in study. Follow the steps below to study, reflect on, and write about the image.

1 **Ask yourself questions.** What does the photo suggest about studying and academic success? What tasks must students perform to be successful? What nonacademic factors, such as job and family responsibilities, may play a role in student success? →

3

2 Brainstorm ideas. Based on your experiences with education until now, make a list of the skills you think contribute to academic success.

3 Write. Draft a paragraph explaining the top three skills that students need to be successful in college. Be detailed and specific.

In your paragraph you may have mentioned being motivated and organized, knowing how to read and study, or knowing how to write papers and take exams. All of these skills, and many others, contribute to academic success. This chapter presents numerous strategies to help you develop the skills you need for a successful academic career. Some of these strategies may surprise you.

Read the following article to understand why some classic study methods may be more effective than modern technologies. As you read, highlight the main points the author makes.

To Remember a Lecture Better, Take Notes by Hand

Robinson Meyer

Robinson Meyer is an associate editor of *The Atlantic*, a well-respected magazine, in which this essay was first published in 2014. Meyer writes about culture and technology for the magazine.

Psych 101 was about to start, and Pam Mueller had forgotten her laptop at home. This meant more than lost Facebook time. A psychology grad student at Princeton, Mueller was one of the class teaching assistants. It was important she have good notes on the lecture. Normally she used her laptop to take notes, but, without it, she'd have to rely on a more traditional approach. So

she put pen to paper—and found something surprising. Class just seemed *better.* "I felt like I had gotten so much more out of the lecture that day," she said. So she shared the story with Daniel Oppenheimer, the professor teaching the class.

"'I had a similar experience in a faculty meeting the other day,'" Mueller remembers him saying. "And we both sort of had that intuition that there might be something different about writing stuff down."

It turns out there is. A new study—conducted by Mueller and Oppenheimer—finds that people remember lectures better when they've taken handwritten notes, rather than typed ones.

YanLev/Shutterstock

4

What's more, knowing how and why typed notes can be bad doesn't seem to improve their quality. Even if you warn laptop-notetakers ahead of time, it doesn't make a difference. For some tasks, it seems, handwriting's just better.

The study comes at a ripe time for questions about laptop use in class. Educators still debate whether to allow students to bring their laptops into the classroom. And while researchers have found that laptop use during class-time tends to be distracting—not only do laptop-using students not perform as well academically, but also they're less happy with their education—Mueller and Oppenheimer's research seems to be the first quantitative attempt to compare laptops disconnected from the Internet with plain-old pencil and paper.

The study was conducted in three parts. At the beginning of each, students watched video of a lecture or a TED talk, and took notes on it either longhand or on laptops. Students watched the video, completed difficult mental tasks for 30 minutes, then took a quiz on the content. In this group, longhand-notetakers outperformed laptop-notetakers on the quiz. Analysis of student notes showed that laptop-notetakers tended to transcribe a lot of the speaker's words verbatim. Mueller and Oppenheimer suspected that this was because those who typed notes were inclined to transcribe lectures, rather than process them. This makes sense: If you can type quickly enough, word-for-word transcription is possible, whereas writing by hand usually rules out capturing every word.

So students in the second group were given a warning. Before the laptop-users watched the lecture or took any notes on it, the study administrator told some of them:

> People who take class notes on laptops when they expect to be tested on the material later tend to transcribe what they're hearing without thinking about it much. **Please try not to do this as you take notes today.** Take notes in your own words and don't just write down word-for-word what the speaker is saying.

The warning seemed to have no effect. The quiz showed that longhand-notetakers still remembered lecture content better than laptop-notetakers. And analyzing the notes that laptop-using students took, the two authors admit: "The instruction to not take verbatim notes was completely ineffective at reducing verbatim content."

The final group of students took the quiz a full week after watching a recorded lecture. Some of these students were allowed to study their notes for 10 minutes before taking the quiz. In this last group, longhand-notetakers who had time to study outperformed everyone else. Longhand-notetakers of any sort, in fact, did better on the quiz than laptop-notetakers. What's more, if someone took verbatim notes on their laptop, then studying seemed more likely to hinder their performance on the quiz. In other words, taking notes on a laptop seems to lead to verbatim notes, which make it tough to study well.

And you can't successfully warn someone to keep them from taking verbatim notes if they're using a laptop.

"We don't write longhand as fast as we type these days, but people who were typing just tended to transcribe large parts of lecture content verbatim," Mueller told me. "The people who were taking notes on the laptops don't have to be judicious in what they write down." She thinks this might be the key to their findings: Take notes by hand, and you have to process information as well as write it down. That initial selectivity leads to long-term comprehension. 9

"I don't think we're gonna get more people to go back to notebooks necessarily," Mueller said. "Tablets might be the best of both worlds—you have to choose what to write down, but then you have the electronic copy." 10

Incidentally, the two researchers might look at tablet use next. (They didn't include them in this study.) But they have busy scientific dockets outside this work, as neither of them specialize in educational psychology. Mueller researches questions of law and morality, and Oppenheimer tends to focus on decision-making and the psychology of democracy. But the two say they've appreciated their foray into note-taking research, which stemmed from a real-life problem. "I think," Mueller said, "that's where the best research comes from, because the questions resonate with other people." 11

Responding to the Reading

1. **Discussion** Have you ever used a laptop computer or other electronic device to take notes? If so, how effective do you think your note-taking was?

2. **Paragraph** Write a one-paragraph summary (in your own words) explaining why taking notes by hand is a more effective study tool than taking notes on a computer.

3. **Essay** The article focuses on one way in which technology may actually decrease learning and recall rather than improve them. Write an essay in which you explore additional ways in which technology can interfere with learning. Alternatively, you may write an essay in which you explore some ways in which technology can aid learning.

Strategies for College Success

Before you read the article, did you know that taking notes by hand is more effective than taking notes on a laptop? This article is just one example of the extensive research that has been done on how college students read, write, study, and learn effectively. The strategies in this chapter and throughout this text have all undergone thorough examination and testing. We know they work. Try them; you'll see!

Manage Your Time

Examine the two student schedules shown in Figures 1.1 and 1.2. Which student is more likely to meet deadlines? Why?

Figure 1.1   Planner with Due Dates

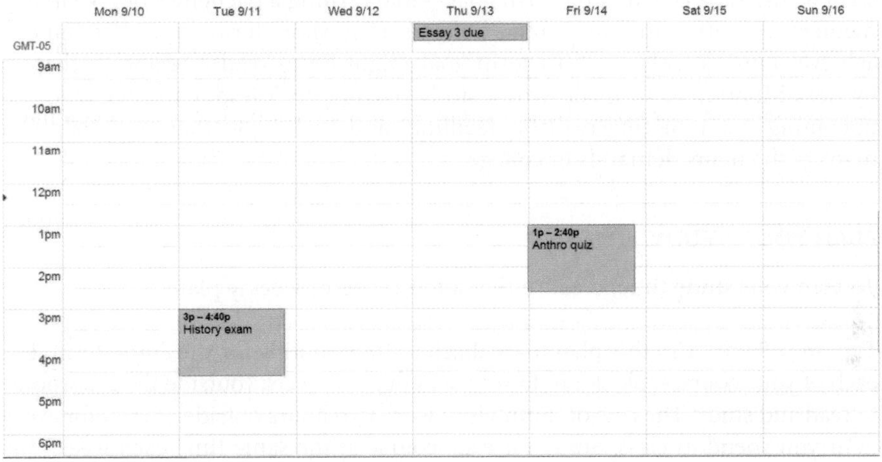

Figure 1.2   Planner with Detailed Schedule

Figure 1.1 shows a planner that lists only test dates and assignment deadlines. Figure 1.2 shows a planner that accounts for the student's work and study schedules. It details how and when the student will meet each deadline. The student who uses the planner in Figure 1.2 is much more likely to complete his or her work with less stress and less worry.

To manage your time effectively, you need to establish realistic short-term goals, plan your study time, and avoid procrastination.

ESTABLISH REALISTIC SHORT-TERM GOALS AND DEADLINES

The first step in managing your time is establishing positive and realistic short-term goals. Set a broad, long-term goal — like earning a bachelor's degree in elementary education in four years — before setting short-term goals that you can achieve more quickly. A short-term goal might be to read a textbook chapter by next Monday or to meet with a study partner on Tuesday to review for an upcoming exam. Setting realistic deadlines and sticking to them will help you manage the many demands of college.

PLAN YOUR STUDY TIME

To plan your study time, create either a term plan or weekly plans.

The Term Plan   Use this plan to establish a study routine for the entire term. For each of your courses, block out four to six hours per week (outside the classroom) to read and study. The rule of thumb is to work two hours outside of class for every hour you spend in class. Study for each course at the same time each week. The weekly tasks will vary, but you will always have enough time to get everything done.

The Weekly Plan   Make a schedule for each week of the term. Take ten minutes at the beginning of each week to specify what you'll work on for each course, taking into account upcoming assignments. Figure 1.2 is a good example of how to organize a weekly plan.

Regardless of which plan you choose, you should use a planner or calendar to record assignments, due dates for papers, and upcoming exams. Purchase a student planner or use one of the many free calendar and scheduling apps offered for computers, tablets, and smartphones. Schedule time for reading, completing assignments, and studying; whether you make your schedule daily, weekly, or for an entire term is up to you. Keep your planner with you at all times and check it regularly. Doing so will help you get and stay organized.

Each time you begin studying, assess what needs to be done and determine the order in which you will complete the required tasks. Tackle the most challenging assignments first, when you are not tired and when your concentration is at its peak.

AVOID PROCRASTINATION

Procrastination is putting off things that need to be done. For example, you know you should work on an assignment, but you log on to Facebook instead.

To avoid procrastination, divide tasks into manageable parts that you can complete one at a time. Look for ways to increase the amount of time you can devote to studying. For example, you might be able to make more time by waking up earlier or postponing a get-together with friends. Also avoid escaping into routine tasks such as shopping, cleaning, or washing your car rather than completing the study task.

Exercise 1.1

Use the suggestions above to create a weekly or term plan. Use your plan for the upcoming week and then evaluate how well it worked. Determine whether you got everything done on time. Look for places in your schedule where you need more or less time. Then revise your plan and try it for another week.

Organize a Reading, Writing, and Study Area

You don't need a lot of room to create an appropriate space for reading, studying, and writing. Just think of how much learning takes place while you are seated at a small desk in a classroom, taking notes by hand (as suggested in the article at the start of this chapter). Use the following suggestions to organize an efficient work area.

- **Choose a setting that is conducive to reading, writing, and studying.** Your work area should be well lit, comfortable, and equipped with all the tools you need — a watch or clock, a computer, a calculator, notebooks, pens, pencils, paper, and so on. Make sure your laptop's battery is fully charged. Better yet, choose a spot with plenty of available electrical outlets.
- **Find a quiet area.** If you live somewhere noisy, consider studying in the library or another quiet place. Libraries offer many spaces where you can work without distractions. Some also provide study rooms for group work or secluded areas with comfortable chairs if you do not need a desk.

At home, find a place where you won't be disturbed by family or roommates. Otherwise, you may waste time setting up your work, figuring out where you left off, and getting started again.

Develop Concentration Skills

Does either of these situations sound familiar?

> *"I just read a whole page, and I can't remember anything I read!"*
>
> *"Every time I start working on this assignment, my mind wanders."*

If so, you may need to improve your concentration. Try the following concentration tips to help you study smarter, not harder.

- **Work at peak periods of attention.** Determine the time of day or night when you are most efficient and best able to concentrate. Do not try to work when you are tired, hungry, or distracted.
- **Vary your activities.** Do not complete three reading assignments consecutively. Instead, alternate assignments. For example, read a portion of a chapter from your textbook, then work on an essay, then work on math problems, then read another assignment, and so on.
- **Monitor your study**. Be sure to devote enough time to each activity, and keep track of how long you take to complete a particular task. Then use that information as you schedule time for future assignments.
- **Write to keep yourself mentally and physically active.** Highlight and annotate as you read. As the reading at the beginning of the chapter suggests, writing is an active process — more physical than typing. (Techniques for highlighting and annotating effectively are found in Chapters 2 and 3.)
- **Avoid electronic distractions.** Turn off the television, your phone, the radio, or anything else that distracts you from your studies.
- **Take a break.** Staring at a textbook or a computer screen for hours at a time can be very draining. Take a short break every half hour; use the time to get a healthy snack or stretch.
- **Reward yourself.** Use fun activities, such as sending a text message to a friend, as a reward when you have completed an assignment (or reached an important milestone toward its completion).

Exercise 1.2

Not all students study the same way; in addition, students study differently for different courses. Make a list of the courses you are taking this term and identify a study strategy for each. Compare your strategies with those of other students and write down any new useful strategies that you learn from them.

Manage Stress

The pressures and obligations of school lead some students to feel overwhelmed. Successful students monitor their stress level and take action to lessen it. Take the quiz in Exercise 1.3 to assess your stress level.

Exercise 1.3

Complete the following stress miniquiz. If you answer "Always" or "Sometimes" to more than two or three items, identify at least two ways you can reduce your stress level.

	Always	Sometimes	Never
1. I worry that I do not have enough time to get everything done.	☐	☐	☐
2. I regret that I have no time to do fun things each week.	☐	☐	☐
3. I find myself losing track of details and forgetting due dates, promises, and appointments.	☐	☐	☐
4. I worry about what I am doing.	☐	☐	☐
5. I have conflicts or disagreements with friends or family.	☐	☐	☐
6. I lose patience over small annoyances.	☐	☐	☐
7. I seem to be late, no matter how hard I try to arrive on time.	☐	☐	☐
8. I have difficulty sleeping.	☐	☐	☐
9. My eating habits have changed.	☐	☐	☐
10. I find myself needing a cigarette, a drink, or a prescription drug.	☐	☐	☐

Here are some effective ways to reduce stress.

- **Establish your priorities.** Decide what is most important in your life. Let's say you decide school is more important than your part-time job. Once you make this decision, you won't feel conflicted about requesting a work schedule to accommodate your study plan because school is your priority.

- **Learn to say no.** Many people try to do too many things for too many people — family, friends, classmates, coworkers. Allow your priorities to guide your willingness to accept new responsibilities.

- **Focus on the positive.** Do not think, I'll never be able to finish this assignment on time. Instead ask yourself, What do I need to do to complete this assignment on time?

- **Separate work, school, and social worries.** Create mental compartments for your worries. Don't spend time in class thinking about a problem at work. Don't think about a conflict with a friend while writing a paper. Deal with problems at the appropriate time and place.
- **Keep a journal.** Taking a few minutes to write in a journal about your worries can go a long way toward relieving stress.

Classroom Skills

What you do in the classroom largely determines your academic success. Do all of the following, and success will follow.

Polish Your Academic Image

Your **academic image** is the way you are perceived by your instructors and other students. How you act and respond in class plays a large part in creating this image.

Do . . .	Don't . . .
Make thoughtful contributions to class discussions.	Read or send text messages during class.
Maintain eye contact with instructors.	Work on homework during class.
Ask questions if information is unclear to you.	Sleep or daydream during class.
Refer to assigned readings in class.	Remain silent during class discussion.
Be courteous to classmates when you speak.	Interrupt others or criticize their contributions.

Don't underestimate the value of communicating — through your words and actions — that you are a hardworking student who takes your studies seriously.

Exercise 1.4

Rate your academic image by checking "Always," "Sometimes," or "Never" for each of the following statements.

	Always	Sometimes	Never
1. I arrive at classes promptly.	☐	☐	☐
2. I sit near the front of the room.	☐	☐	☐
3. I look and act alert and interested in class.	☐	☐	☐
4. I make eye contact with instructors.	☐	☐	☐
5. I complete reading assignments before class.	☐	☐	☐
6. I ask thoughtful questions.	☐	☐	☐
7. I participate in class discussions.	☐	☐	☐
8. I complete all assignments on time.	☐	☐	☐
9. I submit neat, complete, well-organized papers.	☐	☐	☐
10. I refrain from carrying on conversations with or texting other students while the instructor is addressing the class.	☐	☐	☐
11. I say "hello" when I meet my instructors on campus.	☐	☐	☐
12. I use my computer in class only for class-related activities and assignments.	☐	☐	☐

Exercise 1.5

Write a brief paragraph about how you think others perceive you as a student. Refer to the list of tips for building a positive academic image on page 12. Which tips do you normally follow? In which areas would you like to improve?

Demonstrate Academic Integrity

Academic integrity — conducting yourself in an honest and ethical manner — is important in all classrooms. At the simplest level, students with academic integrity do not engage in such obvious forms of dishonesty as copying homework, buying a paper on the Internet, and cheating on exams or helping others do so.

Students with academic integrity also avoid both deliberate and unintentional intellectual **plagiarism**, which occurs when you use others' ideas or language without giving them credit. An example of **intentional plagiarism** is cutting and pasting information from the Internet into your paper without indicating that it is borrowed. **Unintentional plagiarism** occurs when you use language too similar to that of the original source or forget to place quotation marks around a direct quotation. Both types of plagiarism are serious academic offenses.

Communicate with Your Instructors

Meeting regularly with your instructors will help you understand and achieve the course objectives. Use the following suggestions to communicate effectively with your instructors.

- **Don't be afraid to approach your instructors.** Take advantage of your instructors' office hours, or speak to them after class. Many instructors give out their email addresses and encourage email communication. At first, some instructors may seem unapproachable, but most instructors are happy to help you if you ask.

- **Use appropriate texting etiquette.** Do not text your instructors unless they have given you permission to do so, and be mindful of the time at which you are sending the text. (No instructor wants to be awakened in the middle of the night by a text from a student.) Use proper spelling and punctuation in your texts, and be polite at all times.

- **Prepare for meetings with your instructors.** Write out specific questions in advance. If you need help with a paper, bring along all the work (drafts, outlines, list of research sources) you have done so far.

- **Stay in touch with your instructors.** If you cannot attend class for a valid reason, notify your instructor and explain the situation. Unexplained absences suggest that you are not taking your studies seriously. If personal problems interfere with your schoolwork, let your instructors know. They can often refer you to counseling services and may grant you an extension for deadlines missed because of an emergency.

Use Electronic Tools Effectively

Email, texts, and electronic message boards are now widely used for academic purposes at many schools. For example, some colleges allow students to text questions to a reference librarian.

Computers are increasingly being used to encourage class participation and collaboration. For example, an instructor might hold "virtual" (online) office hours. Instructors and students can communicate in real time through course management systems that allow students to take courses completely online. Use the following guidelines for participating in online discussions and collaborations.

- **Become familiar with the software or course management system before you attempt to post messages.** If you need assistance, use the software's Help function, try to find print instructions, look for an online demo, or ask classmates or staff at the computer center.

- **Read all previous posts before posting your comments.** Make sure not to repeat something a classmate has already said.

- **Think through what you want to post before you post it.**

- **Be considerate.** Make it easy for your classmates and instructor to read your postings. Use correct spelling and grammar, and format your comments so that they are easy to read.

- **Place your comments within a context.** Make it clear whether you are responding to another posting (if so, give the date and poster's name), a reading assignment (give the chapter or page), or a lecture (give the date).

Listen Carefully and Critically

Did you know that your brain can process information faster than speakers can speak? As a result, your mind has time to wander while you are listening. Use the following suggestions to maintain your attention in the classroom.

- **If you are easily distracted, sit in the front of the room.** Doing so helps you focus on the speaker.

- **Take notes.** Writing will help you concentrate. As "To Remember a Lecture Better, Take Notes by Hand" (pp. 4–6) points out, taking notes also helps you process and learn information better.

- **Try to anticipate what the speaker will say next.** This keeps your mind engaged.

- **Maintain eye contact with the speaker.** You will feel more personally involved and will be less likely to drift off.

- **Avoid sitting with friends.** You will be tempted to talk to them. If you chat with classmates, you risk missing information.

In many classes, you are expected to understand everything the speaker says and to respond to it. Here are a few suggestions for developing your critical-listening skills.

- **Maintain an open mind.** It is easy to shut out ideas and opinions that do not conform to your values and beliefs. Avoid evaluating a message until you have all the information.

- **Avoid selective listening.** Some listeners hear what they want to hear; they do not remember ideas with which they disagree. Attempt to understand the speaker's viewpoint. Take notes or create an informal outline of the speaker's main points.
- **Avoid oversimplification.** When listening to difficult, emotional, or complex messages, it is tempting to simplify them by eliminating details, reasons, or supporting evidence. Focus on the details in order to comprehend the speaker's message.
- **Focus on the message, not the speaker.** Try not to be distracted by the speaker's clothing, mannerisms, speech patterns, or quirks.

Exercise 1.6

Working with a classmate, evaluate your listening skills. What are your strengths? In which areas would you like to improve?

Ask and Answer Questions

You will learn more from your classes if you actively ask and answer questions. Use the following tips to strengthen your questioning and answering skills.

- **Conquer your fear of speaking in class.** Don't worry about what your friends and classmates will think. Speak out. Other students probably have the same questions but may be reluctant to ask.
- **While reading an assignment, jot down questions as they occur to you.** Bring your list to class, and use it when your instructor invites questions.
- **Ask your questions concisely.** Don't ramble.
- **Focus on critical questions.** While it is perfectly acceptable to ask factual questions, instructors particularly appreciate questions that center on how the information can be used, how ideas fit together, how things work, and the long-term significance of the information.
- **Think before responding.** When answering questions, compose your response in your head before volunteering to answer.

Exercise 1.7

Working with a classmate, brainstorm a list of questions you could ask about the content presented in this chapter.

Work with Classmates

Many assignments and activities require you to work with other students. Some groups are assembled to discuss problems; others carry out an activity, such as examining a piece of writing; others research a topic and present their findings.

UNDERSTANDING THE ASSIGNMENT'S PURPOSE

To benefit most from group projects, be sure you understand the task. Ask yourself, What am I expected to learn from this assignment? You will get more out of an assignment if you focus on its purpose and desired outcomes.

KEEPING GROUPS FUNCTIONING EFFECTIVELY

Some students find group projects to be time-consuming and unproductive. If you feel this way about a group project, take a leadership role and make the project work. Set a good example, and (if you are given the choice) choose to work with serious, energetic classmates. Assign tasks according to each member's strengths, and establish a firm schedule for completion (with checkpoints along the way). Stay focused on the project during group meetings.

Despite your best efforts, problems may arise. Because your grade on the project may depend on every other member's work, you must address problems quickly and effectively when they occur. Use the following suggestions to do so.

- If members miss work sessions, offer to remind everyone of the time and place.
- If the work is not getting done, establish a more detailed timetable.
- Ask questions that may stimulate unproductive members' ideas and interest.
- Suggest that uncommunicative members share their ideas in written form.
- Encourage the students who are causing the problem to propose solutions.

If you are unable to resolve problems or conflicts, discuss them with your instructor.

Take Effective Notes in Class

Research has shown that most people retain far more information when they interact with the information using more than one sense. For instance, if you simply listen to a lecture or discussion, you will probably forget most of it within a couple of weeks, well before the next exam. However, if you take accurate notes and review them regularly, you are more likely to retain the main points and key examples needed. Following are some useful note-taking tips.

- **Read assignments before class.** Read any related textbook material *before* going to class. Familiarity with the topic will make note-taking easier.
- **Don't attempt to record everything.** Record only main ideas and key details. Avoid writing in complete sentences. Use words and phrases instead. As you learned in the reading at the start of this chapter, do not simply transcribe the instructor's words. Rather, write your notes in a way that demonstrates your understanding of the lecture.
- **Develop a system of abbreviations, signs, and symbols to aid in note-taking.** For example, you might use a star to mark key information.

- **Pay attention to your instructor's cues regarding what is important.**
  These cues include repetition of key points, changes in voice or speaking rate, listing or numbering of items, and use of a whiteboard or visuals such as graphs, photos, or PowerPoint slides.

- **Don't rewrite your notes.** Your time is valuable; rewriting is time-consuming. You can better use the time reviewing and studying your notes.

- **Leave plenty of blank space in your notes.** Use this space to add examples or fill in information you missed during the lecture or class discussion.

- **When you must miss a class, borrow notes from a classmate who is a good student.**

- **Review and study your notes immediately after the lecture.** While the class is still fresh in your mind, clarify relationships and cement your understanding. If you wait a day or more, your memory of the class will fade. Spending even ten minutes per week reviewing class notes can improve your retention and reduce the stress of "cramming" for tests.

- **Take notes by hand, rather than by computer.** As emphasized by the reading that opened this chapter, "To Remember a Lecture Better, Take Notes by Hand," handwriting seems to facilitate retention and recall.

Two of the most popular and efficient methods of taking notes are the two-column method and the modified outline method.

USING THE TWO-COLUMN METHOD

All students can benefit from using the two-column note-taking method illustrated in Figure 1.3. Draw a vertical line from the top of a piece of paper to the bottom. The left-hand column should be about half as wide as the right-hand column.

Figure 1.3   Two-Column Method of Note-Taking

Writing Process	Prewriting—taking notes, writing ideas, drawing a cluster diagram, researching, writing questions, noting what you already know, outlining, etc. Writing—drafting
(How many drafts does the average writer complete?)	Rewriting—revision = "to see again" 2 types: global = major overhaul (reconsidering, reorganizing); local = rewording, correcting grammar (editing for correctness & style)
NOT linear	Writing is not a linear process. May go back to prewrite after writing, etc.

In the wider, right-hand column, record ideas and facts as your instructor presents them or as they arise in a discussion group. In the narrower, left-hand column, add your own questions as they arise during the class. When you review your notes later, add summaries of major concepts and sections to the left-hand column. This method allows you to quickly review key information by reading the left-hand column and to study specific information and examples in the right-hand column.

USING THE MODIFIED OUTLINE METHOD

As Figure 1.4 shows, the modified outline method uses symbols and indentations instead of numbers and letters to separate ideas and suggest relative importance. This sample uses bullets for main ideas and dashes for detailed information within a section. Less important details are simply indented farther. The more detailed the information, the farther to the right you indent your outline entries.

Figure 1.4   Modified Outline Method of Note-Taking

Writing is a process.
- Prewriting
  — Taking notes
  — Writing ideas
  — Drawing a cluster diagram
  — Researching
  — Writing questions
  — Noting what you already know
  — Outlining
- Writing
  — First drafts
    On paper
    On cards
    On computer
  — Later drafts
- Rewriting, or revision (means "to see again")
  — Global
    Major revision
    Reconsidering ideas
    Reorganizing
  — Local
    Rewording for style
    Rewriting for correct grammar, spelling, punctuation

Manage Online Course Work

Online courses are growing in popularity. Although convenient, they require more self-direction and more discipline than traditional classes do. They also require a great deal of online writing, reading, and research. Here are some tips for succeeding in online courses.

- **Avoid taking online courses in your first college term.** First learn what is expected in college courses by attending traditional classes. When you are familiar with the expectations of a typical college course, you will be better prepared to take an online course.

- **Set aside specific, regular hours to devote to your online course.** Otherwise, it becomes easy to put off class work.

- **Keep up with the work.** Most students who fail online courses do so because they fall hopelessly behind on readings and assignments.

- **Plan to do a lot of reading.** You will need to read your textbooks, as well as communications from your instructor and other students. Your instructor may also put supplemental (additional) materials online and require you to read them.

- **Maintain your concentration.** Turn off your phone, music, Skype, Facebook, and email while working on your computer.

- **Make sure all your contributions are appropriate and useful.** Comments should be specific and add to the conversation. Avoid posts that simply say "I agree" or "Good job."

These tips and strategies will help you achieve your immediate and long-term college goals. In the rest of Part 1 you will learn how to build the skills that will help you read and write successfully throughout your academic career.

2

Active Reading

In this chapter, you will learn to

- Develop active reading techniques.

- Use prereading strategies.

- Identify topics, main ideas, and thesis statements.

- Highlight and annotate.

- Review a text after reading it.

- Use specialized reading strategies.

© Michael Goulding/Corbis

Reflect on a Visual Text

This photograph shows two women dressed in pink, a color associated with breast cancer awareness and the need for funding to study the disease.

1 **Ask yourself questions.** Study the photograph and consider its meanings. What does it portray? Where was it taken? Who are the subjects in the photo and what are they doing? →

2 **Brainstorm ideas.** What qualities of this photograph make it effective? List at least three memorable aspects of the photo.

3 **Write.** Now write a paragraph explaining what you think is happening in this photograph. Be detailed and specific.

The first step in comprehending the chapter opening photo is to gain a basic understanding of its content. Reading also begins with the process of **understanding**, or comprehending, what the writer says. **Active reading** is a process of getting involved with what you read and taking steps to understand, recall, and respond to what you read. It involves thinking about, questioning, reacting to, and evaluating the author's ideas. This chapter will give you the tools to understand what you read and what you see.

Strategies for Active Reading

Active reading is essential for academic success. It is the primary means through which you acquire ideas and gather information. To read actively, keep the following suggestions in mind.

Assume Responsibility for Reading Assignments Some courses require a heavy reading load. Instructors assume that you are keeping up with reading assignments and that you are learning the material. However, most instructors won't tell you *how* to learn. Consequently, you will have to discover how best to learn each subject. Use the time-management suggestions in Chapter 1 (pp. 7–9) to organize your workload, and experiment with different methods — taking notes, preparing study sheets, highlighting (see pp. 34–35), outlining (see pp. 47 and 49), and annotating (see pp. 35–36).

Pay Attention to Visual Aids Much of what you read will be accompanied by visual aids (for example, drawings, photographs, charts, and graphs) designed to clarify or emphasize ideas, condense information, explain a complicated process, or illustrate a specific viewpoint (see pp. 40–43). Think about the writer's purpose for including them and how they relate to the text that accompanies them.

Adapt Your Reading Skills to Different Materials In your studies, you will encounter a wide range of reading materials. In addition to reading textbooks, you may read articles, professionally written essays, student essays, critiques, field reports, and scientific studies. For each type, begin by noticing how the reading is organized and what its purpose might be. Then devise a strategy for identifying what you should learn and remember.

 **LaunchPad Solo**
macmillan learning
Visit **LaunchPad Solo for Readers and Writers > Overview: Reading** for extra practice in the skills covered in this chapter.

Reading ⊕ Writing   Using Reading to Develop Your Writing Skills

The Reader's Perspective	The Writer's Perspective
By studying the writing of others, you can improve your own writing. As you read an article, essay, or textbook assignment, take note of the writer's techniques for presenting information. For example, notice how the writer organizes paragraphs, how she uses language to express ideas, and how she develops ideas throughout the work.	When you sit down to write, your readers' needs should be uppermost in your mind. Most forms of writing are intended to be read by others. Good writers think about their readership, or *audience*, each time they begin a new piece of writing.

Become an Active Reader   When you attend a baseball game, do you get actively involved? Baseball fans cheer some players and criticize others, evaluate plays and calls, and offer advice and analysis. Like fans with their sports, active readers get involved with the material they read. They question, think about, and react to ideas. Table 2.1 summarizes the differences between active and passive readers. ⧲

Table 2.1   Active vs. Passive Readers

Passive Readers	Active Readers
Passive readers simply begin reading.	Active readers begin by reading the title, learning about the author, and thinking about what they already know about the subject. Then they decide what they need to know before they begin reading.
Passive readers read the material only because it is assigned.	Active readers look for key points and answers to questions while they read the material.
Passive readers read but do not write.	Active readers highlight or underline, annotate, and write notes as they read.
Passive readers quickly move on to the next task or assignment.	Active readers review, analyze, and evaluate what they've read.

⧲ **LaunchPad Solo**
macmillan learning   Visit **LaunchPad Solo for Readers and Writers > Active Reading** for extra practice in the skills covered in this section.

To achieve maximum comprehension, you should generally follow a three-step active-reading process.

1. Preview and form prereading questions *before* reading.
2. Read for meaning *during* the reading process.
3. Review the material *after* reading it.

Figure 2.1 shows these steps graphically and in more detail.

Figure 2.1   Strategies for Active Reading

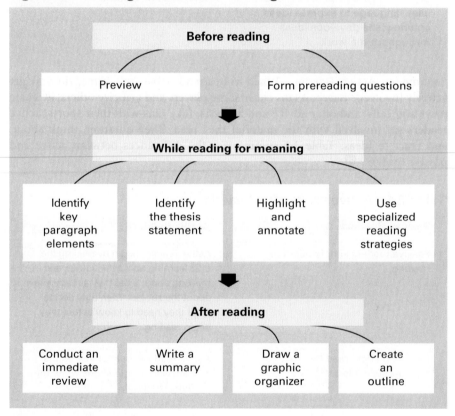

Before Reading: Previewing and Forming Prereading Questions

An effective technique for improving your reading comprehension is to *preview* the reading assignment before you read it. Before you read the following article, which compares traditional and online education, read only the highlighted sections, which indicate what to read while previewing. Next, complete Exercise 2.1 on page 28. Then read the entire article. How well did the preview prepare you to understand the content?

Comparing Online and Traditional Education

Morgan Lowrie

In 2008, I completed my bachelor's degree in English literature by taking advantage of my school's distance-education program. I had completed the first two years of study in the conventional, traditional manner: I had attended classes, participated in discussions, and sat for exams. Two years into my four-year degree, I was offered a job which took me away from home, and I was fortunate enough that my school had a significantly large distance-education program that I was able to finish my degree online.

Having experienced both methods of attending school, my preference is for traditional education. Nevertheless, it is worth weighing the benefits and disadvantages of each.

Online Education—Benefits

Without the option of online classes, I would not have been able to both take my dream job and finish my degree. One or the other would have had to have been sacrificed. And therein lies the beauty of online education: It is tremendously flexible.

The traditional classroom is not always particularly accommodating to working adults. Most classes take place in the daytime, and there are not always multiple sections to choose from. Even schools that offer night classes are inconvenient for people who work rotating schedules, such as retail workers. Distance-education course work can usually be accomplished whenever and wherever it suits the student, as long as deadlines are met. Not everybody can afford to take four years out of their lives to attend school, and not everyone has a trust fund set up to pay for their education. Working one's way through school allows a person to graduate without the crippling debt that burdens so many graduating students. Online learning is also an excellent choice for stay-at-home mothers with young children and people with certain disabilities who might need a little more accommodation in order to thrive. Many people who otherwise would not be able to attend college are given the option to do so because of online classes.

Commuting time is also a factor. When I attended traditional classes, I traveled an hour and a half to get to my school. (I was living at home to save money.) Although I managed to do a lot of reading on the two buses and the train that I took, one cannot say that this was a particularly productive or efficient use of time. Even a fifteen or twenty minute drive each way adds up to hours per week spent traveling—time that an online student could put into his or her course work.

Furthermore, as technology improves, so do the conditions for the online   6
student. Most online classes have forums and chat rooms where students
can engage in discussions and complete assignments with fellow students.
Lectures can be recorded and played back at will by the student. Professors are
accessible through email, by phone, and via interactive chats. One geography
class I took even included a virtual field trip, thanks to the satellite imagery
of Google Earth. Technologies like these ensure that the distance-education
student is less isolated than ever before.

Online Learning—Disadvantages

Although the benefits of online learning are numerous, there are also   7
many disadvantages that some students do not consider before enrolling.

The number-one problem that I encountered was that not all classes were   8
offered online. I would have enjoyed my education much more had I been
able to choose the classes that interested me most; instead, I had to take the
classes that were offered online. In the end, I had to change my major and
drop my minor altogether because my school just didn't offer enough courses
for me to complete the major I wanted. This was partially because my school
was a traditional one with an online component, but even fully online schools
tend to have a narrower curriculum and fewer classes to choose from than
their traditional counterparts. For example, it is difficult to take a quality
language course online. It is equally difficult for science classes with a lab
component to be properly taught online. The online student is limited in the
type of degree that can be earned.

Second, because there is less classroom interaction and no time spent in   9
class, the online courses I took placed much more emphasis on writing papers
and exams. Since there were no (or few) marks given for elements such as
participation, group projects, or oral presentations, the courses I took included
very heavy reading loads and several large papers and had a final exam

that was usually worth at least 30% of the final grade. For me, this was not a problem, since I am a good writer and tend to test extremely well (although I did have trouble finding quality research materials without access to a good college library). Students who are not strong in these subjects might have more difficulty with online classes.

Third, most of the classes that I took still included a final exam. As I was   10 not able to physically make it to the school to write the exam, I had to find a proctor to supervise me as I wrote. Usually, a proctor has to be a college faculty member or administrator, or a librarian. I was lucky enough to work with someone who met these qualifications and who was happy to assist me, but I have known several people who have expressed surprise at the great difficulty they had finding proctors. Many colleges and libraries charge large fees for this service or else refuse altogether. This can be one of the big hassles of distance education.

Finally, there is the obvious problem: Even with all the technological   11 advances being made, taking a course online is still much less interactive than attending a traditional class. Students who take online classes need to be self-motivated, have good time-management skills, and be able to learn independently. Usually there is far less spoon-feeding of material in distance courses, and there are no lively discussions, anecdotes, or jokes during lectures to make the material more interesting. Perhaps in the future, as online courses become more and more common, some of these hurdles will be overcome. But at the moment, online students need to be prepared to work mostly on their own.

Online or Traditional: Which Is Better?

I will be forever grateful for the existence of online learning, as it gave   12 me the opportunity to take my dream job without having to sacrifice my education. Nevertheless, if personal factors had not intervened, I would have preferred the traditional classroom setting.

Let me put it this way: I think that if a person can attend college   13 traditionally, they should.

When I switched to online education, I missed out on a good chunk   14 of the college experience. To me, the best parts of college were listening to lectures by terrific professors and participating in discussions with other young, intelligent people. Once I became a distance student, I missed out on all of these exchanges of ideas. I missed out on making great friends, on taking some terrific classes, on joining clubs, and on writing for the student newspaper. These are very important parts of a college education, and they are parts that simply cannot be experienced through a computer monitor. I put my education second, behind my job and my personal life. Perhaps, for only a couple of years, I should have put it first.

Online classes can be a godsend for some students, and I think that they   15
provide an incredibly valuable service in opening up the world of college
education to some people who otherwise wouldn't be able to earn degrees
without great sacrifice. But, take it from someone who has been on both sides
of the fence: It isn't the same. It truly isn't.

Exercise 2.1

Based on your preview of the essay, mark the following statements either "T" for
true or "F" for false. If most of your answers are correct, you will know that previewing helped you gain a sense of the essay's context and organization. (For the
answers to this exercise, see p. 49.)

_____ 1. The author believes an online education is the equivalent of a traditional
education.

_____ 2. The author is thankful for the opportunities that distance education
provided her.

_____ 3. The author has not yet completed her college degree.

_____ 4. The author stopped attending traditional classes so that she could accept
her dream job.

_____ 5. The author believes that online classes are valuable.

Never start any reading assignment without preparation. Instead, use *previewing* and *prereading questions* to discover what the reading is about and to
focus your mind on the topic.

Preview

As you discovered, **previewing** is a quick way of familiarizing yourself with a
reading's content and organization. Previewing helps you to decide what you
need to learn, and it has a number of other benefits as well.

- It helps you get interested in the material.
- It helps you understand the structure of the material and focus your
concentration.
- It helps you remember more of what you read.

To preview a reading assignment, use the guidelines in Table 2.2. Read *only*
the materials that are listed.

Form Prereading Questions

Before you begin reading, you can improve your **intent to remember**. That is, you
can remind yourself that your goal is to remember what you've read. One way to

Table 2.2　Guidelines for Previewing

Guidelines	Tips
Read the title, subtitle, and author's name.	The title and subtitle may tell you what the reading is about. Check the author's name to see if it is one you recognize. (Most readings in this book include a **headnote** that provides background information about the author or the reading.)
Read the introduction and / or the first paragraph.	These sections often provide an overview of the reading.
Read any headings and the first sentence following each one.	Headings, taken together, often form a mini-outline of the reading. The first sentence following a heading often explains the heading.
If a reading does not include headings, read the first sentence of a few of the paragraphs on each page.	This strategy can be very helpful for readings that are not divided by headings.
Look at any photographs, tables, charts, and drawings.	Ask yourself, What is the key point of this visual aid?
Read the conclusion or summary.	A conclusion (usually found in the reading's last paragraph) brings the reading to a close and may provide a summary of the piece.
***Before* you begin reading the assignment, read any questions you will be expected to answer *after* you've read the assignment.**	These questions will help focus your attention on what is important and on what you are expected to know after you have read the assignment.

improve retention is to use the reading selection's title and headings to form questions before you begin reading. Then, as you read, answer those questions, thereby strengthening your comprehension and memory of the material. The following guidelines will help you start devising prereading questions.

- **Use the title to devise questions, and then read to find the answers.** Here are two examples of titles and relevant questions.

Title	Question
"Part-time Employment Undermines Students' Commitment to School"	Why does part-time employment undermine commitment to school?
"Wounds That Can't Be Stitched Up"	What kinds of wounds cannot be repaired?

- **Use headings to devise questions.** For example, an essay titled "Territoriality" includes two headings, "Types of Territoriality" and "Territorial Encroachment." Each of these headings can easily be turned into a prereading question.

> What are the types of territoriality?
> What is territorial encroachment and how does it occur?

Not all readings lend themselves to using the title and headings to form prereading questions. For some readings, you may need to dig into the introductory and final paragraphs to form questions. Or you may find the subtitle more useful than the title for forming a question.

Exercise 2.2

Return to the essay "Comparing Online and Traditional Education," and use the title and headings to write three questions you expect the essay to answer.

Reading for Meaning: The Thesis Statement and Key Elements of Paragraphs

All essays have a central thought or thesis statement, and most paragraphs within an essay contain a topic, a main idea or topic sentence, supporting details, and transitions. Being able to identify these key elements will help you focus your attention and improve your comprehension while you read.

Identify the Key Elements of Paragraphs

All readings are composed of paragraphs. A **paragraph** is a group of sentences that explain or develop one idea. Some paragraphs are as short as one sentence;

others go on for pages. As you read, look for the key elements in each paragraph. These include

- the topic
- the main idea and topic sentence
- supporting details
- transitions

DETERMINE THE TOPIC

The one general subject discussed in the paragraph is its **topic**. Every sentence in the paragraph somehow explains, discusses, or evaluates this topic. Consider paragraph 14 from "Comparing Online and Traditional Education."

Topic sentence	When I switched to online education, I missed out
Topic	on a good chunk of [the college experience]. To me, the
	best parts of college were listening to lectures by terrific
	professors and participating in discussions with other
Transitions	young, intelligent people. Once I became a distance
	student, I missed out on all of these exchanges of ideas.
Examples	I missed out on making great friends, on taking some
	terrific classes, on joining clubs, and on writing for the
	student newspaper. These are very important parts of a
	college education, and they are parts that simply cannot
	be experienced through a computer monitor. I put my
	education second, behind my job and my personal life.
	Perhaps, for only a couple of years, I should have put it
	first.

The topic of this paragraph — that is, the *general subject* of the entire paragraph — is the college experiences the author missed as a result of pursuing her education online. To find the topic, ask yourself, What is the one thing the writer discusses throughout the entire paragraph?

FIND THE MAIN IDEA AND TOPIC SENTENCE

A paragraph's **main idea** is the most important point it is trying to make. The main idea expresses the writer's viewpoint on the topic, and it is often found in a single **topic sentence**. In the paragraph above, the main idea is expressed in the

LaunchPad Solo
macmillan learning
Visit **LaunchPad Solo for Readers and Writers > Topic Sentences and Supporting Details** for extra practice in the skills covered in this section.

first sentence. The rest of the paragraph supports the main idea. The topic sentence is often the first sentence in a paragraph, but sometimes it can be found at the end of the paragraph or buried in the middle of the paragraph.

The main idea of a paragraph is sometimes not expressed in a single sentence. As an example, look at paragraph 10 of "Comparing Online and Traditional Education." The main idea of this paragraph can be stated as follows: "Taking exams for online courses can be inconvenient and expensive." Not all writers include clear topic sentences; be prepared to state the paragraph's main idea in your own words. A correct statement of the main idea takes the entire paragraph into account.

To state the main idea, ask yourself, What is the most important point of this paragraph? If you have difficulty stating the main idea, try the following suggestions.

1. **Determine the topic.** That is, determine the *one general subject* that the whole paragraph discusses.

2. **Look for the topic sentence.** This will be the most general sentence in the paragraph and will tell you the one important idea the writer wants you to know about the topic.

3. **If you cannot find a topic sentence, study the rest of the paragraph.** Formulate a main idea that conveys the paragraph's key point and takes into account all the information provided in the paragraph.

LOOK FOR SUPPORTING DETAILS AND TRANSITIONS

To fully explain the point they are trying to make, writers provide facts, ideas, and examples. Without these **supporting details**, a paragraph would be undeveloped and unconvincing. The main idea is a *general* statement; the paragraph details provide *specific* support for the main idea. Supporting details can fall into any of the following categories:

- examples
- descriptions
- facts
- statistics
- reasons

- anecdotes (stories that illustrate a point)
- personal experiences and observations
- quotations from or references to authorities and experts

In paragraph 14 of "Comparing Online and Traditional Education," the author provides a number of examples to support her main idea: She gives six examples of things she missed by switching to online education, shaded blue on p. 31.

Supporting details are often signaled by **transitions**, which are words, phrases, clauses, or sentences that help readers link ideas and follow the author's train of thought. Transitions can signal time sequence (*first, later, next, finally,* *in the end*); examples (*for instance, to illustrate, for example*); comparison (*like, similarly*); contrast (*on the other hand, in contrast, however, instead*); or cause and effect (*because, thus, therefore*). The sample paragraph on p. 31 shows two transitions, highlighted in gray.

Reading Ⓘ Writing   Paragraph Elements

Paragraph Element	The Reader's Perspective	The Writer's Perspective
Topic	Identifying the topic of each paragraph enables you to build a mental framework for the reading. As you read, your knowledge of the topic increases.	Developing a clear topic for each paragraph is often the key to writing an effective essay. (See pp. 82–85 for help with choosing and narrowing a topic.)
Main Idea / Topic Sentence	To understand a paragraph, look for a topic sentence and the paragraph's main idea. Many exams test your understanding of main ideas.	Use a topic sentence to state a paragraph's most important point for the reader — that is, its main idea. (See pp. 110–14 for help with writing topic sentences.)
Supporting Details	Supporting details clarify, explain, and provide additional details about the main idea. If the main idea is abstract or difficult to understand, supporting details may help you make connections and increase your comprehension.	Use supporting details to strengthen your case and to provide specific support for your topic sentence. If you do not provide interesting, relevant supporting details, you will not be able to convince your readers that your ideas or conclusions are valid. (See pp. 114–19 for help with including support.)
Transitions	Transitions are signals to readers; they help you follow the writer's train of thought or hint that a line of thought is about to change.	Transitions help to connect your ideas. They also prevent your essay from sounding choppy or disconnected. (See pp. 120–22 for help with writing transitions.)

Exercise 2.3

Reread paragraph 8 of "Comparing Online and Traditional Education" and then complete each item below.

1. What is the topic of the paragraph?
2. What is the topic sentence?
3. State the main idea in your own words.
4. List at least three supporting details provided by the author.
5. Underline the transitional words or phrases.

Identify the Central Thought or Thesis Statement

The single main point of a reading (whether an essay, a textbook chapter, or any other source) is called the **central thought** or **thesis statement**. While each paragraph in the reading will have a topic and a main idea, the reading as a whole has only one central idea. It is often found in the first paragraph of the reading, but it may appear anywhere in the selection. It is often, but not always, a single sentence. In "Comparing Online and Traditional Education," the thesis statement appears in the second paragraph: "Having experienced both methods of attending school, my preference is for traditional education. Nevertheless, it is worth weighing the benefits and disadvantages of each."

Note that the thesis statement covers *every aspect of the entire reading*: the advantages and disadvantages of online education as well as the author's conclusion that a traditional education is preferable.

Highlighting and Annotating

As you read, you will find that some ideas are more important than others. Part of your job as you read is to sort ideas, identifying what is important to learn and remember. Highlighting will provide a visual record of this sorting process. As you read, you will have questions, reactions, and responses. Use annotating to record these thoughts so that you do not lose them as you continue reading.

Highlight Key Points

Highlighting is an active reading strategy in which you sort and sift more important ideas from less important ones. In other words, it helps you distinguish main ideas from supporting details at a glance. Use the guidelines in Table 2.3 to make your highlighting as useful as possible.

LaunchPad Solo
macmillan learning

Visit **LaunchPad Solo for Readers and Writers > Topics and Main Ideas** for extra practice in the skills covered in this section.

Table 2.3   Guidelines for Highlighting

Guidelines	Tips
Use a light-colored highlighter (for example, yellow).	Do not use a color that will interfere with your ability to reread the text.
Decide what kinds of information to highlight before you begin.	What types of tasks will you be doing as a result of your reading? Will you write a paper, participate in a class discussion, or take an exam? Think about what you need to know and tailor your highlighting to the task.
Be selective. Do not highlight too much or too little.	If you highlight every idea, none will stand out. Highlighting too much means you are not distinguishing between main ideas and details. Highlighting too little means you are missing key information.
Read first; then highlight.	First read a paragraph or section; then go back and mark what is important within it. This approach will help you control the tendency to highlight too much.
Highlight key elements, words, and phrases.	Highlight the thesis statement, the topic sentence in each paragraph, important terms and definitions, and key words and phrases.

Exercise 2.4

Using the suggestions above, highlight "To Remember a Lecture Better, Take Notes by Hand" in Chapter 1, pp. 4–6.

Use Annotations

Annotations record your responses to the writer's ideas. When you annotate, you jot down your impressions, reactions, and questions directly in the margins. Later, when you are ready to discuss or write about the reading, your annotations will help you focus on major issues and questions. Here is a list of what you might annotate when reading essays:

- the thesis statement and other important points
- sections about which you need or want further information
- sections in which the author reveals his or her reasons for writing

- ideas you agree or disagree with
- inconsistencies
- questions you want to ask your instructor
- particularly meaningful visuals and images

You can use symbols as well as words. Draw arrows connecting ideas, put asterisks in the margin next to key concepts or important examples, or number causes, reasons, etc. When reading textbooks, in addition to the items listed above, you might mark or annotate

- good test questions (material you expect to be covered on an exam)
- unfamiliar or confusing ideas
- connections with lecture content
- new terminology

The following is a set of annotations for a portion of the essay "Comparing Online and Traditional Education."

Annotation	Text
Disagree — best part of college is knowing I will eventually become a nurse	When I switched to online education, I missed out on a good chunk of the college experience. To me, the best parts of college were listening to lectures by terrific professors and participating in discussions with other young, intelligent people. Once I became a distance student, I missed out on all of these exchanges of ideas. I missed out on making great friends, on taking some terrific classes, on joining clubs, and on writing for the
"thesis Virtual reality may eventually change this!!	student newspaper. [These are very important parts of a college education, and they are parts that simply cannot be experienced through a computer monitor.] I put my education second, behind my job and my personal life. Perhaps, for only a couple of years, I should have put it first.
?? Ask opinion of people who took these courses	Online classes can be a godsend for some students, and I think that they provide an incredibly valuable service in opening up the world of college education to some people who otherwise wouldn't be able to earn degrees without great sacrifice. But, take it from someone who has been on both sides of the fence: It isn't the same. It truly isn't.

Exercise 2.5

Write annotations for "Comparing Online and Traditional Education."

Specialized Reading Strategies

In college, you will encounter a wide range of reading materials, and you will need specialized skills to handle them. This section shows you how to deal with unfamiliar terminology, handle difficult reading material, use the special features of your textbooks as learning tools, and recognize the importance of visual aids.

Look Closely at Unfamiliar Words

If you were to use a dictionary to look up every unfamiliar word you encountered, you might not have enough time to complete all your assignments. You can often figure out a word's meaning by using one of the following strategies. All the examples are drawn from "Comparing Online and Traditional Education." 📷

- **Look for context clues in surrounding text.** You can often figure out a word or phrase's meaning from the way it is used in its sentence or in surrounding sentences. Sometimes the author provides a brief definition or synonym; other times a less obvious context clue reveals meaning.

  Brief Definition

  One cannot say that this was a particularly *productive* or efficient use of time.

  [*Productive* means "efficient."]

  Context Clue

  One geography class I took even included a *virtual field trip*, thanks to the satellite imagery of Google Earth.

  [GoogleEarth is an online application that provides images from around the world. A *virtual field trip* is, therefore, a field trip in which the "traveler" is sitting in front of a computer and seeing images from the destination.]

- **Try pronouncing the word out loud.** Hearing the word will sometimes help you grasp its meaning. By pronouncing the word *godsend* (paragraph 15), you may hear the words *god* and *send* and know a godsend is something "sent by God."

📷 **LaunchPad Solo** Visit **LaunchPad Solo for Readers and Writers > Vocabulary** for extra
macmillan learning practice in the skills covered in this section.

- **Look at parts of the word.** If you break a word down into its parts, you may be able to figure out its meaning. For example, in the word *disadvantage* (paragraph 7) you can see the root word "advantage" and the prefix "dis-," which usually signifies something negative. So you know that a *disadvantage* is the opposite of an advantage. You can find a comprehensive list of word parts at **www.learnthat.org/pages/view/roots.html**.
- **Use a dictionary when necessary.** Sometimes you won't be able to continue reading until you understand a particular word. Be sure you have a collegiate dictionary available where you read and study, be it in print or online. Merriam-Webster (**www.merriam-webster.com**) and Dictionary.com (**dictionary.reference.com**) are two reliable, free dictionary Web sites.

Exercise 2.6

Using the suggestions above, define each of the following words, found in "Comparing Online and Traditional Education."

1. conventional (paragraph 1)
2. accommodating (paragraph 4)
3. curriculum (paragraph 8)

4. proctor (paragraph 10)
5. anecdote (paragraph 11)

Learn to Handle Difficult Reading Material

In college and at work, you'll have to read many different types of materials, from essays to textbooks to visual materials (such as graphs and charts). Expect some materials to be difficult and complicated. Table 2.4 outlines suggestions for dealing with material you find especially challenging.

Table 2.4   Troubleshooting Guide for Difficult Readings

Problems	Strategies for Solving Them
You cannot concentrate.	1. Take limited breaks. 2. Tackle the assignment at peak periods of attention. 3. Divide the material into sections. Make it your goal to complete one section at a time. 4. Give yourself a reasonable deadline for completing the assignment.
The sentences are long and confusing.	1. Read aloud. 2. Divide each sentence into parts and analyze the function of each part. 3. Express each sentence in your own words.

Table 2.4   (continued)

Problems	Strategies for Solving Them
The ideas are complicated and hard to understand.	1. Reread the material several times. 2. Rephrase or explain each idea in your own words. 3. Create a detailed outline. 4. Study with a classmate; discuss difficult ideas. 5. Look up the meanings of unfamiliar or technical words in a dictionary.
The material seems disorganized or poorly organized.	1. Study the introduction for clues to organization. 2. Pay more attention to headings. 3. Read the summary or conclusion. 4. Try to discover the organization by drawing a graphic organizer (see pp. 46–48) or creating an outline (see pp. 47 and 49).
The material contains many unfamiliar words.	1. Look for clues to meaning in the surrounding text. 2. Try pronouncing words aloud to see if they remind you of related words. 3. Break words into parts whose meanings you know. 4. Use a dictionary when necessary.
You cannot get interested in the material.	1. Think about something you've experienced that is related to the topic. 2. Work with a classmate or study group, discussing each section as you go.
You cannot relate to the writer's ideas or experiences.	1. Find some background information about the writer. 2. Imagine yourself having the writer's experiences. How would you react?
The subject is unfamiliar; you lack background information on the subject.	1. Obtain a more basic text or other source that moves more slowly, offers more explanation, and reviews fundamental principles and concepts. 2. For unfamiliar terminology, consult a specialized dictionary within the field of study. 3. Ask your instructor to recommend useful print or online resources and references.

Use the Special Features of Your Textbooks

Textbooks are an essential part of most college courses. (For this reason, one reading in each chapter in Part 2 of this book is taken from a college textbook.) To get the most from your textbook reading assignments, become familiar with the many features textbooks provide. You can often find a list of features in the book's preface. The following are some of the most common textbook features.

Learning objectives. These appear at the beginning of the chapter and outline the student's learning goals for the chapter. Upon completing the chapter, revisit the learning objectives to make sure you can accomplish them. If you can't, go back and reread the relevant sections of the chapter.

Chapter headings. Each chapter in a textbook provides headings to emphasize the chapter's structure and organization. Before reading, conduct a thorough preview of all the headings, formulating prereading questions as you do so.

Key definitions. Each academic discipline (or subject) has its own special vocabulary. To learn the subject, you must learn many new words and definitions. Key terms frequently appear in **boldface** or *italic* type or as marginal notes. You can create flash cards from these key terms to help you study their meanings. Most textbooks also include at the end a **glossary** that lists all the key terms (along with their definitions) in alphabetical order.

Visual aids. Many textbooks contain visual aids. Text and visual aids are designed to work together, so read the visual aid when the text tells you to. (See "Guidelines for Reading Visual Aids," p. 43.)

End-of-chapter material. Most textbook chapters end with a summary of key points, a list of key terms, and exercises. Use the end-of-chapter material to help you conduct an immediate review of the chapter. If your instructor has assigned specific exercises, read them *before* you start the chapter. Doing so will give you a sense of what to look for as you read.

Answers or solutions. Some, but not all, textbooks include an answer section. Use this section wisely. It is intended to help you check your work after you have completed it; don't use it as a shortcut.

Recognize the Importance of Visual Aids

Writers often use **visual aids** (photographs, maps, charts, graphs, etc.) to clarify or emphasize ideas, reveal trends, condense information, or illustrate a point of view. For example, two photos are included with "Comparing Online and Traditional Education" (p. 26). These photos help readers visualize the single greatest difference between online and traditional education: the ability to participate in a classroom and learn alongside other students. Visual aids can also help readers visualize a place or setting, understand a complicated process, or remember important information.

Visual aids are often classified in two categories: (1) **images** and image-based visual aids, such as photographs, cartoons, advertisements, and illustrations, and (2) **graphics**, which generally present or summarize information. Table 2.5 summarizes the most common types of graphics (pie charts, bar graphs, line graphs, tables, and diagrams and flowcharts).

Table 2.5   Types of Graphics

Type of Graphic	Purpose	Example
Pie (Circle) Charts	To show the relationships among parts of a whole; to show how given parts of a unit are divided or classified	A chart showing the proportions of different racial and ethnic groups in the U.S. population
Bar Graphs	To make comparisons between quantities or amounts	A graph showing college enrollments (in millions) for men and women for selected years between 1970 and 2000
Line Graphs	To show changes in a variable over time; to compare relationships between two or more variables	A graph showing the change in median and average prices of new homes sold in the United States for selected years
Tables	To organize and condense data; to compare and classify information	A table showing how many calories men and women in various age groups need daily
Diagrams and Flowcharts	To explain processes or procedures; to show how things work	A diagram showing the process by which the U.S. Constitution can be amended

Writers often include image-based visuals, such as photographs, with their writing to provoke an emotional response or support their thesis. For example, an essay arguing for increased U.S. aid to poor countries may use a photograph of a malnourished child to elicit the reader's sympathy.

To achieve a basic comprehension of the visual aids, preview them when you preview the reading. As you read the text, follow cues in the writing to look at visuals: Many readings will tell you when to look at the visual aid, using a phrase like "As the photograph below illustrates." (Finish reading the sentence before jumping to the graphic.) To understand complicated graphics, you may need to go back and forth several times between the text and the visual aid.

As you read the visual aid, consider the questions in Table 2.6.

Exercise 2.7

For each of the following situations, discuss which type of graphic might be used to advance the writer's purpose and help the reader grasp the material most easily.

1. To show the percentage of Americans belonging to each of the four major religions in 2015

2. To show percentages of registered voters who participated in each presidential election from 1988 to 2016 for five age groups

3. To compare percentages of African Americans, whites, Latinos, and Asian Americans who divorced in each decade from 1970 to 2010

4. To show the process by which a legal immigrant can become a citizen

5. To show which regions of the United States have average, below-average, and above-average divorce rates

After Reading: Reviewing the Material

To improve your comprehension and recall, you can use four strategies after reading:

1. Conduct an immediate review.

2. Write a summary.

3. Draw a graphic organizer.

4. Create an outline.

Choose the strategies that fit your purpose for reading and the nature of the material.

Table 2.6 Guidelines for Reading Visual Aids

Questions	Tips
What is your first reaction?	What is the visual aid's general subject? What did you notice first, and how did it affect you?
Is the visual aid accompanied by a title, caption, or other explanatory text?	Read any surrounding information and determine how it relates to the visual aid. Do the title and caption fully explain the visual? What is stated and what is left unstated?
What exactly does the visual aid show?	Examine the visual aid closely to determine what exactly is being shown. Do any particular parts of the visual aid stand out? Is there an action that is taking place or has taken place? If the image is primarily informative, what type of information is being presented? Examine the foreground, background, main subject, and details of photographs. How do these elements relate to one another? Do any details stand out?
How is the visual aid organized?	Read all column headings, labels, and other text used to organize the visual aid. Use the *legend* (a guide to the colors, symbols, terms, and other information in the visual aid) to understand the image's key elements.
What is the purpose of the visual aid?	Identify why the writer has included a visual aid and what it contributes to the reading. For example, has the writer included it to illustrate or emphasize a particular point?
What does the visual aid mean?	Interpret the meaning of the image, both alone and within the context of the reading. What is the intended message? If words are used within the image, how do they shape the visual aid's overall meaning?
What impact does the visual aid make?	The visual aid's effect on the reader is an important part of the reading experience. Consider what questions or issues the image raises or answers.

Conduct an Immediate Review

If you spend a few minutes reviewing what you read *immediately after you finish the reading*, you can dramatically increase the amount of information you remember.

To review material after reading, use the same steps you used to preview the reading (see pp. 28–29). Reviewing does not take much time. Your goal is to quickly touch on each main point once again. Pay particular attention to the following elements of the reading:

- the headings
- your highlighting
- the conclusion

As you read each heading, look at the prereading questions you composed and see if you can answer them. If you cannot, reread the appropriate section until you can. Also look over your annotations and highlighted material. Think of immediate review as a way of solidifying in your mind what you have just learned.

Write a Summary

As part of your review, it is helpful to write a summary of the reading. A **summary** is a brief statement of the reading's major points with no supporting details. You may not realize it, but you probably compose summaries frequently. For example, when a friend asks, "What was the movie about?" you reply with a summary of the plot but do not include specific scenes or dialogue.

Summarizing is an excellent way of checking your understanding. If you have difficulty writing a summary, you most likely do not fully understand what is important in the reading. A good summary is also an excellent study tool to help you review for exams.

In general, a summary should be less than one-fifth the length of the original (and can be much shorter than that for long readings). Table 2.7 provides guidelines for writing an effective summary. ☙

The following is an effective summary of "Comparing Online and Traditional Education."

> Morgan Lowrie completed her college degree by taking a mixture of on-campus and online courses. In "Comparing Online and Traditional Education," she outlines the pros and cons of distance-learning courses. Online courses have a flexibility that helps working adults and

LaunchPad Solo
macmillan learning   Visit **LaunchPad Solo for Readers and Writers > Summarizing** for extra practice in the skills covered in this section.

Table 2.7   Guidelines for Writing an Effective Summary

Guidelines	Tips
Complete the entire reading assignment before attempting to write anything.	Begin writing your summary only during your second reading.
Use your highlighting and notes.	Any highlighting or marginal notes you made while reading will help you choose the important points to include in your summary.
Write your summary as you reread the assignment.	Work paragraph by paragraph, reading and then writing your summary.
Early in the summary, include a sentence that states the author's thesis (the reading's single most important idea) in your own words.	Being able to state the thesis in your own words shows that you fully understand the thesis.
To avoid plagiarism, be sure to express the author's ideas in your own words.	If you want to include the author's words, be sure to use quotation marks.
Include all — and only — the reading's key points.	Your summary should be a factual, brief reporting of the key idea. Do not include your own impressions, reactions, or responses.
Present the ideas in the order in which they appear in the original.	Be sure to use transitional words and phrases as you move from one idea to another.
Read your summary to determine if it contains sufficient information.	Would your summary be understandable and meaningful to someone who had not read the original? If not, revise your summary to include additional information.

parents fit their studies into their lives, schedules, and family duties. With online classes, students do not waste precious time commuting. The technologies used in distance education are improving and help students record important information and stay in touch with instructors and classmates. However, distance learning has drawbacks.

First, not all courses are offered online, which may limit students to particular majors and classes. Second, online courses require a great deal of reading and writing. Students weak in these areas may find distance learning challenging. Third, it can be difficult and expensive to find someone to oversee the final exam for an online course. Fourth, online classes require students to work independently. Because they're not on a college campus, online learners miss the classroom experience. So, despite the advantages of online courses, Lowrie would have preferred taking courses on campus, even though distance learning helped her complete her degree. She believes distance-education students miss too many of the opportunities that traditional students have (meeting new people and getting involved in student activities). She recommends campus courses over distance courses whenever possible, even if this choice requires sacrifices. Lowrie concludes that the online college experience is very different from, and not as rewarding as, the campus college experience.

Notice that the writer expresses Lowrie's thesis in his own words and that the order of ideas parallels the order in Lowrie's essay.

One good way to identify what to include in a summary is to write a **summary note** for most or all paragraphs. Summary notes are marginal annotations that briefly state the key issue presented in each paragraph. You can easily convert these notes into sentences for your summary. For example, a summary note for paragraph 6 of Lowrie's article might read, "technology promotes communication and lecture recording." This note could then be used to create the following sentence in the summary: "The technologies used in distance education are improving and help students record important information and stay in touch with instructors and classmates."

Exercise 2.8

Read "Talking a Stranger through the Night" (Chapter 10, p. 200) and write a summary of it.

Draw a Graphic Organizer

A **graphic organizer** is a diagram of the reading's structure and main points. Think of a graphic organizer as a visual means of tracking the author's flow of ideas. You will see that graphic organizers are used throughout this text as a tool for both readers and writers.

Figure 2.2 shows the format of a graphic organizer. When you draw a graphic organizer, be sure it includes all the key elements shown here. This is a general format that you can adapt to individual readings. An example of a graphic organizer for "Comparing Online and Traditional Education" appears in Figure 2.3. As you work through the organizer in Figure 2.3, reread the essay, paragraph by paragraph.

Figure 2.2   Key Elements to Include in a Graphic Organizer

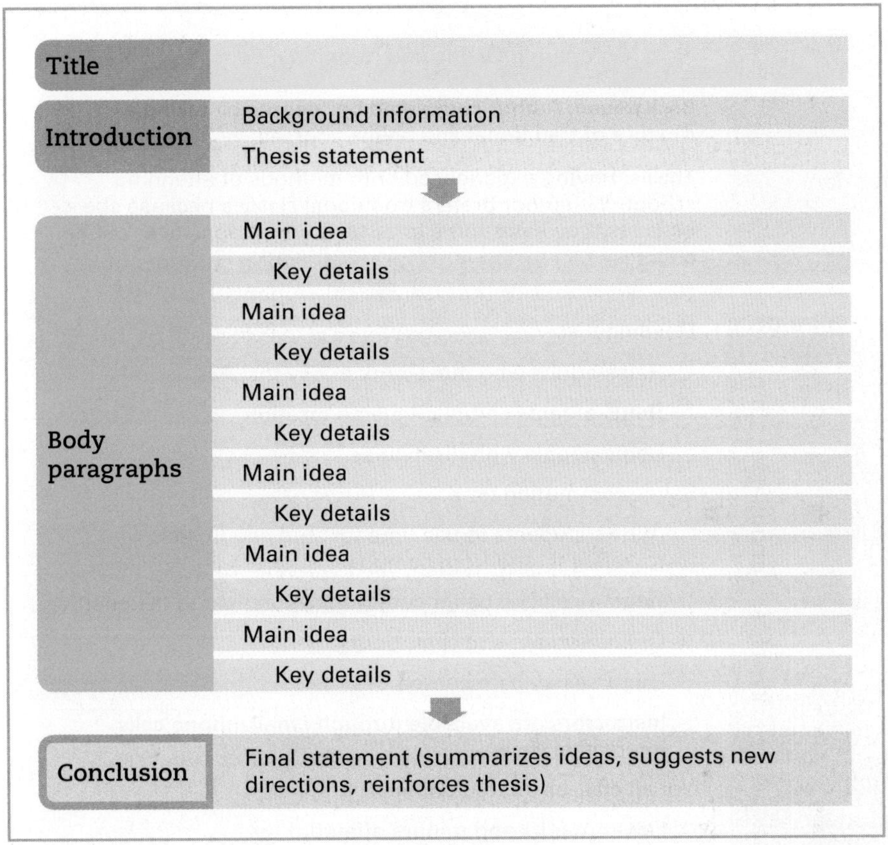

Title	
Introduction	Background information
	Thesis statement

(downward arrow)

Body paragraphs	Main idea
	Key details
	Main idea
	Key details
	Main idea
	Key details
	Main idea
	Key details
	Main idea
	Key details
	Main idea
	Key details

(downward arrow)

Conclusion	Final statement (summarizes ideas, suggests new directions, reinforces thesis)

Create an Outline to Help You Study

Outlining is an effective way of organizing information and discovering relationships between ideas. To be effective, an outline must show the relative importance of ideas. The easiest way to achieve this goal is to use the following format.

I. **First Major Topic**
   A. First major idea
      1. First important detail
      2. Second important detail
   B. Second major idea
      1. First important detail
         a. Minor detail or example
         b. Minor detail or example
      2. Second important detail

II. **Second Major Topic**
   A. First major idea

Figure 2.3   **Graphic Organizer for "Comparing Online and Traditional Education"**

Title	Comparing Online and Traditional Education
Introduction	**Background:** Author completed her degree by taking a mixture of traditional and online courses.
	Thesis: Having experienced both methods of attending school, the author prefers traditional classes because she believes they have some important advantages over online courses.

Body paragraphs	**Benefits of online education**	Flexibility
		Helps adults who must work to pay the bills
		Helps parents complete their education
		Helps people with disabilities
		Saves commuting time
		Allows students to use time for studying instead of traveling to and from campus
		Technology allows better communication than in the past
		Online forums and chat rooms
		Lectures can be recorded
		Instructors are available through email, phone calls, interactive chats
	Disadvantages of online education	Not all classes offered online
		Fewer majors and minors offered
		Narrower curriculum
		Fewer classes to choose from
		Heavy emphasis on reading and writing
		No credit for participation, group projects, oral presentations
		Difficult and expensive to find proctor for final exam
		Less interactivity
		Need for self-motivation and good time-management skills
		No lively discussions, anecdotes, jokes

Conclusion	Author believes in the value and opportunity of online education but believes that students are better off attending traditional classes and spending time on campus, which allows for greater social development and a richer college experience.

Notice that the most important ideas are closest to the left margin, while more minor ideas and supporting details are found toward the middle of the page. In textbooks, headings often form the basis for an effective outline.

Exercise 2.9

Read "The Nature of Stress" in Chapter 13 on page 351, and prepare an outline of it.

Answers to Exercise 2.1: 1. False; 2. True; 3. False; 4. True; 5. True

- Understand what critical reading and critical thinking are.
- Analyze what you read by considering purpose, style, audience, and language features.
- Evaluate what you read by examining bias, source, reliability, relevance, sufficiency, and underlying assumptions.
- Analyze and evaluate visual aids.
- Respond to texts and visual aids using journal entries and response papers.

3

Critical Reading and Thinking Strategies

Rawpixel.com/Shutterstock

Reflect on a Visual Text

The photo shows one way many people get news these days. Suppose you are taking a course in mass media and your instructor asks you to examine one or more online publications and consider how the news is reported and how different viewpoints are expressed.

1 **Ask yourself questions.** What types of news stories do you think deserve reporting? Who decides? Are all stories reported fairly and objectively? What photos and graphics are chosen to accompany news stories? Can they influence readers' responses to the stories themselves?

2 **Brainstorm ideas.** Write a list of several current issues in the news. Choose one and think of several different photographs or graphics that could be used to accompany a news report on the issue. Try to think of photographs or graphics that represent different views on the issue. →

3 **Write.** Write a paragraph explaining how two different photographs or graphics may create different responses to the same news story.

To write about the influence of the photographs or graphics you had to think and react critically; you had to go beyond basic understanding by analyzing and evaluating the photos or graphics. This process is known as **critical thinking**. A related process, **critical reading**, involves reacting to what you read and evaluating and responding to the author's ideas. All of the critical-reading strategies you'll learn in this chapter build on the basic comprehension and understanding skills you learned in Chapter 2, "Active Reading." ✿

What Is Critical Thinking?

In college, you are expected not only to memorize facts but also to analyze them, develop your own opinions, and conduct your own research. College instructors expect you to *think critically* and not simply accept something you've read or heard as "the truth." Thinking critically also means not rejecting an idea just because it contradicts what you currently believe or previously learned. In this case, *critical* does not mean "negative." Rather, it means "thoughtful and analytical" — in other words, thinking deeply about the information and ideas you encounter.

Developing your critical-thinking and critical-reading skills has many benefits. Critical thinking will help you

- distinguish good information from incomplete, inaccurate information
- become a savvy consumer who compares options and avoids scams
- weigh social issues, examine politicians' campaign platforms and promises, and analyze the political and economic motives of people and businesses
- recognize trends, analyze causes and effects, and solve problems
- determine whether research sources and Internet sites are reliable or unreliable

The section that follows provides numerous strategies for analyzing what you read.

✿ **LaunchPad Solo** Visit **LaunchPad Solo for Readers and Writers > Critical Reading** for
macmillan learning   extra practice in the skills covered in this chapter.

Strategies for Analyzing What You Read

Analyzing a piece of writing involves examining how the author wrote it. It involves considering why the author wrote it, for whom it was written, what the writer didn't say as well as what he or she said, and how the writer used language to achieve his or her purpose. It is also important to consider what the author suggests but does not directly state.

Examine the Author's Purpose, Style, and Intended Audience

Writers have many different **purposes** for writing. Sometimes their purpose is to entertain; other times their purpose may be to educate, to advocate for a particular cause, or to elicit a particular emotion from the reader. The writer's purpose determines the words she uses, the details she provides, and the style in which she writes. **Style** is a general term for the characteristics that make a piece of writing unique. For example, one writer's style may be very spare, with short sentences and common words. Another writer's style may be more flowery, with very elaborate descriptions and complicated words.

The writer's **intended audience** is the group of people the writer expects to read his work. Writers often adjust their style and content to meet the needs of different audiences. For example, a sports writer may write two different essays about the most recent Super Bowl. If his intended audience is devoted football fans, the writer will likely refer to specific plays and highly publicized stories about the personal lives of the players and coaches, assuming that the audience already knows about the players. Such an essay might appear in *Sports Illustrated*, a magazine read by sports fans. If the intended audience is people who would rather read a book than watch a football game, the writer will likely focus on different aspects of the game. For example, he might talk about why Super Bowl Sunday has become a great American tradition and why football is so important in American culture. He will probably explain football terms, rather than assume the audience knows them. Such an essay might appear in a general-interest newspaper or magazine like *USA Today* or *Time*.

Exercise 3.1

Based on each of the following essay titles, predict the author's purpose and intended audience.

1. Three Simple Ways to Stay Healthy
2. Ten Reasons We Need a New Mayor
3. IRA or 401(k): Which Is the Better Retirement Solution?

Examine Word Choice

Words are powerful. Words can inspire, comfort, educate, and calm. But they can also inflame, annoy, and deceive. Professional writers understand that word choices influence readers and listeners, and they choose words that will help them achieve their objectives. Consider the following aspects of word choice.

DENOTATIONS AND CONNOTATIONS

A **denotation** is a word's literal meaning. For example, the denotation of *obese* is "very fat." A **connotation** is an additional meaning or association that a word has taken on. Often, a word's connotation has a much stronger effect on readers or listeners than its denotation does. A politician with a stocky build might be described as "pleasingly plump" (which carries a pleasant or jolly connotation), as "quite a bit overweight" (which is an objective-sounding statement), or as "morbidly obese" (which gives readers a negative impression).

Reading ⓘ Writing   Vocabulary and Language

The Reader's Perspective	The Writer's Perspective
Pay close attention to the words that a writer chooses. Often they reveal his or her attitudes and feelings toward the subject. They may also reveal bias (see p. 63).	Words are the most fundamental tool in a writer's toolbox. By choosing the correct word you can convey not only a specific meaning, but also many additional associations that will produce the desired effect on the reader.

Exercise 3.2

For each of the following words, provide one word with a similar denotation but a positive connotation and another word with a similar denotation but a negative connotation.

> **Example:** Group (of people)   Positive: *audience*
>
> Negative: *mob*

1. choosy
2. cheap
3. boss

4. bold
5. walk

EUPHEMISMS, DOUBLESPEAK, AND OTHER TYPES OF FIGURATIVE LANGUAGE

A **euphemism** is a word or phrase used to avoid an unpleasant, embarrassing, or otherwise objectionable word. For example, a used-car dealer may advertise that it sells "pre-owned fleet vehicles." **Doublespeak** is a type of euphemism that uses deliberately unclear or evasive language. For example, a company may say that it is "moving into international sourcing" when it eliminates jobs in the United States and sends them overseas. Euphemisms and doublespeak seek to sugarcoat an unpleasant reality, and as a critical thinker you should always be alert for them, particularly when reading about politics and business.

Euphemisms and doublespeak are just two of the many types of colorful figures of speech in the English language. Table 3.1 summarizes the figures of speech you will encounter in your reading.

Table 3.1   Figures of Speech and Other Features of Language

Figure of Speech	Explanation	Example
Allusion	A reference to a person, place, thing, or literary work	Jackson displayed *Herculean* strength. (Hercules is a Greek hero known for strength and courage.)
Cliché	An overused expression that seldom carries specific meaning	Don't count your chickens before they are hatched.
Connotative Meaning	The feelings and associations that accompany a word	Both *untidy* and *grubby* mean "messy," but *grubby* suggests something dirty as well.
Doublespeak	Deliberately unclear or evasive language	The company is *downsizing its staff.* (firing employees)
Euphemism	Words or phrases used in place of others that would be unpleasant, embarrassing, or otherwise objectionable	The newspaper advertised *previously owned vehicles.* (used cars)
Foreign Words and Phrases	Words that are taken directly, without translation, from another language, often French or Latin	The visiting dignitary committed a *faux pas.* (social blunder or mistake)

Table 3.1   (continued)

Figure of Speech	Explanation	Example
Hyperbole	A deliberate and obvious exaggeration	I could eat 40 pounds of that chocolate!
Idiom	Phrase that has a meaning other than what the words literally mean	My role in the debate was to serve as *devil's advocate*. (one who takes a position for the sake of argument, not necessarily believing in it)
Imagery	Language that creates an impression by appealing to the reader's physical senses, most often sight	The rich carpet of green grass glinted and rippled in the gentle breeze.
Jargon	Specialized words used in particular academic fields or by particular groups and not readily understood by the general public	Publishing language: trim size and bulk. (trim size = book pages' length and width; bulk = book pages' thickness)
Metaphor	An implied comparison, suggesting some likeness between two things without using the word *like* or *as*	The woman spoke politely to the gardener, but *icicles were hanging on her every word*. (she spoke in a cold, unfriendly manner)
Personification	Attributing human traits to nonhuman beings or inanimate objects	As we walked through the jungle, the vines grabbed at our ankles with their wiry fingers.
Restrictive Word Meaning	A meaning of a commonly used word that is unique to a particular field or discipline	The word *foul* in baseball has a specific meaning.
Simile	An explicit comparison between two things, typically introduced by the word *like* or *as*	The surface of the wooden table shone *like a mirror*.

Exercise 3.3

1. Much media coverage is devoted to people who come to the United States from other countries without permission from the U.S. government or who stay after their permission to visit has expired. Two terms are often used to refer to these people: *illegal aliens* and *undocumented immigrants*. Discuss which term has a more negative connotation and which seems more neutral. Why does each term carry the connotations it does? Are they euphemisms? Why or why not?

2. Brainstorm a list of euphemisms and doublespeak currently in use in business, politics, or the media.

Distinguish Fact from Opinion

Sources of information, including textbooks and essays, often differ greatly in their presentation of **facts** and **opinions**. Table 3.2 summarizes the differences between fact and opinion.

Textbooks present factual information that has been checked and rechecked, often over many years, and is, therefore, highly reliable. In addition, when textbook authors write about controversial topics, they usually explain different viewpoints. For example, a marketing textbook that discusses the value of packaging will usually describe the benefits of good packaging (it grabs consumers' attention and makes them more willing to buy the product) as well as the drawbacks (much packaging is expensive, wasteful, and bad for the environment).

In contrast, essays and other reading materials—newspapers, magazines, advertisements, Web sites, books—often present a mixture of fact and opinion without distinguishing between the two. For example, an advertisement may

Table 3.2 Fact and Opinion

Facts . . .	Opinions . . .
. . . are objective statements of information that can be verified—that is, their truth can be established with evidence. Facts can be checked in trustworthy sources such as online dictionaries and Web reference sources like refdesk.com.	. . . are subjective—that is, they differ by individual. They make a claim based on attitudes, feelings, or beliefs. These claims cannot be established definitely as either true or false, at least at the present time. Often they put forth a particular position or agenda.
Examples	**Examples**
• Many people who smoke marijuana do not go on to use more dangerous drugs.	• Marijuana use will probably be legalized in all fifty states by 2020.
• Texting while driving has caused many accidents.	• People who text while driving should be fined and have their driver's licenses revoked.

follow some facts about a car's warranty with the opinion that the car maker offers the best warranty coverage.

Reading ⊕ Writing   Fact and Opinion

The Reader's Perspective	The Writer's Perspective
Much of what you read will be factual information, and the reading will include evidence that the stated facts are indeed true. When you read an opinion, recognize that you have the right to disagaree with it. Be sure to look for evidence the writer uses to support his or her opinion and feel free to dismiss the opinion when evidence is not provided.	When you seek to inform, you will generally fill your writing with facts. When you seek to persuade, you will often combine fact and opinion. Sometimes writers signal opinion statements with words and phrases such as "in my opinion," "I think," "it seems," or "perhaps."

Exercise 3.4

For two of the following topics, write one statement of fact and one statement of opinion. Use the Internet to locate factual information.

1. Voter turnout rates in presidential elections
2. Cell-phone use in classrooms
3. Alternative energy solutions
4. Social media (for example, Facebook)

Analyze the Author's Tone

Have you ever noticed that people can use the same words to mean different things in different situations? The *tone* of the words in two situations can convey very different meanings. Consider a police officer who pulls you over for speeding and says, "Could you please step out of the car?" His tone is likely to be different from that of an employee at a car wash who says the same words so that he can vacuum your car's interior.

A reading's **tone** refers to the way it sounds to readers, and it is influenced by the writer's approach to her topic and audience. Recognizing a writer's tone will help you analyze and evaluate the message and its effect on you.

Writers reveal tone primarily through word choice and stylistic features, such as sentence patterns and length. The following are some examples of tone.

- **Disapproval.** You really need to discipline your children better.
- **Surprise.** I was sitting there, minding my own business, when this stranger came up to me and asked me how old I am!

- **Admiration.** I am amazed by your patience, kindness, and generosity.
- **Gratitude.** My mother and I were very touched by the beautiful flowers you sent when my father passed away.

Table 3.3 lists some words commonly used to describe tone.

Table 3.3   Words Commonly Used to Describe Tone

angry	disapproving	informative	persuasive
apathetic	earnest	instructive	pessimistic
arrogant	flippant	ironic	playful
assertive	forgiving	irreverent	reverent
bitter	formal	joyful	righteous
caustic	frustrated	loving	sarcastic
cheerful	hateful	malicious	satiric
compassionate	humorous	mocking	serious
condemning	impassioned	nostalgic	sympathetic
condescending	incredulous	objective	vindictive
cynical	indignant	optimistic	worried
detached			

Many writers and speakers are passionate about their beliefs, and sometimes they have a personal charisma that makes their audience more receptive to their message. Be sure not to let yourself be distracted by a writer or speaker's tone or commitment to a cause. As a critical thinker, your job is to analyze words, facts, and tone to determine their effect on you and whether you are being told the complete story. It is also important to watch for subtle or hidden tones within a message. For example, although a writer may use an apparently sympathetic tone in describing a political candidate's recent questionable financial deals ("Poor Mayor Jones must not have realized that taking money for political favors is illegal"), the apparent sympathy may really be sarcasm — the writer's way of criticizing the candidate.

Reading ⓘ Writing   Tone

The Reader's Perspective	The Writer's Perspective
As a reader, you often form a brief "relationship" with the writer, thinking about whether the writer is fair, funny, smart, a person who would make a good friend, and so on. The writer's tone is what creates these impressions and helps you form this brief relationship.	Before beginning to write, you must determine your attitude toward the topic. You convey that attitude to your readers through your tone and choice of words.

Exercise 3.5

Describe the tone of each of the following statements. Refer to Table 3.3 for specific descriptors if necessary. Circle the words in each statement that provide clues to its tone.

1. When you are backpacking, you can reduce the risk of back injury by adjusting your pack so that most of its weight is on your hip belt rather than on your shoulder straps.

2. Do you eat canned tuna? Then you are at least partially responsible for the deaths of thousands of innocent dolphins, who are mercilessly slaughtered by fishermen in their quest for tuna.

3. The penalty for creating and launching a computer virus should include a personal apology to every person who was affected by the virus, and each apology should be typed — without errors! — on a manual typewriter.

4. Piles of solid waste threaten to ruin our environment, pointing to the urgent need for better disposal methods and strategies for lowering the rate of waste generation.

5. All poets seek to convey emotion and the complete range of human feeling, but the only poet who fully accomplished this goal was William Shakespeare.

Exercise 3.6

Consider the following situation: A developer has received permission to bulldoze an entire city block of burned-out tenement buildings and abandoned factories. In their place, the developer plans to build a community of three hundred upscale condominiums for people who work in the city and want to live close to their jobs.

Write three different sentences (or paragraphs) that react to this news. Make the tone of your first sentence outraged. Make the tone of your second sentence joyful. Make the tone of your third sentence nostalgic.

Look for Purposeful Omissions

Writers and speakers sometimes mislead by omission — that is, by what they do *not* say. They may leave out essential background or context, include only details that favor their position, or ignore contradictory evidence. They may also use the passive voice ("damage was done") to avoid taking or assigning responsibility for an action, or they may use vague nouns and pronouns ("someone did it") to avoid specifying exactly to what or whom they are referring.

Consider an essay written by a woman who has homeschooled her children. As an advocate of homeschooling, she is likely to emphasize her children's educational progress. However, she may not address arguments made by opponents of homeschooling — for example, that homeschooled children sometimes feel lonely or isolated from their peers. She also may summarize a research study that details the academic excellence of homeschooled children. But she may not mention other studies that have found that homeschooled children do not differ in academic achievement from traditionally educated students.

Ask yourself the questions in Table 3.4 to be sure you are getting full and complete information. To answer these questions, you may need to do some additional reading or research.

Table 3.4   Questions to Determine Purposeful Omissions

- Has any important information been omitted? What, if anything, am I not being told?

- Has the writer or speaker failed to report any evidence that contradicts his or her position?

- Has the writer or speaker selectively reported details to further his or her cause?

- Is there another side to this argument or aspect of this topic that I should consider?

- On the basis of my own experiences, how do I evaluate this material?

Exercise 3.7

Read the following common scenarios. In each situation, what information is being withheld from you? In other words, what other information do you need to evaluate the situation?

1. You see a TV ad for a fast-food restaurant that shows a huge hamburger topped with pickles, onions, and tomatoes. The announcer says, "For a limited time, get your favorite burger for only ninety-nine cents!"
2. You open your mailbox and find a letter from a credit-card company. The letter invites you to open a charge account with no annual fee and offers you instant credit if you return the attached form in a postage-paid envelope.
3. You get an offer from an online health food store that appears to be a good deal. As part of your introductory package, you can order five vitamin supplements for only fifteen dollars, plus shipping and handling.

Make Reasonable Inferences

In some reading materials, such as textbooks and scholarly journals, the writers spell everything out clearly so that you don't have to guess at their conclusions. In other types of reading materials — particularly essays, articles, and advertising copy — writers directly state some ideas but hint at, or **imply**, others. You, the reader, must pick up on the clues and determine the writer's unstated messages.

An **inference** is an educated, reasonable guess based on available facts and information, your own experiences, and the content provided in the reading. Inferences are logical connections between what the writer states directly and what he or she implies. Consider the following situation.

> You are walking down a dark city street when you notice someone following you. When you cross the street, so does he. When you turn a corner, so does he. As you run to get to your apartment, the man picks up speed and starts gaining on you.

In this situation, you can reasonably infer that the man is a criminal who is following you and may wish to rob you. It would not be reasonable to infer that the man is a long-lost friend or a lottery agent who wants to tell you that you've won a million dollars.

Making inferences requires active reading and critical thinking. Developing your inference skills requires practice, but here are some suggestions for getting started.

1. **First, understand the author's purpose and the literal meaning.** Before you can make reasonable inferences, you need a clear understanding of the author's purpose and a reading's thesis statement, its main ideas, and the supporting details.

2. **Pay attention to details.** Sometimes a specific detail provides a hint regarding what the writer has left unsaid. When you notice a striking or unusual detail (whether in a description, an image, or a reported conversation), ask yourself, Why is this detail included? For example, read the following passage.

> Susan attends college, works a part-time job, takes care of her two children, and cooks dinner for her husband every night. You'd never know she has MS (multiple sclerosis). She is planning to become an attorney specializing in environmental law, so she's attending a community college now, and plans to transfer to the university.

What is the writer's reason for including the detail about Susan's medical condition? She is implying that people who have MS can still maintain normal lives.

3. **Look at the facts.** Consider the complete set of facts provided by the writer. Ask yourself, What is the writer trying to suggest with all of these facts? What conclusion does the complete set of facts support? Suppose a writer presents the following facts.

> It's extremely difficult to get in touch with anyone from Sam's Landscaping Service. Nobody answers the phone or returns messages. Technicians do not show up to conduct lawn maintenance on any specific

schedule. The bills sent by Sam's Landscaping Service to customers often include charges for services never performed.

From these sentences, the inference is clear: Sam's Landscaping Service is an unreliable, unethical business that you should never hire.

4. **Examine word choice.** A writer's choice of words often conveys his or her feelings toward the subject. Look for words with numerous connotations and ask yourself why the writer chose these words.

5. **Make sure you can support your inference.** Valid inferences are based on fact, context, and personal experiences. Be sure you have ample evidence to back up any inference you make.

Reading ⓘ Writing   Infer vs. Imply

The Reader's Perspective	The Writer's Perspective
As a reader, you *infer* by "reading between the lines" of what the author has written.	As a writer, you *imply* (as opposed to state outright) through your choice of words and the details you provide.

Exercise 3.8

Read the following selection, and then answer the questions that follow.

Dissatisfied with your current life? Would you like to become someone else? Maybe someone rich? Maybe someone with no responsibilities? You can. Join a world populated with virtual people and live out your fantasy.

For some, the appeal is strong. Second Life, one of several Internet sites that offer an alternative virtual reality, has exploded in popularity. Of its 8 million "residents," 450,000 spend twenty to forty hours a week in their second life.

—James Henslin, *Sociology: A Down-to-Earth Approach*, 11th edition

1. What is the purpose of this brief passage?
2. What can you infer from the phrase "live out your fantasy"?
3. Why does the author put the word *residents* in quotation marks?
4. What can you infer from the statistics quoted in the passage?

Strategies for Evaluating What You Read

Once you have understood and analyzed a reading, you will be prepared to take the final step in the critical-thinking process: evaluation. When you evaluate a reading, you form your own judgment regarding its validity and the strength of its argument. Has the writer presented convincing support for the thesis statement and main ideas?

Understanding, analysis, and evaluation often take place simultaneously. In other words, you may be analyzing and evaluating the reading while you read it. To evaluate what you read, you need to do the following:

- Identify bias.
- Evaluate information sources.
- Evaluate the reliability of information.
- Examine the relevance and sufficiency of evidence.
- Recognize assumptions.

For additional coverage of how to evaluate sources, refer to Chapter 19, pp. 612–14.

Identify Bias

Bias refers to a writer's prejudice in favor of or against the topic he is writing about. Writers are biased when they present only one side of an argument, without considering other viewpoints. For example, an essay biased against amnesty programs for undocumented immigrants will not recognize the benefits of allowing these people to become U.S. citizens. Similarly, an essay biased in favor of such amnesty programs will not recognize the drawbacks of granting privileges to those who have broken the law.

In some reading materials, the author's bias is obvious. In other materials, the bias may be hidden or subtle. In these cases, it is up to you to discover the writer's agenda. To determine if a reading selection is biased, ask yourself the questions in Table 3.5.

Exercise 3.9

Review the brief passage about virtual reality and Second Life in Exercise 3.8. Do you detect bias in this selection? If you do, point to specific elements in the passage that show bias. If you do not, explain why you feel the selection is not biased.

Table 3.5   Guidelines for Identifying Bias

Questions	Tips
Is the writer acting as an objective reporter, presenting well-documented facts on all sides of the argument?	If the answer to this question is *yes*, then the author likely is *not* biased.
Does the writer present only one side of the story? Is he providing only positive or only negative information?	If the answer to either of these questions is *yes*, the author likely *is* biased.
Does the writer feel strongly about the issue?	Analyze the writer's tone to determine her attitude toward the subject. The stronger the author's feelings about the subject, the more biased she is likely to be.
Do the words used in the reading generate a strongly positive or strongly negative impression in the reader?	Pay close attention to word connotations. Writers who repeatedly use words with exclusively positive or exclusively negative connotations tend to be biased.

Evaluate Information Sources

We live in a world of sensory overload. We are surrounded by news, opinions, advertisements, and other kinds of information everywhere we look (or listen). You need to evaluate this avalanche of information. Begin by thinking about the sources of the information you read. Ask yourself the following questions about each.

- How factually accurate is it trying to be?
- Is it written by people with valid experiences?
- Has it been reviewed by editors or experts in the field?
- Is it biased in favor of or against a particular person or viewpoint?

TEXTBOOKS

Textbooks are usually very reliable sources of information. For basic information on any topic, a textbook is often the best place to start.

ESSAYS

Because essays usually reflect the writer's viewpoint, they often have a built-in bias. When reading an essay, identify the writer's purpose and agenda. The author's background and credentials will provide clues.

NEWSPAPERS

Newspapers vary in the quality of their reporting. Some newspapers are meticulous about obtaining accurate and complete information and checking facts before publishing a story. Other newspapers are little more than gossip sheets.

Most newspapers have an editorial page or opinion section in which the paper's editors and contributors offer their views on current issues and other topics. Look for biases as you read these sections. Also keep in mind that some newspapers tend to be liberal in their views while others are conservative. These tendencies often show up not just on the editorial page but also in the way news stories are presented.

A newer category of news reporting, *advertorial*, combines a paid advertisement with factual reporting. For example, a local business may pay a newspaper to write a story about the business, describe its services, and present information about the owners. Advertorial content looks just like the content of traditional news stories, so ask yourself, Is it possible that this "article" is actually a paid advertisement? If it seems as if it might be an ad, look closely at the layout; often, there's a small heading stating that the content is an advertisement.

MAGAZINES

Although magazines can be excellent sources of information, their content, like that of newspapers and television, is influenced by the perspectives and biases of their editors and writers. Magazines also vary in their attention to careful reporting and fact-checking.

THE INTERNET

Because it is free and easy to access, the Internet is the first place many people go for breaking news and research. However, anyone can create a Web site and post anything on it, whether accurate or not. Be particularly cautious when reading blogs (online diaries or columns), which contain personal opinions that are not reviewed by editors. For more information on evaluating Internet sources, see Chapter 19, "Finding and Using Sources."

SCHOLARLY JOURNALS

Scholarly journals report research and developments in a particular academic or professional field. Examples include the *Journal of Psychology* and the *Journal of the American Medical Association*. Journals tend to be highly trustworthy sources because the journals' editors accept only articles that have been evaluated and approved by other authorities in the field.

Exercise 3.10

On your own or as part of a class discussion, evaluate the reliability of each of the following information sources. If necessary, do some research to learn more about them. How seriously should you take each source? Which exist solely for entertainment? Which are likely to be biased? Which would be acceptable as references in an academic research paper?

1. An opinion column in the *Washington Post* (newspaper)
2. A feature story in the *National Enquirer* (newspaper / magazine)
3. An editorial in the *Wall Street Journal* (newspaper)
4. *Meet the Press* (a TV news program)
5. www.thesmokinggun.com
6. www.census.gov
7. www.tmz.com
8. An article in the *Journal of Economic Research*
9. Wikipedia (www.wikipedia.org)
10. A feature article in *InStyle* magazine (a women's fashion magazine)

Evaluate the Reliability of Information

In general, the most reliable information is based on solid **evidence**. Just as police look for evidence to discover who committed a crime, you must look for the evidence that supports an assertion made by a writer. If the writer offers little or no evidence, you should question the assertion. Table 3.6 summarizes common types of evidence and the pros and cons of each.

Exercise 3.11

Consider each of the following statements and the context in which it is made. What types of information are missing that would help you weigh the evidence and evaluate the claim being made? What further types of evidence would you need to accept or reject the claim?

1. On the label of a bag of cookies: "CONTAINS 45% LESS FAT and 0 grams of TRANS FAT!"
2. In a printed campaign flyer for mayoral candidate Mary Johnson: "My opponent, Joe Smith, has been accused of serious conflicts of interest in the awarding of city contracts during his term as mayor."
3. In large print on the cover of a novel you see at the supermarket checkout: "This novel is a . . . wild and exciting . . . ride through the rough-and-tumble days of the Gold Rush . . . full of . . . adventure and excitement. . . . Memorable." — *New York Times*

Table 3.6 Common Types of Evidence

Type	Pros	Cons
Personal Experience or Examples	• Can be powerful: No one understands cancer, for example, like a person who has survived the disease.	• Is subjective: Two people can experience the same event very differently. • May not offer enough examples to support a broad generalization.
Eyewitness Reports	• May be powerful: Witnesses often have strong convictions that their memories are reliable.	• Are often inaccurate: Many studies have shown that memory is easily influenced. • May be subjective: If two people see a man running from a burning building, one may think, "What a lucky man! He escaped from the burning building," while the other may think, "That man started the fire."
Surveys	• May be highly reliable when conducted by experienced researchers who collect responses from a wide array of subjects.	• May be misleadingly worded or administered inconsistently, or may include responses from too narrow a spectrum of respondents.
Data and Statistics	• May be collected by academic researchers and members of professional research organizations who try to be as objective and accurate as possible.	• Can be used in ways that hide the truth. Example: A soda company may claim that "90% of the people in a taste test preferred our cola to the competitor's." This may be true, but consider how many subjects were tested, whether the test was run in a neutral location, and so on.
Evidence from Scientific Experiments and Studies	• Usually considered highly reliable because experiments and studies are based on the scientific method, a set of procedures that researchers follow to investigate their hypotheses and test the results of other experiments and studies.	• May apply to only a narrow range of cases. • Can be influenced by uncontrollable factors. Example: Studies on drug safety are often contradictory. • May reflect the economic or political biases of scientists conducting the study; occasionally, results may be falsified or outcomes misrepresented.

Examine the Relevance and Sufficiency of Evidence

In general, the more evidence a writer provides to support a thesis statement, the more convincing her writing is likely to be. Suppose an essay includes the following thesis statement:

> College graduates lead happier lives than those who have only a high-school diploma.

Now suppose the writer includes just one fact to support this statement: "Research shows that most people with college degrees earn substantially more money than people without a college diploma."

Does this one piece of evidence provide enough support for the thesis statement? Most likely, you would agree that it does not. Money is not the only factor that contributes to happiness, so further evidence on other factors that make college graduates happier would be needed.

Now consider an essay that supports the thesis statement with the following pieces of evidence.

- College graduates tend to have access to better medical care and therefore live longer.

- College graduates usually have greater job stability and therefore less financial stress in their lives.

- College graduates have lower rates of divorce than people without college degrees.

- College graduates on average earn more money throughout their working lives than those who do not have a college degree.

Each of these points on its own may not be enough to provide sufficient evidence for the thesis statement, but taken together they greatly strengthen the writer's argument.

When evaluating a piece of writing, ask yourself the questions in Table 3.7.

Recognize Assumptions

An **assumption** is an idea that a writer believes to be true but does not try to prove. In many cases, assumptions are not directly stated. For example, if someone says to you, "You learned your lesson last time, didn't you?" the unstated assumption is that you made a mistake in the past and the speaker is hoping you won't make the same mistake again. Assumptions can be based on facts, opinions, beliefs, experiences, or any combination of these. They can deal with

Table 3.7   Guidelines for Evaluating the Relevance and Sufficiency of Evidence

Questions	Tips
Has the writer provided sufficient data and evidence?	Be careful about accepting the writer's conclusions if he has not given ample evidence.
Has the writer provided relevant information?	It is easy to be distracted by interesting tidbits that are not relevant to the writer's argument or thesis statement. For example, it is interesting that Harvard University's tuition is over $45,000 per year, but this fact is not relevant to the thesis statement "College graduates lead happier lives than those who have only a high-school diploma."
Is the evidence up to date?	When evaluating the relevance of information, check the year of its publication. For example, an article published in 1992 is likely to include outdated information, while an article published in 2015 is much more likely to contain information still relevant today.

what is right or wrong, good or bad, or important to the writer specifically or to society in general. For example, if a writer argues that the sale of handguns should be banned, she is assuming that the availability of handguns does more harm than good.

Reading ⊕ Writing   Assumptions

The Reader's Perspective	The Writer's Perspective
As a reader, it is your responsibility to identify the author's assumptions and then decide whether they are realistic and reasonable. Once you've identified the assumptions, you can evaluate whether essays (or other reading materials) based on these assumptions make sense and can withstand thorough critical analysis and evaluation.	Often, writers believe that readers will agree with their assumptions because the reader and the writer share a common background or set of values. For example, someone writing an article for a Christian magazine might assume that the reader shares his Christian beliefs. To determine which assumptions your readers are likely to agree with, you must first understand your intended audience.

Exercise 3.12

Answer each of the following questions.

1. You read an editorial about aggressive and violent behavior by prisoners in overcrowded prisons. The writer suggests extending the prison terms of those who behave violently as the solution to the problem. What is the author assuming about prisoners and their behavior?

2. You read a newspaper article that begins, "Now that you've retired, what will you do with the rest of your life?" What is the writer assuming about the age of her readers?

3. You read a Web article titled "Dieting with a Difference: How to Get Rid of Those Pesky Ten Pounds." What is the author assuming about his readers?

Analyzing and Evaluating Visual Aids

As discussed in Chapter 2, visual aids include images (photographs, cartoons, advertisements, illustrations) and graphics (charts, graphs, diagrams). As an active and critical reader, you should not only understand each visual aid but also analyze and evaluate all visual aids carefully. The following are some suggestions for doing so.

Photographs and Other Images

To critically evaluate photos and other images, ask yourself the questions in Table 3.8.
    Figure 3.1 is a public service advertisement from the World Wildlife Fund. Let's use the guidelines in Table 3.8 to analyze and evaluate it. What do you notice

Table 3.8 Questions for Analyzing and Evaluating Photos and Other Images

- What do you notice first?

- Are the images typical or representative of the situation or subject, or do they show exceptions to the rule?

- What is the purpose of the images? In other words, why has the author included them?

- What immediate emotional effects do the images produce?

- Would you feel as strongly about the topic of the reading if the images were not included?

- Do the images achieve their intended purpose?

- What other images might the writer have used to support key points?

- What is the role of the caption, title, or words used in or with the image?

Figure 3.1   Sample Advertisement: World Wildlife Fund

There are as few as 3,200 tigers left in the wild.
Don't wait until they're gone.

Protect the future of nature.

WWF
worldwildlife.org/tigers

World Wildlife Fund 2010 PSA "Don't wait until they're gone." Deforestation image: © Alain Compost/WWF; Tiger image: Frédy Mercay.

first? Your eye probably goes to the tiger in a lush jungle setting in the small framed snapshot, and you recognize this as a common kind of nature photograph demonstrating the magnificence and beauty of jungle animals. Then you realize that the photograph is surrounded by a larger one showing a natural habitat destroyed by deforestation. When you then consider the words that accompany the images, you realize the ad's purpose: to warn against the human destruction of natural habitats and the animals that live there. This ad makes a dramatic and compelling statement that nature is at risk of being destroyed and is worth protecting. The dual images with their corresponding text deliver a strong and effective message.

Exercise 3.13

Discuss what types of images might be useful to include in each of the following writing tasks.

1. An essay opposing the whaling industry
2. An essay describing problems faced by victims of cyberbullying
3. A research paper on graffiti
4. An argumentative essay opposing casino gambling
5. A report about unhealthy fast-food menu items

Graphics and Tables

Information-laden graphics can take extra work to understand. As discussed in Chapter 2, your first step should be to carefully read all parts of the graphic, in order to understand its purpose and its organization. To then analyze and evaluate the graphic, use the guidelines in Table 3.9.

Let's use the guidelines in Table 3.9 to analyze Figure 3.2. First, you may note that the percentage of students nationwide who score at or above the basic level

Table 3.9 Guidelines for Analyzing and Evaluating Graphics and Tables

Guidelines	Tips
Analyze the data to identify trends or patterns.	Note unexpected changes (such as sudden increases or decreases), surprising statistics, or unexplained variations.
Make a brief summary note about any trends or patterns you find.	Writing a summary note will crystallize the idea in your mind, and your note will be useful for review.
Critically evaluate the graphic.	Consider these questions: • Are the data from a reputable source? • Is the information current (timely) and accurate? • How objective (unbiased) is the graphic? • Are the data presented fairly? • Is the meaning of the data clear? • Is anything vague or confusing? • Is the scale (as shown in the units of measurement) misleading in any way? • Could the information be presented differently to show a different trend or outcome?

Figure 3.2   Sample Graphic: U.S. Educational Expenditures, 1990–2015

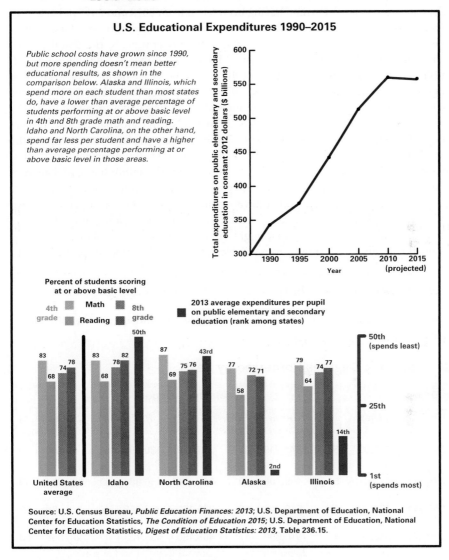

drops from fourth grade to eighth grade for math while increasing for reading. A summary note for Figure 3.2 might read as follows:

> Spending on elementary and secondary public schooling increased considerably from 1990 to 2015. Test scores in 2015 for 4th- and 8th-graders in four states (Idaho, North Carolina, Alaska, and Illinois) all seem fairly similar to the average scores for the United States, even though two of the states (Alaska, Illinois) spend much more per pupil than the other two (Idaho, North Carolina).

The data for Figure 3.2 come from government sources, which are considered among the most reputable: the U.S. Census Bureau and the U.S. Department of Education. The data are also fairly current, having been taken from 2013 and 2015 publications. Notice, however, that the graphic might not be objective and unbiased. First, look at the line graph showing the increase in expenditures over time. Notice that the numbers along the vertical axis start not at $0 billion but rather at $300 billion, which misleadingly makes the expenditures at the beginning of the period look lower than they actually were and the increase, therefore, look greater. Second, in the bar graphs at the bottom, the purple bars for ranking state spending make spending in Alaska and Illinois look lower than spending in Idaho and North Carolina, because the bars for Alaska and Illinois are much shorter. But by reading the labels at the tops of the purple bars, we see that the opposite is true: Alaska and Illinois spend much more per student than Idaho and North Carolina do. Worse, the author has used data from only four states. There are fifty states, and perhaps some other higher-spending states have better results than some other lower-spending states. The author has also failed to address the larger context: Are test scores good measures of learning? Are there factors in addition to learning that might influence test scores? In short, as a critical evaluation of Figure 3.2 shows, even reliable data can be distorted to "prove" a point.

Exercise 3.14

Using the guidelines presented above, study Table 3.10 and answer the following questions.

Table 3.10   Academic Degrees Conferred by Sex

Bachelor's Degree						Master's Degree				
Year	Total	Men	%	Women	%	Total	Men	%	Women	%
1970	792,316	451,097	57	341,219	43	213,589	130,799	61	82,790	39
1980	929,417	473,611	51	455,806	49	305,196	156,882	51	148,314	49
1990	1,051,344	491,696	47	559,648	53	330,152	158,052	48	172,100	52
2000	1,237,875	530,367	43	707,508	57	463,185	196,129	42	267,056	58
2010	1,650,014	706,633	43	943,381	57	693,025	275,197	40	417,828	60
2012	1,791,046	765,317	43	1,025,729	57	754,229	302,191	40	452,038	60
2020*	1,953,000	808,000	41	1,145,000	59	935,000	361,000	39	575,000	61
2024*	2,061,000	842,000	41	1,219,000	59	1,032,000	385,000	37	647,000	63

*Projected

Source: U.S. Department of Education, National Center for Education Statistics, *Digest of Education Statistics: 2013*, Table 318.10.

1. How is the table organized?

2. What is the table's purpose?

3. What trends and patterns are evident for bachelor's degrees? For master's degrees? For both degrees? What other trends and patterns do you see?

4. Write a brief summary note for the table.

5. Do you consider the source of the data to be reliable?

6. Note that the table reports data in ten-year intervals from 1970 to 2010 and then in two-, eight-, and four-year intervals. Consider possible reasons for this variation. Does an increased frequency of reporting make the changes seem less dramatic?

Responding to Texts and Visual Aids with Journals and Response Papers

Active reading (understanding, analyzing, and evaluating) also involves **responding**, or reacting, to the material you read. When you respond to material, you understand and remember it better.

Responses to a reading can take many formats. Sometimes you'll make informal notes, called **annotations**, while you read. (Refer to Chapter 2, pp. 35–36, for more on how to annotate.) Other times you'll record your reactions in an informal personal journal. Sometimes, your instructor will ask you to write a formal response paper.

Keep a Journal

A **journal** is a notebook or computer file in which you record and explore ideas and observations. Experiment with the following two methods of organizing a journal response to a reading assignment.

THE OPEN-PAGE FORMAT

On a blank page, write, outline, draw, or create a diagram to express your reactions to a reading. The open-page format encourages you to let your ideas flow freely. Figure 3.3 shows one student's open-page journal entry for "Comparing Online and Traditional Education" (Chapter 2, pp. 25–28). This entry suggests several possible topics to write about — for example, the college experience, the benefits of in-person lectures, and educational options for people with disabilities.

THE TWO-COLUMN FORMAT

Divide several pages of your journal into two columns. If you keep your journal on a computer, you can insert a table with two columns. Label the left column "Quotations" and the right column "Responses." Under "Quotations," jot down five to ten quotations from the text. Choose remarks that seem important — sentences that state an opinion, summarize a viewpoint, offer an important example, and so forth.

Figure 3.3   Sample Open-Page Journal Format

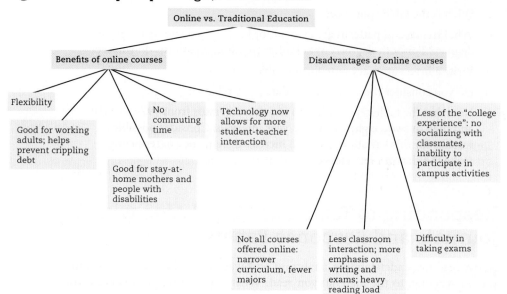

In the right column, next to each quotation, write your response to the quotation. You might explain it, disagree with or question it, relate it to other information in the reading or in another reading, or tie it to your own experiences. The structure of the two-column format forces you to think actively about the reading while you question what you have read and draw connections.

You may find it useful to **paraphrase** a quotation (that is, rewrite it in your own words) before writing your response. Paraphrasing forces you to think about the meaning of the quotation, and ideas for writing may come to mind as a result. To use paraphrasing, add a "Paraphrases" column to your journal between the "Quotations" column and the "Responses" column.

Figure 3.4 shows the two-column format. In this journal entry, the writer has uncovered two possible topics for future writing, related to how the author's experience differs from that of a typical student.

Write in Response to a Reading

When an instructor assigns a reading, some form of response is always expected. You might be expected to participate in a class discussion, summarize the information on an essay exam, or research the topic further and report your findings. Some instructors assign a **response paper**, which requires you to read a selection, analyze it, and write about some aspect of it. In some assignments, your instructor will suggest a particular direction for the paper. Other times, you decide how to respond to the reading. Table 3.11 provides guidelines for writing a response paper.

For example, suppose your instructor asks you to write a paper in response to an essay titled "Advertising: A Form of Institutional Lying," which argues that

Figure 3.4 Sample Two-Column Journal Format

Quotations	Responses
"Without the option of online classes, I would not have been able to both take my dream job and finish my degree."	This writer is extremely lucky. How many of us get offered our dream job before we get our degree? Her experience seems like a rare case, not an example of a typical student's experiences.
"Not everybody can afford to take four years out of their lives to attend school, and not everyone has a trust fund set up to pay for their education."	She is so right about this! Many of us have to work to support ourselves, and it can be very stressful to juggle school and work. This is probably a much more common situation than having to take online courses because you've been offered your dream job.

advertisements deceive consumers by presenting half-truths, distortions, and misinformation. In writing this response paper, you might take one of the following approaches:

- Discuss how you were once deceived by an advertisement, as a way of confirming the author's main points.
- Evaluate the evidence and examples the author provides to support her claim; determine whether the evidence is relevant and sufficient.
- Discuss the causes or effects of deceptive advertising that the writer has overlooked. (You may need to consult other sources to take this approach.)

Table 3.11 Guidelines for Writing a Response Paper

- Before beginning any response paper, make sure you understand the assignment. If you are uncertain about your instructor's expectations, ask for clarification.

- If you have trouble getting started, check with classmates to find out how they are approaching the assignment.

- If your instructor does not mention length requirements, ask how long the response paper should be.

- A response paper may include a brief summary as part of the introduction, but your main focus should be analyzing and evaluating what you have read.

- Do not attempt to discuss all of your reactions to the reading. Instead, choose one key idea, one question the selection raises, or one issue it explores.

For an assignment like this one or for any response paper, how do you decide which facet of the issue to write about? There are several ways to start.

- **Review any summary you've written, as well as your annotations and journal entries.**
- **Think about how the reading relates to your own experiences.** Brainstorming ideas builds a bridge between your ideas and the writer's and suggests ideas to write about.
- **Look for useful information that you can apply or relate to real-life situations.** For example, for "Comparing Online and Traditional Education" you might write a response paper about your experiences with an online course or about your conversation with a friend who has taken a distance-learning course.
- **Think beyond the reading.** Recall other material you have read and events you have experienced that relate to the reading. In thinking about "Comparing Online and Traditional Education," for example, you might recall an article in the student newspaper about the new history, literature, and sociology courses that will be offered online next term.
- **Use the key-word response method for generating ideas.** Choose one or more key words that describe your initial response to the reading, such as *angered, amused, surprised, confused, annoyed, curious,* or *shocked.* For example, fill in the following blank with key words describing your response to "Comparing Online and Traditional Education."

After reading the essay, I felt _____.

The key-word response you just wrote will serve as a point of departure for further thinking. Start by explaining your response, and then write down ideas as they come to you, trying to approach the reading from several different perspectives. Here is the result of one student's key-word response to "Comparing Online and Traditional Education."

After reading "Comparing Online and Traditional Education," I felt informed and enlightened. Sometimes I get frustrated with all the hassles of getting to and from campus, having to participate in class, and working on group projects when I'd rather just work on my own. I always thought online classes would be the easy way out. Just read the textbook and take the exams, and it would be that simple. Now I realize that online courses are just as challenging as traditional courses, but in different ways.

Exercise 3.15

Using the guidelines presented above, write a response paper to the reading in Chapter 1 ("To Remember Lectures Better, Take Notes by Hand," pp. 4–6) or in Chapter 2 ("Comparing Online and Traditional Education," pp. 25–28).

4

Prewriting: How to Find and Focus Ideas

In this chapter, you will learn to

- Choose a topic for your essay.

- Narrow your essay topic.

- Consider your purpose, audience, and point of view as you plan your essay.

- Use seven strategies for discovering ideas to write about.

Photographer's Choice/Getty Images

Reflect on a Visual Text

Suppose you see the photo above in a psychology textbook chapter that discusses the range of human emotions. Examine the photo closely.

1 Ask yourself questions. What is happening in the photo? What do you think the man might be reacting to? ➔

2 **Brainstorm ideas.** Brainstorm a list of words that could describe how this man is feeling.

3 **Write.** Choose one of the words you wrote for Step 2. Think about times when you felt the same emotion the man may be expressing, or consider times when you saw others express a strong emotion in public. Try to write nonstop for at least five minutes, recording all your ideas. Don't stop to evaluate your writing or to phrase your ideas in complete sentences with perfect grammar. Just record your thoughts.

You have just used *freewriting*, a method of discovering ideas about a topic. Read over what you wrote. Suppose you were asked to write an essay about joy or exuberance. Do you see some starting points and usable ideas in your freewriting?

In this chapter, you will learn more about freewriting and other methods that will help you find ideas to write about. You will also learn how to focus an essay by considering why you are writing (your purpose), for whom you are writing (your audience), and the perspective you are using to approach your topic (point of view). These are the first steps in the process of writing an essay, as illustrated in Figure 4.1.

Figure 4.1 Overview of the Writing Process

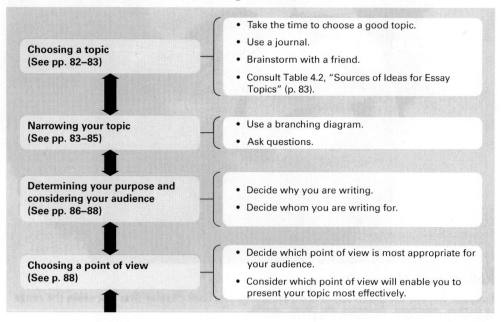

Choosing a topic
(See pp. 82–83)
- Take the time to choose a good topic.
- Use a journal.
- Brainstorm with a friend.
- Consult Table 4.2, "Sources of Ideas for Essay Topics" (p. 83).

Narrowing your topic
(See pp. 83–85)
- Use a branching diagram.
- Ask questions.

Determining your purpose and considering your audience
(See pp. 86–88)
- Decide why you are writing.
- Decide whom you are writing for.

Choosing a point of view
(See p. 88)
- Decide which point of view is most appropriate for your audience.
- Consider which point of view will enable you to present your topic most effectively.

LaunchPad Solo
macmillan learning   Visit **LaunchPad Solo for Readers and Writers > Overview: Writing** for more practice with the writing process.

Figure 4.1 (continued)

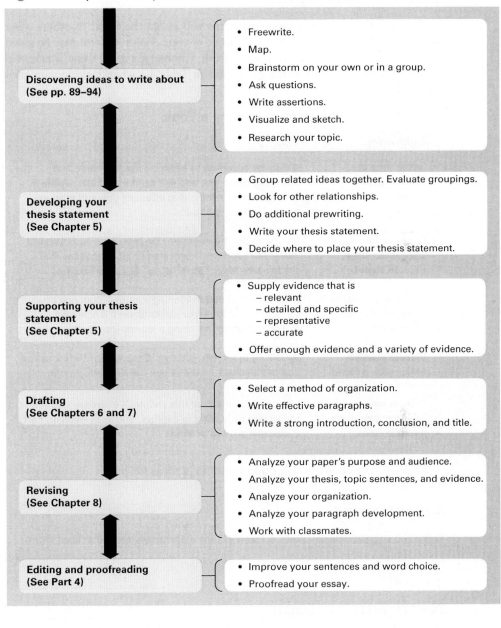

Discovering ideas to write about
(See pp. 89–94)

- Freewrite.
- Map.
- Brainstorm on your own or in a group.
- Ask questions.
- Write assertions.
- Visualize and sketch.
- Research your topic.

Developing your
thesis statement
(See Chapter 5)

- Group related ideas together. Evaluate groupings.
- Look for other relationships.
- Do additional prewriting.
- Write your thesis statement.
- Decide where to place your thesis statement.

Supporting your thesis
statement
(See Chapter 5)

- Supply evidence that is
  – relevant
  – detailed and specific
  – representative
  – accurate
- Offer enough evidence and a variety of evidence.

Drafting
(See Chapters 6 and 7)

- Select a method of organization.
- Write effective paragraphs.
- Write a strong introduction, conclusion, and title.

Revising
(See Chapter 8)

- Analyze your paper's purpose and audience.
- Analyze your thesis, topic sentences, and evidence.
- Analyze your organization.
- Analyze your paragraph development.
- Work with classmates.

Editing and proofreading
(See Part 4)

- Improve your sentences and word choice.
- Proofread your essay.

Choosing a Topic

In some writing situations, your instructor will assign the topic. In others, your instructor will allow you to write on a topic of your choice. Or you may be given a number of possible topics to choose from. Choosing a good topic is essential to writing a good essay. Use the guidelines in Table 4.1 when picking your own topic.

Table 4.1   Guidelines for Choosing a Topic

Guidelines	Tips
Invest time in making your choice.	It may be tempting to settle on the first topic that comes to mind, but you will produce a better essay if you work with a topic that interests you and that you know something about.
Focus on questions and ideas rather than on topics.	For example, the question "Do television commercials really sell products?" will lead to a better essay than the broader topic "advertising" or "commercials."
Use your journal as a source of ideas.	If you have not begun keeping a journal, start one now; try writing in it for a few weeks to see if it is helpful. Chapter 3 has tips on using a journal (pp. 75–76).
Discuss possible topics with a friend.	By talking to friends, you may discover worthwhile topics and get feedback on topics you have already thought of.
Consult your course materials for possible ideas.	For instance, many of this chapter's exercises include topics you may want to explore, and each essay in Part 2 includes writing prompts.

Table 4.2 summarizes some good sources of ideas for topics.

Essay in Progress 1

Using the suggestions in Tables 4.1 and 4.2 for inspiration, record at least three broad topics.

Narrowing a Topic

Once you have chosen a topic, the next step is to narrow it so that it is manageable within an essay of the length your instructor has assigned. For example, a broad topic such as divorce is too large for a two- to four-page paper. However,

LaunchPad Solo
macmillan learning

Visit **LaunchPad Solo for Readers and Writers > Topic, Audience, and Purpose** for extra practice in the skills covered in this section.

Table 4.2   Sources of Ideas for Essay Topics

Source	What to Look For	Example
Your Classes	Listen for issues, controversies, and new ideas that might be worth exploring.	A discussion in your education class leads you to the topic of standardized testing.
Daily Activities	Take note of incidents at work and at sporting or social events.	A health inspector's visit at work suggests an essay on restaurant-food safety.
Newspapers and Magazines	Flip through recent issues; look for articles that might lead to promising topics.	You find an interesting article on a hip-hop musician and decide to write about her career.
Radio, Television, and the Internet	Listen to your favorite radio station for a thought-provoking song, or look for ideas in television programs and commercials or on the Web.	Commercials for diet soda suggest an essay on the diet-food industry.
The World around You	Notice people, objects, and interactions inside your household or outside.	You observe family members reading books and decide to write about the value of leisure time.

you might write about one specific cause of divorce or its typical emotional effects on children.

To narrow a topic, limit it to a specific part or aspect. Two techniques — branching and questioning — will help you do so. Later in the chapter, you will learn idea-generating techniques (pp. 89–94) that may also be used to narrow a broad topic.

Using a Branching Diagram

Start by writing your broad topic at the far left side of your paper or computer screen. Then subdivide the topic into three or more subcategories or aspects. Here is an example of a **branching diagram** for the broad topic of wild-game hunting.

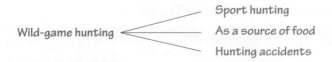

Then choose one subtopic and subdivide it further. Continue narrowing the topic in this way until you believe you have found a topic that is both interesting and manageable. Keep in mind that once you begin planning, researching, and drafting the essay, you may need to narrow your topic even further. The following example shows additional limiting from sport hunting to an even narrower subtopic, "effects on environment."

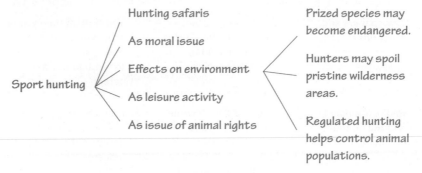

Notice that as the narrowing progresses, the topics change from words and phrases to statements of ideas.

Exercise 4.1

Use branching diagrams to narrow three of the following broad topics to more manageable topics for a two- to four-page essay.

1. Divorce
2. Human space travel
3. School lunches
4. Air-travel safety measures
5. Campaign-finance rules
6. Alternative energy sources

Essay in Progress 2

Narrow one of the broad topics you chose in Essay in Progress 1 to a topic manageable for a two- to four-page essay.

Asking Questions to Narrow a Broad Topic

Use questions that begin with *who, what, where, when, why,* and *how* to narrow your topic. Doing so will help you consider specific aspects of the topic. Here is an example of questions for the broad topic of divorce.

Questions	Narrowed Topics
Why does divorce occur?	• Lifestyle differences • Infidelity
How do couples divide their property?	• Division of assets
Who can help couples work through a divorce?	• Role of friends and family • Marital counselor's or attorney's role
What are the effects of divorce on children?	• Emotional • Financial
When might it be advisable for a couple considering divorce to remain married?	• For the sake of their children • Financial benefit of remaining married

As you can see, the questions about divorce produced several workable topics. Ask additional questions to get to a topic that is sufficiently limited. The topic "emotional effects of divorce on children," for example, is still too broad for an essay. Asking questions such as "What are the most typical emotional effects on children?" and "How do divorcing parents prevent their children from developing emotional problems as a result of the divorce?" would lead to more specific topics.

Exercise 4.2

Use questioning to narrow three of the following subjects to topics that would be manageable within a two- to four-page essay.

1. Senior citizens
2. Mental illness
3. Environmental protection
4. Cyberbullying
5. Television programming

Reading 🔵 Writing   Topics

The Reader's Perspective	The Writer's Perspective
Think about picking up a magazine and flipping through it. How do you decide which articles to read? Most likely, you read the titles and choose one that captures your attention. As a reader, you have responded positively to the topic.	It is important to write a good essay, but it's equally important to write an essay that people will *want* to read. Writers typically choose topics that they find interesting, but before deciding on a topic, ask yourself, Would other people find this topic interesting, too?

Thinking about Your Purpose, Audience, and Point of View

As you work through finding and narrowing a topic, you also need to determine your purpose and consider your audience.

Determining Your Purpose

A well-written essay has a specific **purpose** or goal. There are three main purposes for writing—to *express* yourself, to *inform* your reader, and to *persuade* your reader. For example, an essay might express the writer's feelings about an incident of road rage that she observed. Another essay may inform readers about the primary causes of road rage. Yet another essay might try to persuade readers that anger management classes are the most effective way of combatting road rage.

To determine your purpose, ask yourself two key questions.

- Why am I writing this essay?
- What do I want this essay to accomplish?

Some essays have more than one purpose. An essay on snowboarding, for example, could be both informative and persuasive: It could explain the benefits of snowboarding and then urge readers to take up the sport because it is good aerobic exercise.

Reading ⬤ Writing Purpose

The Reader's Perspective	The Writer's Perspective
As you read, try to determine the author's purpose. Doing so will help you discover the writer's attitude toward his or her subject, allow you to detect bias, and enable you to examine whether the writer was successful in achieving his or her purpose.	Your purpose as a writer should generally match the reader's. For example, readers of romance novels generally read to be *entertained,* and a romance novelist would generally seek to *entertain* readers.

Considering Your Audience

Considering your **audience**—the people who read your essay—is an important part of the writing process. Many aspects of your writing—how you express yourself, your word choice, the details and examples you include, and your attitude toward the topic—all depend on the audience. Your **tone**—how you sound to your audience—is especially important. If you want your audience to feel comfortable with your writing, be sure to write in a manner that appeals to them.

As you consider your audience, keep the following points in mind.

- Your readers are not present and cannot observe or participate in what you are writing about. Therefore, you need to describe events, objects, and conversations accurately and in detail.
- Your readers probably do not know everything that you do about your topic.
- Your readers may not share your opinions and values.
- Your readers may not respond the same way that you do to situations or issues.
- If your audience is your instructor, do not automatically assume that he or she is an expert on your topic. Write as if your instructor were unfamiliar with your topic. He or she wants to see if you understand the topic and can write and think clearly about it. Include background information, definitions of technical terms, and relevant details to make your essay clear and understandable.

Table 4.3 lists the questions you should ask when analyzing your audience.

Table 4.3   Guidelines for Analyzing Your Audience

Questions	Tips
What does your audience know or not know about your topic?	If you are proposing a community garden project to city residents who know little about gardening, capture their interest by describing the pleasures and benefits of gardening. Include some basic information.
What are the education, background, and experience of your audience?	If you are writing your garden project proposal for an audience of low-income residents, you might emphasize how much money they could save by growing vegetables. For middle-income residents, you might stress instead how relaxing gardening can be.
What attitudes, beliefs, opinions, or biases is your audience likely to hold?	For example, if your audience believes that most urban development is harmful to the environment, consider emphasizing how the garden will benefit the environment.
What tone do your readers expect you to take?	Suppose you are writing to your local city council urging council members to approve the community garden. Your tone should be serious, as community leaders expect to be treated with respect.

Exercise 4.3

1. Write a one-paragraph description of a current television commercial for a particular product. Your audience is another college student.

2. Now write about the same commercial for one of the following audiences.

   a. For a business marketing class, analyze the factors that make the advertisement interesting and appealing to consumers. Your audience is your business marketing instructor.

   b. Describe your response to the advertisement in a letter to the company that makes the product. Your audience is the consumer-relations director of the company.

   c. Comment favorably on or complain about the advertisement to a local television station. Your audience is the station director.

Choosing a Point of View

Point of view is the perspective from which you write an essay. There are three possible points of view — *first*, *second*, and *third person*. In choosing a point of view, consider your topic, your purpose, and your audience.

Think of point of view as the "person" you become as you write:

- For some essays, you may find first-person pronouns (*I, me, mine, we, ours*) effective and appropriate, such as in an essay narrating an event in which you participated.

- For other types of essays, second-person pronouns (*you, your, yours*) are appropriate, as in an essay explaining how to build a fence: "First, *you* should measure . . . ." Sometimes the word *you* may be understood but not directly stated, as in "First, measure . . . ." Many textbooks, including this one, use the second person to address students.

- In academic writing, the third-person point of view is prevalent. The third-person point of view is more formal than the first person and the second person. The writer uses people's names and third-person pronouns (*he, she, they*). Think of the third person as public rather than personal. The writer reports what he or she sees.

Exercise 4.4

Working with a classmate, discuss which point of view (first, second, or third person) would be most appropriate in each of the following writing situations.

1. An essay urging students on your campus to participate in a march against hunger to support a local food drive

2. A description of a car accident on a form that your insurance company requires you to submit in order to collect benefits

3. A paper for an ecology course on the effects of air pollution caused by a local industry

Discovering Ideas to Write About

Many students report that one of the most difficult parts of writing an essay is finding enough to say about a narrowed topic. The following sections describe a number of useful strategies for discovering ideas to write about. Experiment to determine which techniques work best for you.

Freewriting

When you **freewrite**, you write nonstop for a specific period of time, usually five to ten minutes. As you learned in the activity that opens this chapter, freewriting involves writing whatever comes to mind. If nothing comes to mind, just write the topic, your name, or "I can't think of anything to write." Then let your mind run free. Explore ideas, make associations, jump from one idea to another. The following tips will help you.

- **Write or type nonstop.** The act of writing itself often forces thoughts to emerge.
- **Don't be concerned with grammar, punctuation, or spelling.**
- **Write fast!** Try to keep up with your thinking. (Most people can think faster than they can write.)
- **Record ideas as they come to you, in whatever form they appear — words, phrases, questions, sentences.**

When you're done, read your freewriting, and highlight or underline ideas that seem useful. Look for patterns and connections. Do several ideas come together to make a point, reflect a sequence, or suggest a larger unifying idea? Here is an excerpt from one student's freewriting on the broad topic of violence in the media.

There seems to be a lot of violence in the media these days, particularly on TV. For example, last night when I watched the news, the cameraman showed people getting shot in the street. What kind of people watch this stuff? I'd rather watch a movie. It really bothered me because people get so turned off by such an ugly, gruesome scene that they won't want to watch the news anymore. Then we'll have a lot of uninformed citizens. There are too many already. Some people do not even know who the vice president of the U.S. is. A negative thing—that is the media has a negative impact on anyone or group who want to do something about violence in the inner city. And they create negative impressions of minority and ethnic groups, too. If the media shows one Latino man committing a crime, viewers falsely assume all Latinos are criminals.

LaunchPad Solo
macmillan learning   Visit **LaunchPad Solo for Readers and Writers > Prewriting** for extra practice in the skills covered in this section.

A number of different subtopics surfaced from this student's freewriting:

- The media's graphic portrayal of violence
- The negative effect of media violence on viewers
- The media's portrayal of minority and ethnic groups

Any one of these topics could be narrowed into a manageable topic for an essay.

Exercise 4.5

Set a clock or timer for five minutes and freewrite on one of the following broad topics. Then review and highlight your freewriting, identifying usable ideas with a common theme that might serve as a topic for an essay. With this new potential topic, freewrite for another five minutes to narrow your topic further and develop your ideas.

1. Music
2. Twitter
3. How to be self-sufficient
4. Pressures on college students
5. Job interviews

Mapping

Mapping, or **clustering**, is a visual way to discover ideas and relationships. Here is how it works.

1. Write your topic in the middle of a blank sheet of paper, and draw a box or circle around it.
2. Think of ideas that are related to or suggested by your topic. As you think of them, write them down in clusters around the topic, connecting them to the topic with lines.
3. Draw arrows and lines or use highlighting to show relationships and connect groups of related ideas.
4. Think of still more ideas, clustering them around the ideas already on your map.
5. If possible, experiment with mapping on a computer, using a graphics program such as the draw function available in Microsoft Word. You can then cut and paste items from your map into an outline or draft of your essay.

The sample map in Figure 4.2 was created by a student working on the topic of the costs of higher education. In this map, the student compared attending a local community college and attending an out-of-town four-year college.

Figure 4.2   Sample Map/Cluster Diagram

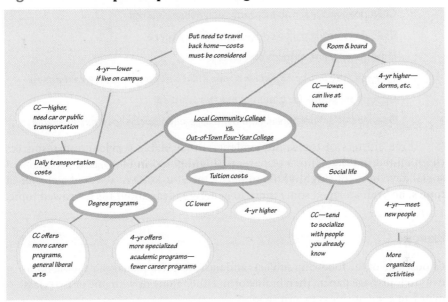

Exercise 4.6

Narrow one of the following topics. Then select one of your narrowed topics and draw a map of related ideas as they come to mind.

1. Presidential politics
2. Daydreaming
3. Tattoos
4. Cable TV
5. Year-round schooling

Brainstorming

When you engage in **brainstorming**, you list everything that comes to mind when you think about your topic — impressions, emotions, and reactions, as well as facts. Record words or phrases rather than sentences, and give yourself a time limit: It will force ideas to come faster. If you use a computer, you might use bullets or the indent function to create lists rather than lines of text.

The following example shows a student's brainstorming on the narrowed topic of the disadvantages of homeschooling.

Topic: Disadvantages of Homeschooling

Parent may not be an expert in each subject

Libraries not easily accessible

Wide range of equipment, resources not available

Child does not learn to interact with other children

Child does not learn to compete against others

Parents may not enforce standards

Parents may not be objective about child's strengths and weaknesses

Special programs (art, music) may be omitted

Services of school nurse, counselors, reading specialists not available

Three clusters of topics are evident — unavailable services and resources (highlighted in pink), limits of parents (highlighted in blue), and problems of social development (highlighted in tan). Once the student selected a cluster of topics, he brainstormed some more to generate ideas about his narrowed topic.

Exercise 4.7

Choose one of the following subjects and narrow it to a manageable topic for a two- to four-page paper. Then brainstorm, either alone or with one or two class-mates, to generate ideas to write about.

1. Value of music
2. National parks
3. Internet fraud
4. Texting
5. Web advertising
6. Violence on campus

Questioning

Questioning is another way to discover ideas about a narrowed topic. Work-ing either alone or with a classmate, write down every question you can think of about your topic. As with other prewriting strategies, focus on ideas, not on grammatical correctness. Don't judge or evaluate ideas as you write. It may help to imagine that you are asking an expert on your topic anything that comes to mind.

Here is a list of questions one student generated on the narrow topic of the financial problems faced by single parents.

Why do many female single parents earn less than male single parents?

Is there a support group for single parents that offers financial advice and planning?

How do single parents find time to attend college to improve their employability?

Beginning a question with "What if" is a particularly good way to extend your thinking and look at a topic from a fresh perspective. Here are a few chal-lenging *What if* questions about the financial situations of single parents.

What if the government provided national day care or paid for day care?

What if single parents were not allowed to deduct more than one child on their income tax?

What if there were financial support groups for single parents?

Exercise 4.8

Working either alone or with a classmate, choose one of the following topics, narrow it, and write a series of questions to discover ideas about it.

1. The campus newspaper
2. Learning a foreign language
3. Student loans
4. Talk radio
5. Government aid to developing countries
6. Presidential campaigns

Writing Assertions

The technique of **writing assertions** forces you to look at your topic from a number of different perspectives. Begin by writing five to ten statements that take a position on or make an assertion about your topic. Here are a few possible assertions for the topic of the growing popularity of health food.

Supermarkets have increased their marketing of health foods.

Health food is popular because buying it makes people think they are hip.

Health food tricks people into thinking they have a healthy lifestyle.

Review your list of assertions, choose one statement, and try brainstorming, freewriting, or mapping to generate more ideas about it.

Exercise 4.9

Working either alone or with one or two classmates, write assertions about one of the following topics.

1. Advertising directed toward children
2. Buying a used car from a private owner
3. Needed improvements in public education
4. Characteristics of a good teacher
5. Attempts to encourage healthier eating on campus

Visualizing or Sketching

Especially if you enjoy working with graphics, **visualizing** or actually **sketching** your topic may be an effective way to discover ideas. If you are writing a description of a person, for example, close your eyes and visualize that person in your mind. Imagine what he or she is wearing; study his or her facial expressions and gestures.

Exercise 4.10

Visualize one of the following situations. Make notes about or sketch what you "see." Include as many details as possible.

1. A traffic jam
2. A couple obviously in love
3. A class you recently attended

4. The campus snack bar
5. A sporting event

Researching Your Topic

Do some preliminary research on your topic in the library or on the Internet. Reading what others have written about your topic may suggest new approaches, reveal issues or controversies, and help you determine what you do and do not already know about the topic. This method is especially useful for an assigned essay on an unfamiliar topic or for a topic you want to learn more about.

Take notes while reading sources. In addition, be sure to record the publication data you will need to cite each source (author, title, publisher, page numbers, and so on). If you use ideas or information from sources in your essay, you must give credit to the sources of the borrowed material. (For more information on finding and using sources, refer to Chapter 19.)

Exercise 4.11

Do library or Internet research to generate ideas on one of the narrowed topics listed here.

1. A recent disaster (hurricane, flood, etc.)
2. Buying clothing on eBay
3. Preventing terrorism in public buildings
4. Controlling children's access to television programs
5. Reducing the federal deficit

Essay in Progress 3

Keeping your audience and purpose in mind, use one of the prewriting strategies discussed in this chapter to generate details about the topic you narrowed in Essay in Progress 2.

Students Write

In this and the remaining four chapters of Part 1, we follow the work of Christine Lee, a student in a first-year writing course who was assigned to write about a recent trend or fad in popular culture.

Lee decided to use questioning to narrow her topic and freewriting to generate ideas about the topic. Here is an example of her questioning.

Sample Questioning

What are some recent fads or trends?

> Political blogging
>
> Extreme sports
>
> Tattooing and body piercing
>
> Reality TV

Lee decided to explore the topic of reality TV further by asking another question.

Why is this trend popular?

Reality TV

> People are more likely to identify with real people, not actors.
>
> The shows are often contests, which keep viewers watching until the last episode.
>
> They are supposedly unscripted and often unpredictable, which builds suspense.
>
> It all started with Survivor, which kept people interested because of the $1 million prize.
>
> Keeping Up with the Kardashians is popular because everyone is curious about the rich, glamorous Hollywood lifestyle.

After looking over the answers to her questions, Lee decided to focus on reality TV's evolution and popularity. The following excerpt from her freewriting shows how she started to develop her topic.

Sample Freewriting

When *Survivor* was first on TV it was new and different, and it was interesting to watch how people started to act when a million dollars was at stake. Everybody had a favorite and someone else they loved to hate. After that season it seemed like every network had two or three competition reality shows they were trying out. *American Idol* was another competition. But then the shows started getting really tacky and distasteful, like *Jersey Shore* and *Big Brother* and *Keeping Up with the Kardashians*. Now I'm getting tired of all of these "real" people as they behave in selfish, immature, and nasty ways. In the end I'll go back to watching *Modern Family* because it's funny (which *The Real Housewives* never is) and *Breaking Bad* on DVD because they talk about serious issues that real people deal with.

As you work through the remaining chapters in Part 1, you will see how Lee develops her tentative thesis statement (Chapter 5), her paragraphs (Chapter 6), her first full draft (Chapter 7), and her final draft (Chapter 8).

To see the next step in Lee's essay (developing a thesis statement), see pages 106–07.

5

Developing and Supporting a Thesis

John Caldwell The New Yorker Collection/The Cartoon Bank

"Go ask your search engine."

Reflect on a Visual Text

Study the cartoon above, which humorously depicts a serious situation.

1 **Ask yourself questions.** What is the setting of the cartoon? What point is the cartoonist trying to make? How does the adult's response differ from the expected response in this type of situation? →

2 Brainstorm ideas. How would you describe the expression on the boy's face? How would you feel if you asked a question and got the response the boy got? What are the benefits of the father's advice? The drawbacks?

3 Write. Working alone or with one or two classmates, write a statement that expresses the main point of the cartoon. Describe what is happening in the cartoon, and state the idea that the cartoonist is trying to communicate to his audience.

The statement you wrote in response to the writing prompt above is an assertion around which you could build an essay. Such an assertion is called a *thesis statement*. In this chapter, you will learn how to write effective thesis statements and how to support them with evidence. Developing a thesis is an important part of the writing process. In Figure 4.1 (pp. 80–81), you can see how developing your thesis fits into the context of the writing process.

What Is a Thesis Statement?

A **thesis statement** (also called the *central thought*) is the main point of an essay. It explains what the essay will be about and expresses the writer's position on the subject. It may also give clues about how the essay will develop or how it will be organized. Usually a thesis statement is expressed in a single sentence. When you write, think of the thesis statement as a promise to your readers. The rest of your essay delivers on that promise.

Here is a sample thesis statement.

> Playing team sports, especially football and baseball, develops skills and qualities that can make you successful in life because these sports demand communication, teamwork, and responsibility.

In this thesis, the writer identifies the topic — team sports — and states the position that team sports, especially football and baseball, equip players with important skills and qualities. After reading this statement, the reader expects to discover what skills and qualities football and baseball players learn and how these contribute to success in life.

Developing a Working Thesis Statement

A thesis statement usually evolves or develops as you explore your topic during prewriting. Do not expect to be able to sit down and simply write a thesis statement as if by magic.

 **LaunchPad Solo** macmillan learning   Visit **LaunchPad Solo for Readers and Writers > Thesis Statements** for extra practice in the skills covered in this chapter.

To come up with a preliminary or working thesis for your paper, reread your prewriting (see Chapter 4) and highlight details that have to do with the same subtopic. Write a word or phrase that describes each group of related ideas.

For example, a student working on the topic of intelligence in dogs noticed in her brainstormed list that the details she highlighted could be grouped into two general categories — details about learning and details about instinct. Here is how she arranged her ideas.

Learning

    follow commands
    perform new tricks
    get housebroken
    serve as guide dogs for blind people
    carry empty water dish to owner

Instinct

    females deliver and care for puppies
    avoid danger and predators
    seek shelter
    automatically raise hair on back in response to aggression

When you've grouped similar details together, the next step is to decide which group or groups of ideas best represent the direction your paper should take. In some instances, one group of details will be enough to develop a working thesis. At other times, you'll need to use two or three groups of details. The student working on a thesis for the topic of intelligence in dogs evaluated her groups of details and decided that instinct was unrelated to her topic. Consequently, she decided to write about learning.

If you are not satisfied with how you have grouped or arranged your details, you probably don't have enough details to come up with a good working thesis. If you need more details, prewrite to generate more. Be sure to try a different prewriting strategy than the one you used previously. A new strategy may help you see your narrowed topic from a different perspective. If your second prewriting does not produce better results, consider refocusing or changing your topic.

Essay in Progress 1

If you used a prewriting strategy to generate details about your topic in response to Essay in Progress 3 in Chapter 4 (p. 94), review your prewriting, highlight useful ideas, and identify several sets of related details among those you highlighted. If you did not yet generate groups of ideas about your topic, do so now.

Writing an Effective Thesis Statement

Use the following guidelines to write an effective thesis statement or to evaluate and revise your working thesis.

1. **Make an assertion.** Unlike a fact, an **assertion** takes a position, expresses a viewpoint, or suggests your approach to the topic.

Lacks an assertion	Hollywood movies, like *American Sniper* and *Black Mass*, are frequently based on true stories.
Revised	Hollywood movies like *American Sniper* and *Black Mass* manipulate true stories to cater to the tastes of the audience.

2. **Be specific.** Try to provide as much information as possible about your main point.

Too general	I learned a great deal from my experiences as a teenage parent.
Revised	From my experiences as a teenage parent, I learned to accept responsibility for my own life and for that of my son.

3. **Focus on one central point.** Limit your essay to one major idea.

Focuses on several points	This college should improve its tutoring services, sponsor more activities of interest to Latino students, and speed up the registration process for students.
Revised	To better represent the student population it serves, this college should sponsor more activities of interest to Latino students.

4. **Offer an original perspective on your topic.** If your thesis seems dull or ordinary, it probably needs more work. Search your prewriting for an interesting angle on your topic.

Too ordinary	Many traffic accidents are a result of carelessness.
Revised	When a driver has an accident, it can change his or her entire approach to driving.

5. **Avoid making an announcement.** Don't use phrases such as "This essay will discuss" or "The subject of my paper is." Instead, state your main point directly.

Makes an announcement	The point I am trying to make is that people should not be allowed to smoke on campus.
Revised	The college should prohibit smoking on campus.

6. **Use your thesis to preview the organization of the essay.** Consider mentioning the two or three key concepts on which your essay will focus, in the order in which you will discuss them.

Does not include a preview	Governments have been using many techniques to deal with a declining birth rate.
Includes a preview	To counter the effects of a declining birth rate, governments have begun allowing more immigrants into the country, using tax incentives to encourage couples to have more children, and sponsoring research into robotics technology that can help care for the elderly.

Exercise 5.1

Working in a group of two or three students, discuss what is wrong with each of the following thesis statements. Then revise each thesis to make it more effective.

1. In this paper, I will discuss the causes of asthma, which include exposure to smoke, chemicals, and allergic reactions.

2. Jogging is an enjoyable aerobic sport.

3. The crime rate is decreasing in American cities.

4. Living in an apartment has many advantages.

5. Children's toys can be dangerous, instructional, or creative.

Essay in Progress 2

Keeping your audience in mind, select one or more of the groups of ideas you identified in Essay in Progress 1 and write a working thesis statement based on those ideas.

Placing the Thesis Statement

Your thesis statement can appear anywhere in your essay, but it is usually best to place it in the first paragraph as part of your introduction. When you place your thesis at the beginning of the essay, your readers will know what to pay attention to and what to expect in the rest of the essay. When you place your thesis later in the essay, you need to build up to the thesis gradually in order to prepare readers for it.

Using an Implied Thesis

In some professional writing, the writer may not state the thesis directly. Instead, the writer may strongly imply the thesis through details and the way they are organized. Although professional writers may use an **implied thesis**, academic writers — including professors and students — generally state their thesis directly. You should always include a clear, direct statement of your thesis in your college papers.

Reading ⊕ Writing   The Thesis Statement/Central Thought

The Reader's Perspective	The Writer's Perspective
Looking for the central thought, or thesis statement, is a way to identify the writer's key point and understand the essay as a whole. It will focus your attention and provide the start of a mental outline you create as you read.	A well-crafted thesis statement provides the organizing principle of your essay. It shows your readers that you have carefully considered the topic and will provide a logical, reasoned discussion of it.

Supporting Your Thesis Statement with Evidence

After you have written a working thesis statement, the next step is to develop evidence that supports your thesis. **Evidence** is any type of information, such as examples, statistics, or expert opinion, that will convince your reader that your thesis is reasonable or correct. This evidence, organized into well-developed paragraphs, makes up the body of your essay. To visualize the basic structure of an essay, look at Figure 7.1 (page 125).

Choosing Types of Evidence

Table 5.1 lists various types of evidence and gives examples of how each type could be used to support a working thesis on acupuncture. Note that many of the types of evidence correspond to the patterns of development discussed in Part 2 of this text.

Analyze your purpose, audience, and thesis to determine which types of evidence will be most effective. If your audience is unfamiliar with your topic, provide definitions, historical background, an explanation of the process, and factual and descriptive details. To persuade, use comparison and contrast, advantages and disadvantages, examples, problems, statistics, and quotations to make your argument.

Exercise 5.2

1. Working in a group of two to three students, discuss and list the types of evidence that could be used to support the following thesis statement for an informative essay.

   The pressure to become financially independent is a challenge for many young adults and often causes them to develop social and emotional problems.

Table 5.1   Types of Evidence Used to Support a Thesis

Working Thesis: Acupuncture, a form of alternative medicine, is becoming more widely accepted in the United States.

Types of Evidence	Example
Advantages and Disadvantages	Describe the pros (nonsurgical, relatively painless) and cons (fear of needles, infection) of acupuncture.
Causes or Effects	Discuss one or two theories that explain why acupuncture works. Offer reasons for its increasing popularity.
Classification	Explain types of acupuncture treatments.
Comparison and Contrast	Compare acupuncture with other forms of alternative medicine, such as massage and herbal medicines. Explain how acupuncture differs from these other treatments.
Definitions	Explain that, in acupuncture, needles are inserted into specific points of the body to control pain or relieve symptoms.
Descriptive Details	Explain what acupuncture needles look and feel like.
Examples	Describe situations in which acupuncture has been used successfully — for dental procedures, for treating alcoholism, for pain control.
Explanation of a Process	Explain the principles on which acupuncture is based and how scientists think it works.
Factual Details	Explain who uses acupuncture, what parts of the body are treated with it, and under what circumstances it is used.
Historical Background	Explain that acupuncture originated in ancient China.
Narrative Story	Relate a personal experience that illustrates the use of acupuncture.
Problems	Explain that acupuncture is not always practiced by medical doctors; licensing and oversight of acupuncturists may thus be lax.
Quotations	Quote medical experts who attest to the effectiveness of acupuncture as well as those who question its value.
Statistics	Indicate how many acupuncturists practice in the United States.

2. For each audience listed here, discuss and record the types of evidence that would offer the best support for the preceding thesis.

   a. Young adults

   b. Parents of young adults

   c. Counselors of young adults

Collecting Evidence to Support Your Thesis

Prewriting may help you collect evidence for your thesis. But try a different prewriting strategy from the one you used to arrive at your working thesis statement. Consider using a strategy from the following list.

1. **Visualize yourself speaking to your audience.** What would you say to convince your audience of your thesis? Jot down ideas as they come to you.

2. **Develop a skeletal outline of major headings with plenty of blank space under each.** Fill in ideas about each heading as they come to you. (For more on outlining, see pp. 130–32 in Chapter 7.)

3. **Draw a graphic organizer for your essay, filling in supporting evidence as you think of it.** (For more on drawing a graphic organizer, see pp. 46–47 in Chapter 2.)

4. **Discuss your thesis statement with a classmate; try to explain why he or she should accept your thesis as valid.**

Essay in Progress 3

Using the preceding list of suggestions, generate at least three different types of evidence to support the working thesis statement you wrote in Essay in Progress 2.

Choosing the Best Evidence

In collecting evidence in support of a thesis, you will probably generate more than you need. Consequently, you will need to identify the evidence that best supports your thesis and that suits your purpose and audience. The guidelines in Table 5.2 will help you select the best evidence to support your thesis.

Choosing Evidence for Academic Writing

Certain types of evidence are preferred for most kinds of academic writing. In general, your personal experiences and opinions are not considered as useful as more objective evidence, such as facts, statistics, historical background, and

Table 5.2   Guidelines for Selecting the Best Evidence

Guidelines	Tips
Make sure the evidence is relevant.	All your evidence must clearly and directly support your thesis. Irrelevant evidence will distract readers and cause them to question the validity of your thesis.
Provide specific evidence.	Avoid general statements that will neither engage your readers nor help you make a convincing case for your thesis. To locate detailed, specific evidence, return to your prewriting or use a different prewriting strategy to generate concrete evidence. You may also need to conduct research to find evidence for your thesis.
Offer a variety of evidence.	Specific evidence is needed to support a general thesis statement. Providing a variety of evidence from different sources helps you prove the generalization in your thesis statement. The variety shows that your thesis applies widely, not just in one particular set of circumstances.
Provide a sufficient amount of evidence.	The amount of evidence you need will vary depending on your audience and your topic. To discover whether you have provided enough evidence, ask a classmate to read your essay and tell you whether he or she is convinced. If your reader is not convinced, ask what additional evidence is needed.
Provide representative evidence.	Be sure the evidence you supply is typical and usual. Do not choose unusual, rare, or exceptional examples as evidence.
Provide accurate evidence.	Gather your information from reliable sources. Do not guess at statistics or make estimates. If you are not certain of the accuracy of a fact or statistic, verify it through research, and cite the source you used.

research evidence. Suppose you are writing an academic paper on the effects of global warming. Your own observations about climate changes in your city would not be considered adequate or appropriate evidence to support the idea of climate change as an effect of global warming. Instead, you would need to provide facts, statistics, and research evidence on climate change in a wide range of geographic areas and demonstrate the relationship of changes in these many locations to global warming.

Essay in Progress 4

Evaluate the evidence you generated in Essay in Progress 3. Select from it the evidence that you could use to support your thesis in a two- to four-page essay.

Using Sources to Support Your Thesis

For many topics, you will need to research sources in a library or on the Internet or interview an expert to collect enough supporting evidence for your thesis. Chapter 19 provides a thorough guide to locating sources in the library and on the Internet and citing them in your paper.

Essay in Progress 5

Locate and consult at least two library or Internet sources to find evidence that supports the working thesis statement you wrote in Essay in Progress 2.

Reading ⊕ Writing Evidence

The Reader's Perspective	The Writer's Perspective
Be sure to examine the amount and types of evidence that a writer offers in support of his or her thesis. It is fine to question a piece of writing as "only an opinion" if it does not include serious, credible evidence from reliable sources.	Using diverse kinds of evidence increases the likelihood that your evidence will convince your readers. It also shows readers that you are knowledgeable and informed about your topic, thus enhancing your credibility.

Students Write

In the Students Write section of Chapter 4, you saw how student writer Christine Lee narrowed her topic and generated ideas for her essay on a contemporary trend or fad. You also saw that she decided to focus on reality TV.

After reviewing her responses to questions about her topic and her freewriting, Lee decided that reality TV had become more distasteful and less interesting. She then wrote the following working thesis statement.

> As the popularity of reality TV continues unabated, shows are becoming both less interesting and more distasteful.

To generate more details to support her thesis, Lee did more freewriting and brainstorming to help her recall details from shows. The following is an excerpt from what she wrote.

- Early shows: Cops and Candid Camera
- MTV's Real World was first recent reality show to become popular.
- The original Survivor was smart and interesting.
- Big Brother just locked people up together and forced us to watch them bicker.
- Reality TV was popular because it was something different, but now there are dozens of these shows each season and few worth watching.
- Shows such as American Idol, America's Got Talent, and America's Next Top Model are a revival of earlier types of TV shows — the talent show and the beauty contest.
- Shows like Top Chef and Project Runway focus on special interests.
- Celebrity reality shows focusing on the lives of real people (Keeping Up with the Kardashians, Kathy Griffin: My Life on the D-List) were the next wave.

To see the next step in Lee's essay (developing paragraphs), see pages 122–23.

6

Writing Effective Paragraphs

Marcio Jose Sanchez/AP Images

Reflect on a Visual Text

Study the photograph to the left.

1 Ask yourself questions. What does the photo show? At what kind of event does it seem to have been taken? What is the likely relationship between the two women in the photo?

2 Brainstorm ideas. Suppose you were assigned to write a paper based on this photograph. What title would you give the paper?

3 Write. Now write a sentence that states the main point of the photograph. Then write several more sentences explaining what is happening in the photograph. Describe what details in the photo enabled you to identify the event.

In much the same way as a photograph does, a paragraph makes an overall impression, or main point, and includes details that support this main point. In a paragraph, the topic sentence states the main idea and the remaining sentences provide the details that support it. The topic sentence is often, but not always, the first sentence in a paragraph. 🔊

This chapter provides the tools you need to create effective paragraphs. Good paragraphs are the building blocks of an effective essay (see Figure 7.1, p. 125).

The Structure of a Paragraph

A **paragraph** is a group of connected sentences that develop an idea about a topic. Each paragraph in your essay should support your thesis and contribute to the overall meaning and effectiveness of your essay. A well-developed paragraph contains

- **a focused topic sentence**
- **relevant, specific supporting details (definitions, examples, explanations, or other evidence)**
- **transitions and repetition that show how the ideas are related**

Here is a sample paragraph with its parts labeled.

Topic sentence	Audiences gather with varying degrees of willingness to hear a speaker. Some are anxious to hear the speaker, and may even have paid a substantial admission price. The
Details and transitions	"lecture circuit," for example, is a most lucrative aspect of public life. But whereas some audiences are willing to pay to hear a speaker, others don't seem to care one way or the other. Other audiences need to be persuaded to listen (or at least to sit in the audience). Still other audiences gather because they have to. For example, negotiations on a union contract may require members to attend meetings where officers give speeches.

—Joseph DeVito, *The Essential Elements of Public Speaking*

In addition to using a focused topic sentence, specific supporting details, and helpful transitions, notice how the writer repeats the words *audience(s)* and *speaker*, along with the synonyms *lecture* and *speeches*, to help tie the paragraph to the idea in the topic sentence.

🔊 **LaunchPad Solo**
macmillan learning
Visit **LaunchPad Solo for Readers and Writers > Topic Sentences and Supporting Details** for extra practice in the skills covered in this chapter.

Figure 6.1   The Structure of a Paragraph

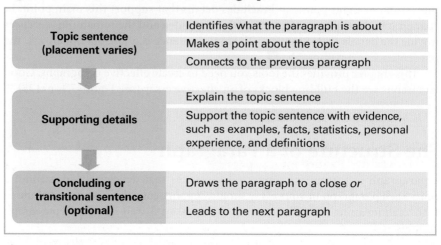

Topic sentence (placement varies)	Identifies what the paragraph is about
	Makes a point about the topic
	Connects to the previous paragraph
Supporting details	Explain the topic sentence
	Support the topic sentence with evidence, such as examples, facts, statistics, personal experience, and definitions
Concluding or transitional sentence (optional)	Draws the paragraph to a close *or*
	Leads to the next paragraph

For a paragraph to develop a single idea, it needs to have **unity**. A unified paragraph stays focused on one idea, without switching or wandering from topic to topic. A paragraph should be of a reasonable length, neither too short nor too long. Short paragraphs look skimpy and are often underdeveloped; long paragraphs are difficult for readers to follow. To visualize the structure of a well-developed paragraph, see Figure 6.1.

Reading ⓘ Writing   Paragraphs

The Reader's Perspective	The Writer's Perspective
When reading a paragraph, look first for its main point, usually expressed in the topic sentence. Then look for details that support the main point.	Before writing a paragraph, ask yourself, What is the one key point I want to make with this paragraph? Answering that question will help you craft the topic sentence and choose the details, transitions, and words or synonyms that should be repeated.

Writing a Topic Sentence

A topic sentence is to a paragraph what a thesis statement is to an essay. Just as a thesis announces the main point of an essay, a **topic sentence** states the main point of a paragraph. In addition, each paragraph's topic sentence must support the thesis of the essay. A topic sentence has several specific functions.

A Topic Sentence Should Focus the Paragraph

A topic sentence should make clear what the paragraph is about (its topic) and express a view or make a point about the topic.

———— topic ————

Shocking behavior by fans, including rudeness to players and violence toward other fans, has become common at many sporting events.

———————— point about the topic ————————

The topic sentence should tell readers what the paragraph is about in specific and detailed language. Avoid vague or general statements. Compare these examples of unfocused and focused topic sentences.

Unfocused	Some members of minority groups do not approve of affirmative action.
Focused	Some members of minority groups disapprove of affirmative action because it implies that they are not capable of obtaining employment based on their own accomplishments.

If you have trouble focusing your topic sentences, review the guidelines for writing an effective thesis statement in Chapter 5 (pp. 100–01). Many of these guidelines also apply to writing effective topic sentences.

A Topic Sentence May Preview the Organization of the Paragraph

A topic sentence may suggest the order in which details will be discussed in the paragraph, thereby helping readers know what to expect.

———— first detail ————

Teaching employees how to handle conflicts through anger management and mediation is essential in high-stress jobs.

second detail

Readers can expect a discussion of anger management first, followed by a discussion of mediation.

Exercise 6.1

Revise each topic sentence to make it focused and specific. At least two of your revised topic sentences should also preview the organization of the paragraph.

1. In society today, there is always a new fad or fashion in clothing.
2. People watch television sitcoms because they find them entertaining.

3. Tattoos are a popular trend.

4. Procrastinating can have a negative effect on your success in college.

5. In our state, the lottery is a big issue.

A Topic Sentence Should Support Your Thesis

Each topic sentence must in some way explain the thesis or show why the thesis is believable or correct. For example, the following sample thesis could be supported by the topic sentences that follow it.

Thesis

Adoption files should not be made available to adult children who are seeking their biological parents.

Topic Sentences

Research has shown that not all biological parents want to meet with the sons or daughters they gave up many years before.

Adult adoptees who try to contact their biological parents often meet resistance and even hostility, which can cause them to feel hurt and rejected.

Both topic sentences support the thesis because they offer valid reasons for keeping adoption files closed.

Exercise 6.2

For each of the following thesis statements, identify the topic sentence that does not support it.

1. To make a marriage work, a couple must build trust, communication, and understanding.
   a. Knowing why a spouse behaves as he or she does can improve a relationship.
   b. People get married for reasons other than love.
   c. The ability to talk about feelings, problems, likes, and dislikes should grow as a marriage develops.
   d. Marital partners must rely on each other to make sensible decisions that benefit both of them.

2. Internet sales are capturing a larger market share relative to in-store sales.
   a. Internet retailers that target a specific audience tend to be most successful.
   b. The convenience of ordering any time of day or night accounts, in part, for increased Internet sales.

   c. Many customers use PayPal for online purchases.

   d. Web sites that locate and compare prices for a specific item make comparison shopping easier on the Internet than in retail stores.

A Topic Sentence Should Be Strategically Placed

Where you place the topic sentence will determine the order and structure of the rest of the paragraph. The topic sentence also may have different effects, depending on its placement.

TOPIC SENTENCE FIRST

The most common, and often the best, position for a topic sentence is at the beginning of the paragraph. A paragraph that opens with the topic sentence should follow a logical sequence: You state your main point, and then you explain it. The topic sentence tells readers what to expect in the rest of the paragraph, making it clear and easy to follow.

Topic sentence	Advertising is first and foremost based on the principle of visibility—the customer must notice the product. Manufacturers often package products in glitzy, even garish, containers to grab the consumer's attention.
Explanatory details	For example, one candy company always packages its candy in reflective wrappers. When the hurried and hungry consumer glances at the candy counter, the reflective wrappers are easy to spot. It is only natural for the impatient customer to grab the candy and go.

TOPIC SENTENCE EARLY IN THE PARAGRAPH

When one or two sentences at the beginning of a paragraph are needed to smooth the transition from one paragraph to the next, the topic sentence may follow these transitional sentences.

Transitional sentence	However, visibility is not the only principle in advertising; it is simply the first. A second and perhaps
Topic sentence	more subtle principle is identity: The manufacturer attempts to lure the consumer into buying a product by linking it to a concept with which the consumer can identify. For instance, Boundaries perfume is advertised on television as the choice of "independent" women. Since independent women are admired in our culture, women identify with the concept and therefore are attracted to the perfume. Once the consumer identifies with the product, a sale is more likely to occur.

TOPIC SENTENCE LAST

The topic sentence can also appear as the last sentence in a paragraph. With this strategy, you first present the supporting details and then end the paragraph with the topic sentence, which usually states the conclusion that can be drawn from the details. Common in argumentative writing, this arrangement allows you to present convincing evidence before stating your point about the issue.

Evidence   The saying "Guns don't kill people; people kill people" always makes me even more certain of my own position on gun control. That statement is deceptive in the same way that the statement "Heroin doesn't kill people; people kill themselves" is deceptive. Naturally, people need to pull the trigger of a gun to make the gun kill other people, just as it is necessary for a person to ingest heroin for it to kill him or her. However, these facts do not excuse us from the responsibility of keeping guns (or heroin) out of people's hands as much as possible. People cannot shoot people

Topic sentence   unless they have a gun. This fact alone should persuade the government to institute stiff gun-control laws.

Reading ⓘ Writing   Topic Sentences

The Reader's Perspective	The Writer's Perspective
The topic sentence is an announcement of what the paragraph is about (its *topic*) and a statement of what the author wants you to know about that topic. Think of it as a promise of what the paragraph will deliver.	Topic sentences help you organize your ideas and keep your writing focused. A topic sentence limits you to a specific topic and requires you to explain that idea before moving on to another topic in a new paragraph.

Essay in Progress 1

Return to the thesis statement you wrote for Essay in Progress 2 in Chapter 5 (p. 101) and write topic sentences for three paragraphs that you will use to support your thesis statement.

Including Supporting Details

In addition to including a focused topic sentence, an effective paragraph provides concrete details that work together to support the main point.

Effective Paragraphs Have Unity

In a unified paragraph, all of the sentences directly support the topic sentence. Irrelevant details make your paragraph unclear and distract your reader from the point you are making. To identify irrelevant details, evaluate each sentence by asking the following questions.

1. Does this sentence directly explain the topic sentence? What new information does it add?

2. Would any essential information be lost if this sentence were deleted? (If not, delete it.)

3. Is this information distracting or unimportant? (If so, delete it.)

The following sample paragraph lacks unity. Sentences that don't relate to the ways the media promote violence should be deleted. These irrelevant sentences are highlighted in yellow.

Paragraph Lacking Unity

Topic sentence   (1) Much of the violence we see in the world today may be caused by the portrayal of violence in the media. (2) More often than not, the front page of the local newspaper contains stories involving violence. (3) In fact, one recent issue of my local newspaper contained seven references to violent acts. (4) There is also violence in public school systems. (5) Television reporters frequently rush to crime and accident scenes and film every grim, violent detail. (6) Violence in video games is another problem. (7) If the media were a little more careful about the ways in which they glamorize violence, there might be less violence in the world today and children would be less influenced by it.

Not related to topic

Not related to topic

Exercise 6.3

Working alone or in a group of two or three students, read each paragraph and identify the sentences that do not support the topic sentence. In each paragraph, the topic sentence is underlined.

1. (a) Today many options and services for the elderly are available that did not exist years ago. (b) My grandmother is eighty-five years old. (c) Adult care for the elderly is now provided in many parts of the country. (d) Similar to day care, adult care provides places where the elderly can go for meals and social activities. (e) Retirement homes for the elderly, where they can live fairly independently with minimal supervision, are another option. (f) My grandfather is also among the elderly at eighty-two. (g) Even many nursing

homes have changed so that residents are afforded some level of privacy and independence while their needs are being met.

2. (a) Just as history repeats itself, fashions have a tendency to do the same. (b) In the late 1960s, for example, women wore miniskirts that came several inches above the knee; fifty years later, the fashion magazines are featuring this same type of dress, and many teenagers are wearing them. (c) The mini-skirt has always been flattering on slender women. (d) I wonder if the fashion industry deliberately recycles fashions. (e) Men wore their hair long in the hippie period of the late 1960s and 1970s. (f) Today, some men are again letting their hair grow. (g) Beards, considered "in" during the 1970s, have once again made an appearance.

Effective Paragraphs Are Well Developed

A unified paragraph provides adequate and convincing evidence to explain the topic sentence. Include enough supporting details to demonstrate that your topic sentence is accurate and believable. Evidence can include explanations, examples, or other kinds of information that help the reader understand and believe the assertion in the topic sentence. The following example shows an underdeveloped paragraph that is revised into a well-developed paragraph.

Underdeveloped Paragraph

Email and text messaging are important technological advances, but they have hidden limitations, even dangers. It is too easy to avoid talking to people face-to-face. Using electronic communications can be addictive, too. Plus, they encourage ordinary people to ignore others while typing on a keyboard.

Developed Paragraph

Email and text messaging are important technological advances, but they have hidden limitations, even dangers. While email and text messaging allow fast and efficient communication and exchange of information, they provide a lower quality of human interaction. It is too easy to avoid talking to people. It is easier to text someone to see if she wants to meet for dinner than it would be to look up her number and actually talk to her. In the workplace, many people use email to avoid face-to-face meetings that would be more efficient and productive. At the same time, electronic communication can become addictive. For example, some people send hundreds or even thousands of text messages a day. They spend their free time texting with acquaintances across the country, while ignoring interesting people right in the same room. Because texting is not face-to-face, text addicts are shortchanging themselves of real human contact. There is something to be said for responding not only to a person's words but also to his or her expressions, gestures, and tone of voice.

These two versions of the paragraph differ in the degree to which the ideas are developed. The first paragraph does include ideas that support the topic sentence, but there are only a few ideas and they are not explained. For example, the first paragraph does not explain why email and text messaging are important or provide any evidence of how or why electronic communication can be addictive. Notice that the second paragraph explains how email and text messaging allow for fast and efficient communication and gives further information about the addictive qualities of texting. The second paragraph also explains the qualities of face-to-face interaction that are absent from electronic communication.

To determine if your paragraphs are well developed, begin by considering your audience. Have you given them enough information to find your ideas understandable and believable? Try reading your essay aloud, or ask a friend to do so. Listen for places where you jump quickly from one idea to another without explaining the first idea. To find supporting evidence for a topic sentence, use a prewriting strategy from Chapter 4. Also note that the same types of evidence used to support a thesis (Table 5.1, p. 103) can be used to develop a paragraph.

Exercise 6.4

Use Table 5.1 (p. 103) to suggest the type or types of evidence that might be used to develop a paragraph to support each of the following topic sentences.

1. Many people have fallen prey to fad diets, risking their health and jeopardizing their mental well-being.
2. One can distinguish experienced soccer players from rookies by obvious signs.
3. To begin a jogging routine, take a relaxed but deliberate approach.
4. The interlibrary loan system is a fast and convenient method for obtaining print materials from libraries affiliated with the campus library.
5. Southwest Florida's rapid population growth poses a serious threat to its freshwater supply.

Exercise 6.5

Create a well-developed paragraph by adding details to the following paragraph.

Although it is convenient, online shopping is a different experience from shopping in an actual store. You don't get the same opportunity to see and feel objects. Also, you can miss out on other important information. There is much that you miss. If you enjoy shopping, turn off your computer and support your local merchants.

Effective Paragraphs Provide Specific Supporting Details Arranged in a Logical Manner

The evidence you provide to support your topic sentences should be concrete, specific, and arranged in a logical manner. For example, you might arrange the details from most to least (or least to most) important, in chronological order, or in spatial order. Specific details will interest your readers and make your meaning clear and forceful. Compare the following two examples.

Vague

Many people are confused about the difference between a psychologist and a psychiatrist. Both have a license, but a psychiatrist has more education than a psychologist. Also, a psychiatrist can prescribe medication.

The example above contains general statements that do not completely explain the topic sentence.

Concrete and Specific

Many people are confused about the difference between psychiatrists and psychologists. Both are licensed by the state to practice psychotherapy. However, a psychiatrist has earned a degree from medical school and can also practice medicine. Additionally, a psychiatrist can prescribe psychotropic medications. A psychologist, in contrast, usually has earned a Ph.D. but has not attended medical school and therefore cannot prescribe medication of any type.

Concrete details make clear the distinction between the two types of professional in the example above. Note that the paragraph is also organized in a logical manner: First it explains what the two professionals have in common. It then explains how they differ.

To make your paragraphs concrete and specific, use the guidelines in Table 6.1.

Exercise 6.6

Working alone or in a group of two or three students, revise and expand each sentence in the following paragraph to make it concrete and specific. Feel free to add new information and new sentences.

I saw a great concert the other night in Dallas. Two groups were performing. The music was great, and there was a large crowd. In fact, the crowd was so enthusiastic that the second group performed one hour longer than scheduled.

Table 6.1   Guidelines for Making Paragraphs Concrete and Specific

Guidelines	Tips
Focus on *who*, *what*, *when*, *where*, *how*, and *why* questions.	Ask yourself these questions about your supporting details, and use the answers to expand and revise your paragraph.
Name names.	Include the names of people, places, brands, and objects.
Use action verbs.	Select strong verbs that will help your readers visualize the action.
Use descriptive language that appeals to the senses (smell, touch, taste, hearing, sight).	Words that appeal to the senses enable your readers to feel as if they were observing or participating in the experience you are describing.
Use adjectives and adverbs.	Including carefully chosen adjectives and adverbs in your description of a person, a place, or an experience can make your writing more concrete and effective.

Reading ⊕ Writing   Supporting Details

The Reader's Perspective	The Writer's Perspective
As you read a paragraph, examine the details to discover how they support the topic sentence. Details often can make a topic sentence clearer and more understandable. In fact, at times, you have to read all the details in order to fully understand the topic sentence.	If you have written a good topic sentence, supporting details should come easily. If you are having difficulty finding evidence to support your topic sentence, carefully re-examine the topic sentence. It likely requires rethinking and revision.

Essay in Progress 2

For each of the topic sentences you wrote for Essay in Progress 1 (p. 114), write a unified paragraph that is logically organized. Be sure to provide concrete, specific details.

Using Transitions and Repetition

All the details in a paragraph must fit together and function as a connected unit of information. When a paragraph has **coherence**, its ideas flow smoothly, allowing readers to follow its progression easily. Two useful devices for linking details are transitions between sentences and repetition of key terms.

As mentioned in Chapter 2, **transitions** are words, phrases, clauses, or sentences that lead your reader from one idea to another. Think of transitional expressions as guideposts, or signals, of what is coming next in a paragraph. Some commonly used transitions are shown in Table 6.2. They are grouped according to the type of connections they show.

Table 6.2   Commonly Used Transitional Expressions

Type of Connection	Transitions
Logical Connections	
Difference / opposition	but, however, on the contrary, nevertheless, neither/nor, on the one/other hand, still, yet
Illustration	for instance, for example, namely, that is
Items in a series	then, first, second, next, another, furthermore, finally, as well as
Restatement	in other words, that is, in simpler terms
Result or cause	consequently, therefore, so, hence, thus, then, as a result
Similarity / agreement	similarly, likewise, in the same way
Summary or conclusion	finally, in conclusion, to sum up, all in all, evidently, actually
Spatial Connections	
Direction	inside/outside, along, above/below, up/down, across, to the right/left, in front of/behind
Distance	beyond, in the distance, away, over there
Nearness	next to, near, nearby, facing, adjacent to

Table 6.2   (Continued)

Type of Connection	Transitions
Time Connections	
At a particular time	at two o'clock, on April 27, in 2010, last Thanksgiving, three days ago
Beginning	before then, at the beginning, at first
Duration	during, briefly, hour by hour
End	finally, at last, eventually, later, at the end, subsequently, afterward
Frequency	often, frequently, now and then, gradually, week by week, occasionally, daily, rarely
Middle	meanwhile, simultaneously, next, then, at that time

In the two examples that follow, notice that the first paragraph is disjointed and choppy because it lacks transitions, whereas the revised version is easier to follow.

Without Transitions

Most films are structured much like a short story. The film begins with an opening scene that captures the audience's attention. The writers build up tension, preparing for the climax of the story. They complicate the situation by revealing other elements of the plot, perhaps by introducing a surprise or additional characters. They introduce a problem. It will be solved either for the betterment or to the detriment of the characters and the situation. A resolution brings the film to a close.

With Transitions

Most films are structured much like a short story. The film begins with an opening scene that captures the audience's attention. Gradually, the writers build up tension, preparing for the climax of the story. Soon after the first scene, they complicate the situation by revealing other elements of the plot, perhaps by introducing a surprise or additional characters. Next, they introduce a problem. Eventually, the problem will be solved either for the betterment or to the detriment of the characters and the situation. Finally, a resolution brings the film to a close.

Notice that the **repetition** of key terms or pronouns that stand in for the key terms also lends coherence to the paragraph. For example, *they* (which stands in for *writers*) appears twice, and the word *film* appears three times.

Reading ⊕ Writing   Transitions

The Reader's Perspective	The Writer's Perspective
Transitions help you follow the writer's train of thought. They lead you from one idea to the next and are often used to signal what is to follow in the paragraph.	While transitions may seem like simple words, they send powerful signals about the material that is to come. For this reason, it is important to choose the best transition to introduce a detail.

Essay in Progress 3

Evaluate your use of transitions and repetition in each paragraph you drafted for Essay in Progress 2 (p. 119). Add transitions and repetition where needed to make the relationships among your ideas clearer and your paragraph more coherent.

Students Write

Chapters 4 to 8 show student writer Christine Lee's progress in planning and drafting an essay on reality television. Below is one of her first-draft paragraphs along with her revised, strengthened paragraph.

First-Draft Paragraph

Reality shows that followed *Survivor* didn't have the interesting elements that it had. *Big Brother* started as the first of the reality TV spin-offs, but audiences didn't have the same things to respond to. It has never been a success because they took the basic concept of *Survivor* and added nothing new or interesting to it. *Big Brother* locked up a bunch of people in a house and forced the audience to watch them bicker over nothing. Viewers were forced to watch bored contestants bicker and fight, locked up in a house with nothing else to do. It didn't seem the kind of competition that *Survivor* was, even though there was a cash prize on the line. The cash prize wasn't large enough anyway. We didn't choose favorites because the players weren't up against anything, except fighting off weeks of boredom. *Big Brother* introduced audience participation with the television audience voting off members, which gave the house members less to do and less motive to scheme and plot their allegiances like the castaways on *Survivor*. Voting members off was an arbitrary and meaningless process. But *Big Brother* had the prize component, and it took away the housemates' access to the outside world.

Revised Paragraph

Reality TV shows that followed *Survivor* had none of the interesting elements that it had. *Big Brother* was the first spin-off reality TV show to try to repeat the success of *Survivor*, but it did not offer the drama, exotic location, or million-dollar prize that *Survivor* did. In *Survivor*, different kinds of real people were the contestants, who developed a sense of camaraderie and teamwork. In *Big Brother*, contestants were locked in a house without any outside contact for weeks. As in *Survivor*, there was a cash prize on the line, but in *Big Brother* there were no competitions or struggles. Contestants were expelled by a viewer phone poll, so the poll gave them no motive to scheme and plot allegiances the way *Survivor* contestants did. In fact, the contestants had little to do except bicker and fight. Viewers lost interest in players who were not up against any challenge except weeks of boredom. In the end, *Big Brother* was simply not interesting.

Analyzing the Writer's Technique

1. How did Lee strengthen her topic sentence?
2. What irrelevant details did she delete?
3. What transitions did she add to provide coherence?
4. What words are repeated that contribute to coherence?
5. What further revisions do you recommend?

To see the next step in Lee's essay (drafting an essay), see pages 141–42.

In this chapter, you will learn to

- Structure an essay based on its parts and functions.

- Organize your supporting details.

- Write the first draft of an essay.

- Use transitions and repetition to connect your ideas.

- Write an effective introduction, conclusion, and title for your essay.

7

Drafting an Essay

M Photo/Exactostock-1527/SuperStock.com

Reflect on a Visual Text

The photograph to the left illustrates a problem many people feel strongly about and are committed to solving.

1 Ask yourself questions. What exactly is the problem? Why does it exist? Does the photograph effectively illustrate this problem?

2 Brainstorm ideas. Working alone or with two or three classmates, write a sentence that states your opinion on why animal rescue is or is not important. Then support this opinion with a list of details (evidence) from your own knowledge and experience or do a quick Google search to locate information. Number your best piece of evidence 1, your second-best piece 2, and so on. Cross out any details that do not support your opinion, or adjust your original sentence if the evidence you gathered contradicts it.

3 Write. Now write a paragraph that begins with the sentence you wrote expressing your opinion and includes your evidence, in order of importance.

The paragraph you wrote could be part of an essay on how animal rescue programs work. To write an essay you would likely need to do additional pre-writing and research on this topic. Then you would write a thesis statement, develop supporting paragraphs, write an effective introduction and conclusion, and choose a good title. This chapter will guide you through developing an essay in support of a thesis statement, yet another part of the writing process (see Figure 4.1, pp. 80–81). 🔀

The Structure of an Essay

Figure 7.1 presents the structure of an effective essay. As the figure shows, an essay has a title and an introduction. It also makes an assertion (the thesis statement) that is explained and supported throughout the body of the essay. The essay ends

Figure 7.1   The Structure of an Essay: Parts and Functions

Title	May announce your subject
	Sparks readers' interest

Introduction	**Paragraph 1** (or introduction can be two or more paragraphs)
	Identifies your narrowed topic
	Presents your thesis
	Interests your readers
	Provides background

Body	**Body paragraphs***
	Support and explain your thesis

Conclusion	**Final paragraph**
	Reemphasizes your thesis (does *not* merely restate it)
	Draws your essay to a close

*There is no set number of paragraphs that an essay should contain. The number depends on your narrowed topic, purpose, and audience.

🔀 **LaunchPad Solo**   Visit **LaunchPad Solo for Readers and Writers > Drafting** for extra
macmillan learning   practice in the skills covered in this chapter.

with a final statement, its conclusion. Each paragraph in an essay is unified and coherent. (For more information about paragraphs, see Chapter 6.)

Organizing Your Supporting Details

The body paragraphs of your essay support your thesis. Before you begin writing these paragraphs, decide on the supporting evidence you will use and the order in which you will present it. (For more on developing a thesis and selecting evidence to support it, see Chapter 5.)

Selecting a Method of Organization

Three common ways to organize ideas are most-to-least (or least-to-most) order, chronological order, and spatial order.

MOST-TO-LEAST (OR LEAST-TO-MOST) ORDER

If you choose the **most-to-least** or the **least-to-most** method of organizing an essay, arrange your supporting details from most to least — or least to most — important, familiar, interesting, or persuasive. You might begin with your most convincing evidence or, alternatively, you might build up to your strongest point. You can visualize these two options by examining Figure 7.2.

Exercise 7.1

For each of the following narrowed topics, identify several qualities or characteristics that you could use to organize details in most-to-least or least-to-most order.

1. Stores in which you shop
2. Friends
3. Members of a sports team
4. Fast-food restaurants
5. Television shows you watched this week

CHRONOLOGICAL ORDER

When you put your supporting details in the sequence in which they happened, you are using **chronological order**. For this method of organization, begin the body of your essay with the first event, and progress through the other events as they occurred or should occur, whether the time increment is in minutes, hours, days, or years. You can visualize chronological order with the help of Figure 7.3.

Figure 7.2 **Essay Organization: Most-to-Least and Least-to-Most Order**

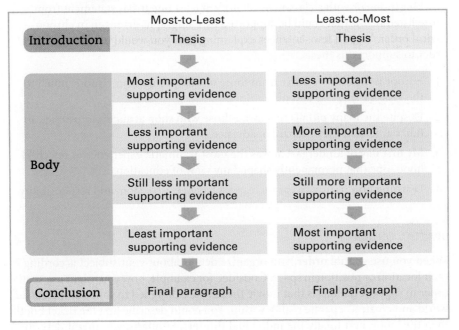

Figure 7.3 **Essay Organization: Chronological Order**

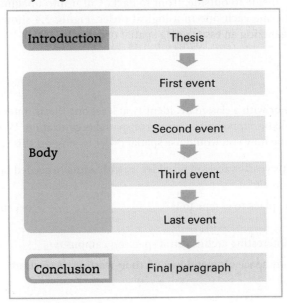

Exercise 7.2

Working alone or with a classmate, identify at least one thesis statement from those listed below that could be supported by paragraphs arranged in chronological order. Write a few sentences explaining how you would use chronological order to support this thesis.

1. European mealtimes differ from those of many American visitors, much to the visitors' surprise and discomfort.

2. Despite the many pitfalls that await those who shop at auctions, people can find bargains if they prepare in advance.

3. My first day of kindergarten was the most traumatic experience of my childhood, one that permanently shaped my view of education.

4. Learning how to drive a car increases a teenager's freedom and responsibility.

SPATIAL ORDER

When you use **spatial order**, you organize details about your subject according to their location or position in space. Consider, for example, how you might use spatial order to support the thesis that movie theaters are designed to shut out the outside world and create a separate reality within. You could describe first the ticket booth, then the lobby, and finally the individual theaters. Similarly, you might describe a basketball court from midcourt to backboard or a person from head to toe.

You can best visualize spatial organization by picturing your subject in your mind or by sketching it on paper. "Look" at your subject systematically—from top to bottom, inside to outside, front to back. Cut it into imaginary sections or pieces and describe each one in a logical order. Figure 7.4 shows two possible options for organizing an essay using spatial order.

Exercise 7.3

Working alone or with a classmate, identify at least one thesis statement listed below that could be supported by means of spatial organization. Write a few sentences explaining how you would use spatial order to support this thesis.

1. Our family's yearly vacation provides us with a much-needed opportunity to renew family ties.

2. My favorite place to escape to is _____ because it _____.

3. The most interesting architectural space on campus is _____.

4. A clear study space can cut down on time-wasting distractions.

Figure 7.4   Essay Organization: Two Ways to Use Spatial Order

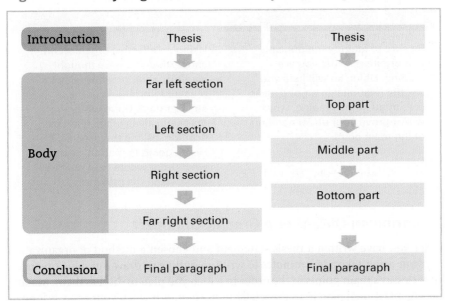

Essay in Progress 1

Choose one of the following activities.

1. Using the thesis statement and evidence you gathered for the Essay in Progress activities in Chapter 5, choose a method for organizing your essay. Then explain briefly how you will use that method of organization.

2. Choose one of the following narrowed topics. Then, using the steps in Figure 4.1 (pp. 80–81), prewrite to produce ideas, develop a thesis, and generate evidence to support the thesis. Next, choose a method for organizing your essay and briefly explain how you will use it.

   a. Positive (or negative) experiences with computers

   b. Stricter (or more lenient) regulations for teenage drivers

   c. Factors that account for the popularity of action films

   d. Discipline in public elementary schools

   e. Advantages (or disadvantages) of text messaging

Reading ① Writing   Order/Method of Organization

The Reader's Perspective	The Writer's Perspective
Be sure to identify the principle that organizes what you are reading. Doing so will help you see the relationship among ideas presented in the reading, which will improve your understanding of the main point.	Using an effective organization shows that you have thought carefully about the best way to present information or make an argument. Good writers put themselves in the reader's position, asking themselves, If I were going to read this essay, what order would help me best understand the material?

Preparing an Outline or a Graphic Organizer

After you have written a thesis statement and chosen a method of organization for your essay, take a few minutes to write an outline or draw a graphic organizer of the essay's main points in the order in which you plan to discuss them. Making an organizational plan is an especially important step when your essay is long or deals with a complex topic.

Outlining or drawing a graphic organizer can help you plan your essay as well as discover new ideas to include. Either method will help you see how ideas fit together and may reveal places where you need to add supporting information.

There are two types of outlines—informal and formal. An **informal outline**, also called a *scratch outline*, uses key words and phrases to list main points and subpoints. An informal outline does not necessarily follow the standard outline format of numbered and lettered headings. Here is an example of one student's informal outline.

Sample Informal Outline

Thesis: Working as a literacy volunteer taught me more about learning and friendship than I ever expected.

Paragraph 1: Learned about the learning process

> Went through staff training program
>
> Learned about words "in context"

Paragraph 2: Discovered the importance of reading for Marie

> Couldn't take bus, walked to grocery store
>
> Couldn't buy certain products
>
> Couldn't write out grocery lists

Paragraph 3: Marie increased her self-confidence

> Made rapid progress
>
> Began taking bus
>
> Helped son with reading

Paragraph 4: Developed a permanent friendship

    Saw each other often

    Both single parents

    Helped each other babysit

Conclusion: I benefited more than Marie did.

A **formal outline** uses Roman numerals (I, II), capital letters (A, B), Arabic numbers (1, 2), and lowercase letters (a, b) to designate levels of importance. There are two categories of formal outline: **Sentence outlines** use complete sentences, and **topic outlines** use only key words and phrases. In either type of formal outline, minor entries are indented, as in the sample formal outline below. Each topic or sentence begins with a capital letter. Here is a format showing the beginning of a formal outline.

Format for a Formal Outline

  I. First main topic
    A. First subtopic of I
    B. Second subtopic of I
      1. First detail about I.B
      2. Second detail about I.B
    C. Third subtopic of I
      1. First detail about I.C
        a. First detail or example about I.C.1
        b. Second detail or example about I.C.1
      2. Second detail about I.C
  II. Second main topic

Here is a sample outline that a student wrote for an essay for her interpersonal communication class.

Sample Formal Outline

  I. Types of listening
    A. Participatory
      1. Involves the listener responding to the speaker
      2. Has expressive quality
        a. Maintain eye contact
        b. Express feelings using facial expressions
    B. Nonparticipatory
      1. Involves the listener listening without talking or responding
      2. Allows speaker to develop his or her thoughts without interruption
    C. Critical
      1. Involves the listener analyzing and evaluating the message
      2. Is especially important in college classes
        a. Listen for instructors' biases
        b. Evaluate evidence in support of opinions expressed

Remember that all items labeled with the same designation (capital letters, for example) should be at the same level of importance, and each must explain or support the topic or subtopic under which it is placed. Also, all items at the same level should be grammatically parallel.

Not parallel	I.	Dietary Problems
		A. Consuming too much fat
		B. High consumption of refined sugar
Parallel	I.	Dietary Problems
		A. Consuming too much fat
		B. Consuming too much refined sugar

If your instructor allows, you can use both phrases and sentences within an outline, as long as you do so consistently. You might write all subtopics (designated by capital letters A, B, and so on) as sentences and all supporting details (designated by 1, 2, and so on) as phrases, for instance.

Begin by putting your working thesis statement at the top of a piece of paper or word-processing document. Then list your main points below your thesis. If you are writing by hand, be sure to leave plenty of space between main points. While you are filling in the details that support one main point, you will often think of details or examples to use in support of a different main point. As these details or examples occur to you, jot them down under or next to the appropriate main point of your outline or graphic organizer. (For more about graphic organizers, see Chapter 2.)

The graphic organizer shown in Figure 7.5, which was made for the same essay as the informal outline on pages 130–31, follows a chronological method of organization.

Essay in Progress 2

For the topic you chose in Essay in Progress 1, write a brief outline or draw a graphic organizer to show the organizational plan of your essay.

Writing a Draft

Once you have collected your ideas and thought about how to organize them, you are ready to write a first draft. A **draft** is a preliminary or tentative version of your essay. Drafting is a process of putting your ideas into sentence and paragraph form. It provides an opportunity to try out your ideas and see if and how they work together. Expect to write several drafts before you end up with one you are satisfied with. Use the guidelines in Table 7.1 for assistance with drafting.

Figure 7.5 Sample Graphic Organizer

Title	The Value of Volunteering
Introduction	**Thesis:** Working as a literacy volunteer taught me more about learning and friendship than I ever expected.
Body paragraphs	Learned about the learning process
	Went through staff training program
	Learned about words "in context"
	Discovered the importance of reading for Marie
	Couldn't take bus, walked to grocery store
	Couldn't buy certain products
	Couldn't write out grocery lists
	Marie increased her self-confidence
	Made rapid progress
	Began taking bus
	Helped son with reading
	Developed a permanent friendship
	Saw each other often
	Both single parents
	Helped each other babysit
Conclusion	I benefited more than Marie did.

Table 7.1 Guidelines for Writing a First Draft

Guidelines	Tips
Start by writing or reviewing your thesis statement.	Make sure your thesis statement is specific and focused. (See Chapter 5 for suggestions on writing a thesis statement.)
Work on developing and expressing ideas that explain your thesis.	Use an outline or a graphic organizer as a guide. Work on ideas that you like best or that will support your thesis particularly well.

Continued >

Table 7.1 (continued)

Guidelines	Tips
Devote one paragraph to each important idea that directly explains your thesis statement.	Refer to Chapter 6 for help with drafting and organizing paragraphs.
Think of drafting as a means of experimenting and testing ideas.	Plan on making changes and writing several drafts. As you draft, you may realize that some ideas do not work. You may think of a better way to organize your ideas. And you may discover new ideas that are better than what you originally started with.
Be prepared to change your topic or focus.	Once in a while, you may realize that your topic isn't working or that you should choose a different thesis statement. If your draft isn't working, do not hesitate to start over.
Focus on ideas first.	As you draft, first be concerned with expressing your ideas. Once you are satisfied that you have said what you want, then focus on correctness — grammar, spelling, punctuation, and so forth.
Allow time between drafts.	You will find that time away from the draft gives you a fresh perspective and allows you to improve on what you have written.
Seek help from classmates or others.	If you think a draft is not working but do not know why, do not hesitate to ask a classmate, a writing center tutor, or your instructor to read and comment on it.

Reading ⬤ Writing   The First Draft

The Reader's Perspective	The Writer's Perspective
Most of the time, you read a final work, not a first draft. However, you may sometimes be asked to review someone else's first draft. Think of this review as an opportunity to help someone else improve his or her writing. The guidelines for peer review in Chapter 8 (pp. 152–53) may be helpful.	It is best to approach the first draft with the expectation that it will not be perfect and will need to be revised. Understanding that a draft is just the first step in writing a good essay may help to reduce any anxiety you feel as you begin a writing assignment.

Using Transitions and Repetition to Connect Your Ideas

To show how your ideas are related, be sure to use transitions between sentences and paragraphs as well as repetition of key words and the synonyms and pronouns that refer to them. Use transitions and repetition both within your paragraphs (see Chapter 6, pp. 120–22) and between paragraphs.

Using Transitional Expressions to Connect Ideas

Recall that a **transitional expression** — which can be a word, phrase, clause, or sentence — shows the reader how a new sentence or paragraph is connected to the one before or after it. A transitional expression may also remind the reader of an idea discussed earlier in the essay. For a list of commonly used transitions and the connections they suggest, see Table 6.2 on pages 120–21.

In the example that follows, the italicized transitional clause connects the two paragraphs by reminding the reader of the main point of the first.

> A compliment is a brief and pleasant way of opening lines of communication and demonstrating goodwill. . . .
>
> *Although compliments do demonstrate goodwill,* they should be used sparingly; otherwise they may seem contrived. . . .

Especially in lengthy essays (five pages or longer), you may find it helpful to include one or more transitional clauses or sentences that recap what you have said so far and suggest the direction of the essay from that point forward. The following example is from a student essay on the invasion of privacy.

> Thus, the invasion of privacy is not limited to financial and consumer information; invasion of medical and workplace privacy is increasingly common. What can individuals do to protect their privacy in each of these areas?

Thus, at the beginning of the first sentence, signals that the sentence is going to summarize the types of invasion of privacy already discussed in the essay. The second sentence signals that the discussion will shift to the preventive measures that individuals can take.

Using Repeated Words to Connect Ideas

Repetition of key words or their **synonyms** (words that have similar meanings) from one paragraph to another helps keep your readers focused on your essay's main point. In the following sentences, the italicized key words focus the readers' attention on the topic of liars and lying.

There are many types of *liars*, but all put forth *dishonest* or *misleading* information. The occasional *liar* is the most common type of *liar* and *lies* to avoid embarrassing or unpleasant situations.

Writing Your Introduction, Conclusion, and Title

When you write an essay, you don't have to start with the title and introduction and write straight through to the end. Some students prefer to write the body of the essay first and then the introduction and the conclusion. Others prefer to write an introduction as a way of getting started. Some students think of a title before they start writing; others find it easier to write the title when the essay is finished. Regardless of when you write them, the introduction, conclusion, and title are important components of a well-written essay.

Writing a Strong Introduction

Your introduction creates a first, and often lasting, impression. It focuses your readers on your topic and establishes the tone of your essay. Based on your introduction, your readers will form an expectation of what the essay will be about and the approach it will take. Because the introduction is crucial, take the time to get it right.

Two sample introductions to student essays follow. Although they are written on the same topic, notice how each creates an entirely different impression and set of expectations.

Introduction 1

Sexual harassment has received a great deal of attention in recent years. It occurs everywhere, from the highest offices of government to factories in small towns. Sexual harassment cases have been tried in court and publicized on national television for all Americans to witness. This focus on sexual harassment has been, in and of itself, a good and necessary thing. However, when a first-grade boy makes national headlines because he kissed a little girl of the same age and is accused of "sexual harassment," the American public needs to take a serious look at the definition of sexual harassment.

Introduction 2

Sexual harassment in the workplace seems to happen with alarming frequency. As a woman who works part-time in a male-dominated office, I have witnessed at least six incidents of sexual harassment aimed at me and my female colleagues on various occasions during the past three months alone. For example, in one incident, a male coworker repeatedly made kissing sounds whenever I passed his desk, even after I explained that his actions made me uncomfortable. A female coworker was invited to dinner several times by her male supervisor; each time she refused. The last time she refused, he made a veiled threat, "You obviously aren't happy working with me. Perhaps a transfer is in order." These incidents were not isolated, did not happen to only one woman, and were initiated by more than one man. My colleagues and I are not the only victims. Sexual harassment is on the rise and will continue to increase unless women speak out against it loudly and to a receptive audience.

In introduction 1, the writer focuses on the definition of sexual harassment. Introduction 2 has an entirely different emphasis — the frequency of incidents of sexual harassment. Each introductory paragraph has a different tone as well. Introduction 1 suggests a sense of mild disbelief, whereas introduction 2 conveys anger, perhaps even outrage. From introduction 1, you expect the writer to examine definitions of sexual harassment and, perhaps, suggest his or her own definition. From introduction 2, you expect the writer to present additional cases of sexual harassment and suggest ways women can speak out against it.

In addition to establishing a focus and tone, your introduction should do the following:

- present your thesis statement
- interest your reader
- provide any background information your reader may need

TIPS FOR WRITING A STRONG INTRODUCTION

The following suggestions will help you write strong introductions that capture your readers' interest.

1. **Ask a provocative or disturbing question.** Also consider posing a series of short, related questions that will direct your readers' attention to the key points in your essay.
2. **Begin with a story or an anecdote.** Choose one that will appeal to your audience and is relevant to your thesis.
3. **Offer a quotation.** The quotation should illustrate or emphasize your thesis.
4. **Cite a little-known or shocking fact or statistic.**
5. **Move from general to specific.** Begin with the category or general subject area to which your topic belongs, and narrow it to arrive at your thesis.
6. **State a commonly held misconception or a position that you oppose.** Your thesis would then correct the misconception or state your position on the issue.
7. **Begin with a striking example.** This example should draw readers in with surprising information or an interesting anecdote that connects to your topic.

MISTAKES TO AVOID

The following advice will help you avoid the most common mistakes in writing introductions.

1. **Do not make an announcement.** Avoid sentences that begin with "I am writing to explain" or "This essay will discuss."

2. **Keep your introduction short.** An introduction that goes beyond two paragraphs will probably sound long-winded and make your readers impatient.

3. **Avoid statements that discourage your readers from continuing.** Statements such as "This process may seem complicated, but . . ." may make your readers apprehensive.

4. **Avoid a casual, overly familiar, or chatty tone.** Openings such as "Whoa, did it surprise me when" or "You'll never in a million years believe what happened" are not appropriate for academic or professional writing.

5. **Be sure your topic is clear and adequately explained.** For example, do not begin an essay by stating, "I oppose Proposition 413 and urge you to vote against it." Before stating your position, explain to readers what Proposition 413 is and what it proposes.

Reading ⏺ Writing   The Introduction

The Reader's Perspective	The Writer's Perspective
A good introduction grabs your attention immediately, making you want to read more. The introduction also sets the tone for the entire essay and tells you what to expect in the paragraphs that follow.	Good writers make sure that their writing fulfills the expectations created by the introduction. However, introductions can be difficult to write. If you have trouble, write a tentative introductory paragraph and return to it later. Once you have written the body of your essay, you may find it easier to complete the introduction.

Writing an Effective Conclusion

A good essay does not end abruptly with the last supporting or body paragraph. Instead, a good essay ends with a concise, effective conclusion—a separate paragraph that (1) reiterates (without directly restating) the importance of your thesis and (2) brings your essay to a satisfying close.

TIPS FOR WRITING AN EFFECTIVE CONCLUSION

In most essays, the conclusion should summarize your main points and reaffirm your thesis. You might also make your conclusion more memorable and forceful by using one of the following suggestions.

1. **Look ahead.** Take your readers beyond the scope and time frame of your essay.

2. **Remind readers of the relevance of the issue.** Suggest why your thesis is important.

3. **Offer a recommendation or make a call to action.** Urge your readers to take specific steps that follow logically from your thesis.

4. **Discuss broader implications.** Point to larger issues not fully addressed in the essay, but do not introduce a completely new issue.

5. **Conclude with a fact, a quotation, an anecdote, or an example that emphasizes your thesis.** These endings will bring a sense of closure and connect your essay to the real world.

MISTAKES TO AVOID

The following advice will help you avoid mistakes commonly made in conclusions.

1. **Avoid a direct restatement of your thesis.** An exact repetition of your thesis will make your essay seem dull and mechanical.

2. **Avoid standard phrases.** Don't use phrases such as "To sum up," "In conclusion," or "It can be seen, then." They are routine and tiresome.

3. **Avoid introducing new points in your conclusion.** All major points should have been discussed in the body of your essay.

4. **Avoid apologizing for yourself, your work, or your ideas.** Do not say, for example, "Although I am only twenty-one, it seems to me."

5. **Avoid weakening your stance in the conclusion.** For instance, if your essay has criticized someone's behavior, do not back down by saying, "After all, she's only human."

Reading ① Writing   The Conclusion

The Reader's Perspective	The Writer's Perspective
Reading a good conclusion gives you a feeling of satisfaction and closure. An effective conclusion also refers back to the thesis, helping fix it firmly in your memory.	A good conclusion usually gives you a feeling of accomplishment. By closing an essay on a strong note, you imply, "I'm satisfied with what I've written. I've stated my key points and supported them strongly. I know my readers are going to respond the way I want them to."

Writing a Good Title

The title of your essay should suggest your topic and spark your readers' interest. Depending on the purpose, intended audience, and tone of your essay, your title may be direct and informative, witty, or intriguing. The following suggestions will help you write effective titles.

1. **Write straightforward, descriptive titles for most academic essays.**

   Lotteries: A Game Players Can Little Afford

2. **Ask a question that your essay answers.**

   Who Plays the Lottery?

3. **Use alliteration.** Repeating initial sounds, or using *alliteration*, often produces a catchy title.

   Lotteries: Dreaming about Dollars

4. **Consider using a play on words or a catchy or humorous expression.** This technique may work well for less formal essays.

   If You Win, You Lose

5. **Avoid broad, vague titles that sound like labels.** Titles such as "Baseball Fans" or "Gun Control" provide your reader with too little information.

Exercise 7.4

Suggest a title for each of the following essays. Try to use each of the above suggestions at least once.

1. An essay explaining the legal rights of tenants
2. An essay opposing human cloning
3. An essay on causes and effects of road rage
4. An essay comparing fitness routines
5. An essay explaining how to choose a primary-care physician

Reading ① Writing   The Title

The Reader's Perspective	The Writer's Perspective
The title is a key to understanding the reading — it offers clues to what to expect from the writer. It often announces the topic and may suggest the writer's approach toward it.	The title offers you the opportunity to summarize your essay's topic, approach, content, and point of view — all in one line.

Essay in Progress 3

Using the outline or graphic organizer you created in Essay in Progress 2 (p. 132), write a first draft of your essay.

Students Write

The first draft of a narrative essay by student writer Christine Lee follows. Lee used her freewriting (see Chapter 4, pp. 95–96) and her working thesis (see Chapter 5, p. 107) as the basis for her draft, adding details after more brainstorming (see Chapter 5, p. 107). You will also notice the paragraph you saw in Chapter 6 (p. 123). Because she was writing a first draft, Lee did not worry about correcting the errors in grammar, punctuation, and mechanics. (You will see her revised draft in Chapter 8.)

First Draft

The Reality of Real TV

Do you remember life before reality TV? One look at a *TV Guide* today shows an overload of reality-based programming, even with the guaranteed failure of most of these shows. Before reality TV there was mostly situational comedies and serial dramas. When *Survivor* caught every viewer's attention, every network in America believed they must also become "real" to keep up its ratings. As the popularity of reality TV continues unabated, shows are becoming both less interesting and more distasteful.

Reality TV shows that followed *Survivor* had none of the interesting elements that it had. *Big Brother* was the first spin-off reality TV show to try to repeat the success of *Survivor*, but it did not offer the drama, exotic location, or million-dollar prize that *Survivor* did. In *Survivor*, different kinds of real people were the contestants, who developed a sense of camaraderie and teamwork. In *Big Brother*, contestants were locked in a house without any outside contact for weeks. As in *Survivor*, there was a cash prize on the line, but in *Big Brother* there were no competitions or struggles. Contestants were expelled by a viewer phone poll, so the poll gave them no motive to scheme and plot allegiances the way *Survivor* contestants did. In fact, the contestants had little to do except bicker and fight. Viewers lost interest in players who were not up against any challenge except weeks of boredom. In the end, *Big Brother* added nothing new and was simply not interesting.

Although nothing seems to capture ratings like the original *Survivor*, networks have continued to use sensational gimmicks to appeal to the audience's basic instincts. Nothing good was carried over from *Survivor*, and the new shows just had extreme situations. *Fear Factor* had contestants commit all sorts of gross and terrifying things like eating worms. Of course, some people liked it, but there will always be weirdoes who like that kind of stuff. But most viewers are disgusted by this.

When these gimmicks did not retain viewers, they turned back to two traditional types of reality TV and put modern twists on them: the talent show and the beauty contest. So were born shows like *American Idol*, *America's Got*

Talent and *America's Next Top Model*. Again, there was no built in drama like in *Survivor* so they tried to create drama with the colorful judges and supportive fans. At first, the shows were exciting with the singing and the beauty, but after a while, audiences lost interest.

The next round of shows had to do with special interests like cooking and shows like *Hell's Kitchen* and *Top Chef*. There were also dance shows like *So You Think You Can Dance* and *Dancing with the Stars*. *The Biggest Loser* was a weight loss competition. *Project Runway* was a fashion designer competition. *The Apprentice* was about business and *Shear Genius* was about hair stylists. These shows appealed to only small numbers of people and had manufactured and contrived situations for the contestants to act in.

Recently reality shows are about everyday lives or celebrities. *The Real World* was the first kind, following young adults as they drank and slept around. *The Simple Life* was a celebrity show with Paris Hilton and Nicole Richie. Soon it seemed every celebrity had a reality show — Ozzy Osbourne, Paula Abdul, Tori Spelling, Bret Michaels, and more. The more minor the celebrity, the more likely he or she was to have a TV show — an example was *Kathy Griffin: My Life on the D-List*. The next wave of shows was people in weird situations like *Jon & Kate Plus Eight*. These programs showed people at their worst. Networks continue to try to find new and different scenarios to find the next big thing in reality TV. The shows just get more specialized and more bizarre. Some real-estate shows follow couples around as they search for a house (boring!) or renovate the house they live in now (a little less boring).

Since *Survivor*, reality shows have gone from terror and violence to talent and beauty to special interest shows and last to shows following real people. It's the viewers who decide what is popular. Reality shows continue to be popular even though they're getting more tasteless and contrived-looking. I hope viewers get tired of all these cheap gimmicks and call for more entertaining programming.

Analyzing the Writer's Technique

1. Evaluate Lee's title and introduction. Which tip for writing a strong conclusion did Lee use?
2. Evaluate Lee's thesis statement. Is it clear? How could it be improved?
3. Does Lee provide adequate details for her essay? If not, what additional information might she include?
4. How does Lee organize her ideas? Is her organization clear and effective?
5. Evaluate her supporting paragraphs. Which paragraphs need more detail? Identify where Lee uses transitional expressions and repetition.
6. Evaluate the conclusion. How does it draw the essay to a close?

To see the next step in Lee's essay (revising), see pages 162–65.

8

Revising Content and Organization

In this chapter, you will learn to

- Use helpful techniques for revising your essay.

- Ask key questions to guide your revision.

- Work with classmates to revise your essay.

- Use your instructor's comments as part of your revision process.

- Edit and proofread your work.

Photo courtesy of the North Dakota National Guard

Reflect on a Visual Text

Carefully look at the photograph above. Start on the left side of the photo and proceed slowly across to the right side, observing everything that is happening.

1 **Ask yourself questions.** What is happening in the photo? What is the likely location? How would you describe the facial expressions and emotions shown in the photo? →

143

2 **Brainstorm ideas.** List everything that is happening in the photo. Then examine your list, looking for ways to make it more understandable to someone who has not seen the photo.

3 **Write.** Now write a paragraph summarizing what you think is going on in the photo. Add details and rearrange sentences as necessary to describe the photo more fully and effectively. Do these changes make it easier for a reader who has not seen the photo to understand what is happening in it?

4 **Collaborate.** Exchange paragraphs with a classmate and examine how your classmate organized ideas. Look for parts that you find confusing or that need more detail. Write down your comments for your classmate. Finally, using your own thoughts and the comments of your classmate, make changes to improve your own description of the photograph.

When you improved on your list in Step 2 above, did you include more details from the photo? Leave some unimportant details out? In doing either of these, you *revised* the description of the photo and improved your content.

Revising an essay works in much the same way. **Revision** is a process of making changes to improve both what your essay says and how it says it. This chapter offers several approaches to revising an essay. It lists some general suggestions, describes how to use a graphic organizer for revision, and offers specific questions to guide your revision. As noted in Figure 4.1 (pp. 80–81), revision is an essential part of the writing process.

Useful Techniques for Revision

A thorough, thoughtful revision can change a C paper to an A paper! Revising can make a significant difference in how well your paper achieves your purpose and how effectively it expresses your ideas to your intended audience. All first drafts require at least some revision. Although revision takes time and hard work, it pays off and produces results.

Revision is not a process of correcting grammatical errors. Rather, revision is a process of looking again at your *ideas* to make them clearer and easier to understand. It may mean adding, eliminating, or reorganizing key elements within the essay. It may even mean revising your thesis statement and refocusing the entire essay.

The techniques in Table 8.1 will help you get the most benefit from the time you spend revising your essays.

 **LaunchPad Solo** macmillan learning Visit **LaunchPad Solo for Readers and Writers > Revising** for extra practice in the skills covered in this chapter.

Table 8.1   Guidelines for Effective Revision

Guidelines	Tips
Allow time between drafting and revising.	Once you have finished writing, set your draft aside for a while, overnight if possible. When you return to your draft, you will be able to approach it from a fresh perspective.
Read your draft aloud.	Hearing what you have written will help you discover main points that are unclear or that lack adequate support. You will notice confusing paragraphs, awkward wording, and vague or overused expressions.
Ask a friend to read your draft aloud to you.	If your reader hesitates, slows down, misreads, or sounds confused, it may be a signal that your message is not as clear as it should be. Keep a copy of your draft in front of you as you listen, and mark places where your reader falters or seems baffled.
Seek the opinions of classmates.	Ask a classmate to read and comment on your paper. This process, called *peer review*, is discussed in detail later in this chapter (see pp. 150–53).
Look for consistent problem areas.	After writing and revising several essays, you may discover consistent problem areas, such as a lack of concrete details.
Use a printed copy.	On a printed copy of your essay, you can see a full page at a time, compared to only a few paragraphs at a time on a computer screen. Also, on a printed copy you can write marginal annotations, circle troublesome words or sentences, and draw arrows to connect details.

One of the best ways to reexamine your essay is to draw a graphic organizer — a visual display — of your thesis statement and supporting paragraphs. A graphic organizer allows you to see how your thesis and topic sentences relate to one another. It also can help you evaluate both the content and the organization of your essay.

As you draw your graphic organizer, record next to it issues you find in the essay, such as an example that does not support a topic sentence, as shown in Figure 8.3 (pp. 160–61). Another option is to write an outline of your draft. (For more information on outlining, see Chapter 7, pages 130–32.)

Key Questions for Revision

The seven key questions listed below will help you identify areas of your essay that need revision. Use the questions to identify broad areas of weakness in your essay.

- **Does your essay clearly convey a purpose and address the appropriate audience?**
- **Does your essay state a thesis?**
- **Do you have enough reasons and evidence to support your thesis?**
- **Are the topic sentences effective?**
- **Do the ideas in your essay fit together? In other words, is your essay well organized?**
- **Does your essay have a strong introduction, conclusion, and title?**
- **Is each paragraph well developed?**

After reading your draft or after discussing it with a classmate, answer each of these seven questions to pinpoint areas that need improvement. Then refer to the flowcharts in the following sections.

Analyzing Your Purpose and Audience

First drafts sometimes lack focus or a clear purpose. For instance, one section of an essay on divorce may inform readers of its causes, while another section may discuss divorce rates in different countries. The two sections do not share a common purpose.

A first draft may also contain sections that appeal to different audiences. For instance, one section of an essay on counseling teenagers about drug abuse might seem to be written for parents; other sections might be more appropriate for teenagers. (For more information about purpose and audience, see Chapter 4, pp. 86–87.)

To find out if your paper has a clear focus, write a sentence stating what your paper is supposed to accomplish. If you cannot write such a sentence, your essay probably lacks a clear purpose. To find a purpose, do some additional thinking or brainstorming, listing as many possible purposes as you can think of.

To find out if your essay is directed to a specific audience, write a sentence or two describing your intended readers. Describe their knowledge, beliefs, and experience with your topic. If you are unable to do so, try to zero in on a particular audience and revise your essay with it in mind.

Essay in Progress 1

Evaluate the purpose and audience of the draft essay you wrote for Essay in Progress 3 in Chapter 7 (p. 140) or of any other essay that you have written. Make notes on your graphic organizer or annotate your outline.

Evaluating Your Thesis Statement, Topic Sentences, and Evidence

Once you have determined if your paper is focused on a specific purpose and audience, your next step is to evaluate your thesis statement and your support for that thesis. Use Figure 8.1 to examine your thesis statement, topic sentences, and evidence.

Essay in Progress 2

Using Figure 8.1, evaluate the thesis statement, topic sentences, and evidence in the draft essay you wrote for Essay in Progress 3 in Chapter 7 (p. 140). Make notes on your graphic organizer or annotate your outline.

Evaluating Your Organization

Your readers will not be able to follow your ideas if your essay does not hold together as a unified piece of writing. To be sure that it does, examine your essay's organization. Your graphic organizer or outline will help you analyze the draft's organization and discover any flaws.

To determine if the organization of your draft is clear and effective, you can also ask a classmate to read your draft and explain how your essay is organized. If your classmate cannot describe your essay's organization, it probably needs further work. Use one of the methods in Chapter 7 (pp. 126–30) or one of the patterns of development described in Table 9.1 (pp. 171–73) to reorganize your ideas.

Essay in Progress 3

Evaluate the organization of your essay in progress. Make notes on your draft copy.

Evaluating Your Introduction, Conclusion, and Title

Once you are satisfied with the draft's organization, analyze your introduction, conclusion, and title. Use the questions in Table 8.2 as guide.

You should also use the suggestions in Chapter 7 to help you revise your introduction (pp. 136–38), conclusion (pp. 138–39), and title (pp. 139–40).

Essay in Progress 3

Evaluate the introduction, conclusion, and title of your draft. Make notes on your draft copy.

Figure 8.1   Flowchart for Evaluating Your Thesis Statement, Topic Sentences, and Evidence

QUESTIONS	REVISION STRATEGIES
1. Thesis Does your essay have a thesis statement that identifies your topic and states your position or suggests your slant on the topic? — **No** →	• Reread your essay and determine the one main point it is mostly concerned with. • Write a thesis statement that expresses that main point. • Revise your paper to focus on that main point. • Delete parts of the essay that do not support your thesis statement.
Yes ↓	
2. Background information Have you given your readers all the background information they need to understand your thesis? — **No** →	• Answer *who, what, when, where, why,* and *how* questions to discover more background information.
Yes ↓	
3. Evidence Have you presented enough convincing evidence to support your thesis? Would *you* accept the thesis? — **No** →	• Use prewriting strategies or do additional research to discover more supporting evidence. • Add the most convincing evidence to your essay.
Yes ↓	
4. Topic sentences Does each topic sentence logically connect to and support the thesis? — **No** →	• Rewrite the topic sentences so that they clearly support the thesis. • If necessary, broaden your thesis to include all your supporting points.
Yes ↓	
5. Supporting details Do you have enough specific supporting details? Do they answer *Who? What? When? Where? Why? How?* — **No** →	• Name names, give dates, specify places. • Use action verbs and descriptive language. • Answer *who, what, when, where, why,* and *how* questions to discover more detailed evidence.

Table 8.2   Guidelines for Evaluating Your Introduction, Conclusion, and Title

Questions	Tips
Does your introduction interest your reader and provide needed background information?	If your essay jumps into the topic without preparing readers for it, your introduction needs to be revised. Ask yourself *who, what, when, where, why,* and *how* questions to determine the background information that you need.
Does your conclusion draw your essay to a satisfactory close and reinforce your thesis statement?	Imagine explaining the significance of your essay to a friend. Use this explanation to rewrite your conclusion.
Does your title accurately reflect the content of your essay?	To improve your title, reread your thesis statement, looking for a few key words that can serve as part of your title. Is your title clear and interesting? Will it motivate readers to read your essay?

Evaluating Your Paragraph Development

In most essays, each paragraph should fully develop a single idea that supports your thesis. In a typical first draft, many paragraphs are weak or loosely structured. They may contain irrelevant information or lack a clearly focused topic sentence. Study each paragraph separately in conjunction with your thesis statement. You may need to delete or combine some paragraphs, rework or reorganize others, or move paragraphs to a more appropriate part of the essay. If you need to supply additional information to support your thesis, you may need to add paragraphs to the draft. Use Figure 8.2 to help you analyze and revise your paragraphs and refer to Chapter 6, "Writing Effective Paragraphs," for more on paragraph development.

Essay in Progress 4

Using Figure 8.2, examine each paragraph of your essay in progress. Make notes on the draft copy of your essay.

Figure 8.2 Flowchart for Evaluating Your Paragraphs

QUESTIONS	REVISION STRATEGIES
1. Topic sentences Does each paragraph have a clear topic sentence that expresses the main point of the paragraph? → No	• Revise a sentence within the paragraph so that it clearly states the main point. • Write a new sentence that states the one main point of the paragraph.
↓ Yes	
2. Supporting sentences Do all sentences in each paragraph support the topic sentence? → No	• Revise supporting sentences to make their connection to the topic sentence clear. • Delete sentences that do not support the topic sentence.
↓ Yes	
3. Supporting details Does the paragraph offer adequate explanation and supporting details? → No	• Add more details if your paragraph seems skimpy. • Use either the *who, what, when, where, why,* and *how* questions or the prewriting strategies in Chapter 4 to generate the details you need.
↓ Yes	
4. Transitions Will it be clear to your reader how each sentence and each paragraph connects to those before and after it? → No	• Add transitions where they are needed. Refer to Table 6.2 (pp. 120–21) for a list of common transitions.

Working with Classmates to Revise Your Essay

In your writing classes and other courses, you may be expected to participate in **peer review**, a process in which two or more students read and comment on each other's papers. Students might work together in class, outside of class, via email, or online. Working with classmates is an excellent way to get ideas for improving your essays. You'll also have the opportunity to discover how other students approach the writing process. The following suggestions will help both the writer and the reviewer get the most out of peer review.

How to Find a Good Reviewer

Selecting a good reviewer is key to getting good suggestions for revision. Your instructor may pair you with another class member or let you find your own reviewer, either a classmate or someone outside of class. If you are permitted to choose your own reviewer, the following guidelines may help you find a good peer reviewer.

- Classmates usually make good reviewers, because they are familiar with the assignment and with what you have learned so far in the course.
- If you need to find someone outside of class, try to choose a person who has already taken the same course and done well.
- Close friends are not necessarily the best reviewers; they may be reluctant to offer criticism, or they may be too critical. Instead, choose someone who is serious, skilled at writing, and willing to spend the time needed to provide useful comments.
- If your college has a writing center, you might ask a tutor to read and comment on your draft.
- Consider using more than one reviewer so that you get several perspectives.

Suggestions for the Writer

To get the greatest benefit from peer review, use the following suggestions.

1. **Provide a readable copy of your essay.** A printed, double-spaced draft is best.
2. **Do some revision yourself first.** If your essay is not very far along, think it through a little more, and try to fix the obvious problems. The more developed your draft is, the more helpful the reviewer's comments will be.
3. **Offer specific questions or guidelines for your reviewer.** A sample set of questions for reviewers is provided in Table 8.3. Give your reviewer a copy of these questions, adding others that you would like answered. (For example, you might also give your reviewer questions from one of the revision flowcharts in this chapter.)
4. **Be open to criticism and new ideas.** As much as possible, try not to be defensive. Instead, look at your essay objectively, seeing it as your reviewer sees it.
5. **Don't feel obligated to accept all the advice you are given.** A reviewer might suggest a change that will not work well in your paper or wrongly identify something as an error. If you are uncertain about a suggestion, discuss it with your instructor.

Table 8.3   Questions for Reviewers

1. What is the purpose of the paper?

2. Who is the intended audience?

3. Is the introduction fully developed?

4. What is the main point or thesis? Is it easy to identify?

5. Does the essay offer evidence to support each important point? Where is more evidence needed? (Be sure to indicate specific paragraphs.)

6. Is each paragraph clear and well organized?

7. Are transitions used to connect ideas within and between paragraphs?

8. Is the organization easy to follow? Where might it be improved, and how?

9. Does the conclusion draw the essay to a satisfying close?

10. What do you like about the draft?

11. What are its weaknesses, and how could they be eliminated? Underline or highlight sentences that are unclear or confusing.

Suggestions for the Reviewer

When you are reviewing someone else's work, be honest but tactful. Criticism is never easy to accept, so keep your reader's feelings in mind. The following tips will help you provide useful comments.

1. **Read the draft through completely before making any judgments or comments.** You will need to read it at least twice to evaluate it.

2. **Concentrate on content; pay attention to what the paper says.** Focus on the main points and how clearly they are expressed and organized. If you notice a misspelling or a grammatical error, you can circle it, but correcting errors is not your primary task.

3. **Offer some positive comments.** Compliments are good motivators.

4. **Be specific.** For instance, instead of saying that more examples are needed, tell the writer which ideas in which paragraphs are unclear without examples, and suggest what kind of example would be most useful in each case.

5. **Use the "Questions for Reviewers" in Table 8.3.** Also use any additional questions that the writer provides to guide your review.

6. **Write notes and comments directly on the draft.** At the end, write a note that summarizes your overall reaction, pointing out both strengths and weaknesses.

7. **If you are reviewing a draft on a computer, type your comments in brackets following the appropriate passage, or highlight them in some other way (for example, by using the "Comment" or "Annotation" feature of the word-processing program).** The writer can easily delete your comments after reading them.

8. **Do not rewrite paragraphs or sections of the paper.** Instead, suggest how the writer might revise them.

Essay in Progress 5

Give your essay in progress to a classmate to read and review. Ask your reviewer to respond to the "Questions for Reviewers" (Table 8.3). Revise your essay using your revision outline, your responses to the evaluation flowcharts in Figures 8.1 and 8.2 (pp. 148 and 150), and your reviewer's suggestions.

Using Your Instructor's Comments

Another resource to use in revising your draft is the commentary your instructor provides. You can use these comments not only to submit a revised version of a particular essay but also to improve your writing throughout the course.

Revising an Essay Using Your Instructor's Comments

Your instructor may want to review a draft of your essay and suggest revisions. Your instructor's comments can provide a road map for you as you begin your revision. Carefully review the comments, looking for recurring problems so that you can focus on eliminating these problems in your future writing. The comments on your essay will often address spelling and grammar errors, as well as problems with organization, clarity, or development of ideas.

Exercise 8.1

If your instructor has returned a marked-up first draft to you, read the comments carefully. Then draw a line down the middle of a blank piece of paper. On the left, write the instructor's comments; on the right, jot down ways you might revise the essay in response to each. Put a check mark next to any problems that recur throughout your essay. These are areas to which you will want to pay particular attention in your future writing.

Table 8.4   Guidelines for Using Your Instructor's Comments to Improve Future Essays

Guidelines	Tips
Reread your returned essay more than once.	Read your essay once to note grammatical corrections, and then read it again to study comments about organization or content. Processing numerous instructor comments on a wide range of topics takes more than one reading.
Make sure you understand any grammar errors.	Check a grammar handbook (see Part 4) or ask a classmate; if you are still unclear about the nature of the error, check with your instructor. Make note of your grammatical errors in an error log. When you proofread your next essay, look carefully for those errors.
If you did not get a high grade, try to determine why.	Was the essay weak in content, organization, or development?
Using the evaluation flowcharts in Figures 8.1 (p. 148) and 8.2 (p. 150), highlight or mark weaknesses that your instructor identified.	When writing your next essay, refer back to these flowcharts. Pay special attention to the identified areas as you evaluate your next paper.
If any of your instructor's comments are unclear, first ask a classmate if he or she understands them.	If your classmate doesn't understand the comments, ask your instructor for clarification.

Using Your Instructor's Comments to Improve Future Essays

When you receive a graded essay back from an instructor, it is tempting to note the grade and then file away the essay. To improve your writing, however, take time to study each comment. Follow the guidelines in Table 8.4 to use your instructor's comments to improve future essays.

Editing and Proofreading

Some of the comments you receive from instructors and classmates will refer not to large issues like ideas, evidence, and organization, which call for thoughtful revision, but to more local issues like style, mechanical and grammatical correctness, and word choice. Reviewing your work for such local issues is generally referred to as *editing*. Giving your revised and edited work a final read-through for any remaining problems, such as transposed letters, missing punctuation, or typographical errors ("typos"), is generally referred to as *proofreading*.

Editing Your Essay

The following sections draw your attention to some key things to keep in mind when you edit and proofread your papers. The editing and proofreading advice we provide here is necessarily brief; Part 4 provides more details on mechanics and punctuation. Use it during the editing process when you have questions about grammar or style issues. Your instructor may also provide other references and resources for further help.

IMPROVING YOUR SENTENCES

To make your sentences stronger and more interesting, use the following questions.

1. **Are your sentences concise?** Look for places where you can use fewer words, avoid saying the same thing twice, or cut unnecessary phrases or clauses.

   ▶ ~~It is my opinion that~~ ^F^ fast-food restaurants should post nutritional information for each menu item.

2. **Are your sentences varied?** Use short sentences only rarely and only for emphasis or clarity. Otherwise, your writing will sound choppy. Use sentences that combine different types of phrases and clauses to show relationships between your ideas.

   ▶ Leon asked a question~~. The~~ ^, and the^ entire class was surprised. OR

   ▶ ^When^ Leon asked a question~~. The~~ ^, the^ entire class was surprised.

3. **Do your sentences have strong, active verbs?** Consider replacing forms of the verb *to be* (*is*, *was*, *were*, etc.) with verbs that are descriptive and help your readers visualize what you're trying to communicate.

   ▶ The puppy ~~was afraid of thunder~~ ^whimpered and quivered during the storm^.

 **LaunchPad Solo**
macmillan learning   Visit **LaunchPad Solo for Readers and Writers > Editing** for extra practice in the skills covered in this section.

4. **Are your sentences parallel in structure?** The parts of a sentence that serve a similar purpose should be expressed with words that have the same grammatical form.

> The children were rowdy and ~~making a great deal of noise~~ *noisy*.

IMPROVING YOUR WORD CHOICE

Each word in your essay has the power to either contribute to or detract from your meaning. Use the following questions to evaluate and improve your choice of words.

1. **Is the tone appropriate, not too formal or too casual?** You should write as naturally as possible, but not the same way you'd talk to friends. Try for the kind of language you'd use in speaking to an instructor who's on the strict side. Avoid slang and any other language you wouldn't use in speaking with this instructor.

2. **Do your words convey the connotations — feelings or attitudes — you intend?** As a test, try setting your writing aside for a bit. Then reread it, preferably aloud, and pay attention to how it sounds or how it makes you feel. If possible, give it to a couple of friends or classmates to read and ask them for their impressions.

3. **Have you used as many specific words as possible and avoided vague, general words?** Try to make your language come to life.

> The ~~red flowers grew~~ *crimson petunias bloomed* in our yard.

4. **Have you avoided clichés and trite expressions?** A *cliché* is an overused phrase like "raining cats and dogs" or "opposites attract." Try inventing descriptions if you can manage it. Otherwise, stick to plain language.

> ~~I felt as sick as a dog~~ *My stomach was a bowl of curdled milk*.

AVOIDING COMMON ERRORS

Table 8.5 lists eight common writing errors. For more details about how to correct these and other errors, see Part 4; Section 1 has a review of the parts of speech, and Sections 11 through 18 cover matters of punctuation (commas, quotation marks, etc.) and mechanics (capitalization, italics, etc.). Be on the lookout for these errors as you revise and edit your essays.

Table 8.5 Common Errors

Error	Explanation	Handbook (Part 4) Section and Page Numbers
Sentence fragments	A sentence fragment lacks a subject, verb, or both and does not express a complete thought.	Section 3 (pp. 656–60)
Run-on sentences	A run-on sentence contains two or more complete thoughts (independent clauses) that run together without a connecting word or correct punctuation.	Section 4 (pp. 660–65)
Errors in subject-verb agreement	Errors in subject-verb agreement occur when the subject and verb of a sentence do not agree in person or number.	Section 5 (pp. 666–69)
Problems with verb forms	Problems with verb forms involve failure to use the correct form of the verb, especially with regard to tense (time).	Section 6 (pp. 669–73)
Pronoun problems	A pronoun problem occurs when the pronoun does not agree with its antecedent in person, number, or gender.	Section 7 (pp. 674–81)
Shifts and mixed constructions	A shift is a sudden, unexpected change in point of view, verb tense, voice, mood, or level of diction. A mixed construction is a sentence containing parts that do not fit together logically.	Section 8 (pp. 681–86)
Problems with adjectives and adverbs	Problems with adjectives and adverbs often involve using an adjective when an adverb is more appropriate, and vice versa, as well as using the incorrect forms of these parts of speech.	Section 9 (pp. 686–89)
Misplaced and dangling modifiers	Misplaced and dangling modifiers occur when a group of words used as a modifier (a description) appears in the wrong place in the sentence or does not describe the sentence at all, creating confusion for the reader.	Section 10 (pp. 689–91)

Table 8.6 Guidelines for Proofreading Your Essay

Guidelines	Tips
Read your essay several times.	Each time focus on *one* error type — spelling, punctuation, grammar, and so on.
Read your essay backward.	Reading from the last sentence to the first will help you concentrate on spotting errors.
Use the spell-check and grammar-check functions regularly but cautiously.	These functions can help you spot many errors, including many spelling errors, but they will miss certain kinds of errors (for example, synonym errors) and are not a reliable substitute for careful proofreading.
Read your essay aloud.	Reading aloud slowly will help you catch problems such as missing words, errors in verb tense, and errors in singular and plural forms of nouns.
Ask a classmate to proofread your paper.	Another reader may spot errors you have overlooked.

Proofreading Your Essay

To proofread, or make a final check for errors, print out a clean double-spaced copy of your essay. Use the suggestions in Table 8.6 to produce an error-free essay.

Students Write

After writing her first draft, which appears in Chapter 7 (pp. 141–42), student writer Christine Lee used the guidelines and revision flowcharts in this chapter to help her decide what to revise. For example, she decided that she needed to add more details about what happened on the TV show *Survivor*. She also decided that she should de-emphasize the uninteresting details of the examples of some other reality TV shows.

Lee asked her classmate Sam to review her essay. A portion of Sam's comments is shown on next page.

Reviewer's Comments

The trend that you have chosen to write about is well known and interesting. Beginning your introduction with a question piques the reader's interest, and your thesis is clear: Reality TV shows are becoming less interesting and more distasteful. You mention that people enjoyed *Survivor* and why they didn't enjoy the other shows. You should provide more details about why television viewers watched *Survivor*. Once that point is clear, many of your ideas might fit better.

I think some specific details about the reality TV shows you mention would help readers who are not familiar with the shows. It would also help prove your point: These shows are getting worse. The title and conclusion could better help make this point too. The title doesn't indicate what the reality of reality TV is, and the conclusion could look ahead to what you think the fate of reality TV will be.

Using her own analysis and her classmate's suggestions, Lee created a graphic organizer (Figure 8.3) to help her decide how to revise her draft. After creating the graphic organizer, Lee revised her first draft. A portion of her revised draft, with her revisions indicated using the Track Changes (in Microsoft Word) function, follows.

Revised Draft

A Trend Taken Too Far: The Reality of Real TV

Do you remember life before the reality TV craze? Before reality TV, television viewers seemed interested only in situational comedies and serial dramas. Characters were played by professional actors, and the shows were written by professional writers. Except for a few early reality-type shows, such as *Cops* and *Candid Camera*, this simple formula was what network television offered. Then came MTV's *The Real World* in 1992. The high ratings that this cable show garnered made network executives take notice of the genre. Eventually *Survivor* debuted in the summer of 2000. When *Survivor* caught the attention of even more viewers, television networks changed their programming. It seems that the networks acted as though they had to become "real" to compete with *Survivor* and maintain viewer interest. The problem with this copycat strategy was that the original *Survivor* offered more interesting elements to its audience than any reality show modeled after it. *Survivor* was engaging and dramatic, but the shows that followed it were both less interesting and more distasteful, lacking drama and relying on gimmicks.

Deleted: One look at a *TV Guide* today shows an overload of reality-based programming, even with the guaranteed failure of most of these shows.

Deleted: there was mostly

Deleted: every viewer's

Deleted: every network in America believed they must also

Deleted: keep

Deleted: up its ratings. As the popularity of reality TV continues unabated, shows are becoming

Figure 8.3   **Graphic Organizer for Christine Lee's Revision Plans**

Introduction	*TV Guide* reveals an overload of reality TV shows.	**Detail to delete:** Mention of *TV Guide*
	Before *Survivor* there were mostly sitcoms and dramas.	**Detail to add:** Mention earlier reality-type shows (*Cops, Candid Camera*).
	Survivor caused networks to become real.	
	Thesis: Shows that followed *Survivor* were less interesting and more distasteful.	**Information to add:** Shows that followed had less drama and relied on gimmicks.

Body paragraphs	**Paragraph 2**	*Big Brother* didn't offer audiences the same things to respond to.	
		No exotic location	**Unnecessary details:** • "Nothing new added" • "Took away access to outside world"
		No competition for million-dollar prize	
		No different kinds of real people playing	
		No development of player camaraderie and sense of teamwork	**Details to add:** • Audience response • Popularity of "getting voted off the island" phrase • Appeal of the drama in *Survivor*
		The audience voted by phone.	
		People bickered over nothing.	
		Participants weren't up against anything.	
		Viewers lost interest.	
	Paragraph 3	Networks have continued to use gimmicks to appeal to the audience's instincts.	
		Shows revolving around gross and terrifying things	**Unnecessary detail:** • "Weirdos" who liked *Fear Factor*
		Pushing limits of good taste	**Detail to add:** • Additional example: *My Strange Addiction*

Continued >

Figure 8.3 **(continued)**

Body paragraphs	**Paragraph 4**	Two types of reality TV became popular.	
		Talent shows	**Details to add:** • Colorful judges • Supportive fans • Long lines for contestants to wait in and too much mascara and bad singing
		Beauty contests	
		There was no built-in drama.	
	Paragraph 5	The next shows were about special interests.	
		Cooking (*Hell's Kitchen* and *Top Chef*)	
		Dancing (*So You Think You Can Dance* and *Dancing with the Stars*)	
		Weight-loss, fashion, business, and hair-styling shows	
	Paragraph 6	Recent shows are about everyday lives or celebrities.	
		Every celebrity seemed to get a show.	**Unnecessary detail:** • Real-estate shows
		Everyday people in weird situations got shows.	**Detail to add:** • *Jersey Shore* • *Keeping Up with the Kardashians*
Conclusion		The popularity of reality shows continues.	
		The viewer decides what's popular.	**Unnecessary detail:** • "I hope"
		Viewers should demand better programming.	**Detail to add:** • Previous shows were copycat spin-offs.

Before Lee submitted her final draft, she read her essay several more times, editing it for sentence structure and word choice. She also proofread it once to catch errors in grammar and punctuation as well as typographical errors. The final version of Lee's essay follows.

Final Draft

Title: A play on words catches the reader's attention.

A Trend Taken Too Far: The Reality of Real TV

Christine Lee

Background information on shows leading up to reality TV

Do you remember life before the reality TV craze? Before reality TV, television viewers seemed interested only in situational comedies and serial dramas. Characters were played by professional actors, and the shows were written by professional writers. Except for a few early reality-type shows, such as *Cops* and *Candid Camera*, this simple formula was what network television offered. Then came MTV's *The Real World* in 1992. The high ratings that this cable show garnered made network executives take notice of the genre. Eventually *Survivor* debuted in the summer of 2000. When *Survivor* caught the attention of even more viewers, television networks changed their programming. It seems that the networks acted as though they had to become "real" to compete with *Survivor* and maintain viewer interest. The problem with this copycat strategy was that the original *Survivor* offered more interesting elements to its audience than any reality show modeled after it. *Survivor* was engaging and dramatic, but the shows that followed it were both less interesting and more distasteful, lacking drama and relying on gimmicks.

The **thesis statement** is focused and detailed.

The **topic sentence** supports part of the thesis: "*Survivor* was engaging and dramatic."

Details offer reasons that support the topic sentence.

Survivor captured the interest of a wide viewing audience because it was fresh and entertaining. The show introduced real participants in a contest where they competed against each other in an exotic location. The participants on *Survivor* were ethnically and socially diverse and represented a variety of ages including young, middle-aged, and older adults. The location was fascinating; a South Pacific island was more interesting than any house full of people on a sitcom. However, the most unique feature of *Survivor* was to make the participants compete for a million-dollar prize. Contestants were divided into two camps that had to compete to win everyday supplies, like food and shelter. At the end of each episode, players voted, and one of them was kicked off the show and lost his or her chance for the million dollars. The last contestant on the island won. To win the game, contestants created alliances and manipulated other contestants. All of these unique elements drew television viewers back each week.

The **topic sentence** continues to support the thesis by explaining engaging aspects of *Survivor*.

The television audience responded favorably to the dramatic elements of *Survivor*. The competition gave viewers something to speculate about as the show progressed. Viewers' allegiance to one team over another or one player over another developed from episode to episode. Viewers were fascinated watching these players struggle in primitive situations, compete in tasks of strength and skill, and decide on how to cast their votes. The phrase "getting voted off the island" became a recognizable saying across America. Although players displayed positive human traits like teamwork, compassion, and camaraderie, they also schemed and plotted to win the allegiance of their fellow players. This situation made *Survivor* dramatic, and the viewers were attracted to the drama. Reality TV shows that followed *Survivor* had none of its interesting elements.

Specific details about dramatic elements support the topic sentence.

The **topic sentence** supports the thesis that later shows were "less interesting."

Big Brother was the first spin-off reality TV show to try to repeat the success of *Survivor*, but it did not offer the drama that *Survivor* did. In *Big Brother*, contestants were locked in a house without any outside contact for weeks. As in *Survivor*, there was a cash prize on the line, but in *Big Brother* there were not any competitions or struggles. Contestants were expelled by a viewer phone poll, but the poll gave them no motive to scheme and plot allegiances the way the *Survivor* contestants did. In fact, the contestants had little to do except bicker and fight. Viewers were not interested in players who were not up against any challenge except weeks of boredom. In the end, *Big Brother* was simply not interesting.

Concrete details about *Big Brother* contestants

The **topic sentence** supports the thesis that later shows relied on gimmicks.

The next wave of reality TV shows tried to use graphic displays of terror and violence to attract viewers. *Fear Factor*, the most successful of these shows, has its contestants commit all manner of gross and terrifying acts, like eating worms or being immersed in a container of live rats. Some viewers may be interested in watching how far the contestants will go, but the majority of viewers regard these acts with disgust. Viewers might tune in once or twice to shows like *My Strange Addiction* (in which people talk about the strange things they are addicted to eating, such as sand, toilet paper, or pieces of a couch) but, disgusted, will not be interested in the long run.

The **topic sentence** identifies other new gimmicks.

When this gimmick did not retain viewers, two traditional types of reality TV were revived with modern twists added—the talent show and the beauty contest. So shows like *American Idol*,

America's Got Talent, and *America's Next Top Model* were born. Again, there was no built-in drama as in *Survivor,* so the shows tried to create drama using colorful judges and supportive fans. At first, these twists provided enough spectacle to engage viewers, but after a while, audiences lost interest. Even footage showing the long lines that contestants had to wait in and the despair of those who did not make the cut did not keep viewers hooked on these types of reality shows. Viewers could only tolerate so much bad singing and mascara.

The next incarnation of reality shows focused on special interests such as cooking, with shows like *Top Chef* and *Hell's Kitchen,* or dance, with shows such as *Dancing with the Stars* and *So You Think You Can Dance.* The net was spread wider with *The Biggest Loser,* a weight-loss competition; *Project Runway,* where fashion designers are pitted against each other; *The Apprentice,* a business competition; and *Shear Genius,* which offered competition among hairstylists. The problems with these shows were that they each appealed to only a very small segment of the population and offered manufactured and increasingly contrived situations for the contestants to act within.

More recently, reality-show programming has turned increasingly to examining the everyday lives of groups of people and showcasing celebrities. *The Real World* was an early example of the first category, simply following the lives of a group of young adults as they drank and slept around. *The Simple Life* was one of the earliest celebrity reality shows, following Paris Hilton and sidekick Nicole Richie in ridiculously contrived situations. Soon it seemed every B-list (or D-list) celebrity had a reality show—Jessica Simpson, Ozzy Osbourne, Paula Abdul, Tori Spelling, Bret Michaels, Kathy Griffin, and more. The next wave of shows featured ordinary people in interesting, strange, or controversial situations, such as *Jon & Kate Plus 8, Dog the Bounty Hunter, The Real Housewives, The Little Couple, Cake Boss, Choppers,* and more. These programs often showed people at their worst, as seen with a recent hit, *The Jersey Shore,* in which a cast of unknowns became famous for carousing and becoming caricatures of themselves. Most notorious, of course, is *Keeping Up with the Kardashians,* which follows the lives of a self-centered, materialistic, attention-hungry Hollywood family who are simply "famous for being famous" and contribute nothing to society. Networks have had to stretch to find new and different scenarios to offer to viewers as these shows have become increasingly tasteless.

Details about talent shows and beauty contests

The **topic sentence** identifies a new focus on special interests.

Details about special-interest shows

The **topic sentence** identifies the latest focus of reality shows.

Details about shows focused on ordinary people and celebrities

Examples continue to support the thesis of "more distasteful."

The conclusion returns to the thesis and calls for more entertaining programming.

In the decade following the advent of *Survivor*, reality shows have evolved from copycat spin-offs to programs featuring terror and violence, talent and beauty contests, special-interest competitions, and finally to shows following the lives of ordinary people or celebrities. In the end, the viewers determine what gets shown on television. Reality shows continue to be popular, despite becoming steadily more contrived and tasteless. One can hope that viewers will tire of all of these cheap gimmicks and call for more entertaining programming. If there were fewer reality shows, viewers could then return to more entertaining situational comedies and serial dramas or perhaps to another form of engaging program that may evolve.

Analyzing the Writer's Technique

1. Identify the major revisions that Lee made from the earlier draft in Chapter 7 (pp. 141–42). How did she carry out the plan indicated in her graphic organizer?

2. Choose one major revision that Lee made, and explain why you think it improved her essay.

3. Evaluate Lee's introduction and conclusion. In what ways are they more effective than the introduction and conclusion in her first draft? What additional improvements could she make?

4. Choose one paragraph, and compare the details provided in it with those in the corresponding paragraph of the first draft. Which added details are particularly effective, and why?

Part

2

Readings
for Writers

9

Patterns: An Introduction

In this chapter, you will learn to

- Recognize the patterns of organization.

- Identify multiple patterns of organization used in essays.

- Write an essay that combines the patterns of organization.

Reflect on a Visual Text

Carefully examine the photographs on this page, noting any details that would help someone who cannot see the images to understand the differences and similarities between the two types of dancing.

1 **Ask yourself questions.** How would you define each type of dancing? How would you describe each style? How is each performed?

2 **Brainstorm ideas.** Working on your own or with a partner, brainstorm answers to these questions: In what ways are the dances shown in the two photos the same? In what ways are they different? Consider also the dancers. How would you describe them? What stories could you construct about the situations pictured? What process did the first set of performers use to learn the dance? What type of dance does each photograph illustrate?

Do you see how each of your answers could be used to create a quite different paragraph about these photographs?

Luca Tettoni/Robert Harding World Imagery/Getty Images

Jasper Mattias/Cultura/Getty Images

169

An Overview of Patterns

The different ways in which you analyzed the photos demonstrate different ways — or patterns — of understanding one topic. You will recall that **essays** present information on a topic from the writer's point of view. Effective essays have a specific topic and provide adequate support for the thesis statement. 🖼

Beyond presenting a specific viewpoint, writers often have different reasons, or *purposes*, for writing. Once a topic has been chosen, the writer selects a particular aspect of that topic to explore. Consider the very general topic *winter*. On which aspect(s) of winter might the writer choose to focus in his essay? How might he focus on that aspect?

- He could tell a story about a memorable ski vacation he took with friends. **(narration)**

- He could describe winter in a particular location. For example, a person writing about winter in New York would write a very different essay than a person writing about winter in Hawaii. **(description)**

- He could outline survival techniques for living in a place with a brutal winter climate, such as Siberia or Alaska. **(illustration)**

- He could focus on a main characteristic of winter — snow — and explain exactly how it forms and falls to earth. **(process analysis)**

- He could examine the similarities and differences between an extremely cold winter and an extremely hot summer. **(comparison and contrast)**

- He could explore how different cultures experience winter. For example, the Saami people of northern Europe have words to describe many different kinds of snow. **(classification and division)**

- He could define and analyze the word *winter*. For instance, the scientific definition of winter refers not to a season but to Earth's position relative to the sun. **(definition)**

- He could discuss how winter affects people. Cold weather causes some people to spend more time indoors, while others spend more time outdoors taking part in winter sports. **(cause and effect)**

- He could make the case that winters are becoming less severe across the world as a result of global climate change. **(argumentation)**

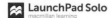 **LaunchPad Solo**
macmillan learning   Visit **LaunchPad Solo for Readers and Writers > Patterns of Organization** for extra practice in the skills covered in Part 2.

An essay using any of these approaches to the general topic of *winter* will have a specific thesis statement and follow a specific pattern. Writing **patterns** are systems for developing and organizing information, and they are extremely helpful for both readers and writers.

Reading ⬤ Writing   Patterns

The Reader's Perspective	The Writer's Perspective
As you read, look closely at the introduction and thesis statement, which often provide signals regarding the author's chosen pattern(s) of organization. Essays that are organized around writing patterns have a clear and specific organization, making them easy to read and remember.	Patterns of organization give you a specific writing plan to follow, helping you present your ideas in a logical, useful manner. Patterns also help readers follow your key points.

Chapters 10 to 18 are devoted to specific patterns. Each chapter presents guidelines for effectively reading and writing works based on a specific pattern and includes professionally written essays that use the pattern.

Table 9.1 summarizes the most common patterns and their purposes. You will find that essay examinations in many college courses ask you to answer questions with a pattern-based essay.

Table 9.1   Writing Patterns and Purposes with Examples

Writing Pattern	Purpose	Sample Thesis Statement	Sample Essay Exam Question
Narration (Chapter 10)	Relates a series of real or imaginary events in an organized sequence	The ski trip I took with three college friends taught me a great deal about friendship and loyalty.	Provide a brief biography of Harriet Tubman's life.
Description (Chapter 11)	Presents information in a way that appeals to one or more of the five senses (sight, smell, touch, taste, or hearing)	Summer in New Jersey can be summarized in three words: hot, humid, and unbearable.	Describe the climate of sub-Saharan Africa.

Continued >

Table 9.1   (continued)

Writing Pattern	Purpose	Sample Thesis Statement	Sample Essay Exam Question
Illustration (Chapter 12)	Uses specific information (examples) to reveal the essential characteristics of a topic or to reinforce the thesis	Minnesotans, who live through extremely cold winters, have developed many coping mechanisms for getting through the coldest months of the year.	List three benefits and three drawbacks of social media like Facebook and Twitter, using examples to explain each.
Process Analysis (Chapter 13)	Explains in a step-by-step fashion how something works, is done, or is made	Snow occurs when water crystallizes into ice in the atmosphere and then falls to earth.	Explain how to administer the flu shot.
Comparison and Contrast (Chapter 14)	Looks at the differences and similarities between two or more ideas, things, or phenomena	Winters in the Northern Hemisphere are often brutal and unpleasant; in the Southern Hemisphere, however, winter means warm, pleasant conditions and maybe even a trip to the beach.	Explore the similarities and differences between the works of Nathaniel Hawthorne and of Mark Twain.
Classification and Division (Chapter 15)	Explains the categories or groups into which a given subject can be divided	The Saami of northern Europe have many words for snow. These include *soalvi* (slushy snow), *luotkku* (loose snow), and *skáva* (a very thin layer of frozen snow).	List and explain the cultural characteristics of the seven key regions within the United States (the Northeast, the Southwest, etc.).

Table 9.1   (continued)

Writing Pattern	Purpose	Sample Thesis Statement	Sample Essay Exam Question
Definition (Chapter 16)	Provides, in detail, the meaning of a specific word, phrase, or term	Winter begins on the winter solstice, which occurs when Earth's axial tilt causes our hemisphere to be farthest away from the sun.	What is the pathetic fallacy? How does Mary Shelley use the pathetic fallacy in *Frankenstein*?
Cause and Effect (Chapter 17)	Analyzes why an event or phenomenon happens (*causes*) and what happens as a result of the event or phenomenon (*effects*)	In general, winter makes humans more likely to stay indoors, gain weight, and go to sleep early.	Describe three causes of the American Civil War.
Argumentation (Chapter 18)	Presents logical, reliable evidence to support a claim	As global warming continues, we can expect to see shorter, warmer winters but, strangely enough, much more snow.	Should teachers be required to assign at least two hours of homework each night? Why, or why not?

Combining Patterns

Many writers find that combining different patterns helps them achieve their purpose. A writer who is *arguing* that the U.S. school year should be extended from ten to twelve months may want to *compare* the U.S. school system to that of countries in Europe and Asia.

Here is an example of a paragraph that combines different writing patterns.

Definition	A nor'easter is a hurricane-like storm that travels along the East Coast of the United States and Canada, starting in the waters of the Southeast (usually off the coast of Florida, Georgia, or the Carolinas) and traveling in a northeastern direction along the coast. Nor'easters are known for their
Cause / Effect	extreme destructiveness. They often cause heavy winds, blizzard conditions, severe flooding, and beach erosion.
Illustration	A particularly devastating nor'easter hit the United States in October 2011, when more than thirty inches of snow fell on
Cause / Effect	parts of the East Coast. The storm disrupted power for about three million people, and winds gusted as high as seventy miles per hour in Massachusetts. In New Jersey, the trees hadn't lost their leaves yet, which allowed wet, heavy snow to collect on them. As a result, heavy branches came crashing down all over the state, causing millions of dollars in damage.

Because writers combine patterns so often, each chapter on a particular pattern (Chapters 10 to 18) includes a textbook excerpt that uses more than one pattern. In your own writing, you should feel free to combine patterns to suit your purpose.

Reading ⏺ Writing   Combining Patterns

The Reader's Perspective	The Writer's Perspective
Combining patterns helps you understand a topic from several different angles. For example, if you are artistic, you may respond well to description; if you are mechanically talented, you may appreciate a detailed, step-by-step process analysis. As you read an essay that combines patterns, note each pattern in the margin and determine how it helps you understand the information better.	Combining patterns allows you to bring more depth to your essay, exploring different (but related) aspects of a topic. When you combine patterns, you will likely find that your essays become richer, fuller, and more interesting.

Writing an Essay That Combines Patterns

Chapters 10 through 18 explore in detail how to use each single pattern. To write an essay that combines patterns, use the following suggestions for each stage of the writing process.

PLANNING AN ESSAY THAT COMBINES PATTERNS

Choose a Topic   When prewriting, use your knowledge of the various patterns to think about your topic in unique, creative, and diverse ways.

Determine Which Patterns to Use   You would not use all the patterns in a single essay, but two or more could be combined effectively to support a thesis statement about, for example, eating organically. The list of questions in Table 9.2, "Using the Patterns of Development to Explore a Topic," can help you consider how your essay may combine different patterns.

Select only those patterns that contribute to the essay by supporting the thesis statement. If you use too many patterns, you may overwhelm the reader and make the essay difficult to follow.

Develop Your Thesis   After deciding how to approach your topic, develop an effective thesis statement. The thesis statement should reveal your primary method of development. It may also suggest other patterns you will use in the essay, but the primary method should be clear to readers. Following is an example of a good thesis statement that combines patterns.

> Student services are divided into two main programs, Health and
> Counseling Services and Disability Services, each providing valuable
> services and support to students and prospective students.

This thesis statement makes it clear that classification (with definitions) is the predominant pattern. It also suggests that cause and effect will be used to explain how these services help students.

Generate Evidence to Support Your Thesis   Understanding the patterns of development can help you generate relevant supporting evidence. For example, while including narrative elements may pique readers' interest, an illustration essay should rely on examples to explain its main topic.

DRAFTING AN ESSAY THAT COMBINES PATTERNS

Determine the Essay's Organization   The way you organize your essay will be determined by the primary pattern and any other patterns you decide to use. In choosing a pattern, consider the nature of your topic and the needs and characteristics of your audience.

Use Transitions between Different Patterns   Transition words and phrases signal that you are moving from one pattern to another, enabling the reader to follow your train of thought easily. Specific transitional words and phrases for each pattern are discussed in Chapters 10 to 18.

Table 9.2   Using the Patterns of Development to Explore a Topic

Pattern of Development	Questions to Ask
Narration (Chapter 10)	What stories or events does this topic remind me of?
Description (Chapter 11)	What does the topic look, smell, taste, feel, or sound like?
Illustration (Chapter 12)	What examples of this topic are particularly helpful in explaining it?
Process Analysis (Chapter 13)	How does this topic work? How does one carry out this process?
Comparison and Contrast (Chapter 14)	To what is the topic similar? In what ways? Is the topic more or less desirable than those things to which it is similar?
Classification and Division (Chapter 15)	Of what larger group of things is this topic a member? What are its parts? How can the topic be subdivided? Are there certain types or kinds of the topic?
Definition (Chapter 16)	How do I define the term? How does the dictionary define it? What is the history of the term? Does everyone agree on its definition? Why, or why not? If not, what points are in dispute?
Cause and Effect (Chapter 17)	What causes the topic? How often does it happen? What might prevent it from happening? What are its effects? What may happen because of it in the short term? What may happen as a result of it over time?
Argumentation (Chapter 18)	What issues surround this topic?

Make Sure Your Introduction and Conclusion Emphasize the Primary Pattern
The introduction should provide necessary background, give the thesis statement, and suggest the primary pattern. The conclusion should draw the essay
to a satisfying close while restating the main ideas, suggesting a new direction,
or making a call to action — again, framed in language that echoes the primary
pattern.

ANALYZING AND REVISING AN ESSAY THAT COMBINES PATTERNS

Set your essay aside for a day or two. Doing so will allow you to revisit your essay
with a fresh, critical eye. As you reread it, pay particular attention to whether your
primary pattern is evident and well developed. Secondary patterns should all be
used to explain or support the primary pattern.

EDITING AND PROOFREADING AN ESSAY THAT COMBINES PATTERNS

For general editing suggestions, use tools from Chapter 8. Also consult the revision flowcharts in Chapters 10 to 18 to analyze the primary pattern used in
your essay. For help with grammar, punctuation, and mechanics, refer to Part 4,
"Handbook: Writing Problems and How to Correct Them." For example, if you
need to know how to correct a sentence fragment or if your instructor notes that
you have numerous subject-verb agreement errors, this handbook will help you
identify these errors as well as show you how to correct them.

Guidelines for Using Chapters 10–18

Chapters 10–18 all follow a specific sequence to help you learn to understand,
analyze, and write paragraphs and essays using each of the patterns. As you proceed through each chapter, you will use the comprehension skills you learned
in Chapter 2, as well as the critical reading and thinking skills you learned in
Chapter 3. Each chapter also takes you through the process of writing an essay
using a specific pattern. In other words, each chapter builds on the prewriting,
drafting, and revising skills you learned in Chapters 4–8.

The following overview will help you understand how to get the most out of
the chapters that follow.

1. Each chapter begins with a definition of the pattern, including its key
   elements. A sample reading selection then demonstrates these elements.
   Take notice of the key elements as you read the essay. Note the writer's
   techniques and ask yourself how you respond to these elements as a reader.

2. The chapter then provides details about the structure and content of each
   pattern, pointing to the details that make an essay particularly effective.
   Each pattern has elements that make it unique. For example, narration

essays often include flashbacks in time, while description essays actively seek to engage the senses (sight, sound, smell, touch, and/or taste). Two graphic organizers are provided: one for the pattern in general and one for the model essay. Use these graphic organizers to visualize the structure of each essay and pattern.

3. Next, the chapter asks you to use the skills you learned in Chapters 2 and 3 to understand, analyze, and evaluate each pattern as a reader. The discussion and questions move you from basic comprehension of key points into critical thinking about the author's techniques and effectiveness.

4. With a full understanding of the pattern in your mind, you will be ready to write your own essay. A sample model essay by a student writer is provided, followed by step-by-step instructions for writing your own essay. This instruction follows the general writing process that you learned in Chapters 4–8.

5. Reading selections make up the bulk of the chapter. One of these is a textbook selection that uses at least two different patterns of organization. The readings demonstrate each pattern at work in a variety of professionally written materials, and opportunities are provided for you to discuss and write about each reading. Finally, the chapter closes with a table that summarizes the reader's perspective and the writer's perspective on each pattern.

Work through each reading selection at your own pace, highlighting and annotating as you read. Note sentences or paragraphs that you find particularly effective and analyze how the writer achieved the intended effect. How can you use the author's techniques to improve your own writing?

10

Narration: Recounting Events

In this chapter, you will learn to

- Recognize the elements of narration.

- Identify the structure and content of narration essays.

- Understand, analyze, and evaluate narration essays.

- Write your own narration essay.

- Work with narration as a reader and a writer.

Howard Kingsnorth/Iconica/Getty Images

Reflect on a Visual Text

This photo shows two people standing in a field and holding hundreds of brightly colored balloons. Follow the steps below to study, reflect on, and write about the image.

1 **Ask yourself questions.** Imagine the events that might have caused the two people in the photo to gather these balloons. Was there a dare? Are they celebrating something? If so, what? Why would they take the balloons to this setting? ➔

2 **Brainstorm ideas.** Working by yourself or with a classmate, construct a series of events that might have led up to the situation shown in the photo.

3 **Write.** Draft a paragraph explaining the events that led up to the photograph. Be detailed and specific.

As you wrote about the events that led up to the scene in the photograph, you probably described a series of events in the order in which they occurred. In short, you constructed a *narrative*: a chronological series of events, real or imaginary, that tells a story to make a point.

What Is Narration?

A **narrative** relates a series of events, real or imaginary, in an organized sequence. It is a *story that makes a point*. It presents actions and details that build toward a **climax**, the point at which the conflict of the narrative is resolved. Most narratives use dialogue to relate selected portions of conversations that move the story along. You probably exchange family stories, tell jokes, read biographies or novels, and watch television sitcoms or dramas — all of which are examples of the narrative form.

Narratives are an important part of the writing you will do in college and in your career. For instance, a sociology instructor may ask you to describe a situation in which you were in conflict with an authority figure. Employers often ask salespeople to submit narrative travel reports that describe the people they meet, meetings they attend, and clients they gain when on business trips.

Narration has many or all of the following elements:

1. It is told from a particular point of view.
2. It makes a point.
3. It presents a conflict and creates tension.
4. It sequences events.
5. It uses dialogue.
6. It uses vivid details that advance the story and the main point.
7. It conveys action and detail.

Narratives use all these techniques to provide human interest, spark curiosity, and draw in readers.

A Model Narration Essay

Now read the following narration essay, looking for how the writer uses narrative techniques. Use the annotations in the margin to guide you.

Right Place, Wrong Face

Alton Fitzgerald White

Alton Fitzgerald White majored in musical theater at Cincinnati's College Conservatory of Music. He made his Broadway debut with *Miss Saigon* in 1991 and has since appeared in five other musicals, including *The Lion King* and *Ragtime*. The following essay, which was first published in *The Nation* in 1999, recounts an ordeal he suffered in New York City.

A narrative is told from a particular point of view: The author speaks directly to the reader using the first-person "I."

As the youngest of five girls and two boys growing up in Cincinnati, I was raised to believe that if I worked hard, was a good person, and always told the truth, the world would be my oyster. I was raised to be a gentleman and learned that these qualities would bring me respect.

A narrative makes a point: The author's point is found in this thesis statement. His experience with the police changes his perspective on them.

While one has to earn respect, consideration is something owed to every human being. On Friday, June 16, 1999, when I was wrongfully arrested at my Harlem apartment building, my perception of everything I had learned as a young man was forever changed—not only because I wasn't given even a second to use the manners my parents taught me, but mostly because the police, whom I'd always naively thought were supposed to serve and protect me, were actually hunting me.

I had planned a pleasant day. The night before was a payday, plus I had received a standing ovation after portraying the starring role of Coalhouse Walker Jr.[1] in the Broadway musical *Ragtime*. It is a role that requires not only talent but also an honest emotional investment of the morals and lessons I learned as a child.

Coalhouse Walker Jr. is a victim (an often misused word, but in this case true) of overt racism. His story is every black man's nightmare. He is hardworking, successful, talented, charismatic, friendly, and polite. Perfect prey for someone with authority and not even a fraction of those qualities. On that Friday afternoon, I became a real-life Coalhouse Walker. Nothing could have prepared me for it. Not even stories told to me by other black men who had suffered similar injustices.

Friday for me usually means a trip to the bank, errands, the gym, dinner, and then off to the theater. On this particular day, I decided to break my pattern of getting up and running right out of the house. Instead, I took my time, slowed my pace, and splurged

---

[1]**Coalhouse Walker Jr.** In the novel *Ragtime,* a black New Yorker in the early twentieth century who snaps under the strain of racist treatment.

by making strawberry pancakes. Before I knew it, it was 2:45; my bank closes at 3:30, leaving me less than 45 minutes to get to midtown Manhattan on the train. I was pressed for time but in a relaxed, blessed state of mind. When I walked through the lobby of my building, I noticed two light-skinned Hispanic men I'd never seen before. Not thinking much of it, I continued on to the vestibule, which is separated from the lobby by a locked door.

A narrative conveys action and detail: The author details his experience using strong verbs that express his sense of violation: "searched, stripped of my backpack, put on my knees, handcuffed, and told to be quiet."

As I approached the exit, I saw people in uniforms rushing toward the door. I sped up to open it for them. I thought they might be paramedics, since many of the building's occupants are elderly. It wasn't until I had opened the door and greeted them that I recognized that they were police officers. Within seconds, I was told to "hold it"; they had received a call about young Hispanics with guns. I was told to get against the wall. I was searched, stripped of my backpack, put on my knees, handcuffed, and told to be quiet when I tried to ask questions.

With me were three other innocent black men who had been on their way to their U-Haul. They were moving into the apartment beneath mine, and I had just bragged to them about how safe the building was. One of these gentlemen got off his knees, still handcuffed, and unlocked the door for the officers to get into the lobby where the two strangers were standing. Instead of thanking or even acknowledging us, they led us out the door past our neighbors, who were all but begging the police in our defense.

A narrative presents conflict: Here the conflict is between the writer (a law-abiding citizen) and the police who mistreat him.

The four of us were put into cars with the two strangers and taken to the precinct station at 165th and Amsterdam. The police automatically linked us, with no questions and no regard for our character or our lives. No consideration was given to where we were going or why. Suppose an ailing relative was waiting upstairs, while I ran out for her medication? Or young children, who'd been told that Daddy was running to the corner store for milk and would be right back? My new neighbors weren't even allowed to lock their apartment or check on the U-Haul.

After we were lined up in the station, the younger of the two Hispanic men was identified as an experienced criminal, and drug residue was found in a pocket of the other. I now realize how naive I was to think that the police would then uncuff me, apologize for their mistake, and let me go. Instead, they continued to search my backpack, questioned me, and put me in jail with the criminals.

A narrative sequences events: This narrative is told in chronological order, one step at a time.

The rest of the nearly five-hour ordeal was like a horrible dream. I was handcuffed, strip-searched, taken in and out for questioning. The officers told me that they knew exactly who I was, knew I was in *Ragtime*, and that in fact they already had the men they wanted.

How then could they keep me there, or have brought me there in the first place? I was told it was standard procedure. As if the average law-abiding citizen knows what that is and can dispute it. From what I now know, "standard procedure" is something that every citizen, black and white, needs to learn, and fast.

A narrative uses vivid details that advance the story and the main point: Notice the contrast here between the narrator's life (he is an employed, successful man) and the way he is treated at the police station. These details emphasize the author's feeling of powerlessness.

I felt completely powerless. Why, do you think? Here I was, young, pleasant, and successful, in good physical shape, dressed in clean athletic attire. I was carrying a backpack containing a substantial paycheck and a deposit slip, on my way to the bank. Yet after hours and hours I was sitting at a desk with two officers who not only couldn't tell me why I was there but seemed determined to find something on me, to the point of making me miss my performance.

It was because I am a black man!

I sat in that cell crying silent tears of disappointment and injustice with the realization of how many innocent black men are convicted for no reason. When I was handcuffed, my first instinct had been to pull away out of pure insult and violation as a human being. Thank God I was calm enough to do what they said. When I was thrown in jail with the criminals and strip-searched, I somehow knew to put my pride aside, be quiet, and do exactly what I was told, hating it but coming to terms with the fact that in this situation I was a victim. They had guns!

A narrative uses dialogue: While the author keeps direct dialogue to a minimum in this essay, this one statement conveys his profound sense of injustice at being arrested in his own home.

Before I was finally let go, exhausted, humiliated, embarrassed, and still in shock, I was led to a room and given a pseudo-apology. I was told that I was at the wrong place at the wrong time. My reply? "I was where I live."

Everything I learned growing up in Cincinnati has been shattered. Life will never be the same.

The Structure and Content of Narration Essays

In this section, you will learn about the structure of a narration essay and practice using the guidelines for understanding, analyzing, and evaluating narration essays. This key information will help you skillfully read and write essays that use narration.

The structure of a narration essay is like that of a short story, novel, or movie. A narration essay contains three elements: an introduction, a body, and a conclusion. Figure 10.1 represents these elements visually.

1. **THE INTRODUCTION CATCHES THE READER'S ATTENTION, PROVIDES BACKGROUND INFORMATION, SETS UP THE SEQUENCE OF EVENTS, ESTABLISHES A POINT OF VIEW, AND USUALLY CONTAINS THE THESIS**

Many narratives use the first-person **point of view**, in which the key participant speaks directly to the reader ("*I* first realized the problem when . . ."). The first person allows the narrator to assume a personal tone and to speak directly to

Figure 10.1   Graphic Organizer for a Narration Essay

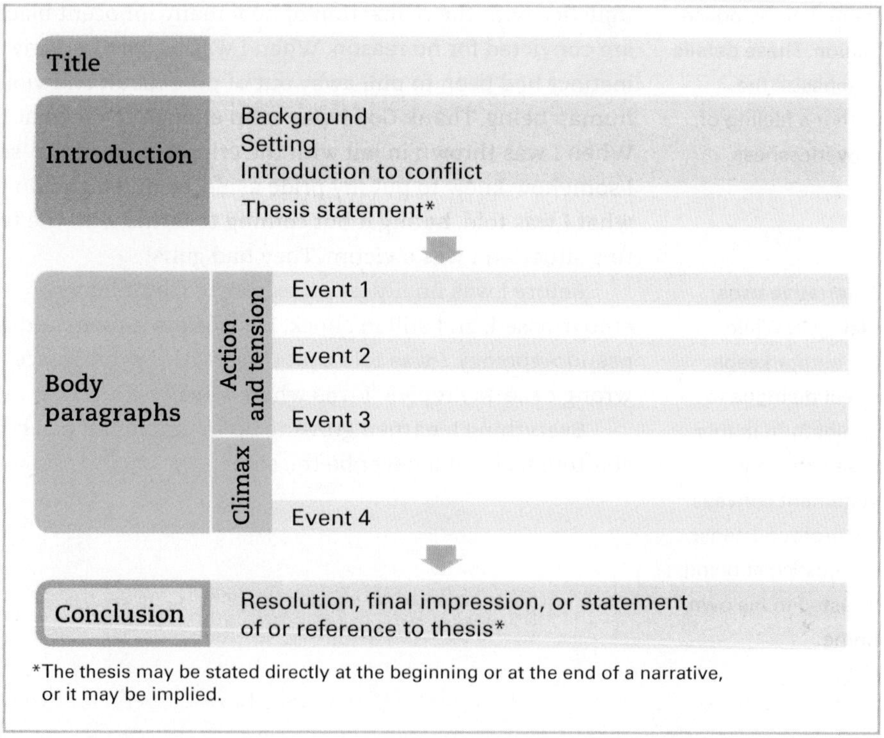

Title	
Introduction	Background Setting Introduction to conflict Thesis statement*
Body paragraphs	Event 1 Event 2 Event 3 Event 4
Conclusion	Resolution, final impression, or statement of or reference to thesis*

*The thesis may be stated directly at the beginning or at the end of a narrative, or it may be implied.

the audience, easily expressing his or her attitudes, feelings, interpretation, and commentary. When you are narrating an event that occurred in your own life, the first person is probably your best choice. In "Right Place, Wrong Face," Alton White speaks directly to the reader using first-person point of view.

Other narratives use the third-person point of view, in which an unknown storyteller describes what happens to the key participants ("The problem began when *Saul* . . ."). The third-person point of view gives the narrator more distance from the action and generally provides a more objective perspective than the first-person point of view. It also allows the narrator to reveal insights about a character's actions or personality.

In a narration essay, the thesis states the purpose of the story being told. Often the writer will state the point directly, using an explicit thesis statement, but at other times he or she will leave the main point unstated, using an implied thesis. The thesis does not necessarily need to appear in the introduction. In "Right Place, Wrong Face," the author directly states his thesis in the second sentence of paragraph 2:

> On Friday, June 16, 1999, when I was wrongfully arrested at my Harlem apartment building, my perception of everything I had learned as a young man was forever changed—not only because I wasn't given even a second to use the manners my parents taught me, but mostly because the police, whom I'd always naively thought were supposed to serve and protect me, were actually hunting me.

White captures the reader's attention by describing his idealistic upbringing and setting the stage for a disturbing sequence of events. The remainder of the essay describes the sequence of events that led to White's altered perception about the police and his questioning of the beliefs with which his parents raised him.

Reading Ⓘ Writing   The Introduction to a Narration Essay

The Reader's Perspective	The Writer's Perspective
When reading a narration essay, start by previewing the text to get an overview of its content and organization.	When writing a narration essay, be sure that your thesis statement clearly states the purpose of the story you will tell. Make sure that you draw readers in and signal your organization.

2. THE BODY PARAGRAPHS TELL THE STORY

The body paragraphs of a narration essay tell a story that makes the point stated in the thesis (or implied if there is no direct thesis). Several elements work together to create effective body paragraphs.

Conflict, Resolution, Tension, and Climax   An effective narrative presents a **conflict** — such as a struggle, question, or problem — and works toward its **resolution**. The conflict can be between participants or between a participant and some external force, such as a law, a value, a moral principle, or an act of nature. **Tension** is the suspense created as the story unfolds and as the reader wonders how the conflict will be resolved. The point just before the conflict is resolved is called the **climax**. In "Right Place, Wrong Face," the conflict is between a law-abiding citizen and the police who treat him like a criminal. Tension mounts as the narrator sits in a jail cell, frustrated and upset by the way he is being treated. The climax occurs when the narrator receives a half-hearted apology and is let go (paragraph 15).

Organization   Organization is important to the effectiveness of a narration essay. The events may all be presented in chronological order from beginning to end, which makes the actions clear. Some narratives create drama or tension by presenting some events as flashbacks or through foreshadowing. Good narratives provide transitions between paragraphs to keep the story flowing.

Vivid Details: Dialogue, Physical Description, and Action   Typically, writers of narratives keep readers involved throughout the body paragraphs in several ways: through vivid details like *dialogue*, *physical description*, and *action*. White uses bits of dialogue to describe his interactions with the police, but his primary focus is recounting what happened during his humiliating encounter with the police. Keep the following points in mind about the use of vivid details in a narrative:

- **The narrative should provide relevant sensory details.** Narration essays include enough detail about the place where the experience occurred to allow readers to feel as if they were there. Details that appeal to the senses work best. For example, White uses physical description to give readers a sense of the setting, describing the vestibule and the lobby (paragraph 5) and the details of his ordeal as he was "handcuffed, strip-searched, taken in and out for questioning" (paragraph 10).

- **The narrative should include details only about the appearance and actions of the main characters.** People who were present but not part of the incident or experience need not be described in detail or even included in the narration. For example, White mentions his neighbors but does not describe them in detail.

- **Key actions should create tension, build it to a climax, and resolve it.** A successful narration essay provides the details about the conflict and answers the following questions.

Questions	Alton White's "Right Place, Wrong Face"
Why did the experience or incident occur?	The incident occurred because someone called the police to report two suspicious men in the lobby of the building in which the author lives.
What events led up to it?	The day began pleasantly for Alton White, but it took a very unpleasant turn when he left his apartment to go to the bank.
How was it resolved?	The incident was resolved when the police finally let the narrator go.
What were its short- and long-term outcomes?	The short-term outcome was the narrator's missing a performance of a Broadway play in which he was starring. The long-term outcome was the narrator's changed perception about the police and about the values his parents had stressed while he was growing up.
What is its significance now?	The narrator will likely never look at police the same way again, and the incident gave him a deeper, more personal understanding of the way black people are sometimes treated by the police.

3. THE CONCLUSION ENDS THE STORY AND CONNECTS TO THE THESIS

The final paragraph of a narrative should finish the story and reinforce the thesis. A summary is usually unnecessary and may detract from the effectiveness of the narrative. An effective conclusion to a narration essay will do one or more of the following things:

- **Make a final observation about the experience or incident.** Alton White's final observation is powerful: "Everything I learned growing up in Cincinnati has been shattered. Life will never be the same."
- **Ask a probing question.** For an essay on adventure travel, a writer might conclude, "Although the visit to Nepal was enlightening for me, do the native people really want or need us there?"
- **Suggest a new but related direction of thought.** For an essay on racial profiling, a writer might conclude by suggesting that sensitivity training for the police might have changed the outcome of the situation.
- **Reveal a surprising piece of information.** For an essay that uses narration to explain the effects of serious phobias, a writer might conclude by stating that less serious phobias also exist — such as arachibutyrophobia, which is the fear of peanut butter sticking to the roof of one's mouth.

- **Refer back to the beginning.** For an essay about home burglary, the writer might return to the beginning of the story, when family members still felt safe and unviolated. The conclusion of Alton White's essay brings it full circle, emphasizing that the incident has dramatically changed his core beliefs.

- **Restate the thesis or broaden its scope.** When restating, be sure to use different words. To broaden the scope of a thesis statement, extend its applicability beyond the immediate situation. For an essay using narration to relate an incident of workplace gender inequality, the writer might refer back to the thesis, either stated or implied, and then comment that the gender inequality illustrated by these events is far too common in numerous other workplace environments as well.

Reading ⓘ Writing   Perspectives on Events and Actions

The Reader's Perspective	The Writer's Perspective
It's a good idea to read a narration essay several times. First, familiarize yourself with the events and action, noting who did what, when, where, and how. Then reread the narrative, this time concentrating on its meaning.	When writing a narration essay, devote a separate paragraph to each major action or distinct part of the story. Use transitional words and phrases — such as *during, after,* and *finally* — to connect events and guide readers along.

Understanding, Analyzing, and Evaluating Narration Essays

In reading and writing narration essays, your goal is to get beyond mere competence. That is, you want to be able to do more than merely understand the content of the essays you read or convey just your basic ideas to the audience you're writing for.

📖 Understanding a Narration Essay

Preview the essay first to get a basic overview of what is happening. When you are reading a narration essay for the first time, it is easy to get lost in the story and overlook its importance. So be sure to reread it, concentrating on its meaning and message. As you read and reread, use the skills you learned in Chapter 2, "Active Reading," and look for the answers to the following questions.

- **What is the writer's thesis?** If the thesis is implied, state it in your own words.
- **What is the role of each participant in the story?** Determine who is important in the story and how the participants interact and relate to one another.

- **What does the dialogue reveal about the characters?** Just as people reveal much about themselves by what they say and how they say it, dialogue can reveal a great deal about the characters in a narrative. In fact, dialogue is often used to dramatize the action, emphasize the conflict, and reveal the personalities or motives of the key participants in a narrative. Much of the dialogue in White's essay is indirect, but the author does include a powerful piece of direct dialogue in paragraph 15: "I was where I live." As you read, consider how the dialogue contributes to the essay's main point.

- **What actions occur within the narrative?** Pay attention to what the participants are doing and where, when, and how they are doing it.

- **What is the conflict?** Consider its causes and observe how the writer builds the conflict.

- **What is the climax?** Determine how, why, and where the conflict is resolved.

- **What is the sequence of events?** The events in a narrative must be arranged in an order that is easy for readers to follow. Often, but not always, a narrative presents events in chronological order. The events in "Right Place, Wrong Face" take place in chronological order. At other times, writers use the techniques of flashback and foreshadowing to make their point. A **flashback** returns the reader to events that took place in the past. White's essay begins with a flashback. **Foreshadowing** hints at events that will happen in the future. Both techniques are used frequently in drama, fiction, and film. A movie, for instance, might start with a pitcher on a baseball field at the end of an important game, flash back to the events that made this game so crucial, and then return to the game. A television show might begin with a wedding reception that foreshadows problems the bride and groom will have in the future. When used sparingly, these techniques can build interest and add variety to a narrative. Especially for lengthy or complex narratives or for those involving flashback or foreshadowing, it is helpful to draw a graphic organizer. Refer to Figure 10.1 before drawing your own diagram.

Reading ① Writing Perspectives on Dialogue

The Reader's Perspective	The Writer's Perspective
When reading a narration essay, ask yourself what each line of dialogue reveals about the person saying it.	When writing a narration essay, include key dialogue that is interesting, revealing, and related to the main point of the story. To make sure the dialogue sounds natural, read the lines aloud or ask a friend to do so. Consider this example: **Natural (from White's essay)** 　　"I was where I live." **Too formal** 　　"I was accosted in the vestibule of my abode."

Understanding in Action

Exercise 10.1

Below is one student's summary of paragraphs 6–8 of "Right Place, Wrong Face."

> He was leaving his building when police officers rushed in. They ordered him against the wall and took his backpack and handcuffed him. Three other innocent black men were also held, along with the real suspects, two light-skinned Hispanic men. They were put in police cars and taken to headquarters. There was no chance to let anyone know what was happening.

Look at Figure 10.2 (the graphic organizer for "Right Place, Wrong Face"), reread the essay, and write your own summary of it. (For advice about writing summaries, see pp. 44–46.)

Figure 10.2   Graphic Organizer for "Right Place, Wrong Face"

Title	Right Place, Wrong Face
Introduction	**Background:** Youngest of seven; raised to be a gentleman **Setting:** June 1999, Harlem Narrator plays Coalhouse Walker Jr., an African American who experiences the injustice of racism, in *Ragtime*.
	Thesis: Narrator's wrongful arrest changes his perception of everything he learned while growing up.

Body paragraphs	**Action and tension**	1. Narrator is on his way to deposit his paycheck.
		2. He notices strange men in his building's lobby.
		3. He opens door for police officers.
		4. Narrator and neighbors (African Americans) are arrested; suspects police seek are Hispanic.
		5. Narrator is jailed, searched, repeatedly questioned.
	Climax	Narrator is finally released; "I was told that I was at the wrong place at the wrong time. My reply? 'I was where I live.'"

Conclusion	"Everything I learned growing up in Cincinnati has been shattered."

📊 Analyzing a Narration Essay

Analyzing a narrative involves examining how and why the story was told and determining the point that the story is making. Use the following questions to guide your analysis of narration essays.

- **What is the author's purpose?** Determine the writer's point or message. Alton White's purpose in "Right Place, Wrong Face" is to explain how his unjustified arrest changed his perception of the police and increased his understanding of matters related to race.

- **Does the point of the story follow logically and clearly from the events in the story?** The story should lead up to and demonstrate the point the writer is attempting to make.

- **How does the writer create tension?** Determine what factors create the tension that leads up to the climax. Does the author give you clues about what is about to happen?

- **How objective is the writer?** Narratives are often personal accounts and, therefore, influenced by the writer's perceptions, attitudes, values, and beliefs. Consequently, different writers may describe the same event differently. If you suspect a writer is one-sided, or biased, seek further information from other sources. For example, how might the arresting officers in "Right Place, Wrong Face" have perceived the situation differently?

Analysis in Action

Exercise 10.2

The following example shows one student's notes analyzing paragraph 14 of the essay.

Connects his experience to other black men's	I sat in that cell crying silent tears of disappointment and injustice with the realization of how many innocent black men are convicted for no reason. When I was handcuffed, my first instinct had been to pull away out of pure insult and violation as a human being. Thank God I was calm
Ties in with lessons from childhood	enough to do what they said. When I was thrown in jail with the criminals and strip-searched, I somehow knew to put my pride aside, be quiet, and do exactly what I was
Would police see this differently?	told, hating it but coming to terms with the fact that in this situation I was a victim. They had guns!

Using the "Analyzing a Narration Essay" questions as a guide, make notes on "Right Place, Wrong Face."

📖 Evaluating a Narration Essay

Evaluating a narration essay involves judging how effectively the writer told the story and determining how well the story conveys its intended point or message. Unless you have reason to believe otherwise, assume that the writer is honest about the events presented. You should also assume, however, that the writer chose details selectively to put forth his or her message. Use the following questions to guide your evaluation of narration essays.

- **Is the story realistic, believable, and well explained?** Consider whether the writer clearly and effectively told the story, maintained your interest, and led you to understand the point of the story.

- **Is the resolution of the conflict believable and well explained?** Determine whether the author has provided adequate detail to help you understand how and why events happened. For example, do you believe that Alton White's encounter with the police was the sole event that changed his perception, or do you think other experiences or conversations may also have played a role?

- **Does the writer leave anything unspoken or unreported?** The writer should report all relevant conversations and actions. Pay attention to what is reported, but also consider what might have been left unsaid.

- **Does the writer reveal his feelings about the incident or events?** Writers often reveal their feelings through their tone, which is established through word choice and other language features (see "Analyze the Author's Tone," pp. 57–58). For example, how does Alton White reveal his feelings through phrases like "Here I was, young, pleasant, and successful, in good physical shape, dressed in clean athletic attire" (paragraph 12) and "I sat in that cell crying silent tears of disappointment and injustice" (paragraph 14)?

Evaluation in Action

Exercise 10.3

The following example is by the same student whose notes appear in the Analysis in Action exercise (p. 191). That student used those notes to write an evaluation of paragraph 14 as it relates to White's thesis.

> In this paragraph White successfully supports and expands on his thesis. He shows how the manners his parents taught him helped him do what the police officers told him to do. He didn't resist them, which would definitely have made the situation worse. He also strengthens his point about how naive he had been to think that the police were there to protect him. Instead he was their victim. He links his experience to the experiences of other black men who have actually been convicted because of police injustice. It is clear why White's youthful hopes were shattered that day.

Use the "Evaluating a Narration Essay" questions, your own summary, and your annotation of the essay to write an evaluation of White's narration.

Writing Your Own Narration Essay

Now that you have learned about the major characteristics, structure, and purposes of a narration essay, you know everything necessary to write your own narrative. In this section, you will read a student's narration essay and get advice on finding ideas, drafting your essay, and revising and editing it. You may want to use the essay prompts in "Readings for Practice, Ideas for Writing" (p. 200) or choose your own topic.

A Student Model Narration Essay

Mina Raine, an education major, wrote this essay for an assignment given by her first-year writing instructor. She had to describe a situation in which her involvement made a difference or affected others. As you read the essay, notice how Raine's narrative creates conflict and tension and builds to a climax and resolution. Highlight the sections where you think the tension is particularly intense.

Title	# Taking Back Control
	Mina Raine
Introduction: Raine gives background about her relationship with Beth.	My friend Beth is soft spoken but strong in faith and character. She is one of those rare people who can light up a room with her smile or make you feel at ease just by simply being near you. We met freshman year at a gathering of mutual friends in the largest dorm on campus. Since then, we've spent our time together
Thesis statement: Raine gives a rationale for her concern.	among a close-knit circle of friends. Beth has always seemed, to me, so mature and composed and so in control of herself and her life, so giving, so caring, so nurturing in all her relationships, which is why I was deeply concerned and very much surprised when I began to notice a drastic change in her.
Transitions help sequence events. **Action** begins with specific detail.	First I noticed that Beth was making a habit out of eating her dinner from a small cereal bowl instead of a plate. I didn't think much of that, at first. Maybe the dining hall had temporarily run out of plates and a bowl was all she could find. Or maybe it was just one of those funny little habits we all find ourselves adopting, eventually. (Later I would learn that the small bowl is a way to monitor and control the amount of food she eats; you can only fit so much food into the shallow dish.)
Tension begins to build.	A few weeks later, my friends and I noticed a dramatic change in Beth's appearance—sunken, tired eyes void of their usual sparkle, a smile that seemed forced, and the clothes that once hugged her lovely curves in a subtle and conservative way now

hanging off her fragile frame. This coupled with her strange cereal bowl habit was finally enough to make us realize something was definitely wrong. Of course, we weren't sure yet if Beth really was struggling with an eating disorder, but it was certainly evident that she was not herself, and from her somewhat depressed and rather distracted demeanor, she seemed to be seriously struggling with something.

Then, on one particular evening in the dining hall, my friends and I overheard Beth discussing her new workout regimen with her boyfriend, Steve. She had recently started fitting in evening running sessions between all of her studies and extracurricular activities. Steve had been running on the treadmill daily and carefully monitoring what he ate in an effort to lose the "freshman fifteen" (or twenty) he had gained. Unfortunately, it seemed his new efforts to live a healthy lifestyle had rubbed off on Beth, in an unhealthy way. My friend, who had been at a perfect weight and had been eating properly, was now eating less and exercising more. It was a sure recipe for disaster. I heard Steve talking to Beth about how many miles they had run that evening and how many more they would run the next day. He had her on the same workout schedule he was on, but she wasn't the one who was overweight. As I sat there listening to him influence her in this way, I felt myself getting angry. I didn't know for sure what was wrong with Beth at that point (though I had a pretty good idea), but it was obvious something was wrong. How could he not see

Tension increases. that? The dark circles under Beth's eyes showed her obvious lack of sleep, and her low energy and lack of focus showed that her body wasn't getting the nutrition it needed.

After listening to the unsettling conversation between Beth and Steve about their strict workout routine, my friends and I began discussing the matter among ourselves and deciding on the best way to address the issue with Beth. I spent a few days wondering how best to approach her or if I even should. What if I upset her and she stopped talking to me? What if we were wrong and Beth was fine? Or worse, what if we were right and she pulled away from us? Then, Beth solved this dilemma for me: *She* came to *me*.

Dialogue leads to a climax. Three weeks after my friend's struggle with food and weight became glaringly obvious, she knocked on my door. "I need to talk to you," she said, "and I think you already know what it's about." I felt unprepared for this moment. Beth responded in a calm, serious tone to my anxious silence: "First, I feel I owe you an apology for making you worry about me. You're a good friend and I'm sorry." Here she broke down, and it was my turn to try to be stoic.

Climax

"It's OK. It's nothing you have to apologize for. But are you OK?"

"Not really," Beth answered in an unsteady voice. "I have an eating disorder."

What do you say to that? You know it happens, but you never think it will be you or someone close to you who will be plagued by a nagging, evil voice in the back of her head telling her she's had enough to eat today (even though she's still very hungry) or that despite the fact that she is a size 5 she really shouldn't enjoy a piece of cake for dessert. "Is it bulimia?" I asked Beth. She had regained her composure now, and spoke matter-of-factly.

"No, I don't make myself sick. It's not really anorexia either because I do eat. I just don't eat much. It's more of a control thing. When I eat my meals out of a cereal bowl, I can control the portion size, keep it small, and I'm aware of exactly how much I am eating."

"When did this start?" I asked, expecting her to say only a few weeks, maybe a few months ago.

"I've struggled with it most of my life, but I had it mostly under control until around a year ago."

A year! She had been fighting this ugly thing for a year, and we, I, had only just noticed in the past few weeks? How could that be? Beth later told me that her now ex-boyfriend had made a trivial but insensitive comment about her weight around a year ago. That was what had triggered the disorder to resurface. I was furious with myself and at a loss for words. All I could do was hug her, tell her that I have absolute faith in her and her ability to fight this thing, this disgusting thing that has taken over her body and her life, and cry into the comfort of my hands when she was finally too far down the hall to hear me.

When I checked in with Beth a couple days after her disconcerting but unsurprising revelation, she broke down and gave me an intimate glimpse into the complicated and disturbing battle being fought within her head. She seemed so defeated but aware of this feeling of defeat, which only made her angry at herself. I did my best to console her with the reassuring fact that her awareness of the problem and the need to make some serious changes in her life was already a giant step toward her recovery. I also told her that while I would always be there for her, to support and encourage her, I'm not qualified to truly help her deal with her disorder.

"I know," she said, a few silent tears sliding down her pale cheeks. "I've made an appointment with the counseling office on campus."

"I'm so proud of you," I responded as I embraced her.

"I'm hoping you'll come with me, at least for the first visit."

"Of course," I answered. "You're strong and smart. You will beat this. You'll get better. And I'm always here if you need to talk or just need a hug. Just please promise me you'll stop working out until you get back to more normal eating habits. That means no more cereal bowls. Unless, of course, you're eating cereal."

Beth laughed a little at this last comment, which is what I had been hoping for. Even if only for a moment, the Beth I knew shone through in that brief smile and soft chuckle. I knew then that though she'll probably have to work on it every day, Beth will regain control of her body and her life.

Conclusion: Raine returns to the idea in her thesis statement—her knowledge of Beth as someone in control of her life.

Responding to Raine's Essay

1. Evaluate the strength of Raine's thesis. How clear and specific is it?
2. What ideas in the essay, if any, do you think should be discussed more fully? Where did you feel more details were needed? Which details — if any — are unnecessary?
3. How does Raine establish conflict and create tension?
4. Where does Raine use foreshadowing? How effective is it?
5. Evaluate the title, introduction, and conclusion of the essay.

Finding Ideas for Your Narration Essay

One way to find ideas to write about is to look for topics *as you read* material in this book, in other classes, or in your spare time. As you read, pay particular attention to the issue, struggle, or dilemma at hand. Try to discover what broader issue the essay is concerned with. For example, a narrative about a worker's conflict with a supervisor is also concerned with the larger issue of authority. Once you've identified the larger issue, you can begin to develop ideas about it by relating it to your own experience.

Choosing an Event or Incident for Your Narration Essay

As you think about an experience or incident to write about, be sure that it is memorable and vivid enough that you can recall the details. After all, you don't want to discover that you are struggling with the first draft because you cannot remember important details about the experience. Make sure you're comfortable writing about the incident. At this stage, you should also decide whether to tell your story in the first or the third person.

Gathering Details about the Experience or Incident

This step involves recollecting as many details about the experience or incident as possible and recording them on paper or in a computer file. Reenact the story, sketching each scene in your mind. Identify key actions, describe the main participants, and express your feelings. Here are a few ways to gather details.

- **Replay the experience or incident in your mind.** Jot down exactly what you see, hear, smell, taste, and feel — colors, dialogue, sounds, odors, flavors, and sensations. Also note how these details make you feel.

- **Write the following headings on a piece of paper, or type them on your computer screen:** *Scene, Key Actions, Key Participants, Key Dialogue,* and *My Feelings.* List your ideas under each heading systematically.

- **Describe the incident or experience to a friend.** Have your friend ask questions as you retell the story. Jot down the details that the retelling and questioning help you recall.

- **Describe the incident or experience aloud while recording it.** Then listen to the recording and make notes.

- **Consider different aspects of the incident or experience by asking *who, what, when, where, how,* and *why* questions.** Record your answers.

Developing and Supporting a Thesis

Once you have enough details, it is time to focus your thesis — the main point of your narrative. You probably have a working thesis in mind. Now is the time to improve it.

A thesis statement may be placed at the beginning or end of a narration essay, or it may be implied. Once you have a thesis, you may need to do some additional prewriting to develop supporting details.

Drafting Your Narration Essay

When you are satisfied with your thesis and your support for it, you are ready to organize your ideas and write the first draft. Decide whether you will put all events in chronological order or whether you will use flashbacks or foreshadowing for dramatic effect. As you write, refer to the graphic organizer in Figure 10.1 (p. 184) to remind yourself of the structure and elements of a narration essay. Use the following guidelines to keep the narrative on track.

1. **The introduction should contain an attention-getting opening, provide any necessary background information, and introduce the conflict.** The introduction should also contain your thesis if you have decided to place it at the beginning of the essay.

2. **The narrative should build tension as it leads up to the final resolution.** Each major action should have its own paragraph. Use transitional words and phrases to help readers understand the sequence of events.

3. **The conclusion should end the essay in a satisfying manner.** Resist providing a summary at the end of the narrative, as it may detract from the impact of the story. Instead, try ending in one of the ways described in "The Structure and Content of Narration Essays" (p. 184).

Revising Your Narration Essay

If possible, set your draft aside for a day or two before rereading and revising it. As you reread, don't worry about errors in spelling, grammar, and mechanics. Focus instead on improving the overall effectiveness of the narrative. Will it interest readers and make them want to know what happens next? Does it make your point clearly? To discover weaknesses in your draft, use the revision flowchart in Figure 10.3.

Editing and Proofreading Your Essay

The last step is to check your revised narrative essay for errors in grammar, spelling, punctuation, and mechanics. In addition, be sure to look for the types of errors that you tend to make in any writing assignments, whether for this class or in other situations. Check the handbook (pp. 645–714) for assistance with common errors in your writing.

Figure 10.3 Revising a Narration Essay

QUESTIONS		REVISION STRATEGIES
1. Main point Is the main point clear?	No	• Make your thesis more explicit.
Yes		
2. Conflict Does the narrative present a clear conflict related to the main point?	No	• Add events specific to the conflict. • Rework your thesis to make it better relate to the conflict.
Yes		
3. Key scenes, people, and action Do they clearly relate to the main point and conflict?	No	• Delete unnecessary scenes, people, or actions.
Yes		
4. Descriptions Is each key scene, person, or action vividly described?	No	• Brainstorm vivid details. • Consider adding dialogue.
Yes		
5. Major events Is the sequence of events clear? Is it clear when you use foreshadowing or flashbacking?	No	• Add missing events. • Consider rearranging the events. • Use transitions to clarify the sequence of events.
Yes		
6. Topic sentences Is each paragraph focused on a separate part of the action?	No	• Be sure each paragraph has a topic sentence and supporting details. (See Chapter 6.) • Combine paragraphs about closely related events and split those that cover more than one event.
Yes		
7. Dialogue Is it realistic when you say it aloud? Does it directly relate to the conflict?	No	• Record yourself telling someone what you want your dialogue to express. Use that recording to revise your dialogue and make it more natural. • Eliminate dialogue that does not add to the story.
Yes		
8. Point of view Do you use a consistent point of view and verb tense?	No	• Reconsider your point of view. • If the tense changes for no reason, revise for consistency.
Yes		
9. Introduction and conclusion Do they address the main point? Does the conclusion resolve the conflict?	No	• Revise your introduction and conclusion. (See pp. 136–39.)

Readings for Practice, Ideas for Writing

Talking a Stranger through the Night

Sherry Amatenstein is an author, a journalist, and a noted relationship expert. She offers advice in an online column and through such books as *The Complete Marriage Counselor: Relationship-Saving Advice from America's Top 50+ Couples Therapists* (2011). The article that follows, which was first published in *Newsweek*, describes her experience volunteering at Help Line, New York City's oldest crisis and suicide hotline.

Reading Tip

As you read, notice how Amatenstein thrusts you immediately into the situation and creates suspense about the crisis. Pay attention to the way her use of dialogue reveals both the caller's and the author's states of mind.

Previewing the Reading

Preview the reading (see pp. 28–29 for guidelines), and then answer the following questions.

1. What experience does the author describe in this reading?
2. What benefit does the author derive from working a hotline?

Talking a Stranger through the Night

Sherry Amatenstein

The call came sixty minutes into my third shift as a volunteer at the crisis hotline. As the child of Holocaust[1] survivors, I grew up wanting to ease other people's pain. But it wasn't until after September 11 that I contacted Help Line, the nonprofit telephone service headquartered in New York. The instructor of the nine-week training course taught us how to handle a variety of callers, from depressed seniors to "repeats" (those who checked in numerous times a day).

We spent two sessions on suicide calls, but I prayed I wouldn't get one until

I felt comfortable on the line. Drummed over and over into the thirty trainees' heads was that our role wasn't to give advice. Rather, we were to act as empathetic[2] sounding boards and encourage callers to figure out how to take action.

My idealism[3] about the hotline's value faded that first night, as in quick succession I heard from men who wanted to masturbate while I listened, repeats who told me again and again about their horrific childhoods, know-nothing shrinks and luckless lives, and three separate callers who railed about

---

[1] **Holocaust** Persecution and mass killing of Jews and other minorities by the Nazis from 1933 to 1945.

[2] **empathetic** Understanding of others' emotions and feelings.

[3] **idealism** The act or practice of envisioning things in the best possible form.

the low intellect of everyone living in Queens (my borough!). Sprinkled into the mix were people who turned abusive when I refused to tell them how to solve their problems.

I tried to remain sympathetic. If I, who had it together (an exciting career, great friends and family) found New York isolating, I could imagine how frightening it was for people so untethered they needed a hotline for company. That rationale didn't help. After only ten hours, I no longer cringed each time the phone rang, terrified it signified a problem I wasn't equipped to handle. Instead I wondered what fresh torture this caller had up his unstable sleeve.

5   Then Sandy's (not her real name) quavering voice nipped into my ear: "I want to kill myself." I snapped to attention, remembering my training. Did she have an imminent plan to do herself in? Luckily, no. Sandy knew a man who'd attempted suicide via pills, threw them up, and lived. She was afraid of botching a similar attempt. Since she was handicapped, she couldn't even walk to her window to jump out.

Sandy's life was certainly Help Line material. Her parents had disowned her forty years before. She'd worked as a secretary until a bone-crushing fall put her out of commission. Years later she was working again and had a boyfriend who stuck with her even after a cab struck Sandy and put her back on the disabled list. They became engaged, and then, soap-opera like, tragedy struck again. Sandy's boyfriend was diagnosed with cancer and passed away last year. Now she was in constant pain, confined to a dark apartment, her only companion a nurse's aide. "There's nothing left," she cried. "Give me a reason to live."

Her plea drove home the wisdom of the "no advice" dictum. How could I summon the words to give someone else's life meaning? The best I could do was to help Sandy fan the spark that had led her to reach out. I tossed life-affirming statements at her like paint on a canvas, hoping some would stick. I ended with "Sandy, I won't whitewash[4] your problems. You've had more than your share of sorrow. But surely there are some things that have given you pleasure."

She thought hard and remembered an interest in books on spirituality. The downside followed immediately. Sandy's limited eyesight made it difficult for her to read. She rasped, "My throat hurts from crying, but I'm afraid if I get off the phone I'll want to kill myself again."

I said, "I'm here as long as you need me."

10   We spoke another two hours. She recalled long-ago incidents—most depressing, a few semi-joyful. There were some things she still enjoyed: peanuts, "Oprah," the smell of autumn. I again broached the topic of spirituality. My supervisor, whom I'd long ago motioned to listen in on another phone, handed me a prayer book. I read, and Sandy listened. After "amen," she said, "I think I'll be all right for the night."

Naturally, she couldn't promise to feel better tomorrow. For all of us, life is one day, sometimes even one minute, at a time. She asked, "When are you on again?"

I said, "My schedule is irregular, but we're all here for you, anytime you want. Thanks so much for calling."

As I hung up, I realized the call had meant as much to me as to Sandy, if not more. Despite having people in my life, lately I'd felt achingly lonely. I hadn't called a hotline, but I'd manned one, and this night had been my best in a long time. Instead of having dinner at an overpriced restaurant or watching HBO, I'd connected with another troubled soul in New York City.

---

[4]**whitewash** Make look less bad than it really is.

Understanding and Reviewing the Reading

1. **Background** What motivated Amatenstein to volunteer for the crisis hotline?

2. **Action** How did Amatenstein respond when she first answered Sandy's call?

3. **Detail** What did Amatenstein find out about Sandy as she spoke to her?

4. **Detail** What important lesson that she had learned during her training did Amatenstein recall during her conversation with Sandy?

5. **Main point** What did Amatenstein learn about herself because of her experience?

6. **Vocabulary** Using context clues (see p. 37) and consulting a dictionary if necessary, briefly define these words: *horrific* (para. 3), *rationale* (4), *signified* (4), *imminent* (5), *botching* (5), and *dictum* (7).

7. **Structure and sequence** To help you see the organization of "Talking a Stranger through the Night," complete the graphic organizer below.

Analyzing the Reading

1. **Conflict** What is the central conflict presented in Amatenstein's narrative? (Hint: *Conflict* can refer to any kind of struggle, not just one involving opposition.)

2. **Tension and suspense** What is the primary source of tension and suspense in "Talking a Stranger through the Night"? What kept you reading?

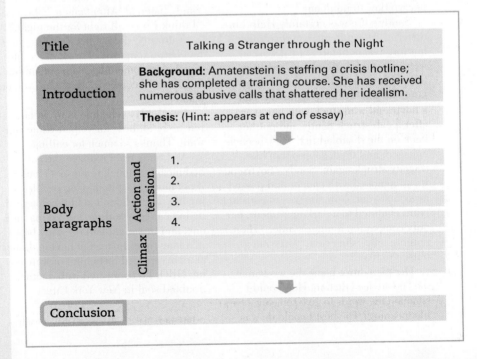

Title	Talking a Stranger through the Night
Introduction	**Background:** Amatenstein is staffing a crisis hotline; she has completed a training course. She has received numerous abusive calls that shattered her idealism.
	Thesis: (Hint: appears at end of essay)

Body paragraphs — Action and tension — Climax

1.
2.
3.
4.

Conclusion

3. **Climax** When and how is the tension resolved, providing the narrative with its climax?

4. **Language** "Fan the spark" (para. 7) is an idiom. Explain its meaning as Amatenstein uses it.

Evaluating the Reading

1. **Character** Evaluate the kinds of detail Amatenstein provides about Sandy—for example, that Sandy enjoyed "peanuts, 'Oprah,' the smell of autumn" (para. 10). How does she make you care about Sandy?

2. **Main point** How do you respond to Amatenstein's implied thesis in her concluding paragraph? Should she have been more specific?

3. **Descriptive detail** What details are particularly vivid and descriptive? Choose several and explain what each contributes to the narrative.

Discussing the Reading

1. Amatenstein gives advice on relationships in her professional life. However, at Help Line she is told not to offer advice to callers. Why might a crisis hotline differ from other resources for people seeking help?

2. In a group discussion or in your journal, explore the various reasons someone might call a crisis hotline. What qualities would you expect a volunteer answering the phone lines to possess?

3. Discuss some of the reasons people choose to volunteer. Are they generally the same as Amatenstein's reasons?

Writing about the Reading

1. **Paragraph** Write a paragraph narrating a situation in which talking to someone helped you solve a problem or provided you with a fresh perspective. Brainstorm about some of the conversations you had with the other person. Pick out the important advice or information that helped you solve your problem and include it in the draft of your paragraph.

2. **Paragraph** Write a paragraph about a situation you had approached idealistically only to find the reality to be less than what you had expected. As you plan your paragraph, be sure to include enough detail to contrast your idealism with the reality of the situation.

3. **Essay** Write a narration essay about a time when, like Amatenstein, you helped another person and found that the experience benefited you as well. Start by brainstorming a list of such experiences. Select the best example and organize a sequence of events relating to it. Be sure to include a thesis statement about some results of helping others.

A New Interpretation of Tears

Roger Porter is a writer and educator from Oakland, California. He has an MFA in creative writing from Mills College. His first book is called *The Souls of Hood Folk*. He blogs at ghettosun.com and also submits writing to publications as a freelancer. "A New Interpretation of Tears" first appeared in the Spring 2014 edition of *Rad Dad* magazine, a quarterly publication that focuses on diverse perspectives on parenting.

Reading Tip

As you read, think about what point Porter wants to make and about how he uses narration to make it.

Previewing the Reading

Preview the reading (see pp. 28–29 for guidelines), and then answer the following questions.

1. What action does Porter describe in the reading?
2. What do you know about Porter based on your preview?

A New Interpretation of Tears

Roger Porter

I learned shortly after my daughter's mother and I separated that by continuing to be in my daughter's life, I was committing a highly subversive act.

It felt as though my ex-girlfriend wasn't prepared to deal with my continued presence, my picking our daughter up on weekends, my asking for her on holidays. It felt as though I wasn't following the script, and she, as well as her family, couldn't understand why I didn't just leave. After all, as a black man wasn't that what I was supposed to do?

My parents' marriage disintegrated not long after I came into the world. I have absolutely no recollection of them being together, but my older brother and sister insist that this was indeed the case for several years. I rarely if ever saw my father. And when I did he was always very serious, even when he smiled. Occasionally, he would pick us up on a Saturday afternoon and take us out to eat. Then we would often go several weeks at a time without seeing him.

Shortly after I turned 7 years old, my father came over to our house one evening and called my two older siblings and me into the living room. Like always he was wearing a collared shirt and a tie, and like always he was very prideful. He told us that he would be moving back to his home state of Tennessee with his new wife to be the pastor of his own church. We didn't believe him. We made him place his hand on the Holy Bible and say it again; after he obliged we knew it was true. He only stayed for a few minutes, and then he left. We smiled and waved goodbye to our father through the window, never fully realizing what was taking place.

5   After that night sometimes we would see him once a year. Other years we wouldn't see him at all. In the beginning he would call, but then the calls began to come in a lot less frequently. I never called him. As a matter of fact, by the time I was a teenager, I became a lot more comfortable with his absence than I was with his presence. In the public schools that I attended not having a father was trendy. It made you normal.

In junior high, whenever I was hanging out with my friends in the hallway or in the gym and the subject of our fathers came up, we all chimed in with different reasons as to why we hated our dads. Why dude was a coward. At least one of us declared that he would beat his father to the ground for what he did to his mother—if he ever saw him again. There could have been a whole room full of black boys and you wouldn't find one of them that wanted to be like his father. No one ever tried to understand his father. We all depended solely on our mothers, or in some cases our grandmothers, for our daily representation of what a man was supposed to be. And we were able to infer from these women's stories that a "real man" was everything that our fathers were not.

At the age of 19, I fell in love with a woman. Three years later she gave birth

Keoni Cabral

to my child. About six months after that she broke up with me. She confronted me one evening and said that she could tell that I was unhappy with the relationship. I couldn't find the words to disagree with her. Two days later she moved out of my house and took my baby girl with her. It was at that point that I realized I had no idea what being a father meant. I needed to find out in a hurry, but there really weren't a lot of role models in my family.

My mother's father was shot in the face the day that she was born and died in the hospital a few days later. The only thing I knew about my paternal grandfather is that he and my father didn't get along. He died before I was born and I have never so much as seen a photograph of him. My mother once said that he was the overbearing type but I've never been able to confirm this with my father. My father has never brought him up.

So each week I approached my ex-girlfriend's house to pick up my daughter, I would be completely confused. I wanted to be in my daughter's life so she could know what it was like to have a father; however, I didn't know how to do it. I had nothing to draw on. My rides to my ex-girlfriend's apartment complex were painful, my walks to her front door were swift, my knocks were violent, and we always exchanged the baby in a visceral silence.

My daughter felt the negative   10 energy. Before I could buckle her down in her car seat for the nearly one-hour drive, she would break out screaming and crying until she lost her breath. After I strapped her in and turned onto Main Street heading toward the freeway the crying would persist. I would look at my baby through the rearview mirror, she'd make eye contact with me and scream louder. One day I became unraveled.

Continued >

I demanded that she stop crying, and told her how much I sacrificed for her. That I had gotten a college degree so I could provide for her. That I was being degraded on a daily basis at a job that I couldn't stand just so I could have enough money to come get her, and she had the nerve to disrespect me. *Cut it out!* I told her. *Stop it!* But she continued to cry. This little brown-skinned girl with light brown eyes like mine, and full eyebrows like mine, was in her car seat openly express-ing all of the sacred things that I had learned to forget, like those trips to the barbershop.

I never liked to get my hair cut as a child. About once every few months my father would take my brother and me to the barbershop for a haircut. By this time I would have a small unkempt Afro with patches of tiny naps on the back of my neck. In preparation for my trip to the barbershop my mother would gently comb my hair with a little plastic comb. She would spray water on the tougher spots so the comb would go through nice and easy, so I wouldn't squirm as much (because I was severely tender-headed). But I still squirmed and all of mother's careful strokes and tedious labor were irrel-evant by the time I got to the barber's chair, because the water had dried, making my hair harder and nappier than ever.

The barber was my father's friend. He was an old guy with glasses, named Will. He never showed me any mercy. My father was always first to get a hair-cut and it always amazed me how he used the barber's chair like a pulpit. He carefully directed the general conversa-tion of the shop to topics that interested him. Somehow he was able to redirect all conversations about sports—which

he had always abhorred—to the need for black people to support black busi-nesses. Conversations about women somehow ended up being about Chris-tianity. My father, although small in stature, was the unofficial maestro of the barbershop . And he never once had to raise his voice.

My brother would go next. He never let his hair get as long and kinky as mine. His hair was so soft and thick the barber almost thanked him for letting him touch it.

Then it was my turn to go. While my 15 father continued to direct conversation and my brother sat in his seat glow-ing with all of the adulation he had just received, Will the barber ripped through my hair with a torturing device known as the "natural comb." A natural comb is a long black comb with metal teeth designed specifically for taming the most savage, unruly naps. As he ran the comb through my hair with so much force that it snapped my head back and I could literally hear the naps popping out, I tried so hard to keep it together, but I could feel the tears coming. I knew that he had to comb my hair so that it wouldn't damage his clippers but I couldn't understand why he had to be so brutal. Why didn't he ask me if I was tender-headed? If he did then maybe he would be able to comb my hair gently like my mother did. Why didn't it bother him that he was hurting me? I could no longer stop the water from trickling down my cheek. I looked at my father, the great composer of conversation, through blurred eyes as I cried. And I remember him finally looking up at me. He did not say any-thing. He was ashamed.

And now this little being was in my backseat screaming so loud and for so long that she lost her breath. I hadn't made it to the freeway before I cracked. She broke me down. I pulled the car into the nearest parking lot, unbuckled her, and held her close to my chest. I let her cry and she did for several minutes. I rocked her and shushed her gently while telling her gently that everything was going to be OK. I kissed her tears away until no more fell, until she went to sleep in my arms.

That was the day I learned to transcend my manhood in order to be a good father. I promised to listen to her cries in order to interpret exactly what she needed. Sometimes it was a bottle, sometimes it was reassurance, and sometimes it was a hug, while other times it was a song. Indeed my daughter was the first female I learned how to effectively communicate with. She became my entire weekend, she was my focus, and she became my identity.

That was the day I promised I would never leave her.

Understanding and Reviewing the Reading

1. **Detail** To whom did Porter look for an idea of what a "real man" should look like?

2. **Background** Describe the role model of fatherhood that Porter had as a child.

3. **Reasons** Why does Porter say that he was "committing a highly subversive act" by staying in his daughter's life?

4. **Vocabulary** Using context clues (see p. 37), briefly define these words: *subversive* (para. 1), *visceral* (9), *unraveled* (10), *abhorred* (13), and *adulation* (15).

5. **Main point** What main point does Porter want to convey to his readers through his narrative? (Hint: Look at paragraph 17.)

Analyzing the Reading

1. **Tension** What actions create tension in the narrative?

2. **Climax** What is the climax of the narrative?

3. **Flashback** Where in the narrative does Porter use the technique of flashback? (Hint: Look for places where Porter recalls his life before he became a father.) Why is flashback useful here? Why does he include it?

4. **Language** What does Porter mean when he refers to his dad as the "unofficial maestro" of the barbershop in paragraph 13?

5. **Dialogue** What does the brief dialogue in paragraph 11 reveal about Porter's emotional state when he was with his baby daughter?

6. **Sequence of events** Why do you think Porter moves back and forth in time as he does in the essay? Was it necessary for him to do so, or could he have told the story strictly in chronological sequence? Explain your answer.

Evaluating the Reading

1. **Evidence** Porter relies on personal experience to make his point in this narrative. Do you think he provides sufficient personal evidence and details to support his ideas? Explain your answer.

2. **Inference** The only information we have about Porter's brother is found in the narrative about the barbershop. What can you infer about the relationship between Porter's father and his brother? What clues does Porter provide in the narrative?

3. **Visual** The photograph that accompanies the piece was provided by Porter. Why do you think he chose to include this particular photo? How does it contribute to the thesis of the essay?

4. **Point of view** Suppose the narrative were told by Porter's father. How would this change in point of view affect the narrative and possibly its message?

5. **Descriptive detail** What details are particularly vivid and descriptive? Choose several and explain what each contributes to the narrative.

Discussing the Reading

1. Porter says that "not having a father was trendy" in public school. He later realizes that what might have been trendy also robbed him and his friends of positive male role models. What are some of the unique challenges faced by young men who grow up in a family without a father? How does or should society address this problem?

2. What is the significance of the title, "A New Interpretation of Tears"? At what points in the narrative does Porter mention tears? Why were the tears being shed? How do these incidents help you to understand the meaning of the title?

3. In paragraph 17, Porter says, "That was the day I learned to transcend my manhood in order to be a good father." What does he mean by this statement? What is your definition of a "good" father?

Writing about the Reading

1. **Paragraph** Porter's baby girl was breathless from crying when he pulled the car off the road and comforted her. Write a narrative paragraph describing a situation in which you were upset and in need of comfort and someone came to your aid.

2. **Essay** Porter writes that he never liked to get a haircut as a child. Write a narration essay describing a particular event or activity that you or someone you know disliked as a child. Be sure to build tension and describe the climax in detail.

3. **Essay** Porter suggests that one's past does not have to rule one's future, and that with determination and persistence, one can rise above one's past and make a better future for oneself. Write a narrative essay describing a situation in which you (or someone you know) overcame negative circumstances and made a better life for yourself.

Excerpt from *In the Skin of a Jihadist: A Young Journalist Enters the ISIS Recruitment Network*

Anna Erelle is a French journalist who writes under a pseudonym for her protection. In 2015, she published a nonfiction account of how she developed a relationship with a French jihadist through a social network. This account is entitled *In the Skin of a Jihadist: A Young Journalist Enters the ISIS Recruitment Network*. The reading below is an excerpt from Erelle's book.

Reading Tip

As you read, pay attention to Erelle's organization. Consider the effect this organization has on her ability to build suspense.

Previewing the Reading

Preview the reading (see pp. 28–29 for guidelines), and then answer the following questions.

1. What event in her life does the author relate in this narrative?
2. What types of technology made this event possible?

Excerpt from *In the Skin of a Jihadist: A Young Journalist Enters the ISIS Recruitment Network*

ANNA ERELLE

Paris, Friday Evening

I was frustrated that Friday night as I left the editorial offices of a magazine where I do freelance work. The paper had received a letter from a lawyer forbidding me to publish an article I'd written about a young female jihadist. I had just spent two days in Belgium with Samira (names have been changed in this story for protection), the girl's mother. Her daughter, naive and blind with emotion, had run away to Syria a year before to join Tarik, the love of her life and a fanatic devoted to the Islamic State's cause. Then a bullet ended his life at 20, but Leila had no intention of coming home. She was furious when Samira mentioned our interview, saying, "If you talk about me to the press," as her panicked mother tearfully reported, "not only will I never come back, you'll never hear from me again. You won't know if I'm dead or alive."

Continued >

I've done a lot of work on radical Islam and tried to interview as many people as I could. I saw the impact of digital propaganda on God's newly minted soldiers, but I still didn't understand what drove them. Over the course of a few weeks, they threw away their lives, convinced they'd never look back.

Social networks contain precious information for those who know how to look. That is why, like many other journalists, I had a fictional account I'd created several years before. I used it to keep an eye on current events. My name on this account was Mélodie. My followers weren't using their real identities, either. Avatars ensure anonymity, which allows users to express themselves more freely and accounts for the growing number of young people attracted to Islamist propaganda.

I spent that Friday night in April on my couch, stewing over the gag order on my article and flicking from account to account. Suddenly I came across a video of a French jihadist who looked to be about 35. The video showed him taking inventory of the items inside his SUV. I smiled wryly at the deplorable images. I wasn't proud of myself, but I couldn't help watching. The man in the video wore military fatigues and called himself Abu Bilel. He claimed to be in Syria. The scene around him, a true no-man's-land, didn't contradict him.

5   In the back of his car, his bulletproof vest sat beside one of his machine guns, an Uzi—a historic gun originally manufactured for the Israeli military. He removed his reflective Ray-Bans, revealing darkly lined black eyes.

I knew that Afghan soldiers used eyeliner to keep their eyes from tearing up when exposed to smoke. Still, seeing a terrorist with eyes made up like my own was surprising. Abu Bilel spoke perfect French, with what sounded to me like a very slight Algerian accent.

I shared his video. I usually kept a low profile on my account, but I occasionally imitated my digital peers in order to carve out a place for myself in their world. My picture was a cartoon image of Princess Jasmine from the Disney movie *Aladdin*. I tended to change my profile location depending on the story I was researching. Now I claimed to be in Toulouse, a city in southwestern France.

Deep in reflection, I was feeling discouraged but unwilling to give up, when my computer alerted me to three messages sent to Mélodie's private in-box from . . . Abu Bilel. It was surreal. There I was, at ten o'clock on a Friday night in spring, sitting on my sofa in my Parisian apartment, wondering how to continue my investigation on European teenagers tempted by Islamic extremism, when a French terrorist based in Syria all of a sudden started writing me.

"Salaam alaikum, sister. I see you watched my video. It's gone viral!" he wrote. "Are you Muslim? What do you think about mujahideen? Last question: Are you thinking about coming to Syria?"

10   He certainly got straight to the point! I didn't know what to do, but I instantly understood that speaking with this jihadist offered a unique opportunity that might lead to a mine of information. I replied, "Walaikum salaam. I didn't think

a jihadist would talk to me. Don't you have better things to do? LOL. I'm not prejudiced against fighters. Anyway, it depends on the person." I also told him I'd converted to Islam, but didn't offer any details. I deliberately included spelling mistakes, and I tried to use teen vocabulary: LOL, LMAO, ROFL. I waited for his reply, a knot in my stomach. I'd interviewed mujahideen before, but never anyone over 20 years old, and never anyone who expressed anything outside of the official propaganda.

Barely three minutes passed before my computer alerted me to a new message. "Of course I have a lot of things to do! But here it's eleven o'clock at night and the fighters are finished for the day. Do you have any questions about the video you shared? We should talk over Skype. I'll give you my user name."

Bilel was direct . . . and authoritative. I ignored his proposal and suggested we talk another time. Mélodie wasn't available now. Abu Bilel understood; he didn't want to bother her. He'd make himself available for her tomorrow whenever she wanted.

"Tomorrow?" I asked, surprised. "Are you sure you'll have Internet access?"

"Of course. I'll be here. I promise." Then, a minute later: "You converted, so . . . you should get ready for your hijrah"—migration. "I'll take care of you, Mélodie."

First Skype, now hijrah! Abu Bilel didn't waste any time!

15

This was our first encounter. We'd only exchanged a few lines. He didn't know anything about this girl except that she'd converted to Islam, and he was already asking her to join him in the bloodiest country on Earth. Bilel was targeting the weak, and whenever they took his bait, he and others like him from the Islamic State tried as hard as they could to reformat them, erasing their pasts as one would clean a disk before recording new information.

What was I getting myself involved in? I sensed it would go much further. But I never imagined that Abu Bilel would continue to impact my life for months, convincing me to set out on a journey to Syria before plans went terribly wrong in Amsterdam, and later tracking me down so that I would have to live in hiding. For the time being, all I could think of was the fact that if I wanted to glean information from this terrorist, Mélodie would really have to exist. As in spy fiction, I needed to craft a story for her. She would step through the looking glass. I would give her traits from all the kids I'd met who'd succumbed to jihadism.

For now, however, it was getting late, and I wanted to stop thinking about Abu Bilel. My boyfriend, Milan, was due to arrive. I called to tell him I wanted to spend the night at his place instead.

Saturday Night

Milan was asleep. His bedroom was calm and quiet. I tossed and turned, my subconscious dragging me into the living room and toward a demon imprisoned

Continued >

behind a retina display. Three new messages from my correspondent awaited me. I hadn't expected so many. I lit a cigarette. He'd sent the first one at 2:30 p.m. in Syria, a surprising time for a zealous fighter to be online. "Salaam alaikum, sister. How are you today? I wanted to let you know that I'm available if you want to talk. I'm around."

20   Around? Around where? His next message grabbed my attention before I could reflect on that question:

"What time will you be online? I really want to talk to you. I have a special surprise for you. . . ."

The "surprise" was a picture of him, armed to the teeth. A gigantic M4 assault rifle was slung across his shoulder. A black bandanna embroidered with the Islamic State's white insignia covered his forehead. He stood erect, puffing out his chest, smiling. What if I was really a cop? Or a journalist searching for reliable information from a solid source? Abu Bilel wasn't concerned. Clearly, he thought he'd caught a fish.

Sunday Night

"Sympathy for the Devil," by the Rolling Stones, crashed against the walls of my living room, resonating like a premonition. I turned on my computer and found new messages from Bilel. I barely had time to read them before he connected and contacted my digital puppet. In his first posts, he struggled to hide his crass insistence. Every other line, the mercenary begged Mélodie to sign off Facebook and continue her conversation with him over Skype. Why was he so obsessed? Did he want to verify my identity? Or did he want to make sure the new fish swimming in his net was appetizing?

"Why do you want to Skype?" I had Mélodie reply awkwardly.

25   "Conversations over Skype are more secure, if you see what I mean."

No, I didn't see. He ended his sentence with a smiley face, a yellow, winking emoticon. It was absurd.

"I see you work for the Islamic State. What's your job? In France, people say it's not a very strong brigade."

I couldn't help using Mélodie to insult him. I also added a blushing smiley face. Bilel was quick to defend his vanity, firmly insisting that ISIS embodied the height of power, not only in Syria but throughout the world. Soldiers came from all corners of the globe to join its ranks.

"There are three types of fighters," my charming interlocutor went on, in teacher mode: "those on the front, those who become suicide bombers, and those who return to France to punish infidels."

30   "Punish? How?"

"You know how . . . like Mohammed. . . ." It was a reference to Mohammed Merah, the perpetrator of a recent shooting spree against soldiers and Jews in Toulouse.

"But Merah killed children. Don't children represent innocence and purity? How can they be enemies?"

"You're so naive, Mélodie. . . . You like children? You know, we have many orphans here in need of mothers. ISIS sisters take care of them; they're remarkable women. You have a lot in common with them."

Although he didn't know Mélodie, Bilel was a master manipulator: Mélodie expressed a certain affection for children, so Bilel suggested she could become a surrogate mother. Then he set about making her feel guilty. "While you're busy eating Snickers bars, watching MTV, buying Wu-Tang Clan albums, and window-shopping at Foot Locker," he continued, "dozens of our people are dying every day so that we Muslims can live in our own state. While we're out risking our lives, you're spending your days doing meaningless activities."

Abu Bilel was diabolical. I examined his profile picture. He was rather good- 35 looking. His stunning grammatical errors barely distracted from the force of his conviction. Bilel acted as a kind of guru who presented war as a divine mission.

"Are you saying that if I don't go to Syria, I'll be a bad Muslim, and I'll never know Heaven?"

"Exactly . . . but you still have time. I'll help you. I have a good feeling about you. But before you go to sleep, answer me something."

It was midnight in Syria, eleven o'clock in France. I was exhausted, and I sensed his next question would finish me off for the night.

"Can I be your boyfriend?"

I logged off Facebook.   40

We'd exchanged 120 messages in the space of two hours. I carefully reread them all. Late in the night, I called Milan.

Monday

I woke up early, which is unusual for me. I rushed to the magazine where I often work, eager to discuss my weekend with one of the editors in chief. Twenty-four hours earlier, I'd forwarded him the video of Bilel showing off the contents of his car. He was stunned by how easily contact had been established. Urging caution, he assigned me a photographer, André, one of my best friends and also a freelancer. I would agree to Bilel's request to meet over Skype, and André would take pictures.

It suddenly struck me as strange to be playing one of two protagonists in a fabricated story, but for the time being, I was preoccupied with a single, urgent detail: how to become Mélodie. I needed to look ten years younger, find a veil, and somehow slip into the skin of a very young woman. Another editor, a former reporter who would also be supervising my investigation, lent me a hijab and a black dress—a kind of djellaba. I was glad to wear the veil. The idea of a terrorist becoming familiar with my face didn't thrill me, especially not when the man in question could return to France, his home country, at any moment.

Continued >

André arrived at my apartment that night around six o'clock. That gave us an hour or so to prepare before Bilel "got home from fighting" and contacted Mélodie. We looked for the best angle from which to take pictures of the computer screen and keep me as indistinct as possible. While André made adjustments in the living room, I pulled on Mélodie's somber clothing over my jeans and sweater.

45   I removed my rings, assuming Bilel wouldn't appreciate such frivolousness, and covered the small tattoo on my wrist with foundation. The hour was approaching. André tried to calm my nerves by talking about something else. To be clear, I wasn't afraid of the terrorist I was about to meet; I'd Skyped with others like him before. Rather, I sensed I was about to learn a lot, and I was afraid Mélodie wouldn't be able to handle it. As soon as I turned on my computer, I saw that Abu Bilel was already logged on to Facebook.

"Mélodie??? . . . You there???"

Monday, 8:00 p.m.

OK. It was time. I sat cross-legged on my sofa. It had a high back, which hid most of my apartment—and any distinctive features—from the camera. André positioned himself in a blind spot behind the sofa.

The Skype ringtone sounded like a church bell tolling in a dreary village. If I pressed the green icon, I would become Mélodie. I took a moment to breathe. Then I clicked the button, and there he was. He saw me, too. For a split second, we didn't speak. Bilel stared. His eyes were still accentuated with dark liner. They smoldered as he gazed at the young Mélodie, as if trying to cast a spell. He was Skyping from his car, using a state-of-the-art smartphone. He lived in a country often deprived of water and electricity, yet he had access to the latest technological devices. He was a proud man, his shoulders pulled back and his chin thrust forward, but I sensed he was nervous meeting Mélodie. After what felt like an eternity, he finally broke the silence:

"Salaam alaikum, my sister."

50   I made my voice as tiny, and as sweet and bright, as I could. And I smiled. My smile instantly became my best defense mechanism, and it remained so throughout my investigation. I would use it whenever I didn't know how to react. Bilel was hanging on Mélodie's every word. He may have been in Syria, and I in France, but our faces were separated by mere inches. I had to be careful not to let my eyes wander from the screen.

"What's new?" he asked.

Seriously? I hadn't expected him to show interest in Mélodie's day. I was so caught off guard by this ordinary request that I couldn't think of anything to say but "So much! But first, tell me about yourself."

"What do you want to know?" he asked, smiling confidently. He took the bait. Mélodie's life didn't seem to interest him much after all. Too bad for her.

Great for me. That said, I didn't want to risk blowing my cover by asking too many questions. Mélodie was 20 years old, and her knowledge of the world needed to match her age.

"It's crazy to be talking to a mujahid in Syria," I said, impressed. "It's like you have easier access to the Internet than I do in Toulouse! I share the computer with my sister, and my mom takes it away from us a lot. Even your phone is newer than mine." In addition to getting into character, I was giving Mélodie a plausible excuse for future unavailability.

"Syria is amazing. We have everything here: It's paradise! A lot of women   55
fantasize about us; we're Allah's warriors."

"But every day people die in your paradise. . . ."

"That's true, and every day I fight to stop the killing. Here the enemy is the devil. You have no idea. The enemy steals from and kills poor Syrians. He rapes women, too. He's attacking us, and we're defending peace."

"Is the enemy the president of Syria?"

"Among others. We have many adversaries."

I sensed the fighter didn't want to elaborate.   60

"You're awfully curious," Bilel said. "Tell me, do you wear your hijab every day?"

Mélodie recited what I'd heard from the majority of girls I'd met who had secretly converted to Islam.

"I dress normally in the morning. I say goodbye to my mom, and when I'm outside the house, I put on my djellaba and my veil."

"Good. I'm proud of you. What you're doing is really brave. You have a beautiful soul. And you're very pretty on the outside, too."

Bilel peered lecherously at Mélodie. I smiled.   65

"Can I ask what your job is?"

"Killing people."

"That's a job?"

"Of course it is! I work hard here. This isn't Club Med!"

"I bet you helped capture Raqqa. There were pictures of the Islamic State   70
everywhere."

The Battle of Raqqa, which took place in March 2013, was one of ISIS's bloodiest victories.

"You make me laugh!" he said. "Yes, of course. We obliterated them. It was crazy. . . . Tell me about you!"

"OK, but I'm too shy! Let me see your car first. It looks like you have a lot of interesting stuff."

Bilel was glad to show off his car, delighted whenever Mélodie—whom he already considered his betrothed—flattered him. Mélodie told him she thought the white submachine gun sitting amid a heap of clutter on the backseat was pretty. "Do you like guns? I'll give you plenty, starting with a lovely Kalashnikov."

Continued >

75   My veil was starting to itch, and when I glanced at André, a man known for his hyperactivity, I noticed that he was stunned. Bilel assumed that everything had been decided. For him, Mélodie would soon arrive in Syria.

"I'm not sure that I want to go—"

"Listen, Mélodie. Among other things, it's my job to recruit people, and I'm really good at my job. You can trust me. You'll be really well treated here. You'll be important. And if you agree to marry me, I'll treat you like a queen."

Understanding and Reviewing the Reading

1. **Background** What motivated the author to set up a fictional account under the name of Mélodie?

2. **Action** What happened when the author watched and then shared the video of Abu Bilel, a thirty-five-year-old French jihadist?

3. **Action** How did Bilel respond to Mélodie's concern for the innocent children in Toulouse who had been killed by Merah?

4. **Main point** What central idea does Erelle communicate in her essay?

5. **Language** In paragraph 23, Erelle asks if Bilel wanted to "make sure that the new fish swimming in his net was appetizing." You know the denotative meaning of the word *appetizing*, but what is the connotation of this word?

Analyzing the Reading

1. **Metaphor** In paragraph 19, Erelle writes that her subconscious dragged her "into the living room and toward a demon imprisoned behind a retina display." What is the meaning of this metaphor? How does it contribute to the author's attitude toward her "correspondent"?

2. **Narrative suspense** How does Erelle create suspense in telling her story, particularly in the paragraphs about the Skype conversation between Bilel and Mélodie? What techniques does she use to keep readers interested?

3. **Foreshadowing** Where in the narrative does Erelle use the technique of foreshadowing? (Hint: Look for places where Erelle writes about her life after the events of this narrative occurred.) Why does the author include foreshadowing?

4. **Climax** When and how is the tension resolved, providing the narrative with its climax? Where does the climax of the narration occur?

5. **Visualizing the reading** Using this chart or a similar one, record several examples of each of the characteristics of narration essays used by Erelle.

Narrative Characteristics	Examples
Makes a point or thesis	
Uses dialogue	
Includes sensory details	
Recounts action	
Builds tension	
Presents a sequence of events	

Evaluating the Reading

1. **Audience** How can you tell that Erelle's intended audience was people who had some knowledge about Islam and Syrian terrorism? To support your answer, give some specific details that she provides.

2. **Character** Why does the author create Mélodie as a curious and naive twenty-year-old girl? How effective is Erelle's presentation of Mélodie? What does this presentation contribute to the narrative? Use examples from the reading to support your answers.

3. **Dialogue** Why do you think Erelle uses so much dialogue in the essay? Does the dialogue she writes seem to echo the way a French jihadist and a twenty-year-old convert to Islam would really speak?

4. **Descriptive detail** What details are particularly vivid and descriptive? Choose several and explain what each contributes to the narrative.

5. **Tone** How do you think Erelle herself comes across in the essay? Do you find her sympathetic, or would you use another word to describe her?

6. **Visuals** Erelle did not include a photograph to accompany this piece. If you were choosing a photograph for this piece, what would it look like? Why would you choose this photograph, and how would it contribute to the overall impression of the narrative?

Discussing the Reading

1. Why do you think that the number of young people being attracted to Islamist propaganda is growing?

2. Erelle states that "social networks contain precious information for those who know how to look." What kind of information can be found on social networks? How can this information be used for good? In what ways can this information be used for illicit purposes?

3. The author, a freelance writer for a magazine, was forbidden by a lawyer to publish an article she had written about a young female jihadist. Do you think this is what should have happened, or do you think she should have been allowed to publish the article? Why or why not? Do you think this could be considered censorship or a violation of the author's rights?

Writing about the Reading

1. **Essay** In her excerpt, Erelle foreshadows the future events that occurred as a result of her involvement with Abu Bilel. We learn that she embarked on a journey to Syria, had a disastrous experience in Amsterdam, and later had to live in hiding for fear of being tracked down by Bilel. Using these events as the basis of your story, write a narrative that picks up where the reading leaves off. Be sure to incorporate the major parts of a narrative — background information, a thesis, conflict, suspense (tension), climax, and conclusion.

2. **Essay** In this reading, Bilel was a master manipulator who preyed on a naive young woman, trying to pressure her into doing something that she wasn't convinced she should do. Write an essay about an experience from your own life when you fell victim to the pressure of an individual or a group that persuaded you to do something that you knew you should not do. (Hint: Don't forget to use dialogue and descriptive language to add interest to your narrative.)

3. **Essay** In her introductory paragraph, Erelle tells the story of Leila, a young girl who ran away to Syria to be with her lover, Tarik, a "fanatic devoted to the Islamic State's cause." Leila had clearly chosen to live a life out of the mainstream. Have you ever chosen to rebel against what was expected of you, to go your own way in spite of what others thought, whether they were your peers, your family, or mainstream society as a whole? Share your experience in a narration essay that explores the development of your decision to pursue a course others didn't expect for you and how you put your decision into practice. (Hint: In planning your narrative, be sure to think about how to present conflict, both with others and within yourself.)

📖 **COMBINING THE PATTERNS | TEXTBOOK EXCERPT: INFORMATION TECHNOLOGY**

History of the Future

Ben Beekman is a writer, Web and multimedia designer, consultant, and technology educator. **George Beekman** is also a writer, teacher, consultant, and multimedia developer. "History of the Future" is an excerpt from their textbook *Digital Planet: Tomorrow's Technology and You*.

Reading Tip

As you read this excerpt, highlight and annotate the reading using the guidelines for active reading discussed in Chapter 2. Consider what information you would need to remember for a class discussion or an in-class exam on the material.

Previewing the Reading

Preview the reading (see pp. 28–29 for guidelines), and write a sentence summarizing what you expect its main point will be.

History of the Future
Ben Beekman and George Beekman

*First we shape our tools, thereafter **they shape us**.*—*Marshall McLuhan*

Today's technology raises fascinating and difficult questions. But these questions pale in comparison to the ones we'll have to deal with as the technology evolves in the coming years. Imagine . . .

The "Meteor" subway line of the Paris Metro is completely automated. The trains have no drivers.

You wake up to the sound of your radio playing songs and news sto-ries that match your personal interest profile. The newscaster is talking about the hacker uprising that has crippled China's infrastructure[1], but you have other things on your mind.

Today's the day of your big trip. You're looking forward to spend-ing time in the same room with Tony, your Italian lab partner. Over the past few months you've become close friends, working and chatting by videophone, conquering virtual reality games together, and creating truly terrible music in those late-night long-distance jam sessions. Still, there's no substitute for being in the same space, especially after Tony's accident. Tony says that the chip implant and the prosthetic hand will make him almost as good as new, but you know he can use some moral support while he recovers.

On the way to the airport, your electric car's computer pipes up, "Ben's Bagels ahead on the right is running a special on cinnamon bagels. Nobody is at the drive-up window, so you can pick up a bagel and still make your flight."

"I thought I told you already: I don't like cinnamon bagels," you 5 *grumble.*

Noting your annoyance, the car responds, "Sorry. I knew you didn't like cinnamon buns. No more cinnamon bagel ads or notifications, either." You wonder if the computer's spam and ad filter needs fixing, or you just forgot to tell it about your bagel preferences. Before you can ask, the computer announces that the next freeway entrance is blocked because of an accident. It suggests another entrance and talks you through the traffic to that entrance.

Once you get on the freeway, you join the "auto train" in the fast lane. Your car, now controlled by a network computer, races along at exactly the same speed as the car that's a few feet in front of it. You take this opportunity to ask your phone, "Which bus do I take to get from Rome airport to Tony's place?" The phone responds, "Bus 64. Watch out for pickpockets." You shiver when you remember what happened the last time you lost your wallet; it took months to undo the damage from that identity thief.

At the airport, you step out of the car near the shuttle station, remove your suitcase, and tell the car to park itself in the long-term lot. It says "Goodbye" and glides away.

On the shuttle you use your phone to try to learn a few Italian phrases. You say "Translate Italian" then "I would like to convert dol-lars into Euros." The phone responds, "Vorrei convertire i dollari in Euro," into your tiny wireless earpiece. You know the phone can trans-late for you on the fly, but you'd like to be able to say a few things without its help.

At the security station, you insert your passport into the slot, 10 *put your hand on the scanner, and put your face into a shielded enclosure. After the system confirms your identity by taking your*

[1]**infrastructure** Fundamental facilities and systems that service a country.

Continued >

Courtesy of KNFB Reading Technology Inc.

The Kurzweil KNFB Mobile Reader makes it possible for a blind person to read signs, menus, and money.

handprint and scanning your retinas, it issues a boarding pass, baggage claim slip, and routing tag. Under the watchful eye of the security guard, you attach the routing tag to your bag and place it on the conveyer belt leading to the baggage handling area. You notice that a nearby passenger is being vigorously questioned, and you hope that she's not the victim of yet another security system error.

You realize you forgot to pack your jet lag medication. You enter the airport gift shop and insert your medical ID card under the pharmacy scanner. A dispenser issues a vial of pills that should work well with your genetic structure. You also download a best-selling book into your phone for the trip. As you leave the store, a sensor detects your two purchases. Your phone tells you that $33.97 has just been deducted from your account and asks if you want to know the remaining balance. You don't answer; you're trying to remember the last time you bought something from a human cashier.

This isn't far-fetched fantasy. Early versions of most of the devices in this story already exist. And exponential growth in computing power . . . makes it likely that you'll see similar technology in your everyday life in just a few years.

For better and for worse, we will be coexisting with information technology until death do us part. As with any relationship, a little understanding can go a long way.

Understanding and Reviewing the Reading

1. **Terminology** Choose five words or phrases in the reading that refer to concepts related to the subject of digital technology. Briefly define each, using context clues or a dictionary.

2. **Meaning** How does the opening quotation by Marshall McLuhan support the point of the excerpt?

3. **Details** Which of the hypothetical examples provided by the authors are particularly close to reality today?

Analyzing the Reading

1. **Purpose** As part of the first chapter in an information technology textbook, what does "History of the Future" communicate to readers? What did you learn from the reading?

2. **Predicting** Predict what will follow this textbook excerpt. What clues in the excerpt helped you to make this prediction?

3. **Combining the patterns** Although the authors of this textbook excerpt use primarily narrative techniques, they also incorporate other patterns into the reading. Identify the other patterns that you see in this writing and provide an example that illustrates each of the patterns.

Evaluating the Reading

1. **Detail** What are some details in the narrative that you find particularly strong and helpful in communicating the main message of the excerpt?

2. **Language** The authors write in paragraph 12 that this is no "far-fetched fantasy" and that what they imagine will result from "exponential growth in computing power." How do you respond to the language they use here?

3. **Application of information** How does this information connect to what you are learning in your other courses?

Discussing the Reading

1. What differences and similarities do you see between this "factual" narrative of the future and science fiction?

2. The narrative suggests both positive and negative aspects of technology. Provide several examples of each. Do the positives outweigh the negatives in your mind? Explain your answer.

3. Which predictions made in the reading do you find most surprising or intriguing? Do you find any disturbing? If so, why do you find the prediction disturbing?

Writing about the Reading

1. **Response paper** Write a narrative of your own in response to this reading. That is, imagine yourself at some point in the future going through your daily life using the technology you predict will be available then — no matter how far-fetched. See "Write in Response to a Reading," on pages 76–78 in Chapter 3, for guidelines.

2. **Summary for class** Assume you are preparing for a class discussion about this essay. Write a summary in which you answer the following question: What will be involved in the future for people "coexisting with information technology"?

3. **Essay assignment** Suppose that, in your Introduction to Technology course, you have been given the following assignment as the culminating project for the course: In an essay, react to the statement by Marshall McLuhan that opens the reading: "First we shape our tools, thereafter **they shape us.**" Discuss how you, and people generally, are "shaped" by currently available technology.

Working with Narration as a Reader and Writer

The following table reviews the key elements of narration essays and explains how these elements are important to both readers and writers.

Reading ⬤ Writing   Narration Essays

Element of a Narration	The Reader's Perspective	The Writer's Perspective
Point of View	When reading narration essays, consider who is telling the story and why. Understanding the viewpoint helps you analyze and critically evaluate the narrative.	When writing narration essays, choose the best viewpoint from which to tell the story. First-person narrative works well for a narrative about the writer's life or experiences. Third-person narrative may be more effective when writing about another person's experiences.
Key Point(s)	As you read, look for the main point the author is trying to make. Try to understand where the narrative is going.	Analyze the elements of the narrative to ensure that there is a deeper meaning that can be taken from the experience.
Conflict and Tension	Take note of what provides suspense in the narrative. How does the author create conflict and tension? What is at stake?	Provide enough information for your readers to identify what is at stake and why. Conflict and tension are necessary to achieve insight, change, and resolution.
Sequence of Events	Follow the narrative's sequence of events as you read. The story may skip around, using foreshadowing and flashbacks, but you should be able to determine the order in which the events actually occurred.	At its heart, a narrative is a story, and the essence of good storytelling is providing a plot (sequence of events) that your readers can easily follow. Mapping out the sequence of events is essential before beginning to write the essay. A beginning, middle, and end (introduction, body, and conclusion) give readers a structure that helps them make sense of the events in the narrative.

Continued >

Dialogue	Reflect on the ways an author uses dialogue to humanize the narrative. What characteristics about the people in the narrative are revealed through dialogue?	Most narratives involve the interaction of at least two people, and dialogue is the most common method of communication between people (even if it takes place through text messages or other media). You can use dialogue to provide a break from long paragraphs while also giving readers insight into the way characters think and express themselves.
Vivid Details	Pay attention to vivid details that advance the story and bring it to life. By contrast, consider how lack of details may cause you to lose interest in a story.	Vivid details bring an essay to life and increase the reader's engagement with the narrative and its characters. The many vivid details may culminate in the essay's key insight.
Action and Detail	Consider how the action and detail in the narrative convey information and keep you involved as a reader. Also think about how action and detail keep the story interesting and realistic.	Telling a good story means providing action and details that will keep the reader involved.

11

Description: Portraying People, Places, and Things

In this chapter, you will learn to

- Recognize the elements of description.

- Identify the structure and content of description essays.

- Understand, analyze, and evaluate description essays.

- Write your own description essay.

- Work with description as a reader and a writer.

Reflect on a Visual Text

Suppose you are moving to a large city and need to sell your car because the apartment you just rented does not include parking. You place the following advertisement on craigslist.com:

Vintage VW van. $4500 or best offer. Call 514-555-2298.

Although the ad runs for two weeks, you get only a few calls and no offers. Then a friend advises you to write a more appealing description of your unique vehicle that will make people want to contact you.

1 Ask yourself questions. Why do you think the original ad is ineffective? If you were looking to buy a van, would this ad motivate you to call? How might the ad be improved?

2 Brainstorm ideas. Working by yourself or with a classmate, identify at least five additional details you might provide about the van. →

© Nomad/Nomad/Superstock.com

3 **Write.** Rewrite the advertisement, describing the van shown in the photograph in a way that will persuade prospective buyers to call you.

The ad you wrote uses description. *Description* presents information in a way that appeals to one or more of the five senses (sight, hearing, smell, taste, touch), usually with the purpose of creating a specific impression or feeling.

What Is Description?

Description makes your ideas vivid so that the audience can almost see, hear, smell, taste, or touch what you are writing about. People use description every day. For example, in a conversation with a friend, you might describe a pair of new shoes you recently bought or a new cuisine you tried last night. In your college courses, you may be asked to describe the odor and appearance of a substance made by combining two chemicals. In the workplace, a nurse at a local burn treatment center might be responsible for recording on each patient's chart the overall appearance of and changes in second- and third-degree burns.

Description has many or all of the following elements:

1. It creates a dominant impression.
2. It uses sensory details.
3. It uses active verbs and varied sentences.
4. It uses connotative language effectively.
5. It uses comparisons.
6. It assumes a vantage point.
7. It is often combined with other patterns.

The first point is particularly important. Successful descriptions offer readers more than a list of sensory details or a catalog of characteristics. In a good description, the details work together to create a single dominant impression.

A Model Description Essay

The following description essay will be used throughout this chapter to demonstrate strategies for reading and writing description essays. Read it now, looking for the ways the writer uses the above descriptive techniques. Use the annotations in the margin to guide you.

Eating Chilli Peppers

Jeremy MacClancy

Jeremy MacClancy is an anthropologist who studies the everyday choices people make and how those choices vary from culture to culture. As a professor of social anthropology at Oxford Brookes University in England, MacClancy has written on a variety of topics, but he has a particular interest in food. The following essay comes from MacClancy's book *Consuming Culture: Why You Eat What You Eat* (1993).

How come over half of the world's population have made a powerful chemical irritant the center of their gastronomic lives? How can so many millions stomach chillies?

Biting into a tabasco pepper is like aiming a flame-thrower at your parted lips. There might be little reaction at first, but then the burn starts to grow. A few seconds later the chilli mush in your mouth reaches critical mass and your palate prepares for liftoff. The message spreads. The sweat glands open, your eyes stream, your nose runs, your stomach warms up, your heart accelerates, and your lungs breathe faster: All this is normal. But bite off more than your body can take, and you will be left coughing, sneezing, and spitting. Tears stripe your cheeks, and your mouth belches fire like a dragon celebrating its return to life. Eater, beware!

As a general stimulant, chilli is similar to amphetamines— only quicker, cheaper, nonaddictive, and beneficial to boot. Employees at the tabasco plant in Louisiana rarely complain of coughs, hay fever, or sinusitis. (Recent evidence, however, suggests that too many chillies can bring on stomach cancer.) Over the centuries, people have used hot peppers as a folk medicine to treat sore throats or inflamed gums, to relieve respiratory distress, and to ease gastritis induced by alcoholism. For aching muscles and tendons, a chilli plaster is more effective than one of mustard, with the added advantage that it does not blister the skin. But people do not eat tabasco, jalapeño, or cayenne peppers because of their pharmacological side effects.

A description assumes a vantage point: The author takes the vantage point of an admirer of chillis who seeks to understand the worldwide appeal of eating chilli peppers.

A description uses sensory details: Note the memorable simile (comparison) and the vivid details that explain the experience of eating a chilli pepper.

A description uses active verbs and varied sentences: The verbs *open, run, warm up, accelerate,* and *breathe* all explain the body's reaction to eating chilli peppers.

A description uses comparisons: Here the author compares a chilli pepper to an amphetamine—a stimulating drug.

They eat them for the taste—different varieties have different flavors—and for the fire they give off. In other words, they go for the burn.

A description uses connotative language effectively: The language here conveys the wild excitement of eating chillis: the *thrill* of anticipation, the *extremity* of the flames, and the *slow descent* back to *normality.*

Eating chillies makes for exciting times: the thrill of anticipation, the extremity of the flames, and then the slow descent back to normality. This is a benign form of masochism, like going to a horror movie, riding a roller coaster, or stepping into a cold bath after a sauna. The body flashes danger signals, but the brain knows the threat is not too great. Aficionados, self-absorbed in their burning passion, know exactly how to pace their whole chilli eating so that the flames are maintained at a steady maximum. Wrenched out of normal routines by the continuing assault on their mouths, they concentrate on the sensation and ignore almost everything else. They play with fire and just ride the burn, like experienced surfers cresting along a wave. For them, without hot peppers, food would lose its zest and their days would seem too dull. A cheap, legal thrill, chilli is the spice of their life.

In the rural areas of Mexico, men can turn their chilli habit into a contest of strength by seeing who can stomach the most hot peppers in a set time. This gastronomic test, however, is not used as a way to prove one's machismo, for women can play the game as well. In this context, chillies are a nonsexist form of acquired love for those with strong hearts and fiery passions—a steady source of hot sauce for their lives.

A description is often combined with other patterns: Here the author combines description with cause and effect.

The enjoyable sensations of a running nose, crying eyes, and dragon-like mouth belching flames are clearly not for the timorous.

A description creates a dominant impression: The final lines of the essay encapsulate the dominant impression of eating chilli peppers: an intense, thrilling, and somewhat painful experience.

More tabasco, anyone?

The Structure and Content of Description Essays

In this section, you will learn about the structure of a description essay and practice using the guidelines for understanding, analyzing, and evaluating description essays. This key information will help you skillfully read and write essays that use description.

The structure of a description essay depends on the subject, but all description essays have a structure that includes a dominant impression, supporting details, and a conclusion. Figure 11.1 represents these major components visually.

Figure 11.1   Graphic Organizer for a Description Essay

Title	
Introduction	Background Setting
	Dominant impression (stated or suggested in thesis)
Body paragraphs	Supporting details
	Supporting details
	Supporting details
Conclusion	Reference to the dominant impression Draws essay to a close

1. THE INTRODUCTION PROVIDES THE BACKGROUND AND SETTING, AND THE THESIS STATES OR SUGGESTS THE DOMINANT IMPRESSION

In a descriptive essay, the introduction provides a context for the description and presents the thesis statement, which states or suggests the dominant impression that will hold the rest of the essay together. The **dominant impression** is a mood or feeling created about the subject, which all the other details in the essay will explain or support. The dominant impression is the **implied thesis** of a description essay; it suggests the author's main point about the subject. Any background information necessary for understanding the description, such as the setting, should also be included in the introduction.

The dominant impression should appeal to the writer's audience, offer an unusual perspective, and provide new insights into the subject. In "Eating Chilli Peppers," Jeremy MacClancy provides insight into the appeal of chilli peppers around the world, not only describing the roller coaster of sensations that accompanies the eating of chilli peppers, but also exploring their health benefits and cultural importance.

Reading ⬤ Writing   The Dominant Impression

The Reader's Perspective	The Writer's Perspective
When reading a description essay, ask yourself, How does the author want me to feel about the subject? The answer will be the dominant impression the writer wants to convey.	When writing a description essay, carefully consider what dominant impression of your subject you would like to convey.

2. THE BODY PARAGRAPHS PROVIDE SUPPORTING DETAILS AND COMPARISONS, WHICH CAN BE ORGANIZED IN SEVERAL DIFFERENT WAYS

The body of a description essay expands on the dominant impression established in the introduction. It uses vivid sensory details, active verbs, strong connotations, varied sentences, and effective comparisons to do so. Good descriptions also establish a vantage point and follow a clear method of organization.

Sensory Details   The details in a description essay should appeal to one or more of the five senses: sight, sound, smell, taste, and touch. Consider how Jeremy MacClancy appeals to the senses in "Eating Chilli Peppers."

Sense	Example from the Model Essay
Sight	"Biting into a tabasco pepper is like aiming a flame-thrower at your parted lips" (para. 2).
Sound	"You will be left coughing, sneezing, and spitting" (para. 2).
Smell	"Your nose runs" (para. 2).
Taste	"They eat them for the taste — different varieties have different flavors — and for the fire they give off" (para. 3).
Touch	"For aching muscles and tendons, a chilli plaster is more effective than one of mustard, with the added advantage that it does not blister the skin" (para. 3).

Active Verbs, Strong Connotations, and Varied Sentences   Sensory details are often best presented with active, vivid verbs; words with strong connotations; and sentences with varied structure. Consider the following sentences from the essay. Each sentence is structured differently. Vivid verbs are in italics, while words or phrases with strong connotations are underlined.

Sentence 1	Tears *stripe* your cheeks, and your mouth *belches* fire like a dragon celebrating its return to life. (para. 2)
Sentence 2	<u>Aficionados</u>, <u>self-absorbed</u> in their <u>burning passion</u>, know exactly how to pace their whole chilli eating so that the <u>flames</u> are maintained at a steady maximum. (para. 4)

Comparisons   When describing a person or an object, writers can help their audience by comparing it to something familiar. Several types of comparison are used in descriptive writing. Table 11.1 defines and provides examples of three of these: a **simile**, a **metaphor**, and an **analogy**.

Another common type of comparison is **personification**, in which an object is given human qualities or characteristics. "The television screen stared back at me" is an example.

Table 11.1   Types of Comparisons

Comparison Type	Definition	Example from the Model Essay
Simile	A direct comparison that is introduced by the word *like* or *as.*	"This is a benign form of masochism, like going to a horror movie" (para. 4).
Metaphor	An indirect comparison, describing one thing as if it were another.	Chillies are "a steady source of hot sauce for their lives" (para. 5).
Analogy	An extended comparison in which one subject is used to explain the other. Often, a more familiar subject is used to explain one that is less familiar.	"As a general stimulant, chilli is similar to amphetamines— only quicker, cheaper, nonaddictive, and beneficial to boot" (para. 3).

Vantage Point   A **vantage point** is the point or position from which a description is written. With a *fixed vantage point*, you describe what you see from a particular position. With a *moving vantage point*, you describe your subject from a number of different positions. Using a fixed vantage point is like using a stationary camera trained on a subject from one direction, whereas using a moving vantage point is like using a handheld camera that moves around the subject, capturing it from many directions. "Eating Chilli Peppers" uses a moving vantage point.

Methods of Organization   Three common methods of organization used in descriptive writing are spatial order, chronological order, and most-to-least or least-to-most order.

- **Spatial order** might be used to systematically describe a subject from top to bottom, inside to outside, or near to far away. Essays start from a focal point and then describe the objects that surround it. For example, a description of a college campus might start with a building at the center of the campus, then turn to the buildings next to it, and conclude with something on the outskirts.

- **Chronological order** works well for describing events or changes that occur in objects or places over a given period. For example, chronological order would be appropriate to describe the changes in a puppy's behavior as it grows.

- **Most-to-least** or **least-to-most order** (see p. 126) might be used to describe the different smells in a flower garden or the sounds of an orchestra tuning up. "Eating Chilli Peppers" uses most-to-least order, starting with the strongest (most immediate) effects of chilli peppers on the eater's body and then moving into details about chillies' medicinal properties, the reasons behind aficionados' love of chillies, and chillies' importance in Mexican culture.

Description essays can also be arranged according to the five senses. For example, an essay describing a chocolate-chip cookie could give details about how it looks, smells, tastes, sounds (its crunch), and feels.

Guidelines for Writing Effective Body Paragraphs   No matter which method of organization the essay follows, the details included in the body paragraphs should be consistent with the guidelines in Table 11.2.

Table 11.2   Guidelines for Writing Effective Body Paragraphs in a Description Essay

Guidelines	Tips
Include only relevant details.	Each detail should enhance the reader's understanding of the event, person, or scene being described.
Keep the description focused.	Select only enough details to make your essential points and dominant impression clear. Readers may become impatient if you include too many details.
Make sure the description fits the essay's tone and point of view.	A personal description, for example, is not appropriate in an essay explaining a technical process.

Reading ⊕ Writing The Body of a Description Essay

The Reader's Perspective	The Writer's Perspective
When reading the body of a description essay, highlight particularly striking details and images that you may want to refer to again or that may help you assess the essay's effectiveness.	When writing the body of a description essay, select striking sensory details that make your point effectively; leave out details that tell the reader little or nothing. Consider providing a few metaphors or similes to make your essay understandable and vivid, but only do so if the comparison comes naturally. A contrived metaphor or simile will lessen the impact of your essay.

3. THE CONCLUSION REFERENCES THE DOMINANT IMPRESSION AND BRINGS THE ESSAY TO A CLOSE

The conclusion draws the description to a close and makes a final reference to the dominant impression. It may offer a final detail or make a closing statement.

Reading ⊕ Writing The Conclusion of a Description Essay

The Reader's Perspective	The Writer's Perspective
When reading the conclusion of a description essay, ask yourself if the writer brings the essay to a satisfying close. Is the conclusion consistent with the dominant impression?	When writing a conclusion to a description essay, ask yourself, Have I provided vivid details that are consistent with the dominant impression? What final statement will make this impression stick in my reader's mind?

Understanding, Analyzing, and Evaluating Description Essays

In reading and writing description essays, your goal is to get beyond mere competence. That is, you want to do more than merely understand the content of the essays you read or convey just your basic ideas to the audience you're writing for.

▥ Understanding a Description Essay

To understand a description essay, focus on the dominant impression and the details, both factual and sensory, that support it. You may find it helpful to read the essay more than once. Read it the first time to get a general sense of what is going on. Then reread it, paying attention to the details and the language used. Use the reading skills you learned in Chapter 2, and answer the following questions:

- **What is the subject, and on what aspect of the subject does the essay focus?** Almost any subject has many aspects or facets. Determine with what trait, characteristic, or part of the subject the essay is concerned.

- **What is the essay's dominant impression?** If the thesis is not directly stated, ask yourself how the author wants you to feel about the subject. Your answer is the dominant impression.

- **How does each paragraph contribute to the dominant impression?** Figure out what new information each paragraph adds.

- **What sensory details are particularly important?** Highlight particularly striking details and images that may be helpful in analyzing the essay.

- **What is the author's vantage point?** The vantage point (see p. 233) will help you understand how the author is looking at the subject.

- **How is the essay organized?** Draw a graphic organizer that shows the structure of the essay. Figure 11.2 provides a graphic organizer of Jeremy MacClancy's "Eating Chilli Peppers." Refer back to the graphic organizer for description essays (Figure 11.1) before starting your own diagram.

Figure 11.2   Graphic Organizer for "Eating Chilli Peppers"

Title	Eating Chilli Peppers
Introduction	Many people like eating chilli peppers despite the possible pain caused by doing so.
	Dominant impression: Chilli acts as stimulant, thrilling the senses.
Body paragraphs	Sensory details and comparisons
	Eating chillies is "like going to a horror movie, riding a roller coaster."
	Eating chillies can become a contest of strength.
	"Biting into a tabasco pepper is like aiming a flame-thrower at your parted lips" "...your mouth belches fire..."
Conclusion	Eating chilli peppers can be painful, exciting, and, in some cases, beneficial to one's health.

Exercise 11.1

Following is one student's brief summary of paragraph 3 of Jeremy MacClancy's "Eating Chilli Peppers."

> Chillies are a "stimulant" more "beneficial" than any drug. They are also a "folk medicine" used to treat many ailments. But that's not really why people eat them. People eat chillies for the "fire" and the "burn" they enjoy in their taste.

Write your own one-paragraph summary for the entire essay, describing the dominant impression created in the essay and quoting specific words that contribute to this impression.

Analyzing a Description Essay

Analyzing a description essay involves examining how the writer describes the subject and shapes your response to it. The words and details that a writer chooses can make a subject sound pleasant or unpleasant, attractive or repellant, and so forth. Consider the difference between a stranger described as having an "impish, childlike grin" and one with "cold, vacant eyes." Use the following questions to analyze description essays:

- **Is the essay intended to be objective, subjective, or both?** An **objective** essay is written to inform—to present information or communicate ideas without bias or emotion. A **subjective** essay, often written in the first person (*I, me, mine*), is intended to create an emotional response. An objective essay describes only what the writer observes or experiences, while a subjective essay includes both observations and the writer's feelings about them. For subjective essays, be sure to ask yourself what attitude the writer is trying to convey.
- **What impression of the subject did the writer create?** Authors choose sensory details carefully and intentionally, usually to make a point. Added together, what feelings, impressions, or responses do the sensory details leave you with? What do they point to, suggest, or imply?
- **What types of language did the writer use to create his or her impression?** To which senses do the sensory images appeal? Examine the comparisons (similes, metaphors, analogies, and personifications) that are used. What do they add to the dominant impression?
- **Why did the writer choose a particular vantage point?** Consider what else you might have learned if the author had used a different vantage point. What does the chosen vantage point emphasize that another would not?

Analysis in Action

Exercise 11.2

Following is an example of a student's analysis of how the language in one paragraph of MacClancy's essay creates an appealing impression of the topic.

> In paragraph 4, MacClancy uses language that describes chillies as a positive experience, at least for people who enjoy them. They make "for exciting times" and create "the thrill of anticipation." The experience is like the fun of seeing a horror movie or riding a roller coaster. For fans they add "zest" and are the "spice of their life." Without chillies everything would be "dull." MacClancy's use of words and phrases that convey excitement and thrills makes the description of the experience of peppers seem like a positive one.

Based on your reading of "Eating Chilli Peppers," answer one of the analysis questions on the previous page.

Evaluating a Description Essay

Evaluating a description essay involves judging how effective the writer's description of the subject is, as well as determining how fair and accurate it is. As you evaluate the essay, ask yourself the following questions:

- **Is the dominant impression fair and accurate?** Determine whether the writer presents a biased or unbiased impression of the subject. If the impression is biased, determine whether the writer openly reveals the bias or whether it is subtle or hidden.

- **What details might the writer have chosen to omit?** As you read, ask yourself, What hasn't the author told me? What else would I like to know about the subject? Authors may omit details because they are not relevant, but they may also omit details that disprove the dominant impression they are trying to convey. To be sure you are getting a complete picture of the subject, do some research, consulting several other sources of information. Then pull together what you have learned and form your own impression.

- **If comparisons or analogies were made, do they work?** That is, are they representative, logical, and effective?

- **Is the writer trying to be convincing or persuasive?** If so, consider whether this intent is up front and obvious, subtle, or hidden.

- **If photographs, graphics, or other visuals are included, why are they used?** Are they used effectively? Are they intended to sway or persuade you to take a particular viewpoint toward the subject?

Evaluation in Action

Exercise 11.3

The following evaluation of the appeal of language in paragraph 4 of Jeremy MacClancy's "Eating Chilli Peppers" is by the same student who wrote the earlier summary and analysis.

> While a lot of the language in paragraph 4 might be meant to create an appealing impression of eating chillies, I'm not convinced. The "extremity of the flames" doesn't appeal to me, and I don't like horror movies or roller coasters. The last thing I want is an "assault" on my mouth when I'm eating that makes me "ignore almost everything else." I don't want to "play with fire," and I don't need a "cheap" thrill like chillies. The description is effective but doesn't appeal to me!

Using your Analysis in Action response from Exercise 11.2, write a paragraph evaluating the aspect of the essay you focused on.

Writing Your Own Description Essay

Now that you have learned about the major characteristics, structure, and purposes of a description essay, you know everything necessary to write your own. In this section, you will read a student's description essay and get advice on finding ideas, drafting your essay, and revising and editing it. You may want to use the essay prompts in "Readings for Practice, Ideas for Writing" (p. 248) or choose your own topic.

A Student Model Description Essay

Madeleine Massey, a student at Wake Technical Community College in Raleigh, North Carolina, wrote the following essay in response to an assignment in one of her classes. She was asked to describe a community event that she had experienced. As you read, study the annotations and pay particular attention to Massey's use of sensory language that helps you see and feel what she experienced.

Small Town New Orleans

Madeleine Massey

The Mardi Gras Festival, in quaint downtown Wake Forest, North Carolina, is a spectacular event that gives visitors and locals a chance to participate in their community and interact with friends and family. The townspeople do their best to make their festival closely resemble the famous Mardi Gras celebration in New Orleans, and people from the community and surrounding towns attend every year for a quasi-authentic taste of a unique culture. The streets are filled with lively music, mouth-watering food, inviting entertainment, and eclectic art that overload the senses and make it a great opportunity for people to do something different from their everyday lives.

This little community celebration lacks the exotic atmosphere that is rumored to captivate the "real" Mardi Gras partiers, but it carries a more subdued and old-fashioned charm that appeals to a slightly more conservative southern community. A few hundred people litter the narrow streets, staring in wonder at the various attractions. Children skirt from one place to the next playing games like corn hole or horse shoe toss, and their little faces light up when they are rewarded with candy for emerging victorious. Their eyes widen and their bodies seem to hum with energy as they bite into the rainbow colored, sticky pieces of sugary delight. These tasty prizes kindle the little ones' competitive natures, causing them to face each new challenge with determination and focus.

Parents work tirelessly to keep their children from scampering off and being swallowed by the crowd. Mothers and fathers hold lively conversations with other families and chat with their spouses while snacking on the various finger foods offered throughout town. Teenage boys run through the streets looking for excitement or girls to flirt with. The entire community has a certain rhythm to it that balances out the otherwise chaotic air. A cold gust of wind rushes through the town, distracting from the intermingling of the excitable townspeople.

This wind brings a soft buzz of jazz music that adds a calming touch to the bustling street festival. As it hums in the revelers' ears, they find themselves stepping to the rhythm of the entrancing melody. The tune has an effect that rivals the power of the Pied Piper. Much like the music, the smell of food floods through the entire town. It is a rich mixture of hot spices, fresh herbs, and a mysterious secret ingredient that would leave anyone journeying to discover the source that brought their senses alive. The smell is so powerful it leaves behind a feeling of warmth and comfort, and is so intoxicating that it makes mouths water and stomachs growl.

Sensory details: Massey describes the sights and tastes of the festival foods.

In the spirit of authenticity, downtown Wake Forest has created an array of dishes that are famous in New Orleans for a rich, appetizing appearance and a taste that screams "home cooked meal." Across the street at a small concession stand, the source of the aroma is discovered. Aspiring chefs serve bowls of steaming hot gumbo. Looking closer, one can see the lively boil of the dark soup splashing in a shiny large pot and can follow the trail of steam leading into the bright blue sky.

Organization: Massey uses spatial order as she seems to roam down the street and take in the sights, sounds, and smells of the festival.

Suddenly, sparkling bubbles overcome the open air, and the bubble machine can be heard puttering in the near distance. A stray orb drifts higher and higher before exploding onto the velvety top hat of a dancer. The dancer's face is covered in white paint and topped with fake rosy cheeks. His multi-color top hat stretches high above his head, balancing out his impossibly long legs covered in pants that are so large they billow like parachutes in the wind. The townspeople strain their necks to get a glimpse of the incredibly tall character who floats over the crowd. Looking closely, they can see the tip of the entertainer's stilts and hear the soft pat of wood meeting concrete as he continues farther down the street. He spins, dances, leaps, and shocks people with his impressive performance while weaving skillfully around chalk artists, like water flows over rocks in a stream.

Vivid words: The connotation of *puttering* supports the dominant impression better than a more formal word would.

Sensory details: Massey describes the sights of the festival.

Sentences vary in length and structure.

Comparison: Massey conveys the ease and skill of the entertainer as he moves among the artists.

Comparison: Massey helps the reader visualize the artists.

The chalk artists are hunched over their designated patch of worn concrete. They concentrate on the ground, with furrowed brows, trying to decide what will most excite their captivated viewers. Stretching their arms out like the wings of a bird, they reach to color the dull pavement. Dazzling gold, red, and purple tones fly out in every direction, curving and curling, until they form an image. The drawings are bound to a two-dimensional surface, but are so skillfully crafted that they leave passersby to wonder when they will spring to life. These artists are fearless masters, in their own rights, who know no bounds, mimicking true fearless Mardi Gras spirit.

Conclusion: Massey references the dominant impression and brings the essay to a close.

It is true that this small town event cannot compare to the real Mardi Gras celebration, in grandeur or exotic flare. This festival does not have gigantic floats, scantily clad dancers, or an audience consisting of thousands of people. This festival achieves a sense of oneness with the community, brings families together, and is a perfect display of homey southern culture that would cause New Orleans citizens to be taken with jealousy.

Responding to Massey's Essay

1. What words does Massey use to describe her hometown? What impression do these descriptive words convey about Wake Forest, North Carolina?

2. How does the final sentence in paragraph 1 predict the essay's organization?

3. What details in paragraph 2 show that the street festival carries an old-fashioned charm?

4. In paragraph 7, Massey describes the street artists as "fearless masters, in their own rights, who know no bounds." What is she trying to convey about the artists by describing them this way?

5. What specific details in the concluding paragraph reemphasize the key points of the essay?

Finding Ideas for Your Description Essay

Because you may be asked to write a response to a description essay, keep an eye out for ideas as you read. Try to think of parallel situations that evoked similar images for and feelings in you. For example, when reading an essay describing the peace and serenity the author experienced while sitting beside a remote lake in a forest, try to think of situations in which you felt peace and serenity or how you felt when you visited a national park or wilderness area. Perhaps you had negative feelings, such as anxiety about being in a remote spot. Negative feelings are as worthy of exploration as positive feelings are.

Choosing a Subject and a Slant for Your Description Essay

Your first step is to choose a subject. Make sure it is one you are familiar with or one you can readily observe. Also be aware that you may need to observe the object, activity, or person several times as you work through your essay.

Because almost any subject will encompass many more details than you could possibly include, you'll need to emphasize a particular *slant* or angle. For example, a description essay about an old storage box in the writer's parents' attic might emphasize, or give a slant to, *memories of childhood*. Given this slant, the writer could describe the box in several different ways, each of which would convey a different dominant impression.

> A box filled with treasures from my childhood brought back memories of long, rainy afternoons playing in our attic.
>
> (The essay goes on to describe those afternoons.)

> Opening the box was like lifting the lid of a time machine, revealing toys and games from another era.
>
> (The essay describes games that the speaker no longer plays.)

> When I opened the box I was eight years old again, fighting over my favorite doll with my twin sister, Erica.
>
> (The essay focuses on describing a sibling relationship.)

Collecting Details That Describe Your Subject

Once you've decided on a slant or an angle, you're ready to collect and record additional sensory details. The following suggestions will help you generate details. Also refer to Table 11.3 to stimulate your thinking.

Table 11.3   Characteristics to Consider in Developing Sensory Details

Sight	Color
	Pattern
	Shape
	Size
Hearing	Volume (loud or soft)
	Pitch
	Quality
Taste	Pleasant or unpleasant
	Salty, sweet, sour, or bitter
Touch	Texture
	Weight
	Temperature
Smell	Agreeable or disagreeable
	Strength

1. **Brainstorm about your subject.** Record any sensory details that support the slant or angle you have chosen.

2. **Describe the subject to a friend, concentrating on your particular slant.** You may discover that details come more easily during conversation. Make notes on what you say and on your friend's responses.

3. **Draw a quick sketch of the subject, and label the parts.** You may recall additional details as you draw.

4. **List the sensory details.** Divide a piece of paper or a computer file into five horizontal sections. Label the sections *sight, hearing, taste, touch,* and *smell.* Work through each section in turn, systematically recording what the subject looks like, sounds like, and so forth.

Finding Comparisons and Choosing a Vantage Point

Look over your list of details. Try to think of appropriate comparisons—similes, metaphors, analogies, personification—for as many details as possible. Jot down your comparisons in the margin next to the relevant details in your list. Don't expect to find a comparison for each detail. Instead, your goal is to discover one or two strong comparisons that will be most effective.

Next, consider whether to use a fixed or a moving vantage point. Think about the aspect of your subject you are emphasizing and how it can best be communicated. Ask yourself the following questions:

- What vantage point(s) will give readers the most useful information?
- From which vantage point(s) can I provide the most revealing or striking details?

Creating a Dominant Impression

Think of the dominant impression as the thesis that conveys your main point and holds the rest of your essay together. It also creates a mood or feeling about the subject, which all other details in the essay explain or support.

The dominant impression you decide on should be the one about which you feel most confident. It should also appeal to your audience, offer an unusual perspective, and provide new insights on the subject. Before drafting your essay, check to see if you have enough sensory details to support your dominant impression. If you don't have enough details, you may need to do additional prewriting to gather support for your dominant impression. This step is similar to collecting evidence for a thesis, except the "evidence" for a description essay consists of sensory details.

Drafting Your Description Essay

Once you are satisfied with your dominant impression and sensory details, you can choose the method of organization that will best support the dominant impression (see p. 234). As you draft the essay, remember that all details must support the dominant impression. For example, if you are describing the way apes in a zoo imitate one another and humans, only details about how the apes mimic people and other apes should be included. Other, unrelated details, such as the condition of the apes' environment and types of animals nearby, do not belong in the essay.

Also be careful about the number of details you include. Too many details will tire your readers, but an insufficient number will leave them unconvinced of your main point. Select striking sensory details that make your point effectively; leave out details that tell the reader little or nothing. For example, instead of selecting five or six ordinary details to describe a concert, choose one revealing detail such as the following:

> As the band performed the final song, the lights dimmed and every single member of the audience of twelve hundred people silently held a lighted candle before his or her face.

Try also to include one or two telling metaphors or similes. If you cannot think of any, however, don't stretch to construct them. Effective comparisons usually come to mind as you examine your subject. Contrived comparisons will only lessen the impact of your essay.

As you write, remember that the sensory language you use should enable readers to re-create the person, object, or scene in their minds. Keep the following three guidelines in mind:

1. **Create images that appeal to the five senses.** Your descriptions should appeal to one or more of the senses.

2. **Avoid vague, general descriptions.** Use specific, not vague, language to describe your subject.

Vague	The pizza was cheaply prepared.
Concrete	The supposedly "large" pizza was miniature, with a nearly imperceptible layer of sauce, a light dusting of cheese, a few paper-thin slices of pepperoni, and one or two stray mushroom slices.

3. **Use comparisons effectively.** Comparisons (similes, metaphors, analogies, and personification) create memorable images that enliven your writing and capture the readers' attention.

   - **Choose fresh, surprising images.** Avoid overused clichés such as "cold as ice" and "it's a hop, skip, and a jump away."

- **Make sure the similarity between the two items being compared is apparent.** If you write "*Peter* looked like an *unpeeled tangerine*," your reader will have to try to guess what characteristics Peter shares with the tangerine. "Peter's *skin* was as dimpled as a *tangerine peel*" gives the reader a better idea of what Peter looks like.
- **Don't mix or combine figures of speech.** Such expressions, called **mixed metaphors**, are confusing and often unintentionally humorous. For example, the following sentence mixes images of a hawk and a wolf: "The fighter jet was a hawk soaring into the clouds, growling as it sought its prey."

Revising Your Description Essay

If possible, set aside your draft for a day or two before rereading and revising. As you reread, focus on overall effectiveness, not on grammar and mechanics. Use the revision flowchart in Figure 11.3 to discover the strengths and weaknesses of your description essay.

Editing and Proofreading Your Essay

The last step is to check your revised essay for errors in grammar, spelling, punctuation, and mechanics. In addition, be sure to look for the types of errors you tend to make in writing assignments, whether for this class or in other situations. Check the handbook (pp. 645–714) for assistance with common errors in your writing.

Figure 11.3   **Revising a Description Essay**

QUESTIONS		REVISION STRATEGIES
1. Dominant impression Does your essay express the dominant impression you wish to convey?	No	• Reread your essay. Make a list of the different impressions it conveys. • Choose one impression that you have the most to say about, and develop additional details that support it.

Yes

| **2. Sensory details** Does each detail support your dominant impression? | No | • Eliminate irrelevant sensory details. |

Yes

| **3. Vivid language** Is there enough vivid language to help your reader visualize the topic? Are the connotations of your language appropriate? | No | • Brainstorm additional sensory details.
• Replace passive verbs with active ones.
• Vary your sentences.
• Replace words with inappropriate connotations with ones that better support your dominant impression. |

Yes

| **4. Comparisons** Is each simile, metaphor, and analogy fresh and effective? | No | • Look for and eliminate clichés.
• Brainstorm new comparisons. |

Yes

| **5. Organization** Are the details arranged in a clear way? | No | • Experiment with several arrangements of details to see which works best.
• Add transitions to connect your ideas. |

Yes

| **6. Topic sentence** Does the topic sentence make clear what the paragraph is describing? | No | • Revise so that each paragraph has a clear topic sentence and supporting details that relate to it. |

Yes

| **7. Introduction and conclusion** Is each effective? | No | • Revise your introduction and conclusion so that they meet the guidelines given in Chapter 7. |

Readings for Practice, Ideas for Writing

The Discus Thrower

Richard Selzer is a former surgeon who has written several books and articles presenting frank descriptions of life as a physician knows it. His works include *Mortal Lessons* (1977), *Raising the Dead* (1994), and, most recently, *Diary* (2011). This essay first appeared in *Harper's* magazine in 1977.

Reading Tip

As you read, notice Selzer's use of detail. These sensory elements create a vivid picture of his patient. Also pay attention to his use of dialogue; it is important for what is *not* said as much as for what *is* said.

Previewing the Reading

Preview the reading (see pp. 28–29 for guidelines), and then answer the following questions.

1. What word does Selzer use to describe his observations of his patients?
2. Who is the subject of this essay?

The Discus Thrower

Richard Selzer

I spy on my patients. Ought not a doctor to observe his patients by any means and from any stance, that he might the more fully assemble evidence? So I stand in the doorways of hospital rooms and gaze. Oh, it is not all that furtive an act. Those in bed need only look up to discover me. But they never do.

From the doorway of Room 542 the man in the bed seems deeply tanned. Blue eyes and close-cropped white hair give him the appearance of vigor and good health. But I know that his skin is not brown from the sun. It is rusted, rather, in the last stage of containing the vile repose within. And the blue eyes are frosted, looking inward like the windows of a snowbound cottage. This man is blind. This man is also legless—the right leg missing from midthigh down, the left from just below the knee. It gives him the look of a bonsai, roots and branches pruned into the dwarfed facsimile of a great tree.

Propped on pillows, he cups his right thigh in both hands. Now and then he shakes his head as though acknowledging the intensity of his suffering. In all of this he makes no sound. Is he mute as well as blind?

The room in which he dwells is empty of all possessions—no get-well cards, small, private caches of food, day-old flowers, slippers, all the usual kickshaws[1] of the sickroom. There is only the bed, a chair, a nightstand, and

[1]**kickshaws** Trinkets.

a tray on wheels that can be swung across his lap for meals.

5 "What time is it?" he asks.

"Three o'clock."

"Morning or afternoon?"

"Afternoon."

He is silent. There is nothing else he wants to know.

10 "How are you?" I say.

"Who is it?" he asks.

"It's the doctor: How do you feel?"

He does not answer right away.

"Feel?" he says.

15 "I hope you feel better," I say.

I press the button at the side of the bed.

"Down you go," I say.

"Yes, down," he says.

He falls back upon the bed awkwardly. His stumps, unweighted by legs and feet, rise in the air, presenting themselves. I unwrap the bandages from the stumps, and begin to cut away the black scabs and the dead, glazed fat with scissors and forceps. A shard of white bone comes loose. I pick it away. I wash the wounds with disinfectant and redress the stumps. All this while, he does not speak. What is he thinking behind those lids that do not blink? Is he remembering a time when he was whole? Does he dream of feet? Of when his body was not a rotting log?

20 He lies solid and inert. In spite of everything, he remains impressive, as though he were a sailor standing athwart a slanting deck.

"Anything more I can do for you?" I ask.

For a long moment he is silent.

"Yes," he says at last and without the least irony. "You can bring me a pair of shoes."

In the corridor, the head nurse is waiting for me.

25 "We have to do something about him," she says. "Every morning he orders scrambled eggs for breakfast, and, instead of eating them, he picks up the plate and throws it against the wall."

"Throws his plate?"

"Nasty. That's what he is. No wonder his family doesn't come to visit. They probably can't stand him any more than we can."

She is waiting for me to do something.

"Well?"

"We'll see," I say.   30

The next morning I am waiting in the corridor when the kitchen delivers his breakfast. I watch the aide place the tray on the stand and swing it across his lap. She presses the button to raise the head of the bed. Then she leaves.

In time the man reaches to find the rim of the tray, then on to find the dome of the covered dish. He lifts off the cover and places it on the stand. He fingers across the plate until he probes the eggs. He lifts the plate in both hands, sets it on the palm of his right hand, centers it, balances it. He hefts it up and down slightly, getting the feel of it. Abruptly, he draws back his right arm as far as he can.

There is the crack of the plate breaking against the wall at the foot of his bed and the small wet sound of the scrambled eggs dropping to the floor.

And then he laughs. It is a sound you have never heard. It is something new under the sun. It could cure cancer.

Out in the corridor, the eyes of the   35 head nurse narrow.

"Laughed, did he?"

She writes something down on her clipboard.

A second aide arrives, brings a second breakfast tray, puts it on the nightstand, out of his reach. She looks over at me shaking her head and making her mouth go. I see that we are to be accomplices.

Continued >

"I've got to feed you," she says to the man.

40 "Oh, no you don't," the man says.

"Oh, yes I do," the aide says, "after the way you just did. Nurse says so."

"Get me my shoes," the man says.

"Here's oatmeal," the aide says. "Open." And she touches the spoon to his lower lip.

"I ordered scrambled eggs," says the man.

45 "That's right," the aide says.

I step forward.

"Is there anything I can do?" I say.

"Who are you?" the man asks.

In the evening I go once more to that ward to make my rounds. The head nurse reports to me that Room 542 is deceased. She has discovered this quite by accident, she says. No, there had been no sound. Nothing. It's a blessing, she says.

I go into his room, a spy looking for 50 secrets. He is still there in his bed. His face is relaxed, grave, dignified. After a while, I turn to leave. My gaze sweeps the wall at the foot of the bed, and I see the place where it has been repeatedly washed, where the wall looks very clean and very white.

Understanding and Reviewing the Reading

1. **Background** According to Selzer, what is wrong with the patient? What don't we know about his medical condition?

2. **Details** In paragraph 25, we learn that the head nurse is upset. What is upsetting her, and how does the doctor react to the nurse's complaints?

3. **Dominant impression** The author does not include a stated thesis. Instead, Selzer uses description to build a single dominant impression. Identify his dominant impression. What might this tell you about his purpose in writing about this patient?

4. **Subject** What emotion does the patient exhibit as he throws his food? Why might he feel this way?

5. **Actions** How does the doctor find out that the patient has died? What is the head nurse's reaction to the patient's death? How does Selzer react to his death?

6. **Vocabulary** Explain the meaning of each of the following words as it is used in the reading: *furtive* (para. 1), *shard* (19), *inert* (20), *athwart* (20), and *hefts* (32). Refer to your dictionary as needed.

7. **Organization** To analyze the descriptive elements used in Selzer's essay, complete the graphic organizer that follows.

Title	The Discus Thrower
Introduction	**Background and setting:** Doctor spies on his patients.
	Dominant impression:

⬇

Body paragraphs: sensory details and comparisons, organized chronologically	1.
	2.
	3.

⬇

Conclusion	

Analyzing the Reading

1. **Vantage point** This story is told from the vantage point of the doctor. What does this vantage point achieve? What do you learn, and what information remains untold?

2. **Conclusion** What does the doctor notice about the patient and his room after the death? How do these details contrast with earlier descriptions of the patient and his room?

3. **Language** What are the connotative meanings of the word *spy* as used in paragraphs 1 and 50?

4. **Tone** How does Selzer's tone affect your reading of the situation described in the essay? How does it make you feel about doctors and nurses? How does it make you feel about the patient?

Evaluating the Reading

1. **Sensory details** Highlight several sections in which sensory details are particularly effective. What makes these details most successful?

2. **Dialogue** How does the author's use of dialogue contribute to the tone of the essay? How does it contribute to your overall impression of the essay's subject?

3. **Figurative language** Evaluate the use of figurative language in this essay. Consider the statements that liken the patient to a cottage (para. 2), a bonsai tree (2), a log (19), and a sailor (20). What do you learn about the patient from each?

Discussing the Reading

1. Suggest how the doctor might have approached the patient differently or offered more help and support.

2. Why does the doctor refer to himself as a spy? Are there certain things about a patient that a doctor should not know or ask about?

3. The discus thrower dies quietly and alone. In class or in your journal, describe a time when you were alone and wished you had a friend or family member nearby.

Writing about the Reading

1. **Paragraph** Selzer focuses on one particular patient in "The Discus Thrower"; but other than the man's medical condition, we know little about him. Using descriptive details, write a paragraph that describes briefly who this man might be and why he might be alone at the hospital.

2. **Paragraph** The patient Selzer describes is, at least in his last stage of life, a pretty unpleasant man, as the head nurse suggests in paragraph 27. Write a paragraph describing a person you know whose personality and actions you find objectionable, even "nasty" —someone you would avoid if you could. (Hint: Begin by explaining your relationship to this person, and then detail specific aspects of his or her personality and behavior that you find distasteful.) Unlike Selzer, you might make your subject the object of some humor.

3. **Essay** Brainstorm a list of reactions and / or feelings you or someone you know experienced when undergoing a medical procedure of some kind. What dominant impression do they suggest? Develop and support this dominant impression by writing an essay that describes the medical treatment and experience.

Rain Is Sizzling Bacon, Cars Are Lions Roaring: The Art of Sound in Movies

Jordan Kisner writes essays, stories, and reviews for numerous publications. Having received a Master of Fine Arts degree in creative nonfiction from Columbia University, she now teaches there in the Undergraduate Writing Program. Her essay, "Rain Is Sizzling Bacon, Cars Are Lions Roaring: The Art of Sound in Movies," appeared in the film section of *The Guardian* magazine in the summer of 2015.

Reading Tip

As you read, think about why the writer is so interested in the man she identifies as Skip Lievsay. Why does she think readers should want to learn about Lievsay?

Previewing the Reading

Preview the reading using the guidelines on pages 28–29, and then answer the following questions.

1. Why is *No Country for Old Men* important in this essay?
2. Based on your preview, what do you know about creating sound for movies?

Rain Is Sizzling Bacon, Cars Are Lions Roaring: The Art of Sound in Movies

Jordan Kisner

Skip Lievsay, an unassuming-looking guy in his mid-60s with highly trained ears, stood before the stacks of speakers and giant movie screen in his office, fussing quietly. Lievsay is one of the preeminent sound designers working in film today, and whatever he does—whether it's fussing or making jokes or padding down the hall of his New York offices to murmur instructions to employees—he does it quietly, as if his personal volume dial operates in inverse correlation to the often noisy task at hand.

On this midwinter afternoon, he was meeting with one of his effects editors, a similarly soft-spoken young man named Larry Zipf, about a film they had been hired to work on: *Miles Ahead*, a forthcoming Miles Davis biopic directed by and starring Don Cheadle. The two men stood with their arms crossed and heads cocked at the same angle, reviewing a scene in which a sound cue they had designed had gone awry. The sound, originally of vintage tape decks turning, had ended up evoking a sci-fi odyssey rather than

Continued >

a jazz biopic. One of the problems, it was agreed, is that to the untrained ear, 1970s tape decks sound a bit like lasers.

On screen, Cheadle entered an elevator and pushed the button for the lobby. The button emitted a soft, innocuous beep. "That's a good beep, Lar," Lievsay muttered. "Good beep." As he said so, Cheadle-as-Miles leaned against the wood-panelled elevator wall, eyes closed. Suddenly, the elevator swung open to reveal a dark room of Miles's imagination, filled only with a piano, a horn, and a spotlight. The moment was intended to feel surreal, as though you were entering Miles's mind, but as the door began to swing, a deep rumble erupted into a volley of zings and swishes—those troublesome tape decks—as if the scene had plunged into a battle in outer space.

Lievsay hit pause and turned to Larry, shaking his head. No good.

5   For research, Lievsay had spent a few months reading biographies and listening through all the recordings in the Miles Davis estate: Miles interviews, Miles in the studio, Miles in concert, Miles on the street. He briefly tried to compile a timeline of every recording Miles ever made, then gave up. The film is set in the 1970s, "which is Bitches Brew Miles," Lievsay explained, a period when Miles favored improvisational rhythms and electric instruments over traditional jazz. The research had led to the idea of experimenting with recording equipment of the sort that Miles would have used. Lievsay thought that they might fit moments that called for more abstract sound design, such as when Cheadle wanted to evoke Miles's agitated mental state. "He was a creature of the studio," Lievsay explained, taking off thin-rimmed glasses and rubbing one eye. "The sounds of his mental landscape would probably have been the sounds you'd hear in a recording studio, like tape decks or the click of instruments."

They had got their hands on some vintage tape decks and spent an afternoon recording the sound of them playing forward and backward, clicking and scrubbing. But when Zipf edited the sounds and played them underneath scenes from the movie, the result sounded like *Battlestar Galactica*, not old-fashioned music equipment. Lievsay sighed. "Probably because sound editors used to use tape decks when they needed space sounds. Bet you *Battlestar Galactica* was tape decks." He threw the noises out and started over.

It is a central principle of sound editing that people hear what they are conditioned to hear, not what they are actually hearing. The sound of rain in movies? Frying bacon. Car engines revving in a chase scene? It's partly engines, but what gives it that visceral, gut-level grist is lion roars mixed in. To be excellent, a sound editor needs not just a sharp, trained ear, but also a gift for imagining what a sound could do, what someone else might hear.

Lievsay is one of the best. He won an Academy award in 2014 for his work on *Gravity*. He was awarded the 2015 Career Achievement award from the Motion Picture Sound Editors society. *Goodfellas, Silence of the Lambs, Do The Right Thing*—his work. He is also the only sound editor the Coen Brothers work with, which means that he is the person responsible for that gnarly wood chipper noise in *Fargo*, the peel of wallpaper in *Barton Fink*, the resonance of The Dude's bowling ball in *The Big Lebowski* and the absolutely chilling crinkle of Javier Bardem's gum wrapper in *No Country for Old Men*.

Trying to sum up what makes Lievsay special, Glenn Kiser, the head of the Dolby Institute and the former head of Skywalker Sounds, told me: "What separates tremendously gifted designers comes down to taste. Skip has an unfailing sense for the right sound, and how to be simple and precise. He's not about sound by the pound." Jonathan Demme, who first worked with Lievsay on *The Silence of the Lambs*, put it more concisely: "He's a genius."

10   The monstrous complexity of Lievsay's work—the quest to make films sound the way the world sounds—may not be immediately apparent. When a movie finishes shooting, it enters the labyrinthine world of post-production, in which the best takes are selected and spliced together into reels—roughly 20-minute segments of film that are worked on and then stitched together at the end of post-production. Each reel goes through picture editing (for such things as visual continuity or color) before being handed off to the sound supervisor, who oversees all the various elements of sound design, editing and mixing.

At the beginning of this process, editors remove the audio recordings taken during filming and break down each scene into four sonic elements: dialogue, effects, music and Foley, which is the term for everyday sounds such as squeaky shoes or cutlery jangling in a drawer. For every scene, each of these four elements needs to be built and then edited separately, and at WBNY, the New York production company Lievsay runs with fellow editor Paul Urmson, each gets its own dedicated editor. Then, Lievsay

or Urmson takes the team's work and layers it to make scenes that sound like the world sounds.

Consider the scene at the end of *No Country for Old Men* when Javier Bardem's character has a car accident. After the crunch of impact, there are a few moments of what might be mistaken for stillness. The two cars rest smoking and crumpled in the middle of a suburban intersection. Nothing moves—but the soundscape is deceptively layered. There is the sound of engines hissing and crackling, which have been mixed to seem as near to the ear as the camera was to the cars; there is a mostly unnoticeable rustle of leaves in the trees; periodically, so faintly that almost no one would register it consciously, there is the sound of a car rolling through an intersection a block or two over, off camera; a dog barks somewhere far away. The faint sound of a breeze was taken from ambient sounds on a street like the one depicted in the scene. When Javier Bardem shoves open the car door, you hear the door handle stick for a moment before it releases. There are three distinct sounds of broken glass tinkling to the pavement from the shattered window, a small handful of thunks as he falls sideways to the ground, his labored breathing, the chug of his boot heel finally connecting with the asphalt—even the pads of his fingers as they scrabble along the top of the window. None of these sounds are there because some microphone picked them up. They're there because Lievsay chose them and put them there, as he did for every other sound in the film. The moment lasts about 20 seconds. *No Country for Old Men* is 123 minutes long.

All this requires a very particular—and somewhat strange—set of talents

Continued >

and fascinations. You need the ability not only to hear with an almost super-human acuity but also the technical proficiency and Job-like patience to spend hours getting the sound of a kettle's hiss exactly the right length as well as the right pitch—and not only the right pitch but the right pitch considering that the camera pans during the shot, which means that the viewer's ear will subconsciously anticipate hearing a maddeningly subtle (but critical) Doppler effect, which means that the tone the kettle makes as it boils needs to shift downward at precisely the interval that a real kettle's hiss would if you happened to walk by at that speed.

The impact a tiny aural cue can have on the brain's understanding of narrative is astonishing. On the third day of the mix, Lievsay and Larry were breezing through a scene of Miles dropping in on one of his wife's dance rehearsals when Cheadle, who had been doing t'ai-chi in one corner to pass the time, paused them. The scene sounded a little too dreamy. Cheadle wanted a more matter-of-fact sound. "The point is that [Miles and his wife Frances] are carving a special moment out of something that's not special," he said.

15   Lievsay nodded and fiddled for a moment. When he replayed the scene, something small but extraordinary happened. I had watched this scene somewhere between one and two dozen times but this time I noticed something I'd never seen before: a young woman passing behind Frances with a stack of papers in her hand. Lievsay had given her footsteps. Without the footsteps, I'd somehow never seen her; now, I saw her, and her presence—along with a few other tweaks by Lievsay—suggested bustling in the room, people at work,

things happening outside the eye contact forged between Miles and Frances. I didn't exactly hear the difference: I just saw the scene differently.

"Is it busy enough now?" Lievsay asked.

In order for that edit to be possible, Lievsay needed the footsteps of that young woman close at hand. He needed not just any footsteps, but ones that sounded like they were made by a low high heel of roughly the sort that women would wear in the mid-1970s crossing a wooden stage. This kind of noise—one that requires precision, but that is intended to blend in to the background—is called Foley. (The work is named after Jack Foley, who first came up with a process for adding quotidian[1] noises, such as footsteps, to films in the 1920s.)

When Lievsay reached for that girl's footsteps, he wasn't going back into some old library—he was reaching into the library of Foley designed and created specifically for Cheadle's film. The Foley house, also known informally at his studio as "the sound castle," where these sounds are made, is in New Jersey, just 15 minutes past the place where the George Washington Bridge connects Manhattan with Fort Lee. It is not so much a castle as a warehouse crammed with more stuff than can be adequately described here.

In its resting moments, the sound console that sits in the middle of Lievsay's office displays a curious screensaver. It is a slideshow of rooms: wine cellars, cathedrals, living rooms, sheds. The photos come from a program called Altiverb, developed by people who record sounds in different spaces

[1]quotidian Everyday, ordinary.

and then calculate the reverb acting on those sounds. The reverb pattern—what happens to noise as it moves through space to our ears—is known as the delta. Lievsay's central mission is to find the right one for every sound, no matter how small. He lives in search of the delta.

20   That he is one of the best in the industry at finding it he attributes mostly to what he calls "seat time," or experience. "The longer you work, the better you are at imagining what something should sound like." At heart, the pursuit of the delta is the pursuit of the viewer's consciousness. The sound editor's question is, at its most essential: how do you experience the world? How can I imagine what it will be like to be you listening to your wife call to you from across a field, or realizing that the car approaching from behind on the dark road is coming too fast? In ways we mostly do not notice, hearing is not just sound—it is sound plus feeling, or sound plus physical sensation, thought, history, and choice of what to hear. To work on sound, then, is not simply about crafting noise—it is about anticipating what it is to be a peculiar, particular sentient creature in the world.

It is a dramatic enterprise, but it does not look like much. On the final day of the *Miles Ahead* mix, Lievsay was still and silent. During the weird philosophical arguments that went on throughout the afternoon—was the sound of that record spinning too loud? If a trumpet came in a half-second later, would it change the entire meaning of the scene? Where was this guy supposed to be in the room when we hear him speaking off-camera?—Lievsay rarely responded. His head bobbed only twice. It appeared, oddly, as though he was doing mostly nothing that afternoon, just clicking in slow, methodical plunks.

Five-thirty arrived, the final hour before Lievsay had to catch a plane to Los Angeles, where he would start working on a documentary about Malala Yousafzai early the next morning. Slowly, Cheadle and the team began gathering, one by one, to stand behind Skip's chair. They looked over his shoulder anxiously, as if watching a finish line approach.

What came next was uncharacteristically theatrical for Skip. He worked until there was only one cue left, a single trumpet bleat that would mark a kind of epiphany for Miles; the film's final turn. It was first too rough, then too bleaty, then too quiet. Lievsay made an alteration. After that, it sounded too far back in the room, too reverby[2].

Six-thirty arrived. Lievsay clicked quietly, dragging a soundwave down on the monitor in front of him, nudging another one up, and then played the cue back again. The trumpet was in the room suddenly, plaintive and ugly and insistent and right. It was the epiphany that the film needed it to be. Lievsay nodded. "That's it," he said.

25   He stood up, shook Cheadle's hand, clapped Zipf on the shoulder, and was gone. Everyone stood around in his wake for a while, dazed and din-drunk. Zipf shook his head, as if clearing his ears. People kept looking reflexively at the screen, where the horn player was frozen mid-stride, as if to see what it was Lievsay had done to that trumpet. After a few minutes this stopped, as if in acknowledgment. The delta is not something you see, anyway.

[2]**reverby** Producing an echoing sound.

Understanding and Reviewing the Reading

1. **Dominant impression** What dominant impression does this description create of the movie sound industry ? How does it primarily do so?

2. **Subject** This description focuses both on Lievsay himself and on the sound editing process. How does the connection between the two of them help make this "double description" work? Of the two, which does the author describe more effectively? Explain your answer.

3. **Descriptive details** Annotate the reading to highlight the specific details that help you "see" Lievsay.

4. **Meaning** According to Kisner, how does the brain have an effect on what the ear hears? (Hint: See paragraphs 14–15 for help with this question.)

5. **Language** Glen Kiser, the head of the Dolby Institute, said that Lievsay was not about "sound by the pound" (para. 9). What does this mean, and how does it set Lievsay apart from other sound specialists in his field?

Analyzing the Reading

1. **Intention** Is this description mainly subjective or objective? How can you tell?

2. **Descriptive detail** Highlight some of the adjectives and verbs Kisner uses in paragraph 12 in describing the car accident in *No Country for Old Men*. What impression of the accident do these descriptive words suggest?

3. **Thinking visually** If you were asked to choose a photo for this reading, what would it look like? What concept in the reading would the photo illustrate?

4. **Language** In paragraph 13, Kisner writes that Job-like patience is required to do Lievsay's job well. What is the author trying to communicate about the type of patience that is needed for the job?

5. **Patterns** What pattern(s) of writing—other than description—does the author use? Explain your answer and support it with examples from the text.

6. **Sensory details** Sensory details are those details that appeal to one or more of the five senses—sight, hearing, smell, taste, and touch. Locate examples for as many of the different senses as possible and organize your examples in a chart.

Evaluating the Reading

1. **Dominant impression** Do you find Kisner's description of Lievsay generally biased or unbiased? Do you think she tries to hide any biases?

2. **Dialogue** How does the author's use of dialogue contribute to the tone of the essay? How does it contribute to your overall impression of the essay's subject?

3. **Intention** What is Kisner trying to persuade readers of in this essay? Do you think she succeeds?

4. **Personal response** In three words, summarize how you respond to Lievsay as he is described here. (For example, fill in the following blanks: "I think that Lievsay is _____, _____, and _____.") Are all your descriptive words similar, or do they reveal some conflict in your attitude? What in the essay makes you feel as you do?

Discussing the Reading

1. The title of the essay suggests that movie sound editing is an art. What does the author mean? Do you agree with this? Can the skills be taught? Can just anyone do it? What makes some people better at it than others? What other professions do you consider to be arts?

2. Kisner writes that Skip Lievsay is a genius. What makes someone a genius? Do you know anyone whom you would classify as a genius? Are people born geniuses, or do they develop into geniuses?

3. Skip Lievsay was not a one-man show; he worked with a team. He was a leader. What do you think are some characteristics of a good leader? What kind of leader was Lievsay?

Writing about the Reading

1. **Paragraph** Like Kisner, describe a person you know whom you consider to be an expert in his/her field. (Hint: Before drafting, make a list of the person's characteristics that support your claim. Use this list as the basis for your paragraph.)

2. **Essay** Write a story, like the one about Lievsay and the trumpet sound, in which you describe yourself (or someone you know well) in terms of how you struggled to solve a problem and then, all of a sudden, had an epiphany that led you directly to the solution. Write freely and conversationally as you draft, but then go back to edit for clarity and to make sure you create a dominant impression. Consider adding an introduction and a conclusion to clarify and give context to your dominant impression.

3. **Essay** Kisner writes, "whether it's fussing or making jokes or padding down the hall of his New York offices to murmur instructions to his employees—he does it quietly." What one word describes you? Write an essay in which you describe yourself. Make sure that your description creates a dominant impression and that all of your details support that impression.

The Secret Latina

Veronica Chambers is a fiction writer, journalist, and former editor at the *New York Times Magazine.* In the acclaimed memoir *Mama's Girl* (1996), she examines her complex relationship with her mother. The following essay, which originally appeared in *Essence* magazine, also explores her family heritage.

Reading Tip

As you read, think about the relationship between the writer and her mother. How does the writer feel about her mother, and how does her mother feel about the writer?

Previewing the Reading

Preview the reading (see pp. 28–29 for guidelines), and then write a sentence summarizing what you have learned about the meaning of the title.

The Secret Latina

Veronica Chambers

She's a platanos-frying, malta Dukesa-drinking, salsa-dancing Mamacita—my dark-skinned Panamanian mother. She came to this country when she was twenty-one, her sense of culture intact, her Spanish flawless. Even today, more than twenty years since she left her home country to become an American citizen, my mother still considers herself Panamanian and checks "Hispanic" on census forms.

As a Black woman in America, my Latin identity is murkier than my mother's, despite the fact that I, too, was born in Panama, and call that country "home." My father's parents came from Costa Rica and Jamaica, my mother's from Martinique. I left Panama when I was two years old. My family lived in England for three years then came to the States when I was five. Having dark skin and growing up in Brooklyn in the 1970s meant I was

Black, period. You could meet me and not know I was of Latin heritage. Without a Spanish last name or my mother's fluent Spanish at my disposal, I often felt isolated from the Latin community. And frankly, Latinos were not quick to claim me. Latinos can be as racist as anybody else, favoring blue-eyed, blond *rubias* over *negritas* like me.

I found it almost impossible to explain to my elementary-school friends why my mother would speak Spanish at home. They would ask if I was Puerto Rican and look bewildered when I told them I was not. To them, Panama was a kind of nowhere. There weren't enough Panamanians in Brooklyn to be a force. Everybody knew where Jamaicans were from because of famous singers like Bob Marley. Panamanians had Ruben Blades, but most of my friends thought he was Puerto Rican, too.

In my neighborhood, where the smell of somebody's grandmother's cooking could transform a New York corner into Santo Domingo, Kingston, or Port-au-Prince, a Panamanian was a sort of fish with feathers—assumed to be a Jamaican who spoke Spanish. The analogy was not without historical basis: A century ago, Panama's Black community was largely drawn to the country from all over the Caribbean as cheap labor to build the Panama Canal.

5 My father didn't mind that we considered ourselves Black rather than Latino. He named my brother Malcolm X, and if my mother hadn't put her foot down, I would have been called Angela Davis Chambers. It's not that my mother didn't admire Angela Davis, but you have only to hear how *Veronica Victoria* flows off her Spanish lips to know that she was homesick for Panama and for those names that sang like *timbales*[1] on carnival day. So between my father and my mother was a Black-Latin divide. Because of my father, we read and discussed books about Black history and civil rights. Because of my mother, we ate Panamanian food, listened to salsa, and heard Spanish at home.

Still it wasn't until my parents divorced when I was ten that my mother tried to teach Malcolm and me Spanish. She was a terrible language teacher. She had no sense of how to explain structure, and her answer to every question was "That's just the way it is." A few short weeks after our Spanish lessons began, my mother gave up and we were all relieved. But I remained intent on learning my mother's language. When she spoke Spanish, her words were a fast current, a stream of

language that was colorful, passionate, fiery. I wanted to speak Spanish because I wanted to swim in the river of her words, her history, my history, too.

At school I dove into the language, matching what little I knew from home with all that I learned. One day, when I was in the ninth grade, I finally felt confident enough to start speaking Spanish with my mother. I soon realized that by speaking Spanish with her, I was forging an important bond. When I'd spoken only English, I was the daughter, the little girl. But when I began speaking Spanish, I became something more—a *hermanita*, a sisterfriend, a Panamanian homegirl who could hang with the rest of them. Eventually this bond would lead me home.

Two years ago, at age twenty-seven, I decided it was finally time. I couldn't wait any longer to see Panama, the place my mother and my aunts had told me stories about. I enlisted my cousin Digna as a traveling companion and we made arrangements to stay with my godparents, whom I had never met. We planned our trip for the last week in February—carnival time.

Panama, in Central America, is a narrow sliver of a country: You can swim in the Caribbean Sea in the morning and backstroke across the Pacific in the afternoon. As our plane touched down, bringing me home for the first time since I was two, I felt curiously comfortable and secure. In the days that followed, there was none of the culture shock that I'd expected—I had my mother and aunts to thank for that. My godmother, Olga, reminded me of them. The first thing she did was book appointments for Digna and me to get our eyebrows plucked and our nails and feet done

[1]**timbales** Drums played with the hands.

Continued >

with Panamanian-style manicures and pedicures. "It's carnival," Aunt Olga said, "and you girls have to look your best." We just laughed.

10   In Panama, I went from being a lone Black girl with a curious Latin heritage to being part of the *Latinegro* tribe or the *Afro-Antillianos*, as we were officially called. I was thrilled to learn there was actually a society for people like me. Everyone was Black, everyone spoke Spanish, and everyone danced the way they danced at fiesta time back in Brooklyn, stopping only to chow down on a smorgasbord of souse[2], rice with black-eyed peas, beef patties, *empanadas*[3], and codfish fritters. The carnival itself was an all-night bacchanal[4] with elaborate floats, brilliantly colored costumes, and live musicians. In the midst of all this, my godmother took my cousin and me to a photo studio to have our pictures taken in *polleras*, the traditional dress. After spending an hour on makeup and hair and donning a rented costume, I looked like Scarlett in *Gone with the Wind*.

Back in New York, I gave the photo to my mother. She almost cried. She says she was so moved to see me in a *pollera* because it was "such a patriotic thing to do." Her appreciation made me ridiculously happy; ever since I was a little girl, I'd wanted to be like my mother. In one of my most vivid memories, I am seven or eight and my parents are having a party. Salsa music is blaring and my mother is dancing and laughing. She sees me standing off in a corner, so she pulls me into the circle of grown-ups and tries to teach me how to dance to the music. Her hips are electric. She puts her hands on my sides and says, "Move these," and I start shaking my hip bones as if my life depends on it.

Now I am a grown woman, with hips to spare. I can salsa. My Spanish isn't shabby. You may look at me and not know that I am Panamanian, that I am an immigrant, that I am both Black and Latin. But I am my mother's daughter, a secret Latina, and that's enough for me.

[2]**souse** Pig parts preserved in brine.
[3]**empanadas** Small pies with meat or other fillings.
[4]**bacchanal** Celebration.

Understanding and Reviewing the Reading

1. **Dominant impression** What main impression does Chambers create of herself and of her mother? What do the final two paragraphs contribute to this dominant impression?

2. **Meaning** What is the point of paragraphs 3–4? What do they contribute to Chambers's underlying point about herself?

3. **Meaning** Why was it important for Chambers to make the trip to Panama she writes about in paragraphs 8–10?

Analyzing the Reading

1. **Attitude** This is obviously a subjective description. What attitude is the writer trying to convey about herself and her mother?

2. **Introduction** Why does the opening paragraph focus only on Chambers's mother? And the why does Chambers shift her focus to herself in paragraph 2?

3. **Subject** This description focuses both on Chambers herself and on her mother. How does the connection between the two of them help make this "double description" work?

4. **Language** In paragraph 3, Chambers writes that in her neighborhood Panamanians were viewed as "fish with feathers." What is her point, and why does she go on to put this analogy in historical context?

5. **Development** What do paragraphs 6–7 contribute to your understanding of Chambers's relationship with her mother? How is this point echoed in the final paragraph?

Evaluating the Reading

1. **Descriptive details** How well do you think Chambers describes her mother? What details do you find most effective? Are there any aspects of her mother about which you would like to learn more?

2. **Language and audience** Throughout the essay, Chambers sprinkles in Spanish vocabulary, which she doesn't always define for a non-Spanish-reading audience: for example, *rubias* (para. 2), *timbales* (5), and *souse* (10). Do you think this is appropriate for the general audience of a publication like *Essence*?

3. **Presentation** How do you respond to Chambers's presentation of herself in the essay? Point to specific details that contribute to your response.

4. **Opening and conclusion** How well do you think the concluding paragraph provides a connection to the opening paragraph? That is, do the opening and conclusion serve to give the essay a sense of cohesion?

Discussing the Reading

1. Why does Chambers make such a point of the fact that her friends in elementary school didn't understand who she was culturally? Do you think this should be an issue in personal relationships?

2. Chambers says that it was important for her to learn Spanish, her mother's native language. In what other ways do children, as they grow up, attempt to connect with their parents?

3. While we generally think about prejudice as occurring across racial and ethnic divides, Chambers writes about prejudice *within* the Latino community regarding skin color. Within your own community, are some "types" valued more highly while other "types" receive prejudicial treatment? Why might this be the case?

Writing about the Reading

1. **Essay** Like Chambers, write an essay of "double description," focusing on both yourself and a significant person in your life whom you mirror in some way: a parent, a sibling, a partner, or a close friend. (Hint: As you plan your essay, use Chambers's organization as a model: how she opens by describing her mother, ends by describing herself to echo that opening description, and uses her body paragraphs to develop the connections between herself and her mother.)

2. **Essay** Chambers could have written an extended description essay just about her experiences during carnival time in Panama (paras. 8–10). Brainstorm a list of holiday celebrations and festivals you have participated in. Then choose one as the basis for a description essay in which you re-create it for readers using as many details of the senses—sight, smell, hearing, touch, taste—as possible.

3. **Essay** In paragraph 4, Chambers writes about the memories created by "the smell of somebody's grandmother's cooking." Write an essay describing a vivid childhood memory of your own that can be called up by something that occurs in the present. It might be positive, as Chambers's example is, or it might be a different kind of memory—one that is unpleasant or even frightening. Be sure to develop your essay by explaining what evokes the memory and using sensory details to communicate the memory vividly.

📖   COMBINING THE PATTERNS | TEXTBOOK EXCERPT: FILM STUDIES

Costumes

Louis Giannetti is an emeritus professor of film studies and English at Case Western Reserve University. His books on the cinema include *Flashback: A Brief History of Film* (2009) and *Masters of the American Cinema* (2010). The selection here comes from *Understanding Movies* (2010), his introductory textbook on the language of film.

Reading Tip

As you read, think about how the caption below the still of Marilyn Monroe from *The Seven Year Itch* relates to the rest of the text discussion and whether you find the two discussions equally informative.

Previewing the Reading

Preview the reading (see pp. 28–29 for guidelines), and list three things you think it will cover in more detail.

Costumes
Louis Giannetti

In the most sensitive films and plays, costumes and makeup aren't merely frills added to enhance an illusion, but aspects of character and theme. Costumes can reveal class, self-image, even psychological states. Depending on their cut, texture, and bulk, certain costumes can suggest agitation, fastidiousness[1], delicacy, dignity, and so on. A costume, then, is a medium, especially in the cinema, where a close-up of a fabric can suggest information that's independent even of the wearer.

Color symbolism is used by Zeffirelli in *Romeo and Juliet.* Juliet's family, the Capulets, are characterized as aggressive parvenues[2]: Their colors are appropriately "hot" reds, yellow, and oranges. Romeo's family, on the other hand, is older and perhaps more established, but in obvious decline. They are costumed in blues, deep greens, and purples. These two color schemes are echoed in the liveries of the servants of each house, which helps the audience identify the combatants in the brawling scenes. The color of the costumes can also be used to suggest change and transition. Our first view of Juliet, for example, shows her in a vibrant red dress. Afer she marries Romeo, her colors are in the cool blue spectrum. Line as well as color can be used to suggest psychological qualities. Verticals, for example, tend to emphasize stateliness and dignity (Lady Montague); horizontal lines tend to emphasize earthiness and comicality (Juliet's nurse).

[1] **fastidiousness** The quality of being excessively particular about details or hard to please.
[2] **parvenues** People who have risen economically or socially but lack the appropriate social skills for their new position.

on
Continued >

Publicity photo of Marilyn Monroe in *The Seven Year Itch* (U.S.A., 1955), directed by Billy Wilder.   Variations of this image have become iconographic[3] in popular culture, replicated millions of times, and recognized by virtually everyone on the planet. Why did this image in particular capture the imagination of so many people? Perhaps it was the costume. (1) The *period* of the garment is 1955, but so classic in its lines that variations of the dress can still be found in stores. (2) The *class* of the dress is middle to upper middle: It's an elegant, well-made party dress. (3) The *sex* is feminine in the extreme, emphasizing such erotic details as a plunging neckline and bare arms and back. (4) The *age* level would be suitable to any mature woman (from the late teens to the mid-forties) in good physical shape. (5) The *silhouette* is form-fitting from the waist up, emphasizing Marilyn's famous breasts. The accordion-pleated flare skirt ordinarily would obscure her shape below the waist, but the updraft from the subway below swooshes the skirt toward her face. Her gesture of holding the skirt down near the crotch suggests a childish innocence and spontaneity. (6) The *fabric* is lightweight, suitable for a summer evening, probably a silk/cotton blend. (7) The *accessories* include only the circular earrings (hard to see in this photo) and the high-heeled strap sandals. The shoes are sexy and delicate, but not very practical. They make her look pampered and vulnerable and easy to catch. (8) The dress's *color* is white—pure, clean, untouched by the city's dirt. (9) There is quite a bit of *body exposure*—the arms, shoulders, back, cleavage, and—at least here—much of the upper thighs. (10) The *function* of the dress is recreational, not work-related. It's meant to attract attention. It's a dress to have fun in. (11) Marilyn's *body attitude* is childish exuberance—she's not in the least ashamed or embarrassed by her body and wears the outfit with confidence. (12) The general *image* suggests innocence, femininity, spontaneity, and a riveting sexual allure.

[3] **iconographic** Serving to represent, as a symbol.

Perhaps the most famous costume in film history is Charlie Chaplin's tramp outfit. The costume is an indication of both class and character, conveying the complex mixture of vanity and dash that makes Charlie so appealing. The moustache, derby hat, and cane all suggest the fastidious dandy. The cane is used to give the impression of self-importance as Charlie swaggers confidently before a hostile world. But the baggy trousers several sizes too large, the oversized shoes, the too-tight coat—all these suggest Charlie's insignificance and poverty. Chaplin's view of humanity is symbolized by that costume: vain, absurd, and—finally—poignantly vulnerable.

In most cases, especially period films, costumes are designed for the performers who will be wearing them. The costumer must always be conscious of the actor's body type—whether he or she is thin, overweight, tall, short, and so on—to compensate for any deficiency. If a performer is famous for a given trait—Dietrich's legs, Marilyn's bosom, Matthew McConaughey's chest—the costumer will often design the actor's clothes to highlight these attractions. Even in period films, the costumer has a wide array of styles to choose from, and his or her choice will often be determined by what the actor looks best in within the parameters[4] defined by the milieu[5] of the story.

During the Hollywood studio era, powerful stars often insisted on costumes and makeup that heightened their natural endowments, regardless of period accuracy. This was a practice that was encouraged by the studio bosses, who wanted their stars to look as glamourous as possible by suggesting a "contemporary look." The results are usually jarring and incongruous[6]. Even prestigious directors like John Ford gave in to this tradition of vanity. In Ford's otherwise superb western *My Darling Clementine* (1946), which is set in a rough frontier community, actress Linda Darnell wore glamourous star makeup and a 1940s-style hairdo, even though the character she was playing was a cheap Mexican "saloon girl"—a coy period euphemism for a prostitute. She looks as though she just stepped out of a hoity-toity beauty salon after receiving the deluxe treatment. She's groomed to within an inch of her life.

In realistic contemporary stories, costumes are often bought off the rack rather than individually designed. This is especially true in stories dealing with ordinary people, people who buy their clothes in department stores. When the characters are lower class or poor, costumers often purchase used clothing. For example, in *On The Waterfront*, which deals with dockworkers and other working-class characters, the costumes are frayed and torn. Costumer Anna Hill Johnstone bought them in used clothing stores in the neighborhood adjoining the waterfront area.

Costumes, then, represent another language system in movies, a symbolic form of communication that can be as complex and revealing

---

[4] **parameters** Boundaries; guidelines.
[5] **milieu** Setting.
[6] **incongruous** Out of place; not fitting together; inconsistent.

Continued >

as the other language systems filmmakers use. A systematic analysis of a costume includes a consideration of the following characteristics:

1. **Period** What era does the costume fall into? Is it an accurate reconstruction? If not, why?
2. **Class** What is the apparent income level of the person wearing the costume?
3. **Sex** Does a woman's costume emphasize her femininity or is it neutral or masculine? Does a man's costume emphasize his virility or is it fussy or effeminate?
4. **Age** Is the costume appropriate to the character's age or is it deliberately too youthful, dowdy, or old-fashioned?
5. **Silhouette** Is the costume form-fitting or loose and baggy?
6. **Fabric** Is the material coarse, sturdy, and plain or sheer and delicate?
7. **Accessories** Does the costume include jewelry, hats, canes, and other accessories? What kind of shoes?
8. **Color** What are the symbolic implications of the colors? Are they "hot" or "cool"? Subdued or bright? Solids or patterns?

Understanding and Reviewing the Reading

1. **Textbook reading** Highlight each of the reading's seven main paragraphs as if you were preparing for an objective exam on the material. Compare your highlighting with that of a classmate.
2. **Language** Reread the long photo caption analyzing Marilyn Monroe's costume in *The Seven Year Itch*. Using your own words, state the meanings of the italicized words and explain why they are italicized.
3. **Understanding details** In paragraph 2, the author includes information on Zeffirelli's use of color symbolism in the film *Romeo and Juliet*. Explain why the color of Juliet's dress changes from red to blue when she marries Romeo.
4. **Dominant impression** Express the essay's dominant impression in your own words.

Analyzing the Reading

1. **Predicting exam questions** To prepare for an essay exam, it can be helpful to predict possible questions your instructor might ask. Suppose you are a student in an Introduction to Film Making class. Write an essay question that might be asked about this reading.
2. **Considering examples** In addition to Marilyn Monroe's costume in *The Seven Year Itch*, what other specific examples does the author describe? What do these examples contribute to the discussion?

3. **Thinking about textbook visuals** Why does the author reproduce this particular photo of Marilyn Monroe in costume? What does this costume represent?

Evaluating the Reading

1. **Language** Choose five words in the caption analyzing Marilyn Monroe's costume that would be important to learn when reading or writing about costume design. Write a definition of each, using your own words.

2. **Technique** How does the topic of paragraph 5 differ from what is covered in the rest of the reading? Is this information necessary? Explain your answer.

3. **Value of information** What did you learn from this textbook excerpt and how will this information be valuable to you in your other courses or in your life outside of school?

Discussing the Reading

1. The author includes examples describing costumes from films student readers may not be familiar with, such as Zeffirelli's *Romeo and Juliet* and *On the Waterfront*. Is this a problem in terms of understanding the points being made? Explain your answer.

2. The author suggests that the image of Marilyn Monroe from *The Seven Year Itch* might be so well known around the world because of the costume. Are you convinced? Why or why not? For what other reasons might the image be famous?

3. In general, how closely do you pay attention to what characters are wearing in films? Has this reading changed how you will look at costumes in movies? Why, or why not?

Writing about the Reading

1. **Essay-exam question** Write a brief essay answering the question you posed for Analyzing the Reading.

2. **Applying the reading** Suppose you are a student in a course entitled The Art of Film Making, and your instructor has given you the following assignment: Watch the video of a film that you regard highly. Take notes about the costumes, and write an essay that both describes and analyzes some of the costumes in terms of what they communicate symbolically about the characters. (Take into consideration the eight characteristics that conclude the reading.)

3. **Thinking on your own** In paragraph 1, the author writes that costumes can reveal "class, self-image, even psychological states" as well as traits such as "agitation, fastidiousness, delicacy, dignity, and so on." Suppose that, in a psychology class where you have been studying social psychology, you have been assigned the following culminating activity: Using the images in paragraph 1 as a guideline, write an essay in which you describe and analyze what people in real life may reveal about themselves by how they dress.

Working with Description as a Reader and Writer

The following table reviews the key elements of description essays and explains how these elements are important to both readers and writers.

Reading ⟲ Writing   Description Essays

Element of a Description Essay	The Reader's Perspective	The Writer's Perspective
Dominant Impression	State the dominant impression in your own words. Several years from now, you may not remember all the details of an essay—but you will likely remember the dominant impression.	From your perspective as a writer, the dominant impression is the thesis. There is no reason to write a description essay if you cannot provide a lasting, dominant impression of the item.
Sensory Details	Reading is more than simply understanding the words on a page or screen. It is an immersive experience that asks you to interact with the text. Use the sensory details to see, hear, feel, touch, and/or taste the topic being described.	Human beings experience the world through the five senses; they are the most effective means of conveying information about any item. Sensory details help you make your writing concrete and specific, as opposed to vague or abstract.
Active Verbs and Varied Sentences	Evaluate the essay's sentence variety and the writer's choice of verbs as you read. Active verbs and varied sentences keep you involved in the reading selection and wanting to read more. Identify any weak verbs that could be replaced with more active, more engaging ones.	Monotony is the result when you do not vary your sentences and do not use active verbs. Take advantage of the richness of the English language to give your essays the kind of sentence variety that will prevent your readers from getting bored.

Connotative Language	Attune yourself to the nuances of the words the author has chosen. Do the words' connotations point to a specific bias on the author's part?	Many English words have multiple synonyms, each with its own connotations and associations. Do not be afraid to use a thesaurus to find exactly the right word to convey the meaning you intend.
Comparisons	In the margin, note the author's use of comparisons: similes, metaphors, analogies, and personification. Evaluate each comparison. Did any give you an "aha!" moment that helped you comprehend a difficult concept or topic?	Comparisons allow you to give free rein to your creativity. Many writers find that creating comparisons is one of the most enjoyable aspects of writing for any audience.
Vantage Point	While reading, put yourself in the author's position and see through his or her eyes. Doing so will help you to better understand the topic and the author's point of view.	The number of details that can be provided about any topic is almost infinite. By choosing a specific vantage point, you narrow your topic (item being described) and give form and structure to your essay.
Combined Patterns	As you read, note in the margins the primary and secondary patterns used. Examine how the use of multiple patterns helps you understand multiple aspects of the topic.	By combining patterns, you can shed light on important components of the topic that do not fit within your essay's primary pattern.

In this chapter, you will learn to

- Recognize the elements of illustration.

- Identify the structure and content of illustration essays.

- Understand, analyze, and evaluate illustration essays.

- Write your own illustration essay.

- Work with illustration as a reader and a writer.

12

Illustration: Explaining with Examples

Folio Images/Getty Images

Reflect on a Visual Text

In a social problems class, the instructor shows the photograph on this page and makes the following statement: "Environmental pollution is a growing global problem." She asks the class to think of situations similar to the one shown in the photo that confirm this view.

1 Ask yourself questions. How does the photo support the instructor's statement? What do you already know about environmental pollution, and how does that knowledge match or conflict with the image in the photo?

2 Brainstorm ideas. With a small group of classmates, brainstorm a list of examples of environmental pollution that you have observed or read about.

3 Write. Now write a paragraph in which you use the instructor's statement as a topic sentence and provide an example of your own to support it.

272

The paragraph you just wrote could be part of an illustration essay. An *illustration essay* uses examples to reveal a topic's essential characteristics and reinforce the thesis statement. Many ideas are meaningful and clear only when they have been fully explained. Providing examples is a simple, effective way to make a concept clear in a lively, interesting manner. For instance, if someone says that a child's behavior is *atrocious*, examples can illustrate the degree of the child's misbehavior (such as "he pulled the cat's tail, broke two plates, and drew on my wall with permanent markers"). Examples bring ideas to life.

What Is Illustration?

Illustration is a technique that uses one or more examples to make a point. For instance, you might argue that two movies have similar plots and give examples of *how* they're similar. Or, if you are making the point that holidays no longer have the same meaning as they used to, you could give several examples of their increasing commercialization. (Note that the last two sentences *illustrate* the definition of *illustration* provided in the first sentence!)

By providing specific examples that make abstract ideas concrete, you help readers connect these abstract ideas to their own experience. Most textbooks are filled with examples, and writers in academic and work situations also commonly use illustration. For example, in a literature course, you might provide examples of the Victorian novelists and their representative work. In the workplace, you might show a possible client several examples of your work.

Illustration has most or all of the following elements:

1. It brings ideas to life.
2. It helps clarify unfamiliar or difficult topics, concepts, or terms.
3. It helps readers and writers connect.

Knowing how writers (and other communicators) use illustration will help you understand, analyze, and evaluate illustration when you read and help you use it in your own writing.

A Model Illustration Essay

The following model illustration essay will be used throughout this chapter to demonstrate strategies for reading and writing illustration essays. Read it now, looking for the ways the writer uses the above illustration techniques. Use the annotations in the margin to guide you.

Snoopers at Work

Bill Bryson

Bill Bryson (b. 1951) grew up in the United States and then lived in England from 1977 to the mid-1990s, where he wrote for newspapers and then branched out to write about travel. The essays in *I'm a Stranger Here Myself* (1999), one of Bryson's nonfiction works about traveling in the United States, began as a column in a British newspaper, the *Mail on Sunday*. In the following piece from that collection, Bryson discusses the invasion of workers' privacy by their employers.

Now here is something to bear in mind should you ever find yourself using a changing room in a department store or other retail establishment. It is perfectly legal—indeed, it is evidently routine—for the store to spy on you while you are trying on their clothes.

I know this because I have just been reading a book by Ellen Alderman and Caroline Kennedy called *The Right to Privacy*, which is full of alarming tales of ways that businesses and employers can—and enthusiastically do—intrude into what would normally be considered private affairs.

The business of changing-cubicle spying came to light in 1983 when a customer trying on clothes in a department store in Michigan discovered that a store employee had climbed a stepladder and was watching him through a metal vent. (Is this tacky or what?) The customer was sufficiently outraged that he sued the store for invasion of privacy. He lost. A state court held that it was reasonable for retailers to defend against shoplifting by engaging in such surveillance.

He shouldn't have been surprised. Nearly everyone is being spied on in some way in America these days. A combination of technological advances, employer paranoia, and commercial avarice means that many millions of Americans are having their lives delved into in ways that would have been impossible, not to say unthinkable, a dozen years ago. . . .

Many companies are taking advantage of technological possibilities to make their businesses more ruthlessly productive. In Maryland, according to *Time* magazine, a bank searched through the medical records of its borrowers—apparently quite legally—to find out which of them had life-threatening illnesses and used this information to cancel their loans. Other companies have focused not on customers but on their own employees—for instance, to check what prescription drugs the employees are taking. One

An illustration brings ideas to life: The examples in this paragraph provide vivid proof that companies are using spying technologies to increase profits or minimize losses.

large, well-known company teamed up with a pharmaceutical firm to comb through the health records of employees to see who might benefit from a dose of antidepressants. The idea was that the company would get more serene workers; the drug company would get more customers.

According to the American Management Association, two-thirds of companies in the United States spy on their employees in some way. Thirty-five percent track phone calls, and 10 percent actually tape phone conversations to review at leisure later. About a quarter of companies surveyed admitted to going through their employees' computer files and reading their email.

Still other companies are secretly watching their employees at work. A secretary at a college in Massachusetts discovered that a hidden video camera was filming her office twenty-four hours a day. Goodness knows what the school authorities were hoping to find. What they got were images of the woman changing out of her work clothes and into a track suit each night in order to jog home from work. She is suing and will probably get a pot of money. But elsewhere courts have upheld companies' rights to spy on their workers.

There is a particular paranoia about drugs. I have a friend who got a job with a large manufacturing company in Iowa a year or so ago. Across the street from the company was a tavern that was the company after-hours hangout. One night my friend was having a beer after work with his colleagues when he was approached by a fellow employee who asked if he knew where she could get some marijuana. He said he didn't use the stuff himself, but to get rid of her—for she was very persistent—he gave her the phone number of an acquaintance who sometimes sold it.

The next day he was fired. The woman, it turned out, was a company spy employed solely to weed out drug use in the company. He hadn't supplied her with marijuana, you understand, hadn't encouraged her to use marijuana, and had stressed that he didn't use marijuana himself. Nonetheless, he was fired for encouraging and abetting the use of an illegal substance.

An illustration helps clarify unfamiliar or difficult topics, concepts, or terms: Here the author introduces and explains the acronym TAD as an example of companies' monitoring of their employees' lives.

Already, 91 percent of large companies—I find this almost unbelievable—now test some of their workers for drugs. Scores of companies have introduced what are called TAD rules—TAD being short for "tobacco, alcohol, and drugs"—which prohibit employees from using any of these substances at any time, including at home. There are companies, if you can believe it, that forbid their employees to drink or smoke at any time—even one beer, even on a

Saturday night—and enforce the rules by making their workers give urine samples.

An illustration helps readers and writers connect: Throughout the essay, the author identifies with his audience by expressing his surprise and dismay about invasive technologies.

He closes with a humorous paragraph that emphasizes his connection with his readers.

But it gets even more sinister than that. Two leading electronics companies working together have invented something called an "active badge," which tracks the movements of any worker compelled to wear one. The badge sends out an infrared signal every fifteen seconds. This signal is received by a central computer, which is thus able to keep a record of where every employee is and has been, whom they have associated with, how many times they have been to the toilet or water cooler—in short, to log every single action of their working day. If that isn't ominous, I don't know what is.

However, there is one development, I am pleased to report, that makes all of this worthwhile. A company in New Jersey has patented a device for determining whether restaurant employees have washed their hands after using the lavatory. Now *that* I can go for.

The Structure and Content of Illustration Essays

In this section, you will learn about the structure of an illustration essay and practice using the guidelines for understanding, analyzing, and evaluating illustration essays. This key information will help you skillfully read and write essays that use illustration.

The structure of an illustration essay is straightforward. Figure 12.1 represents the major structural components visually.

1. THE INTRODUCTION PRESENTS THE TOPIC, PROVIDES BACKGROUND INFORMATION, AND INCLUDES THE THESIS STATEMENT

The introduction of an illustration essay should

- present the topic
- state the thesis
- suggest why the topic is worth reading about

Background information should include relevant material to help orient readers to the topic. In "Snoopers at Work," Bill Bryson orients his readers to his topic in the first two paragraphs, warning them about an important trend that they should "keep in mind." He also notes that he became aware of the topic as a result of reading a book, *The Right to Privacy*, by Ellen Alderman and Caroline Kennedy.

Figure 12.1   Graphic Organizer for an Illustration Essay

Title	
Introduction	Background
	Thesis statement*

Body paragraphs	**Example 1**		**One extended example with details**
	Detail		
	Detail	**or**	
	Detail		
	Example 2		
	Detail		
	Detail		
	Detail		
	Example 3		
	Detail		
	Detail		
	Detail		

Conclusion	Final statement

*In some essays, the thesis statement may be implied or appear in a different position.

As you learned in Chapter 5 (p. 100), the heart of every essay is its thesis—the point or main idea that a writer wants to persuade his or her audience to accept. In essays that use illustration, the thesis is often a **generalization**—a broad statement offered as a general truth—that the writer attempts to make specific and concrete through the use of examples. In "Snoopers at Work," the thesis comes at the end of paragraph 4:

> A combination of technological advances, employer paranoia, and commercial avarice means that many millions of Americans are having their lives delved into in ways that would have been impossible, not to say unthinkable, a dozen years ago.

Here are two other sample thesis statements that also make generalizations:

> Teenagers use various forms of self-expression, including clothing, body art, and hairstyles, to establish their identity.

(The body of the essay would give examples of each form.)

Effective decision making in the workplace requires two essential skills: planning and assessment.

(The body of the essay would give examples of situations in which each skill is used.)

Reading ⓘ Writing   Thesis Statements and Generalizations in an Illustration Essay

The Reader's Perspective	The Writer's Perspective
When reading an illustration essay, identify the thesis or generalization and observe how it is supported and explained through examples.	When writing an illustration essay, focus on composing a clear and effective statement of your thesis or the generalization you're making. Highlight the thesis/generalization and refer back to it often as you revise, checking to make sure that each example in your essay supports it.

2. THE BODY PARAGRAPHS CONTAIN SUPPORTING EXAMPLES IDENTIFIABLE THROUGH A CLEAR ORGANIZATION AND TRANSITIONS

To maintain readers' interest, writers must select their examples carefully, and they must provide a sufficient number of examples to make their points understandable and believable. Examples in illustration essays should be relevant, representative, detailed, complete, and striking. They should also be appropriate in length and number, and they should be suited to the purpose and intended audience. They may explore unfamiliar topics or help to explain difficult concepts or terms. Finally, the examples must be ordered logically and introduced to the reader by logical transitions.

Examples Should Be Relevant   Examples should clearly demonstrate the point or idea the essay illustrates. For instance, the thesis that publicly funded and operated preschool programs should be expanded should be supported with examples of public programs, not private ones. If you reread Bryson's essay, you will notice that every example is relevant to the topic of business snooping.

Examples Should Be Representative   Typical cases, not specialized or unusual ones, often best support an essay's main point. In many essays, several representative examples are necessary. Note that Bryson's essay talks about the common or typical types of everyday snooping—in retail stores, in office buildings, at a college, in workers' everyday lives—and provides specific examples of each.

Examples Should Be Detailed and Complete   For readers to understand the connection between the generalization and the examples, the examples must be thoroughly explained. Illustration essays that report statistics should do so objectively and provide enough information so that readers can evaluate the reliability of the data. Bryson provides specific statistics in paragraphs 6 and 10: Two-thirds of U.S. companies spy on their employees, 35 percent track phone calls, 10 percent tape phone conversations, and 91 percent test some of their workers for drugs.

Examples Should Be Striking   A good illustration essay includes examples that capture readers' attention and make a vivid impression.

Generic example	snooping on campus
Vivid example	A secretary at a Massachusetts college discovered a hidden video camera was filming her office twenty-four hours a day. Goodness knows what the school authorities were hoping to find. What they got were images of the woman changing out of her work clothes and into a track suit each night in order to jog home from work.

Examples Should Be Appropriate in Length and Number   The appropriate number of examples depends on how complex the generalization—or thesis—is. For a focused thesis statement, a single, extended example may be sufficient.

In New York, a wealthy city, pollution can be severe in poor neighborhoods. Consider the South Bronx.

An extended discussion of conditions in the South Bronx would clearly explain and support the thesis. Consider, on the other hand, the thesis of Bryson's essay. It contains three distinct generalizations—technological advances, employer paranoia, and commercial avarice—that require multiple examples.

Either method (a single example or multiple examples) can be effective, as long as the material included serves to adequately support the thesis.

Examples Should Be Suited to the Purpose and Audience   Audience and purpose are key factors in deciding what types of examples to include. Suppose you want to persuade readers that the Food and Drug Administration should approve a new cancer drug. If your audience is composed of physicians, the most effective examples would include clinical studies and technical explanations of how the drug works and what the potential side effects are. But if your audience is the general public, it would be better to include personal anecdotes about lives being saved because of the drug's effectiveness. Note that the intended audience of Bryson's essay is the "common person" or "everyday traveler"—the examples are intended to convey the message "In the United States, this could happen to you."

Examples May Explore Unfamiliar Topics or Help to Explain Difficult Concepts or Terms   Examples may be particularly useful in helping the reader explore a new topic or understand a challenging idea. Note that Bryson's essay explores two key terms that readers are likely not acquainted with: *TAD* (paragraph 10) and *active badge* (paragraph 11).

Reading ⬤ Writing   Examples in an Illustration Essay

The Reader's Perspective	The Writer's Perspective
When reading an illustration essay, be sure you understand how the example or examples support the thesis. Also analyze and evaluate the examples using the criteria explained in "Understanding, Analyzing, and Evaluating Illustration Essays" (pp. 281–84).	When writing an illustration essay, select examples that best support your thesis. As you review your examples, don't hesitate to revise or entirely change your thesis.

Examples Should Be Organized Effectively   All good essays use a clear method of organization. Often, illustration essays employ one of the organization methods discussed in Chapter 7: most-to-least, least-to-most, chronological, or spatial order. For instance, in an essay explaining how teenagers today typically dress, the examples might be arranged spatially, starting with footwear (such as flip-flops) and moving upward to facial piercings and hairstyles.

In some instances, illustration essays use a secondary pattern of development, such as definition, classification and division, or comparison and contrast. Bryson's essay includes many descriptions, but he also uses definition (to explain TAD and active badges) and cause/effect (to explore the effects of snooping on individual workers and the companies themselves, which are sometimes sued for invasion of privacy).

Examples Should Make Use of Transitions   Effective illustration essays use clear **transitions** to guide the reader from example to example or from one aspect of an extended example to the next. Transitional words and phrases particularly useful for illustration essays include the following:

another example	for instance	such as
for example	in another situation	to illustrate

Reading ⬤ Writing   Organization and Transitions in an Illustration Essay

The Reader's Perspective	The Writer's Perspective
When reading an illustration essay, examine how the essay is organized and use the organization to guide you through the reading. Watch for transitions that signal the next example.	When writing an illustration essay, use an outline or graphic organizer to help you plan and organize your examples and transitions.

3. THE CONCLUSION PRESENTS A FINAL STATEMENT AND REINFORCES THE THESIS

The conclusion usually returns to or references the generalization and makes a final statement that draws the essay to a close. Bryson ends his essay on a humorous note, pointing to the one example of employee snooping that he supports—probably because it affects him directly, and in a positive way. (But would he feel the same way if he were a restaurant employee?)

Reading ⊕ Writing The Conclusion of an Illustration Essay

The Reader's Perspective	The Writer's Perspective
As a reader, pay attention to whether the writer has logically connected the examples and whether the examples lead to the stated conclusion.	As a writer, be sure to give your readers a sense of unity and closure, perhaps by referring back to one or more examples. Be sure to refer to your generalization by restating it, suggesting further directions to pursue, or expanding on it.

Understanding, Analyzing, and Evaluating Illustration Essays

In reading and writing illustration essays, your goal is to get beyond mere competence. That is, you want to do more than merely understand the content of the essays you're reading or convey just your basic ideas to the audience you're writing for.

📊 Understanding an Illustration Essay

To understand an illustration essay—that is, to understand the point it's making—focus on the thesis and the examples used to support the thesis. Use the reading skills you learned in Chapter 2, as well as the following questions, to assist you.

- **What is the essay's thesis?** Read the essay to identify the thesis or generalization.
- **What examples does the author use to illustrate the thesis?** As you read, take note of each example offered to support that generalization. Highlight the examples as you read. If the author uses one extended example, be sure to identify all aspects of that example.
- **How is the essay organized?** Draw a diagram that shows the structure of the essay and the sequence of ideas. Figure 12.2 provides a diagram of the structure of Bryson's essay. Refer back to the model graphic organizer for illustration essays (Figure 12.1) before starting your own.

Figure 12.2   Graphic Organizer for "Snoopers at Work"

Title	Snoopers at Work

| Introduction | **Background:** Example of changing-room surveillance; reference to book *The Right to Privacy* |
| | **Thesis:** Technology, employer paranoia, and commercial greed have resulted in increasing invasions of privacy for many Americans. |

Body paragraphs	**Example 1:** Medical-record surveillance
	Example 2: Phone and computer surveillance
	Example 3: Video surveillance
	Example 4: Drug-use entrapment
	Detail: Personal anecdote about a friend who experienced entrapment
	Example 5: TAD rules
	Example 6: "Active badge" tracking

| Conclusion | Humorous approval of surveillance of restaurant employees washing hands after using lavatory |

Understanding in Action

Exercise 12.1

Following is one student's brief summary of paragraph 3 of Bill Bryson's "Snoopers at Work" (pp. 274–76).

> The issue of spying on customers changing their clothes in department store dressing rooms began when a man in a dressing room was observed by a store worker and sued the store, claiming his right to privacy had been violated. A state court ruled that it was legal for the store to conduct surveillance.

Use the completed graphic organizer in Figure 12.2 to write your own brief summary of Bryson's entire essay.

📊 *Analyzing an Illustration Essay*

Analyzing an illustration essay involves investigating *how* the essay works, not just the message it conveys. Whether you're reading someone else's essay or your own, analysis requires you to look closely at the examples and study their relationship to the thesis (or generalization). You may need to reread the essay, perhaps several times, considering each example first by itself and then in conjunction with the other examples. Here are key questions to ask:

- **How does each example illustrate the thesis?** As you read, note in the margin the aspect of the thesis that each example illustrates.

- **What kinds of examples did the author choose? Why? How do the examples suit the intended audience and the author's purpose?** Study the examples to discover how they appeal to the intended audience. Consider whether different examples might produce different results.

- **What is the emotional impact of the examples?** If an example stirs your emotions or evokes a response, ask how and why the writer chose this example. What was he or she attempting to accomplish?

- **What is the author's tone? How does the tone contribute to the essay's intended effect?** How does the author present the examples? Does he or she treat them seriously, comically, or in some other manner?

- **What type of evidence other than examples, if any, does the author offer in support of the thesis? What effect does this evidence have?** In many situations, a thesis can be supported effectively with facts, details, statistics, and expert opinion.

Analysis in Action

Exercise 12.2

Following are one student's annotations of an excerpt from Bill Bryson's essay.

Stat supports claim.	Already, 91 percent of large companies—I find this almost unbelievable—now test some of their workers for drugs.
Example would appeal to general audience—everyone works!	Scores of companies have introduced what are called TAD rules—TAD being short for "tobacco, alcohol, and drugs"—which prohibit employees from using any of these substances at any time, including at home. There are companies, if you can believe it, that forbid their
Author sounds upset here.	employees to drink or smoke at any time—even one beer, even on a Saturday night—and enforce the rules by making their workers give urine samples.

Using the Analyzing an Illustration Essay questions given above, make notes on Bryson's essay.

▥ Evaluating an Illustration Essay

Evaluate how well the examples in an illustration essay support the thesis by answering the following questions:

- **Is each example accurate and clearly presented?** That is, are the examples believable and documented, if necessary? Are all relevant aspects of the example well explained?

- **Are the examples representative or exceptional?** That is, are the examples used to support the thesis typical, or are they rare or unusual? If they are *not* typical, do they negatively affect the essay's persuasiveness?

- **Are all the examples relevant?** Do they relate specifically to the thesis?

- **Are there enough examples to fully explain the generalization?** Are more examples needed to demonstrate that the generalization applies to a wide variety of situations?

- **Can you think of any examples that have been omitted that would contradict the author's thesis and should have been taken into account?** Be sure the writer offers fair and objective examples, not examples that show only one side of an issue or viewpoint.

Evaluation in Action

Exercise 12.3

The student whose annotations are shown in Analysis in Action used them to write the following evaluation of that same paragraph.

> This paragraph is relevant to Bryson's thesis that employers invade employees' privacy. It shows that companies force employees to behave in certain ways even when they're not at work. He uses a statistic to make the example seem common, which is persuasive. However, he doesn't say how many companies forbid alcohol and smoking on the weekend. His examples appeal to his audience. As newspaper readers, they are likely to be employed and would probably not like the idea of their employer spying on them.

Using Figure 12.2 (p. 282), the Evaluating an Illustration Essay questions above, and your annotations analyzing Bill Bryson's "Snoopers at Work," write an evaluation of the whole piece.

Writing Your Own Illustration Essay

Now that you have learned about the major characteristics, structure, and purposes of an illustration essay, you know everything necessary to write your own. In this section, you will read a student's illustration essay and get advice on finding ideas, drafting your essay, and revising and editing it. You may want to use the essay prompts in "Readings for Practice, Ideas for Writing" (p. 292) or choose your own topic.

A Student Model Illustration Essay

Assigned to write an essay about a current issue in the United States for a writing course, Kaitlyn Frey decided to focus on food waste, an issue that is especially problematic in light of the number of people in the United States who desperately need food to eat. Frey used her personal experience, her observations, and some research-based information to write this illustration essay. As you read, pay attention to how she uses her examples to illustrate three major groups who contribute to this issue.

Title: Frey indicates the topic and suggests the focus of the essay.

Introduction: Frey provides background information and explains the seriousness of food waste.

Thesis: Frey presents the main idea she will illustrate.

Example 1: ordered but uneaten food in restaurants

Waste, Away!

Kaitlyn Frey

Have you ever looked down after a big meal, only to see a significant amount of food still left on your plate? Do you ever order more than you know you can eat, just so you can have a little bit of everything? Do you know that saying "your eyes are bigger than your stomach"? These are all illustrations of a growing problem in the United States: food waste. But the problem is not confined to the United States. With an ever-increasing global population, food scarcity is one of the primary issues facing the world today. According to the USDA, the United States alone wastes more than 130 billion pounds of food per year, which is in excess of $160 billion down the drain. Food waste is a problem that has many contributors; the consumer, the vendors, and even the producers play a key role in the issue.

Perhaps the most apparent example of food waste is ordered but uneaten food in restaurants. Imagine a person sitting in a McDonald's with a tray full of half-eaten food. Chances are, when he ordered his food, he believed that he could eat the entire burger, all the fries and his shake. He might even convince himself that he must finish the food before he leaves, even if he is not hungry

Detail: Consumers with uneaten food must decide whether to take it home or waste it.

anymore. However, more likely, he does not finish his meal and must decide whether he has enough to take home for leftovers or whether he even wants to take part in the leftovers. To put this into perspective, "1 in 4 calories intended for consumption is never actually eaten" due to consumer food waste (United Nations).

Detail: Frey suggests alternatives to food waste.

Now imagine a scene in which not a single morsel from the meal mentioned above went to waste. There are initiatives being designed by organizations like the Food Waste Alliance, which is developing and publishing literature to educate consumers on how to reduce the amount of food waste they produce each year. Practices like composting organic materials, recycling cooking oil, and even bulk donating fruit and vegetable scraps to farmers to feed animals are just a few of the methods the Food Waste Alliance is promoting to create better habits around food and food waste for the average consumer. Educating consumers on how to reduce their food waste is the first step in solving the problem.

Example 2: vendors' contribution to food waste

The consumer is not the only one at fault; vendors are also contributing to the problem of food waste. Vendors play a key role in the oversupply of portions and eventual waste of leftovers.

Detail: Food service establishments waste food that cannot be re-served.

Restaurants and other establishments where food is served waste a high volume of perfectly decent and often untouched portions of meals because they cannot serve this food back to someone else once it has been discarded by the original recipient. Think about the dining hall on a University campus, catering to over 25,000 students. There are calculations that go into the amount of food prepared for every meal; however, there is always human error, which leads to food waste. At the end of the meal, inevitably there is food that is left unserved but cannot be salvaged or saved to serve at another meal.

Transition:

Transitions keep reader on track.

In the dining hall scenario, what if that food left over at the end of the day was donated to a food bank or a homeless shelter? What if it could be packaged up and given as take-away meals at a church? Universities across the country have pondered this question. Stanford University's SPOON has volunteers take the uneaten food from campus eateries and cafeterias to a freezer center, where it is then distributed to families who need it most. Stanford is not unique. The Campus Kitchens Project has chapters all across the country devoted to reducing the amount of food waste universities produce by redistributing the unused food back into the needy sections of the community.

Example 3: misunderstanding of expiration and sell-by dates

The third example of food waste is a product of the expiration and sell-by dates that are placed on products by producers and manufacturers. In fact, these dates are often not regulated by the Food and Drug Administration (FDA). Furthermore, the laws

Detail: Shoppers throw out edible food because of the date.

that the FDA administers do not preclude the sale of food that is past the expiration date indicated on the label, as these dates are entirely determined by the manufacturer (FDA). Often, this date is the date the item must be sold by, rather than when the food is no longer edible, so the shopper throws out perfectly good food because of a date. For example, let's say a gallon of milk has a sell-by date of August 12. In reality, that gallon of milk is good until August 19—a full week after the sell-by date—but chances are that by August 12 that gallon of milk has been pulled both from the shelf in the store and off the shelf of the refrigerator of the buyer.

Detail: Frey uses research to further support example 3.

The Food Waste Alliance has done some research on these sell-by dates as well as the consumers' role in food waste. It seems the date posted on the food is more about the quality than the ability for the food to be eaten or donated. Rather than throwing that food away, many grocery stores, such as Walmart and Trader Joe's, are partnering with organizations like Food Finders and Feed America to get the food to those who need it most.

Conclusion: Frey sums up the food waste issue and calls for change.

While food waste continues to be a problem in our society, the major issue seems to be that people are uneducated or unwilling to contribute to the solution. Hunger is 100% preventable in the United States. If consumers take a look at their daily habits and consumption, they may find small ways to adjust their eating habits in order to prevent food from being left over or thrown out. Restaurants and grocers alike can take into account what to do with left-over or excess food that is still good and work to get it to those who need it. There are steps that everyone needs to take to reduce waste, and many of them do not require a high level of commitment. With more attention to the subject, and realistic ways to create change, the entire world can benefit from the discontinuation of wasteful practices. It's time to do away with waste and work toward more sustainable living.

Sources: Frey properly cites sources in MLA format.

Works Cited

United Nations Environment Programme, Regional Office of North America. "Food Waste: The Facts." *World Food Day*, United Nations, 16 Oct. 2015, www.worldfooddayusa.org/food _waste_the_facts.

United States, Food and Drug Administration (FDA). "Did You Know That a Store Can Sell Food Past the Expiration Date?" *FDA Basics*, U.S. Department of Health and Human Services, 28 Sept. 2015, www.fda.gov/AboutFDA/Transparency/Basics /ucm210073.htm.

Responding to Frey's Essay

1. What is Frey's purpose in opening the essay with three questions?
2. How does Frey's thesis statement predict the essay's organization?
3. For what purpose does Frey use research in her essay?
4. Explain the double meaning of the title.
5. What specific details in the conclusion reemphasize the key points of the essay?

Finding Ideas for Your Illustration Essay

When you are asked to write an illustration essay, keep an eye out for ideas to write about as you read. While reading "Snoopers at Work," for instance, you might have thought about your own experience with surveillance. What surveillance issues concern you? What type of surveillance is acceptable? What's your stance on antiterrorism-related wiretapping in the United States? How do you feel about parental surveillance of children, especially their Internet use? When does that surveillance violate children's privacy, and when is it for their own good? Each of these examples could lead you to a thesis and ideas for writing.

Choosing a Subject for Your Illustration Essay

Your first step is to choose a subject and then narrow it to a manageable topic that can be supported by one or more examples. Use the characteristics of an illustration essay described in this chapter to help you find a topic that is specific, yet expansive enough that you can make a generalization and support it with detailed, relevant evidence.

Gathering Examples for Your Illustration Essay

Once you are satisfied with your subject, you'll need to generate examples that illustrate it. As you do so, begin to think about the generalization that will become your thesis. As you work, you may think of situations that illustrate a different or more interesting thesis than the one you first had in mind. Take advantage of such developments, which will make your thesis and essay better.

Here are a few techniques you can use to generate examples.

- **Brainstorm examples that relate to your subject.** Jot down all instances or situations you can think of that are relevant to your subject and that illustrate your tentative thesis.

- **Visualize situations that illustrate your subject.** Close your eyes and imagine situations, images, stories, or scenes that relate to your subject.

- **Use your memory.** Systematically review your life—year by year, place by place, or job by job—to recall situations that illustrate the topic.
- **Talk to someone else.** Discuss your tentative thesis with a classmate. Try to match or improve on each other's examples.
- **Research your topic.** At the library or on the Internet, search to discover examples outside your own experience.

Developing and Supporting Your Thesis

The next step is to develop a working thesis about the narrowed topic by making a generalization about it. The thesis in an illustration essay expresses the idea that all your examples will support. For examples of thesis statements for an illustration essay, see "The Introduction Presents the Topic, Provides Background Information, and Includes the Thesis Statement" on page 276.

Drafting Your Illustration Essay

As you draft your essay, refer to the graphic organizer in Figure 12.1 (p. 277) to remind yourself of the elements of an illustration essay. Use the following suggestions to write effective drafts.

1. **Begin with a clear introduction and thesis statement.** In most illustration essays, the thesis is stated in the first paragraph. In addition to stating the generalization the essay will illustrate, your introduction should spark readers' interest and include background information about the topic.

2. **Remember that each paragraph should express one key idea; the example(s) or details in that paragraph should illustrate that key idea.** Develop the body paragraphs so that each one presents a single example or a group of closely related examples or details about the extended example.

3. **Use the topic sentence in each paragraph to identify the particular point that each example or set of examples or details makes.**

4. **Provide sufficient detail about each example.** Explain each one with vivid descriptive language. Your goal is to make readers feel as if they were experiencing or observing the situation themselves.

5. **Use transitions to move from one idea to another.** Without transitions, your essay will seem choppy and disconnected. Use transitions such as *for example* and *in particular* to keep readers on track when you move to a new example or detail.

6. **End with an effective conclusion.** Your essay should conclude with a final statement that pulls your ideas together and reminds readers of your thesis. In less formal writing situations, you may end with a final example—as Bryson does in "Snoopers at Work"—as long as it effectively concludes the essay and reminds readers of the thesis.

Revising Your Illustration Essay

If possible, set aside your draft for a day or two before rereading and revising it. As you reread and review, concentrate on organization, level of detail, and overall effectiveness—not on grammar or mechanics. Use the flowchart in Figure 12.3 to discover the strengths and weaknesses of your illustration essay.

Editing and Proofreading Your Essay

The last step is to check your revised essay for errors in grammar, spelling, punctuation, and mechanics. In addition, look for the types of errors you commonly make in writing assignments, whether for this class or in other situations. Check the handbook (pp. 645–714) for assistance with common errors in your writing.

Figure 12.3 Revising an Illustration Essay

QUESTIONS	REVISION STRATEGIES

1. Thesis statement Does your thesis clearly indicate the generalization that your examples support?

No →
- Revise your thesis so that the generalization fits your examples.

Yes ↓

2. Audience Will your examples appeal to your audience? After eliminating those that do not, do you have enough left?

No →
- Brainstorm examples that will appeal to your audience, and add them to your essay.

Yes ↓

3. Purpose Do all of your examples fulfill your purpose? After eliminating those that do not, do you have enough left?

No →
- Brainstorm examples that are more appropriate to your purpose, and add them to your essay.

Yes ↓

4. Examples Is each one relevant, representative, detailed, and striking? Are they varied?

No →
- Eliminate irrelevant, unrepresentative, or dull examples.
- Brainstorm or conduct research to discover better examples.
- Add details to vague examples.
- Omit misleading examples.
- Consider adding other kinds of examples.

Yes ↓

5. Topic sentences Does each paragraph have a topic sentence that clearly states the point that the paragraph develops?

No →
- Add a topic sentence or revise the existing one to clearly indicate the paragraph's point.
- Reorganize examples according to the idea they demonstrate.

Yes ↓

6. Organization Is your organization clear and effective? Do you use transitional phrases to make it clear?

No →
- Add or revise transitions to make your organization clear.
- Consider using a different organization strategy from Chapter 7.

Yes ↓

7. Introduction and conclusion Is each effective?

No →
- Revise each so that they meet the guidelines on pages 136–39.

Readings for Practice, Ideas for Writing

What Happened to Innovation?

Michael Hanlon was a British science journalist who wrote for *The Sunday Times* and *The Daily Telegraph.* He also authored several popular science books, one being *Including Eternity: Our Next Billion* Years. "What Happened to Innovation?" was first published in *Aeon Magazine.* The excerpt included in this chapter appeared in the January 16, 2015 issue of *The Week,* a British online and print news magazine.

Reading Tip

As you read, identify the thesis statement and notice whether each example directly supports it. Also notice whether Hanlon provides adequate details about each example.

Previewing the Reading

Preview the reading (see pp. 28–29 for guidelines), and then answer the following questions.

1. What is the subject of the essay?
2. What innovative event in space travel is discussed throughout the essay?
3. What question about progress does the author seek to answer in the essay?

What Happened to Innovation?

Michael Hanlon

We live in a golden age of technological, medical, scientific, and social progress. Look at our computers! Look at our phones! Twenty years ago, the Internet was a creaky machine for geeks. Now we can't imagine life without it. Life expectancy in some rich countries is improving by five hours a day. A day! Surely immortality, or something very like it, is just around the corner.

The notion that our 21st-century world is one of accelerating advance is so dominant that it seems churlish to challenge it. Almost every week, we read about "new hopes" for cancer sufferers, developments in the lab that might lead to new cures, talk of a new era of space tourism, and superjets that can fly around the world in a few hours. Yet a moment's thought tells us that this vision of unparalleled innovation can't be right, that many of these breathless reports of progress are in fact mere hype, speculation—even fantasy.

Yet there once was an age when speculation matched reality. It spluttered to a halt more than 40 years ago. Most of what has happened since has been merely incremental improvements upon what came before. That true age of innovation—I'll call it the Golden Quarter—ran from approximately 1945 to 1971. Just about everything that defines the modern world either came about or had its seeds sown during this time. The pill. Electronics. Computers and the birth of the Internet. Nuclear power. Television. Antibiotics. Space travel. Civil rights.

There is more. Feminism. Teenagers. The green revolution in agriculture. Decolonization. Popular music. Mass aviation. The birth of the gay rights movement. Cheap, reliable, and safe automobiles. High-speed trains. We put a man on the moon, sent a probe to Mars, beat smallpox, and discovered the double-spiral key of life.

5   Today, progress is defined almost entirely by consumer-driven, often banal improvements in information technology. Sure, our phones are great, but that's not the same as being able to fly across the Atlantic in eight hours or eliminating smallpox. As the technologist Pete Thiel once put it: "We wanted flying cars; we got 140 characters."

But surely progress today is real? Well, take a look around. The airliners you see are basically updated versions of the ones flying in the 1960s— slightly quieter Tristars with better avionics. In 1971, a regular airliner took eight hours to fly from London to New York City; it still does. And in 1971, there was one airliner that could do the trip in three hours. Now, Concorde is dead. Our cars are faster and safer and use less fuel than they did in 1971, but there has been no paradigm shift.

And yes, we are living longer, but this has disappointingly little to do with any recent breakthroughs. Since 1970, the U.S. government has

NASA

We landed on the moon in 1969, and then began retreating from space.

spent more than $100 billion in what President Richard Nixon dubbed the War on Cancer. Far more has been spent globally. Despite these billions of investment, this has been a spectacular failure. In the U.S., the death rates for all kinds of cancer dropped only 5 percent in the period 1950–2005. The blunt fact is that, with most kinds of cancer, your chances of beating it in 2014 are not much better than they were in 1974. In many cases, your treatment will be pretty much the same.

For the past 20 years, as a science writer, I have covered such extraordinary medical advances as gene therapy, cloned replacement organs, stem-cell therapy, life-extension technologies, the promised spin-offs from genomics and tailored medicine. None of these new treatments is yet routinely available. The paralyzed still cannot walk, the blind still cannot see. The human genome was decoded (one post-Golden Quarter triumph) nearly 15 years ago, and we're still waiting to see the benefits that, at the time, were confidently asserted to be "a decade away."

Continued >

There has been no new green revolution. We still drive steel cars powered by burning petroleum spirit or, worse, diesel. There has been no new materials revolution since the Golden Quarter's advances in plastics, semiconductors, new alloys, and composite materials. After the dizzying breakthroughs of the early to mid-20th century, physics seems (Higgs boson aside) to have ground to a halt. And nobody has been to the moon for 42 years.

10   But why *has* progress stopped?

One explanation is that the Golden Age was the simple result of economic growth and technological spin-offs from the Second World War. It is certainly true that the war sped the development of several weaponizable technologies and medical advances. The *Apollo* space program probably could not have happened without the aerospace engineer Wernher von Braun and the V-2 ballistic missile. But penicillin, the jet engine, and even the nuclear bomb were on the drawing board before the first shots were fired. They would have happened anyway.

Conflict spurs innovation, and the Cold War played its part—we would never have gotten to the moon without it. But someone has to pay for everything. The economic boom came to an end in the 1970s with the collapse of the 1944 Bretton Woods trading agreements and the oil shocks. So did the great age of innovation. Case closed, you might say.

And yet, something doesn't quite fit. The 1970s recession was temporary; we came out of it soon enough. What's more, in terms of Gross World Product, the world is two to three times richer now than it was then. There is more than enough money for a new *Apollo*, a new Concorde, and a new green revolution. So if rapid economic growth drove

innovation in the 1950s and '60s, why has it not done so since?

It is possible that the advances we saw in the period 1945–1971 were quick wins and that further progress is much harder. Going from the prop-airliners of the 1930s to the jets of the 1960s was, perhaps, just easier than going from today's aircraft to something much better.

But history suggests that this explanation is fanciful. During periods of   15 technological and scientific expansion, it has often seemed that a plateau has been reached, only for a new discovery to shatter old paradigms completely. The most famous example was when, in 1900, Lord Kelvin declared physics to be more or less over, just a few years before Einstein proved him comprehensively wrong.

Lack of money, then, is not the reason that innovation has stalled. What we do with our money might be, however. Today, wealth is concentrated in the hands of a tiny elite. The richest 1 percent of humans own half the world's assets. That has consequences. Firstly, there is a lot more for the hyperrich to spend their money on today than there was in the golden age of philanthropy in the 19th century. The superyachts, fast cars, private jets, and other gewgaws of Planet Rich simply did not exist when people such as Andrew Carnegie walked the earth and, though they are no doubt nice to have, these fripperies don't much advance the frontiers of knowledge.

As success comes to be defined by the amount of money one can generate in the very short term, progress is defined not by making things better but by rendering them obsolete as rapidly as possible so that the next iteration of phones, cars, or operating systems can be sold to a willing market.

In particular, when share prices are almost entirely dependent on growth (as opposed to market share or profit), built-in obsolescence becomes an important driver of "innovation." Half a century ago, makers of telephones, TVs, and cars prospered by building products that their buyers knew (or at least believed) would last for many years. No one sells a smartphone on that basis today; the new ideal is to render your own products obsolete as fast as possible.

But there is more to it than inequality and the failure of capital.

20   During the Golden Quarter, we saw a boom in public spending on research and innovation. Nearly all the advances of this period came either from tax-funded universities or from popular movements. The first electronic computers came not from the labs of IBM but from the universities of Manchester and Pennsylvania. The early Internet came out of the University of California, not Bell or Xerox. In short, the great advances in medicine, materials, aviation, and spaceflight were nearly all pump-primed by public investment. But since the 1970s, an assumption has been made that the private sector is the best place to innovate.

And yet we cannot pin the stagnation of ingenuity on a decline in public funding. Tax spending on research and development has, in general, increased in real and relative terms in most industrialized nations even since the end of the Golden Quarter. There must be another reason why this increased investment is not paying more dividends.

Could it be that the missing part of the jigsaw is our attitude toward risk? Nothing ventured, nothing gained, as the saying goes. Many of the achievements of the Golden Quarter just

The life spans of machines keep getting shorter.

wouldn't be attempted now. The assault on smallpox, spearheaded by a worldwide vaccination campaign, probably killed several thousand people, but it saved tens of millions more. In the 1960s, new medicines were rushed to market. Not all of them worked, and a few (thalidomide) had disastrous consequences. But the overall result was a medical boom that brought huge benefits to millions. Today, this is impossible.

The time for a new drug to gain approval in the U.S. rose from less than eight years in the 1960s to nearly 13 years by the 1990s. Many promising treatments now take 20 years or more to reach the market.

Apollo almost certainly couldn't happen today. That's not because people aren't interested in going to the moon anymore but because the risk—calculated at a couple-of-percent chance of astronauts' dying—would be unacceptable. Boeing took a huge risk when it developed the 747, an extraordinary 1960s machine that went from drawing board to flight in under five years. Its modern equivalent, the Airbus A380, first flew in 2005—15 years after the project go-ahead. Scientists and technologists were generally celebrated 50 years ago, when people

Continued >

remembered what the world was like before penicillin, vaccination, modern dentistry, affordable cars, and TV. Now, we are distrustful and suspicious—we have forgotten just how dreadful the world was pre–Golden Quarter.

25   Does any of this really matter? So what if the white heat of technological progress is cooling off a bit? The world is, in general, far safer, healthier, wealthier, and nicer than it has ever been. The recent past was grim; the distant past disgusting. Levels of violence in most human societies were falling well before the Golden Quarter and have continued to decline since.

We are living longer. Civil rights have become so entrenched that gay marriage is being legalized across the world, and any old-style racist thinking is met with widespread revulsion. The world is better in 2014 than it was in 1971.

And yes, we have seen some impressive technological advances. The modern Internet is a wonder, more impressive in many ways than *Apollo*. We might have lost Concorde, but you can fly across the Atlantic for a couple days' wages— remarkable. Sci-fi visions of the future often had improbable spacecraft and flying cars but, even in *Blade Runner*'s Los Angeles of 2019, Rick Deckard had to use a pay phone to call Rachael.

But it could have been so much better. If the pace of change had continued, we could be living in a world in which Alzheimer's was treatable, where clean nuclear power had ended the threat of climate change, where the brilliance of genetics was used to bring the benefits of cheap and healthy food to the bottom billion, and where cancer really was on the back foot. Forget colonies on the moon; if the Golden Quarter had become the Golden Century, the battery in your magic smartphone might even last more than a day.

Understanding and Reviewing the Reading

1. **Topic** What is the main topic of the selection?

2. **Main idea** What is the main idea Hanlon is trying to convey about the topic?

3. **Detail** Give three examples of what we now consider modern progress that Hanlon says are not progress at all. (Hint: See paragraphs 6 through 9.)

4. **Detail** Explain why lack of money is not the reason that progress and innovation have stalled. (Hint: See paragraphs 12 through 16.)

5. **Detail** Hanlon writes of products that are created to become obsolete as quickly as possible. What are some of the relatively newly created products that fit into this category? (Hint: See paragraphs 17 and 18.)

6. **Detail** What examples of risks that led to innovations does Hanlon discuss? (Hint: See paragraphs 21 and 22.)

7. **Vocabulary** Using context clues (see Chapter 2, p. 37), write a brief definition of each of the following words as it is used in the reading, checking a dictionary if necessary: *banal* (para. 5), *paradigm* (6), *obsolescence* (18), *ingenuity* (20), and *entrenched* (24).

8. **Organization** To analyze the examples used in Hanlon's essay, complete the graphic organizer that follows.

Title	What Happened to Innovation?
Introduction	**Background**: Examples of why we think our current age is so innovative
	Thesis statement: Just about everything that defines the modern world either came about or had its seeds sown during this time [1945–1971].

▼

Body paragraphs	**Example 1:**
	Example 2:
	Example 3:
	Example 4:

▼

Conclusion	Our current age has many positive aspects, especially social ones, but Hanlon asserts that our lives could be even better with the spirit of technological innovation that drove what he calls the "Golden Quarter."

Analyzing the Reading

1. **Audience** To whom do the examples used by Hanlon appeal? Describe his intended audience.
2. **Evidence** How does each example support Hanlon's thesis?

Evaluating the Reading

1. **Evidence** Are all Hanlon's examples relevant to his claim that innovation and progress have stalled?
2. **Tone** Describe the tone of the piece. How does it help or hinder the author's thesis?

Discussing the Reading

1. With your classmates, discuss whether you agree or disagree with Hanlon's assertion that we don't have many innovations today outside of technology. Give your reasons.
2. Hanlon asks the question "Does any of this [lack of innovation] really matter?" (para. 23). What do you think? Discuss this question with your

classmates. Be sure to back up your answer with examples from your own experience.

3. Hanlon writes, "We [Americans] landed on the moon in 1969, and then began retreating from space." Since then, our space travel budget has been cut and our explorations have been less than spectacular. Do you consider the lack of or stall in space exploration to be a problem in the United States? Should we more aggressively extend our reach to outer space, or should we be content to rest with the knowledge we already have? Discuss this topic with your classmates and support your position with valid reasons.

Writing about the Reading

1. **Paragraph** Brainstorm a list of the innovations/inventions that have come about during your lifetime. Then write a paragraph in which you present the innovation/invention that you think has had the most impact on the world and explain the reasons you believe it to be so important. Your topic sentence might begin, "Although there have been many inventions during my lifetime, I believe that the single most important invention is . . . ." Draft your paragraph using the strong and logical reasons to support your topic sentence.

2. **Paragraph** You may not be an inventor, a computer genius, or an aerospace engineer, but you do have the capacity to make your world a better place in which to live. Write a paragraph explaining what you can do to improve your world. Your draft should include examples of why doing this would benefit others.

3. **Essay** Michael Hanlon says, "There has been no green revolution" in our world. As stewards of our resources, it's up to us to begin the revolution in our little spheres of influence—our homes, schools, communities, etc. Devise a green initiative for your school, and write an essay describing the details of your plan. Begin by brainstorming possible plans and their details. Choose the plan that seems most workable. Write a clear thesis statement, such as "[Name of your program] is a campus-wide recycling plan designed to build student interest and commitment through competition." Then draft your essay, being sure to include examples of how your plan would work.

Hey Mom, Dad, May I Have My Room Back?

Cristina Rouvalis's essays and articles have appeared in such magazines as *Inc., AARP Bulletin, Pittsburgh Quarterly, Carnegie Mellon Today*, and *Carnegie Magazine*. She has also been a staff writer for the *Pittsburgh Post-Gazette*, where the following piece appeared in August 2008.

Reading Tip

As you read the selection, look for and highlight the examples Rouvalis uses to support her thesis.

Previewing the Reading

Preview the reading (see pp. 28–29 for guidelines), and then answer the following questions.

1. What trend among college graduates does this reading address?
2. Why is this trend necessary or popular?

CRISTINA ROUVALIS

Hey Mom, Dad, May I Have My Room Back?

Bobby Franklin Jr., confident and energetic, seemed on a trajectory to an independent life—going to college, moving into an off-campus apartment, and jumping into the banking industry just weeks after his last final exam. Only, the Clarion University graduate circled back home like a boomerang[1]. Inside his parents' elegant five-bedroom house in Plum, he has settled into a roomy bedroom, with its own staircase leading outside. His return home has raised nary an eyebrow with his peers. After all, he said, most of his friends have moved home, too. "Everyone is doing it. No one says, 'Why are you still at home?'" said the twenty-four-year-old. "I never get that. It is

[1] **boomerang** A wooden object that can be thrown so as to return to the thrower.

more like, 'Stay at home as long as you can and save.'"

Some parents who pondered the loneliness of empty-nest syndrome are facing a surprising new question. When will their young adult children leave home—and this time for good? The sight of a college graduate moving into his or her childhood bedroom, filled with dusty high school trophies and curling rock-star posters, is no longer an oddity. A sour economy, big college loans, and sky-high city rents have made some new graduates defer their plans to strike out on their own.

Boomerangers, as they are called, are everywhere you look. Some 14.5 million children age eighteen to twenty-four lived at home in 2007, up from 6.4 million in 1960, according to U.S. Census figures. To be sure, much of the increase simply reflects overall population growth—as the actual percentage of men living at home is up only slightly, from 52% in 1960 to 55% in 2007. The bigger change has occurred with women. Nearly half in this age range were living at home in 2007, up from 35% nearly a

Continued >

half century ago—a shift attributed in part to the delay in marriage.

Other reports suggest the number of boomerangers is even higher—and has grown as a tough economy has made it harder for debt-laden college grads to find jobs. Some 77% of college graduates who responded to an unscientific readers' survey by the online entry job site CollegeGrad.com said they were living with mom and dad in 2008, up from 67% in a 2006 survey. "We see a larger percentage of Gen-Yers or Millennials, or whatever tag we want to use, have a closer relationship to their parents and feel more comfortable relying on parental support," said Heidi Hanisko, director of client services for CollegeGrad.com. "There is less of a stigma than there was five or ten years ago. We see that as a good thing that college grads are willing to go to their parents for support, but we encourage students to stand on their own. It seems

the reliance can be too much and spill over on their ability to do the job."

Others also wonder if this gen- 5 eration is coasting and letting their parents do too much. But Jeffrey Jensen Arnett, author of *Emerging Adulthood: The Winding Road from the Late Teens through the Twenties*, is tired of hearing all the judgments against the Boomerang generation. Most of them move home for a year or two while they go through a transition and a period of self-discovery— waiting for graduate school, looking for a fulfilling career option, paying down a huge loan, or saving enough so they can afford big-city rent. "People jump to the conclusion that they are lazy and irresponsible and pampered and self-indulgent," said Dr. Arnett, a research professor at Clark University in Worcester, Massachusetts. "It is not true. Think about the ones you know. Are they lazy? Do they stand around

Laptop in hand, Bobby Franklin moves about his room at his parents' home in Plum. A recent graduate of Clarion, Mr. Franklin says his dream job would be in pharmaceutical sales.

in their underwear watching TV? No. They are out working their bottoms off trying to make money in these crummy jobs available to them in their twenties."

"Grandma's Boy"

Mike Masilunas's old childhood bedroom—the one with photos of him fly-fishing and Jerome Bettis playing football—was converted into an office inside his family's Peters house. So when Mr. Masilunas, a graduate of Penn State Erie, moved home in May of 2007, he had to share a room with his older brother. In the musical bedrooms of his household, Mr. Masilunas later took over his younger sister's bedroom when she headed off to college. "We joke about the movie *Grandma's Boy*, hanging out all the time, sleeping on the couch," said Mr. Masilunas, referring to the comedy about the guy who gets evicted from his apartment and moves in with his grandmother.

The twenty-three-year-old financial consultant said it made sense to live at home because it is close to his office. Plus, there is the matter of $40,000 in student loans. "I can put $600 toward school loans instead of rent," he said. "Rather than living for right now, I am thinking about a house and retirement. I can put up with this for a few years." Most of his friends understand because they are at home too. Sometimes he catches flak. "You gotta get out of there," one friend told him recently. "The ones who give me flak are the ones spending money like idiots," he said. "They are also the same ones who complain about not having money."

And there are trade-offs to his rent-free existence. He gets along well with his parents and pitches in with chores, but it is an adjustment to go from total freedom to being under his mother's watch. "A mother will always be a mother. They only want the best for you. They are always nagging you. I kind of zone it out. 'Do this. Do that.' The first month it was like, 'Let's pull back the reins a little bit.'" Plus there is the culture shock of going from a college campus to a quiet residential neighborhood—something Brenna O'Shea experienced after graduating from West Virginia University and heading back to her parents' home in Mt. Lebanon.

Even though the twenty-one-year-old Ms. O'Shea has plenty of company—most of her friends from elementary school have done the same thing—she misses the energy of the campus. Her first night back in Mt. Lebanon, she caught herself yelling a little on the street. "I had to check myself." "It can be a hard adjustment both ways," Dr. Arnett said. "If children regret coming home, it is not because of the stigma. They like their parents and their parents like them. But they want to make their own decisions without parental commentary. Parents aren't that crazy about it either. They like not knowing. If they don't have any idea what time their kids come home or who they are with, ignorance is bliss."

In the Franklin home, Jan and 10
Bobby Franklin, parents of Bobby Jr., can't help but worry about their son when he is out. Even so, they like having him around, especially since he follows the house rules of picking up after himself. Mrs. Franklin knows another mother who put her thirty-year-old son's mattress on the porch, a not-so-subtle hint to fly on his own. "I could never do that to my son—as long as he is not causing any problems." Still mother and son have a standing joke about his boomerang back home.

"When are you going to move out?" she asks Bobby Jr.

Bobby, who plans to leave in a year or two, quips back, "I am not going anywhere until I am at least thirty."

Understanding and Reviewing the Reading

1. **Detail** What difficulties do boomerangers experience when they move back home?

2. **Detail** How do parents respond to their children moving back in?

Analyzing the Reading

1. **Audience** What audience is Rouvalis addressing? How do her examples address this audience?

2. **Evidence** What other types of supporting evidence, in addition to examples, does Rouvalis use?

3. **Tone** What is the author's attitude toward boomerangers?

4. **Evidence** Analyze Rouvalis's use of examples by completing the following chart. For each example, indicate what information it adds to the author's thesis.

Example	What It Contributes
Franklin (paras. 1, 10–12)	
Masilunas (paras. 6–8)	
O'Shea (paras. 8–9)	

5. **Visuals** Look carefully at the photograph that accompanies the essay. How is the subject presented in the photo? What does it suggest about the author's tone? How is the tone of the photo similar to or different from the tone of the essay itself?

Evaluating the Reading

1. **Purpose** Express Rouvalis's thesis in your own words. Is it directly stated in the essay? If not, should it be?

2. **Evidence** The essay opens with an example that illustrates the topic and then returns to it in the final paragraph. Why is this an effective technique?

3. **Evidence** Does Rouvalis provide enough examples to support her thesis? Are these examples fair and representative of the situation that college graduates face?

4. **Evidence** Rouvalis includes statistics from the U.S. Census and from an "online entry job site." How trustworthy do you consider each of these sources to be?

5. **Evidence** What information, if any, is not presented that would help you understand the situation more completely?

Discussing the Reading

1. What would be the most compelling reason for you or someone you know to live with parents after college?

2. With your classmates, discuss what adult children and parents could do to make living together easier.

3. Brainstorm options, other than moving back home, for adult children who cannot afford to live on their own.

4. Given current economic conditions, do you expect the numbers of boomerangers to increase or decrease in the next year? Justify your answer.

Writing about the Reading

1. **Essay** Mike Masilunas explains that he's willing to put up with some of the problems of living with his parents in order to get the benefits of the situation. Describe a decision you made to put up with the problems associated with something (other than living with your parents) in order to experience the benefits. Use the benefits as examples to support your thesis.

2. **Essay** Family members of different generations have often been forced or chosen to live together; elderly parents moving in with their adult children (and often with their grandchildren as well) is an example of one such arrangement. Write an essay discussing either the problems or the benefits of multigenerational households, other than those containing boomerangers. Give examples from your own experience or observations to support your thesis.

3. **Essay** Write an essay describing and giving examples of the long-term effects on boomerangers of moving back in with their parents. How will their lives be affected? (Hint: You might consider how delaying marriage and childbearing will affect them and how their feelings of independence and self-worth will be affected.)

Just Walk On By: A Black Man Ponders His Power to Alter Public Space

Brent Staples (b. 1951) is a journalist who has written numerous articles, essays, and editorials, as well as a memoir, *Parallel Time: Growing Up in Black and White* (1994). Staples holds a Ph.D. in psychology and is currently a member of the editorial board at the *New York Times.* This essay was first published in *Harper's* magazine in 1986.

Reading Tip

As you read the selection, highlight or underline the author's thesis and the examples he uses to support it.

Previewing the Reading

Preview the reading (see pp. 28–29 for guidelines) to discover what the public space referred to in the title is and how the author has the power to "alter" it.

Just Walk On By: A Black Man Ponders His Power to Alter Public Space

Brent Staples

My first victim was a woman—white, well dressed, probably in her early twenties. I came upon her late one evening on a deserted street in Hyde Park, a relatively affluent neighborhood in an otherwise mean, impoverished section of Chicago. As I swung onto the avenue behind her, there seemed to be a discreet, uninflammatory distance between us. Not so. She cast back a worried glance. To her, the youngish black man—a broad six feet two inches with a beard and billowing hair, both hands shoved into the pockets of his bulky military jacket—seemed menacingly close. After a few more quick glimpses, she picked up her pace and was soon running in earnest. Within seconds she disappeared into a cross street.

That was more than a decade ago. I was twenty-two years old, a graduate student newly arrived at the University of Chicago. It was in the echo of that terrified woman's footfalls that I first began to know the unwieldy inheritance I'd come into—the ability to alter public space in ugly ways. It was clear that she thought herself the quarry of a mugger, a rapist, or worse. Suffering a bout of insomnia, however, I was stalking sleep, not defenseless wayfarers. As a softy who is scarcely able to take a knife to a raw chicken—let alone hold one to a person's throat—I was surprised, embarrassed, and dismayed all at once. Her flight made me feel like an accomplice in tyranny. It also made it clear that I was indistinguishable from

Continued >

the muggers who occasionally seeped into the area from the surrounding ghetto. That first encounter, and those that followed, signified that a vast, unnerving gulf lay between nighttime pedestrians—particularly women—and me. And I soon gathered that being perceived as dangerous is a hazard in itself. I only needed to turn a corner into a dicey situation, or crowd some frightened, armed person in a foyer somewhere, or make an errant move after being pulled over by a policeman. Where fear and weapons meet—and they often do in urban America—there is always the possibility of death.

In that first year, my first away from my hometown, I was to become thoroughly familiar with the language of fear. At dark, shadowy intersections, I could cross in front of a car stopped at a traffic light and elicit the *thunk, thunk, thunk, thunk* of the driver— black, white, male, or female— hammering down the door locks. On less traveled streets after dark, I grew accustomed to but never comfortable with people crossing to the other side of the street rather than pass me. Then there were the standard unpleasantries with policemen, doormen, bouncers, cabdrivers, and others whose business it is to screen out troublesome individuals *before* there is any nastiness.

I moved to New York nearly two years ago and I have remained an avid night walker. In central Manhattan, the near-constant crowd cover minimizes tense one-on-one street encounters. Elsewhere—in SoHo, for example, where sidewalks are narrow and tightly spaced buildings shut out the sky— things can get very taut indeed.

5   After dark, on the warrenlike streets of Brooklyn where I live, I often see women who fear the worst from me.

They seem to have set their faces on neutral, and with their purse straps strung across their chests bandolier-style, they forge ahead as though bracing themselves against being tackled. I understand, of course, that the danger they perceive is not a hallucination. Women are particularly vulnerable to street violence, and young black males are drastically overrepresented among the perpetrators of that violence. Yet these truths are no solace against the kind of alienation that comes of being ever the suspect, a fearsome entity with whom pedestrians avoid making eye contact.

It is not altogether clear to me how I reached the ripe old age of twenty-two without being conscious of the lethality nighttime pedestrians attributed to me. Perhaps it was because in Chester, Pennsylvania, the small, angry industrial town where I came of age in the 1960s, I was scarcely noticeable against a backdrop of gang warfare, street knifings, and murders. I grew up one of the good boys, had perhaps a half-dozen fistfights. In retrospect, my shyness of combat has clear sources.

As a boy, I saw countless tough guys locked away; I have since buried several, too. They were babies, really—a teenage cousin, a brother of twenty-two, a childhood friend in his mid-twenties—all gone down in episodes of bravado[1] played out in the streets. I came to doubt the virtues of intimidation early on. I chose, perhaps unconsciously, to remain a shadow— timid, but a survivor.

The fearsomeness mistakenly attributed to me in public places often has a perilous flavor. The most frightening of

[1] **bravado** Display of courage and self-confidence.

these confusions occurred in the late 1970s and early 1980s, when I worked as a journalist in Chicago. One day, rushing into the office of a magazine I was writing for with a deadline story in hand, I was mistaken for a burglar. The office manager called security and, with an ad hoc posse[2], pursued me through the labyrinthine[3] halls, nearly to my editor's door. I had no way of proving who I was. I could only move briskly toward the company of someone who knew me.

Another time I was on assignment for a local paper and killing time before an interview. I entered a jewelry store on the city's affluent Near North Side. The proprietor excused herself and returned with an enormous red Doberman pinscher straining at the end of a leash. She stood, the dog extended toward me, silent to my questions, her eyes bulging nearly out of her head. I took a cursory look around, nodded, and bade her good night.

10   Relatively speaking, however, I never fared as badly as another black male journalist. He went to nearby Waukegan, Illinois, a couple of summers ago to work on a story about a murderer who was born there. Mistaking the reporter for the killer, police officers hauled him from his car at gunpoint and but for his press credentials would probably have tried to book him. Such episodes are not uncommon.

Black men trade tales like this all the time.

Over the years, I learned to smother the rage I felt at so often being taken for a criminal. Not to do so would surely have led to madness. I now take precautions to make myself less threatening. I move about with care, particularly late in the evening. I give a wide berth to nervous people on subway platforms during the wee hours, particularly when I have exchanged business clothes for jeans. If I happen to be entering a building behind some people who appear skittish, I may walk by, letting them clear the lobby before I return, so as not to seem to be following them. I have been calm and extremely congenial on those rare occasions when I've been pulled over by the police.

And on late-evening constitutionals[4] I employ what has proved to be an excellent tension-reducing measure: I whistle melodies from Beethoven and Vivaldi and the more popular classical composers. Even steely New Yorkers hunching toward nighttime destinations seem to relax, and occasionally they even join in the tune. Virtually everybody seems to sense that a mugger wouldn't be warbling bright sunny selections from Vivaldi's *Four Seasons*. It is my equivalent of the cowbell that hikers wear when they know they are in bear country.

---

[2] **ad hoc posse** Group formed for a special purpose.
[3] **labyrinthine** Intricate, mazelike.

[4] **constitutionals** Regular walks, often for health benefits.

Understanding and Reviewing the Reading

1. **Detail** Explain how Staples alters public space and why it happens.
2. **Detail** Staples considers himself a "survivor" (para. 7). To what does he attribute his survival?
3. **Language** Explain the analogy of cowbells and hikers used in the last sentence of the essay.
4. **Language** Beginning with the word *victim* in paragraph 1, Staples uses a number of terms that relate to hunting or pursuit. Find several other words or phrases that carry this connotation. How do they shape the reader's attitude toward Staples's subject?

Analyzing the Reading

1. **Organization** In addition to illustration, what other patterns does Staples use to organize his essay? Explain how the pattern or patterns are used.
2. **Language** Staples uses descriptive language to make his examples engaging and striking. Find several places where he does so. In each place, how does the descriptive language contribute to the effectiveness of the example?
3. **Structure** Staples opens and closes his essay with examples. Is this an effective way to begin and end? What other ways might be equally or more effective?
4. **Evidence** Staples's essay is based on personal experiences. What other types of evidence could he have used to support his thesis?
5. **Tone** How do Staples's tone and attitude change as the essay progresses? What could account for this change?

Evaluating the Reading

1. **Inference** What advice might Staples offer to others at risk of racial profiling?
2. **Voice** If the incidents in this essay were reported by an uninvolved third-person narrator rather than told by Staples in the first person, how would the essay's impact change?
3. **Evidence** What additional details might have made the essay even more realistic, convincing, or compelling?
4. **Themes** This essay was written several decades ago. Evaluate how closely it reflects current reality with regard to the issues Staples raises. To what extent, if at all, have public perceptions of black men and their effect on public space changed since Staples wrote this piece?

5. **Audience** Define Staples's intended audience. Are the examples that Staples provides appealing to and appropriate for this audience? (Hint: *Harper's* magazine is a general-interest periodical that explores issues of national concern, including politics, society, the environment, and culture.)

Discussing the Reading

1. Staples's "unwieldy inheritance" gives him the power to alter public space. Discuss some other ways that people can alter public space and how they use that power.

2. Why do you think whistling tunes by Beethoven or Vivaldi makes Staples's presence less threatening? Analyze his choice of music in relation to his purpose and audience. According to your analysis, what other strategies might work to make him less intimidating?

3. Why does Staples mention his upbringing on the mean streets of Chester, Pennsylvania? How does his experience growing up in a tough neighborhood affect his perspective on the issues he raises in this essay? Discuss this with your classmates.

Writing about the Reading

1. **Essay** Staples describes himself as a "survivor" (para. 7) of the streets he grew up on. In a sense, everyone is a survivor of certain decisions or circumstances that, if they had played out differently, might have resulted in misfortune or, at least, a different direction in life. Using illustration, write an essay that explains a situation in which you were a survivor.

2. **Essay** Rewrite Staples's essay from the point of view of his "first victim," using illustrative techniques. Include a thesis that makes a generalization, and provide supporting examples. (Tip: You might begin with a thesis statement such as "An experience that I had on a December night in Chicago made me realize the extent to which I engage in racial stereotyping.") You might include the woman's background, past experiences, and emotional state. Discuss how encountering Staples on the street affects her and whether she changes her behavior as a result of the experience.

3. **Using Internet research** Visit the part of the American Civil Liberties Union Web site that deals with racial profiling (www.aclu.org/racialjustice /racial-profiling) or another site of your choice that deals with the topic. Using what you learn from the Web site, along with your own knowledge and experience, write an essay that takes a position or makes a recommendation on racial profiling. Be sure to include examples to support your thesis.

📖 **COMBINING THE PATTERNS | TEXTBOOK EXCERPT: ART APPRECIATION**

Issue-Oriented and Street Art

Patrick Frank is adjunct professor of visual and public art at California State University, Monterey Bay. He is the author of *Prebles' Artforms: An Introduction to the Visual Arts,* the textbook from which this reading was taken. His recent scholarly work is devoted to Latin American graphic artists.

Reading Tip

As you read this textbook excerpt, look for language that is particular or unique to the field of visual arts.

Previewing the Reading

Preview the reading (see pp. 28–29 for guidelines), and write a list of three things you expect to learn from it.

Issue-Oriented and Street Art

Patrick Frank

Today the public accepts most modern art. Exhibitions of work by such former rule-breaking radicals as Henri Matisse, Paul Gauguin, Paul Cézanne, and Claude Monet fill museums with visitors. Nine of the ten most expensive paintings ever sold at auction are modern works (three each by Picasso and van Gogh; one each by Cézanne, Renoir, and Jackson Pollock). The modern-style Vietnam Veterans Memorial is a national shrine. Modern art is no longer controversial.

The impact of this situation is not yet clear. Art of our own time is always the most difficult to evaluate. In general, most artists of the present generation do not appear intent on perfecting form, creating beauty, or fine-tuning their sense of sight. They mostly want to comment on life in all of its aspects. They want to create work that illuminates the relationships between what we see and how we think. Rather than being objects of timeless beauty, most art since the 1980s consists of objects laden with information about the period in which we live. This article will present two movements of the present generation.

Issue-Oriented Art

Many artists in the past twenty years have sought to link their art to current social questions. Issue-oriented artists believe that if they limit their art to aesthetic[1] matters, then their work will be only a distraction

---

[1] **aesthetic** Concerned with what is beautiful or pleasing in appearance.

from pressing problems. Furthermore, they recognize that what we see influences how we think, and they do not want to miss an opportunity to influence both.

Photographer Richard Misrach presents new kinds of landscape in new ways. His photograph *Submerged Lamppost, Salton Sea* captures the silent yet ironic beauty of a small town in California that was flooded by a misguided irrigation system. In other works he has documented in chilling detail the bloated carcasses of animals killed on military proving grounds in Nevada. His brand of nature photography is the opposite of the common calendars that include soothing views of pristine landscapes. He wants us to know that such scenes are fast disappearing.

Barbara Kruger. *Untitled* (*I Shop Therefore I Am*). 1987. Photographic silkscreen/vinyl. 111″ × 113″. Courtesy Mary Boone Gallery, New York.

5

Barbara Kruger was trained as a magazine designer, and this profession shows in her piece *Untitled* (*I Shop Therefore I Am*). She invented the slogan, which sounds as though it came from advertising. The position of the hand, too, looks like it came from an ad for aspirin or sleeping medication. Do our products define us? Are we what we shop for? Often we buy a product because of what it will say about us and not for the thing itself. These are some of the messages present in this simple yet fascinating work. Perhaps its ultimate irony is that the artist had it silkscreened[2] onto a shopping bag.

Artists who create works about racism and class bias show how common practices of museum display contribute to such problems. In 1992, the Maryland Historical Society invited African American artist Fred Wilson to rearrange the exhibits on one floor to create an installation[3] called *Mining the Museum*. He spent a year preparing for the show, rummaging through the Society's holdings and documentary records; the results were surprising. He found no portraits, for example, of noted African American Marylanders Benjamin Banneker (who laid out the boundaries of the District of Columbia), Frederick Douglass (noted abolitionist and journalist), or Harriet Tubman (founder of the Underground Railroad). He found instead busts of Henry Clay, Andrew Jackson, and Napoleon Bonaparte, none of whom ever lived in Maryland. He exhibited those three busts next to three empty pedestals to symbolize the missing African Americans. He set out a display of colonial Maryland silverware and tea utensils, and included a pair of slave shackles. This lesser-known form of

---

[2] **silkscreened** Printed using a special stencil process.
[3] **installation** A work of art made up of multiple components, often in different media, and exhibited in an arrangement specified by the artist.

Continued >

metalwork was perhaps equally vital to the functioning of nineteenth-century Maryland. He dusted off the Society's collection of wooden cigar-store Indians and stood them, backs to the viewers, facing photographs of real Native Americans who lived in Maryland. In an accompanying exhibition brochure he wrote that a museum should be a place that can make you think. When *Mining the Museum* went on display, attendance records soared.

The Swiss-born Thomas Hirschhorn took up the issue of the Iraq war, but only indirectly, in the context of today's media-saturated society. His 2006 installation *Superficial Engagement* filled the entire gallery space with a *dizzying* array of objects that resembled a parade float on drugs, or a cross between an insane asylum and a grocery store. Photos of mangled war dead competed for space with coffins, nail-studded mannequins, blaring headlines, and reproductions of abstract artworks. The nailed bodies refer to traditional African magic sculptures, and the abstract art was mostly copied from the Austrian mystic Emma Kunz in what the artist called "friendly piracy." The headlines shout the aimless alarmism of cable news channels: "Decision Time Approaches," "Broken Borders," "An Assault on Hypocrisy," "The Real Crisis." The artist used only cheap materials (cardboard, plastic, plywood, package tape) in an effort to avoid art-world pretense and make it more accessible. He said of his brash style, "Art is a tool, a tool to encounter the world, to confront the reality and the time I am living in." The shrill volume of this exhibition only paralleled the strident intensity of today's news, where a disaster might follow a fashion show. At the opening reception, the artist provided hammers and screwdrivers, and the crowd joined in attaching nails and screws, thus finishing the piece.

Street Art

In the late 1990s, many galleries in various cities began to exhibit work by artists who had previously made illegal graffiti. Many of these "street artists" were based in the culture of skateboards and Punk music, and they used materials bought at the hardware store rather than the art supply house. Their creations were only rarely related to gang-oriented graffiti, which usually marks out territories of influence. Nor were they autobiographical or personal. Rather, the street artists made much broader statements about themselves and the world in a language that was widely understandable. The ancestors of the movement in the 1980s were Keith Haring and Jean-Michel Basquiat, both of whom worked illegally for years before exhibiting in galleries. By the turn of the twenty-first century, Street Art was a recognized movement, and most of its main practitioners work both indoors and out.

The career of Shepard Fairey is exemplary. He studied at the Rhode Island School of Design, but was never satisfied in the art world, which seemed to him closed-off and elitist. He began working outdoors, and quickly acquired notoriety for posting dozens of signs and stickers with the single word "Obey" below the ominous-looking face of wrestler Andre the Giant. His vocabulary soon expanded to include advertising symbols, propaganda posters, and currency, even as the scale of his work increased to billboard size.

His 2006 work *Revolution Girl* is an antiwar mural created on a legal wall for a three-month show in West Hollywood. The dominant motif is a huge female Communist soldier from the Vietnam War that the artist borrowed from Chinese propaganda, but her rifle has a flower protruding; her weapon has become an elaborate vase. Other motifs from Chinese propaganda decorate the center right, repurposed for a peace campaign. In the lower corner, posters of a female face with flowery hair symbolize nurturing. The message of the mural is antiwar, but the artist made the statement positive rather than negative, expressing the hope that we can convert our weapons into flower holders. His friend and fellow street artist Blake Marquis provided the vivid leafy patterns at the left. . . .

Some of today's most skillful street art is created by Swoon, a woman who uses the pseudonym to avoid prosecution. She carves large linoleum blocks and makes life-sized relief prints from them, usually portraits of everyday people. She prints them on large sheets of cheap (usually recycled) newsprint and pastes them on urban walls, beginning on the Lower East Side of Manhattan but now in cities on every continent. Her *Untitled* installation at Deitch Projects was a recent indoor work. Against objections that her work is mostly illegal, she replies that her creations are far easier to look at than advertising, that they lack any persuasive agenda, and that they glorify common people. Moreover, the newsprint that she uses decays over time so that her work is impermanent. Although she works mostly outdoors, she sometimes

Dan De Kleined/Alamy

Continued >

shows in galleries because, she admits, "I have to make a living," but she charges far less for her work than most other artists of wide repute.

Probably the most famous street artist is Banksy (who also uses a pseudonym). He placed his own art in the collections of several major museums in 2005 by merely entering the galleries and sticking his pieces to the wall. His street graffiti is generally witty, as we see in his *Graffiti Removal Hotline, Pentonville Road*. There is no such thing as a graffiti removal hotline; the artist stenciled the words and then created the youth who seems to paint out the phone number. Banksy is currently one of the most popular artists in England, and many of his outdoor works have been preserved. When a prominent work of his was recently defaced by another graffiti artist, protests ensued and the defacer was arrested for vandalism! Thus street artists often blur the line between legal and illegal.

Understanding and Reviewing the Reading

1. **Textbook reading** In the reading, highlight important information you would need to learn for an art-history exam based, in part, on it.

2. **Language** What terminology specific to the art field is used in this reading? Select five words (other than those defined in the footnotes) that would be important in an art-history course. Write the meaning of each.

3. **Organizing textbook information** Other than highlighting, what strategies might you use to organize information from this reading about the artists and their works so as to better learn and recall it for an exam? Use one of these strategies to create a study guide for this piece.

Analyzing the Reading

1. **Combining the patterns** Although Frank organizes this piece of writing using the pattern of illustration, he also infuses his writing with vivid description. Identify at least five particularly descriptive phrases that contribute to the effectiveness of the essay. Explain what image or feeling each creates.

2. **Predicting exam questions** A useful way to prepare for an essay exam is to predict possible questions your instructor might ask and then to practice answering them. Compose several essay-exam questions that would likely appear on an exam covering "Issue-Oriented and Street Art."

3. **Similarities and differences** In what ways is this textbook excerpt similar to and different from other illustration essays included in this chapter?

4. **Expert opinion** The opinion of experts is known as "informed" opinion. Patrick Frank, the author of this textbook reading, is an expert in the field of art, and an example of his informed opinion is that the "shrill volume of

[Hirschhorn's] exhibition only paralleled the strident intensity of today's news, where a disaster might follow a fashion show" (para. 7). While considered trustworthy, different experts may present differing opinions on an issue. Identify several other statements of informed opinion in the reading. For each, discuss what further evidence might be helpful in analyzing the opinion.

Evaluating the Reading

1. **Visuals** How important and useful are the visuals included in this chapter? Choose one and explain how it is used.

2. **Value of information** Do you think that this selection taught you something useful? Explain your answer.

3. **Evidence** Write a paragraph evaluating the effectiveness of illustration as it is used in this reading. Consider each of the characteristics of illustration explained on pages 276–81; discuss whether the characteristic is evident in the reading and, if so, what it contributes or what problems you see with it.

Discussing the Reading

1. Do you agree with Frank's interpretation of Kruger's *Untitled* (*I Shop Therefore I Am*)? Do you think that the products we purchase define us? Are there exceptions to this generalization?

2. In what circumstances can you envision art being "only a distraction from pressing problems" (para. 3)?

3. What is the author's attitude toward modern artists in contrast to classic art masters?

4. What similarities and differences do you observe between issue-oriented art and street art? How does the notion of "impermanent art" fit with your definition of art?

Writing about the Reading

1. **Essay-exam question** Choose one of the questions you predicted in Analyzing the Reading question 2 (p. 314) and write an essay answering it.

2. **Response paper** In art classes, students are often asked to understand, analyze, evaluate, and respond to a particular work. Choose one of the pieces of art included in this excerpt and write a response to it. Explain what it accomplishes and how it affects you or what feelings or ideas it draws out.

3. **Using Internet research** Explore the Los Angeles street art gallery at lastreetartgallery.com, or locate other sites that focus on such art. View some examples of street art and form a thesis about the value, function, or purpose of this art form. Write an essay explaining your thesis and supporting it with examples drawn from the art you viewed.

Working with Illustration as a Reader and Writer

The following table reviews the key elements of illustration essays and explains how these elements are important to both readers and writers.

Reading ⊕ Writing   Illustration Essays

Element of an Illustration Essay	The Reader's Perspective	The Writer's Perspective
Bringing Ideas to Life	As you read, take note of particularly vivid examples that help you connect the topic to your own life and experiences.	An illustration essay offers you an opportunity to generate excitement about, or interest in, a topic about which the reader has little knowledge or curiosity.
Clarifying Unfamiliar or Difficult Topics, Concepts, or Terms	Underline or highlight key terms and concepts as you read, and then mark the examples used to explain the topic. In the margin, write additional examples from your own experience to help cement the terms and concepts in your mind.	When writing to inform, your key goal is to explain information that may be unknown to the reader. Well-chosen examples are an extremely effective tool for making an abstract concept into something specific and concrete.
Connecting Readers and Writers	Active reading is a process of engaging with a text, of "talking back" to the author through active questioning and annotating. As you read, look for examples that provide common ground between you and the author. These are access points that can bridge the gap between reader and writer.	To be a good writer, you must actively seek to make connections with your readers—to use the tools of writing to provide a rewarding experience for your readers. Examples are one of the most important tools in your writing toolbox.

13

Process Analysis: Explaining How Something Works or Is Done

In this chapter, you will learn to

- Recognize the elements of process analysis.

- Identify the structure and content of process analysis essays.

- Understand, analyze, and evaluate process analysis essays.

- Write your own process analysis essay.

- Work with process analysis as a reader and a writer.

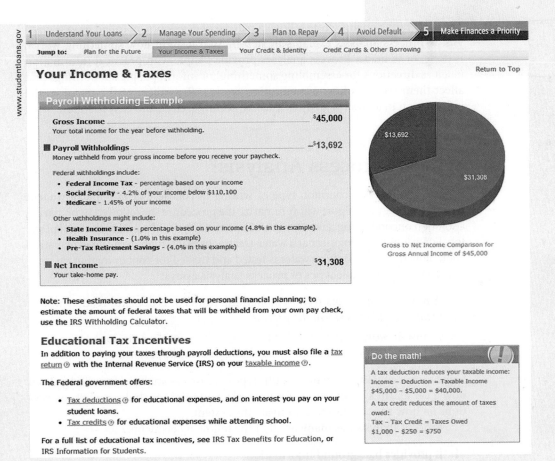

1 Understand Your Loans	2 Manage Your Spending	3 Plan to Repay	4 Avoid Default	5 Make Finances a Priority

Jump to: Plan for the Future   Your Income & Taxes   Your Credit & Identity   Credit Cards & Other Borrowing

Your Income & Taxes

Return to Top

Payroll Withholding Example

Gross Income — $45,000
Your total income for the year before withholding.

■ **Payroll Withholdings** — –$13,692
Money withheld from your gross income before you receive your paycheck.

Federal withholdings include:
- **Federal Income Tax** - percentage based on your income
- **Social Security** - 4.2% of your income below $110,100
- **Medicare** - 1.45% of your income

Other withholdings might include:
- **State Income Taxes** - percentage based on your income (4.8% in this example).
- **Health Insurance** - (1.0% in this example)
- **Pre-Tax Retirement Savings** - (4.0% in this example)

■ **Net Income** — $31,308
Your take-home pay.

$13,692

$31,308

Gross to Net Income Comparison for
Gross Annual Income of $45,000

Note: These estimates should not be used for personal financial planning; to estimate the amount of federal taxes that will be withheld from your own pay check, use the IRS Withholding Calculator.

Educational Tax Incentives

In addition to paying your taxes through payroll deductions, you must also file a tax return ⑦ with the Internal Revenue Service (IRS) on your taxable income ⑦.

The Federal government offers:

- Tax deductions ⑦ for educational expenses, and on interest you pay on your student loans.
- Tax credits ⑦ for educational expenses while attending school.

For a full list of educational tax incentives, see IRS Tax Benefits for Education, or IRS Information for Students.

Do the math!

A tax deduction reduces your taxable income:
Income – Deduction = Taxable Income
$45,000 – $5,000 = $40,000.

A tax credit reduces the amount of taxes owed:
Tax – Tax Credit = Taxes Owed
$1,000 – $250 = $750

Reflect on a Visual Text

This screen shot is from a Web site (**www.studentloans.gov**) that offers college students help managing their finances. As you know, the process of earning, saving, budgeting, and spending money involves important skills and has serious consequences.

1 **Ask yourself questions.** To which elements of the screen is your eye drawn first? Which part of the Web page would you read first? Does the Web page provide useful and practical information to help you understand income and taxes? Does it provide enough detail? Does it provide adequate examples?

2 **Brainstorm ideas.** Working alone or with a classmate, compile a list of the items and services on which you spend money in a typical week. (Be sure to include necessities like housing and utilities.) Which expenses take up the bulk of your income?

3 **Write.** Now write a paragraph describing your own process in deciding how to spend and/or save money. Include the steps you follow when budgeting each week or month.

The paragraph you just wrote follows a pattern of development called *process analysis*. A process analysis explains in step-by-step fashion how something works, is done, or is made. Process analyses provide people with practical information (such as directions for assembling something) or inform people about things that affect them (such as how a medication works). Regardless of the purpose, the information in a process analysis must be accurate, clear, and easy to follow.

What Is Process Analysis?

Process analysis is a common type of writing in college. For example, a student writing a biology lab report will summarize the procedure she followed in preparing a solution or conducting an experiment. Process analysis is helpful in the workplace, too. For example, an engineer at a water-treatment plant might write an explanation about how the city's drinking water is tested and treated for contamination.

There are two basic types of process analysis essays:

- A **how-to essay** explains how something works or is done for readers *who want or need to perform the process.*

- A **how-it-works essay** explains how something works or is done for readers *who want to understand the process but not actually perform it.*

Some essays contain elements of both types of process analysis. In writing about how a car alarm system works, for example, you might include explicit instructions on how to activate and deactivate the system.

Process analysis has many or all of the following elements:

1. It provides background information.
2. It defines technical terms.

3. It describes necessary equipment.

4. It anticipates trouble spots and offers solutions.

5. It provides an appropriate level of detail.

A Model Process Analysis Essay

The following essay will be used throughout this chapter to demonstrate strategies for reading and writing process analysis essays. Read it now, looking for the ways the writer uses the above process analysis techniques. Use the annotations in the margin to guide you.

How to Make Money with YouTube

Eric Rosenberg

Eric Rosenberg is a blogger who holds an MBA in finance. He has worked as a bank manager and in corporate finance and accounting. He is based in Portland, Oregon.

Process analysis provides background information: In the first paragraph, the author provides background information about YouTube as a source of revenue for people who make videos.

Most people think of YouTube as a place to find instructional videos, watch music videos, or waste time. Another group of people, however, look at YouTube as a major revenue  source for their online business. In fact, the highest paid YouTube channel is DC Toys Collector, who has earned $4.9 million with her channel DC Toys Collector. Making money with YouTube takes some time and effort, but those efforts can pay off with big money.

Create an Account and Turn on AdSense

The first step to making money with YouTube is to sign up for an account. If you have a Gmail account, or use any products that require a Google account, you already have an account to use that you just need to link to YouTube via the YouTube account page. Once your YouTube account is up and running, your next step is to link to an AdSense account. AdSense is the primary advertising engine Google uses on its own sites and partner sites, including YouTube. When you create your AdSense account, you will need to input payment information and provide tax reporting information such as a social security number or employer ID number (EIN) for your business.

Process analysis defines technical terms: Here the author defines a key term in the Internet world: *AdSense.*

Make Videos

Your next step is creating the actual videos. There is no universal model for what works and what doesn't work on YouTube. Some of the most popular content includes professionally produced music videos and impromptu family videos recorded with a smart phone. If you want to record with a phone, you likely already have your camera in your pocket. Recording in HD will produce a better quality video, so be sure to use the highest quality possible on your phone. If you want an even more professional video, you can use a DSLR camera and external microphone.

Process analysis describes necessary equipment: The author describes the equipment necessary to shoot and edit YouTube videos.

Once you finish recording, you can edit your video with a desktop program like the free Windows Movie Maker or iMovie, which comes with new computers, or a paid program like Adobe Premiere for more robust features. YouTube also has a free editor with basic features. As you edit your video, be sure you don't use copyrighted music. If you do, your videos won't be eligible for YouTube advertising.

Process analysis anticipates trouble spots and offers solutions: The author warns readers against using copyrighted music, which will make videos ineligible for YouTube advertising.

Upload to YouTube and Configure for SEO

Now that your video is complete, it is time to upload your video to the YouTube servers. You can drag and drop videos from your computer into the uploader, or you can add them individually by clicking on the upload arrow. Depending on the size of your video and your Internet connection, uploading could last anywhere from a few seconds to a few hours. You can upload multiple videos at a time as long as you do not close the upload page in your browser.

When your video is uploaded, or while it is uploading, you can fill out information about it. Be as detailed as possible when creating a title, description, category, and tags. YouTube is the second largest search engine in the world, and good search engine optimization (SEO) can be the difference between a few views and a few million views.

Promote Your Video

Process analysis provides an appropriate level of detail: In these two paragraphs, the author provides just enough detail to explain why the most popular videos make the most money and why promotion is important.

Now that your video is online, it's time to get the word out. Share your video on social networks, blogs, forums, message boards, and anywhere else you can online. You can embed your video on other sites or link to the video so viewers can watch it on YouTube. Just be careful to avoid spamming because that would result in fewer views for your videos.

Your AdSense earnings are determined by the number of views the video receives, which advertisers show up on your video, and how many times the ads are clicked. High engagement and clicks are more important than total views, but the more views you receive, the higher likelihood of clicks. Depending on your video's engagement levels, you can earn anywhere from 30 cents to $10 per 1,000 views. Making videos that people will actively watch until the end will earn you more than a video where people click away after only a few seconds.

The Bottom Line

As long as your videos are being watched, YouTube income is passive after the video is posted. Keep track of which videos perform the best and create videos with a similar topic. As your video library and views grow, so will your income.

The Structure and Content of Process Analysis Essays

In this section, you will learn about the structure of a process analysis essay and practice using the guidelines for understanding, analyzing, and evaluating process analysis essays. This key information will help you skillfully read and write essays that use process analysis.

A process analysis essay is structured so that the reader will understand or be able to perform the process after reading the essay. The introduction provides background, identifies the process, and usually includes an explicit thesis statement. Body paragraphs are often organized chronologically to present a clear, step-by-step description of the process. A conclusion draws the essay to a close and refers back to the thesis. Figure 13.1 represents these major structural components visually.

Figure 13.1   Graphic Organizer for a Process Analysis Essay

Title	
Introduction	Background information
	Thesis statement*

(arrow pointing down)

Body paragraphs: steps in the process	Step 1**
	Substep 1
	Substep 2
	Step 2
	Step 3
	Step 4

(arrow pointing down)

Conclusion	Draws essay to a close and refers back to the thesis

* In some essays, the thesis statement may be implied or may appear in a different position.
** In some essays, substeps may be included.

1. THE INTRODUCTION PROVIDES BACKGROUND, IDENTIFIES THE PROCESS, AND INCLUDES A THESIS STATEMENT

The introduction to a process analysis often contains background information that readers must have in order to understand the process being described. Eric Rosenberg's essay on making money with YouTube begins with background information about YouTube's popularity and the income it generates for people who upload videos. The author grabs the reader's attention with the example of DC Toys Collector, who has earned almost $5 million from YouTube.

The introduction usually contains a clear thesis that identifies the process to be discussed and suggests the writer's attitude or approach toward it. The thesis statement also tells why the process is important or useful. In Rosenberg's essay, the thesis appears in the last sentence of the first paragraph: "Making money with YouTube takes some time and effort, but those efforts can pay off with big money." This thesis statement implies that the essay will explain the process of using YouTube to make money.

Thesis statements for how-to process analyses suggest the usefulness or importance of the process. In a how-it-works essay, the writer either reveals why the information is worth knowing or makes an assertion about the nature of the process itself. "How to Make Money with YouTube" is a how-to essay. In fact, the words "how to" even appear in the title.

> **How-To Thesis:** Switching to a low-carbohydrate diet can improve weight control dramatically.
>
> (The body of the essay will inform readers of the steps to take to change their diets.)
>
> **How-It-Works Thesis:** Although understanding the grieving process will not lessen the grief that you experience after the death of a loved one, knowing that your experiences are normal does provide some comfort.
>
> (The body of the essay will explain the intricacies of the grieving process.)

Reading ⬤ Writing   Thesis Statement in a Process Essay

The Reader's Perspective	The Writer's Perspective
When reading a process essay, identify the process being explained and look for clues in the thesis statement about the value of the process. This will help you determine the most important information as you read.	When writing a process essay, be sure to make clear to your readers why they should care about and want to read the essay. Point out the value, importance, or usefulness of becoming familiar with the process.

2. THE BODY PARAGRAPHS EXPLAIN EACH STEP IN THE PROCESS, DEFINE TECHNICAL TERMS, DESCRIBE NECESSARY EQUIPMENT, AND POINT TO POSSIBLE TROUBLE SPOTS

All process essays must explain each step in the process. Some process essays also define technical terms, describe necessary equipment, and anticipate possible trouble spots.

Steps in the Process   The steps or events in a process analysis are usually organized in chronological order—that is, the order in which they are completed. Think of process analysis as being organized by the clock or calendar. A process essay presents what happens first in time, then what happens next in time, and so forth. Rosenberg's article follows a strict chronological order that begins with shooting the video and ends with earning money on YouTube. Note that the steps in the process correspond to the headings in the essay.

Step	Heading	Paragraph(s)
Step 1	Create an Account and Turn on AdSense	2
Step 2	Make Videos: • Shoot the video • Edit the video	3–4
Step 3	Upload to YouTube and Configure for SEO	5–6
Step 4	Promote Your Video	7–8

On occasion, the steps of a process may not have to occur in any particular order. For example, in an essay on how to resolve a dispute between two coworkers, the order may depend on the nature of the dispute. In this type of situation, recommended actions should be presented in some logical order, such as starting with informal or simple steps and progressing to more formal or complex ones.

The steps in a process analysis essay should provide just enough detail to satisfy the audience — not too much, not too little. The essay should not overwhelm readers with too many technical details. For example, an essay about how to perform CPR would be highly technical if written by and for physicians, but it would be less technical if written for paramedics and even less so if written for restaurant staff who need to be prepared for emergencies. No matter the circumstance, the analysis must include enough detail to show readers how to perform the steps of the CPR process.

Reading ⊕ Writing   The Steps in a Process

The Reader's Perspective	The Writer's Perspective
When reading a process essay, use transitional words and phrases as guides or markers. For complicated processes, stop after each step to mentally review what the process has involved thus far and consider what the new step contributes to the process. If a visual aid of the process is provided, use it to keep track of the steps in the process.	When writing a process essay, be sure to make it easy for your readers to identify and follow the steps. For complicated or lengthy processes, consider grouping the steps into stages, such as *before, during,* and *after* or *setting up, carrying out,* and *following up.* Use transitional words and phrases to guide your reader from step to step.

Technical Terms   In most cases, a writer will assume her audience is not familiar with technical terms associated with the process she is describing. In a process essay, it is necessary to define specialized terms. In describing how cardiopulmonary resuscitation (CPR) works, for instance, an essay would need to include meanings of such terms as *airway*, *sternum*, and *cardiac compression*. Note that Rosenberg's essay includes a couple of technical terms with which readers may not be familiar: *employer ID number (EIN)*, *search engine optimization (SEO)*. Because this essay is intended for a general readership, it might have benefited from a fuller explanation of these terms.

Necessary Equipment   When special equipment is needed to perform or understand the process, the writer must describe the equipment. If necessary, he should also mention where to obtain it. In an essay about how to make chili for a large group, for example, the writer should describe the specific materials necessary for cooking in bulk, as follows:

Special size pot for the particular task	To start off, you'll need a huge pot with a lid. Mine's a 32-quart monstrosity you could boil a cow's head in. (Don't ask how I know.) Cooking the chili in several smaller pots results in different kinds of chili — great, but not what
Additional equipment needed	we're looking for here. Beg, borrow, or rent a good large pot and lid for this one. Also essential are a knife, a cutting board, a cool drink (never cook without refreshment), and
Specific types of equipment that work best for the task	something for stirring the chili. A wooden spoon works great, as does a silicone spatula. Just don't use anything that'll melt in bubbling chili.

In his essay, Eric Rosenberg discusses the equipment needed to create videos: a smart phone or other camera; editing software like Windows Movie Maker, iMovie, or Adobe Premiere; and the YouTube servers.

Trouble Spots and Possible Solutions   Process analysis essays, especially how-to essays, must anticipate potential trouble spots or areas of confusion for readers and offer advice on how to avoid or resolve them. A how-to essay should also alert readers to difficult, complicated, or critical steps. In the following paragraph, the author anticipates problems readers might have doing sit-ups.

> Begin [the sit-up] by lying on your back with your arms crossed on your chest. Your knees should be bent at approximately 90-degree angles, with your feet flat on the floor. The complete sit-up is performed by bringing your chest up to touch your knees and returning to the original

Precaution 1: neck stress	lying position. . . . Two precautions should be mentioned. First, avoid undue stress on your neck during the "up" phase of the exercise. That is, let your abdominal muscles do the work; do not whip your neck during
Precaution 2: hitting head	the sit-up movement. Second, avoid hitting the back of your head on the floor during the "down" phase of the
Advice: Use a mat.	sit-up. Performance of the [exercise] on a padded mat is helpful.

> —Scott K. Powers and Stephen L. Dodd, *Total Fitness and Wellness*, 3rd ed.

Note that Eric Rosenberg cautions against using copyrighted music in paragraph 4 and against spamming in paragraph 7.

3. THE CONCLUSION DRAWS THE ESSAY TO A CLOSE AND SUMMARIZES THE VALUE OF THE PROCESS

Especially in how-it-works essays, simply ending with the final step in the process may leave readers with the feeling that the essay is incomplete. Therefore, a successful process analysis will emphasize the value or importance of the process, describe particular situations in which it is useful, or offer a final emphatic or amusing comment or anecdote. Rosenberg's essay introduces the conclusion with a heading, "The Bottom Line," leaving readers with the upbeat impression that they will be able to make good money by uploading videos to YouTube. The following conclusion to a different process analysis essay, describing why leaves change color in the fall, gives that process much more meaning:

Concluding step	At last the leaves leave. But first they turn color and thrill us for weeks on end. Then they crunch and crackle underfoot. They shush, as children drag their small feet through leaves heaped along the curb. Dark, slimy
Process provides a valuable reminder about life.	mats of leaves cling to one's heels after the rain. . . . Sometimes one finds in fossil stones the imprint of a leaf, long since disintegrated, whose outlines remind us how detailed, vibrant, and alive are the things of this earth that perish.

> —Diane Ackerman, *A Natural History of the Senses*

Reading ⓘ Writing   **The Conclusion of a Process Analysis**

The Reader's Perspective	The Writer's Perspective
When reading process essays, use the conclusion to gauge your understanding of the process. Mentally review the entire process, making sure you understand why or how each step is done. Doing so will help you remember it and be able to carry it out or discuss it with others.	When writing process essays, use your conclusion to set the importance or usefulness of the process firmly in your reader's mind. You might conclude with an interesting example that describes a situation in which knowing the process was helpful or essential. Another option is to condense the steps into a summary statement that will help your readers understand the information.

Understanding, Analyzing, and Evaluating Process Analysis Essays

In reading and writing process analysis essays, your goal is to get beyond mere competence. That is, you want to do more than merely understand the content of the essays you read or convey just your basic ideas to the audience you're writing for.

📊 *Understanding a Process Analysis Essay*

Begin by previewing the essay to find out what process is being explained and to get an overall sense of how complicated or complex it may be. Then consider how much, if anything, you already know about the process. These tasks will help you determine how to read the essay and what to look for.

Read complicated essays about unfamiliar topics slowly — and perhaps several times — highlighting each step. You may be able to read an essay that is about a familiar topic and offers general advice much faster, with less or no rereading. As you read and reread, use the skills you learned in Chapter 2 and look for the answers to the following questions:

- **What process is being explained, and what is the author's thesis?** The writer's view of why the topic is important or useful may suggest what parts of the process to pay most attention to.

- **Is it a how-to or how-it-works essay?** Your answer will determine what types of information are important to remember. For how-to essays, you need exact, detailed comprehension because you will be performing the process. For how-it-works essays, you need to understand the logic of the process, mechanical and technical aspects of executing it, and how steps relate to one another.

- **Can steps be grouped into larger categories?** For complicated or lengthy processes, categorize the steps and label those groupings in the margin.
- **Does the essay include cautions or warnings about difficult or troublesome steps?** You might highlight these in a different color.
- **Can you visualize the process?** For a how-to essay, imagine yourself carrying out the process. For a complex how-it-works essay, draw the object and label working parts. These techniques will cement the steps of the process in your memory and improve your recall. If a visual aid is provided, use it to aid your comprehension as you read.
- **Can you summarize the process?** To test whether you understand the process, try to summarize it without looking back at the essay. If you cannot, then you have not learned the process fully.

Figure 13.2 is a visual representation of Eric Rosenberg's "How to Make Money with YouTube."

Figure 13.2   Graphic Organizer for "How to Make Money with YouTube"

Title	How to Make Money with YouTube
Introduction	**Background**: Most people think of YouTube as a source of entertainment, but others see YouTube as an opportunity to make money.
	Thesis: Making money with YouTube takes some time and effort, but those efforts can pay off with big money.
Body paragraphs: steps in process	**Step 1**: Create an account and turn on AdSense
	Step 2: Make videos
	Step 3: Upload to YouTube and configure for search engine optimization (SEO)
	Step 4: Promote your video
Conclusion	Your income grows as more people watch your videos. To make more money, create more videos similar to your most popular videos.

Exercise 13.1

Following is one student's understanding of the main idea of
Eric Rosenberg's process analysis.

> Many of us see YouTube as a way to pass the time or find information, but
> Eric Rosenberg points out that a lot of people make money by creating
> videos and uploading them to YouTube. The more people who watch your
> videos and the ads that go with them, the more money you make.

Write a summary of the stages described in Eric Rosenberg's process analysis.
Use the graphic organizer in Figure 13.2 to help structure your summary.

Analyzing a Process Analysis Essay

Analyzing a process analysis essay involves assessing how clearly and accurately
the writer presented the process. Use the following questions to guide your
analysis of process essays:

- **Does the writer explain why the process is important and useful?**
  Determine whether the reasons are sound, practical, and logical.

- **Are the steps clear, sequential, and distinct?** Steps should be explicit,
  should be sequentially or logically arranged, and should not overlap.

- **Does the writer provide sufficient background information?** Assess
  whether the writer adequately explains unfamiliar terminology, unusual
  equipment, and complicated techniques.

- **Is the level of detail appropriate for the intended audience?** Writers
  should neither assume knowledge that readers lack nor tire them by
  explaining things they already know.

Exercise 13.2

Following is an analysis of how Rosenberg presents the first stage of
the process in his essay (paras. 2–3), written by the student who wrote
the summary in Understanding in Action.

> The first stage of the process is signing up for a YouTube account. The
> author explains that YouTube and Google are linked, which is helpful
> for anyone who already uses Google or its services (such as Gmail). He
> then goes on to discuss the need for an AdSense account into which
> earnings will be deposited, explaining the types of information that
> are required to set up an account.

Write your own analysis of how Rosenberg presents the subsequent stages.

⊞ Evaluating a Process Analysis Essay

Although most process analysis essays are straightforward and informative, you should still consider the author's motives for writing, the author's qualifications to write about the topic, and the quality, accuracy, and completeness of the information presented. Use the following questions to guide your evaluation of process analysis essays:

- **What are the writer's motives?** As you read, ask yourself, Why does the writer want me to understand or carry out this process? A writer may have a particular motive for explaining a process. For example, a writer opposed to the death penalty may use graphic details about the process of execution to shock readers and persuade them to actively oppose the death penalty. Sometimes a writer may have a hidden agenda, even in an article on a noncontroversial topic. For example, an essay titled "How to Lose Ten Pounds" written by the owner of a weight-loss clinic may be attempting to sell the clinic's services.

- **Is the writer knowledgeable and experienced?** Always consider whether the writer has sufficient knowledge, training, education, or experience to write about the topic. This question is particularly important for how-to essays in which you will learn how to perform a task. Following the advice of someone unqualified could be a waste of time or even dangerous. Check the author's credentials and determine if he or she is an expert in the field. Also consider whether the writer supports his or her assertions by referring to outside sources or mentioning or quoting other experts in the field.

- **Is the information complete and sufficiently detailed?** Authors writing for a particular audience make assumptions about what readers do and do

Evaluation in Action

Exercise 13.3

Based on his analysis (p. 329), our student writer composed the following evaluation of the presentation of the first stage of Rosenberg's process analysis:

> To give the reader background information, the author briefly explains what AdSense is, but he doesn't provide other key information, such as the difference between a social security number and an employer ID number (EIN). Those who are trying to set up an AdSense account will likely need to search elsewhere for more information about what is involved. Overall, though, this lack of information doesn't affect the quality of the essay, which is intended as a very broad overview of the process.

Write your own evaluation of the presentation of the rest of the process.

not know. If writers do not correctly assess their readers' level of knowledge, readers may not be able to understand or carry out the process. For example, in explaining how to prepare for an interview, a writer may advise readers to research a company beforehand, assuming they know what information to look for and how to find it. But if readers are unfamiliar with this research process, they will be unable to complete the step.

Writing Your Own Process Analysis Essay

Now that you have learned about the major characteristics, structure, and purposes of a process analysis essay, you know everything necessary to write your own process analysis essay. In this section, you will read a student's process analysis essay and get advice on finding ideas, drafting your essay, and revising and editing it. You may want to use the essay prompts in "Readings for Practice, Ideas for Writing" (p. 339) or choose your own topic.

A Student Model Process Analysis Essay

Aurora Gilbert wrote the following essay in response to an assignment that asked her to explain a process that she had mastered. As you read the essay, consider whether the steps described in the essay clearly explain the process of planning a fund-raising event.

Title: Gilbert identifies the process.

The Pleasures and Particulars of Philanthropy: How to Publicize Your Fund-Raising Event

Aurora Gilbert

Introduction: Gilbert explains importance of the topic.

One of the most useful and enjoyable skills someone can learn in college is that of organizing and publicizing a philanthropic event. Putting on such an event certainly requires hard work and dedication, yet the enthusiasm it spreads in your community and support it generates for your charity are invaluable rewards.

Thesis: identifies steps in the process

For the occasion to be successful, it is important to start planning about a month before the event, following a four-step process that includes settling on basic details of the event, gathering the materials for the event, fund-raising, and publicizing the event. In describing these steps, I will discuss an annual all-you-can-eat cupcake event, sponsored by my service group, which raises money for a summer camp for the children of parents affected by cancer.

Body paragraphs

Step 1: Name the event, pick a date, and communicate these to group members. Topic sentence previews step discussed.

The first step in putting on an event is taking care of the basic details: the name and the date. Choose a name that is simple yet appealing and informative. Make sure it is catchy and at the same time refers to the main attraction of the event. We chose the name Eat Your Heart Out because it utilizes a simple, well-known phrase to indicate that our event centers around both food ("eat") and charity ("heart"). At the same time that you name the event, finalize the date, location, and time, and notify all members of your group of these details. For instance, in early September, an email announced to my service group that Eat Your Heart Out was to be held on October 10th at Artopolis Espresso from 8 to 11 p.m.

Transitions help readers keep track of process.

Step 2: Gather materials.

Next, begin gathering the materials, which include T-shirts and raffle prizes, that you will need to publicize and run the event. Do this about three and a half weeks before the event; in this time, your committee must design and order publicity T-shirts and ask members to start collecting raffle prizes for the event. Like the event name, T-shirts must be simple yet informative. Design your T-shirts in a style that reflects the tone of your event and make sure to include the names of your organization and event, as well as the event's logo. Our shirts, for example, were emblazoned with a silver heart and the phrase "Eat Your Heart Out" in white and blue script on the front; the back read "Philanthropy 2011" in white script. The sleek black of the shirts implied professionalism while the aesthetically pleasing detail promised entertainment and satisfaction.

Specific details about T-shirts

Step 3: Solicit raffle donations for fund-raising efforts.

Detailed advice for complex stage in process

If your event will include a raffle, you should begin gathering prizes at the same time that you design your T-shirts. By selling raffle tickets for fun prizes, many organizations entice people to attend a charity event and donate. At this time, you must require all members of your organization to begin soliciting businesses to donate these prizes. Among these donations, try to receive a particularly exciting one that gives people an incentive to buy raffle tickets; for Eat Your Heart Out, we received an iPad that we advertised constantly in the weeks leading up to our event. Create and distribute a flyer that outlines the details and purpose of the event that members can give to businesses. This flyer should display the logo and name of your event, the date, location, and time, raffle ticket prices, a paragraph about planned activities, and a description of your featured charity. Make sure to play up the importance of the charity in order to ensure that the businesses know they are donating to a good cause.

Step 4: Publicize event in three substeps.
Substep 1: initial publicity

Publicizing your event in several stages is key to having a well-attended, successful event. Two weeks before the event, your group should begin publicizing the event and selling tickets. One great way to reach students on a college campus and maximize attendance is to create a Facebook event and start selling tickets to prospective attendees. Use your event name as the title of the Facebook page and upload an image of your logo. Include

Effective example illustrates this stage.

the same information that you provided to businesses. Invite all organization members to "attend" the Facebook event and encourage them to invite all their Facebook friends to attend as well. At the same time, create tickets with the event name, date, location, and charity printed on them and distribute them among group members. Require each member to sell a certain number of tickets (for Eat Your Heart Out, it was three), and ask them to generate enthusiasm for the event in the weeks leading up to it.

Substep 2: Distribute flyers and display banners.

Everything starts to come together one week before the event; your group must post its flyer around campus, create and display a banner advertising the event, collect raffle prizes from the businesses donating them, and have members sign up for time slots to staff the event. The publicity flyers must be simpler than the raffle flyers and more aesthetically pleasing; make sure all the necessary information is included and presented in a way that will excite and motivate people to attend your event. The flyer for Eat Your Heart Out consisted of

Detailed examples

our logo and the information from the tickets in a creative font arranged neatly on the page. We enticed potential attendees by emphasizing the cupcakes, raffle prizes, and charitable aspect of the event, using a larger font size for "All you can eat cupcakes for only $5!!!" "Raffle GRAND PRIZE: iPad," and "All proceeds go to the Camp Kesem Chapter at Columbia University." Each

Reminder of other important, simultaneous tasks

group member should be assigned a dorm or building in which to post flyers within one day of his or her assignment. Your group should also create a banner to display in a public place on campus; like the other publicity material, this banner should be informative, easy to read, and pleasing to the eye. All raffle prizes donated by businesses should be collected by this time, and a spreadsheet should be sent out to the group by email that allows members to sign up for time slots during which they will staff the event. It is important to require each member to sign up for at least one slot to ensure that the work is distributed evenly.

In the four days before the event comes the last extreme publicity push. Four days before the event, all group members must wear their event shirts on campus and change their Facebook profile pictures to the event's logo; this will remind the campus of your upcoming event and inspire enthusiasm and anticipation in your prospective attendees. Remind your members to keep selling tickets and inviting all their friends to the event in the following days.

Substep 3: final push

Step 5: Hold fund-raiser (the result is a successful event).

The last step is to hold your event. On the day of the event, members should wear their shirts again and post Facebook statuses linking viewers to the event. Have your group meet early to set up equipment and decorations, make sure each member is present for his or her time slot, have fun, and watch all your careful planning pay off with a great event.

While planning a fund-raising event can be time-consuming and stressful, using these steps will make it both successful and rewarding. There is little that surpasses the joy and satisfaction one can gain from arranging an event that not only provides entertainment for those involved but also generates support and funds for a worthy cause.

Conclusion emphasizes importance of process.

Responding to Gilbert's Essay

1. Do you think the essay's introduction helps engage readers in wanting to learn about the fund-raising process? Why or why not?

2. The writer's key example is the process used for a fund-raising event that her own campus organization sponsored. Do you find the use of this example effective throughout the essay?

3. Do the steps of the process as the writer presents them follow clearly from the thesis?

4. Do you find the level of detail adequate? Could you follow the instructions here to create a successful fund-raising event?

5. How well do you think the two final paragraphs conclude this process analysis?

Finding Ideas for Your Process Analysis Essay

Look for ideas to write about *as you read*. Record your ideas and impressions as marginal annotations. Think about why you want or need to understand the process. Consider situations in which you can apply the information. Consider also how other processes are the same as and / or different from the one in the essay. If metaphors or analogies come to mind, such as the similarity of a dream catcher to a spider's web, make a note of them. Finally, evaluate the usefulness and completeness of the information provided.

Choosing a Process for Your Essay

The first step is to select a process to write about. Be sure to keep the following tips in mind.

- For a how-to essay, choose a process that you can visualize or actually perform as you write. Keep the object or equipment nearby for easy reference. In explaining how to scuba dive, for example, it may be helpful to have your scuba equipment near you.

- For a how-it-works essay, choose a topic about which you have background knowledge or for which you can find adequate information. Unless you are experienced in woodworking, for example, do not try to explain how certain stains produce different effects on various kinds of wood.

- Choose a topic that is useful and interesting to readers. For example, unless you can find a way to make an essay about how to do the laundry interesting, do not write about it.

Developing and Supporting Your Thesis

Once you have chosen a process to write about, the next step is to develop a working thesis. The thesis of a process analysis essay should tell readers *why* the process is important, beneficial, or relevant to them. In a how-to essay on jogging, for instance, your thesis might be "Jogging, an excellent aerobic activity, provides both exercise and a chance for solitary reflection." Note how the benefits of the activity are clearly stated in the thesis statement.

Considering your audience is especially important in developing a thesis for a process analysis because what may be of interest or importance to one audience may be of little interest to another audience.

Listing the Steps and Gathering Details

Once you are satisfied with your working thesis statement, it is time to list the steps in the process and to gather appropriate and interesting details. You will probably need to do additional prewriting at this point to generate ideas and details that help explain the process. Use the following suggestions:

1. **List the steps in the process as they occur to you, keeping these questions in mind:**

   - What separate actions are involved?

   - What steps are obvious to me but may not be obvious to someone unfamiliar with the process?

   - What steps, if omitted, will lead to problems or failure?

2. **Record the process aloud, and then take notes as you play back the recording.**

3. **Discuss the process with classmates to see what kinds of details they need to know about it.**

4. **Generate details for the steps you are describing by doing additional prewriting or conducting research online or in the library.** Make sure you have sufficient detail about unfamiliar terms, equipment, and trouble spots. If you are explaining how to hike in the Grand Canyon, for example, you might include details about carrying sufficient water and dressing in layers.

Drafting Your Process Analysis Essay

Once you have an effective thesis and enough details to explain the steps in the process, it is time to organize your ideas and draft the essay. For a process that involves fewer than ten steps, you can usually arrange the steps in chronological order, devoting one paragraph to each. However, for a process with ten or more steps, divide the steps into three or four major groups.

After organizing the steps, you are ready to write a first draft. Use the following guidelines:

1. **Write an effective introduction.** The introduction usually presents the thesis statement and includes necessary background information. It should also capture the readers' interest and focus their attention on the process. For some essays, you may want to explain that the process you are describing is related to other processes and ideas (for example, the process of jogging is related to running). For a lengthy or complex process, consider including an overview of the steps or providing a brief introductory list.

2. **Include reasons for the steps.** Unless the reason is obvious, explain why each step or group of steps is important and necessary. In explaining why a step is important, consider including a brief anecdote as an example.

3. **Consider using graphics.** For a process involving many complex steps, consider using a drawing or diagram to help readers visualize each step. Remember, however, that a graphic is no substitute for a clearly written explanation.

4. **Consider adding headings.** Headings divide the body of a lengthy or complicated process analysis into manageable segments. They also call attention to the main topics and signal readers that a change in topic is about to occur.

5. **Use transitions.** To avoid writing a process analysis that sounds monotonous, use transitions such as *before*, *next*, and *finally*.

6. **Use an appropriate tone.** Your tone should be appropriate for your audience and purpose. In some situations, a direct, matter-of-fact tone is appropriate; at other times, an emotional or humorous tone may be suitable.

7. **Write a satisfying conclusion.** Remind readers of the importance of the process or explain situations in which it would be useful.

Review "The Structure and Content of Process Analysis Essays" (pp. 321–27) for the characteristics of each part of a process analysis essay.

Revising Your Process Analysis Essay

If possible, wait at least a day before rereading and revising your draft. As you reread, concentrate on the organization and your ideas, not on grammar or mechanics. Use the flowchart in Figure 13.3 to guide your analysis.

Editing and Proofreading Your Essay

The last step is to check your revised essay for errors in grammar, spelling, punctuation, and mechanics. In addition, be sure to look for errors that you tend to make in any writing assignments, whether for this class or in other situations. Check the handbook (pp. 645–714) for assistance with common errors in your writing.

Figure 13.3   Revising a Process Analysis Essay

QUESTIONS		REVISION STRATEGIES
1. Thesis Is the importance of the process clear?	No	• Consider why readers want or need to know this process and its importance. Incorporate the answer into your thesis statement.
Yes		
2. Organization Are the steps of the process in chronological or another logical order? Is the order clear?	No	• Use your graphic organizer or outline to determine if any steps are out of order. • Visualize or perform the process to discover the best order in which to do it. • Rearrange the steps into the right order. • Add transitions if necessary.
Yes		
3. Background information Is it sufficient? Have you provided an overview of the process, if needed?	No	• Give an example of a situation in which the process might be used. • Explain that related processes and ideas depend on the process.
Yes		
4. Unfamiliar or technical terms Is each term clearly defined?	No	• Ask a classmate to read your draft and identify any missing or unclear definitions. • Add or revise definitions as needed.
Yes		
5. Equipment Have you described all necessary equipment? Will it all be familiar to readers?	No	• Mention equipment you have overlooked. • Describe potentially unfamiliar equipment.
Yes		
6. Key details Have you included an appropriate level of detail for your readers?	No	• Add or delete background information, definitions of technical terms, or other details.
Yes		
7. Potential difficulties For a how-to essay, have you anticipated all likely trouble spots? Are these sections clear and reassuring?	No	• Add more detail about critical steps. • Add warnings about confusing or difficult steps. • Offer advice on what to do if things go wrong.
Yes		
8. Introduction and conclusion Is each effective?	No	• Revise your introduction and conclusion so that they meet the guidelines given in Chapter 7, pages 136–39.

Readings for Practice, Ideas for Writing

8 Steps to Pay Off $81,000 of Debt in Less Than 3 Years

Austin Netzley graduated from college in 2008 with a degree in mechanical engineering and debt of $81,000. Since that time, he has become an investor, an entrepreneur, a speaker, and an author, and he now considers himself to be "retired." In his bestselling book *Make Money, Live Wealthy,* Netzley presents ten steps to true wealth based on the experiences and advice of 75 entrepreneurs. The how-to process essay below, which first appeared on yoprowealth.com, is the account of how he erased $81,000 worth of debt in just three years.

Reading Tip

As you read this how-to essay, think about the kind of connection the author creates between himself and his potential audience, as well as how he establishes that connection. Also, determine whether the author gives you sufficiently detailed information to actually complete the process of paying off student loan debt.

Previewing the Reading

Preview the reading (see pp. 28–29 for guidelines), and then answer the following questions.
1. What process is described in this essay?
2. What are the main steps in the process?

---

yoprowealth.com

8 Steps to Pay Off $81,000 of Debt in Less Than 3 Years

By Austin Netzley

Do you remember your first major bill? Perhaps you were a senior in college and soon headed off to the corporate world. You were filled with excitement and looking forward to that first big paycheck until you went to the mailbox. There it was—a letter from Sallie Mae, the source of your funds for college. Upon opening the letter, you realized for the first time exactly how much debt you had racked

Austin Netzley graduated from college with $81,000 in debt.

Austin Netzley, ONE Press Publishing, LLC

Continued >

up over the past four years. How in the world would you be able to repay the eight different student loans that Sallie Mae had so generously loaned you? Reeling from the sickening feeling, you began to mentally calculate the amount you would have to repay. When you added in the $9,000 car loan, you were now facing $81,000 in debt. You were broke; in fact, you were worse than broke!

But take heart. There is a way to attack the debt you have accrued. In under three years, you can be debt-free and on your way to achieving financial freedom in your mid-20s. Here's how you do it.

Step 1: Make the decision.

This sounds like a simple first step, because we all say that we really want to be debt-free, but our actions don't follow our words. When you truly make the decision, it becomes real. You fully commit and develop a belief that ensures that it is not a matter of if you will achieve your goals; it is only a matter of when.

You are probably sick of being broke—and, more important, feeling broke. You are sick of worrying about money every single day. So well before graduation, make the decision that some way, somehow, you are soon going to be rich.

Step 2: Stop getting into additional debt.

5   When your friends in other similar jobs are buying brand-new sports cars, you must stick to your used car with high mileage and keep your expenses to a minimum.

The biggest challenge that people have is getting out of the vicious debt cycle that becomes harder and harder to escape. Sticking to this step is absolutely critical.

Step 3: Define the situation.

You can't fix what you don't know, so you will need to get very clear on all of your loan details, including all of the debt balances, lender information, interest rates, and the required monthly payment amounts and start dates.

The best ways to find all of this information are via your loan statements and a credit report. When you run your first credit report, you may find some additional accounts that you thought were closed that were not, so it's important to do this on an annual basis.

Put all of your loan information on a spreadsheet and update it regularly. This will allow you to get a clear picture of what you owe and how to attack it.

Step 4: Look at your debt-relief options.

If you have a high salary, you may not qualify for any debt relief, but you should   10
definitely look into it. This simple step can save you thousands of dollars. The bad
thing is that there are a lot of scams out there, so you have to tread lightly.

Debt-relief options include loan-forgiveness programs, consolidating all of your loans
into something more manageable, debt settlement, or credit counseling (reducing the
interest rates). It is absolutely worth making the calls to see what your options are,
but be sure to consult a financial adviser before agreeing to anything.

Step 5: Pick your strategy.

There are two core debt repayment strategies.
- **Debt Snowball:** Pay the minimums on all loans, but pay off as much as you can on the
  loan with the smallest balance. This works because you start to see progress as you
  reduce the number of loans you have, and we're psychological creatures—we typically
  need to trick ourselves into success.
- **Debt Stacking:** Pay the minimums on all loans, but pay off as much as you can on
  the highest-interest-rate loan. By paying off the highest interest rate first, you pay less
  interest. Logically speaking, if it makes dollars, it makes sense.

If you have trouble staying disciplined, choose the Snowball method. Otherwise,
option B is your best bet.

Step 6: Make more money!

This is the most exciting step, but it also requires the most amount of work. Seventy-
five wealthy entrepreneurs were interviewed for the book *Make Money, Live Wealthy*,
and a surprising number of them found themselves in over $75,000 worth of debt at
one point.

Each one of them had the same secret for overcoming massive debt in a short   15
period of time: hard work. Whether it's working a lot more hours, getting a second
job, or learning how to invest, it is well worth the sacrifice to be able to be debt-free
much earlier than you otherwise would.

. . .

From day one on the job, you should start investing in your retirement fund, and then
also start investing in a taxable account more and more. This may not be the best
advice for most people, but once you start making a higher return in the stock market
than you are paying on your 3–8% loans, you can start paying the minimum payments
each month while you watch your investments grow even faster.

Continued >

yoprowealth.com

This is an ultra-risky method that can cause you a lot more harm than you're in (see Step 2), but if you are confident that you can get more than double the return (after taxes) of a debt, no one will stand in your way to stop you. Again, if it makes dollars, it makes sense.

Step 7: Delete debt.

Finally, after three years of receiving bill after bill, you may be sick of having the cloud of debt over your head. You may still feel strapped, and every time you see an email from Sallie Mae, you may remember that sickening feeling you got from opening the envelope back in college. So, at the age of 24 with a $35,000 balance remaining, you might decide to pull your money out of the stock market and pay the rest of your student loans off in full . . .

. . . and immediately start to tear up.

20   Every single day to that point you have been worried about money. However, as you press "submit" on that last payment, a rush will surge through your body, and you will never forget it. For the first time in your adult life, you will feel completely free. They say that paying off debt is a "weight off your shoulders," and you will agree that in fact it is.

Step 8: Celebrate.

Paying off debt is an accomplishment worth celebrating. Millions upon millions of people are burdened by debt, and it's definitely a challenge to get ahead if it is constantly holding you back. By escaping the debt trap, you can start to really have compound interest work in your favor, and that is when you can really build wealth. As a result, it should be financial priority number one on your way to financial freedom.

Set goals, celebrate your milestones, and go about getting out of debt in a strategic manner by using these eight steps. If you combine a plan with some focus and sacrifice, you are on your way to massive wealth.

You will be able to testify from experience: It is all well worth it.

Understanding and Reviewing the Reading

1. **Thesis** What is Netzley's thesis, and where does he state it?
2. **Audience** Throughout the essay, Netzley writes to "you." What specific audience does he have in mind?

3. **Purpose** Is this a how-to essay or a how-it-works essay? How does Netzley hope readers will benefit from his essay? Where does he state this idea specifically?

4. **Detail** How long does Netzley say this process should take?

5. **Meaning** What does Netzley say is the most exciting step in the process but also the one that requires the most work? What advice does he give for getting through this stage?

6. **Detail** What challenge does Netzley say people encounter in Step 2 of the process? What setback do they encounter?

7. **Paraphrasing** In your own words, explain debt stacking.

8. **Vocabulary** Using context clues (p. 37), write a brief definition of each of the following words as it is used in the reading, checking a dictionary if necessary: *reeling* (para. 1), *accrued* (2), *consolidating* (11), *strapped* (18), *surge* (20), and *strategic* (22).

9. **Organization** To help understand the organization of the essay, complete the graphic organizer that follows.

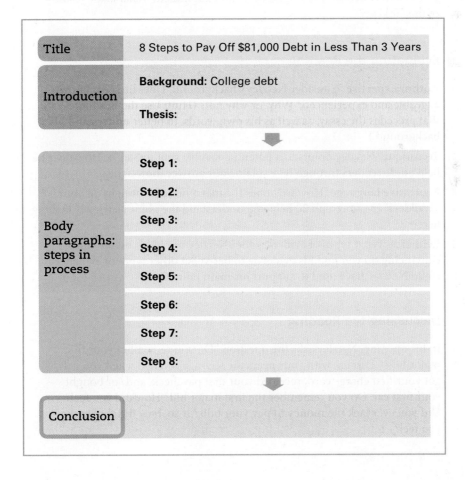

Title	8 Steps to Pay Off $81,000 Debt in Less Than 3 Years
Introduction	**Background:** College debt
	Thesis:
Body paragraphs: steps in process	**Step 1:**
	Step 2:
	Step 3:
	Step 4:
	Step 5:
	Step 6:
	Step 7:
	Step 8:
Conclusion	

Analyzing the Reading

1. **Background information** Netzley doesn't begin to focus on the process he describes until paragraph 3. What is the point of his two introductory paragraphs?

2. **Level of detail** Is Netzley's level of detail appropriate for the intended audience? Could you use the eight steps to actually reduce your debt? What details, if any, are missing from the process? Explain your answer thoroughly.

3. **Fact versus opinion** Is Netzley's essay predominantly fact or opinion? Explain your answer. Give an example of a fact and an opinion from the reading.

4. **Purpose and audience** Is Netzley's advice pertinent to someone who is not currently in massive debt? Why, or why not?

5. **Introduction and conclusion** How are the introduction (paragraphs 1 and 2) and conclusion (paragraphs 22 and 23) linked? What is the result of this linkage?

Evaluating the Reading

1. **Author expertise** Consider Netzley's background. Does he seem knowledgeable and experienced? Why, or why not? (Hint: Use the headnote that precedes the essay, as well as his own words, to better understand his background.)

2. **Technique** Netzley points to a potential trouble spot in Step 4. How does he help guide readers through it? Explain your answer thoroughly.

3. **Figurative language** How well does the metaphor of a "weight off your shoulders" in paragraph 20 help you understand the point Netzley is making here?

4. **Evidence** What types of evidence does Netzley use in his essay? How convincing do you find his evidence to be? What other types of evidence could Netzley have used to support his main points?

Discussing the Reading

1. In his opening, Netzley asks the question "Do you remember your first major bill?" Discuss with your peers the feelings you had when you got your first charge card, received your first paycheck, and/or bought your first car. Do you remember the first major bill? How did you feel? Did you ever lack the money to pay your bills? If so, how did that make you feel?

2. Most of Netzley's debt came from student loans. Do you have student loan debt awaiting you when you graduate? Do you have any idea of what the final amount of indebtedness will be? Have you given any thought to how you will repay your loans and / or how long it will take you to repay them? What will your strategy be?

3. Netzley's immediate goal was erasing debt from his life, but when he accomplished that goal, he set another goal for himself—building wealth. At this point in your life, what are your immediate goals and what are your long-term goals?

Writing about the Reading

1. **Paragraph** Summarize the eight steps of Netzley's process analysis in your own words. Start with a topic sentence and perhaps some further information to introduce the process. (Hint: Use transitional words, such as *first*, to replace *Step* headings in the essay.)

2. **Paragraph** For Netzley, paying off $81,000 worth of debt was a life-changing experience. Brainstorm a list of changes you would like to make in your life. Then choose one that seems challenging but doable. Write a paragraph in which you describe the process you would follow to accomplish that change. Make sure you start with a topic sentence explaining your goal before describing the steps.

3. **Essay** Imagine you have a friend who is burdened by the weight of massive debt and sees no way out of his / her situation. Write an essay describing for that friend the steps to take in achieving financial freedom. (Hint: Draw on the advice Netzley offers, tailoring it to your friend, but also include information from your own experience and observations.)

How Does Google Search Really Work?

Scott Matteson is a freelance technical writer for trade publications such as *TechRepublic,* an online publication devoted to areas of interest and advice for IT professionals. In addition to being a writer, Matteson is also a systems adminis-trator, project manager, and IT consultant. The how-it-works process essay below first appeared in *TechRepublic* on December 11, 2013.

Reading Tip

As you read this how-it-works essay, use one color of highlighting to indicate sections that focus on process analysis and another color to identify sections that focus on explaining cause-and-effect relationships. Also, consider whether the essay adequately explains the Google search process.

Previewing the Reading

Preview the reading (see pp. 28–29 for guidelines), and then answer the follow-ing questions.

1. What is the purpose of the reading?
2. Do you predict that this reading will be technical and specialized or practical and readable?

How Does Google Search Really Work?

Scott Matteson

I recently wrote an article about change management in the data center and needed to provide some examples of related software, so I consulted Google to see what I could find. Evolven was one of the top listed results so I examined their products and included a reference in the article.

That got me thinking later: "How exactly was Evolven near the top of the search results? Is it because they're most closely identified with change management software? Do they have the highest customer satisfaction? Are more people searching for them than other companies? Did they recently update their website? How does this Google Search stuff really work, anyhow? Why am I asking myself this when I can go find out on Google?" And so I did.

Google provides what is inarguably the most popular and effective search engine (the only one which has become a verb, such as when people say they will "Google" a topic to find out more). Many of us take it for granted that Google Search just works and the results are valid without bothering to wonder what's going on behind the curtain or how things are arranged. However, since you're reading this on *TechRepublic*, chances are you're the type of person who likes to see what's behind that curtain, especially if you own or work in a business on which Google returns search results for the public. Let's pull it back, shall we?

Note there are related elements to Google Search such as Instant Search and the "I'm Feeling Lucky" function but for the purpose of this article I'll focus on the underlying structure and how results are returned.

In the beginning . . .

5   Let's start with the basics. According to Wikipedia, Google Search was created in 1997 by Larry Page and Sergey Brin and it now performs more than three billion daily searches for users. These searches are conducted across 60 trillion web pages using an index (a directory of data) which Google reports is 95 petabytes in size—approximately 100 million gigabytes!

Step 1: Exploring the Web

Google provides an interesting explanation of the search process which states that they use special software (known as "Googlebot") running on a large number of computers to crawl the web, following links "from page to page" (this reminds me of the eerily efficient spider robots from the 2002 film *Minority Report*—perhaps it's more comforting to think of the Minions from *Despicable Me*). Googlebot starts from its last crawl status and busily looks for new sites, changes to current sites and invalid links.

Google stresses they do not accept money to favor one page or another by crawling it more often, but site owners can specify to some extent how their sites are crawled (or whether they are crawled at all). For instance, they can prevent summaries from appearing in results or keep their sites from being cached on Google servers.

Step 2: Organizing the data

Now that they've scouted out the territory, Google's web crawlers report on the pages they visited, and that ginormous 95 petabyte index is updated. To put things in perspective, this is 95,000,000,000,000,000 bytes in size—almost twice the amount of information ever written by mankind. That's not even all they could potentially index, however—Google says "Googlebot can process many, but not all, content types. For example, we cannot process the content of some rich media files or dynamic pages."

Step 3: Presenting the data

A Google search doesn't just dive into this index and fish around for what it needs. That would take a long time and return a lot of garbage. Several factors are used to present the most relevant search results, and this is where the "Coca Cola recipe" lies. Some of these factors are known and others are kept confidential to thwart malcontents who might try to unfairly rig the system (read: spammers and other scum and villainy).

What are the known factors?

- Type of content (how relevant the data on the site is to the search terms)   10
- Quality of content (spell check is used to separate professional sites from sloppy wannabes)

Continued >

- Freshness of content (sites from 1996 are less likely to be returned before sites from 2013)
- The user's region (no sense returning web pages in another language)
- Legitimacy of the site (whether the page is deemed likely to be spam-related)
- Name and address of the website
- Search word synonyms
- Social media promotions
- How many links point to a particular web page
- The value of those links

These last two involve a crucial process called "PageRank." PageRank rates web pages based on a score. Sites are assigned these scores based on whether links to them come from important or "higher authority" sites—high-traffic, well-established pages. These sites are then presented higher in the search result list, allowing the searcher to hit the right target.

Note that PageRank is intelligent enough to differentiate by focusing on quantity and quality. If one site has 5 high-quality links to it from important sites and another has 10 low-quality links from unimportant sites, the first site will end up with a higher PageRank score.

For instance, if the *New York Times* contains several links to my writing blog, my blog will be given a higher PageRank than if one person, Joe-Bob Taylor of Huckaloosa, Arkansas, links to my blog from his nearly extinct fishing web page (sorry, Joe-Bob!). This means if someone searches for writing topics and my blog contains relevant information that meets their criteria, they're more likely to see my page in the results thanks to those *New York Times* links.

Similarly, in the case of Evolven, I would guess their site came up among the top search results for "change management software" because of the relevance and freshness of their content, the links pointing to their site, and the importance of the sites providing those links.

It sounds simple, but there's still way more behind that curtain. Wikipedia's entry on PageRank presents a "simplified" algorithm:

15

Wikipedia

If you like equations this page has them a'plenty!

How can I improve my PageRank score?

Naturally, there have been attempts to raise website PageRank scores through sneaky tactics such as Google Bombs and Link Farms. Getting Joe-Bob and all his siblings and cousins to link to your site won't help much either, as we've seen. However, there are legitimate ways to improve your website's PageRank score. That's where search engine optimization (SEO) comes in. In my next article I'll discuss how SEO works and cover principles you can apply to your business.

📊 Understanding and Reviewing the Reading

1. **Thesis** Matteson suggests his thesis in paragraphs 3 and 4. How would you summarize this thesis?

2. **Background** What prompted Matteson to research the topic of the reading and then write about it?

3. **Purpose** Is this a how-to essay or a how-it-works essay? Explain your answer. How does Matteson hope readers will benefit from his essay?

4. **Detail** In paragraph 6, Matteson writes about Googlebot. What is it, and what is its purpose in the search process?

5. **Detail** In paragraphs 11 and 12, the author explains PageRank. How does a web page end up with a high PageRank score?

📊 Analyzing the Reading

1. **Purpose and audience** "How Does Google Search Really Work?" was originally published in *TechRepublic*. What does this tell you about Matteson's purpose and audience?

2. **Combining patterns** Where in the essay does Matteson use process analysis? Where does he focus on a relationship between cause and effect?

3. **Process** What techniques does the author use to make the process of explaining how Google search really works interesting and understandable? What level of knowledge and skill does the author assume his readers possess?

4. **Tone** Based on the language the author uses and the style of his writing, what do you think the tone of the essay is? Explain your answer.

📊 Evaluating the Reading

1. **Language** Evaluate the metaphors of pulling back the curtain (para. 3) and the "Coca Cola recipe" (para. 9). How effective are they in helping you understand the concept being described?

2. **Language** In paragraph 13, Matteson writes about "Joe-Bob Taylor of Huckaloosa, Arkansas" while trying to make a point about a high-quality link and its effect on a PageRank score. How effective do you find this example to be? Explain your answer.

3. **Evidence** Matteson uses several different Web sites as sources of supporting evidence. How convincing do you find his sources to be? Do you find the sources to be equally reliable? Explain your answer.

4. **Author expertise** Consider Matteson's background. Does he seem knowledgeable and experienced? Why, or why not? (Hint: Use the headnote that precedes the essay, as well as his own words, to help you answer this question.)

5. **Value of information** Do you think that this essay taught you something useful? Do you think you could now explain this process to someone else? Why, or why not?

6. **Visuals** What is the purpose of Figure 1? Does it effectively communicate its purpose? Why, or why not?

Discussing the Reading

1. Matteson uses humor to discuss difficult technical information. How does this help or hinder readers as they try to comprehend the information?

2. Matteson writes in paragraph 3 that "Google provides what is inarguably the most popular and effective search engine." What is your response to this statement? What other search engines are available, and which one do you prefer?

3. Do you think that it is necessary to understand the inner workings of a computer in order to be able to derive maximum benefit from using it? Why, or why not?

4. How might this reading change how you use Google or how you appreciate it?

Writing about the Reading

1. **Paragraph** Suppose the person sitting beside you in class is a novice at using a computer. After reading Matteson's article, your peer admits that he / she does not care about what goes on behind the curtain. He / She simply wants to know how to use Google Search. In a paragraph, explain the steps that one must follow in order to conduct a Google search. (Hint: Start with a topic sentence and perhaps some further information to introduce the process. Define and simplify technical terms. Use transitional words, such as *first,* instead of *Step* headings. End your paragraph with a concluding sentence that effectively summarizes the value of the process.)

2. **Essay** Rewrite the process of how Google Search works. (Hint: To start, you'll need to reread Matteson's essay carefully. Be sure to personalize the introductory paragraph, use examples from your experience as support, and write a concluding paragraph that links with the introduction.)

3. **Internet research** Write a how-it-works process analysis essay explaining how a machine that you use every day works. For example, you could explain how a microwave oven operates. Think of a process about which you have some background knowledge. Then use a search engine to look for articles that address your topic / process and expand your understanding. Be sure to include a thesis and an explanation of the steps in the process, using relevant and appropriate details. Personalize your essay by describing how the item influences your life.

📖 COMBINING THE PATTERNS | TEXTBOOK EXCERPT: PSYCHOLOGY

The Nature of Stress

Carole Wade is a cognitive psychologist, an author, and a former professor of psychology at the University of New Mexico, San Diego Mesa College, College of Marin, and, most recently, Dominican University of California. **Carol Tavris** is a social psychologist, an author, a lecturer, and a former professor of psychology at UCLA and the New School for Social Research. **Maryanne Garry** is a cognitive psychologist, an author, a researcher, and a professor of psychology at Victoria University of Wellington. The following selection is from the eleventh edition of their book *Psychology*, an introductory textbook that emphasizes the principles of scientific and critical thinking.

Reading Tip

As you read, highlight each of the phases in the process the authors discuss, and when you have finished reading, briefly summarize the whole process that the human body goes through when it responds to stress.

Previewing the Reading

Preview the reading (see pp. 28–29 for guidelines), and determine whether it is a how-to essay or a how-it-works essay.

The Nature of Stress
Carole Wade, Carol Tavris, and Maryanne Garry

Emotions can take many forms, varying in complexity and intensity, depending on physiology, cognitive processes, and cultural rules. These same three factors can help us understand those difficult situations in which negative emotions become chronically stressful, and in which chronic stress can create negative emotions.

When people say they are "under stress," they mean all sorts of things: They are having recurring conflicts with a parent, are feeling frustrated and angry about their lives, are fighting with a partner, are overwhelmed with caring for a sick child, can't keep up with work obligations, or just lost a job. Are these stressors linked to illness—to migraines, stomachaches, flu, or more life-threatening diseases such as cancer? And do they affect everyone in the same way?

Stress and the Body

The modern era of stress research began in 1956, when physician Hans Selye published *The Stress of Life*. Environmental stressors such as heat, cold, toxins, and danger, Selye wrote, disrupt the body's

Continued >

equilibrium. The body then mobilizes its resources to fight off these stressors and restore normal functioning. Selye described the body's response to stressors of all kinds as a **general adapation syndrome**, a set of physiological reactions that occur in three phases:

1. **The alarm phase**, in which the body mobilizes the sympathetic nervous system to meet the immediate threat. The threat could be anything from taking a test you haven't studied for to running from a rabid dog. As we saw earlier, the release of adrenal hormones, epinephrine and norepinephrine, occurs with any intense emotion. It boots energy, tenses muscles, reduces sensitivity to pain, shuts down digestion (so that blood will flow more efficiently to the brain, muscles, and skin), and increases blood pressure. Decades before Selye, psychologist Walter Cannon (1929) described these changes as the "fight-or-flight" response, a phrase still in use.

Stress hormones elevated

Blood flow increases
Heart rate speeds up
Digestion slows
Muscles tense

Printed and Electronically reproduced by permission of Pearson Education, Inc., NEW YORK, NEW YORK

2. **The resistance phase**, in which your body attempts to resist or cope with a stressor that cannot be avoided. During this phase, the physiological responses of the alarm phase continue, but these very responses make the body more vulnerable to other stressors. When your body has mobilized to deal with a heat wave or pain from a broken leg, you may find you are more easily annoyed by minor frustrations. In most cases, the body will eventually adapt to the stressor and return to normal.

3. **The exhaustion phase**, in which persistent stress depletes the body of energy, thereby increasing vulnerability to physical problems and illness. The same reactions that allow the body to respond effectively in the alarm and resistance phases are unhealthy as long-range responses. Tense muscles can cause headache and neck pain. Increased blood pressure can become chronic hypertension. If normal digestive processes are interrupted or shut down for too long, digestive disorders may result.

Selye did not believe that people should aim for a stress-free life. Some stress, he said, is positive and productive, even if it also requires the body to produce short-term energy: competing in an athletic event, falling in love, working hard on a project you enjoy. And some negative stress is simply unavoidable; it's called life.

CURRENT APPROACHES

One of Selye's most important observations was that the very biological 5 changes that are adaptive in the short run, because they permit the body to respond quickly to danger, can become hazardous in the long run (McEwen, 2007). Modern researchers are learning how this happens.

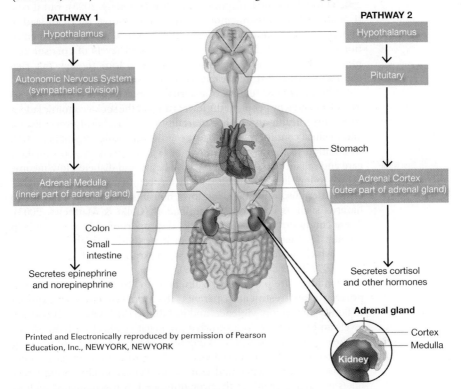

Printed and Electronically reproduced by permission of Pearson Education, Inc., NEW YORK, NEW YORK

Figure 1. The brain and body under stress. When a person is in danger or under stress, the hypothalamus sends messages to the endocrine glands along two major pathways. In one, the hypothalamus activates the sympathetic division of the autonomic nervous system, which stimulates the adrenal medulla to produce epinephrine and norepinephrine. The result is the many bodily changes associated with "fight or flight." In the other pathway, messages travel along the HPA axis to the adrenal cortex, which produces cortisol and other hormones. The result is increased energy and protection from tissue inflammation in case of injury.

When you are under stress, your brain's hypothalamus sends messages to the endocrine glands along two major pathways. One, as Selye observed, activates the sympathetic division of the autonomic nervous system for "fight or flight," producing the release of epinephrine and norepinephrine from the inner part (medulla) of the adrenal glands. In addition, the hypothalamus initiates activity along the **HPA axis** (HPA stands for hypothalamus–pituitary–adrenal cortex). The hypothalamus releases chemical messengers that communicate with

Continued >

the pituitary gland, which in turn sends messages to the outer part (cortex) of the adrenal glands. The adrenal cortex secretes **cortisol** and other hormones that elevate blood sugar and protect the body's tissues from inflammation in case of injury (see Figure 1).

One result of HPA axis activation is increased energy, which is crucial for short-term responses to stress (Kemeny, 2003). But if cortisol and other stress hormones stay high too long, they can lead to hypertension, immune disorders, other physical ailments, and emotional problems such as depression. Elevated levels of cortisol also motivate animals (and presumably humans, too) to seek out rich comfort foods and store the extra calories as abdominal fat.

The cumulative effects of external sources of stress may help us to understand why people at the lower rungs of the socioeconomic ladder have worse health and higher mortality rates for almost every disease and medical condition than do those at the top (Adler & Snibbe, 2003). In addition to the obvious reasons of lack of access to good medical care and reliance on diets that lead to obesity and diabetes, low-income people often live with continuous environmental stressors: higher crime rates, discrimination, rundown housing, and greater exposure to hazards such as chemical contamination (Gallo & Matthews, 2003). These conditions affect urban blacks disproportionately and may help account for their higher incidence of hypertension (high blood pressure), which can lead to kidney disease, strokes, and heart attacks (Clark et al., 1999; Pascoe & Richman, 2009).

Children are particularly vulnerable to stressors associated with poverty or maltreatment by parents: The more years they are exposed to family disruption, violence, and instability, the higher their cortisol levels and the greater the snowballing negative effect on their physical health, mental health, and cognitive abilities (especially working memory, the ability to hold items of information in memory for current use) in adolescence and adulthood. Persistent childhood stress takes its toll on health both through biological mechanisms, such as chronically elevated cortisol, and behavioral ones. Children living with chronic stress often become hypervigilant to danger, mistrust others, have poor relationships, are unable to regulate their emotions, abuse drugs, and don't eat healthy food. No wonder that by the time they are adults, they have an elevated risk of cardiovascular disease, autoimmune disorders, diabetes, and early mortality (Evans & Schamberg, 2009; Miller, Chen, & Parker, 2011).

10   Because work is central in most people's lives, the effects of persistent unemployment can threaten health for people at all income levels, even increasing their vulnerability to the common cold. In one study, heroic volunteers were given either ordinary nose drops or nose drops containing a cold virus, and then were quarantined for five days. The people most likely to get a cold's miserable symptoms were those who had been underemployed or unemployed for at least

a month. The longer the work problems lasted, the greater the likelihood of illness (Cohen et al., 1998).

Nonetheless, the physiological changes caused by stress do not occur to the same extent in everyone. People's responses to stress vary according to their learning history, gender, preexisting medical conditions, and genetic predisposition for high blood pressure, heart disease, obesity, diabetes, or other health problems (Belsky & Pluess, 2009a; McEwen, 2000, 2007). This is why some people respond to the same stressor with much greater increases in blood pressure, heart rate, and hormone levels than other individuals do, and their physical changes take longer to return to normal. These hyperresponsive individuals may be the ones most at risk for eventual illness.

Understanding and Reviewing the Reading

1. **Textbook reading** Write a summary of the three phases of the physiological reaction to stressors.

2. **Language** According to the authors, stress can produce a "fight-or-flight" response in the body. What does "fight or flight" mean to you? How do the authors explain this response?

3. **Details** According to the authors, why are animals and humans drawn to comfort food during a stressful situation?

4. **Thesis** Do you think this excerpt has a thesis? Explain your answer. Summarize one overall point that the authors make about how the human body responds to stress.

5. **Organizing information** Create a chart, table, or map of the human body's response to stress. Be sure to include more than just the three phases of physiological reaction.

Analyzing the Reading

1. **Predicting exam questions** A useful way to prepare for an exam is to predict possible questions your instructor might ask and then to practice answering them. Compose two essay-exam questions that would likely appear on an exam covering the excerpt "The Nature of Stress."

2. **Combining patterns** Where in the reading selection do the authors use process analysis? Where do they focus on explaining cause-and-effect relationships?

3. **Difficulty of text** What sections of the excerpt were most challenging for you? Why were they challenging? What strategies could you use to help you more clearly understand the selection?

Evaluating the Reading

1. **Strategy** How useful do you find the process analysis as presented here? Do you think each phase is explained in enough detail to answer most students' questions?

2. **Writer's voice** How do you respond to the way the authors write to you, the reader? How is the authors' approach different from that employed in textbooks in other subject areas?

3. **Value of information** Do you think this textbook excerpt taught you anything? Explain your answer.

4. **Visuals** How useful is Figure 1 to you? What additional information do you need to use the figure to help you study?

Discussing the Reading

1. The authors write that "when people say they are 'under stress,' they mean all sorts of things." What does "under stress" mean to you, and what stressors do you have in your life?

2. The excerpt suggests both positive and negative aspects of stress. Point to several examples of each. Do the positives outweigh the negatives or vice versa?

3. What is the most valuable information you take away from this reading? How might you actually apply it to your own life?

Writing about the Reading

1. **Writing essay-exam answers** Choose one of the questions you predicted in Analyzing the Reading question 1 (p. 355) and write an essay answering it.

2. **Essay** In an essay, write about a stressful experience in your life, how the stress affected you, and the steps you took to effectively relieve yourself of stress.

3. **Internet research** This textbook excerpt addresses how stress works in our bodies, but it does not address how to manage stress effectively. First read several different online articles on the how-to's of managing stress. Then write a process analysis essay in which you explain the steps to managing stress more effectively.

Working with Process Analysis as a Reader and Writer

The following table reviews the key elements of process analysis essays and explains how these elements are important to both readers and writers.

Reading ⊕ Writing   Process Analysis Essays

Element of a Process Analysis Essay	The Reader's Perspective	The Writer's Perspective
Background Information	While reading, pay close attention to the introduction, which likely provides background information. You may wish to reread the introduction if you do not have a high level of familiarity with the topic.	When writing, help to "set the stage" for your analysis by providing important background information and explaining why the information in your essay is useful or important.
Technical Terms	As you read, highlight technical terms and their definitions. After reading, quiz yourself on each definition. If you still do not understand the term, check another source for more information.	When writing, anticipate the technical terms with which readers are likely unfamiliar, and research the accurate definition of each term. Whenever possible, try to provide clear, careful definitions in plain, simple English. You may sometimes have to "translate" technical definitions into something easier to read.
Descriptions of Necessary Equipment	As you read, try to envision the equipment. If diagrams are included, study them along with the written description.	When describing the necessary equipment, provide tips and pointers on how to use the equipment correctly or possible problems to guard against. Your readers will thank you.

Continued >

Possible Trouble Spots	As you read, underline or highlight possible trouble spots. Keep a list of them and refer to the list before you attempt to perform the process.	When writing, clearly signal possible problem areas by using such phrases as "here's a warning," "be careful not to," or "make sure that you."
Appropriate Level of Detail	As you read, check to make sure you fully understand each step in the process. That is, evaluate whether the author has provided an appropriate level of detail. Write marginal notes if you still have questions about a step in the process. Your notes will remind you to consult other sources for additional information.	To provide the appropriate level of detail, carefully analyze your intended audience and the number of steps involved in the process. For example, changing a light bulb involves only a few steps. But learning a new word-processing program may require entire chapters of detailed (and welcome) step-by-step instructions.

14

Comparison and Contrast: Showing Similarities and Differences

In this chapter, you will learn to

- Recognize the elements of comparison and contrast.

- Identify the structure and content of comparison-and-contrast essays.

- Understand, analyze, and evaluate comparison-and-contrast essays.

- Write your own comparison-and-contrast essay.

- Work with comparison and contrast as a reader and a writer.

Reflect on a Visual Text

Study this photograph of a young man watching a basketball game on TV. Think about how watching a sport on TV is similar to and different from actually playing the sport.

1 Ask yourself questions. If this man is watching basketball on TV, why is he holding a basketball? Does he wish he were out on the court playing basketball himself rather than sitting in front of the TV? What does his expression suggest about his engagement with the game?

2 Brainstorm ideas. Working on your own or with a small group of classmates, make two lists—one of the similarities between watching sports on TV and playing them, and one of the differences. Base your lists on basketball or on some other sport of your choice. You can include details about the degree of physical activity, nature of interaction with others, setting, emotions, and so on. →

Exactostock-1527/Superstock

3 Write. Now write a paragraph comparing the experiences of playing a sport and watching it on television.

As you discovered in writing your paragraph, using *comparison and contrast* involves looking at both similarities and differences. When writers use comparison and contrast, they consider subjects with characteristics in common, examining similarities, differences, or both. Whether used as the primary pattern of development or alongside another pattern, comparison and contrast can help writers achieve a specific purpose and make a clear point about their subjects.

What Is Comparison and Contrast?

Comparison and contrast typically involves detailing the similarities or differences between two items, or subjects, on key criteria. For example, when you compare and contrast two used cars, you might consider how they are similar in terms of size, body type, and gas mileage and how they are different in terms of price, color, and engine size. Comparison and contrast is used widely in college assignments and on the job. For instance, for a course in criminal justice, an instructor might ask students to compare organized crime in three countries: Italy, Japan, and Russia. On the job, a computer technician for a pharmaceutical firm may have to compare and contrast several notebook computers and recommend which one the company should purchase for its sales force.

There are two basic types of comparison-and-contrast essays:

- A **subject-by-subject essay** describes the key points or characteristics of one subject before moving on to those of the other subject.
- A **point-by-point essay** moves back and forth between two subjects, comparing or contrasting them on the basis of several key points.

Comparison and contrast has all or most of the following elements:

1. It considers subjects that can be compared.
2. It has a clear purpose.
3. It fairly examines similarities, differences, or both.
4. It considers a sufficient number of significant characteristics and details.
5. It makes a point.

Knowing how writers (and other communicators) use comparison and contrast will help you understand, analyze, and evaluate this pattern when you read and help you use it in your own writing.

A Model Comparison-and-Contrast Essay

The following model essay will be used throughout this chapter to demonstrate strategies for reading and writing comparison-and-contrast essays. Read it now, looking for the ways the writer uses the above comparison-and-contrast techniques. Use the annotations in the margin to guide you.

We've Got the Dirt on Guy Brains

Dave Barry

Dave Barry began his professional writing career covering local events for a Pennsylvania newspaper. In 1983, he began writing a humor column for the *Miami Herald* that appeared in more than five hundred newspapers; Barry stopped writing the column in 2004. Barry has written thirty books; plays guitar in the Rock Bottom Remainders, a rock band made up of well-known writers such as Stephen King and Amy Tan; and received a Pulitzer Prize for Commentary in 1988. "We've Got the Dirt on Guy Brains" originally appeared in November 2003.

I like to think that I am a modest person. (I also like to think that I look like Brad Pitt naked, but that is not the issue here.)

There comes a time, however, when a person must toot his own personal horn, and for me, that time is now. A new book has confirmed a theory that I first proposed in 1987, in a column explaining why men are physically unqualified to do housework. The problem, I argued, is that men — because of a tragic genetic flaw — cannot see dirt until there is enough of it to support agriculture. This puts men at a huge disadvantage against women, who can detect a single dirt molecule twenty feet away.

This is why a man and a woman can both be looking at the same bathroom commode, and the man — hindered by Male Genetic Dirt Blindness (MGDB) — will perceive the commode surface as being clean enough for heart surgery or even meat slicing; whereas the woman can't even *see* the commode, only a teeming, commode-shaped swarm of bacteria. A woman can spend two hours cleaning a toothbrush holder and still not be

> **Comparison and contrast considers subjects that can be compared:** The essay uses a light-hearted tone to set up the comparison between men and women that follows. As you continue reading, you will notice that the tone becomes slightly more serious as the author considers real scientific evidence.

totally satisfied; whereas if you ask a man to clean the entire New York City subway system, he'll go down there with a bottle of Windex and a single paper towel, then emerge twenty-five minutes later, weary but satisfied with a job well done.

When I wrote about Male Genetic Dirt Blindness, many irate readers complained that I was engaging in sexist stereotyping, as well as making lame excuses for the fact that men are lazy pigs. All of these irate readers belonged to a gender that I will not identify here, other than to say: Guess what, ladies? There is now scientific proof that I was right.

This proof appears in a new book titled *What Could He Be Thinking? How a Man's Mind Really Works*. I have not personally read this book, because, as a journalist, I am too busy writing about it. But according to an article by Reuters[1], the book states that a man's brain "takes in less sensory detail than a woman's, so he doesn't see or even feel the dust and household mess in the same way." Got that? We can't see or feel the mess! We're like: "What snow tires in the dining room? Oh, *those* snow tires in the dining room."

And this is only one of the differences between men's and women's brains. Another difference involves a brain part called the "cingulate gyrus," which is the sector where emotions are located. The Reuters article does not describe the cingulate gyrus, but presumably in women it is a structure the size of a mature cantaloupe, containing a vast quantity of complex, endlessly recalibrated emotional data involving hundreds, perhaps thousands, of human relationships; whereas in men it is basically a cashew filled with NFL highlights.

In any event, it turns out that women's brains secrete more of the chemicals "oxytocin" and "serotonin," which, according to biologists, cause humans to feel they have an inadequate supply of shoes. No, seriously, these chemicals cause humans to want to bond with other humans, which is why women like to share their feelings. Some women (and here I am referring to my wife) can share as many as three days' worth of feelings about an event

Comparison and contrast has a clear purpose: Barry's purpose here is clear: to share the results of a scientific study that compares men's brains and women's brains—and also to justify his own beliefs on the topic.

Comparison and contrast fairly examines similarities, differences, or both: While Barry takes a comic approach, he fairly looks at scientific evidence regarding men's and women's brain chemicals.

[1]**Reuters** An international news and financial information service providing reports and stories to the media.

Comparison and contrast considers a sufficient number of significant characteristics and details: Throughout the essay, the author makes several points of comparison: men's and women's perceptions of dirt, their different brain chemicals, their approaches to sharing their feelings.

that took eight seconds to actually happen. We men, on the other hand, are reluctant to share our feelings, in large part because we often don't have any. Really. Ask any guy: A lot of the time, when we look like we're thinking, we just have this low-level humming sound in our brains. That's why, in male-female conversations, the male part often consists entirely of him going "hmmmm." This frustrates the woman, who wants to know what he's really thinking. In fact, what he's thinking is, literally, "hmmmm."

So anyway, according to the Reuters article, when a man, instead of sharing feelings with his mate, chooses to lie on the sofa, holding the remote control and monitoring 750 television programs simultaneously by changing the channel every one-half second (pausing slightly longer for programs that feature touchdowns, fighting, shooting, car crashes, or bosoms) his mate should *not* come to the mistaken conclusion that he is an insensitive jerk. In fact, he is responding to scientific biological brain chemicals that require him to behave this way for scientific reasons, as detailed in the scientific book *What Could He Be Thinking? How a Man's Mind Really Works*, which I frankly cannot recommend highly enough.

Comparison and contrast makes a point: The author closes by jokingly reinforcing his key point: that men are always going to be more interested in sports than in cleaning or talking about their emotions.

In conclusion, no *way* was that pass interference.

The Structure and Content of Comparison-and-Contrast Essays

In this section, you will learn about the structure of a comparison-and-contrast essay and practice using the guidelines for understanding, analyzing, and evaluating such essays. This key information will help you skillfully read and write essays that use comparison and contrast.

A comparison-and-contrast essay follows a clear structure to help the reader follow and understand the points of comparison. Figures 14.1 and 14.2 represent these major components visually.

When choosing a topic for a comparison-and-contrast essay, writers need to keep two key points in mind.

Figure 14.1   Graphic Organizer for a Subject-by-Subject Comparison-and-Contrast Essay

Title	
Introduction	Background information
	Subjects: A comparison/contrast of Houses A and B
	Thesis statement
Body paragraphs: subject by subject	Subject A (House A)
	Point 1 applied to Subject A (Layout of House A)
	Point 2 applied to Subject A (Size of House A)
	Point 3 applied to Subject A (Building materials used in House A)
	Point 4 applied to Subject A (Landscaping around House A)
	Subject B (House B)
	Point 1 applied to Subject B (Layout of House B)
	Point 2 applied to Subject B (Size of House B)
	Point 3 applied to Subject B (Building materials used in House B)
	Point 4 applied to Subject B (Landscaping around House B)
Conclusion	Reinforces thesis
	Summarizes main points

Comparison and Contrast Must Have a Clear Purpose   A comparison-and-contrast essay usually has at least one of three purposes: *to express ideas, to inform,* or *to persuade.* Dave Barry tries to achieve all three purposes in his essay. He is not only *expressing* his own ideas; he is also *informing* his readers about key differences between women's brains and men's brains while trying to *persuade* readers that he was right all along.

Comparison and Contrast Must Consider Subjects That Can Be Reasonably Compared   When choosing a topic for a comparison, a writer needs to choose subjects that have some *basis of comparison*—that is, one or more characteristics on which they can reasonably be compared. You would not, for example, write an essay that compares a cotton ball and the Soviet Union. But you *could* write an essay that compares a cotton ball and a Q-Tip or an essay that compares the governmental structure of Russia and the governmental structure of the United States.

Figure 14.2   Graphic Organizer for a Point-by-Point Comparison-and-Contrast Essay

Title	
Introduction	Background information
	Subjects: A comparison/contrast of Houses A and B
	Thesis statement
	▼
Body paragraphs: point by point	Point 1 (Layout)
	Subject A (House A)
	Subject B (House B)
	Point 2 (Size)
	Subject A (House A)
	Subject B (House B)
	Point 3 (Building materials)
	Subject A (House A)
	Subject B (House B)
	Point 4 (Landscaping)
	Subject A (House A)
	Subject B (House B)
	▼
Conclusion	Reinforces thesis
	Summarizes main points

1. THE INTRODUCTION ESTABLISHES THE COMPARISON OR CONTRAST AND INCLUDES A THESIS STATEMENT

The introduction should identify the subjects being compared or contrasted and present the thesis statement. It should also provide any background information readers may need to understand the comparison.

Most comparison-and-contrast essays include an explicit thesis statement in the introduction. The thesis has three functions:

1. It identifies the *subjects* being compared or contrasted.
2. It suggests whether the focus is on *similarities, differences,* or *both.*
3. It states the *main point* of the comparison and contrast.

Dave Barry's introduction is longer than the typical introduction, mostly because he spends several paragraphs providing background information about a previous column he wrote. His thesis statement is split between two paragraphs. Paragraph 4 concludes with the thesis statement "There is now scientific proof that I was right." What was he right about? The second part of the thesis comes in paragraph 5 and states the main point: "The book states that a man's brain 'takes in less sensory detail than a woman's, so he doesn't see or even feel the dust and household mess in the same way.'" The subject being compared is men's and women's perceptions of dirt, and the focus is on the differences.

Here are two additional examples of thesis statements that make clear the main point of the comparison or contrast.

Although different in purpose, weddings and funerals each draw families together and confirm family values.

(The essay would go on to compare the effects of weddings and funerals.)

The two cities Niagara Falls, Ontario, and Niagara Falls, New York, demonstrate two different approaches to appreciating nature and preserving the environment.

(The essay would go on to contrast the two cities' environmental preservation methods.)

Reading ⏺ Writing   The Introduction of a Comparison-and-Contrast Essay

The Reader's Perspective	The Writer's Perspective
When reading a comparison-and-contrast essay, study the introduction to get a sense of what the writer knows about the subjects and determine how detailed or complex the essay will be. Also determine how much you already know about the subjects. This information will help you determine how slowly and carefully you should read the essay and what strategies (such as highlighting, annotating, or summarizing) may be most useful for understanding and recalling the information.	When writing a comparison-and-contrast essay, be sure your introduction speaks directly to your audience, indicating why the comparison and contrast is relevant to them. Explain the benefits or advantages of knowing how the subjects are similar or different.

2. THE BODY PARAGRAPHS COMPARE OR CONTRAST THE SUBJECTS

In writing the body paragraphs in a comparison, you should organize your material in a way that suits your topic and purpose. In addition, you should *fairly* examine similarities, differences, or both. Finally, you should provide a sufficient number of significant characteristics and details to support your thesis.

Organization

Comparison-and-contrast essays are organized in one of two ways: subject by subject or point by point. For example, a writer who is going to compare two houses (A and B) on the basis of layout, size, building material, and landscaping has two options for organizing the essay: subject by subject or point by point.

Subject-by-Subject Organization   Using *subject-by-subject organization*, the writer would first discuss all points about House A—its layout, size, building materials, and landscaping. Then the writer would do the same for House B. This pattern is shown in the graphic organizer in Figure 14.1 (p. 364).

Point-by-Point Organization   Using *point-by-point organization*, the writer would first discuss the layouts of the houses, then their sizes, then their building materials, and finally their landscaping. The writer would go back and forth between the two houses, noting similarities and differences on each point of comparison. This pattern is shown in the graphic organizer in Figure 14.2 (p. 365).

Each organization is appropriate for certain topics and purposes.

1. The subject-by-subject method tends to emphasize the larger picture, whereas the point-by-point method emphasizes details and specifics.
2. The point-by-point method often works better for lengthy essays if you want to keep both subjects current in your reader's mind. Dave Barry's essay uses the point-by-point method.
3. The point-by-point method is often preferable for complicated or technical subjects. For example, if you were comparing two computer systems, it would be easier to explain the functions of a memory card once and then describe the memory cards in each of the two systems.

Fair Examination of Similarities, Differences, or Both

Whether you focus on similarities, differences, or both in an essay, you should strive to treat your subjects fairly. Relevant information should not be purposely omitted to show one subject in a more favorable light. In his essay, Dave Barry does not say that one set of brain chemicals is better than another; nor does he imply that men are superior to women (or vice versa). He simply examines the differences and expresses them in a humorous way.

Reading ⓘ Writing   Organization of a Comparison-and-Contrast Essay

The Reader's Perspective	The Writer's Perspective
When reading a comparison-and-contrast essay, identify whether the method of organization is subject by subject or point by point as soon as possible. It may be suggested in the introduction, but it will definitely be evident as you begin reading the body paragraphs. Knowing the chosen method will help you begin to construct a mental outline as you read, slotting in details as you encounter them. Understanding the organization will also help you draw a graphic organizer or write an outline as a study tool.	When writing a comparison-and-contrast essay, carefully define your purpose for writing, since it will determine, in part, which method of organization you choose—subject by subject or point by point. Consider your audience: Which method are they likely to respond to better and find easier to follow?

A Sufficient Number of Significant Characteristics and Details

A comparison-and-contrast essay should consider various points of comparison to support the essay's purpose and thesis. Although the number of points of comparison will vary by topic, usually at least three or four significant points are needed to support a thesis. Each point should be fully described or explained so that readers can completely grasp the thesis. Note that Barry's essay offers various points of comparison: men's and women's awareness of dirt, differences in men's and women's brain structures and chemicals, and men's and women's desire or willingness to talk about feelings.

3. THE CONCLUSION REINFORCES THE THESIS AND SUMMARIZES THE MAIN POINTS

The conclusion should draw the essay to a satisfying close. You might offer a final comment on your comparison or contrast, as well as sum up and remind your readers of your thesis. Barry's essay closes with a humorous reminder of the way the male brain works.

Reading 🔄 Writing   **The Conclusion of a Comparison-and-Contrast Essay**

The Reader's Perspective	The Writer's Perspective
When reading a comparison-and-contrast essay, use the conclusion to help you pull together the entire essay to understand points of similarity and difference. Also, for an essay discussing both similarities and differences, consider whether the subjects are mostly similar or mostly different. Finally, consider whether the author achieved his or her purpose: Did he or she convince you of the relevance and importance of comparing or contrasting the subjects?	When writing a comparison-and-contrast essay, you might refer back to the introduction by mentioning again the usefulness or value of the comparison or contrast. For lengthy or complicated comparisons, you might want to summarize the main points as well.

Understanding, Analyzing, and Evaluating Comparison-and-Contrast Essays

In reading and writing comparison-and-contrast essays, your goal is to get beyond mere competence. That is, you want to do more than merely understand the content of the essays you read or convey just your basic ideas to the audience you're writing for.

📊 *Understanding a Comparison-and-Contrast Essay*

Reading a comparison-and-contrast essay is somewhat different from reading other kinds of essays. First, the essay addresses two (or more) subjects instead of just one. Second, the subjects are being compared, contrasted, or both, so you must follow the writer's points of comparison between them. These differences make comparison-and-contrast essays more difficult to read, so plan on reading them several times.

Begin by previewing the essay to determine the subjects being considered and whether the writer is concerned with similarities, differences, or both. Also consider your familiarity with the subjects, as your familiarity will determine, in part, how difficult the essay will be to read. Then, as you read, use the skills you learned in Chapter 2 and look for the answers to the following questions.

- **What is the author's purpose?** Determine whether the essay is written to express ideas, inform, or persuade. Depending on the purpose, you will be looking for different things as you read. If the purpose is to express ideas, you will be looking for the author's attitudes, opinions, and beliefs. If the purpose is to inform, you will be looking for factual statements and their support. If the purpose is to persuade, you will be looking for reasons and evidence.

- **What method of organization is used?** Determine the method of organization as soon as possible, because your mind-set and focus will depend on it. Both methods can present the same information, but what you expect to come next will depend on whether you are reading a point-by-point or subject-by-subject essay.

- **What is the basis of comparison?** Identifying the basis of comparison will help you focus your attention and identify the most important supporting details.

- **What are the points of comparison?** The points of comparison are the key ideas of the essay. Be sure to highlight each as you identify it. The points of comparison are usually directly tied to the writer's purpose, so be sure to connect the two. For example, if a writer's purpose is to express ideas about two popular films, the points of comparison are likely to be subjective—expressing the writer's preferences. If, however, the purpose is to inform, the author is more likely to make factual points of comparison.

Understanding in Action

Exercise 14.1

Following is one student's summary of the second paragraph of Dave Barry's "We've Got the Dirt on Guy Brains."

> The author praises himself by explaining his theory that men lack the qualifications to do household chores. Barry claims that men just cannot see dirt, unlike women, who do have the capacity to spot small amounts of dirt at great distances.

Write your own brief summary of Barry's entire essay. Be sure to include his thesis, the body of the comparison, and the conclusion. Use the Understanding a Comparison-and-Contrast Essay guidelines and Figure 14.3 (p. 371) to make sure you include all the important points.

📖 Analyzing a Comparison-and-Contrast Essay

Analyzing a comparison-and-contrast essay involves assessing how effectively and clearly the writer explains similarities and/or differences between two or more subjects. Use the following questions to guide your analysis of comparison-and-contrast essays:

- **Does the thesis statement identify whether the writer intends to express ideas, inform, or persuade?** Good writers help their readers form a mind-set and know what to expect. If the writer does not have a clear purpose

Figure 14.3   Graphic Organizer for "We've Got the Dirt on Guy Brains"

Title	We've Got the Dirt on Guy Brains
Introduction	**Background:** The author wrote an article in which he argued that men have a tragic genetic flaw called Male Genetic Dirt Blindness, which prevents them from seeing household dirt. Various readers criticized him for being sexist.
	Topic: Men's and women's perceptions of dirt
	Thesis: There is now scientific proof that I was right . . . a man's brain takes in less sensory detail than a woman's.

Body paragraphs: point by point	**Point 1:** Perceptions of dirt and other stimuli
	Women's brains: Take in more sensory detail
	Men's brains: Take in less sensory detail
	Point 2: Brain structure and chemicals
	Women's brains: Produce more oxytocin and serotonin, which cause humans to want to bond with other humans
	Men's brains: Produce less of these chemicals, making men less communicative

Conclusion	Reinforces the idea that men would rather watch sports than engage in meaningful conversation

in mind or does not express it clearly, you might notice a mixed basis of comparison or overlapping points of comparison.

- **Is the basis of comparison clear, and does it fulfill the writer's purpose?** If the writer's purpose is to inform readers about two football players' athletic skills, he or she should not, for example, discuss the players' off-field behavior.

- **Do the points of comparison cover some of the major similarities and differences?** For many subjects, it would be impossible to cover all similarities or differences, but at least some of the major ones should be covered. In comparing two musical groups, it would be important to identify the type of music each plays, for instance.

- **Are the points of comparison relevant to the thesis statement?** Writers should choose points that are common and typical and that support the thesis statement. For example, in an essay about two medical specialties, contrasting them according to the ethnicities of their practitioners would not be pertinent, whereas comparing types of training and uses of surgery would be appropriate.

Analysis in Action

Exercise 14.2

The student who wrote the summary in Understanding in Action made notes as she read the introduction to Dave Barry's "We've Got the Dirt on Guy Brains."

Ha! Author's tone is humorous	I like to think that I am a modest person. (I also like to think that I look like Brad Pitt naked, but that is not the issue here.)
	There comes a time, however, when a person must toot his own personal horn, and for me, that time is now. A new book has confirmed a theory that I first proposed
Ridiculous & exaggerated, but pretty funny	in 1987, in a column explaining why men are physically unqualified to do housework. The problem, I argued, is that men—because of a tragic genetic flaw—cannot see dirt until there is enough of it to support agriculture. This puts men at a huge disadvantage against women, who can detect a single dirt molecule twenty feet away.
	This is why a man and a woman can both be looking at the same bathroom commode, and the man—hindered by Male Genetic Dirt Blindness (MGDB)—will perceive the commode surface as being clean enough for heart surgery or even meat slicing; whereas the woman can't even *see* the commode, only a teeming, commode-shaped swarm of bacteria. A woman can spend two hours cleaning a toothbrush holder and still not be totally satisfied; whereas
Definitely stereotypical, but maybe there's some truth in it?	if you ask a man to clean the entire New York City subway system, he'll go down there with a bottle of Windex and a single paper towel, then emerge twenty-five minutes later, weary but satisfied with a job well done.

Choose a two- or three-paragraph section of the essay. Use the "Analyzing a Comparison-and-Contrast Essay" questions on pages 370–71 to analyze the section you chose. Write marginal notes recording your thoughts.

Evaluating a Comparison-and-Contrast Essay

Comparison-and-contrast essays written to inform can be direct and straightforward. However, when the purpose is to express ideas or to persuade, closer evaluation is needed. Use the following questions to guide your evaluation of comparison-and-contrast essays:

- **Does the writer treat each subject fairly and provide balanced coverage of all subjects?** Determine whether the writer gives equal and objective coverage to each subject. If one of the subjects seems to be favored or given special consideration (or if one subject seems not to be treated fairly, fully, or adequately), the writer might be biased—that is, introducing his or her own values and attitudes into the comparison.

- **How does the organization affect meaning?** The two methods of development provide different emphases. Point-by-point organization provides a steady back and forth between subjects, keeping the reader's attention focused on both subjects simultaneously. Subject-by-subject organization tends to allow in-depth consideration of each subject separately. To present one subject more positively than another, a writer may choose to discuss the favored subject and all its characteristics first, thereby shaping the reader's impression in a positive way before the reader encounters the second subject. Or a writer may present the less-favored subject first, bringing out its faults, and then move to the more-favored second subject, pointing out its merits and leaving the reader with a final positive impression of the second subject.

- **What points of comparison are omitted?** Be sure to ask yourself what other points of comparison could have been included that were not. For example, in an essay comparing landlines and cell phones, it would be odd if convenience and accessibility were not discussed.

Evaluation in Action

Exercise 14.3

A student wrote the following evaluation of Barry's introduction after reviewing her notes analyzing the piece.

> The author's opening story is funny and works so well because it is really exaggerated. Barry appeals to the reader by being so honest about the stereotypes that he is perpetuating—and that he believes are backed up by science! It's important to note that while Barry does play on stereotypes, he is not being offensive to either sex; he is just trying to write a humorous essay that has some fun with some of the many differences between men and women.

Use the questions above to help you write your own evaluation of the rest of the essay.

Writing Your Own Comparison-and-Contrast Essay

Now that you have learned about the major characteristics, structure, and purposes of a comparison-and-contrast essay, you know everything necessary to write your own. In this section, you will read a student's comparison-and-contrast essay and get advice on finding ideas, drafting your essay, and revising and editing it. You may want to use the essay prompts in "Readings for Practice, Ideas for Writing" (p. 381) or choose your own topic.

A Student Model Comparison-and-Contrast Essay

Heather Gianakos was a first-year student when she wrote the following comparison-and-contrast essay for her composition course. Although she had always enjoyed the two styles of cooking she chose to discuss, she needed to do some research in the library and on the Internet to learn more about their history. As you read the essay, observe how Gianakos integrates information from sources into her essay.

Border Bites

Heather Gianakos

Introduction
indicates essay
examines similarities
and differences
but focuses on
differences.
Subject A:
Southwestern food
Subject B: Mexican
food
Thesis

Chili peppers, tortillas, tacos: All these foods belong to the styles of cooking known as Mexican, Tex-Mex, and southwestern. These internationally popular styles often overlap; sometimes it can be hard to tell which style a particular dish belongs to. Two particular traditions of cooking, however, play an especially important role in the kitchens of Mexico and the American Southwest—native-derived Mexican cooking ("Mexican") and Anglo-influenced southwestern cooking, particularly from Texas ("southwestern"). The different traditions and geographic locations of the inhabitants of Mexico and of the Anglo American settlers in the Southwest have resulted in subtle, flavorful differences between the foods featured in Mexican and southwestern cuisine.

Body paragraphs:
point by point
Point 1: the physical
conditions in which
the two styles
developed

A: difficult conditions
B: fresh foods available
Notice the use of
transitions and
sources.

Many of the traditions of southwestern cooking grew out of difficult situations—cowboys and ranchers cooking over open fires, for example. Chili, which can contain beans, beef, tomatoes, corn, and many other ingredients, was a good dish to cook over a campfire because everything could be combined in one pot. Dry foods, such as beef jerky, were a convenient way to solve food storage problems and could be easily tucked into saddlebags. In Mexico, by contrast, fresh fruits and vegetables such as avocados and tomatoes were widely available and did not need to be dried or stored. They could be made into spicy salsa and guacamole. Mexicans living in coastal areas could also enjoy fish and lobster dishes (Jamison and Jamison 5).

Point 2: the use of
corn and wheat

Corn has been a staple in the American Southwest and Mexico since the time of the Aztecs, who made tortillas (flat, unleavened bread, originally made from stone-ground corn and water) similar to the ones served in Mexico today (Jamison and Jamison 5). Southwesterners, often of European descent, adopted the tortilla but often prepared it with wheat flour, which was easily available to them. Wheat-flour tortillas can now be found in both Mexican and southwestern cooking, but corn is usually the primary grain in dishes with precolonial origins. Tamales (whose name derives from a word in Nahuatl, the Aztec group of languages) are a delicious example: A hunk of cornmeal dough, sometimes combined with ground meat, is wrapped in corn husks and steamed. In southwestern cooking, corn is often used for leavened corn bread, which is made with corn flour rather than cornmeal and can be flavored with jalapeños or back bacon.

> **A and B:** in tortillas
>
> **B:** corn especially important; example: tamales
>
> **A:** corn bread

Meat of various kinds is often the centerpiece of both Mexican and southwestern tables. However, although chicken, beef, and pork are staples in both traditions, they are often prepared quite differently. Fried chicken rolled in flour and dunked into sizzling oil or fat is a popular dish throughout the American Southwest. In traditional Mexican cooking, however, chicken is often cooked more slowly, in stews or baked dishes, with a variety of seasonings, including ancho chiles, garlic, and onions.

> **Point 3:** the use of chicken
> **A:** fried
>
> **B:** stewed or baked

Ever since cattle farming began in Texas with the early Spanish missions, beef has been eaten both north and south of the border. In southwestern cooking, steak—flank, rib eye, or sirloin—grilled quickly and served rare is often a chef's crowning glory. In Mexican cooking, beef may be combined with vegetables and spices and rolled into a fajita or served ground in a taco. For a Mexican food purist, in fact, the only true fajita is made from skirt steak, although Mexican food as it is served in the United States often features chicken fajitas.

> **Point 4:** the use of beef
> **A:** grilled
>
> **B:** fajita or taco

In Texas and the Southwest United States, barbecued pork ribs are often prepared in barbecue cook-offs, similar to chili-cooking competitions. Such competitions have strict rules for the preparation and presentation of the food and for sanitation (Central Texas Barbecue Assn.). However, while the BBQ is seen as a southwestern specialty, barbecue ribs as they are served in southwestern-themed restaurants today actually come from a Hispanic and Southwest Mexican tradition dating from the days before refrigeration: Since pork fat, unlike beef fat, has a tendency to become rancid, pork ribs were often marinated in vinegar and spices and then hung to dry. Later the ribs were basted with the same sauce and grilled (Campa 278). The resulting dish has become a favorite both north and south of the border, although

> **Point 5:** the use of pork
> **A:** BBQ
>
> **B:** originated BBQ; chorizo

Conclusion:

Gianakos returns to the idea of overlap mentioned in the introduction and makes clear her purpose—to inform readers about the differences between the two cuisines.

in Mexican cooking, where beef is somewhat less important than in southwestern cooking, pork is equally popular in many other forms, such as chorizo sausage.

Cooks in San Antonio or Albuquerque would probably tell you that the food they cook is as much Mexican as it is southwestern. Regional cuisines in such areas of the Southwest as New Mexico, Southern California, and Arizona feature elements of both traditions; chimichangas—deep-fried burritos—actually originated in Arizona (Jamison and Jamison 11). Food lovers who sample regional specialties, however, will note—and savor—the contrast between the spicy, fried or grilled, beef-heavy style of southwestern food and the richly seasoned, corn- and tomato-heavy style of Mexican food.

Works Cited

Campa, Arthur L. *Hispanic Culture in the Southwest*. U of Oklahoma P, 1979.

Central Texas Barbecue Association. "CTBA Rules." *Central Texas Barbecue Association*, 1 Feb. 2016, www.ctbabbq.com/Home/Rules.

Jamison, Cheryl Alters, and Bill Jamison. *The Border Cookbook*. Harvard Common Press, 1995.

Responding to Gianakos's Essay

1. What is Gianakos's purpose in writing the essay? How effectively does she present and support her thesis?

2. What method of organization does Gianakos use?

3. Consider Gianakos's points of comparison. How effective is she in presenting details to support each point? What types of examples and sensory details describe each characteristic?

4. How does Gianakos's use of sources contribute to the essay?

Finding Ideas for Your Comparison-and-Contrast Essay

To write a comparison-and-contrast essay, consider the following strategies.

- If you read an essay that interested you, try comparing its subjects by using a different basis of comparison. If, for example, an essay compared or contrasted athletes in two sports on the basis of salary, you could compare them according to the training required.

- If an essay that interested you emphasized differences between its subjects, consider writing about their similarities, or vice versa. For example, in response to an essay on the differences between two late-night television hosts, you might write about their similarities.

- If a reading has a point of comparison that you would like to develop in more depth, you might do research to discover further information or interview an expert on the topic.

Choosing a Basis of Comparison and a Purpose

The first step is to choose specific subjects to write about. You may want to compare subjects that are concrete (such as two public figures) or abstract (such as teaching styles or views on an issue). Be sure, in any case, to choose subjects with which you have some firsthand experience or that you can learn about through research. Also choose subjects that interest you. It will be more fun writing about them, and your enthusiasm will enliven your essay.

After selecting your subjects, you need to establish a basis of comparison and a purpose for writing. To compare or contrast two well-known football players—a quarterback and a linebacker—you could use as a basis the positions they play, describing the skills and training needed for each position. Your purpose in this instance would be to *inform* readers about the two positions. Alternatively, you could base the comparison on their performances on the field; in this case, your purpose might be to *persuade* readers to accept your evaluation of both players and your opinion on who is the better athlete. Other bases of comparison might be the players' media images, contributions to their respective teams, or service to the community.

Once you have a basis of comparison and a purpose, try to state them clearly in a few sentences. Refer to these sentences throughout the process of writing your essay to keep on track.

Discovering Similarities and Differences and Generating Details

The next step is to discover how your two subjects are similar and how they are different. You can approach this task in a number of ways.

1. **Create a two-column list of similarities and differences.** Jot down ideas in the appropriate column.
2. **Ask a classmate to help you brainstorm aloud, mentioning only similarities and then countering each similarity with a difference.** Take notes as you brainstorm, or record your session.
3. **If your subjects are concrete, try visualizing them.** Take notes on what you "see," or draw a sketch of the subjects.
4. **Create a scenario in which your subjects interact.** For example, if your topic is automobiles of the 1920s and 2016, imagine taking your great-grandfather, who owned a Model T Ford, for a drive in a 2016 luxury car. How would he react? What would he say?
5. **Do research on your two subjects at the library or on the Internet.**

Keep in mind that your readers will need plenty of details to grasp the similarities and differences between the subjects. Vivid descriptions, interesting examples, and appropriate facts will bring your subjects to life.

To maintain an even balance between the two subjects, do some brainstorming, freewriting, or library or Internet research to gather roughly the same amount of detail on each. This guideline is especially important if your purpose is to demonstrate that Subject A is preferable to or better than Subject B. Readers will become suspicious if you provide plenty of detail about Subject A and only sketchy information about Subject B.

Developing and Supporting Your Thesis

The thesis statement for a comparison-and-contrast essay needs to fulfill the three criteria noted earlier: It identifies the subjects; suggests whether you will focus on similarities, differences, or both; and states your main point. In addition, the thesis should tell why your comparison and contrast of the two subjects is important or useful. Look at the following sample thesis statements.

Weak	The mystery novels of Robert Parker and Sue Grafton are similar.
Revised	The mystery novels of Robert Parker and Sue Grafton are popular because readers are fascinated by the intrigues of witty, independent private detectives.

The first thesis is weak because it presents the two subjects in isolation, without placing the comparison within a context or giving readers a reason to care about it. The second thesis provides a basis for comparison and indicates why the similarity is worth reading about. As you develop your thesis, consider what large idea or worthwhile point the comparison demonstrates.

Selecting Points of Comparison

With your thesis in mind, review your notes and try to identify the points or characteristics by which you can best compare your subjects. For example, if your thesis involved evaluating the performance of two football players, you would probably select various facts and details about their training, the plays they made, and their records. Think of points of comparison as the main similarities or differences that support your thesis. Make sure to have enough points of comparison to support the thesis and enough details to develop those points. If necessary, do additional brainstorming.

Drafting Your Comparison-and-Contrast Essay

Before you begin writing, decide whether you will use a point-by-point or a subject-by-subject organization. To select a method of organization, consider the complexity of your subjects and the length of your essay. You may also need to experiment with the two approaches to see which one works better. It is a good idea to make an outline or draw a graphic organizer at this stage. To experiment with different methods of organization, create a new computer file for each possibility and try each one out. (For more details on the benefits of each type of organization, see p. 367.)

After choosing a method of organization, your next step is to write a first draft. Use the following guidelines:

1. **Write an effective introduction.** The introduction should spark readers' interest, present your subjects, state your thesis, and include any background information that readers may need.

2. **For a point-by-point essay, work back and forth between the two subjects, mentioning the subjects in the same order.**

3. **For a point-by-point essay, arrange the points of comparison carefully.** Start with the clearest, simplest points and then move on to more complex ones.

4. **For a subject-by-subject essay, cover the same points for both subjects.** Address the points of comparison for each subject in the same order in both halves of your essay.

5. **Use transitions to alert readers to the organization of the essay and to shifts between subjects or to a new point of comparison.** To move between subjects, use transitional words and phrases such as *similarly, in contrast, on the one hand . . . on the other hand,* and *not only . . . but also.*

6. **Write a satisfying conclusion.** The conclusion should offer a final comment on the comparison and contrast, reminding readers of your thesis. For a lengthy or complex essay, it is a good idea to summarize the main points as well.

Revising Your Comparison-and-Contrast Essay

If possible, set your draft aside for a day or two before rereading and revising it. As you reread, concentrate on your ideas and not on grammar or mechanics. Use the flowchart in Figure 14.4 to guide your analysis of the draft's strengths and weaknesses.

Editing and Proofreading Your Essay

The last step is to check your revised essay for errors in grammar, spelling, punctuation, and mechanics. In addition, be sure to look for errors that you tend to make in any writing assignment, whether for this class or in other situations. Check the handbook (pp. 645–714) for assistance with common errors in your writing.

Figure 14.4 Revising a Comparison-and-Contrast Essay

QUESTIONS	REVISION STRATEGIES

1. Thesis Does it identify the subjects being compared and state your main point? Does it or do nearby sentences express a clear purpose?

 No

- Brainstorm a list of reasons for making the comparison. Make the most promising reason your purpose.

 Yes

2. Basis of comparison Is it clear? Does it relate to your thesis?

No

- Brainstorm a clear or new basis of comparison with a friend or classmate.

Yes

3. Points of comparison Have you included all significant points of comparison and fairly examined them? Does each support your thesis?

 No

- Delete any insignificant similarities or differences or ones that do not support your thesis.
- Add any significant points of comparison from your prewriting that you have not already included.
- Conduct research or talk to a classmate to find new points of comparison.

Yes

4. Topic sentences Does each paragraph have a clear topic sentence? For a point-by-point comparison, is each paragraph focused on a single point or shared characteristic?

No

- Consider splitting paragraphs that focus on more than one point or characteristic and combining paragraphs that focus on the same one.

Yes

5. Details Are there enough details to make your comparisons vivid and interesting? Is there roughly the same amount of detail for each subject?

 No

- Add or delete details as necessary.
- Review your prewriting to see if you overlooked any significant details.
- Conduct research to come up with additional details.

Yes

6. Organization Did you use either point-by-point or subject-by-subject organization consistently? Is your organization clear to your reader?

 No

- Study your graphic organizer or outline to find inconsistencies or gaps.
- Reorganize your essay using one method of organization consistently.
- Add transitions if necessary.

Yes

7. Introduction and conclusion Does the introduction provide a context for your comparison? Is the conclusion satisfying and relevant to the comparison?

 No

- Revise your introduction and conclusion to meet the guidelines in Chapter 7.
- Consider proposing an action or a way of thinking that is appropriate in light of the comparison.

Readings for Practice, Ideas for Writing

What Kind of H₂O Should You Drink? We Asked L.A.'s Only Water Sommelier

Sara Rashkin is a writer based in Los Angeles. She contributed this article to the *L.A. Weekly*, a free alternative-weekly tabloid that covers cultural events and topics of interest to local residents.

Reading Tip

As you read, think about the quotations the author includes and how these contribute to her comparison and contrast.

Previewing the Reading

Preview the reading (see pp. 28–29 for guidelines), and then answer the following questions.

1. What three things are compared in the essay?
2. What are the four major areas of comparison that the author addresses?

SARA RASHKIN

What Kind of H₂O Should You Drink? We Asked L.A.'s Only Water Sommelier

The act of drinking water seems to have become unnecessarily confusing. What is the average person to make of advertisements for "alkaline water" and discussions of "total dissolved solids"? How different can water taste? And what environmental impact do our decisions about bottled water have?

For guidance, we turned to water expert Martin Riese, who has been a certified water sommelier since 2010 and has studied water for more than a decade. He's also developed extensive water menus for restaurants, including fine-dining destination Patina and Ray's & Stark Bar at LACMA, and regularly teaches Water 101 classes for those who want to learn more.

Riese believes it's important to educate people about the differences in water types and to bring an increased sense of value to water. "People say 'only in L.A.' about having a water menu," he admits, "but we are wasting water like crazy in the city, and I say it's 'only in L.A.' that we live in the desert and no one cares about water."

From tap water to infused waters, here's the lowdown on source, taste, health and possible environmental implications of all kinds of H₂O.

Los Angeles Tap Water

Providing citywide safe drinking water 5 requires disinfecting the water to kill harmful bacteria. Over the course of the past year, the Los Angeles Department of Water and Power made the

Continued >

REUTERS/Mario Anzuoni

Water sommelier Martin Riese with spring and mineral bottled waters.

switch from chlorine to chloramine (a combination of ammonia and chlorine) as its disinfectant. Chloramine is not a new treatment, but it is new to L.A. On the LADWP website, the switch is explained as an effort "to improve taste and odor, and to comply with more stringent water-quality regulations."

The city follows legal guidelines to keep the chloramine at an acceptable level for human consumption, although chloramine-treated water is not suitable for people on dialysis or for use in fish tanks. For those who are sensitive to it or don't like the taste, chloramine presents a challenge because it's notoriously difficult to filter out. Those who do like the taste are in luck, since this is the least expensive and most eco-friendly drinking water option, unless you have access to well water.

Riese says he does taste a difference in our tap water since the switch. "The chlorine is not as overpowering now," he says, "but I'm still not really a fan.

You still can taste it, but at the same time I totally understand why they have to do it. They have to make sure it's safe."

. . .

Purified Water

Without access to glacier-fed tap water, many people in L.A. choose to use purified water for drinking, showering and even brewing. Purified water is simply water that has been processed to remove minerals and chemicals, resulting in a very low TDS, or Total Dissolved Solids, in parts per million— a measurement of the mobile charged ions in water including dissolved minerals, salts and metals. Magnesium, calcium, sodium and potassium are some of the minerals commonly found naturally occurring in water, absorbed from the surroundings, along with trace elements like zinc and fluoride. Purified water that has had these minerals removed can refer to both distilled water (where water is vaporized, which leaves the minerals behind, and then condensed into water again) and heavily filtered water.

Riese is among the many experts who believe purified water is not a healthy drinking water choice. "People think it's just clean and sounds so good for you," Riese explains, "but it's actually very harmful water. This water is good for machines. In Europe it's labeled 'do not drink.'" He adds: "The body runs on minerals, that's the reason we're eating and drinking." The UN's World Health Organization has published a report entitled "Health Risks of Drinking Demineralized Water," which includes a warning that this water is "highly aggressive" and can leach metals from pipes and minerals from food.

10   Many purified-water products have a few minerals added back in to improve taste and to address health concerns about drinking "empty" water. At Intelligentsia Coffee locations, you can try reverse osmosis–filtered tap water that has been blended with water that retains some minerals—this is the water they currently use for everything from brewing coffee to the dispenser of complimentary drinking water. Many bottled water brands on the market are reverse osmosis–filtered tap water with minerals added. Coca-Cola and Pepsi long ago admitted that their water brands, Dasani and Aquafina, are filtered tap water. (Dasani bottles, for instance, are labeled "purified water enhanced with minerals" and the ingredients read: purified water, magnesium sulfate, potassium chloride, salt.) Nestlé Pure Life brand also uses municipal water and has a plant in Sacramento.

. . .

Spring and Mineral Waters

If taste is your priority in drinking water, it's easy to see why spring and mineral waters are such big business. With a fascinating variety of water from all over the world, you can drink Iskilde one day, a still water with a rare mineral profile from an isolated aquifer in Denmark, and Vichy Catalan the next, a strong-tasting, naturally carbonated hot springs water from Spain that has been bottled since 1889.

It's the difference in the mineral amounts (the TDS measurement), as well as the specific minerals present, that gives each water a unique taste. Consider that Iskilde has a TDS of 426 while Vichy has an astounding TDS of 3,052. (TDS levels for a single brand can vary from bottle to bottle.) Voss, a naturally low-mineral spring water from Norway, has a low TDS of about 22.

To be labeled mineral water, a water source must have a relatively constant TDS level of 250 parts per million or higher. Spring water must come from an underground aquifer that either pushes to the surface naturally (referred to as an artesian spring) or is tapped so the water can be pumped up. The ground prevents contact with air and naturally filters many contaminants from the water while imparting minerals. Spring and mineral waters must be bottled at the source, and this water can be minimally processed to remove elements such as iron, but the bottled product must reflect the same composition as the original water.

Riese feels that many people no longer appreciate water varieties and their health properties, and he points out that everything from mineral deficiencies to overeating to headaches can be linked to dehydration and poor

Continued >

water choices. He traces the history of bottled water to the early popularity of healing mineral springs—when people couldn't get to the springs, bottled water brought the springs to people. Roi, a Slovenian mineral water with the highest TDS Riese has ever encountered (7,500), is labeled the most magnesium-rich water in the world (you can even see the sediment on the glass), and it has been bottled since 1647.

15   As for bottles, Riese prefers glass ones, which are better than plastic at protecting water and do not affect taste the way plastic can. The shelf life of a glass bottle is three years, while it's just one year for a plastic bottle.

And therein lies the catch: To enjoy these waters anywhere but their place of origin, you must buy bottles. If you want to avoid disposable bottles and pollution from bottling and shipping, tap water is the safer environmental choice (not to mention the economical one). But if you are choosing among all your bottled beverage options like juice and soda, bottled water has the least environmental cost. "Nobody is saying something about wine and beer, and those are much worse [in environmental impact]," Riese points out.

▥ Understanding and Reviewing the Reading

1. **Thesis** What is Rashkin's thesis, and where does she state it most directly?

2. **Basis of comparison** What characteristics do L.A. tap water, purified water, and spring and mineral water share that allow a comparison among them to be made?

3. **Contrasts** According to water sommelier Martin Riese, what are the strengths of L.A. tap water, purified water, and spring and mineral water?

Strengths of Tap Water	Strengths of Purified Water	Strengths of Spring and Mineral Water
1.	1.	1.
2.	2.	2.
3.	3.	3.

4. **Language** Using context clues (p. 37), write a brief definition of each of the following words as it is used in the reading, checking a dictionary if necessary: *infused* (para. 4), *stringent* (5), *notoriously* (6), *leach* (9), and *imparting* (13).

5. **Details** What other international waters are cited in the essay? What point is Rashkin making by mentioning them?

6. **Organization** Complete the graphic organizer to better understand the structure of the piece.

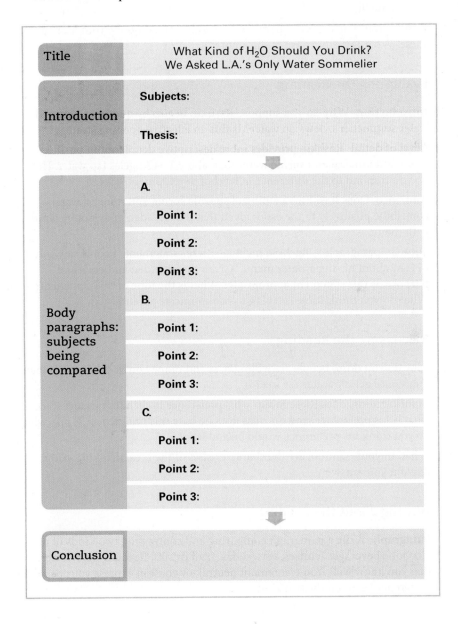

Title	What Kind of H_2O Should You Drink? We Asked L.A.'s Only Water Sommelier
Introduction	**Subjects:**
	Thesis:

	A.
	Point 1:
	Point 2:
	Point 3:
	B.
Body paragraphs: subjects being compared	Point 1:
	Point 2:
	Point 3:
	C.
	Point 1:
	Point 2:
	Point 3:

Conclusion	

Analyzing the Reading

1. **Purpose** Is Rashkin's purpose mainly to inform or to persuade? Why do you think as you do?

2. **Sources** List the sources Rashkin quotes or paraphrases in the essay. Why might she have included all these sources?

3. **Visual** Why do you think the photograph that accompanies this reading was included?

4. **Conclusion** Rashkin's last paragraph includes a final quote from Martin Riese. What is the purpose of this quote?

Evaluating the Reading

1. **Introduction** Why do you suppose Rashkin begins by quoting a certified water sommelier's views on water? Is this an effective opening strategy?

2. **Level of detail** Rashkin provides more descriptive details about purified water and mineral and spring water than about Los Angeles tap water. How do you respond to the difference in level of development?

3. **Audience** Does Rashkin's naming of specific spring and mineral waters contribute positively to the essay, given that most readers may not be familiar with them?

4. **Tone** In paragraph 3, Rashkin includes Riese's statement "People say 'only in L.A.' about having a water menu." Given the intended audience and purpose, is this statement appropriate? What is the tone of this statement? What do you think Riese is trying to communicate about L.A.?

Discussing the Reading

1. Why do you think people are willing to spend money on bottled water when they could get tap water for free?

2. In this reading, does Riese indicate his preference in drinking water? If so, what is his preference, and on what does he base this preference? If not, what do you think his preference would be and why?

3. What, in your opinion, are the characteristics of the ideal drinking water? Explain your answer.

Writing about the Reading

1. **Paragraph** Write a paragraph comparing and contrasting two kinds of non-alcoholic beverages (coffees, teas, sodas, fruit drinks, flavored waters, etc.) that you know well. You can remain neutral, or you can express your personal preference between the two kinds.

2. **Paragraph** In the reading, Rashkin highlights rare spring and mineral waters that are served in high-end restaurants around the world. Most of us do not know much about high-end restaurants around the world, but we are experts when it comes to casual dining restaurants and fast-food chains. Brainstorm a list of casual dining restaurants or fast-food chains. Then choose two specific establishments to compare and contrast in a paragraph. (Hint: Make sure that the two have enough commonalities to provide a basis of comparison but also enough differences to develop in the paragraph.)

3. **Essay** In an essay, describe how your personal tastes—perhaps in terms of food, clothing, music, movies, hobbies, or political views—are similar to and different from those of someone with whom you are close. (Hint: Before drafting, think about whether a subject-by-subject or point-by-point organization will be more effective.)

Sex, Lies, and Conversation

Deborah Tannen holds a Ph.D. in linguistics and is currently a professor at Georgetown University. Tannen has written several books about communication and language, including *I Only Say This Because I Love You* (2001), in which she examines communication between family members. The following essay first appeared in the *Washington Post* in 1990.

Reading Tip

Notice how the author begins with a personal example, immediately catching the reader's interest. Pay attention also to her use of supporting evidence.

Previewing the Reading

Preview the reading (see pp. 28–29) and then answer the following questions.

1. What is Tannen comparing and contrasting in this essay?
2. Identify at least one point of comparison.
3. Why does Tannen think understanding is important?

DEBORAH TANNEN

Sex, Lies, and Conversation

I was addressing a small gathering in a suburban Virginia living room—a women's group that had invited men to join them. Throughout the evening, one man had been particularly talkative, frequently offering ideas and anecdotes, while his wife sat silently beside him on the couch. Toward the end of the evening, I commented that women frequently complain that their husbands don't talk to them. This man quickly concurred. He gestured toward his wife and said, "She's the talker in our family." The room burst into laughter; the man looked puzzled and hurt. "It's true," he explained. "When I come home from work I have nothing to say. If she didn't keep the conversation going, we'd spend the whole evening in silence."

This episode crystallizes the irony that although American men tend to talk more than women in public situations, they often talk less at home. And this pattern is wreaking havoc with marriage.

The pattern was observed by political scientist Andrew Hacker in the late '70s. Sociologist Catherine Kohler Riessman reports in her new book *Divorce Talk* that most of the women she interviewed—but only a few of the men—gave lack of communication as the reason for their divorces. Given the current divorce rate of nearly 50%, that amounts to millions of cases in the United States every year—a virtual epidemic of failed conversation.

In my own research, complaints from women about their husbands most often focused not on tangible inequities such as having given up the chance for a career to accompany a husband to his, or doing far more than their share of daily life-support work like cleaning, cooking, social arrangements, and errands. Instead, they focused on communication: "He doesn't listen to me." "He doesn't talk to me." I found, as Hacker observed years before, that most wives want their husbands to be, first and foremost, conversational partners, but few husbands share this expectation of their wives.

5   In short, the image that best represents the current crisis is the stereotypical cartoon scene of a man sitting at the breakfast table with a newspaper held up in front of his face, while a woman glares at the back of it, wanting to talk.

Linguistic Battle of the Sexes

How can women and men have such different impressions of communication in marriage? Why the widespread imbalance in their interests and expectations?

In the April issue of *American Psychologist*, Stanford University's Eleanor Maccoby reports the results of her own and others' research showing that children's development is most influenced by the social structure of peer interactions. Boys and girls tend to play with children of their own gender, and their sex-separate groups have different organizational structures and interactive norms[1].

I believe these systematic differences in childhood socialization make talk between women and men like cross-cultural communication, heir to all the attraction and pitfalls of that enticing but difficult enterprise. My research on men's and women's conversations uncovered patterns similar to those described for children's groups.

For women, as for girls, intimacy is the fabric of relationships, and talk is the thread from which it is woven. Little girls create and maintain friendships by

[1] **norms** Standards of behavior that are typical of a group or culture.

exchanging secrets; similarly, women regard conversation as the cornerstone of friendship. So a woman expects her husband to be a new and improved version of a best friend. What is important is not the individual subjects that are discussed but the sense of closeness, of a life shared, that emerges when people tell their thoughts, feelings, and impressions.

Bonds between boys can be as intense   10 as girls', but they are based less on talking, more on doing things together. Since they don't assume talk is the cement that binds a relationship, men don't know what kind of talk women want, and they don't miss it when it isn't there.

Boys' groups are larger, more inclusive, and more hierarchical, so boys must struggle to avoid the subordinate position in the group. This may play a role in women's complaints that men don't listen to them. Some men really don't like to listen, because being the listener makes them feel one-down, like a child listening to adults or an employee to a boss.

But often when women tell men, "You aren't listening," and the men protest, "I am," the men are right. The impression of not listening results from misalignments in the mechanics of conversation. The misalignment begins as soon as a man and a woman take physical positions. This became clear when I studied videotapes made by psychologist Bruce Dorval of children and adults talking to their same-sex best friends. I found that at every age, the girls and women faced each other directly, their eyes anchored on each other's faces. At every age, the boys and men sat at angles to each other and looked elsewhere in the room, periodically glancing at each other. They were obviously attuned to each other, often mirroring each other's movements. But

Continued >

the tendency of men to face away can give women the impression they aren't listening even when they are. A young woman in college was frustrated: Whenever she told her boyfriend she wanted to talk to him, he would lie down on the floor, close his eyes, and put his arm over his face. This signaled to her, "He's taking a nap." But he insisted he was listening extra hard. Normally, he looks around the room, so he is easily distracted. Lying down and covering his eyes helped him concentrate on what she was saying.

Analogous to the physical alignment that women and men take in conversation is their topical alignment. The girls in my study tended to talk at length about one topic, but the boys tended to jump from topic to topic. The second-grade girls exchanged stories about people they knew. The second-grade boys teased, told jokes, noticed things in the room, and talked about finding games to play. The sixth-grade girls talked about problems with a mutual friend. The sixth-grade boys talked about fifty-five different topics, none of which extended over more than a few turns.

Listening to Body Language

Switching topics is another habit that gives women the impression men aren't listening, especially if they switch to a topic about themselves. But the evidence of the tenth-grade boys in my study indicates otherwise. The tenth-grade boys sprawled across their chairs with bodies parallel and eyes straight ahead, rarely looking at each other. They looked as if they were riding in a car, staring out the windshield. But they were talking about their feelings. One boy was upset because a girl had told him he had a drinking problem, and the other was feeling alienated from all his friends.

15   Now, when a girl told a friend about a problem, the friend responded by asking probing questions and expressing agreement and understanding. But the boys dismissed each other's problems. Todd assured Richard that his drinking was "no big problem" because "sometimes you're funny when you're off your butt." And when Todd said he felt left out, Richard responded, "Why should you? You know more people than me."

Women perceive such responses as belittling and unsupportive. But the boys seemed satisfied with them. Whereas women reassure each other by implying, "You shouldn't feel bad because I've had similar experiences," men do so by implying, "You shouldn't feel bad because your problems aren't so bad."

There are even simpler reasons for women's impression that men don't listen. Linguist Lynette Hirschman found that women make more listener-noise, such as "mhm," "uhuh," and "yeah," to show "I'm with you." Men, she found, more often give silent attention. Women who expect a stream of listener-noise interpret silent attention as no attention at all.

Women's conversational habits are as frustrating to men as men's are to women. Men who expect silent attention interpret a stream of listener-noise as overreaction or impatience. Also, when women talk to each other in a close, comfortable setting, they often overlap, finish each other's sentences, and anticipate what the other is about to say. This practice, which I call "participatory listenership," is often perceived by men as interruption, intrusion, and lack of attention.

A parallel difference caused a man to complain about his wife, "She just wants to talk about her own point of view. If I show her another view, she gets mad at me." When most women talk to each other, they assume a conversationalist's job is to express agreement and support.

But many men see their conversational duty as pointing out the other side of an argument. This is heard as disloyalty by women, and refusal to offer the requisite support. It is not that women don't want to see other points of view, but that they prefer them phrased as suggestions and inquiries rather than as direct challenges.

20   In his book *Fighting for Life*, Walter Ong points out that men use "agonistic" or warlike, oppositional formats to do almost anything; thus discussion becomes debate, and conversation a competitive sport. In contrast, women see conversation as a ritual means of establishing rapport. If Jane tells a problem and June says she has a similar one, they walk away feeling closer to each other. But this attempt at establishing rapport can backfire when used with men. Men take too literally women's ritual "troubles talk," just as women mistake men's ritual challenges for real attack.

The Sounds of Silence

These differences begin to clarify why women and men have such different expectations about communication in marriage. For women, talk creates intimacy. Marriage is an orgy of closeness: You can tell your feelings and thoughts, and still be loved. Their greatest fear is being pushed away. But men live in a hierarchical world, where talk maintains independence and status. They are on guard to protect themselves from being put down and pushed around.

This explains the paradox of the talkative man who said of his silent wife, "She's the talker." In the public setting of a guest lecture, he felt challenged to show his intelligence and display his understanding of the lecture. But at home, where he has nothing to prove and no one to defend against, he is free to remain silent. For his wife, being home means she is free from the worry that something she says might offend someone, or spark disagreement, or appear to be showing off; at home she is free to talk.

The communication problems that endanger marriage can't be fixed by mechanical engineering. They require a new conceptual framework about the role of talk in human relationships. Many of the psychological explanations that have become second nature may not be helpful, because they tend to blame either women (for not being assertive enough) or men (for not being in touch with their feelings). A sociolinguistic approach by which male–female conversation is seen as cross-cultural communication allows us to understand the problem and forge solutions without blaming either party.

Once the problem is understood, improvement comes naturally, as it did to the young woman and her boyfriend who seemed to go to sleep when she wanted to talk. Previously, she had accused him of not listening, and he had refused to change his behavior, since that would be admitting fault. But then she learned about and explained to him the differences in women's and men's habitual ways of aligning themselves in conversation. The next time she told him she wanted to talk, he began, as usual, by lying down and covering his eyes. When the familiar negative reaction bubbled up, she reassured herself that he really was listening. But then he sat up and looked at her. Thrilled, she asked why. He said, "You like me to look at you when we talk, so I'll try to do it." Once he saw their differences as cross-cultural rather than right and wrong, he independently altered his behavior.

25   Women who feel abandoned and deprived when their husbands won't

Continued >

listen to or report daily news may be happy to discover their husbands trying to adapt once they understand the place of small talk in women's relationships. But if their husbands don't adapt, the women may still be comforted that for men, this is not a failure of intimacy. Accepting the difference, the wives may look to their friends or family for that kind of talk. And husbands who can't provide it shouldn't feel their wives have made unreasonable demands. Some couples will still decide to divorce, but at least their decisions will be based on realistic expectations.

In these times of resurgent ethnic conflicts, the world desperately needs cross-cultural understanding. Like charity, successful cross-cultural communication should begin at home.

Understanding and Reviewing the Reading

1. **Thesis** What is Tannen's thesis about gender communication?

2. **Introduction** What does the opening anecdote about the man at a women's group illustrate?

3. **Contrasts** What differences in communication are observable between young girls and boys?

4. **Contrasts** In what ways does body language differ between men and women? How do these differences affect communication between the sexes?

5. **Organization** What method of organization does Tannen use?

Analyzing the Reading

1. **Thesis** Is Tannen's thesis effectively placed? Why, or why not?

2. **Points of comparison** Identify the points of comparison that Tannen uses to support her thesis. Does she focus on similarities, differences, or both? Does she treat her subjects fairly? Explain.

3. **Evidence** In explaining the communication differences between men and women, Tannen explores the causes of these differences. How does this information strengthen the essay?

4. **Language** What sort of image does the phrase "wreaking havoc" (para. 2) bring to mind?

5. **Analyzing evidence** Tannen includes different types of evidence to support her thesis. Analyze the purpose of the supporting evidence by completing the chart on page 393. The first entry has been done for you.

Evaluating the Reading

1. **Organization** Why do you think Tannen chose the organization she used? Would the essay be as effective with a different organizational plan? Explain.

Evidence	Purpose
Reference to political scientist Andrew Hacker (para. 3)	Gives legitimacy to the thesis and demonstrates that the thesis is not a new idea
Sociologist Catherine Kohler Riessman's observations from her book *Divorce Talk* (para. 3)	
The author's own research (para. 4)	
American Psychologist article by Stanford University's Eleanor Maccoby (para. 7)	
Psychologist Bruce Dorval's videotapes (para. 12)	
The author's own research (paras. 13–16)	
Linguist Lynette Hirschman's research (para. 17)	
Reference to *Fighting for Life* by Walter Ong (para. 20)	

2. **Language** Tannen, a linguist, uses some linguistic jargon even though she is writing for the general public. Highlight these terms and evaluate their effectiveness. Are they a benefit or a detriment to your understanding of the essay?

3. **Original sources** Sometimes when authors are reporting on research for a general audience, they do not provide full citations for the work—that is, the original sources—they mention. Review the chart of sources above. Next to each source, indicate whether full (i.e., author, title, date, publisher), incomplete (e.g., author and title but no date or publisher), or no source information has been given. Then jot down your ideas on how to find the original sources mentioned in the essay. For example, you might use your library catalog to locate Catherine Kohler Riessman's book *Divorce Talk*.

4. **Evidence** Use Tannen's essay as a basis for observing how men and women communicate around you. Observe the men and women with whom you attend class, participate in extracurricular activities, live, or work. Make a chart or list of your observations in relation to Tannen's descriptions. For each of Tannen's points of comparison, decide whether you agree or disagree with her findings based on this exercise and on your own knowledge and experience.

5. **Purpose** At the end of the piece, Tannen provides a reason we should work toward better communication between men and women. Evaluate her reasoning. Does it follow logically from the rest of her essay? Does her evidence (the comparisons and contrasts she offers) relate to her conclusion? Defend your answer using specific examples from the essay.

Discussing the Reading

1. Discuss the importance of clear communication in a relationship you have experienced.

2. Discuss how Tannen's findings are similar to or different from those of Dave Barry as expressed in "We've Got the Dirt on Guy Brains" (p. 361).

3. In class or in your journal, describe an incident from your own experience that confirms or contradicts Tannen's findings.

Writing about the Reading

1. **Essay** Tannen provides many points of comparison to support her thesis. Choose one of them and expand it into a comparison-and-contrast essay of your own. Develop the point of comparison by using information from your own experiences. For example, you could show how differences in body language do, indeed, reflect a common communication pattern.

2. **Essay** Tannen's essay addresses differences in communication between men and women. Consider how communication is similar or different between two other groups—parents and teenagers, employers and employees, or twenty-year-olds and forty-year-olds, for example. Then write an essay that defines each group and discusses their differences or similarities. Include descriptive details and narration to help readers "see" your subjects. Conclude with possible reasons for the differences you observed.

3. **Internet research** Using a search engine, look for articles on communication between men and women. For example, the *Purdue News* includes a short article on this subject at http://news.uns.purdue.edu/UNS/html4ever /2004/040217.MacGeorge.sexroles.html. After choosing an article, write an essay that compares and contrasts it with Tannen's report. Are their findings similar or different? If they disagree, why might their findings differ?

Why Chinese Mothers Are Superior

Amy Chua is a professor at Yale Law School whose expertise includes international business transactions and globalization. Her personal account of extreme parenting, *Battle Hymn of the Tiger Mother*, propelled her onto *Time* magazine's 2011 list of the "100 Most Influential People in the World." The following excerpt comes from *Battle Hymn*.

Reading Tip

This essay is relatively long. As you read, look specifically for the point at which the author begins to focus most directly on comparing and contrasting her two subjects.

Previewing the Reading

Preview the reading (see pp. 28–29 for guidelines) to learn what two specific subjects the author is comparing.

Why Chinese Mothers Are Superior

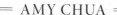

AMY CHUA

A lot of people wonder how Chinese parents raise such stereotypically successful kids. They wonder what these parents do to produce so many math whizzes and music prodigies, what it's like inside the family, and whether they could do it too. Well, I can tell them, because I've done it. Here are some things my daughters, Sophia and Louisa, were never allowed to do:

- attend a sleepover
- have a playdate
- be in a school play
- complain about not being in a school play
- watch TV or play computer games
- choose their own extracurricular activities
- get any grade less than an A
- not be the No. 1 student in every subject except gym and drama
- play any instrument other than piano or violin
- not play piano or violin

I'm using the term "Chinese mother" loosely. I know some Korean, Indian, Jamaican, Irish, and Ghanaian parents who qualify too. Conversely, I know some mothers of Chinese heritage, almost always born in the West, who are

Continued >

Amy Chua with her daughters, Louisa and Sophia, at their home in
New Haven, Connecticut.

not Chinese mothers, by choice or otherwise. I'm also using the term "Western
parents" loosely. Western parents come in all varieties.

All the same, even when Western parents think they're being strict, they
usually don't come close to being Chinese mothers. For example, my Western
friends who consider themselves strict make their children practice their instruments for thirty minutes every day. An hour at most. For a Chinese mother, the
first hour is the easy part. It's hours two and three that get tough.

Despite our squeamishness about cultural stereotypes, there are tons of
studies out there showing marked and quantifiable differences between Chinese
and Westerners when it comes to parenting. In one study of fifty Western
American mothers and forty-eight Chinese immigrant mothers, almost 70% of
the Western mothers said either that "stressing academic success is not good
for children" or that "parents need to foster the idea that learning is fun." By
contrast, roughly 0% of Chinese mothers felt the same way. Instead, the vast
majority of the Chinese mothers said that they believe their children can be "the
best" students, that "academic achievement reflects successful parenting," and
that if children did not excel at school then there was "a problem" and parents
"were not doing their job." Other studies indicate that compared to Western
parents, Chinese parents spend approximately ten times as long every day drilling academic activities with their children. By contrast, Western kids are more
likely to participate in sports teams.

5   What Chinese parents understand is that nothing is fun until you're good
at it. To get good at anything you have to work, and children on their own never
want to work, which is why it is crucial to override their preferences. This often
requires fortitude on the part of the parents because the child will resist; things

are always hardest at the beginning, which is where Western parents tend to give up. But if done properly, the Chinese strategy produces a virtuous circle. Tenacious practice, practice, practice is crucial for excellence; rote repetition is underrated in America. Once a child starts to excel at something—whether it's math, piano, pitching, or ballet—he or she gets praise, admiration, and satisfaction. This builds confidence and makes the once not-fun activity fun. This in turn makes it easier for the parent to get the child to work even more.

Chinese parents can get away with things that Western parents can't. Once when I was young—maybe more than once—when I was extremely disrespectful to my mother, my father angrily called me "garbage" in our native Hokkien dialect. It worked really well. I felt terrible and deeply ashamed of what I had done. But it didn't damage my self-esteem or anything like that. I knew exactly how highly he thought of me. I didn't actually think I was worthless or feel like a piece of garbage.

As an adult, I once did the same thing to Sophia, calling her garbage in English when she acted extremely disrespectfully toward me. When I mentioned that I had done this at a dinner party, I was immediately ostracized. One guest named Marcy got so upset she broke down in tears and had to leave early. My friend Susan, the host, tried to rehabilitate me with the remaining guests.

The fact is that Chinese parents can do things that would seem unimaginable— even legally actionable—to Westerners. Chinese mothers can say to their daughters, "Hey fatty—lose some weight." By contrast, Western parents have to tiptoe around the issue, talking in terms of "health" and never ever mentioning the f-word, and their kids still end up in therapy for eating disorders and negative self-image. (I also once heard a Western father toast his adult daughter by calling her "beautiful and incredibly competent." She later told me that made her feel like garbage.)

Chinese parents can order their kids to get straight As. Western parents can only ask their kids to try their best. Chinese parents can say, "You're lazy. All your classmates are getting ahead of you." By contrast, Western parents have to struggle with their own conflicted feelings about achievement, and try to persuade themselves that they're not disappointed about how their kids turned out.

I've thought long and hard about how Chinese parents can get away with 10 what they do. I think there are three big differences between the Chinese and Western parental mind-sets.

First, I've noticed that Western parents are extremely anxious about their children's self-esteem. They worry about how their children will feel if they fail at something, and they constantly try to reassure their children about how good they are notwithstanding a mediocre performance on a test or at a recital. In other words, Western parents are concerned about their children's psyches. Chinese parents aren't. They assume strength, not fragility, and as a result they behave very differently.

Continued >

For example, if a child comes home with an A-minus on a test, a Western parent will most likely praise the child. The Chinese mother will gasp in horror and ask what went wrong. If the child comes home with a B on the test, some Western parents will still praise the child. Other Western parents will sit their child down and express disapproval, but they will be careful not to make their child feel inadequate or insecure, and they will not call their child "stupid," "worthless," or "a disgrace." Privately, the Western parents may worry that their child does not test well or have aptitude in the subject or that there is something wrong with the curriculum and possibly the whole school. If the child's grades do not improve, they may eventually schedule a meeting with the school principal to challenge the way the subject is being taught or call into question the teacher's credentials.

If a Chinese child gets a B—which would never happen—there would first be a screaming, hair-tearing explosion. The devastated Chinese mother would then get dozens, maybe hundreds of practice tests and work through them with her child for as long as it takes to get the grade up to an A.

Chinese parents demand perfect grades because they believe that their child can get them. If their child doesn't get them, the Chinese parent assumes it's because the child didn't work hard enough. That's why the solution to substandard performance is always to excoriate, punish, and shame the child. The Chinese parent believes that their child will be strong enough to take the shaming and to improve from it. (And when Chinese kids do excel, there is plenty of ego-inflating parental praise lavished in the privacy of the home.)

15   Second, Chinese parents believe that their kids owe them everything. The reason for this is a little unclear, but it's probably a combination of Confucian filial piety and the fact that the parents have sacrificed and done so much for their children. (And it's true that Chinese mothers get in the trenches, putting in long grueling hours personally tutoring, training, interrogating, and spying on their kids.) Anyway, the understanding is that Chinese children must spend their lives repaying their parents by obeying them and making them proud.

By contrast, I don't think most Westerners have the same view of children being permanently indebted to their parents. My husband, Jed, actually has the opposite view. "Children don't choose their parents," he once said to me. "They don't even choose to be born. It's parents who foist life on their kids, so it's the parents' responsibility to provide for them. Kids don't owe their parents anything. Their duty will be to their own kids." This strikes me as a terrible deal for the Western parent.

Third, Chinese parents believe that they know what is best for their children and therefore override all their children's own desires and preferences. That's why Chinese daughters can't have boyfriends in high school and why Chinese kids can't go to sleepaway camp. It's also why no Chinese kid would ever dare say to their mother, "I got a part in the school play! I'm Villager Number Six. I'll have to stay after school for rehearsal everyday from 3:00 to 7:00, and I'll also need a ride on weekends." God help any Chinese kid who tried that one.

Don't get me wrong. It's not that Chinese parents don't care about their children. Just the opposite. They would give up anything for their children. It's just an entirely different parenting model.

Here's a story in favor of coercion, Chinese-style. Lulu was about seven, still playing two instruments, and working on a piano piece called "The Little White Donkey" by the French composer Jacques Ibert. The piece is really cute—you can just imagine a little donkey ambling along a country road with its master—but it's also incredibly difficult for young players because the two hands have to keep schizophrenically different rhythms.

Lulu couldn't do it. We worked on it nonstop for a week, drilling each of   20
her hands separately, over and over. But whenever we tried putting the hands together, one always morphed into the other, and everything fell apart. Finally, the day before her lesson, Lulu announced in exasperation that she was giving up and stomped off.

"Get back to the piano now," I ordered.

"You can't make me."

"Oh yes, I can."

Back at the piano, Lulu made me pay. She punched, thrashed, and kicked. She grabbed the music score and tore it to shreds. I taped the score back together and encased it in a plastic shield so that it could never be destroyed again. Then I hauled Lulu's dollhouse to the car and told her I'd donate it to the Salvation Army piece by piece if she didn't have "The Little White Donkey" perfect by the next day. When Lulu said, "I thought you were going to the Salvation Army, why are you still here?" I threatened her with no lunch, no dinner, no Christmas or Hanukkah presents, no birthday parties for two, three, four years. When she still kept playing it wrong, I told her she was purposely working herself into a frenzy because she was secretly afraid she couldn't do it. I told her to stop being lazy, cowardly, self-indulgent, and pathetic.

Jed took me aside. He told me to stop insulting Lulu—which I wasn't even   25
doing, I was just motivating her—and that he didn't think threatening Lulu was helpful. Also, he said, maybe Lulu really just couldn't do the technique—perhaps she didn't have the coordination yet—had I considered that possibility?

"You just don't believe in her," I accused.

"That's ridiculous," Jed said scornfully. "Of course I do."

"Sophia could play the piece when she was this age."

"But Lulu and Sophia are different people," Jed pointed out.

"Oh no, not this," I said, rolling my eyes. "Everyone is special in their own   30
special way." I mimicked sarcastically. "Even losers are special in their own special way. Well don't worry, you don't have to lift a finger. I'm willing to put in as long as it takes, and I'm happy to be the one hated. And you can be the one they adore because you make them pancakes and take them to Yankees games."

I rolled up my sleeves and went back to Lulu. I used every weapon and tactic I could think of. We worked right through dinner into the night, and I wouldn't

Continued >

let Lulu get up, not for water, not even to go to the bathroom. The house became a war zone, and I lost my voice yelling, but still there seemed to be only negative progress, and even I began to have doubts.

Then, out of the blue, Lulu did it. Her hands suddenly came together—her right and left hands each doing their own imperturbable thing—just like that.

Lulu realized it at the same time I did. I held my breath. She tried it tentatively again. Then she played it more confidently and faster, and still the rhythm held. A moment later, she was beaming.

"Mommy, look—it's easy!" After that, she wanted to play the piece over and over and wouldn't leave the piano. That night, she came to sleep in my bed, and we snuggled and hugged, cracking each other up. When she performed "The Little White Donkey" at a recital a few weeks later, parents came up to me and said, "What a perfect piece for Lulu—it's so spunky and so *her*."

35   Even Jed gave me credit for that one. Western parents worry a lot about their children's self-esteem. But as a parent, one of the worst things you can do for your child's self-esteem is to let them give up. On the flip side, there's nothing better for building confidence than learning you can do something you thought you couldn't.

There are all these new books out there portraying Asian mothers as scheming, callous, overdriven people indifferent to their kids' true interests. For their part, many Chinese secretly believe that they care more about their children and are willing to sacrifice much more for them than Westerners, who seem perfectly content to let their children turn out badly. I think it's a misunderstanding on both sides. All decent parents want to do what's best for their children. The Chinese just have a totally different idea of how to do that.

Western parents try to respect their children's individuality, encouraging them to pursue their true passions, supporting their choices, and providing positive reinforcement and a nurturing environment. By contrast, the Chinese believe that the best way to protect their children is by preparing them for the future, letting them see what they're capable of, and arming them with skills, work habits, and inner confidence that no one can ever take away.

Understanding and Reviewing the Reading

1. **Thesis** What is Chua's thesis, and where does she state it most directly?
2. **Meaning** What is Chua's point in paragraph 4? How does she go on to illustrate this point at length later in the essay?
3. **Meaning** Summarize paragraphs 5–8. What does the brief anecdote about the Western father and daughter at the end of paragraph 8 contribute to Chua's meaning?
4. **Points of comparison** What three main points of distinction does Chua make between Chinese and Western parents?

5. **Patterns** In addition to comparison and contrast, what other pattern(s) does Chua use to develop her essay? Explain how the pattern or patterns are used.

Analyzing the Reading

1. **Audience** Would you say Chua is writing primarily for Western readers or readers of Asian heritage? What makes you think so?

2. **Technique** Chua opens with a list of things she doesn't allow her daughters to do. What effect does she expect this list to have on readers?

3. **Evidence** Early in the essay, Chua offers statistical data from several different sources. What role do these statistics serve?

4. **Argument** Without quite saying so directly, Chua is arguing a point as she contrasts Chinese and Western parents. What is this argument, and where in the essay does she suggest it clearly?

5. **Structure** Why do you suppose Chua relates in such detail the story of her struggle with her daughter over learning the piano piece (paras. 18–33)?

6. **Visual** How does the photograph of Chua and her daughters contribute to the thesis of this essay?

Evaluating the Reading

1. **Opening** Evaluate Chua's four opening paragraphs. How do they create interest in her topic?

2. **Bias** How fairly do you think Chua represents Western parents? Might your own biases contribute to your response?

3. **Strategy** Why do you think Chua gives voice to her non-Asian husband in paragraph 15 and when she tells about her struggle with Lulu (paras. 25–29)? Do you think she presents his views adequately?

4. **Argument** How well do you think Chua makes her case for her Chinese parenting philosophy and methods? Are you convinced that they work as she claims?

Discussing the Reading

1. Chua writes in paragraph 4 that "practice, practice, practice is crucial for excellence; rote repetition is underrated in America." How do you respond to this statement?

2. Chua has no qualms about parents referring to their children as "garbage," "fatty," "lazy," "cowardly," "self-indulgent," even "pathetic." Can she really believe this and still consider herself a loving parent?

3. In not allowing her daughters to participate in extracurricular activities of their own choosing, is Chua limiting her daughters' lives? Or do parents know best?

4. Chua writes of telling her husband that she's "happy to be the one hated" and to allow him to be the parent their daughters "adore" (para 29). What does this suggest to you about Chua as a person?

Writing about the Reading

1. **Essay** Write an essay comparing and contrasting the parenting styles of two parents—or sets of parents—that you know. You might choose your own parents and a friend's parents, yourself as a parent and your parents when you were a child, or perhaps a mother and a father with different parenting styles. While planning, be sure to focus on types of parental differences, as Chua does in paragraphs 9–17.

2. **Essay** Just as parents have different approaches to child rearing, teachers have different approaches to educating. Think of two teachers you've had whose ways of dealing with students and presenting material differ, at least in some respects. Then write an essay comparing and contrasting the two styles. Like Chua, you might cast your essay as a comparison not so much of individuals but of the more general types they represent. (Another possibility might be to focus on two different coaching styles.)

3. **Combined patterns** Using either of the previous two suggestions, write an essay in which you both compare and contrast your subjects and make the argument that one style is preferable to the other.

📖 COMBINING THE PATTERNS | TEXTBOOK EXCERPT: PSYCHOLOGY

Dealing with Cultural Differences

Carole Wade holds a Ph.D. in cognitive psychology from Stanford University. She and **Carol Tavris**, a writer and public lecturer on psychology, have co-authored four books. Among their collaborations is *Invitation to Psychology*, from which the following selection is taken.

Reading Tip

As you read, consider what the authors mean by *critical thinking*, a term they use several times in the selection, and why they think critical-thinking skills are important.

Previewing the Reading

Preview the reading (see pp. 28–29 for guidelines), and then list three questions you expect it to answer.

Dealing with Cultural Difference
Carole Wade and Carol Tavris

A French salesman worked for a company that was bought by Americans. When the new American manager ordered him to step up his sales within the next three months, the employee quit in a huff, taking his customers with him. Why? In France, it takes years to develop customers; in family-owned businesses, relationships with customers may span generations. The American manager wanted instant results, as Americans often do, but the French salesman knew this was impossible and quit. The American view was, "He wasn't up to the job; he's lazy and disloyal, so he stole my customers." The French view was, "There is no point in explaining anything to a person who is so stupid as to think you can acquire loyal customers in three months."

Both men were committing the fundamental attribution error: assuming that the other person's behavior was due to personality rather than the situation, in this case a situation governed by cultural rules. Many corporations now realize that such rules are not trivial and that success in a global economy depends on understanding them. But you don't have to go to another country to encounter cultural differences; they are right here at home.

If you find yourself getting angry over something a person from another culture is doing or not doing, use the skills of critical thinking to find out whether your expectations and perceptions of that person's

Continued >

behavior are appropriate. Take the time to examine your assumptions and biases, consider other explanations of the other person's actions, and avoid emotional reasoning. For example, people who shake hands as a gesture of friendship and courtesy are likely to feel insulted if a person from a non-hand-shaking culture refuses to do the same, unless they have asked themselves the question, "Does everyone have the custom of shaking hands the way I do?"

Similarly, people from Middle Eastern and Latin American cultures are used to bargaining for what they buy; Americans and northern Europeans are used to having a fixed price. People who do not know how to bargain, therefore, are likely to find bargaining an exercise in frustration because they will not know whether they got taken or got a great deal. In contrast, people from bargaining cultures will feel just as exasperated if a seller offers a flat price. "Where's the fun in this?" they'll say. "The whole human transaction of shopping is gone!"

5   Learning another culture's rule or custom is hard enough, but it is much more difficult to comprehend cultural differences that are deeply embedded in its language. For instance, in Iran, the social principle of *taarof* describes the practice of deliberate insincerity, such as giving false praise and making promises you have no intention of keeping. Iranians know that they are supposed to tell you what you want to hear to avoid conflict or to offer hope for a compromise. To Iranians, these practices are a part of good manners; they are not offended by them. But Americans and members of other English-speaking cultures are used to "straight talking," to saying directly and succinctly what they want. Therefore they find *taarof* hard to learn, let alone to practice. As an Iranian social scientist told the *New York Times* (August 6, 2006), "Speech has a different function than it does in the West"—in the West, "yes" generally means yes; in Iran, "yes" can mean yes, but it often means maybe or no. "This creates a rich, poetic linguistic culture," he said. "It creates a multidimensional culture where people are adept at picking up on nuances. On the other hand, it makes for bad political discourse. In political discourse people don't know what to trust."

You can see why critical thinking can help people avoid the tendency to stereotype and to see cultural differences in communication solely in hostile, negative ways. "Why are the Iranians lying to me?" an American might ask. The answer is that they are not "lying" in Iranian terms; they are speaking in a way that is completely natural for them, according to their cultural rules for communication.

To learn the unspoken rules of a culture, you must look, listen, and observe. What is the pace of life like? Do people regard brash individuality and loud speech as admirable or embarrassing? When customers enter a shop, do they greet and chat with the shopkeeper or ignore the person as they browse? Are people expected to be direct in their speech or evasive? Sociocultural research enhances critical thinking by teaching us to appreciate the many cultural rules that govern people's behavior, values, attitudes, and ways of doing business. Before you write off someone from a culture different from your own as being rude, foolish, stubborn, or devious, consider other interpretations of that person's behavior—just as you would want that person to consider other, more forgiving, interpretations of yours.

Understanding and Reviewing the Reading

1. **Textbook reading** Explain the cultural difference that the authors present between the American manager and the French salesman in paragraph 1.

2. **Summary** In a sentence or two, summarize the main point of the reading.

3. **Textbook terminology** In paragraph 2, the authors define the term *attribution error*. Where else in the reading are terms used and then defined? Highlight them and define them in your own words. Being able to explain words / terms in your own words is a true measure of understanding.

4. **Textbook reading** In paragraph 6, the authors write, "To learn the unspoken rules of a culture, you must look, listen, and observe." In your own words, explain what the authors mean by this statement.

Analyzing the Reading

1. **Similarities and differences** In what way does the use of comparison and contrast in this textbook reading differ from that in other essays in this chapter? How does the subject of the reading account for this difference?

2. **Technique** What is the point of the opening example? How does it function in making the larger point of the reading?

3. **Organization** In addition to comparison and contrast, what other pattern or patterns are used in the reading? Explain what the pattern or patterns contribute to the reading.

4. **Textbook reading** This reading is from a featured section called "Taking Psychology with You" at the end of a psychology textbook chapter titled "Behavior in Social and Cultural Context." What does this suggest about the purpose of this section in terms of the rest of the chapter?

Evaluating the Reading

1. **Value of information** Do you think that this textbook selection taught you something useful? How or when would you use this information?

2. **Examples** The authors present four examples of specific cultural behavior in paragraphs 1, 3, 4, and 5. Do you think these examples are sufficient to communicate the point being made? Why, or why not?

3. **Technique** In paragraphs 1, 3, 4, and 6, the authors create imaginary quotations from people they suppose are experiencing cultural miscommunication. Are these quotations realistic? Explain your answer.

Discussing the Reading

1. The authors' underlying assumption is that "success in a global economy" (para. 2) requires understanding differences among cultures. Give two examples from the reading that support this assumption.

2. The authors write in paragraph 7 that learning "the unspoken rules of a culture" requires one to "look, listen, and observe." What would you add to this advice?

3. Paragraph 5 suggests that, unlike Iranians, English speakers are "straight talking" and don't practice "deliberate insincerity." In your experience, is this the case? Further, is political discourse in the United States, therefore, basically trustworthy?

Writing about the Reading

1. **Response paper** Suppose that, in your psychology class, you have been given the following assignment for a take-home exam to conclude a unit on cultural differences: Write an essay responding to the examples of cultural difference described in paragraphs 1, 3, 4, and 5. Which behavior, in each case, does your background lead you to view more favorably, and why do you feel as you do?

2. **Applying the reading** Suppose that, in your sociology class, you have just completed a study on conflicts and interpersonal relationships. Based on your own experience, write an essay in which you describe either a cultural misunderstanding that you have had with a friend or family member or a cultural misunderstanding that you have observed between two people.

3. **Essay assignment** Suppose that, in a psychology class where you have been studying stereotypical behavior, you have been given the following assignment: "Dealing with Cultural Difference" considers "the tendency to stereotype." Write an essay comparing and/or contrasting a widely held cultural stereotype with the reality as you know it. Potential topics might include an ethnic stereotype, a regional stereotype, or a stereotype based on people's activities and interests.

Working with Comparison and Contrast as a Reader and Writer

The following table reviews the key elements of comparison-and-contrast essays and explains how these elements are important to both readers and writers.

Reading ⊕ Writing Comparison-and-Contrast Essays

Element of a Comparison-and-Contrast Essay	The Reader's Perspective	The Writer's Perspective
Subjects for Comparison	When reading a comparison-and-contrast essay, first identify the subjects of comparison. Look for insights into the subjects or approaches to the topic that you had not considered before reading the essay.	When writing a comparison-and-contrast essay, the key is to make your subjects interesting for your readers. Good writers explain why they've chosen their subjects for comparison and explain the benefits of this comparison for the reader.
Purpose	As you read, identify the author's purpose for writing. Often the purpose will be obvious in the introduction. Use the purpose to guide your reading. For example, if the author is writing to express herself or to amuse her readers, you can expect the essay to be entertaining.	To determine your purpose, first conduct an audience analysis to understand what readers want and expect from your comparison. Next, be sure to have a clear goal specifying what you hope to achieve with your writing.
Similarities and Differences	When reading a comparison-and-contrast essay, underline key points of similarity or difference, and write marginal notes that will help you create a graphic organizer of the essay after you've completed the reading. Identify whether the author has used subject-by-subject or point-by-point organization.	When writing a comparison-and-contrast essay, choose *meaningful* similarities and differences to write about. It makes no sense to write about characteristics that readers already know about. The goal of a comparison-and-contrast essay is to provide information that readers do *not* already know.

Continued >

Sufficient Number of Characteristics and Details	As you read, check to make sure that the author has included a sufficient number of detailed examples to support the thesis statement. Then evaluate the thesis statement itself: Has the author convinced you that the thesis is correct?	Providing a good number of characteristics and details helps you support your thesis. Just as importantly, examining a good number of characteristics and details *before* you write will help you formulate a thesis that readers will accept.
Point of the Comparison and Contrast	When you have finished reading the essay, ask yourself, What is the author's key point? To be sure you understand the key point, write a summary of the key point in your own words.	Before you sit down to write a comparison-and-contrast essay, you must have your key point in mind. Without a key point to hold it together, a comparison-and-contrast essay will read like a list of vaguely related information. As a writer, your goal is to pull all the points of comparison together into a key statement that makes an important point about the items being compared.

15

Classification and Division: Explaining Categories and Parts

In this chapter, you will learn to

- Recognize the elements of classification and division.

- Identify the structure and content of classification and division essays.

- Understand, analyze, and evaluate classification and division essays.

- Write your own classification or division essay.

- Work with classification and division as a reader and a writer.

fiphoto/Shutterstock

Reflect on a Visual Text

1 Ask yourself questions. Study this photograph of a clothing store. Notice how similar items are grouped together on the shelves.

2 Brainstorm ideas. Think of other ways you have seen items in a clothing store arranged. Did some seem more logical and easy to use than others? Why? →

Think of a store that you frequent, and write a paragraph describing for someone who has never been there how the different categories of merchandise are arranged. Be sure to clearly identify all the categories.

The paragraph you just wrote uses *classification*, a method of development that puts items into categories or groups.

What Are Classification and Division?

Classification is the process of sorting people, things, or ideas into groups or categories. You use classification every day to organize things and ideas. Your dresser drawers and kitchen cabinets are probably organized by categories—with socks and sweatshirts in different drawers and pots and glasses in different cabinets. Your college classifies course offerings by schools, divisions, and departments.

Division is similar to classification, but instead of grouping items into categories, division breaks *one* item down into parts. For example, the humanities department at your college (one item) may be divided into English, modern languages, and philosophy; the modern language courses (one item) might be further divided into Spanish, French, Chinese, and Russian.

A classification or division essay explains a topic by describing its categories or parts. For example, a classification essay might explore types (categories) of advertising: direct mail, radio, television, magazine, online, and so forth. A division essay might describe the parts of an art museum: exhibit areas, museum store, visitor-services desk, and the like. You will use these patterns of development frequently in the writing you do in college and the workplace. For instance, for a course in anatomy and physiology, you might be asked to review the structure and parts of the human ear by identifying the function of each part. In the workplace, a facilities planner might conduct a feasibility study of several new sites by sorting them into categories such as within state, out of state, and out of country.

A successful classification or division essay has all or most of the following elements:

1. It groups or divides ideas according to one principle.
2. It develops a principle meaningful to the audience.
3. It fully explains each category or part.

Knowing how writers (and other communicators) use classification and division will help you understand, analyze, and evaluate this pattern when you read and help you use it in your own writing.

A Model Classification Essay

The following model classification essay will be used throughout this chapter to demonstrate strategies for reading and writing classification and division essays. Read it now, looking for the ways the writer uses the above classification and division techniques. Use the annotations in the margin to guide you.

Online Dating—Five Things to Avoid

Joshua Fruhlinger

As editor in chief of *TapOnline*, **Joshua Fruhlinger** helped create the first twenty-four-hour online reality show. He later joined AOL and served as editorial director of *Engadget*, a Web magazine covering electronics and technology. This article appeared in 2007 on *Switched*, a Web site devoted to the intersection of the digital world and popular culture that is now part of the technology section of the *Huffington Post*.

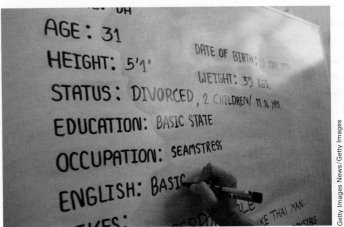

Everyone's doing it—over 40% of U.S. singles are finding matches online. That's more than 40 million single Americans cruising the Internet looking for love (based on census results that say there are over 100 million single Americans).

So the Internet *must* be a great place to find true love, right? Not so fast. While online dating can be a great way to find someone new, dating *sites* are littered with scam artists, cheaters, and straight-up liars.

Now, this doesn't mean you should avoid online dating altogether—just don't believe everything you see out there.

Classification and division group or divide ideas according to one principle that is meaningful to the audience: The one organizing principle of this essay is "types of online daters you should avoid." Given the popularity of online dating, many readers will find this classification meaningful.

Classification and division use categories or parts that are clearly and easily identified: This essay's heading structure clearly identifies the five categories that will be discussed: liars, photo fakes, fixer-uppers, membership fishers, and cheaters.

In order to help sort out the winners from the losers, we've compiled a list of the top five types of online daters you should definitely avoid, along with some tips to help you save some heartache. Be careful out there, and good luck!

1. Liars

In a recent survey, it was found that most online profiles contain some sort of lie, whether it's the person's age or—in some cases—relationship status. White lies—adding an inch to height or dropping a couple pounds—are the most common and not a big deal to most people.

Consider these facts according to the April 2007 issue of *Proceedings of Computer/Human Interaction*:

- About 52.6% of men lie about their height, as do 39% of women.
- Slightly more women lie about their weight (64.1%) than men (60.5%).
- When it comes to age, 24.3% of men lie compared with 13.1% of women.

When it comes to misrepresentations of age or relationship status, be careful or you could get seriously burned. In one recent case, a woman met a man on a popular dating site with whom she immediately hit it off. She even put her life on hold to go with him to Dubai when he was transferred for work. Eleven months into the relationship, she came across an email—from his son! What's more, the email said something about "Mom" saying hi. In one fell swoop, our poor girl found out the man she met online was not only a father—he was married! She moved back to the United States and has given up on online dating since.

How to Avoid Them: Ask questions. Though it may be listed on someone's profile, someone's age is fair game in the questions department, so feel free to ask your potential date how old (or young!) they are. You may find that thirty-five suddenly becomes forty-two. While you don't want to ask too many questions and scare the person away, it's perfectly fair to verify the big things: age, weight, height, and—most of all—whether or not that person is, in fact, single. Half the time, people lie on their profiles to get people interested—nine times out of ten, someone will level with you about their stats once you show some real interest, since they know they might have a chance of meeting you in person.

2. Photo Fakes

Dating-site traffic analyses show that profiles with pictures are clicked on twice as much as those without. Having a good picture of yourself can be the difference between getting seen and getting lost. However, some people take the notion of "looking good" a little too far. They post misleading pictures that can trap you into thinking you're meeting your dreamboat only to find a shipwreck waiting for you. Let's face it, not everyone looks as good as George Clooney or Angelina Jolie.

Joan, a woman from New Jersey, had thought she met Mr. Right. He was charming and—according to the picture on his profile—quite handsome. She looked forward to seeing his auburn hair and deep eyes when it turned out that Mr. Right had gone gray. He also hadn't seen a gym in years. Turns out that his profile picture was over five years old. While there's nothing wrong with gray hair or a couple extra pounds, people who misrepresent their looks aren't being honest.

How to Avoid Them: Look for profiles with more than one picture. People who choose only flattering angles could be hiding something. Ask for a recent picture, and if the person refuses, you could be looking at that person's high school yearbook photo. And if someone looks as good as George Clooney or Angelina Jolie, you need to double-check that it's for real.

Classification and division fully explain each part: In this section, the author fully explains how fixer-uppers operate and provides good suggestions for avoiding them. He uses the same strategy for the other four categories of online daters to avoid.

3. Fixer-Uppers

Most marriages end in divorce—that's just a fact of life. But many people on the rebound make their profiles about what they *don't* want. The truth is, these people are on the rebound and are likely to still be living with the wounds of their last relationship. You may be in for some serious scrutiny, criticism, and baggage handling, so beware. Imagine, for example, what any of Sir Paul McCartney's new lovers must think as he talks about his past relationships!

Consider these recent profile headlines:

- Cheaters Need Not Apply
- Tired of Meeting Women in Bars
- No Manipulative B*tches, please!
- Please Don't Be a Liar
- Felons, Potheads, and Jerks Need Not Apply

What we have here are jilted lovers. Run. Run away. While it's a good idea to learn from your past relationships, no one wants to date a bitter, angry person. By telling people what you don't want, you're scaring off potential mates.

On the other side, if you're reading profiles, avoid these singles as they are either recently out of relationships or still getting over something pretty big. They're not ready, and you don't want to be their fixer-upper.

How to Avoid Them: To steer clear of the fixer-upper at all costs, watch out for the aforementioned profile headlines. While you may hate the same things these rebounders do, you still shouldn't pursue a relationship with them. Having something in common can be great, but those things should be positive, not negative. As the old saying goes, You must love yourself before you love another.

4. Membership Fishers

You finally got a response to your profile, and she's hot! You're all set to respond to the beauty queen, but there's one problem: Her profile happens to be over at some other site.

Of course, before you can send her a note on her profile, you're asked by the new dating site she's listed with to sign up. Before you know it, you're a member of a new dating site, and it has your credit card info, and, it turns out, your new love doesn't exist.

Dating sites make their money on membership dues, and with thousands of them competing for daters, they're in a vicious fight to get you to sign up. Some wily sites have taken to trolling single people from other sites, making them think that a new lovely wants to meet them . . . at a new site that requires signing up.

How to Avoid Them: Make sure anyone you hear from is already signed up with the online dating site you're signed up with. If someone responds to your profile, it means they already have a profile at the site you are using. Don't fall for the "meet me over here" tactic. If they really like you, they'll come talk to you where you are.

5. Cheaters

How is it possible that this new, wonderful person is still single? In fact, he or she may not be. While there are some great singles out there waiting to steal your heart away, some of them are not, in fact, single. Surprise, surprise, it turns out that some people use dating sites as a way to get a little something on the side when they're out of town.

Consider this story about Jill, a twenty-seven-year-old Washington, D.C., marketing executive, who met the "man of her dreams" online:

"Since he lived in a different city—Roanoke, Virginia—it was easy for him to sneak around." She told iVillage, "Although he made excuse after excuse about why he continually had to cancel a date at the last minute—one time claiming he'd been in a car accident—I got suspicious only after I knew everything." There had been numerous red flags. For instance, he only called from his cell phone while driving in his car. It turns out that Joe (not his real name) was talking to several women online. According to his wife, Jill was the only one he'd met and kissed.

How to Avoid Them: Look out for people who can only talk to you during the day, will only talk online or via text message, or who mysteriously disappear at night and on weekends. Other warning signs include out-of-town lovers who happen to be in town a lot. And be especially cautious of people who live thousands of miles away, since you have no real way of verifying what's actually going on with them day-to-day. There's a good chance you could be on the back burner. Also, look out for people who list their status as "separated"—they could be separated in mind, only.

The Structure and Content of Classification and Division Essays

In this section, you will learn about the structure of classification and division essays and practice using the guidelines for understanding, analyzing, and evaluating classification and division essays. This key information will help you skillfully read and write essays that use classification and division.

The structure of a classification or division essay is usually straightforward. Figure 15.1 presents the typical structure visually.

1. THE INTRODUCTION EXPLAINS THE CLASSIFICATION OR DIVISION AND PRESENTS THE THESIS STATEMENT

The introduction provides background information and explains or justifies the principle of classification or division used. It also states or suggests the essay's purpose: why the classification or division is significant, important, or worth knowing. The thesis statement identifies the topic and may reveal the principle used to classify or divide it. The categories or parts may also be briefly identified.

In the introduction to "Online Dating—Five Things to Avoid," Joshua Fruhlinger provides background information about the number of Americans who are dating online. He also suggests why the classification is worth knowing ("dating sites are filled with scam artists, cheaters, and straight-up liars").

Figure 15.1   Graphic Organizer for a Classification or Division Essay

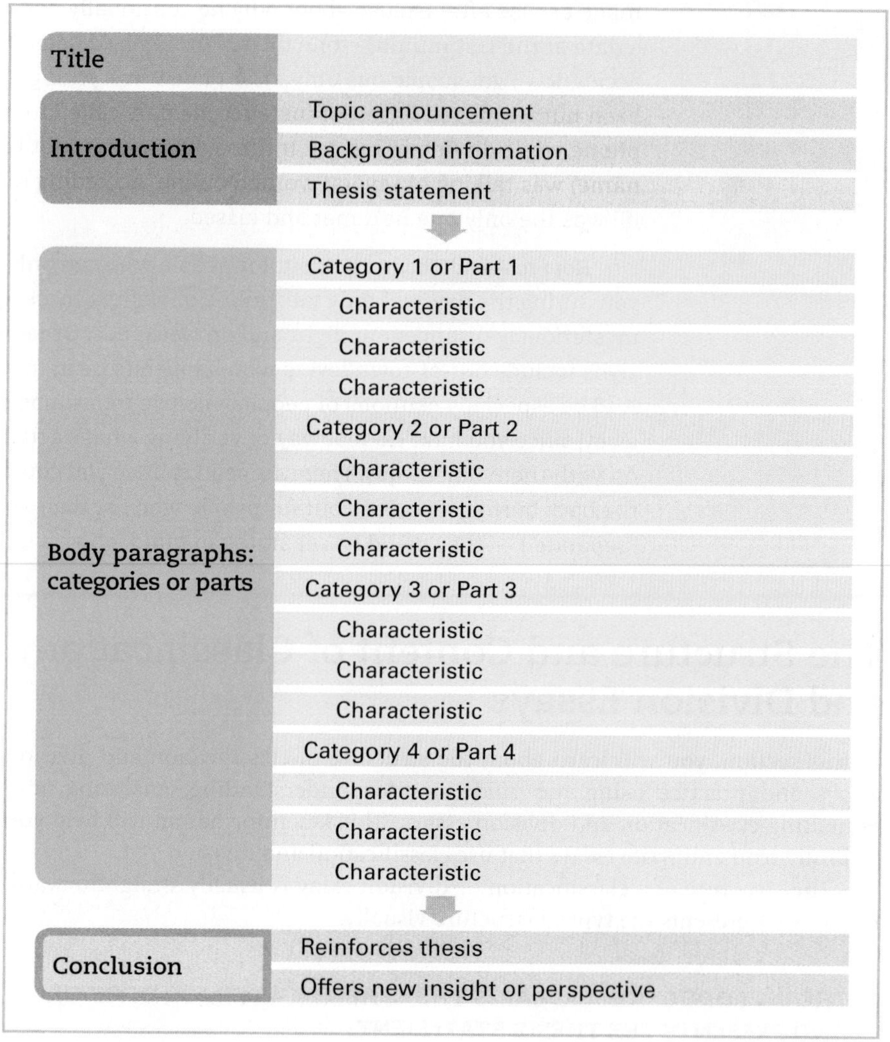

Title	
Introduction	Topic announcement
	Background information
	Thesis statement
	⬇
Body paragraphs: categories or parts	Category 1 or Part 1
	Characteristic
	Characteristic
	Characteristic
	Category 2 or Part 2
	Characteristic
	Characteristic
	Characteristic
	Category 3 or Part 3
	Characteristic
	Characteristic
	Characteristic
	Category 4 or Part 4
	Characteristic
	Characteristic
	Characteristic
	⬇
Conclusion	Reinforces thesis
	Offers new insight or perspective

The Principle of Classification or Division   To develop an effective set of categories or parts, a writer must choose *one principle of classification or division* and use it consistently throughout the essay. For instance, a college president might classify professors by experience or teaching style, but he or she would not mix categories by classifying some professors by experience and others by teaching style. The president could, however, classify all professors by experience in the first part of a report and then by teaching style in another part. Once the writer has chosen an appropriate principle of classification or division, the next step is to identify a manageable number of categories or parts. An essay classifying birds according to diet, for example, might address five or six types of diet, not twenty. There are many types of online daters to avoid, but Joshua Fruhlinger focuses on only five types.

The Purpose of Classification or Division   To develop a meaningful classification or division, writers must focus on their purpose for writing. When the purpose is to inform, essays should use a principle of classification or division that will be of interest to readers. For instance, if a writer wishes to inform parents about the types of day-care centers in the area, she could classify the centers according to the services they offer because readers would be looking for that information. A writer who divides the day in a kindergarten into time spent on active play, imaginative play, and formal learning might be writing to inform an audience of parents considering the kindergarten for their children.

The intended audience of Fruhlinger's essay is obvious: single people who are serious about online dating and want to avoid negative experiences. Fruhlinger's purpose is equally clear: to inform readers about online "scam artists, cheaters, and straight-up liars" and to provide tips on how to avoid them.

The Thesis Statement   Most classification and division essays provide a specific thesis statement. The thesis statement appears in the third paragraph of "Online Dating—Five Things to Avoid":

> In order to help sort out the winners from the losers, we've compiled a list of the top five types of online daters you should definitely avoid, along with some tips to help you save some heartache.

Here are two additional examples of thesis statements.

Classification essay	Most people consider videos a form of entertainment; however, videos can also serve educational, commercial, and political functions.
	(The essay goes on to classify the subject, the functions of videos, into three types in addition to entertainment.)
Division essay	The Grand Canyon is divided into two distinct geographical areas, the North Rim and the South Rim; each offers different views, facilities, and climatic conditions.
	(The essay goes on to discuss the differences between the two parts of the Grand Canyon.)

2. THE BODY PARAGRAPHS EXPLAIN AND DESCRIBE THE CATEGORIES OR PARTS

The body paragraphs each deal with a category or part. These categories or parts result from the principle of classification or division and its purpose. An essay discussing highway drivers might classify them by driving habit; its purpose

Reading ⊕ Writing The Introduction to a Classification or Division Essay

The Reader's Perspective	The Writer's Perspective
When reading a classification or division essay introduction, identify the subject and examine how it is classified or divided. Then assess how familiar you are with the subject and decide how carefully you need to read the essay, what you need to look for and remember, and what strategies you will use to read it effectively.	When writing a classification or division essay introduction, draw your readers in by explaining why the classification or division is important. For example, you might describe a situation in which familiarity with the classification or division was useful.

might be to point out that there are many annoying or unsafe drivers on the road. Categories and parts should be kept clear, specific, and comprehensive. Each category or part should be fully explained.

Keeping Categories and Parts Clear, Specific, and Comprehensive Categories or parts should not overlap in a way that may lead to confusion. A familiar example is age ranges: The age categories 25 to 30 and 30 to 35 are not effective because someone who is 30 years old would fit into both. The second category should be changed to 31 to 35. In an essay about the nutritional value of pizza, you could divide the topic into carbohydrates, proteins, and fats, but you would not add a separate category for saturated fat because that is already contained in the fats category.

Categories or parts should also be comprehensive. In a division essay, all the major parts of an item should be included. In a classification essay, the categories must be able to include all the items related to the topic. For example, an essay classifying fast-food restaurants according to type of food served would have to include a category for pizza parlors, because many fast-food establishments fall into this category.

Sometimes, multiple categories in a classification fit a particular person or item. For example, based on the categories defined in "Online Dating—Five Things to Avoid," it is quite possible that a person may be a liar, a photo faker, *and* a cheater.

Fully Explaining Each Category or Part A classification or division essay should contain adequate detail so that each category or part can be well understood. Note that Joshua Fruhlinger devotes at least two body paragraphs to each category: liars, photo fakers, fixer-uppers, membership fishers, and cheaters. He also provides a full paragraph explaining how to avoid people in each of these categories.

Reading ⓘ Writing   The Body of a Classification or Division Essay

The Reader's Perspective	The Writer's Perspective
When reading the body of a classification or division essay, pay attention to the organization, noting when it moves from category to category or part to part. Creating an outline or a graphic organizer can help you track the organization. Highlight categories or parts and the features of each category or part, using one color to identify categories or parts and another to identify the features of each. Also mark important definitions and useful examples for future reference. If you find a category or part confusing, make a marginal annotation and then, later, reread, research, or check with a classmate or your instructor.	When writing the body of a classification or division essay, focus on developing and explaining each category or part, offering roughly the same amount of detail and description for each. To help your readers follow your classification or division, use transitional words and phrases to signal when you are moving on to a new category or part.

3. THE CONCLUSION REINFORCES THE THESIS AND MAY OFFER NEW INSIGHT OR PERSPECTIVE

The conclusion should do more than just repeat categories or parts. It should bring the essay to a satisfying close, reemphasizing the thesis or offering a new insight or perspective on the topic. Joshua Fruhlinger's essay does not include an explicit conclusion, but it does end with some general advice.

Reading ⓘ Writing   The Conclusion of a Classification or Division Essay

The Reader's Perspective	The Writer's Perspective
When reading the conclusion of a classification or division essay, take a moment to summarize the categories or parts presented and their importance. If you find that you can't recall the major points, reread the essay and review your outline or graphic organizer to better understand the topic.	When writing a conclusion for a classification or division essay, reread your essay. Then ask yourself, Will my readers care about the topic? Make sure your conclusion addresses this question by reasserting the thesis or shedding new light on the topic.

Understanding, Analyzing, and Evaluating Classification and Division Essays

In reading and writing classification and division essays, your goal is to get beyond mere competence. That is, you want to do more than merely understand the content of the essays you read or convey just your basic ideas to the audience you're writing for.

Understanding a Classification or Division Essay

Preview the essay before reading to identify the subject being classified or divided and, if possible, to identify the categories or parts. Then read to become familiar with specifics about each category or part. As you read and reread, use the skills you learned in Chapter 2 and look for answers to the following questions.

- **What is the writer's thesis?** State it in your own words. Why is the classification or division important? When might you use it or need to explain it to someone else?
- **What is the principle of classification?** If the author does not explicitly state the principle, try explaining it in your own words. Identifying the principle is the key to understanding the entire essay.
- **What are the categories or parts?** Mark or highlight each as you encounter it. Creating a graphic organizer can help you identify the categories or parts. Figure 15.2 shows a graphic organizer for "Online Dating—Five Things to Avoid."

Understanding in Action

Exercise 15.1

Following is one student's summary of the introduction to "Online Dating—Five Things to Avoid" and the first category it describes. Using it as a model, write a summary of the whole essay.

> While online dating sites can be a good way to meet possible matches, there is also a lot to beware of. The first thing to look out for is people who lie in their profile. Some lies may be minor, like age or height. Others can be major, like marital status. To protect yourself, ask questions. Make sure in particular that the person is actually single.

Figure 15.2   Graphic Organizer for "Online Dating—Five Things to Avoid"

Title	Online Dating—Five Things to Avoid
Introduction	**Topic:** Online-dating-site profiles
	Background: A large percent of singles today are looking for matches online. Online dating sites can be helpful, but there are also potential problems to consider.
	Thesis: Here are five types of online daters to avoid.
Body paragraphs: categories or parts	**Category 1:** Liars
	May lie about little or major things about themselves in their profiles.
	Can be avoided by asking questions.
	Category 2: Photo fakes
	Post photos that are misleadingly good.
	Can be avoided by asking for recent photos and multiple photos.
	Category 3: Fixer-uppers
	Make negative comments and are really just on the rebound.
	Can be avoided by looking for positive things in common.
	Category 4: Membership fishers
	Post phony profiles to get you to pay to sign up at another site; the person does not exist.
	Can be avoided by sticking with people on the site you're signed up with.
	Category 5: Cheaters
	Pretend to be single and may often be unavailable.
	Can be avoided by watching for people who aren't available on nights or weekends.

Analyzing a Classification or Division Essay

Analyzing a classification or division essay involves examining how and why the classification or division was made. Use the following questions to guide your analysis:

- **Is each category or part clearly named or titled?** The author should make it easy for the reader to identify each and to move from one category or part to another.

- **Is each category or part distinct from the others?** The author should make clear how each differs, using details, descriptions, examples, comparisons or contrasts, or personal experiences.
- **Is each category or part explained clearly and understandably?** Each description should be clear, with key terms defined, and should not require background knowledge the reader does not have.

Analysis in Action

Exercise 15.2

The student who wrote the summary for Understanding in Action wrote the following analysis of the author's purpose in "Online Dating—Five Things to Avoid." Using it as a starting point, write a brief analysis of the essay's intended audience and how the author tries to connect with the audience.

> The author of "Online Dating—Five Things to Avoid" wants to help readers recognize that you have to be careful when you're reading profiles on dating sites. To do so, he lists five types of postings that could be iffy. For each type he also offers tips to avoid being burned.

Evaluating a Classification or Division Essay

Evaluating a classification or division essay involves judging how accurately and effectively the author has classified or divided the subject. Use the following questions to guide your evaluation of such essays:

- **Is the classification or division comprehensive and complete?** Determine whether all essential categories or all essential parts are included. It would be misleading, for example, for a writer to classify unemployed workers into only two groups—those who have been laid off or downsized and those who lack skills—because many people are out of work for other reasons. Such a classification fails to consider, for example, those who are unable to work because of illness or those who have recently completed college and have not yet found a job.
- **Does each category or part have fair and equal coverage?** Each category or part should be given roughly the same amount of coverage and include the same level of detail. To provide many details for some categories and just a few for others suggests bias. For example, if a writer classifying how high school students spend their time goes into great detail about leisure activities and offers little detail on part-time jobs or volunteer work, the writer may create a false impression that students care only about having fun and make few meaningful contributions to society.

Exercise 15.3

The student who wrote the summary and analysis of "Online Dating—Five Things to Avoid" wrote this brief evaluation of the essay's strengths and weaknesses. Read it and then write your own evaluation of the essay.

> I think the best thing about the essay is that it doesn't just classify the iffy types of postings to dating sites. It goes further and offers specific advice about what to do to avoid being fooled by them. This is helpful information. The only negative I see is that several of the categories overlap, but then again it is difficult to place most people into just one category.

Writing Your Own Classification or Division Essay

Now that you have learned about the major characteristics, structure, and purposes of classification and division essays, you know everything necessary to write your own. In this section you will read a student's classification essay and get advice on finding ideas, drafting your essay, and revising and editing it. You may want to use the essay prompts in "Readings for Practice, Ideas for Writing" (p. 431) or choose your own topic.

A Student Model Classification Essay

For her introductory sociology course, Maris Vasquez was asked to write an essay about people's use of technology. She chose to discuss Facebook users. As you read the essay, notice how Vasquez uses classification as her primary method of organization.

Title: identifies subject

A Profile of Facebook Users

Maris Vasquez

Introduction: Vasquez establishes expertise on the topic.

As a college student, I have spent a good amount of my life on Facebook. I use it to procrastinate, discover what friends are doing at other colleges, or determine who a person is. Facebook is a great Web site from which to observe human activity. In my travels across all kinds of profiles, I have drawn one conclusion.

Thesis lists categories and includes basis of classification.

Based on posts, photos, profile pictures, likes, comments, and other Facebook activities, users can generally be grouped into five categories that characterize their purpose in using Facebook: creepers, socialites, politicians, philosophers, and amateur photographers.

Category 1: creepers

The first category is what I like to call the creepers. When one hears the word *creeper*, one might think of bugs and other sorts of creepy, crawly creatures. That is just what this kind of Facebook user does. She (this user often happens to be female) makes her way across Facebook profiles, discovering bits and pieces about the users she observes, much like a bug crawling across the

Characteristic 1: rarely comments

earth. The creeper rarely comments on the things she observes or leaves clues that she was reading along. She simply takes in the information and adds it to her repertoire of gossip. Her own

Characteristic 2: prevents others from finding out her information

Facebook page is often creeper proof. She spends a great deal of time perfecting her privacy settings so that no one can peek in on her. What she does post is perfectly edited, be it a picture or a

Characteristic 3: judges others in her messages

status, so that no one can make any false judgments. Her status is often about how dumb other people are. This status is usually posted after a thorough thirty-minute creeping session. The word *stalking* is often synonymous with *creeping*.

Category 2: socialites

The socialites are, in many ways, the opposite of the creepers.

Characteristic 1: frequently posts party photos

The socialite (also known as the partier) posts every picture from every party she goes to. She is not discreet in her postings and makes it quite clear that she doesn't particularly care what other people did on their weekend. She tags herself in pictures that the nightclubs post and is known for a certain type of status, which often includes at least three other users, who are tagged, and lists their location. Themed parties are her favorite. Before, during, and after photos are a must, even if the evidence turns undignified.

Characteristic 2: posts status updates while intoxicated but deletes them later

An intoxicated word-salad status is quite common, but finding them later can be difficult as they're often deleted the next morning. Morning-after statuses often say something like "Last night was crazy! Love my girls." Profile pictures are never "selfies" but always show her with at least two other people, preferably at

Characteristic 3: is not concerned with the impression her profile makes

Category 3: politicians

Characteristic 1: posts news articles and partisan political information

Characteristic 2: purposefully starts debates online

Characteristic 3: posts photos relating to his politics

Category 4: philosophers

Characteristic 1: posts romantic quotes

Characteristic 2: posts black-and-white photos

Category 5: amateur photographers

Characteristic 1: posts photos of objects

Characteristic 2: posts answers to questions about camera equipment

Characteristic 3: uses pictures rather than words

Conclusion: Categories may overlap, but each type exists.

a nightclub. The socialite does not particularly care if potential employers see photos of her drinking because she assumes that, as former college kids, they'll excuse her actions.

The politician uses Facebook for a completely different type of self-promotion. He posts provocative articles on recent news developments, campaign videos from his favorite professional politicians, and his own witty responses to the day's events. His status is often controversial; it attracts many "likes" from his political followers and angry comments from his detractors. It isn't really a successful month on Facebook unless he's started at least one Facebook fight in which he must defend his position against users of the opposite political persuasion. The politician's profile frequently features a campaign logo or a photograph of himself posing with an actual politician.

Similar to the politician, but deserving of her own category, is the philosopher. She posts sappy quotes about life or song lyrics, which are usually thinly disguised comments on her love interests. Her profile pictures are often in black and white and never feature her smiling. The caption usually includes one of her sappy quotes, occasionally with a heart or other symbol featured prominently.

Finally, the photographer uses Facebook like his second Tumblr account. He posts albums of completely random objects like his cat, his shoe laces, and his pens. He favors black and white, and his profile picture is often of him taking a picture of something, sometimes of the person taking the picture of him. He uses Facebook to convince others how artsy he is. He posts statuses about whether or not he should get a fisheye lens and answers any questions anyone posts about cameras, whether he knows the person or not. His statuses are few and far between because he prefers to speak through pictures. When he does post a status, his words often resemble those of the philosopher.

Most people on Facebook are probably a combination of all these categories, but when you see one of these stereotypical Facebook users, you know it. Statuses, photos, profile pictures, comments, and the like can tell a lot about a person. In combination, these things can inform you as to a user's ultimate intention in using Facebook.

Responding to Vasquez's Essay

1. How well does the writer's opening paragraph create interest in her classification essay? Does her thesis make you want to read on?
2. Are Vasquez's categories equally well developed? How clearly do you understand each?
3. How well do Vasquez's topic sentences make transitions from one category to the next?
4. Do you think her mentioning in the conclusion that the categories she has established can often be combined helps or hurts Vasquez's essay?

Finding Ideas for Your Classification or Division Essay

One way to find ideas to write about is to look for topics *as you read* material from this book, for other classes, or in your spare time. As you read classification or division pieces, think of other ways of classifying or dividing the topic. For example, consider an essay that classifies exercise programs according to their health benefits. Alternatively, exercise programs could be classified according to cost, degree of strenuousness, types of exercise, and so forth. A classification or division essay provides the reader with one particular viewpoint on the subject. Be sure to keep in mind that it is only *one* viewpoint. Once you have identified alternative viewpoints, choose one to write about.

Planning Your Classification or Division Essay

Your first step is to choose a subject to classify or divide. Once you've done so, you need to come up with details about the subject and its categories or parts. Often it works best to generate details first and then use the details to identify categories or parts. Begin with one or more of the following strategies for generating details about your topic.

1. **Visit a place where you can observe the topic or the people associated with it.** For example, to generate details about sports fans, attend a sporting event or watch one on television. Take notes on what you see and hear. Be specific; record conversations, physical characteristics, behaviors, and so forth.
2. **Discuss the topic with a classmate or friend.** Focus on the qualities and characteristics of the topic. Allow the perspective of your classmate or friend to open your mind to new details on your topic.
3. **Brainstorm a list of all the features or characteristics of the topic.** Jot down everything that comes to mind; one feature will serve as a springboard for further characteristics.
4. **Draw a map or diagram that illustrates the topic's features and characteristics.** This map or diagram will help you discover relationships and connections among the characteristics.

5. **Conduct library or Internet research to discover facts, examples, and other details about the topic.** Research will suggest new possibilities and help you expand on your own ideas.

Choosing a Principle of Classification or Division

Your next task is to decide on the principle or basis on which to classify or divide the subject. Read through your details, thinking about the kinds of categories that might be relevant to discussing your subject or the parts into which you could usefully divide it. If the topic is highway drivers, for instance, you could classify them by gender, age, type of car driven, or driving habits. If the topic is a sports team, you could divide it into coaches, assistants, primary players, back-up players, and so forth. Experiment with several principles of classification or division until you find one that fits your purpose and audience.

Choosing Categories or Parts

With your principle of classification or division in mind, use the following suggestions to determine categories or parts.

1. **Make sure that your categories or parts are comprehensive—that your categories can include all items or that you haven't left out any parts.** For example, in a division essay about parts of a baseball stadium, you would not exclude the infield or the bleachers.

2. **Be sure the categories do not overlap.** For example, in a classification essay about preschool, you shouldn't use the categories preschoolers and pre-K(indergarten) students, because they mean the same thing.

3. **Create categories or parts that will engage your readers.** For example, a division essay on players' facilities in a baseball stadium—dugout, locker room, and bullpen—would be more interesting to sports fans than an essay describing different seating sections of the stadium.

4. **Once you establish categories or parts, you may need to do additional brainstorming or some other type of prewriting to generate enough details to explain each category or part adequately.**

5. **Choose names that effectively describe the categories or parts.** For example, in an essay classifying highway drivers with annoying habits, you might assign names like "I-own-the-road" drivers and "I'm-busy-texting" drivers.

Identifying the Key Features of Each Category or Part

Once you have a workable list of categories or parts, go back to the details and identify key features. These are the features that you will use to explain and differentiate each category or part. Consider again the categories of annoying highway drivers. You might distinguish each type of driver by the key characteristics listed here.

"I-own-the-road" drivers	Inconsiderate of other drivers; weave in and out of traffic; honk horns or flash lights to intimidate others into letting them pass
"I'm-busy-texting" drivers	Are selfish and addicted to their smart phones; endanger themselves and others because they are not paying attention to the road

As you identify characteristics for each category or part, you may find that two categories or parts overlap or that a category or part is too broad. Do not hesitate to create, combine, or eliminate categories or parts as you work.

Developing and Supporting Your Thesis

The next step is to develop a working thesis that identifies your topic and reveals your principle of division or classification. The thesis should also suggest why your classification or division is useful or important. For examples of thesis statements for classification and division essays, see "The Introduction Explains the Classification or Division and Presents the Thesis Statement" on page 415.

Drafting Your Classification or Division Essay

After evaluating categories or parts and reviewing your thesis, you are ready to organize your ideas and draft the essay. Choose the method of organization that best suits your purpose. One method that works well in classification essays is the least-to-most arrangement, in which categories are addressed in increasing order of importance or from least to most common, difficult, or frequent. Spatial order often works well in division essays, as does order of importance. In describing the parts of a baseball stadium, you might move from stands to playing field (spatial order). In writing about the parts of a hospital, you might describe the most important areas first (operating rooms and emergency room) and then move to less important facilities (waiting rooms and cafeteria).

Once you decide how to organize your categories or parts, the next step is to write a first draft. Use the following guidelines:

1. **Write an effective introduction.** See "The Structure and Content of Classification and Division Essays" (p. 415) for advice on introductions.

2. **Explain each category or part.** Begin by defining each category or part, taking into account the complexity of the topic and the audience's background knowledge. For example, in a division essay about a baseball stadium, you might need to define *infield* and *outfield* if the audience includes a large number of people who are not sports fans.

3. **Provide details that describe each category or part.** Be sure to show how each category or part is distinct from the others. Include a wide range of details—sensory details, personal experiences, examples, and comparisons and contrasts.

4. **Generally, allow one or more paragraphs for each category or part.**

5. **Use transitions.** Your readers need transitions to keep on track as they move from one category or part to another. Transitions such as "the *third* category of . . . ," "an *additional* characteristic of . . . ," and "it *also* contains . . ." will help distinguish key features between and within categories or parts.

6. **Provide roughly the same amount and kind of detail and description for each category or part.** For instance, if you give an example of one type of mental disorder, then you should give an example for every other type discussed in the essay.

7. **Consider adding headings or lists to make the categories or parts clear and distinct.** Headings or lists can be especially useful if you will be explaining a large number of categories or parts.

8. **Consider adding a visual such as a diagram or flowchart to help your readers visualize your system of classification or division.**

9. **Write a satisfying conclusion.** If you have trouble finding an appropriate way to conclude, return to your statement about why the classification or division is significant and try to elaborate on it.

Revising Your Classification or Division Essay

If possible, set your draft aside for a day or two before rereading and revising it. As you review the draft, focus on content and ideas, not on grammar, punctuation, or mechanics. Use the flowchart in Figure 15.3 to guide your analysis of the strengths and weaknesses in your draft essay.

Editing and Proofreading Your Essay

The last step is to check your revised essay for errors in grammar, spelling, punctuation, and mechanics. In addition, watch out for the types of errors you tend to make in writing assignments, whether for this class or in other situations. Check the handbook (pp. 645–714) for assistance with common errors in your writing.

Figure 15.3 Revising a Classification or Division Essay

QUESTIONS		REVISION STRATEGIES

1. Thesis and introduction Do they explain your principle of classification or division and suggest its importance?
→ No →
- Revise your thesis to make your justification stronger or more apparent.
- Add explanatory information to your introduction.

↓ Yes

2. Principle of classification Do you use it consistently throughout the essay? Does it fit your audience and purpose and clearly relate to your thesis?
→ No →
- Brainstorm other possible principles of classification of your topic that better fit your audience and purpose.
- Revise your categories and parts to fit either your existing principle or a new one.
- Rewrite your thesis to reflect your principle of classification.

↓ Yes

3. Categories or parts Do they cover all or most members of the group or all major parts of the topic? Are your categories or parts exclusive (not overlapping)?
→ No →
- Brainstorm or do research to add categories or parts.
- Revise your categories or parts so that each item fits into one group only.

↓ Yes

4. Details of each category Does your essay use details to fully explain each category? (If it reads like a list, answer "No.")
→ No →
- Brainstorm or do research to discover more details.
- Add examples, definitions, facts, and expert testimony to improve your explanations.

↓ Yes

5. Organization Is the organization clear? Does the method you use suit your audience and purpose? Have you followed it consistently?
→ No →
- Refer to Chapter 7 to discover a more appropriate organizing plan.
- Revise the order of your categories or parts.
- Add transitions to make your organization clear.

↓ Yes

6. Topic sentences Is each paragraph focused on a separate category or part?
→ No →
- Consider combining paragraphs that cover a single category or part and splitting paragraphs that cover more than one.

↓ Yes

7. Conclusion Does it offer a new insight or perspective on the topic?
→ No →
- Build the importance of the classification or division into the conclusion.

Readings for Practice, Ideas for Writing

Types of Women in Romantic Comedies Who Are Not Real

Mindy Kaling is an Emmy-nominated writer, actress, and producer and is well known for her work on NBC's sitcom *The Office*. This excerpt from her book *Is Everyone Hanging Out Without Me? (And Other Concerns)* (2011) classifies the types of female characters that appear in Hollywood films.

Reading Tip

As you read, identify the author's attitude toward the characters she classifies. Summarize her attitude in a word or two.

Previewing the Reading

Preview the reading (see pp. 28–29 for guidelines), and then name several types of female characters said by Kaling to appear in romantic comedies.

Types of Women in Romantic Comedies Who Are Not Real

====== MINDY KALING ======

When I was a kid, Christmas vacation meant renting VHS copies of romantic comedies from Blockbuster and watching them with my parents at home. *Sleepless in Seattle* was big, and so was *When Harry Met Sally*. I laughed along with everyone else at the scene where Meg Ryan fakes an orgasm at the restaurant without even knowing what an orgasm was. In my mind, she was just being kind of loud and silly at a diner, and that was hilarious enough for me.

I love romantic comedies. I feel almost sheepish writing that, because the genre has been so degraded in the past twenty years or so that admitting you like these movies is essentially an admission of mild stupidity. But that has not stopped me from watching them.

I enjoy watching people fall in love on-screen so much that I can suspend my disbelief for the contrived situations that only happen in the heightened world of romantic comedies. I have come to enjoy the moment when the normal lead guy, say, slips and falls right on top of the hideously expensive wedding cake. I actually feel robbed when the female lead's dress *doesn't* get torn open at a baseball game while the JumboTron is on her. I simply regard romantic comedies as a subgenre of sci-fi, in which the world created therein has different rules than my regular human world. Then I just lap it up. There is no difference between Ripley from

Continued >

Alien and any Katherine Heigl character. They're all participating in the same level of made-up awesomeness, and I enjoy every second of it.

So it makes sense that in this world there are many specimens of women who I do not think exist in real life, like Vulcans or UFO people or whatever. They are:

The Klutz

5   When a beautiful actress is in a movie, executives wrack their brains to find some kind of flaw in her that still allows her to be palatable. She can't be overweight or not perfect-looking, because who would want to see that? A not 100-percent-perfect-looking-in-every-way female? You might as well film a dead squid decaying on a beach somewhere for two hours.

So they make her a Klutz.

The 100-percent-perfect-looking female is perfect in every way, except that she constantly falls down. She bonks her head on things. She trips and falls and spills soup on her affable date. (Josh Lucas. Is that his name? I know it's two first names. Josh George? Brad Mike? Fred Tom? Yes, it's Fred Tom.) Our Klutz clangs into stop signs while riding a bike, and knocks over giant displays of expensive fine china. Despite being five foot nine and weighing 110 pounds, she is basically like a drunk buffalo who has never been a part of human society. But Fred Tom loves her anyway.

The Ethereal Weirdo

The smart and funny writer Nathan Rabin coined the term *Manic Pixie Dream Girl* to describe a version of this archetype[1] after seeing Kirsten Dunst in the movie *Elizabethtown*. This girl can't be pinned down and may or may not show up when you make concrete plans. She wears gauzy blouses and braids. She decides to dance in the rain and weeps uncontrollably if she sees a sign for a missing dog or cat. She spins a globe, places her finger on a random spot, and decides to move there. This ethereal[2] weirdo abounds in movies, but nowhere else. If she were from real life, people would think she was a homeless woman and would cross the street to avoid her, but she is essential to the male fantasy that even if a guy is boring, he deserves a woman who will find him fascinating and pull him out of himself by forcing him to go skinny-dipping in a stranger's pool.

The Woman Who Is Obsessed with Her Career and Is No Fun at All

I, Mindy Kaling, basically have two full-time jobs. I regularly work sixteen hours a day. But like most of the other people I know who are similarly busy,

---

[1] **archetype** Perfectly typical example or model.
[2] **ethereal** Extremely delicate or refined; heavenly.

I think I'm a pleasant, pretty normal person. I am slightly offended by the way busy working women my age are presented in film. I'm not, like, always barking orders into my hands-free phone device and telling people constantly, "I have no time for this!" I didn't completely forget how to be nice or feminine because I have a career. Also, since when does having a job necessitate women having their hair pulled back in a severe, tight bun? Often this uptight woman has to "re-learn" how to seduce a man because her estrogen leaked out of her from leading so many board meetings, and she has to do all sorts of crazy, unnecessary crap, like eat a hot dog in a libidinous[3] way or something. Having a challenging job in movies means the compassionate, warm, or sexy side of your brain has fallen out.

The Forty-Two-Year-Old Mother of the Thirty-Year-Old Male Lead

I am so accustomed to the young mom phenomenon, that when I saw the poster   10 for *The Proposal* I wondered for a second if the proposal in the movie was Ryan Reynolds suggesting he send his mother, Sandra Bullock, to an old-age home.

However, given the popularity of teen moms right now, this could actually be the wave of the future.

The Sassy Best Friend

You know that really horny and hilarious best friend who is always asking about your relationship and has nothing really going on in her own life? She always wants to meet you in coffee shops or wants to go to Bloomingdale's to sample perfumes? She runs a chic dildo store in the West Village? Nope? Okay, that's this person.

The Skinny Woman Who Is Beautiful and Toned but Also Gluttonous and Disgusting

Again, I am more than willing to suspend my disbelief during a romantic comedy for good set decoration alone. One pristine kitchen from a Nancy Meyers movie like in *It's Complicated* is worth five Diane Keatons being caught half-clad in a topiary[4] or whatever situation her character has found herself in.

But sometimes even my suspended disbelief isn't enough. I am speaking of the gorgeous and skinny heroine who is also a disgusting pig when it comes to food. And everyone in the movie—her parents, her friends, her boss—are all complicit in this huge lie. They are constantly telling her to stop eating and being such a glutton. And this actress, this poor skinny actress who so clearly lost

---

[3] **libidinous** Full of sexual lust; lewd.
[4] **topiary** Tree or bush trimmed in a decorative shape.

Continued >

weight to play the likeable lead, has to say things like "Shut up you guys! I love cheesecake! If I want to eat an entire cheesecake, I will!" If you look closely, you can see this woman's ribs through the dress she's wearing—that's how skinny she is, this cheesecake-loving cow.

15   You wonder, as you sit and watch this movie, what the characters would do if they were confronted by an actual average American woman. They would all kill themselves, which would actually be kind of an interesting movie.

The Woman Who Works in an Art Gallery

How many freakin' art galleries are out there? Are people constantly buying visual art or something? This posh-smart-classy job is a favorite in movies. It's in the same realm as kindergarten teacher in terms of accessibility: Guys don't really get it, but the trappings of it are likeable and nonthreatening.

> ART GALLERY WOMAN: Dust off the Rothko[5].We have an important buyer coming into town and this is a really big deal for my career. I have no time for this!

This is one of the rare clichés that actually has a male counterpart. Whenever you meet a handsome, charming, successful man in a romantic comedy, the heroine's friend always says the same thing. "He's really successful—he's an . . . (say it with me)

20   . . . architect!"

There are like nine people in the entire world who are architects, and one of them is my dad. None of them look like Patrick Dempsey[6].

---

[5] **the Rothko** A painting by the twentieth-century American painter Mark Rothko.
[6] **Patrick Dempsey** A well-known American actor.

📊 Understanding and Reviewing the Reading

1. **Thesis** What is Kaling's thesis, and where does she state it most directly?

2. **Principle of classification** What is Kaling's main principle of classification? That is, on what basis does she compare the members of each category?

3. **Categories** Briefly summarize each of Kaling's categories using your own words. How does her final category explanation differ somewhat from those preceding it?

4. **Supporting details** What types of supporting details does Kaling offer to explain each category?

5. **Vocabulary** Using context clues (p. 37), write a brief definition of each of the following words as it is used in the reading, consulting a dictionary if necessary: *sheepish* (para. 2), *degraded* (2), *contrived* (3), *heightened* (3), *palatable* (5), *complicit* (14), and *posh* (16).

6. **Organization** Complete the graphic organizer to understand the structure of Kaling's essay.

Title	Types of Women in Romantic Comedies Who Are Not Real
Introduction	**Topic:** Women in romantic comedies
	Background: Explains why she likes romantic comedies
	Thesis: Romantic comedies have ridiculously fake female characters, but just like sci-fi films, which also have ridiculously fake characters, the movies can still be excellent.
Body paragraphs: types of women in romantic comedies (who do not exist in real life)	**Category 1:**
	Characteristic:
	Category 2:
	Characteristic:
	Category 3:
	Characteristic:
	Category 4:
	Characteristic:
	Category 5:
	Characteristic:
	Category 6:
	Characteristic:
	Category 7:
	Characteristic:
Conclusion	The essay ends with a memorable joke, which reinforces the idea that romantic comedies are nothing like real life.

Analyzing the Reading

1. **Introduction** What do the first four paragraphs contribute to introducing Kaling's topic?

2. **Audience** How would you define Kaling's intended audience? In your answer, highlight several references she makes that she expects readers to be familiar with.

3. **Purpose** What is Kaling's purpose? Is this essay basically informative, or does it have another purpose?

4. **Language** In paragraph 4, how does Kaling's reference to "Vulcans" and "UFO people" relate to her thesis?

5. **Technique** Why does Kaling begin paragraphs 12 and 16 with a series of questions? What do these questions and those used throughout the piece contribute to her thesis?

Evaluating the Reading

1. **Audience** Based on your response to Analyzing the Reading question 2, how well do you think Kaling appeals to her intended audience?

2. **Voice** Do you agree with Kaling's claim in paragraph 2 that saying one likes romantic comedies is "an admission of mild stupidity"? Why might she say this about herself?

3. **Language** In paragraph 3, Kaling uses the phrase "suspend my disbelief" and calls romantic comedies a "subgenre of sci-fi" in which "the world created therein has different rules than my regular human world." How well do you think she carries through with this idea? Is there consistency in the language she uses? How effective is this idea?

4. **Categories** Based on your movie-watching experience, which of Kaling's types of romantic-comedy characters make most sense to you? Do any not correspond with the female characters you've seen in such comedies?

Discussing the Reading

1. Kaling does not provide a traditional conclusion to this essay. How do you think she should conclude it? Which ideas—either stated or implied—are most important and the ones that readers should be reminded of at the end?

2. Kaling briefly mentions the male characters who appear in romantic comedies. What do you think her attitude is toward these characters? Is it similar to or different from her attitude toward female characters? What might this say about how men and women are presented in movies?

3. What is your attitude toward romantic comedies? Do you agree with Kaling that they have nothing to do with the "regular human world"?

Writing about the Reading

1. **Paragraph** In a paragraph, summarize "Types of Women in Romantic Comedies Who Are Not Real." Write a brief introduction, and then in just a sentence or two describe each of Kaling's seven categories. (Hint: Note that Kaling's formal classification begins with para. 5.)

2. **Paragraph** In a paragraph, classify three types of male characters in romantic comedies. (Hint: Kaling mentions the "boring" guy [para. 8], the male lead son [10], and the "architect" [20] and also refers specifically to the actors Ryan Reynolds [10] and Patrick Dempsey [21]. Use these references to help you develop categories based on your own movie viewing.)

3. **Essay** Kaling likens romantic comedies to science-fiction films and refers specifically to Vulcans and UFO people (para. 4). Write a classification essay about science-fiction films. You might focus on different types of films, various sorts of characters, or even kinds of plot devices. (Hint: Start by brainstorming a list of films, characters, and so forth in the science-fiction genre. Then separate appropriate individual examples according to a clear basis of classification.)

A Brush with Reality: Surprises in the Tube

David Bodanis is a journalist and an academic trained in mathematics, physics, and economics. He has taught social science courses at Oxford University, consulted with businesses on energy policy and sustainable development, and written several books. The following essay is from *The Secret House* (1986), his examination of the foods eaten and products consumed by a family over the course of a day.

Reading Tip

In this piece, Bodanis examines the substances that are put together to make toothpaste. Notice the deadpan tone he uses to describe the ingredients and the words he chooses in order to leave a particular impression on readers.

Preview the Reading

Preview the reading (see pp. 28–29 for guidelines), and then decide what the author's purpose is in writing this division essay.

A Brush with Reality: Surprises in the Tube

═══ DAVID BODANIS ═══

Into the bathroom goes our male resident, and after the most pressing need is satisfied it's time to brush the teeth. The tube of toothpaste is squeezed, its pinched metal seams are splayed, pressure waves are generated inside, and the paste begins to flow. But what's in this toothpaste, so carefully being extruded out?

Water mostly, 30 to 45% in most brands: ordinary, everyday simple tap water. It's there because people like to have a big gob of toothpaste to spread on the brush, and water is the cheapest stuff there is when it comes to making big gobs. Dripping a bit from the tap onto your brush would cost virtually nothing; whipped in with the rest of the toothpaste the manufacturers can sell it at a neat and accountant-pleasing $2 per pound equivalent. Toothpaste manufacture is a very lucrative occupation.

Second to water in quantity is chalk: exactly the same material that schoolteachers use to write on blackboards. It is collected from the crushed remains of long-dead ocean creatures. In the Cretaceous[1] seas chalk particles served as part of the wickedly sharp outer skeleton that these creatures had to wrap around themselves to keep from getting chomped by all the slightly larger other ocean creatures they met. Their massed graves are our present chalk deposits.

[1] **Cretaceous** Dating from the last part of the age of dinosaurs, 144 to 65 million years ago.

The individual chalk particles—the size of the smallest mud particles in your garden—have kept their toughness over the aeons[2], and now on the toothbrush they'll need it. The enamel outer coating of the tooth they'll have to face is the hardest substance in the body—tougher than skull, or bone, or nail. Only the chalk particles in toothpaste can successfully grind into the teeth during brushing, ripping off the surface layers like an abrading wheel[3] grinding down a boulder in a quarry.

The craters, slashes, and channels that the chalk tears into the teeth will 5 also remove a certain amount of built-up yellow in the carnage, and it is for that polishing function that it's there. A certain amount of unduly enlarged extra-abrasive chalk fragments tear such cavernous pits into the teeth that future decay bacteria will be able to hunker down there and thrive; the quality control people find it almost impossible to screen out these errant super-chalk pieces, and government regulations allow them to stay in.

In case even the gouging doesn't get all the yellow off, another substance is worked into the toothpaste cream. This is titanium dioxide. It comes in tiny spheres, and it's the stuff bobbing around in white wall paint to make it come out white. Splashed around onto your teeth during the brushing it coats much of the yellow that remains. Being water soluble it leaks off in the next few hours and is swallowed, but at least for the quick glance up in the mirror after finishing it will make the user think his teeth are truly white. Some manufacturers add optical whitening dye—the stuff more commonly found in washing machine bleach—to make extra sure that that glance in the mirror shows reassuring white.

These ingredients alone would not make a very attractive concoction. They would stick in the tube like a sloppy white plastic lump, hard to squeeze out as well as revolting to the touch. Few consumers would savor rubbing in a mixture of water, ground-up blackboard chalk, and the whitener from latex paint first thing in the morning. To get around that finicky distaste the manufacturers have mixed in a host of other goodies.

To keep the glop from drying out, a mixture including glycerine glycol—related to the most common car antifreeze ingredient—is whipped in with the chalk and water, and to give that concoction a bit of substance (all we really have so far is wet colored chalk) a large helping is added of gummy molecules from the seaweed Chondrus Crispus. This seaweed ooze spreads in among the chalk, paint, and antifreeze, then stretches itself in all directions to hold the whole mass together. A bit of paraffin oil (the fuel that flickers in camping lamps) is pumped in with it to help the moss ooze keep the whole substance smooth.

With the glycol, ooze, and paraffin we're almost there. Only two major chemicals are left to make the refreshing, cleansing substance we know as

---

[2] **aeons** Eons; an eternity.
[3] **abrading wheel** Tool that wears down material by applying friction and pressure from a rotating disk.

Continued >

toothpaste. The ingredients so far are fine for cleaning, but they wouldn't make much of the satisfying foam we have come to expect in the morning brushing.

10   To remedy that, every toothpaste on the market has a big dollop of detergent added too. You've seen the suds detergent will make in a washing machine. The same substance added here will duplicate that inside the mouth. It's not particularly necessary, but it sells. The only problem is that by itself this ingredient tastes, well, too like detergent. It's horribly bitter and harsh. The chalk put in toothpaste is pretty foul-tasting too for that matter. It's to get around that gustatory discomfort that the manufacturers put in the ingredient they tout perhaps the most of all. This is the flavoring, and it has to be strong. Double rectified peppermint oil is used—a flavorer so powerful that chemists know better than to sniff it in the raw state in the laboratory. Menthol crystals and saccharin or other sugar simulators are added to complete the camouflage operation.

Is that it? Chalk, water, paint, seaweed, antifreeze, paraffin oil, detergent, and peppermint? Not quite. A mix like that would be irresistible to the hundreds of thousands of individual bacteria lying on the surface of even an immaculately cleaned bathroom sink. They would get in, float in the water bubbles, ingest the ooze and paraffin, maybe even spray out enzymes to break down the chalk. The result would be an uninviting mess. The way manufacturers avoid that final obstacle is by putting something in to kill the bacteria. Something good and strong is needed, something that will zap any accidentally intrudant bacteria into oblivion. And that something is formaldehyde—the disinfectant used in anatomy labs.

So it's chalk, water, paint, seaweed, antifreeze, paraffin oil, detergent, peppermint, formaldehyde, and fluoride (which can go some way towards preserving children's teeth)—that's the usual mixture raised to the mouth on the toothbrush for a fresh morning's clean. If it sounds too unfortunate, take heart. Studies show that thorough brushing with just plain water will often do as good a job.

Understanding and Reviewing the Reading

1. **Division** What are the ingredients in toothpaste?
2. **Background information** Why did Bodanis include information about the origins of chalk?
3. **Division** What is put in toothpaste to inhibit the growth of bacteria?
4. **Conclusion** What does the author present as a final thought on the subject?

Analyzing the Reading

1. **Thesis** Analyze the effectiveness of using an implied thesis. Is the author's purpose in writing clear? Why, or why not?

2. **Parts** How successful is Bodanis in presenting his parts? Is the division of the ingredients in toothpaste complete? Do any parts overlap?

3. **Details** Name some especially effective details that are included for each category. Are some parts better explained than others? Explain your answer.

4. **Conclusion** What does Bodanis's conclusion imply about his feelings about toothpaste?

5. **Language** What does the author mean by the phrase "reassuring white" in paragraph 6?

Evaluating the Reading

1. **Drawing conclusions** When drawing conclusions, one makes reasoned decisions or forms opinions on the basis of available facts. What conclusion does Bodanis draw about the fact that water is the most plentiful ingredient in toothpaste?

2. **Drawing conclusions** Throughout the essay, Bodanis refers repeatedly to the consumers of toothpaste. Reread paragraphs 6, 7, and 10. What conclusion is he drawing about consumers?

3. **Implied conclusion** Just as the thesis is implied, the main conclusion is not stated directly. Based on his use of details, what conclusion do you think Bodanis is drawing about the use of toothpaste?

4. **Conclusion** Did you find the conclusion satisfying? Is there additional information that you would find helpful?

5. **Language** Evaluate the expressions "finicky distaste" and "host of other goodies" (para. 7). What is the author trying to express? How effective is he at making his point?

6. **Organization** To better understand the structure Bodanis uses in this essay, create a graphic organizer or outline that shows all the major divisions, plus the thesis and conclusion. Then evaluate how effective this organization is. How might you have organized the essay differently?

Discussing the Reading

1. Discuss the role of dental hygiene in our society. Why do we place such great importance on our teeth?

2. Discuss the strategies that manufacturers use to make their products appealing to consumers.

3. In class or in your journal, explore the various reasons some people choose to buy "natural" personal-care products.

Writing about the Reading

1. **Essay** Conduct a study of one advertising medium: TV, radio, the Internet, newspapers, or magazines. Take notes on what you see, hear, and read. Then write a classification essay describing the different types of ads with respect to aspects such as content, intended audience, or placement. Be sure to indicate what effect the ads had on you.

2. **Essay** How much do people know about what they consume and use? Choose a common processed food or household product, and ask three to five friends to tell you what they think it contains; take notes on their comments. Then compare their answers to the actual ingredients. Write a classification or division essay describing the degrees of knowledge people have about this food or product. Make recommendations about how consumers can learn more about what they eat and use.

3. **Internet research** Choose a product that you use daily, such as shampoo or deodorant. Using the label of ingredients as a starting point, consult the Internet to research what the product really contains. Then write a division essay that identifies the product's components and explains each, as Bodanis does for toothpaste in his essay.

📖 **COMBINING THE PATTERNS | TEXTBOOK EXCERPT: HEALTH**

Addiction

This selection is excerpted from the textbook *Health: Making Choices for Life*, by April Lynch, Barry Elmore, and Jerome Kotecki. **April Lynch** is an award-winning author and journalist who frequently writes about health and science. **Barry Elmore** is on the faculty at East Carolina University; **Jerome Kotecki** is professor of health sciences at Ball State University. The chapter in which this excerpt appears is titled "Compulsive Behaviors and Psychoactive Drugs: Understanding Addiction."

Reading Tip

As you read, identify and highlight the characteristics of addiction.

Previewing the Reading

Preview the reading (pp. 28–29), and then list as many behavioral addictions as you can recall.

Addiction
April Lynch, Barry Elmore, and Jerome Kotecki

From time to time, we all do things for fun even though we know they might cause us trouble in the long term: We cut classes, eat that extra slice of pizza, or buy those concert tickets that we "really can't afford." Such behavior is normal—and reflects the fact that the pleasure centers in our brains evolved for short-term survival, not for the kind of long-term planning that leads to academic success, healthy weight maintenance, or financial security. But why do some people repeatedly engage in problematic behaviors that have long since stopped providing any real pleasure? Why, in short, do some people develop addictions? To explore this perplexing question, let's first take a look at what an addiction really is.

What Is Addiction?

The American Society of Addiction Medicine defines **addiction** as a chronic disease of brain reward, motivation, memory, and related circuitry. Dysfunction in these brain circuits is reflected in the individual pathologically pursuing reward and/or relief by substance use or other behaviors.

Perhaps the most fundamental characteristic of addiction is craving. The person experiences an uncontrollable compulsion to engage in the behavior, and seeks it out even in the face of significant negative consequences. Often, these negative consequences are entirely clear

addiction:
A chronic, progressive disease of brain reward, motivation, memory, and related circuitry characterized by uncontrollable craving for a substance or behavior despite both negative consequences and diminishment or loss of pleasure associated with the activity.

Continued >

SGO/AGE Fotostock

People who experiment with drugs at early ages are more likely to become addicted later in life.

to loved ones, but the addict may have a diminished capacity to recognize the problems caused by his or her behavior. Denial of both the negative consequences and the addiction itself is common.

Another characteristic of addiction is loss of pleasure. Although the person originally may have engaged in the activity for pleasurable recreation, he or she now derives very little satisfaction from it. Instead, the addict's motivation becomes an increasingly powerful compulsion to relieve the physical discomfort and emotional anguish experienced when abstaining. As a result, the person experiences an escalating loss of control over the act and comes to feel increasingly controlled by it.

Without treatment, addiction is progressive; that is, the behavior becomes more fre-

5   quent and/or severe. Depending on the type of addiction, this escalation can eventually lead to loss of intimate relationships, impoverishment, imprisonment, disability, or premature death. Recovery is often preceded by one or more cycles in which the person abstains from the behavior, then relapses; however, with treatment, full recovery from addiction is possible.

Behavioral Addictions

behavioral addiction: A form of addiction involving a compulsion to engage in an activity such as gambling, sex, or shopping rather than a compulsion to use a substance.

In 2013, the American Psychiatric Association (APA) will publish the fifth edition of its manual of clinical diagnoses. The working draft of this manual, which is referred to as the *DSM-5,* includes a new category of diagnoses called **behavioral addictions** that could be applied to patients who are addicted not to a substance, but rather to an activity such as gambling. The rationale for this category is that the patient's subjective experience, the brain networks involved, the progression of the disorder, and the effective treatment are equivalent to those for substance addictions. Not all experts agree, and many are calling for more research to evaluate the validity of "behavioral addictions."

Currently, the working draft of the *DSM-5* classifies two types of behavioral addiction as true psychiatric disorders: pathological gambling and hypersexual disorder (commonly called sex addiction). In addition, the working draft includes a proposed diagnosis for a behavioral addiction "not otherwise specified" that psychiatrists could use for patients with behaviors such as compulsive shopping, texting, and Internet use.

Pathological Gambling

About 85% of adults in the United States have gambled at least once in their life. For the vast majority of us, a night at the casino or the occasional game of poker does not pose a problem. However, for an estimated 2 million people in the United States, roughly 1% of adults, gambling is an addiction. Although gambling is illegal for anyone under age 21 in many states, most addicted gamblers get their start in high school, and young adults are especially vulnerable. Studies estimate that 3–11% of American college students have a serious gambling problem that can result in psychological difficulties, unmanageable debt, and failing grades.

The APA considers a gambling habit *pathological* (harmful) when players experience destructive traits such as:

- Being preoccupied with thoughts and plans related to gambling
- Needing to gamble with increasing amounts of money in order to achieve the desired excitement
- Feeling restless or irritable when attempting to cut back or stop gambling, or being unable to do so
- Using gambling to escape feelings of helplessness, guilt, anxiety, or depression

Other telltale signs include lying to friends and family to hide the extent of the problem and borrowing from others or stealing to finance the habit. 10

Both industry and public policy-making can help reduce the number of people who develop a gambling addiction. For example, many casinos have policies that physically ban from their facilities players who are unable to control their gambling. But whereas casinos can screen out compulsive gamblers, websites cannot, and Internet gamblers can lose thousands of dollars in minutes. Thus, in 2006, the U.S. Congress passed a law prohibiting transfer of funds between financial institutions and online gaming sites. This effectively outlawed Internet gambling; however, most companies have found ways to evade the regulations and continue business. In 2011, the U.S. Justice Department issued indictments against the founders of three of the largest Internet poker companies. It remains to be seen if these indictments will quash the activity of all online gaming sites.

Continued >

Like drug addiction, pathological gambling can be successfully treated. Cognitive-behavior therapy has proven effective in long-term abstinence from gambling. Some studies suggest that the use of anti-depressants or other medications along with therapy may be helpful.

Hypersexual Disorder

A variety of sources estimate that between 3% and 5% of the U.S. population could meet the criteria for sexual addiction, which the APA refers to as *hypersexual disorder*. The disorder is characterized by recurrent and intense sexual fantasies, urges, and behavior that consume excessive time and cannot be controlled, despite negative consequences such as sexually transmitted infections, unintended pregnancy, broken relationships, and financial problems. The person typically gains very little satisfaction from sexual activity and in fact may experience feelings of deep guilt and shame that cause tremendous emotional distress. Treatment may include education, individual or family counseling, group therapy, and medications, typically antidepressants.

Other Potential Behavioral Addictions

Some psychotherapists believe that working, credit card spending, blogging, and many other behaviors can develop into true addictions—which can be successfully treated. Others argue against assigning "disorder status" to behaviors that they say are within the range of normal. Concerned by the inadequate research into such "addictions," they ask whether any behavior—watching TV? sunbathing? tracking your favorite pop star?—can qualify as an addiction and, if so, at what point? Of the many potential "not otherwise specified" behavioral addictions, probably the most widely debated are compulsive spending and the use of the Internet, cell phones, or another form of technology.

COMPULSIVE SPENDING

15   Compulsive spending (also referred to as compulsive buying or shopping) is thought to affect more than 1 in 20 U.S. adults. Most "shopaholics" are young and have incomes under $50,000. Most are also four times less likely than the average person to pay off their credit card balances in full.

When a compulsive spender buys something, the act triggers the release of certain chemicals in the brain that cause a rush of euphoria. This may explain why, in a national survey, researchers found that people addicted to spending "took greater pleasure in shopping and buying." Compulsive spenders were also more likely to experience uncontrollable buying binges, make senseless and impulsive purchases, and feel depressed after shopping. Other preliminary studies suggest that compulsive spenders may suffer from abnormally high levels of depression and anxiety, as well as substance abuse and eating disorders.

ADDICTION TO TECHNOLOGY

The average American adult spends 13 hours per week online, not including e-mail, but one in seven are online for 24 or more hours each week. Does this level of Internet use suggest addiction? Some sources suggest that about 4% to 8% of regular Internet users do become addicted; that is, their Internet use interferes with their academic success, work, relationships, hours of sleep, or exercising. Moreover, the addict turns to Internet use to alter his or her mood, especially to escape from depression or anxiety.

Technology addictions are becoming a concern in this gadget-friendly age.

Blend Images/Alamy

Another use of technology that's increasingly getting media attention is "addiction" to texting. Undoubtedly, Americans love to text: We send or receive about 5 billion text messages per day. Most of these messages are sent by people of college age; a national survey found that, whereas just 3% of adults over 25 send more than 200 messages a day, 18% of adults aged 18 to 24 send that many messages. If you subtract 8 hours per day for sleep, that's 12.5 messages every waking hour. Does this level of texting constitute an addiction? Those who say it does point to brain scans showing that the same areas of the brain light up when people text and when they use psychoactive drugs. Moreover, many people continue to text excessively despite serious negative consequences—including damage to the tendons in their hands. Other addiction experts say that, although frequent texting is a bad habit, before we can classify it as an addiction, more research is needed.

Understanding and Reviewing the Reading

1. **Meaning** What are two fundamental characteristics of addiction?
2. **Categories** Identify the types of behavioral addictions discussed in the reading. Which ones are classified as true psychiatric disorders?
3. **Organizing information** Create an outline for this reading that would help you learn and remember it.
4. **Textbook terminology** How does the American Society of Addiction Medicine define the term *addiction*? How is the term *behavioral addiction* defined?

Analyzing the Reading

1. **Introduction** What is the purpose of the opening paragraph?

2. **Combining patterns** Where in the selection do the authors use definition? Where do the authors use classification?

3. **Visuals** This textbook excerpt includes two photographs. What does each of these photographs illustrate about addiction?

4. **Annotations** Go back to the reading and annotate it in preparation for a class discussion on the following question: What are the consequences of untreated addiction?

5. **Audience** Do you think the authors are writing primarily to students studying for a career in health care? Or is a broader audience intended? What makes you think so?

6. **Predicting exam questions** If an instructor were to give a pop quiz on this selection, what three questions might be included? How would you answer each?

Evaluating the Reading

1. **Details** What types of details did the authors use to explain addiction and behavioral addictions? Were these details sufficient?

2. **Visual** Do you think that the photograph of young women looking at their phones effectively illustrates the concept of a technology addiction? Why, or why not?

3. **Categories** What other types of addictions could the authors have included? Do you think these other types of addictions are covered elsewhere in the chapter?

4. **Learning aids** How were the headings and highlighted / marginal definitions helpful?

5. **Applying information** How does this information connect to what you are learning in other courses?

Discussing the Reading

1. Discuss industry policies that address gambling addiction. Do you think the casino policy that bans compulsive gamblers is an effective approach? Why, or why not?

2. What other topics do you think are discussed in this chapter? Consider the title of the textbook from which the excerpt is taken (*Health: Making Choices for Life*) and predict the authors' approach in the rest of the chapter.

3. Discuss the statistics quoted in the section about addiction to technology. How accurate do these statistics seem to you? What is typical for college students? Do you think your level of texting constitutes an addiction?

Writing about the Reading

1. **Essay** Were you surprised by anything you learned in this reading? What information did you find most useful or relevant to your own life? What was least surprising to you in this reading? Why? Write an essay addressing these questions.

2. **Essay** Did this excerpt give you any insight into your own habits or behaviors? Consider the discussion among psychotherapists regarding other potential behavior addictions: At what point does a behavior qualify as an addiction? Write an essay describing one of your own habits or behaviors (or a habit or behavior of someone you know) that could become problematic. Using the information you have learned in this reading, explain at what point you would consider the behavior an addiction.

3. **Essay** The reading addresses two forms of technology—texting and Internet use—in the section on addiction to technology. How many different forms of technology can you think of? Write an essay in which you use classification to describe at least four forms of technology or an essay in which you use division to explain any one form of technology. Assume that some members of your audience are not frequent users of technology, and be sure to include enough details, descriptions, and examples so that your readers can understand the purpose and most appropriate use of each form of technology.

Working with Classification and Division as a Reader and Writer

The following table reviews the key elements of classification and division essays and explains how these elements are important to both readers and writers.

Reading ⬤ Writing   Classification and Division Essays

Element of a Classification or Division Essay	The Reader's Perspective	The Writer's Perspective
Grouping or Division According to One Meaningful Principle	As you read, look for the key principle on which the essay is based. This understanding will provide a schema (mental framework) for following the essay and the writer's logic.	As a writer, you must identify a basis for classification or division that makes sense logically *and* that readers will find helpful or informative. Without a good basis for classification or division, your essay will be confusing or (worse) useless.
Categories or Parts That Are Clearly and Easily Identified	As you read, try to relate the categories or parts to your own life and experiences and jot down examples in the margin. Ask yourself, Has the writer left out any key parts or categories? If so, what are they?	If you are struggling with identifying categories or parts, you have likely chosen a topic that is beyond your capacity to write about effectively. You might consider conducting more research or choosing another topic.
Full Explanations of Each Category or Part	As you read, remember that the names of the categories have little meaning on their own—it is the explanatory information that appears with each category that makes the category memorable and fun to read about.	To demonstrate your credibility as a writer, provide a full explanation of each category or part you have identified. Remember that your goal is to educate and inform readers about your topic.

16

Definition: Explaining What You Mean

In this chapter, you will learn to

- Recognize the elements of definition.

- Identify the structure and content of definition essays.

- Understand, analyze, and evaluate definition essays.

- Write your own definition essay.

- Work with definition as a reader and a writer.

David Davis Photoproductions RF/Alamy

Reflect on a Visual Text

Examine the photograph above, which shows someone painting a picture on the side of a building.

1 Ask yourself questions. Do public images like this one count as art? Does art need to appear in a museum? Does art include graffiti? Who creates art? →

451

2 **Brainstorm ideas.** Alone or in a small group, brainstorm the characteristics of art.

3 **Write.** Now use your brainstorming list to create a definition of the term *art*. Use examples and sensory details to help define exactly what you think constitutes art.

The paragraph you just wrote is an example of a *definition*. Your paragraph goes beyond a simple dictionary definition; it explores art in greater detail to arrive at a richer, fuller definition of the word *art*.

What Is a Definition?

A **definition** explains what a term means or which meaning is intended when a word has several different meanings. Definitions are an important part of daily communication. For instance, you might need to define *slicing* to someone unfamiliar with golf or *koi* to someone unfamiliar with tropical fish. If you call a friend a *nonconformist*, she might ask you for your definition of that word. You and a friend might disagree over what constitutes *feminism* even though you have similar politics.

When members of a group share a set of terms with commonly understood meanings, communication is simplified. For example, many sports and hobby enthusiasts have their own special vocabulary: Hockey fans know terms such as *high-sticking, icing, puck,* and *blueline*; cooking enthusiasts know terms such as *sauté, parboil,* and *fillet.* Members of professions and academic fields also have specialized terminology. For example, a surgeon asks for the *scalpel,* not for "the small, straight knife with the thin, sharp blade." As you can see, specialized terms make communication precise, helping to prevent misunderstandings and confusion.

Many academic and work situations require that you write or learn definitions. On an exam for a health and fitness course, you might find the short-answer question "Define the term *wellness.*" As a chemical engineer responsible for your department's compliance with company standards, you might be asked to write a brief memo to your staff defining the terms *safety* and *work efficiency.*

There will be many occasions to use definition in your writing. For example, when you suspect your reader may not understand a key term, you will offer a brief definition. Often, however, a standard definition is not sufficient to explain a complex idea. At times, you may need a paragraph or an entire essay to define a single term. For instance, if you had to define *happiness,* you would probably have trouble coming up with a brief definition because the emotion is experienced in a variety of situations and in different ways. In an essay-length piece of writing, however, you could explore the term and explain some of its many meanings. Such a lengthy, detailed definition is an **extended definition**.

A successful definition essay has all or most of the following elements:

1. It includes a brief explanation of the term.
2. It makes a point.
3. It may use negation and address misconceptions.
4. It is specific and focused.
5. It uses other patterns of development.

Knowing how writers (and other communicators) use definition will help you understand, analyze, and evaluate this pattern when you read and help you use it in your own writing.

A Model Definition Essay

The following model essay will be used throughout this chapter to demonstrate strategies for reading and writing definition essays. Read it now, looking for the ways the writer uses the above definition techniques. Use the annotations in the margin to guide you.

The Satori Generation

Roland Kelts

Roland Kelts is a Japanese-American writer who divides his time between Tokyo and New York. He is the author of *Japanamerica: How Japanese Pop Culture Has Invaded the U.S.*, as well as a novel, *Access*. He is a frequent commentator on National Public Radio and the BBC (British Broadcasting Corporation). This essay originally appeared in *Adbusters*, a not-for-profit magazine devoted to contemporary issues such as media and the environment.

A definition essay includes a brief definition of the term: Here the author introduces and briefly defines the term *satori generation*. He will expand on this definition throughout the article.

They don't want cars or brand name handbags or luxury boots. To many of them, travel beyond the known and local is expensive and potentially dangerous. They work part-time jobs—because that is what they've been offered—and live at home long after they graduate. They're not getting married or having kids. They're not even sure if they want to be in romantic relationships. Why? Too much hassle. Oh, and too expensive.

In Japan, they've come to be known as *satori sedai*—the "enlightened generation." In Buddhist terms: free from material desires, focused on self-awareness, finding essential truths. But another translation is grimmer: "generation resignation," or those

A definition essay is specific and focused: The author concisely and specifically explains the key characteristics of the satori generation.

without ideals, ambition or hope. They were born in the late 1980s on up, when their nation's economic juggernaut, with its promises of lifetime employment and conspicuous celebrations of consumption, was already a spent historical force. They don't believe the future will get better—so they make do with what they have. In one respect, they're arch-realists. And they're freaking their elders out.

A definition essay may use negation and address misconceptions: This paragraph defines the satori generation by what its members do *not* want. Note that the first paragraph of the essay uses the same strategy.

"Don't you want to get a nice German car one day?"—asked one flustered 50-something guest of his 20-something counterpart on a nationally broadcasted talk show. The show aired on the eve of Coming of Age Day, a national holiday in Japan that celebrates the latest crop of youth turning 20, the threshold of adulthood. An animated graphic of a smiling man wearing sunglasses driving a blonde around in a convertible flashed across the screen, the man's scarf fluttering in the wind. "Don't you want a pretty young woman to take on a Sunday drive?" There was some polite giggling from the guests. After a pause, the younger man said, "I'm really not interested, no."

Critics of the satori youths level the kinds of intergenerational accusations time-honored worldwide: they're lazy, lacking in willpower, potency and drive. Having lectured to a number of them at several universities in Tokyo, I was able to query students directly. "We're risk-averse," was the most common response. We were raised in relative comfort. We're just trying to keep it that way.

Is this enlightened, or resigned? Or both? Novelist Genichiro Takahashi, 63, addressed the matter in an essay 10 years ago. He called the new wave of youth a "generation of loss," but he defined them as "the world's most advanced phenomenon"—in his view, a generation whose only desires are those that are actually achievable.

A definition essay uses other patterns of development: In this paragraph, the author uses illustration and comparison/contrast. Paragraph 9 uses cause-effect. Which other patterns can you find in the article?

The satori generation are known for keeping things small, preferring an evening at home with a small gathering of friends, for example, to an upscale restaurant. They create ensemble outfits from so-called "fast fashion" discount stores like Uniqlo or H&M, instead of purchasing top-shelf at Louis Vuitton or Prada. They don't even booze. "They drink much less alcohol than the kids of my generation, for sure," says social critic and researcher Mariko Fujiwara of Hakuhodo. "And even when they go to places where they are free to drink, drinking too much was never 'cool' for them the way it was for us."

Fujiwara's research leads her to define a global trend—youth who have the technological tools to avoid being duped by phony needs. There is a new breed of young people, she says, who have outdone the tricksters of advertising.

"They are prudent and careful about what they buy. They have been informed about the expensive top brands of all sorts of consumer goods but were never so impressed by them like those from the bubble generation. We have identified them as those who are far more levelheaded than the generations preceding them as a result of the new reality they came to face."

The new reality is affecting a new generation around the world. Young Americans and Europeans are increasingly living at home, saving money, and living prudently. Technology, as it did in Japan, abets their shrinking circles. If you have internet access, you can accomplish a lot in a little room. And revolution in the 21st century, as most young people know, is not about consumption—it's about sustainability.

Waseda University professor Norihiro Kato points to broader global phenomena that have radically transformed younger generations' sense of possibility, calling it a shift from "the infinite to the finite." Kato cites the Chernobyl meltdown and the fall of communism in the late 1980s and early 90s; the September 11 terrorist attacks in the early 2000s; and closer to home, the triple earthquake, tsunami and ongoing nuclear disasters in Japan. These events reshaped our sense of wisdom and self-worth. The satori generation, he says, marks the emergence of a new "'qualified power,' the power to do and the power to undo, and the ability to enjoy doing and not doing equally. Imagine a robot with the sophistication and strength to clutch an egg without crushing it. The key concept is outgrowing growth toward degrowth. That's the wisdom of this new generation."

In America and Europe, the new generation is teaching us how to live with less—but also how to live with one another. Mainstream media decry the number of young people living at home—a record 26.1 million in the US, according to recent statistics—yet living at home and caring for one's elders has long been a mainstay of Japanese culture.

In the context of shrinking resources and global crises, satori "enlightenment" might mean what the young everywhere are telling us: shrink your goals to the realistic, help your family and community and resign yourself to peace. What Takahashi called "the world's most advanced phenomenon" may well be coming our way from Japan. But this time it's not automotive or robotic or electronic. It's human enlightenment.

A definition essay makes a point: The author makes his key point in his conclusion: The satori generation gives priority to what matters over materialistic consumption.

The Structure and Content of a Definition Essay

In this section, you will learn about the structure of a definition essay, read a sample essay, and practice using the guidelines for understanding, analyzing, and evaluating definition essays. This will help you skillfully read and write essays that use definition.

Definition essays follow a familiar pattern. The introduction presents the term, provides background information, and includes the thesis statement. The body paragraphs use one or more patterns of development to describe the distinguishing characteristics of the term and the supporting details. The conclusion refers back to the thesis and brings the essay to a satisfying close. Figure 16.1 represents these major components visually.

1. THE INTRODUCTION IDENTIFIES THE TERM BEING DEFINED AND GIVES THE THESIS STATEMENT

The introduction to a definition essay identifies the term being defined, provides a strong thesis statement that reflects a point of view, suggests the importance of understanding the term, and may use negation to explain what the term does *not* mean.

Figure 16.1   Graphic Organizer for a Definition Essay

Title	
Introduction	Introduces the term
	Provides background information
	Thesis statement: Gives standard definition and reveals the importance or significance of the term
Body paragraphs: organized using one or more patterns of development	Distinguishing characteristic(s)
	Supporting details
	Distinguishing characteristic(s)
	Supporting details
	Distinguishing characteristic(s)
	Supporting details
Conclusion	Refers back to thesis
	Draws essay to a satisfying close

Essential Definition and Background Information   The introduction identifies the term being defined and provides necessary background information. It then offers a brief definition of the term that the essay will expand on. A brief or standard definition (the kind found in a dictionary) consists of three parts:

- the *term* itself
- the *class* to which the term belongs
- the *characteristics or details* that distinguish the term from all others in its class

For example, a *wedding band* is a piece of jewelry. "Jewelry" is the **class**, or group, of objects that includes wedding bands. To show how a wedding band differs from other members of that class, you would need to identify its **distinguishing characteristics** — the features that make it different from other types of jewelry. In "The Satori Generation," Roland Kelts provides a standard definition of *satori generation* in the second paragraph: He explains that the *satori generation* is a subgroup of the larger Japanese population (the class) that was born in the late 1980s or after, is free from material desires, is focused on self-awareness, and is interested in finding essential truths (characteristics that distinguish the term from all others in its class).

Thesis Statement   The introduction usually includes a strong thesis statement that signals the author's perspective or point of view on the term being defined. In "The Satori Generation," the thesis statement comes at the end of the second paragraph: "They're arch realists. And they're freaking their elders out." The thesis statement hints that the author approves of the satori generation and suggests the importance or value of understanding the term: The author implies that having a greater understanding of the satori generation will help bridge the generation gap.

Notice how the following weak thesis statement can be revised to reveal a main point.

Weak	Wireless cable is a means of transmitting television signals through the air by microwave.
Revised	The future of wireless cable, a method of transmitting television signals through the air using microwaves, is uncertain.

Negation and Misconceptions   In introducing a term, it can be helpful to use **negation**, explaining what the term is *not*. Notice that the first paragraph of Kelts's essay is all about negation, describing what the satori generation does *not* want.

In addition, an extended definition may address popular misconceptions about the term. In an essay defining *plagiarism*, for instance, you might correct the mistaken idea that plagiarism involves only passing off another writer's entire paper as your own, because plagiarism also includes using other writers' quotes or general phrases without giving them credit. Although he does it in the fourth paragraph of his essay rather than in the introduction, Roland Kelts addresses common misconceptions about the satori generation, noting that many critics view them as "lazy, lacking in willpower, potency and drive."

Reading ◑ Writing   The Introduction to a Definition Essay

The Reader's Perspective	The Writer's Perspective
When reading the introduction to a definition essay, identify the term and determine how much, if anything, you already know about it. Your familiarity with the term will shape how you read the essay. If the term is completely unfamiliar, you will need to read and reread, perhaps several times. If you are well acquainted with the term, you may read with the purpose of learning new or additional information.	When writing an introduction for a definition essay, consider the knowledge and experience of your audience and choose an appropriate level of background information. Make sure that, in addition to defining your term, you include in your thesis a statement about your perspective on or point of view about that term.

2. THE BODY PARAGRAPHS OFFER DETAILS TO MAKE THE TERM UNDERSTANDABLE

The body of a definition essay explains the term's class and presents characteristics that distinguish the term from others in the class. The body paragraphs must be specific and focused, presenting facts, examples, and descriptions to make the term understandable. The writer's goal is to provide sufficient information to enable readers to understand each characteristic. The body may also use other patterns of development to provide additional insight into the term being defined.

Specific and Focused Details   An **extended definition** focuses on a specific term, and the body paragraphs discuss its characteristics in detail. For instance, an essay that explored *freeganism*, an environmental movement whose members live primarily on things that other people throw away, would go beyond a simple definition (like the one in this sentence). In order to help readers better understand the lifestyle, the author would present the term and then, in the body paragraphs, go on to describe the philosophy behind the movement, how and where freegans find food, and the safety measures they take. The body of "The Satori Generation" talks about the generation's realistic expectations, their care in making purchases, and their definition of "enlightenment." All of these details help readers better understand the members of the satori generation.

Other Patterns of Development   To explain the meaning of a term, writers of definition essays usually integrate one or more patterns of development, depending on the type of supporting information being used. Here are some examples of how other patterns might be used in an extended definition of *lurking*.

Pattern of Development	Defining the Term *Lurking*
Narration (Chapter 10)	Relate a story about learning something important by lurking.
Description (Chapter 11)	Describe the experience of lurking.
Illustration (Chapter 12)	Give examples of typical situations involving lurking.
Process Analysis (Chapter 13)	Explain how to lurk in an Internet chat room.
Comparison and Contrast (Chapter 14)	Compare and contrast lurking and other forms of observation.
Classification and Division (Chapter 15)	Classify the reasons people lurk — for information, entertainment, and so on.
Cause and Effect (Chapter 17)	Explain what might lead to lurking and what its benefits or outcomes might be.
Argumentation (Chapter 18)	Argue that lurking is an ethical (or unethical) practice.

For a brief overview of these patterns, see Chapter 9, "Patterns: An Introduction." In the Kelts essay, notice that the author uses several other patterns of organization, including illustration (paragraphs 3 and 6), comparison/contrast (paragraph 6), and cause-effect (paragraph 9).

Reading ⊕ Writing   The Body of a Definition Essay

The Reader's Perspective	The Writer's Perspective
When reading the body of a definition essay, be sure to identify and highlight each distinguishing characteristic. Make sure you understand how each characteristic is unique and how it relates to the term.	When writing the body of the essay, be sure to make your definition easy for your reader to follow. Consider devoting one paragraph to each characteristic and using transitions to move from one distinguishing characteristic to another.

3. THE CONCLUSION BRINGS THE ESSAY TO A SATISFYING CLOSE

The conclusion should pull together information presented in the essay and leave the reader with a final impression of the term. Note that the conclusion to Kelts's essay is very optimistic. He suggests that the satori generation is more enlightened than previous generations and has the power to advance human society and understanding. Rather than placing his key point in the introduction, Kelts decided to place it in his conclusion. Why? After reading about the characteristics of the satori generation, readers will have a better sense of their potential.

Reading ⊕ Writing   The Conclusion of a Definition Essay

The Reader's Perspective	The Writer's Perspective
When reading the conclusion of a definition essay, be sure to test yourself. If you can define the term in your own words, without looking back at the essay, then you understand it. If you cannot, continue to work with the essay until you are able to do so, consulting with classmates or doing further research if necessary.	When writing the conclusion of a definition essay, you may find it helpful to first read through your essay again. Look for points or ideas that need repetition or review.

Understanding, Analyzing, and Evaluating Definition Essays

In reading definition essays, you want to be able to do more than merely understand the content. Truly skillful reading and writing require the abilities to understand, analyze, *and* evaluate material. These abilities are important to you as a reader because they give you a systematic, thorough method of examining a reading. They're important to you as a writer because they help you decide what to revise, rewrite, drop, and replace, allowing you to produce a well-written, engaging essay.

▥ *Understanding a Definition Essay*

Preview the essay before reading to identify the subject being defined and its general definition. Then read it slowly, using the skills you learned in Chapter 2, and look for answers to the following questions.

- **What term is being defined and in what context?** An essay may define the term *green computing*, but as the reader, it is up to you to determine whether the term is being defined from an industrial/manufacturing viewpoint, an environmental viewpoint, or a business sales perspective.

- **Why is the term useful or important to know?** Understanding this will give you a purpose for reading and will help you maintain your interest.

- **To what class does the term belong?** Knowing the class will help you place the term within a framework of your knowledge and experience. If an essay defines the practice of *paying forward*, helping others because someone helped you, knowing that the practice belongs to the general class of Good Samaritan activities may help you set it in your mind.

- **What are the distinguishing characteristics?** These will help you understand how the term is unique and distinct from other members of the same class. Creating a graphic organizer can help you identify the distinguishing characteristics. Figure 16.2 shows a graphic organizer for "The Satori Generation."

- **What examples or other practical explanations are provided?** These supporting details are useful for making the term real and understandable.

- **How does the term differ from similar terms?** This question is especially important if similar terms are presented. If a textbook or an article does not explain sufficiently how two or more terms differ, check the terms in a standard dictionary. If the difference is still unclear, check the terms in a specialized subject dictionary.

Understanding in Action

Exercise 16.1

Following is one student's summary of the opening paragraph of "The Satori Generation."

> The author begins by stating what the satori generation does *not* want. Members of that generation do not desire expensive cars, purses, or shoes. They don't want to travel abroad, or get married, or have children. The author cites two reasons. First, all of these things are too much trouble. Second, the satori generation cannot afford them.

Write your own summary of the rest of the essay. Refer to page 45 for help with summary writing.

Figure 16.2 Graphic Organizer for "The Satori Generation"

Title	The Satori Generation
Introduction (2 paragraphs)	**Paragraph 1** begins with negation, explaining what the satori generation does *not* want: fancy cars, handbags, boots, marriage, children. (Negation is picked up again in paragraph 3.)
	Paragraph 2 contains the standard definition: The satori generation is composed of people born in the late 1980s and after.
	Thesis: "They're arch-realists. And they're freaking their elders out."
Body paragraphs: distinguishing characteristics of the satori generation	**Defining characteristic 1:** They make do with what they have.
	Defining characteristic 2: They are accused of being lazy or lacking in drive, but they define themselves as "risk-averse."
	Defining characteristic 3: They have only desires that are actually achievable.
	Defining characteristic 4: They keep things small, preferring an evening at home with friends to a night on the town.
	Defining characteristic 5: They shop at discount stores and don't drink much alcohol.
	Defining characteristic 6: They have the intellectual tools to think critically about advertisements, which makes them careful about what they buy. They are level-headed.
	Defining characteristic 7: They care about sustainability.
	Defining characteristic 8: They have learned how to live with less while living at home and helping to care for their elders.
Conclusion	The satori generation may help the human race achieve enlightenment about what really matters.

📊 *Analyzing a Definition Essay*

Analyzing a definition essay involves examining how clearly, thoroughly, and effectively the term is defined. Use the following questions to guide your analysis:

- **Is the term's class described clearly and specifically?** The class should be broad enough to be recognizable and meaningful but not so broad that you are unable to place it in a context.

- **Do the characteristics make the term distinguishable from other similar terms or other members of the same class?** Together, the characteristics should define the term uniquely, so that it doesn't overlap with any other term.

- **Is each characteristic named or titled?** The author should make it easy for you to identify each characteristic and to follow along as he or she moves from one characteristic to another.

- **Is each characteristic distinct?** The author should make it clear how each characteristic differs from others, using details, descriptions, examples, comparison or contrast, or personal experiences to make those distinctions throughout the essay.

- **Is each characteristic understandable?** Each characteristic should be clearly explained; understanding it should not require background knowledge the reader does not have.

Analysis in Action

Exercise 16.2

The student who wrote the summary for Understanding in Action also annotated paragraph 9 of "The Satori Generation."

a global trend	The new reality is affecting a new generation
somewhat true — I know a lot of people who still live with their parents, but not necessarily saving money	around the world. Young Americans and Europeans are increasingly living at home, saving money, and living prudently. Technology, as it did in Japan, abets their shrinking circles. If you have internet access, you can accomplish a lot in a little room. And revolution in the 21st
Sustainability is important, but is this conclusion an overstatement? The U.S. is still a consumer society.	century, as most young people know, is not about consumption — it's about sustainability.

Using these annotations as a model, annotate paragraphs 9–11 of the essay.

Evaluating a Definition Essay

Evaluating a definition essay involves judging how accurately and effectively the author has explained the term. Use the following questions to guide your evaluation of definition essays:

- **Is the definition comprehensive and complete?** Determine whether the author covers all the important characteristics.
- **Does each characteristic have fair and equal coverage?** Each characteristic should be given roughly the same amount of coverage and described at the same level of detail.
- **Are the writer's definitions objective or subjective?** In some essays, the purpose is to persuade the reader to take a particular action or accept a specific viewpoint. In such essays, subjective or emotional language may be used to influence the reader. For example, a writer who defines the term *liberal* as "someone who wants to allow criminals to run free on the streets while sacrificing the rights of innocent victims" reveals a negative bias toward liberals and probably intends to make the reader dislike them.
- **Do you agree with the writer's definition of the term?** Determine whether it is accurate, correct, and consistent with what you already know about the term.
- **Do you think the characteristics the author identified apply to all members of the group that the term covers?** Evaluate whether the characteristics commonly apply in a wide variety of situations. For example, if a writer defining *college students* states that a characteristic of college students is that they are "attending school primarily to please their parents," you might rightly question whether this characteristic accurately applies to most college students.

Evaluation in Action

Exercise 16.3

Below is an evaluation of the opening paragraph of "The Satori Generation," written by the student who summarized it in Understanding in Action.

> The opening example is an example of negation, a technique in which the writer defines what something is by describing what it is *not*. This opening grabs the reader's attention because we're used to advertisements for exotic travel and ways to find a mate on Match.com. The reader thinks: It will be interesting to read about a generation that rejects conspicuous consumption as well as marriage.

Write your own evaluation of this definition essay. Use your annotations from Exercise 16.2 to help you.

Writing Your Own Definition Essay

Now that you have learned about the major characteristics, structure, and purposes of a definition essay, you know everything necessary to write your own. In this section, you will read a student's definition essay and get advice on finding ideas, drafting your essay, and revising and editing it. You may want to use the essay prompts in "Readings for Practice, Ideas for Writing" (p. 472) or choose your own topic.

A Student Model Definition Essay

In the following essay, Sarah Frey explores the meaning of the term *FLOTUS*. As you read, notice the ways in which Frey extends the definition beyond a simple explanation to discuss the term's relevancy. Also take note of the sources she uses and her citations of those sources.

Title: Frey captures the reader's interest.

Woman of Many Talents

Sarah Frey

Introduction: The class of the subject is *new dictionary entries.*

    There has been a new term added to the English language this year. This term describes a person who is in the news almost daily. This person assumes her role only by association, rather than being elected or appointed. The term is a companion to POTUS, President of the United States, and it is FLOTUS, or First Lady of the United States. The United States is a country like no other, and one of the most important roles anyone can assume is that of First Lady. Because there are very few comparable positions in the world to that of the First Lady, her role is constantly being defined by the women who fill it. The First Lady of the United States of America is many things. She can be the wife or daughter of the President, or she can be the niece or the granddaughter of the President. She is a woman who is trusted and loved by the President. She is committed to the well-being of the United States. She is the right hand of one of the most powerful men in the world. She is,

Thesis: Frey provides a brief definition.

Defining characteristic 1: Frey describes the First Lady as the hostess of the United States.

Specific details

much of the time, overlooked and underappreciated. However, and perhaps most importantly, the First Lady of the United States of America is a hostess, a politician, and a volunteer.

    Since the inception of the United States, it seems as if the First Lady's primary role is to be the hostess of the United States. Martha Washington, although she did not live in the White House, was tasked with hosting events in both New York and Philadelphia. Dolly Madison set the precedent for the next two hundred years for the First Lady to balance her image as an

Sources: Frey uses sources throughout the paper.

average citizen and queen ("The Role of First Lady"). It became the First Lady's duty to uphold the President's image at state dinners and to foreign diplomats, all the while being a gracious hostess. Her job as hostess allows her to do so much more than just entertain small talk; she has the opportunity to meet with foreign leaders from all over the world. The First Lady can discuss politics, budgets, foreign matters, and much more, with those who have direct influence on these issues.

Defining characteristic 2: Frey describes the First Lady as a politician with her own agenda.

In addition to hosting parties and meeting foreign dignitaries in the White House, the First Lady is a politician, pushing her own agenda forward to make the country a better place. Perhaps the most notable of these politician–First Ladies was Eleanor Roosevelt, who expanded her role not only so she could be President Franklin Roosevelt's eyes and ears across the country, but also because she had a strong sense of autonomy and wished to be involved as more than just a hostess confined to the White House ("Eleanor Roosevelt"). Her involvement across the country, as an advocate for young people, women, African Americans and even government programs for artists and writers, set the stage for all the First Ladies after her. More recently, First

Specific details

Ladies like Hillary Clinton and Michelle Obama also have political platforms of their own, taking stands on issues like the Children's Insurance Policy and childhood obesity. For Hillary Clinton, what began as political involvement as the First Lady became a platform for a presidential candidacy in the 2016 election ("Hillary Rodham Clinton").

Defining characteristic 3: Frey describes the First Lady as a volunteer.

Perhaps the most important characteristic of the First Lady is that she is a volunteer. No one runs for First Lady, and she does not get paid to do it. She volunteers to stand alongside her husband, her father, or her uncle. She did not sign up for the role of First Lady; more often than not, it is just expected that she will fill that role. Over the course of the presidency, the First Lady defines her own role (Vallely). There is no official list of duties or of expectations for her; there is only what has been done before her and what needs to be done in front of her. She is, by very definition, a volunteer; she

Specific details

gives her time and her talents selflessly for the betterment of her country. No one swears her into this role, and yet the whole world holds her accountable for everything that she does in it.

As of late, First Ladies, however different, have become hard to ignore. Each First Lady brings something different to the table, but they all share attributes that bind them together. They are setting standards and making an impact not only on the country, but also across the world. And it is because of the combined impact of women like Dolly Madison, Eleanor Roosevelt, Hillary Clinton, and Michelle Obama that the First Lady of the United States is now

Conclusion: Frey suggests that the role of First Lady is constantly changing.

receiving the attention she deserves, as the acronym FLOTUS has been added to the *Oxford English Dictionary*.

There is no First Lady who fills the role better than another, but rather the title in itself molds and changes to fit the woman who fills it. There are a few things that remain constant even with the changes in women over the last two hundred years. Characteristics such as being the hostess, a politician, and a volunteer exemplify the First Lady's uniquely defined position and provide her the vehicle to inspire change not just among the citizens of the United States, but among the citizens of the world. The First Ladies are undoubtedly some of the most influential women in human history; it will be interesting to see what the role of the First Gentleman will be, when there eventually is one.

Sources: Frey properly cites sources in MLA format.

Works Cited

"Eleanor Roosevelt." *History.com*, A&E Television Networks, www
.history.com/topics/first-ladies/eleanor-roosevelt. Accessed 9
Sept. 2015.

"Hillary Rodham Clinton." *History.com*, A&E Television Networks,
www.history.com/topics/first-ladies/hillary-rodham-clinton.
Accessed 9 Sept. 2015.

"The Role of First Lady and Origin of the Title 'First Lady.'" *National
First Ladies' Library*, FirstLadies.org, www.firstladies.org
/firstladiesrole.aspx#RoleFirstLady. Accessed 9 Sept. 2015.

Vallely, Paul. "The Big Question: What Is the Role of a First Lady,
and Can She Have Political Significance?" *The Independent*,
Independent Digital News and Media, 27 Mar. 2008, www
.independent.co.uk/news/world/politics/the-big-question
-what-is-the-role-of-a-first-lady-and-can-she-have-political
-significance?-801716.html.

Responding to Frey's Essay

1. Is Frey's description of FLOTUS in her introduction sufficient for you to understand the position? What further information, if any, would be helpful?

2. In the introductory paragraph, Frey states that the role of a First Lady "is constantly being defined by the women who fill it." Cite two examples from the essay that support this statement.

3. Did this essay spark your interest in the FLOTUS? Why, or why not? If it did not, how could the essay be improved to build or sustain interest?

4. Highlight the transitional words or phrases that Frey uses to guide her readers.

5. Explain why the concluding paragraph is effective. How does it bring the essay to a close?

Finding Ideas for Your Definition Essay

As you read an extended definition or an article containing brief definitions, jot down any additional characteristics or examples that come to mind. When responding to the article, you might indicate how the definition could be expanded to include these additional characteristics or examples. You might also try the following strategies:

- **Think of other terms in the same class.**
- **Try to relate the definitions to your own experience.** Where or when have you observed the characteristics described? Your personal experiences might be useful in an essay in which you agree with or challenge the writer's definitions.
- **If the writer has not already done so, use negation to expand the meaning of the term or explore the term's etymology (origin).**

Planning Your Definition Essay

The first step is to select a topic and narrow it to a more specific term. For example, *celebrity* is probably too broad a topic for a brief essay, but it can be narrowed to a particular type of celebrity, such as *sports celebrity, Hollywood celebrity, local celebrity,* or *political celebrity.* Consider your readers as well. When the audience is unfamiliar with the term, you will need to explain it in greater detail than when the audience is already familiar with it.

The following suggestions will help you identify distinguishing characteristics and supporting details for the term you intend to define.

1. **Define the term out loud for a classmate.** Then discuss the term with your classmate, making notes about anything that was unclear.

2. **Brainstorm a list of (a) words that describe your term, (b) people and actions that might serve as examples of it, and (c) everything a person would need to know to fully understand it.**

3. **Observe a person who is associated with the term or who performs some aspect of it.** Take notes on your observations, including the qualities and characteristics of what you see.

4. **Look up the term's etymology, or origin, in the *Oxford English Dictionary, A Dictionary of American English,* or *A Dictionary of Americanisms,* all of**

which are available in the reference section of your library. Take notes; the word's etymology may indicate some of its characteristics and details, which might give you ideas on how to organize the essay.

5. **Think of incidents or situations that reveal the meaning of the term.**

6. **Think of similar and different terms with which your readers are likely to be more familiar.**

7. **Do a search for the term on the Internet.** Visit three or four Web sites, and take notes on what you discover.

Developing and Supporting Your Thesis

The next step is to develop a working thesis that provides a standard definition of the term and expresses a point of view. The thesis should also suggest why your definition is useful or important. For examples of thesis statements for definition essays, see "The Introduction Identifies the Term Being Defined and Gives the Thesis Statement" on page 456.

Drafting Your Definition Essay

Once you have evaluated your term's distinguishing characteristics, your supporting details, and your thesis, it is time to organize your ideas and draft your essay.

To a considerable extent, the organization of a definition essay depends on the other pattern(s) of development you decide to use (see the examples on p. 459). With your pattern(s) firmly in mind, think about how to organize your term's characteristics and details. For example, consider an essay defining *marathon runner*. An essay that focused on *classifying* different types of marathon runners would probably follow a least-to-most or most-to-least organization, whereas an essay *narrating* a story about marathon runners might be most effectively presented in chronological order.

Once you have decided on a method of organization, use the following guidelines to draft the essay:

1. **Describe the class as specifically as possible.** Narrowing the class will make it easier for readers to understand the term. For example, in an essay defining *Dalmatian*, the class should be not the broad category "animal" or "mammal" but rather the more specific "breed of dog."

2. **Do not use the term (or forms of the term) as part of your definition.** Synonyms may be helpful as substitutes for a term. For example, do not write, "*Mastery* means that one has *mastered* a skill." In place of *mastered*, you could use *truly learned*.

Continued >

3. **Include enough distinguishing characteristics so that readers will not mistake the term for something similar within the class.** If you defined *answering machine* as "a machine that records messages," your definition would be incomplete because other machines (such as computers) also record messages.

4. **Do not limit the definition so much that it becomes inaccurate.** A definition of *bacon* as "a smoked, salted meat from a pig that is served at breakfast" would be too limited because bacon is also served at other mealtimes (at lunch, for instance, as part of a bacon, lettuce, and tomato sandwich).

5. **Use transitions.** When moving from characteristic to characteristic, be sure to use transitional words or phrases to signal each change. The transitions *another*, *also*, and *in addition* are especially useful in extended definitions.

6. **Consider including the etymology of the term.** The etymology, or origin, of a term may be of interest to readers. Alternatively, you might include a brief history of the term in your introduction or elsewhere in your essay.

Revising Your Definition Essay

If possible, set your draft aside for a day or two before rereading and revising it. As you review it, concentrate on your ideas and organization, not on grammar or mechanics. Use the flowchart in Figure 16.3 to discover the strengths and weaknesses of your definition essay.

Editing and Proofreading Your Essay

The final step is to check your revised essay for errors in grammar, spelling, punctuation, and mechanics. In addition, look for the types of errors you commonly make in any writing, whether for this class or in other situations. Check the handbook (pp. 645–714) for assistance with common errors in your writing.

Figure 16.3 Revising a Definition Essay

QUESTIONS	REVISION STRATEGIES

1. Thesis Does it include a brief definition of the term? Does it indicate why your definition is useful, interesting, or important? → No →
- Incorporate the distinguishing characteristics of your term and a standard definition into your thesis.
- In your thesis, answer the question Why is this definition worth reading about?

 Yes

2. Distinguishing character-istics Do they make your term distinct from similar terms? Is each characteristic true in all cases? → No →
- Do additional research or prewriting to discover more characteristics and details to add.
- Eliminate characteristics and details that limit the definition too much.

 Yes

3. Patterns of development Identify the patterns you use in your definition. Does each clearly connect your details and help explain the distinguishing characteris-tics of your term? → No →
- Review the patterns (Chapter 9) and consider substituting or adding one or more of them to enhance your definition.

 Yes

4. Negation and misconcep-tions Does each section eliminate possible misun-derstandings? Are there other places where you need to do so? → No →
- Revise your explanation of what your term is not.
- Add facts or expert opinion to correct readers' mistaken notions about the term.

 Yes

5. Topic sentences Does each paragraph have a clear topic sentence and focus on a particular characteristic? Is each paragraph well developed? → No →
- Consider combining paragraphs that cover the same characteristic or splitting paragraphs that cover more than one.
- Add or revise topic sentences and supporting details.

 Yes

6. Introduction and conclusion Does the introduction pro-vide necessary background information? Does your conclusion bring the essay to a satisfying close? → No →
- Add background information that sets a context for the term you are defining.
- Revise your introduction and conclusion so that they meet the guidelines presented in Chapter 7.

Readings for Practice, Ideas for Writing

On Dumpster Diving

Lars Eighner began writing essays and fiction after graduating from the University of Texas at Austin. The following selection is an abridged version of a nonfiction piece originally published in the *Threepenny Review*. His works include *Travels with Lizbeth* (1993), a book about the homelessness he experienced after losing his job at a mental hospital.

Reading Tip

Eighner's essay is written in the first person. Notice how this point of view gives added depth and intimacy to the topic. Also, pay attention to the author's tone and his attitude toward Dumpster diving.

Previewing the Reading

Preview the reading using the guidelines on pages 28–29, and then answer the following questions.

1. What is Dumpster diving?
2. Give some examples of items the author collects from Dumpsters.

On Dumpster Diving

Lars Eighner

I began Dumpster diving about a year before I became homeless.

I prefer the word *scavenging* and use the word *scrounging* when I mean to be obscure. I have heard people, evidently meaning to be polite, use the word *foraging*, but I prefer to reserve that word for gathering nuts and berries and such, which I do also according to the season and the opportunity. *Dumpster diving* seems to me to be a little too cute and, in my case, inaccurate because I lack the athletic ability to lower myself into the Dumpsters as the true divers do, much to their increased profit.

I like the frankness of the word *scavenging*, which I can hardly think of without picturing a big black snail on an aquarium wall. I live from the refuse of others. I am a scavenger. I think it a sound and honorable niche, although if I could I would naturally prefer to live the comfortable consumer life, perhaps—and only perhaps—as a slightly less wasteful consumer, owing to what I have learned as a scavenger.

While Lizbeth and I were still living in the shack on Avenue B as my savings ran out, I put almost all of my sporadic income into rent. The necessities of daily life I began to extract from Dumpsters. Yes, we ate from them. Except for jeans, all my clothes came from Dumpsters. Boom boxes, candles, bedding, toilet paper, a virgin male love doll, medicine, books, a typewriter, dishes, furnishings, and change, sometimes amounting to many dollars—I acquired many things from the Dumpsters.

5   After all, the finding of objects is becoming something of an urban art. Even respectable employed people will sometimes find something tempting sticking out of a Dumpster or standing beside one. Quite a number of people, not all of them of the bohemian type, are willing to brag that they found this or that piece in the trash. But eating from Dumpsters is what separates the dilettanti from the professionals. Eating safely from the Dumpsters involves three principles: using the senses and common sense to evaluate the condition of the found materials, knowing the Dumpsters of a given area and checking them regularly, and seeking always to answer the question "Why was this discarded?"

Perhaps everyone who has a kitchen and a regular supply of groceries has, at one time or another, made a sandwich and eaten half of it before discovering mold on the bread or got a mouthful of milk before realizing the milk had turned. Nothing of the sort is likely to happen to a Dumpster diver because he is constantly reminded that most food is discarded for a reason. Yet a lot of perfectly good food can be found in Dumpsters.

Canned goods, for example, turn up fairly often in the Dumpsters I frequent. All except the most phobic people would be willing to eat from a can, even if it came from a Dumpster. Canned goods are among the safest of foods to be found in Dumpsters but are not utterly foolproof.

For myself I have few qualms about dry foods such as crackers, cookies, cereal, chips, and pasta if they are free of visible contaminates and still dry and crisp. Most often such things are found in the original packaging, which is not so much a positive sign as it is the absence of a negative one.

Raw fruits and vegetables with intact skins seem perfectly safe to me, excluding of course the obviously rotten. Many are discarded for minor imperfections that can be pared away. Leafy vegetables, grapes, cauliflower, broccoli, and similar things may be contaminated by liquids and may be impractical to wash.

10   Students throw food away around breaks because they do not know whether it has spoiled or will spoil before they return. A typical discard is a half jar of peanut butter. In fact, non-organic peanut butter does not require refrigeration and is unlikely to spoil in any reasonable time. The student does not know that, and since it is Daddy's money, the student decides not to take a chance. Opened containers require caution and some attention to the question "Why was this discarded?" But in the case of discards from student apartments, the answer may be that the item was thrown out through carelessness, ignorance, or wastefulness. This can sometimes be deduced when the item is found with many others, including some that are obviously perfectly good.

Yogurt, cheese, and sour cream are items that are often thrown out while they are still good. Occasionally I find a cheese with a spot of mold, which of course I just pare off, and because it is obvious why such a cheese was discarded, I treat it with less suspicion than an apparently perfect cheese found in similar circumstances. Yogurt is often discarded, still sealed, only because the expiration date on the carton had passed. This is one of my

Continued >

favorite finds because yogurt will keep for several days, even in warm weather.

No matter how careful I am I still get dysentery[1] at least once a month, oftener in warm weather. I do not want to paint too romantic a picture. Dumpster diving has serious drawbacks as a way of life.

I learned to scavenge gradually, on my own. Since then I have initiated several companions into the trade. I have learned that there is a predictable series of stages a person goes through in learning to scavenge.

At first the new scavenger is filled with disgust and self-loathing. He is ashamed of being seen and may lurk around, trying to duck behind things, or he may try to dive at night. (In fact, most people instinctively look away from a scavenger. By skulking around, the novice calls attention to himself and arouses suspicion. Diving at night is ineffective and needlessly messy.)

15   Every grain of rice seems to be a maggot. Everything seems to stink. He can wipe the egg yolk off the found can, but he cannot erase from his mind the stigma of eating garbage.

That stage passes with experience. The scavenger finds a pair of running shoes that fit and look and smell brand-new. He finds a pocket calculator in perfect working order. He finds pristine ice cream, still frozen, more than he can eat or keep. He begins to understand: People throw away perfectly good stuff, a lot of perfectly good stuff.

At this stage, Dumpster shyness begins to dissipate. The diver, after all, has the last laugh. He is finding all manner of good things that are his for the taking. Those who disparage his profession are the fools, not he.

He may begin to hang on to some perfectly good things for which he has neither a use nor a market. Then he begins to take note of the things that are not perfectly good but are nearly so. He mates a Walkman with broken earphones and one that is missing a battery cover. He picks up things that he can repair.

At this stage he may become lost and never recover. Dumpsters are full of things of some potential value to someone and also of things that never have much intrinsic value but are interesting. All the Dumpster divers I have known come to the point of trying to acquire everything they touch. Why not take it, they reason, since it is all free? This is, of course, hopeless. Most divers come to realize that they must restrict themselves to items of relatively immediate utility. But in some cases the diver simply cannot control himself. I have met several of these pack-rat types. Their ideas of the values of various pieces of junk verge on the psychotic. Every bit of glass may be a diamond, they think, and all that glistens, gold.

20   I find from the experience of scavenging two rather deep lessons. The first is to take what you can use and let the rest go by. I have come to think that there is no value in the abstract. A thing I cannot use or make useful, perhaps by trading, has no value however rare or fine it may be. I mean useful in a broad sense—some art I would find useful and some otherwise.

I was shocked to realize that some things are not worth acquiring, but now I think it is so. Some material things are white elephants that eat up the possessor's substance. The second lesson

---

[1]**dysentery** An intestinal infection marked by abdominal pain, fever, and diarrhea.

is the transience[2] of material being. This has not quite converted me to a dualist[3], but it has made some headway in that direction. I do not suppose that ideas are immortal, but certainly mental things are longer lived than other material things.

Once I was the sort of person who invests objects with sentimental value. Now I no longer have those objects, but I have the sentiments yet.

Many times in our travels I have lost everything but the clothes I was wearing and Lizbeth. The things I find in Dumpsters, the love letters and rag dolls of so many lives, remind me of this lesson. Now I hardly pick up a thing without envisioning the time I will cast it aside. This I think is a healthy state of mind. Almost everything I have now has already been cast out at least once, proving that what I own is valueless to someone.

Anyway, I find my desire to grab for the gaudy bauble has been largely sated. I think this is an attitude I share with the very wealthy—we both know there is plenty more where what we have came from. Between us are the rat-race millions who nightly scavenge the cable channels looking for they know not what.

I am sorry for them.   25

[2]**transience** Quality of being temporary or short lived.
[3]**dualist** One who believes that substances are either material or mental.

Understanding and Reviewing the Reading

1. **Background information** According to Eighner, what stages do people go through before becoming "professional" Dumpster divers?

2. **Detail** What risks associated with Dumpster diving does the author mention?

3. **Main point** What lessons does Eighner reveal about his experiences Dumpster diving?

4. **Detail** What attitude does Eighner say he shares with the wealthy?

5. **Language** According to Eighner, what is the difference between *scavenging* and *foraging* (paras. 2–3)?

6. **Vocabulary** Using context clues, define each of the following words as it is used in the essay, consulting a dictionary if necessary: *niche* (para. 3), *bohemian* (5), *dilettanti* (5), *phobic* (7), *pristine* (16), *dissipate* (17), and *disparage* (17).

7. **Organization** To analyze Eighner's organization, complete the graphic organizer that follows. Keep in mind that he doesn't use only definition as a pattern.

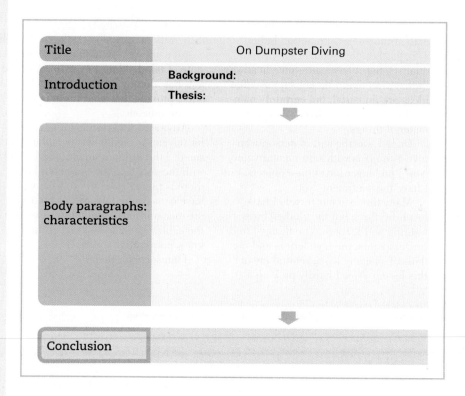

Title	On Dumpster Diving
Introduction	**Background:**
	Thesis:
Body paragraphs: characteristics	
Conclusion	

Analyzing the Reading

1. **Technique** The primary pattern of development in Eighner's essay is definition. To make Dumpster diving clear to his readers, Eighner uses other patterns as well. What other patterns does he use? (See Chapter 9, "Patterns: An
   Introduction," for a brief overview.)

2. **Details** What kinds of sensory details does Eighner include? Highlight several particularly effective examples. What do these details contribute to the
   essay?

3. **Conclusion** Eighner begins his conclusion in paragraph 20. How does he
   signal the transition to his conclusion?

Evaluating the Reading

1. **Purpose** Did this essay alter your opinion of the homeless? Did any of your
   preconceptions about the homeless affect your response? Why, or why not?

2. **Presentation** How did you react to learning that Eighner eats out of Dumpsters? Does this reaction affect your response to the writer?

3. **Technique** Eighner's essay both opens and closes with a single-sentence paragraph. Do you find these effective? Explain.

4. **Definition** Does the essay give you a good sense of what Dumpster diving is and what it involves? How would you evaluate the level of detail here?

Discussing the Reading

1. Discuss Eighner's attitude toward materialism, wealth, and personal possessions. How do these correspond to your own?

2. Does *scavenging* have a positive or negative connotation? Is shopping at garage sales and thrift stores a form of scavenging?

3. In class or in your journal, discuss the possible reasons for homelessness.

Writing about the Reading

1. **Paragraph** Using Eighner's essay as a source for information, write a paragraph defining Dumpster diving. (Hint: Eighner writes in the first person about himself. In your paragraph, write in the third person using the subject "Dumpster divers.")

2. **Paragraph** Brainstorm a list of activities that are important to you on an everyday basis. Then choose one that you can define in detail in a paragraph entitled "On _____" (for example, "On Text-Messaging"). (Hint: As Eighner has done in his essay, use a variety of personal examples to develop your definition.)

3. **Essay** Eighner comments on American values and the emphasis on acquiring and owning goods. He also explains how he provides for his own daily needs. Write an essay in which you explain your view on consumerism, defining that term as you see it. How important is consumption as an American value?

Gullible Travels

Bethe Dufresne is a freelance journalist based in Connecticut. In 2009, she traveled to Kenya to report on the launch of the first free school for girls in East Africa's largest slum. The following article, first published in the Catholic magazine *Commonweal*, grew out of her experience there.

Reading Tip

The author of this definition essay offers different names for her topic. What are they, and how does her inclusion of them relate to her purpose?

Previewing the Reading

Preview the reading using the guidelines on pages 28–29. Then answer the following questions.

1. What, specifically, is the author defining in this essay?
2. List one fact you learned about this topic.

Gullible Travels[1]

Bethe Dufresne

In the lobby of Nairobi's Boulevard Hotel you'll see signs promoting all manner of tourist sites, from a Maasai crafts market to animal parks. For now, at least, you're unlikely to see any signs promoting tours of Nairobi's infamous Kibera slum, the largest in East Africa. Yet such tours aren't difficult to find.

As a reporter covering the debut of Kibera's first free school for girls in 2009, I made multiple visits to the massive slum, where an estimated 1.5 million people eke out an existence mostly without basic services such as electricity, running water, sanitation, and police protection. I was shocked to learn that this was a popular tourist destination.

Kibera is one of the leading attractions of "poverty tourism"—a trend that has been given many names, including "slum safaris" and "poverty porn." From Soweto to São Paulo, Jakarta to Chicago, urban "slumming" has become a global phenomenon, even as a lively debate rages about the ethics of what promoters call "reality tourism."

The fuss over slum tours may be just a footnote to the great international-aid debate, but the same hot-button issues arise: Who really reaps the economic benefits? What are the long-term effects? And where—for the poor who are the prime attraction—is the protection and oversight?

[1] **Gullible Travels** The title is a reference to *Gulliver's Travels*, the classic novel by Jonathan Swift, which is a traveler's narrative but also pokes fun at human nature.

© Beth Stirnaman/Corbis

Tourists flock to the Dharavi slum in Mumbai, which was featured in the movie Slumdog Millionaire.

5   Of course, no one who promotes slum tours actually says, "Come with us to gawk at desperately poor people."

The typical pitch targets travelers' desire for authentic experiences, as if authenticity can only be found in suffering. But the broader appeal is to travelers' charitable impulses: Take this tour and help slum dwellers in the process, because—it is claimed—part of the profits go to schools, orphanages, and other worthy projects.

Prices vary. A short tour of Mumbai's Dharavi slum can be had for $11, while a private tour that includes interaction with residents costs $71. Alex Ndambo, who books all types of tours for Real Adventures Africa from Nairobi's Boulevard Hotel, told me a day tour of Kibera costs $50 to $80. He said he'd "heard" that 35 to 45% goes to the community, where most people live on less than a dollar a day.

Slum tours have existed in some form for a long time. Nineteenth-century New Yorkers toured the Bowery to satisfy their curiosity, and perhaps to stimulate their charitable instincts. Today, however, the Internet has helped popularize the concept as never before: Travelers in almost any major city can find or arrange a tour of the urban underbelly. A 2009 article in *National Geographic Traveler* called reality tourism "the latest frontier in travel" and credited its growth to tourists' eschewing "indulgent vacations in favor of more meaningful travel experiences." The same article gave tips for "the right way to slum it," like inquiring about how much of the cost goes to the slum community, but it neglected to mention how difficult that information is to verify.

All tour promoters claim the best intentions. Most tours have rules for patrons: No photos without permission

Continued >

from the subject, no peering into windows, and no handing out treats or money to the children who chant "How are you?" while reaching out to brush white skin. After tours end, guides typically solicit donations of cash or goods on behalf of residents, pledging to pass along the loot.

10   The biggest markets for slum tours are Kibera, Rio de Janeiro's favelas (shantytowns), and the Dharavi district of Mumbai. The obvious reasons are their scale, both in square footage and degree of human misery, and the fact that all three have been featured prominently in major films. For Kibera, it was *The Constant Gardener* (2005); for Rio, *City of God* (2002); and for Mumbai, *Slumdog Millionaire* (2008). Those films didn't create slum tourism, but they have certainly bolstered it.

Kennedy Odede, a cofounder of Kibera's first free girls' school, wrote an opinion piece for the *New York Times* . . . describing how, as a teenager outside his Kibera shack, he spied a white woman taking his picture and "felt like a tiger in a cage." He recalled another occasion when a tour guide— someone he knew—led a group into a private home to photograph a woman giving birth.

For my part, I had a job to do in Kibera and an invitation to be there. Yet I have to wonder what made me so different from slum tourists, driven as I was by curiosity, seeking the satisfaction of doing good, and attracted, like many journalists, to danger and despair.

My husband and I traveled around Kibera under the guidance of a resident named Bangkok, a nickname he acquired after a trip to Thailand as part of a youth boxing team. With a scar on one cheek and long, muscular limbs, Bangkok moved with leonine grace and assurance. Kibera is said to have

"a thousand corners," and every time we rounded another it was plain from the deference we were accorded that no one messed with Bangkok. "You get into any trouble," he said, "just say Bangkok."

Each time we returned to Kibera, the residents seemed less beaten down and foreign, and we appreciated their resourcefulness and vitality more. Once we got over the initial shock of the place, we could begin to see Kibera as a community, not just a slum. But this takes time, and a tour is by definition a glimpse, a chance to skim the surface.

Bangkok also led commercial   15 slum tours, and in the midst of such extreme poverty I questioned my right to criticize how he made a living. He told me he made sure Kibera residents got a cut of the profits. Perhaps they did. But to date there appears to be no real accounting, there or anywhere else, of how much tourism money actually makes its way into slums.

Robert Frank, blogging for the *Wall Street Journal's Wealth Report* in February 2010, wrote that the slum tourism debate has so far been "fueled by emotion and politics, with little research." That may change, he added, with a study by British researcher Fabian Frenzel, who is attempting to quantify the economic impact of tourism in Rio's favelas.

When I asked Ndambo in Nairobi what Kenyan lawmakers thought about Kibera tours, he said they encourage them because it inspires charitable giving. You could also say it helps let the leaders off the hook when it comes to addressing the poverty in their midst.

Brazil is trying a different approach with "Rio Top Tour: Rio de Janeiro in a Different Perspective," through which the government partners with slum residents to promote tours celebrating local arts and culture, and marketing something other than poverty to tourists. A bit of shrewd politics in advance of hosting the 2016 Summer Olympics, perhaps, but it also shows how slum tours could evolve into something genuinely beneficial to residents.

Curious about the demographics of slum tourists, I asked Ndambo who is most apt to book a Kibera tour. "Americans," he answered without hesitation. Asked why he thought that was the case, he replied, "I suppose it's because Americans are so kind."

20   "Thoughtless" is more like it, if you ask Wayne and Emely Silver, cofounders of American Friends of Kenya (AFK). Since 2004 their Connecticut-based nonprofit has provided partnership on projects driven by Kenyans. No one associated with AFK is paid. Twice I've joined the Silvers in an ethics class at Three Rivers Community College in Norwich, Connecticut, to discuss working in developing nations. Slum tours were a hot topic, and I found the "reality television" generation primed to give them a chance. Most tourists probably want to help, students theorized, and as long as they are respectful, where is the harm?

Wayne Silver insisted that the tours are "inherently disrespectful" because there can be "no real zone of privacy" where homes are shacks and all neighborhood life is on the streets. Students listened respectfully, but not all were convinced. "Eyes are being opened," one said. "It all depends on what you do with what you see," said another.

To this Emely Silver offered a challenge. The plane ticket alone makes any trip to Africa an expensive proposition, she said, "so if you can afford to go to Africa to take a slum tour, you can afford to go and work with us."

Understanding and Reviewing the Reading

1. **Thesis** Where in the essay does Dufresne state the thesis that introduces her definition?

2. **Characteristics** What term does Dufresne define? What are the primary characteristics of the term?

3. **Meaning** What is the "broader appeal" of slum tours (para. 6)? What is Dufresne's response to this stated goal?

4. **Meaning** How has the Brazilian government modified the idea of slum tours?

5. **Vocabulary** Using context clues (p. 37), define each of the following words as it is used in the reading, consulting a dictionary if necessary: *infamous* (para. 1), *debut* (2), *urban underbelly* (8), *eschewing* (8), *leonine* (13), *shrewd* (18), *demographics* (19), and *inherently* (21).

Analyzing the Reading

1. **Combining patterns** In her extended-definition essay, what patterns of development in addition to definition does Dufresne use? Annotate the reading to identify the various patterns of development. (See Chapter 9, "Patterns: An Introduction," for a brief overview.)

2. **Technique** Does Dufresne put her term in a larger class? What is that class? Does she state it implicitly or explictly?

3. **Viewpoint** What is Dufresne's personal connection to her subject? How does she compare herself to others who tour slum areas?

4. **Technique** Dufresne uses quotation throughout the essay. Why, in particular, does she use quotation in paragraphs 5, 8, 11, 21, and 22?

5. **Voice** How does Dufresne characterize herself in terms of slum tourists in paragraphs 2, 12, 14, and 15? Why does she make it a point to do so in these parts of the essay?

Evaluating the Reading

1. **Definition** Do you think Dufresne succeeds in fully defining her subject? Does she provide sufficient detail?

2. **Bias** Is Dufresne's definition objective? Do you think her personal feelings color the presentation? Explain your answer with specific examples from the essay.

3. **Visuals** Why was the photograph of an Indian slum included in the essay? What message does it convey?

4. **Language** In paragraph 9, Dufresne writes that slum-tour operators solicit donations from tourists and promise "to pass along the loot." Is this a fair use of language?

Discussing the Reading

1. Would you have any interest in participating in a slum tour? Why, or why not?

2. What do you think of the claim that slum tours open people's eyes in a way that ultimately benefits slum dwellers? In your view, is the attraction to such tours primarily "charitable"?

3. How do you respond to Emely Silver's challenge quoted in the final paragraph? How does what she suggests relate to slum-tour operators' offer of "reality tourism"?

Writing about the Reading

1. **Paragraph** Write a paragraph in which you define Dufresne's subject in your own words. (Hint: You'll first need to choose the term that you wish to define. Dufresne primarily uses the term *slum tourism*, but she also offers alternatives such as *poverty porn* and *reality tourism*. Your choice of term will influence the basis of your definition.)

2. **Essay** Dufresne quotes Wayne Silver as criticizing slum tourism as "disrespectful" because there is "no real zone of privacy" in slums. Do you think our society values respect and privacy? Is there a trend toward the acceptance of disrespectful behavior and/or the loss of privacy? Write an essay in which you define respectful (or disrespectful) behavior or in which you define privacy or its loss. Think about how your definition of the concept you choose is or is not reflected in situations you see around you.

3. **Essay** Dufresne writes in paragraph 14 about being able to see Kibera "as a community, not just a slum." Write an essay in which you define a particular "community" that you are familiar with. Begin by brainstorming examples of different kinds of communities, and then choose one and brainstorm its characteristics.

Can You See Me Now? Deaf America

Stefany Anne Golberg is a multimedia artist, musician, and writer, and she teaches at the Maryland Institute College of Art. She is also a cofounder of the Flux Factory, a nonprofit that fosters art innovation. The following piece is excerpted from *The Smart Set*, a Web magazine that covers culture, ideas, and everything in between. In this essay, Golberg defines the deaf culture.

Reading Tip

As you read, consider why the author, who is not deaf, holds the "Deaf-World," as she terms it, in such high regard.

Previewing the Reading

Preview the reading (see pp. 28–29 for guidelines), and then list two things you already learned about the deaf culture.

---

thesmartset.com

Can You See Me Now?
Deaf America

By Stefany Anne Golberg

Blair Kelly

For most deaf Americans, being deaf is not the inability to hear but rather the ability to perceive life in a different way from hearing people. For many, it's a blessing.

I first decided to take up American Sign Language as a teenager. Sadly, I had no deaf friends or family members with whom to practice ASL. I didn't know any deaf people at all, in fact. I was driven mostly by fascination with the silent language itself, which is powered by a clarity and expressiveness absent from everyday spoken English.

There is an illustrated diagram in my ASL textbook explaining that to properly ask a question in ASL you first make a statement and then shrug your shoulders, cock your head to one side, and open your eyes wide, perhaps adding an inquisitive expression to your face. To a hearing person, this feels like overkill—like donning a Greek theater mask every time you need to find the bathroom. But communicating with your whole body is a fundamental part of ASL. It's a visual idiom, a language of the eye.

Modern deaf poetry is filled with intense imagery, as in J. Schuyler Long's "The Poetry of Motion":

> In the poetry of motion there is music if one sees,
> In the soaring birds above us there are moving symphonies.
> There is music in the movement of a ship upon the wave
> And the sunbeams dancing o'er it, that the minstrels never gave.
>
> . . . in harmony of motion there are songs that Nature sings.
> And there is music all around us if we have the eyes to see.

What deaf people have realized about themselves in the past century is that being deaf opens up a new mode of experience. ASL is the language of that experience. They are creating their own world. But it's a world they have to defend. 5

Deaf activists have argued for decades that deafness is not a defect but a character trait, even a benefit. In their 2011 book *The People of the Eye*, authors Harlan Lane, Richard C. Pillard, and Ulf Hedberg go one step further. They assert that deafness is an ethnicity that, like all officially classed ethnicities, must be given its due politically and culturally [and grammatically, which is why the classification is capitalized throughout the rest of this piece].

Deaf identity is based not on religion, race, or class, say the authors, but "there is no more authentic expression of an ethnic group than its language." And language is the core of American Deaf life. With the emergence of Deaf schools, literacy allowed Deaf people to better communicate in the hearing world. As ASL developed, Deaf Americans could better communicate with each other, and with this came the creation of a Deaf culture, even a new way of being.

ASL signers say that they spend much more time thinking about and dealing with language than most Americans, resulting in a rich and independent tradition of Deaf literature, theater, and journalism. Deaf people have their own clubs, their own rituals, their own places of worship, their own newspapers, and their own sense of humor. In *The People of the Eye*, readers learn how the fully embodied language of ASL and Deaf pride created a culture of storytelling in the Deaf-World, and how this storytelling developed a unique narrative structure based on the particularities of ASL.

Continued >

thesmartset.com

American signers also share a common history and even ancestry. Indeed, *The People of the Eye* is chock-full of ancestral accounts and pedigree diagrams that would make a Mormon genealogist proud.

Americans have been searching for ways to eliminate deafness for a long time. These remedies have ranged from the abusive to the absurd, from so-called oralism (forcing Deaf people to speak and lip-read instead of sign); to sticking twigs, urine, or electricity in the ears; to divine intervention. Charles Lindbergh reportedly would charge $50 to take Deaf people up in a little plane and perform acrobatic stunts to "rouse the slumbering hearing apparatus."

10   Today, thanks to the cochlear implant, deafness can, in effect, be "cured." An estimated 71,000 adults and children have had the treatment, and daytime television is rife with heartwarming stories about people whose lives have been dramatically changed by the device.

The cochlear implant resembles a sea parasite escaped from Radio Shack and looks like it is feasting on the side of the human head. But unlike a hearing aid, which rests outside the ear and amplifies sound, the implants are surgically attached to the cochlea[1]. On its Web site, the National Institute on Deafness and Other Communication Disorders explains that cochlear implants "bypass damaged portions of the ear and directly stimulate the auditory nerve. Signals generated by the implant are sent by way of the auditory nerve to the brain, which recognizes the signals as sound."

Recognizing signals as sound is not a restoration of complete hearing capacity, but cochlear implants do seem to help those who want to better perceive sound, as well as increase their ability to communicate orally. And the technology is improving all the time.

It seems as if all of this progress is good progress. For adults who have grown up in the Deaf-World and live in it as happy citizens, though, the suggestion that they should get a cochlear implant can sound downright insulting, prejudiced even. After all, the authors of *The People of the Eye* posit, if one accepts the argument that Deaf is an ethnicity, aren't plans to eradicate it to be seen as an act of genocide[2]? And even if deafness is a choice, does this make it any less valid than, say, Judaism? Many of the qualities we hold inviolable[3], as true to our identities, to our "ethnicities," are mutable[4], after all. (As the Inquisition[5] demonstrated, even white Protestants can be cured.) But because they can be changed does not mean they must be.

---

[1] **cochlea** Part of the inner ear that converts sound vibrations into nerve impulses.
[2] **genocide** The deliberate extermination of a group of people.
[3] **inviolable** Not able to be changed, broken, or destroyed.
[4] **mutable** Able to be changed.
[5] **Inquisition** Group of institutions within the Roman Catholic Church justice system that tried and punished heretics (disbelievers).

These are tough, uncomfortable questions. Are cures an acceptable way to address human diversity? Are deviations from the norm to be embraced, with education and social sensitivity, or eliminated? What of Deaf children, who are too young to understand the implications of the potential loss of their Deaf identity? Or who may not want to grow up in the Deaf-World but are unable to make the choice? And what of the hearing parents of a Deaf child? How could they encourage their child to be Deaf, especially given the option of a cochlear implant? Even the most permissive, who might accept their Deaf child's different ethnicity as one would for an adopted child, would have to come to terms with leaving their child to the unfamiliar Deaf-World. In doing so, would they lose their own connection to the world of their child?

What authors Lane, Pillard, and Hedberg want hearing people to understand is that most Deaf Americans would not assimilate[6] even if they could. Deaf people tend to marry other Deaf people, go to Deaf schools, have Deaf friends and even surrogate[7] Deaf parents when hearing parents are insufficient to bolster a Deaf identity (or who threaten that identity by attempting to cure them). The Deaf-World, born of necessity, has now become a fortress against the invading hordes of the hearing. There are ASL signers who dream of a Deaf homeland, where visual communication is the norm. Deaf people who gain too much success in the hearing world or marry into it can be looked on with suspicion.   15

In *Understanding Deaf Culture: In Search of Deafhood*, author Paddy Ladd draws a distinction between deafness and what he calls Deafhood. Deafness, says Ladd, is a term given by the hearing. It presents being Deaf as a finite state. "Deafhood is not, however, a 'static' medical condition like 'deafness,'" Ladd writes. "Instead, it represents a process—the struggle by each Deaf child, Deaf family, and Deaf adult to explain to themselves and each other their own existence in the world. In sharing their lives with each other as a community, and enacting those explanations rather than writing books about them, Deaf people are engaged in a daily praxis[8], a continuing internal and external dialogue."

When we look at it this way, maybe considering Deaf as an ethnicity is itself a process of reconsidering what a Deaf person is or can be. Maybe it's not an end but a beginning, for hearing and Deaf alike.

[6]**assimilate** Be or become absorbed.
[7]**surrogate** Person acting for another; substitute.
[8]**praxis** Regular activity involving a skill.

⬛ Understanding and Reviewing the Reading

1. **Thesis** What is the thesis of this definition essay, and where does Golberg state it directly?

2. **Meaning** Why does Golberg write about deafness being a "choice" (para. 13)? What larger point is she making?

3. **Meaning** What does Golberg suggest defines deaf culture and qualifies it as an "ethnicity"?

4. **Language** What distinction is made between "deafness" and "Deafhood" in paragraph 16?

⬛ Analyzing the Reading

1. **Introduction** What specific words in Golberg's opening paragraph serve to summarize the main point of her definition?

2. **Audience** Who are Golberg's intended readers? What effect does she seem to hope her essay will have on these readers?

3. **Technique** Why does Golberg write in such detail about American Sign Language in paragraph 3?

4. **Technique** Paragraph 14 consists almost completely of a series of questions. What is the function of this paragraph in terms of the audience to whom Golberg is appealing?

5. **Technique** How do the final three paragraphs of the essay deal with the questions raised in paragraph 14?

6. **Language** Consider Golberg's use of vocabulary in describing cochlear implants in paragraphs 10–11: "cured" (in quotation marks), "heartwarming stories," "sea parasite . . . feasting on the side of the human head," and "recognizes the signals as sound." What do these words and phrases contribute to the impression she hopes to create?

⬛ Evaluating the Reading

1. **Effectiveness** How effective do you find Golberg's essay as a definition? Do you think she makes her point fully and clearly? Does she convince you of her thesis?

2. **Evidence** Golberg writes in paragraph 2 that ASL "is powered by a clarity and expressiveness absent from everyday spoken English." Do you think she offers sufficient evidence to support this point?

3. **Visuals** Consider the drawing that accompanies this piece. How does it contribute to the definition Golberg presents? From whose perspective does it seem to be drawn? What does it contribute to the tone of the essay?

4. **Language** Paraphrasing defenders of deaf culture, Golberg writes in paragraph 13 that attempts to cure deafness medically and technologically can be seen "as an act of genocide." Do you think this language is appropriate?

5. **Language** Golberg writes of the "Deaf-World" as a "fortress against the invading hordes of the hearing" (para. 15). Does her essay make you sympathize with this description?

Discussing the Reading

1. Golberg asserts in paragraph 15 that most deaf people don't want to "assimilate." Do you think that assimilation into mainstream culture is generally a good thing or a bad thing? Why?

2. In paragraph 13, Golberg writes that just because innate personal qualities "can be changed does not mean they must be." How broadly do you think this statement can be applied?

3. How do you answer the questions Golberg poses in paragraph 14?

Writing about the Reading

1. **Essay** Write an essay in which you define a primary culture, subculture (group of people who share a common interest or characteristic), or ethnicity you see yourself belonging to. You may belong to several cultures or subcultures. You belong to the subculture of college students, for example, but you may also belong to a subculture consisting of members of a particular community service organization or players of a particular sport. (Hint: As you plan your essay, think about stereotypes of your culture versus the reality you see.) You may take a humorous approach to this assignment if you wish.

2. **Essay** Golberg uses the term *ethnicity* throughout her essay. Write an essay of extended definition in which you consider the concept of ethnicity, using Golberg's definition of the term as a starting point.

3. **Essay** Write an essay about the various aspects of assimilation. Choose a subculture (group of people who share a common interest or characteristic) that you are familiar with or part of. You might choose a work, school, or sport subculture. Briefly define what the subculture is and explain its characteristics. Then discuss what is involved in assimilating to the group — that is, in becoming part of that group.

📖 **COMBINING THE PATTERNS | TEXTBOOK EXCERPT:
PUBLIC RELATIONS**

The Cult of Celebrity

Dennis L. Wilcox is professor emeritus of public relations and past director of the School of Journalism and Mass Communications at San Jose State University. **Glen T. Cameron** is Gregory Chair in Journalism Research and founder of the Health Communication Research Center at the University of Missouri. **Bryan H. Reber** is professor of public relations at the University of Georgia's Grady College of Journalism and Mass Communication. Wilcox, Cameron, and Reber are coauthors of the textbook *Public Relations: Strategies and Tactics*, which is the source of the following selection.

Reading Tip

As you read, identify and highlight the characteristics of celebrities.

Previewing the Reading

Preview the reading, keeping in mind that it is from a chapter in a public relations textbook focusing more generally on entertainment, sports, and tourism. Why do you think celebrities are an important component of these industries?

The Cult of Celebrity

Dennis Wilcox, Glen Cameron, and Bryan Reber

According to historian Daniel Boorstin, a celebrity can be defined as a person well known in one of a wide variety of fields such as science, politics, or entertainment. In other words, Barack Obama, Pope Francis, and even Lady Gaga are legitimate celebrities. Being a celebrity today, however, doesn't necessarily mean that it's based on some sort of outstanding achievement or accomplishment.

The entertainment industry, in particular, is fueled by the constant publicizing and glorification of personalities. Individuals such as movie stars, pop music divas, television personalities, and talk show hosts generate a great deal of publicity in the media and on the Web, but today's celebrity status is often only temporary, as there are continually new celebrities who try to take the place of established icons in the public's esteem and interest.

Stephen Cave, reviewing a number of books about fame and celebrity in the *Financial Times*, makes several observations. First, he says, "Fame is a product of certain industries — most notably the mass entertainment business — not a gold star given by the good fairy to the deserving." He goes on, "Fame is not what it used to be . . . Now it is heaped on anyone who is runner-up in a television talent show, subsequently strips for a lads' magazine, then writes their life story age 25 while on day-release from rehab." Cave continues, "But the fame trade has indeed changed. The rise of instant communications, digital media and mass literacy have all fueled the market for stars. Dedicated TV channels, websites, and magazines such as *Heat* and *People* have exponentially increased the speed and volume of celebrity gossip—and the number of celebrities."

An example of the media's fixation on celebrity was the coverage of the death of pop star Michael Jackson in mid-2009. In the 24 hours after his death, the Pew Research Center for Excellence in Journalism found that 60 percent of the total news coverage was devoted to his death, his life story, and his legacy. The coverage eclipsed all other major news stories such as health care reform, major political violence in Iran, and the greenhouse gas bill. The three-hour memorial service for Jackson at Staples Center in Los Angeles, however, seemed to confirm the media's assessment that there was tremendous public interest in the story. The *New York Times* dubbed it "one of the most watched farewells in history" because the service attracted a television audience of 31 million and almost 8 million online viewers. Later that day, 20 million watched the prime-time specials offered by the major TV networks.

The death of a celebrity, particularly under unusual circum-   5
stances, generates massive media coverage, but so does the birth of a child to the "right" celebrity couple. Angelina Jolie and Brad Pitt, for example, received $14 million from *People* magazine for an exclusive interview and photos of their newborn twins in 2008. It was the best-selling issue of *People* in seven years.

More recently, the birth of Britain's Prince George in 2013 also generated a media frenzy. On a more somber note, the passing of Nelson Mandela in December 2013 generated more than two weeks of worldwide coverage about his life and march to freedom from 27 years in prison to becoming the first Black president of a new South Africa in 1994.

The Public's Fascination with Celebrities

Psychologists offer varied explanations of why the public becomes impressed—"fascinated" might be the more accurate word—by highly publicized individuals. In pretelevision days, the publicity departments of the motion picture studios promoted their male and female stars as glamorous figures that lived in a special world of privilege and wealth. The studios catered to the universal need for fairy tales, which often have a rags-to-riches theme. Dreaming of achieving such glory for themselves, young people with and without talent go to Hollywood to try to crash through the magical gates, almost always in vain.

Continued >

Many ordinary people leading routine lives also yearn for heroes. Professional and big-time college sports provide personalities for hero worship. Publicists emphasize the performances of certain players, and television sports announcers often build up the stars' roles out of proportion to their actual achievements; this emphasis is supposed to create hero figures for youthful sports enthusiasts to emulate, but the doping scandal of Lance Armstrong and other athletes, including the scandal of Tiger Woods having multiple affairs while married, has somewhat diminished the idea that professional athletes are good role models.

Athletic teams, however, still retain public esteem and loyalty—especially if they are winning. Sports enthusiasts develop a vicarious sense of belonging that creates support for athletic teams. To signify their loyalty, both children and adults gobble up expensive baseball caps, sweatshirts, and other clothing that advertise the team and let others know they are loyal fans. Indeed, a major revenue stream for most professional teams is the sale of merchandise. The NFL teams make about $3 billion annually on merchandise.

10   Still another factor behind the public's fascination is the desire for entertainment. Reading fan magazines or listening to TMZ report on the personal lives and troubles of celebrities gives fans a look behind the curtain of celebrity. Such intimate details provide fuel for discussion among friends or even something to tweet about. And talking about Hollywood's latest couple break-up is certainly more fun than discussing tax reform.

Understanding and Reviewing the Reading

1. **Thesis** Summarize the overall point about celebrities that the authors make.

2. **Definition** Identify the term being defined, the class to which it belongs, and the characteristics that distinguish it from all others in its class.

3. **Examples**. What examples do the authors give to make the term real and understandable?

4. **Vocabulary** Define the following words as they are used in the reading: *fueled* (para. 2), *exponentially* (3), *eclipsed* (4), *somber* (6), *emulate* (8), and *vicarious* (9). Consult a dictionary if needed.

5. **Meaning** What does Stephen Cave mean when he says that fame is "not a gold star given by the good fairy to the deserving" (para. 3)?

6. **Organization** Create an outline for this reading that would help you learn and remember it.

Analyzing the Reading

1. **Patterns** The authors open by using the definition pattern. What other pattern or patterns do they use in this reading?

2. **Source** Consider that the source of this excerpt is a public relations textbook. How do the authors address the role of publicists and public relations in this reading?

3. **Negation** How do the authors use negation as part of the definition in paragraph 1?

4. **Conclusion** What final impression do the authors establish about the appeal of celebrities?

5. **Annotation** Go back to the reading and annotate it in preparation for a class discussion. Assume your instructor has asked you to prepare to answer the following question: What observations does Stephen Cave make about fame and celebrity?

Evaluating the Reading

1. **Details / examples** Evaluate the types of supporting evidence in this reading. Which details or examples did you find most effective? Why?

2. **Complexity** Which parts of this excerpt do you find most accessible, and which parts are difficult to follow? Which reading techniques did you use to ensure that you understood the complex parts of the piece?

3. **Language** Can you find examples of subjective or emotional language in this reading? How do the authors reveal their attitude toward the subject?

4. **Completeness** Based on this excerpt, evaluate how well you understand the idea of celebrity. What further information would be helpful?

Discussing the Reading

1. Do you think the media's coverage of events like Michael Jackson's death and the birth of a famous baby is excessive? Why, or why not? Does it matter that news coverage of such events "eclipses" other major news stories?

2. The authors state that today's celebrity status is often only temporary. Can you think of celebrities who have extended their status beyond temporary? How have they done so?

3. Discuss the reasons given for the public's fascination with celebrities. Which reasons do you find most compelling? Why?

4. Should professional athletes or other celebrities be considered role models? Why, or why not?

Writing about the Reading

1. **Summary** Using the information in this excerpt, write a summary of the authors' definition of celebrity in your own words.

2. **Essay** Consider the examples of world-famous celebrities given in this reading and the authors' discussion of heroes. Who are the local heroes in your world? Think of people you know (or know of) who have achieved respect or renown in their fields. You may want to consider people from your family, your community, your college, or your local sports teams. Choose one and create your own definition of *celebrity* (or *hero*) with this person in mind. Then write an essay describing him or her.

3. **Essay** Terms that are related to but different in meaning from *celebrity* are *fame*, *infamy*, *icon*, and *reputation*. Choose one of these terms or another along these lines, and write an essay giving an extended definition of the term. Be sure that you include a brief or standard definition in which you state the term itself, the class to which it belongs, and its distinguishing characteristics. Present facts, examples, descriptions, and any other supporting details that will make the term understandable, and conclude your essay by leaving readers with a final impression of the term.

Working with Definition as a Reader and Writer

The following table reviews the key elements of definition essays and explains how these elements are important to both readers and writers.

Reading ⊕ Writing   Definition Essays

Element of a Definition Essay	The Reader's Perspective	The Writer's Perspective
Brief Explanation	While reading, underline the key term and its brief definition. Also identify the class to which the term belongs.	When writing a definition essay, begin by looking up your term in a dictionary, encyclopedia, or other reference work. You will then have a good brief definition on which to expand in your essay. (Be sure to credit your source.)
Key Point	Look for a sentence or two that summarizes the author's key point about the definition. Often you can find the key point in the introduction or conclusion.	Before writing, ask yourself, Why have I chosen to define this term? Why is it significant for my audience? What key point do I want to make about it? Then structure your essay so that it begins with or leads up to your key point.
Negation and Correction of Misconceptions	Note whether the author uses negation or addresses any common misconceptions about the term, and consider whether you held any misconceptions about the term yourself. Determine if the author's techniques have helped you understand the term better (and increased your enjoyment of the essay).	When writing, look for opportunities to use negation and to correct misconceptions. Both techniques can be very helpful to readers. But use them only when doing so matches your purpose or addresses the readers' need for relevant, specific information.

Continued >

Specific, Focused Characteristics	As you read, underline or highlight the characteristics or details that distinguish the item from other items in its class. After reading the essay, write a paragraph-length summary of the author's definition in your own words.	Before you begin writing, identify the item's class as specifically as possible and brainstorm a list of distinguishing characteristics. Then focus on the best, most specific characteristics that are not too broad for your definition.
Other Patterns of Development	As you encounter other patterns of organization, note them in the margins. Determine how each pattern contributes to the author's purpose.	Determine other appropriate patterns during your prewriting, and then make note of them in the outline that will guide your first draft.

17

Cause and Effect: Using Reasons and Results to Explain

In this chapter, you will learn to

- Recognize the elements of cause and effect.

- Identify the structure and content of cause-and-effect essays.

- Understand, analyze, and evaluate cause-and-effect essays.

- Write your own cause-and-effect essay.

- Work with cause and effect as a reader and a writer.

© Bill Stormont/Alamy

Reflect on a Visual Text

Examine the photo above, which was taken by someone with a smart phone who was watching on the sidelines.

1 Ask yourself questions. What is happening in the photo? What sequence of events do you think led up to the event shown? What may happen as a result of it? →

2 **Brainstorm ideas.** Working alone or with a classmate, make up a plausible account of a sequence of events that may have led up to the scene depicted in the photograph. (You may base your brainstorming on stories you've heard or read in the past.)

3 **Write.** Suppose you are a journalist for your local newspaper reporting on a disaster that occurred in a nearby town. Your task is to write a brief article to accompany the photo. Write a paragraph telling readers why the disaster occurred and what happened as a result of it.

The paragraph you just wrote is an example of a *cause-and-effect* analysis because it considered *causes* (why the fire occurred) and *effects* (what happened because of the fire). A cause-and-effect essay generally shows how one event or phenomenon brings about another—for example, how losing your car keys (the cause) led you to be late for class (the effect).

What Are Causes and Effects?

A **cause-and-effect** essay, also called a *causal-analysis* essay, analyzes (1) **causes**—why an event or phenomenon happens, (2) **effects**—what happens because of the event or phenomenon, or (3) both causes and effects.

Many everyday occasions require the use of causal analysis. If your child is injured in an accident, the doctor may ask you to describe how the accident happened and its effects on the child. You will have many occasions to use causal analysis in college and on the job, too. For example, in an essay exam in your twentieth-century history course, you might be required to discuss the causes of U.S. involvement in the Korean conflict. If you become an insurance salesperson, you might need to explain to a potential client the effects of not having life insurance.

Causal analysis has all or most of the following elements:

1. It has a clear purpose.
2. It explains causes, effects, or both.
3. It may recognize or dispel readers' assumptions about the topic.
4. It explains each cause or effect fully.

Knowing how writers (and other communicators) use cause-and-effect analysis will help you understand, analyze, and evaluate this pattern when you read and help you use it in your own writing.

A Model Cause-and-Effect Essay

The following model cause-and-effect essay will be used throughout this chapter to demonstrate strategies for reading and writing cause-and-effect essays. Read it now, looking for the ways the writer uses the above cause-and-effect techniques. Use the annotations in the margin to guide you.

A cause-and-effect essay may recognize or dispel readers' assumptions about the topic: Tan begins by dispelling readers' assumption that ice cubes are always free of germs.

A cause-and-effect essay has a clear purpose: Amy Tan's purpose is to make readers aware that dangerous bacteria may be lurking in the ice cubes served at restaurants.

A cause-and-effect essay explains causes, effects, or both: Amy Tan explores two key causes in this paragraph: E. coli can live on ice (primary cause), and people who do not wash their hands transfer bacteria to ice (secondary cause). In paragraph 5, she explores the effects: People may unknowingly transfer bacteria, and she has changed her habits based on this new information.

E. coli on the Rocks

Amy Tan

Amy Tan has written two children's books and several novels, including *The Joy Luck Club.* She has also contributed articles to such magazines as the *New Yorker* and *National Geographic.* Her work has been translated into French, Finnish, and thirty-three other languages.

If you're like me, you've assumed that anything frozen is naturally germ free. The cold would kill the nasties. Furthermore, the only bad ice cubes are those made with dirty water. Tap water in China, for example. Clean water from U.S. taps makes for worry-free clean ice cubes. Wrong.

Just when you thought Purell solved all your public hygiene needs, now there's news that the lovely crystalline form of water you get in a restaurant may be dirtier than water from your toilet. The specific culprit is E. coli. The chilling reason your drink may be afloat with this bacteria stems purely from people's lack of toilet hygiene. Simply put, a lot of people in a lot of restaurants who handle ice don't wash their hands.

This is very mysterious to me—this dirty-hand syndrome. Whenever I have been in a public restroom, I have never seen anyone exit a toilet stall and not wash their hands. This leads me to think that some people wash their hands only when someone is watching.

One of the news reports mentioned how many colonies were found on a single ice cube. Colonies! I thought it would be only a few rogue E. coli microbes. But colonies made me imagine an ice floe with a thousand swaying porta-potties and no sinks.

A cause-and-effect essay examines each cause or effect fully: Here the author fully explains how bacteria are transferred to ice cubes. She also presents a vivid result: "an ice floe with a thousand swaying porta-potties and no sinks."

I started recalling friends who had come over to our house and said, "I can help myself," and they helped themselves to ice by grabbing the cubes with their bare hands rather than using the ice scoop. I have no doubt that they wash their hands. But what if they were just in a store to pick up a bottle of wine to bring to our house? What if that bottle had been handled by someone who washed their hands only when someone was watching? That is why I'm emptying out my freezer and starting over. Fresh ice. Ice scoops firmly planted in full view. No more packages of Boca Burgers and edamame near the ice tray.

The next time you order a drink, do what my mainland Chinese relatives and friends do. Hold up your hand, palm out, and say: "No ice." Two simple words. They can save your life.

The Structure and Content of Cause-and-Effect Essays

In this section, you will learn about the structure of a cause-and-effect essay and practice using the guidelines for understanding, analyzing, and evaluating cause-and-effect essays. This key information will help you skillfully read and write essays that use this pattern.

The structure of a cause-and-effect essay can take many different forms depending on your purpose for writing it. There are three types of cause-and-effect essays.

- Figure 17.1 shows the organization of an essay with multiple causes or multiple effects.
- Figure 17.2 shows how an essay with both multiple causes and multiple effects is organized.
- Figure 17.3 presents the organization of an essay concerned with a chain of causes and effects.

Notice that causes are presented before effects. Although this is the typical arrangement, writers sometimes reverse it, discussing effects first and then causes.

No matter what your purpose, a cause-and-effect essay should always have an introduction, body paragraphs, and a conclusion.

1. THE INTRODUCTION IDENTIFIES THE EVENT, PROVIDES BACKGROUND INFORMATION, AND STATES THE THESIS

The introduction identifies the event on which the essay will focus. Often, it provides background information about the event, such as where, when, why, or

Figure 17.1   Graphic Organizer for an Essay on Multiple Causes or Multiple Effects

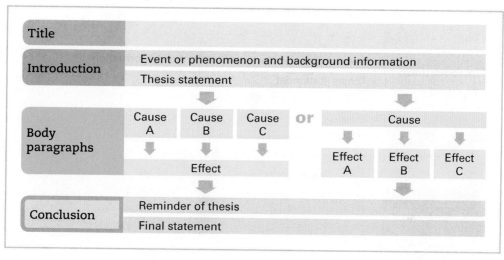

Figure 17.2   Graphic Organizer for an Essay on Multiple Causes and Multiple Effects

Title	
Introduction	Event or phenomenon and background information
	Thesis statement

	Arrangement 1	or	Arrangement 2
Body paragraphs	Cause A		Cause A
	Cause B		Effect A
	Cause C		
			Cause B
			Effect B
	Effect A		
	Effect B		Cause C
	Effect C		Effect C

Conclusion	Reminder of thesis
	Final statement

Figure 17.3   Graphic Organizer for an Essay on a Chain of Causes and Effects

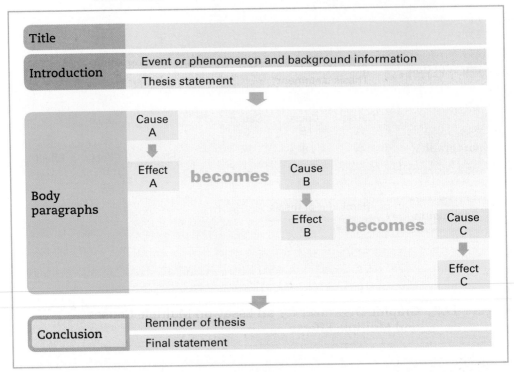

under what circumstances it occurred. It also makes the essay's purpose obvious and provides a clear thesis statement that asserts causes, effects, or both. The introduction may also recognize and dispel assumptions.

Considering Purpose   Like all other essays, a cause-and-effect essay must have a purpose. A cause-and-effect essay may be expressive, but more often it is informative, persuasive, or both. For example, in an essay about the effects of the death of a close relative, you would express your feelings about the person by showing how the loss has affected you. However, an essay describing the sources (*causes*) of the pollution of a local river could be primarily informative, or it could be informative and persuasive if it also stresses the positive results (*effects*) of enforcing antipollution laws.

Some cause-and-effect essays have more than one purpose. For example, an essay may examine the causes of academic cheating (*informative*) and propose policies that would alleviate the problem (*persuasive*).

Tan's purpose in "E. coli on the Rocks" is clear: She wants to *inform* readers of the dangers lurking in restaurant ice cubes and *persuade* her readers to say "No ice" when they place their drink orders at a restaurant.

Asserting Causes, Effects, or Both in a Thesis Statement   The thesis statement should identify the topic—the event or phenomenon discussed—and make an assertion about its causes, effects, or both. This example shows the parts of a strong thesis statement:

topic   *assertion about effect*

The high cost of medicine in the United States forces many elderly to go without their prescriptions or to seek medicines from questionable sources abroad.

The thesis statement should make clear the cause-and-effect relationship. Here is an example of a weak and a revised thesis statement.

Weak	Breathing paint fumes in a closed environment can be dangerous for people suffering from asthma and other lung disorders.
Revised	Breathing paint fumes in a closed environment can be dangerous for people suffering from asthma and other lung disorders because their lungs are especially sensitive to irritants.

The revised thesis statement makes the cause-and-effect connection explicit by using the word *because* and by including necessary information about the problem.

When you write cause-and-effect essays for college classes, you should try to express your thesis in a single sentence. Professional writers, however, sometimes express their theses in a less direct way, using two or more sentences, as Amy Tan does in paragraph 2 of "E. coli on the Rocks":

> Just when you thought Purell solved all your public hygiene needs, now there's news that the lovely crystalline form of water you get in a restaurant may be dirtier than water from your toilet. The specific culprit is E. coli. The chilling reason your drink may be afloat with this bacteria stems purely from people's lack of toilet hygiene. Simply put, a lot of people in a lot of restaurants who handle ice don't wash their hands.

Recognizing and Dispelling Readers' Assumptions   Some cause-and-effect essays recognize or dispel popular ideas that readers assume to be true. For example, an essay on the effects of capital punishment might attempt to dispel the notion that it is a deterrent to crime. Amy Tan's essay dispels American readers' assumption that "anything frozen is naturally germ free."

Recognizing the causes or effects that readers assume to be most important, regardless of whether you support or refute them, lends credibility to your writing. In an informative essay, recognizing assumptions shows your readers that you have not overlooked anything important. In a persuasive essay, it reassures readers that you have considered other viewpoints.

Reading 🔵 Writing The Introduction of a Cause-and-Effect Essay

The Reader's Perspective	The Writer's Perspective
When reading the introduction of a cause-and-effect essay, be sure to identify the topic and assess your familiarity with it. Your knowledge and experience, or lack of such, will determine how closely you need to read the essay.	When writing the introduction of a cause-and-effect essay, help your readers by making it clear whether your essay will be concerned with causes, effects, or both.

2. BODY PARAGRAPHS CONNECT THE CAUSES AND EFFECTS OF THE EVENT AND SUPPORT THE THESIS USING A LOGICAL ORGANIZATION

The body paragraphs of a cause-and-effect essay focus on causes or effects or both. In deciding whether to consider causes, effects, or both, it is important to distinguish the causes from the effects. To do this, think of causes as the *reasons that something happened* and effects as the *results of the thing that happened.*

cause   *effect*

Event X happened because . . .   ← EVENT X →   The result of Event X was . . .

Sometimes causes and effects are relatively easy to identify. In complex situations, causes and effects are often less clear. For example, the causes of a weight problem are complex, and the causes may not be clearly separable from the effects. Some people have an obsession with dieting (*effect*) because they have a poor body image (*cause*). Yet an obsession with dieting (*cause*) can lead to a poor body image (*effect*).

One Cause and Effect   In some cases, there is a single cause, which has one effect.

cause   *effect*

You get a flat tire. ───────────────→ You are late for work.

Multiple Causes and/or Effects   Causal analysis can be complex when it deals with an event or a phenomenon that has multiple causes, multiple effects, or both. Several causes may produce a single effect. For example, you probably chose the college you attend now (*one effect*) for a number of reasons, including the availability of courses in your major, the cost of tuition, the reputation of the school, and its distance from your home (*multiple causes*).

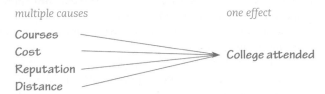

Alternatively, one cause may have several effects. For instance, the decision to quit your part-time job (*one cause*) will result in more study time, less pressure, and less spending money (*multiple effects*).

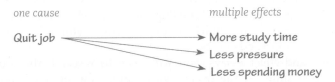

Related events or phenomena may have both multiple causes and multiple effects. For instance, an increase in the number of police officers patrolling the streets in urban areas along with the formation of citizen watch groups (*multiple causes*) will result in less street crime and the growth of small businesses (*multiple effects*).

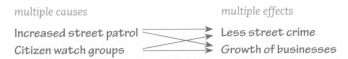

Amy Tan's article presents multiple causes (ability of E. coli to live on ice, a lack of sanitation) and multiple effects (people unknowingly transferring bacteria, her changed behavior, explained in the few sentences of paragraph 5).

Chain of Events   In some cases, a series of events forms a chain in which each event is both the effect of what happened before it and the cause of the next event. In other words, a simple event can produce a chain of consequences.

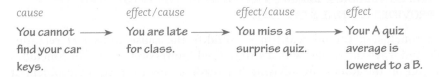

Once you have clearly separated causes and effects, you can decide whether to focus on causes, effects, or both.

Primary and Secondary Causes   The body paragraphs should focus on **primary causes** (more important, more directly related causes) and may discuss **secondary causes** (less important or less directly related causes) as well, depending on the author's purpose and the audience's levels of knowledge and sophistication. In Amy Tan's essay, the primary cause of germ-filled ice is the ability of E. coli to live on ice, and the secondary cause is the fact that people do not wash their hands, thus transferring bacteria to ice.

Two additional items to consider in the body paragraphs are the level of detail and the method of organization.

Sufficient Detail   A causal analysis presents each cause or effect in a detailed and understandable way, using examples, facts, descriptions, comparisons, statistics, and/or anecdotes. Each cause and effect should be well and fully explained, with sufficient evidence provided to indicate that the casual relationship exists. Note that Amy Tan provides vivid, sufficient, and sometimes stomach-turning detail in presenting her causes and effects.

For many cause-and-effect essays, you will need to research the topic to locate evidence that supports the thesis. For example, for an essay about the effects on children of viewing violence on television, you might need to locate research or statistics that document changes in children's behavior after they've watched violent programs. In addition to statistical data, expert opinion is often used as evidence. For example, to support the thesis that reading aloud to preschool children helps them develop prereading skills, you might cite the opinions of reading specialists or psychologists who specialize in child development.

Method of Organization   A cause-and-effect essay often presents causes or effects in chronological order—the order in which they happened. However, it may instead use a most-to-least or least-to-most order to sequence the causes or effects. Amy Tan begins with the effect (germ-riddled ice cubes) and works backwards to the cause. She then moves ahead to consider another effect—her changed behavior at home.

For more information on methods of organization, see pages 171–73 in Chapter 9, "Patterns: An Introduction."

3. THE CONCLUSION REMINDS READERS OF THE THESIS AND PROVIDES A FINAL STATEMENT

The conclusion should reaffirm or solidify the cause-and-effect relationship and leave the reader with a strong final impression. Amy Tan concludes "E. coli on the Rocks" by advising her readers how to solve the problem at hand.

Reading ⬤ Writing   The Body of a Cause-and-Effect Essay

The Reader's Perspective	The Writer's Perspective
When reading the body of a cause-and-effect essay, work on distinguishing causes from effects. You might highlight causes in one color and effects in another. Also annotate causes or effects that are unclear or that you have questions about.	When writing the body of a cause-and-effect essay, be sure to give special consideration to your audience. Your level of detail will be determined by the complexity of the topic as well as by your audience's familiarity with it. If your audience is unfamiliar with the topic, you need to focus on primary, obvious causes or effects. If your audience is familiar with the topic, you can go into greater detail about secondary causes or effects.

Reading ⬤ Writing   The Conclusion of a Cause-and-Effect Essay

The Reader's Perspective	The Writer's Perspective
When reading the conclusion of a cause-and-effect essay, check that you understand the relationship discussed by writing a two-column list of causes and of effects or by drawing a graphic organizer. If you cannot clearly express or draw the cause-and-effect relationship, reread the essay and discuss it with a classmate if necessary. Testing your recall will also help you remember what you read for later analysis or class discussion.	When writing the conclusion of a causal-analysis essay, concentrate on leaving your readers with a concise review or summary of the cause-and-effect relationship.

Understanding, Analyzing, and Evaluating Cause-and-Effect Essays

In reading and writing cause-and-effect essays, your goal is to get beyond mere competence. That is, you want to do more than merely understand the content of the essays you read or convey just your basic ideas to the audience you're writing for.

📖 *Understanding a Cause-and-Effect Essay*

Preview the essay before reading it to identify the event or situation being explained and, if possible, to determine whether the essay will focus on causes, effects, or both. Then read it slowly, to identify specific causes and effects. As you read and reread, use the skills you learned in Chapter 2 and look for answers to the following questions:

- **What is the author's thesis?** Determine what point or assertion the thesis makes about the topic.

- **What is the event or situation being explained?** Think about what you already know about the event or situation and use that information to maintain your interest and to formulate questions.

- **What are the primary causes and primary effects?** Recall that *primary causes* are those that are most directly related to the effect and are considered most important. Identify each and begin to think about how and why they are connected. Drawing a graphic organizer can help you determine the primary causes and effects (as well as secondary causes and effects) when reading or writing. Figure 17.4 shows a graphic organizer for Amy Tan's "E. coli on the Rocks."

- **What are the secondary causes and/or effects?** Secondary causes and effects are less important than primary causes and effects. Determine how the author distinguishes primary causes/effects from secondary causes/effects and look for their relationship to the primary causes/effects.

Figure 17.4   Graphic Organizer for "E. coli on the Rocks"

Title	E. coli on the Rocks
Introduction	**Background information** on water: Common conception that ice made with clean water is free of germs. Wrong.
Body paragraphs	**Cause A**: E. coli can live on ice.
	Cause B: People do not wash their hands.
	Effect A: People may unknowingly transfer bacteria.
	Effect B: The author changes her habits based on new information.
Conclusion	**Advice**: Always say you want no ice when ordering a drink.

Exercise 17.1

Below is one student's summary of the first two paragraphs of Tan's essay.

> Tan has always assumed that ice cubes made with clean water are germ free because the cold would kill any possible germs. But it turns out that ice handled by servers in restaurants may be covered in the bacteria E. coli because those servers haven't washed their hands after going to the bathroom.

Using this summary as a model, write your own summary of the entire essay.

Analyzing a Cause-and-Effect Essay

Analyzing a cause-and-effect essay involves examining how the events or situations presented are related and how the selection is organized. Use the following questions to guide your analysis:

- **Is the assertion in the thesis statement fully explained and supported?** The assertion should be focused and limited so that it is fully and completely covered in the remainder of the essay.

- **Is the causal relationship clearly explained?** Determine whether the author provided sufficient evidence that the causal relationship exists and examine the types of evidence provided.

- **Is the sequence of events clear?** Not all essays are organized chronologically. Some authors may discuss the effect(s) before presenting the cause(s). Other authors may not mention key events in the order in which they occurred. Understanding a causal relationship sometimes requires putting events in order.

- **Does the author use a clear method of organization to help you follow the essay?** The author may devote a separate paragraph to each cause or effect and may arrange the paragraphs using one of the methods of organization shown in Figures 17.1 (p. 501), 17.2 (p. 501), and 17.3 (p. 502).

- **Does the author use transitions to help you move from one cause or effect to another?** Transitional words, phrases, or sentences work as guideposts, helping you anticipate what the author will discuss next.

Analysis in Action

Exercise 17.2

Below is Tan's first paragraph, annotated by the same student who wrote the summary for Understanding in Action.

Appeals directly to readers	If you're like me, you've assumed that anything frozen is naturally germ free. The cold would kill the nasties.
Casual tone emphasizes "ick" factor	Furthermore, the only bad ice cubes are those made with dirty water. Tap water in China, for example. Clean water from U.S. taps makes for worry-free clean ice cubes.
Interesting way to introduce thesis	Wrong.

Use annotations of your own to analyze the remainder of the essay.

Evaluating a Cause-and-Effect Essay

Evaluating a cause-and-effect essay involves judging how accurately and effectively the author has established and demonstrated the causal relationship. Use the following questions to guide your evaluation of cause-and-effect essays:

- **Does the writer cover all major causes or effects?** Consider whether the author presents a fair description of the causal relationship. For instance, a writer arguing in favor of using animals for medical research might fail to mention the painful effects of the testing on the animals.

- **Does the writer provide sufficient evidence for the causal relationship?** Look closely at the supporting evidence and determine whether it is sufficient to show that the relationship exists. For example, suppose a writer asserts that medical doctors often order unnecessary medical tests to prevent possible lawsuits and supports the assertion using only personal experience. A few personal anecdotes are not sufficient evidence to support the assertion.

- **What is the writer's purpose?** Does the writer describe certain causes or effects to urge you to accept a particular viewpoint or position? For example, a graphic description of the physical effects of an experimental drug on laboratory animals may strengthen a writer's argument against the use of animals in medical research.

- **Does the author make assumptions?** If so, are they supported by the reasons given and the evidence? For example, a writer may assume that cosmetics should be tested on animals to assure their safety for humans. But unless the author explains and documents this assumption, you are not obliged to accept or agree with it.

Exercise 17.3

This evaluation of the two opening paragraphs of Tan's "E. coli on the Rocks" was written by the same student who summarized and annotated the essay in the Understanding in Action and Analysis in Action boxes.

> I like that Tan pulls me in as a reader with her first sentence. I also think that it's effective in the first paragraph that she sounds like she's speaking directly to her readers, almost as if they were friends. The final "Wrong" really makes me want to read on. Then saying that ice in restaurants may be "dirtier than water from your toilet" is also effective in making clear how disgusting it is that people don't wash their hands after going to the bathroom.

Use this evaluation as a model for writing your own evaluation of the essay.

Writing Your Own Cause-and-Effect Essay

Now that you have learned about the major characteristics, structure, and purposes of a cause-and-effect essay, you know everything necessary to write your own causal analysis. In this section, you will read a student's cause-and-effect essay and get advice on finding ideas, drafting your essay, and revising and editing it. You may want to use the essay prompts in "Readings for Practice, Ideas for Writing" (p. 520) or choose your own topic.

A Student Model Cause-and-Effect Essay

Nathan Nguyen was a first-year liberal arts major when he wrote this essay in response to an assignment for his writing class. He was asked to explain the causes and effects of a current social problem. As you read, notice how Nguyen presents a chain of causes and effects, in which an initial cause has an effect, which in turn becomes a cause of another effect, and so on.

Title: suggests importance of topic.

Gambling on Our Future

Nathan Nguyen

Introduction: Opening example catches readers' interest.

Marge Simpson is a junkie. Are you surprised? Marge has always been the moral anchor that kept *The Simpsons* squarely in the mainstream. She was the stay-at-home mom who tempered Lisa's progressive politics, the sober wife who supported Homer during his drunken misadventures, and the upstanding citizen who taught Bart how to live in society. If Marge had an intravenous drug habit, Americans everywhere would be up in arms. But it's just gambling, and in this day and age, few things are more mainstream. In fact, inspired by the huge revenues generated by Las Vegas, states are turning to gambling to boost their post-recession economies and their ailing educational systems and urban centers. As states open up their laws to all kinds of gambling, it has become more widespread and convenient, leading to an increase in addiction and problem gambling.

Thesis suggests essay will focus on chain of events.

Cause A: Nevada legalizes gambling.

The passage of the 1931 bill allowing gambling in Nevada was originally designed to generate revenue for the state and its ailing educational system. The result was little less than a phenomenon, establishing Las Vegas as a tourist playground and a symbol of American decadence but also changing forever the way politicians tax the people. Recently, the Las Vegas tourism and hospitality industry, which includes gambling, has accounted for 46% of the state's income and yielded $16 billion a year ("How Gaming Benefits Nevada"; "2011 Las Vegas"). The economic boon to the state was watched enviously by lawmakers around the country; over time, what was once viewed as sinful has captured the dreams and imaginations of politicians and constituents alike.

Effect A / Cause B: Las Vegas becomes popular; economic boom.

Source

Effect B / Cause C: Seeing the boom, other states legalize gambling.

Use of quote from **source**

Even before the nation's most recent economic struggles, cities and states had entered the business of gambling, desperate to re-create the rags-to-riches story of Las Vegas. According to the journal *American Family Physician,* "in 1978 only two states had legalized gambling; in 1998, however, only two states had not legalized gambling" (Unwin et al. 741). The business of legalized gambling takes many forms. For example, a landmark Supreme Court decision in 1987 opened up the door to Native American gaming on tribal lands. The ensuing increase to economic development on some of these lands has caught the imagination of other impoverished areas. Struggling urban centers, such as Detroit and St. Louis, have opened large luxury casinos in the hopes of bringing money in from the wealthy suburbs to revitalize decaying downtown districts.

Effect C / Cause D: Once legal, access to gambling becomes widespread.

But gambling is not confined to casinos alone. Forty-three states now have casinos of a sort in every grocery, convenience store, and gas station, in the form of the lottery. Moreover, because hopeful lawmakers eased limitations on Internet gambling to boost state revenues, there are opportunities for "casinos" to be reached legally from every household and office in the country (Berzon). The problem now is not how to find legal gambling, but how to escape it.

Effect D / Cause E: Lotteries and the Internet have increased the acceptance of gambling.

The dramatic acceptance of state lotteries and Internet gaming across the nation has had the largest impact on how Americans view gambling. The lottery, like its big brother Las Vegas, was originally set up to subsidize state educational systems. Since 1964 when New Hampshire began its lottery, states have turned to lotteries as a way of increasing revenues without raising taxes and now they expect Internet gaming to do the same. While the revenues of state-run lotteries are often lauded, according to the final report by the National Gambling Impact Study Commission, the "actual contributions are exceedingly modest" (ch. 2, 4). Furthermore, the American Gaming Association predicted that Internet gaming, such as poker, "would generate . . . a fraction of what states get from their lotteries" (Cooper). Despite this, Americans continue to support the lottery, making it one of the top forms of gambling in the country. Even before the economic downturn, 86% of Americans had admitted to gambling at least once in their lives ("National Gambling Impact" ch. 1, 1). But as "states have become active agents for the expansion of gambling," public welfare has taken a backseat to revenue raising (ch. 3, 4).

Sources: statistic and expert opinion cited

Effect E / Cause F: With acceptance of gambling, addiction is common.

The abundance of opportunities to gamble has created more compulsive gamblers by exposing people to an "illness" they might not otherwise have developed and by giving reformed gamblers more chances to fall off the wagon. While most gamblers are able to do it healthily, a majority of the benefit derived from gambling is at the expense of the ill. A study by Duke University professors Charles Clotfelter and Philip Cook found that "5% of lottery players account for 51% of total lottery sales." Their research indicates that those who make under $10,000 spend "more than any other income group" and that lotteries rely on players who are "disproportionately poor, black, and have failed to complete a high school education" ("National Gambling Impact" ch. 7, 10). People joke that it is a tax on the stupid, but in fact it is a tax on hope, especially with the rise of online gambling.

Sources: Research study documents appeal of gambling to the poor.

Effect F: increase in social problems associated with gambling addiction

Regarding the effects of Internet gaming, Keith Whyte, executive director of the National Council on Problem Gambling, argues that pathological gambling "definitely can be heightened" in this "immersive environment where you can lose track of time and money" (Berzon). College students are particularly vulnerable, precisely because they are more prone to taking risks than other groups and because people who begin gambling at a young age are at a much higher risk for developing a gambling problem later in life ("National Gambling Impact" ch. 4, 12). The rising rates in problem gambling correspond to the growth of legalized gambling across the country.

Conclusion restates chain of events and emphasizes thesis. Use of gambling jargon suggests author's opinion of the trend.

The promise of a Las Vegas miracle has lured states into expanding gambling and putting a mini Vegas in every 7-11 store and Internet device. As states increasingly turn to gambling, more people are exposed to it, a cycle that leads to ever-rising rates of problem gambling and addiction. The hope of a Vegas miracle lures people, often poor and occasionally very sick, to a casino, to the lottery, or to online betting. The trickle-down effect from this is the often unseen side to the promise of the big jackpot: Bankruptcy, job loss, divorce, alcoholism, drug addiction, and welfare are just some of the costs associated with gambling addiction. The question then is, are states willing to gamble with our future? For now, the trend continues, but the odds of winning are a million to one.

Sources: Nguyen documents sources.

Works Cited

Berzon, Alexandra. "States Cleared for Online Bets." *The Wall Street Journal*, 27 Dec. 2011, www.wsj.com/articles/SB10001424052970 203391104577123024019184502#:XNd6kOv0xhNf2A.

Cooper, Michael. "As States Weigh Online Gambling, Profit May Be Small." *The New York Times*, 17 Jan. 2012, www.nytimes.com /2012/01/18/us/more-states-look-to-legalize-online-gambling .html?_r=0.

"How Gaming Benefits Nevada." *Nevada Resort Association*, nevadaresorts.org/benefits/. Accessed 28 Feb. 2012.

"National Gambling Impact Study Commission Final Report." National Gambling Impact Study Commission, 3 Aug. 1999. *Cyber Cemetery*, University of North Texas Libraries, 2 Feb. 2009, govinfo.library.unt.edu/ngisc/reports/fullrpt.html.

"2011 Las Vegas Year-to-Date Executive Summary." *Las Vegas Convention and Visitors Authority*, www.lvcva.com/stats-and -facts/visitor-statistics/. Accessed 28 Feb. 2012.

Unwin, Brian K., et al. "Pathologic Gambling." *American Family Physician*, vol. 61, no. 3, 1 Feb. 2000, pp. 741–48.

Responding to Nguyen's Essay

1. Suggest an alternative title that would more directly reflect the essay's thesis.

2. Evaluate Nguyen's introduction. Is the opening reference to Marge Simpson an effective strategy? How would it come across to those who are unfamiliar with *The Simpsons?* Discuss alternative ways to introduce the topic.

3. Nguyen does not include examples of real people and their gambling addictions. Would such examples strengthen the essay? Why, or why not?

4. Nguyen concludes by reiterating his thesis. What alternative ways might he have chosen to end the essay?

Finding Ideas for Your Cause-and-Effect Essay

Look for ideas for cause-and-effect essays as you do your reading for this and other classes. By thinking critically about—understanding, analyzing, and evaluating—the texts you read, you can find inspiration for your own writing. Here are a few approaches to take.

- When reading an essay that discusses the causes of an event or a phenomenon, consider writing about the effects. When reading about the effects of an event or a phenomenon, consider writing about the causes.

- Think of possible causes or effects other than those given in an essay you have read.

- For a chain-of-events essay, imagine what might have happened if the chain had been broken at some point.

- Consider the secondary causes or effects the writer does not mention.

- Write about a cause-and-effect relationship from your own life that is similar to one in the essay.

Selecting an Event or Phenomenon to Write About

The first step is to select an event or a phenomenon to write about. Be sure to choose one with which you are familiar or about which you can find information in the library or on the Internet. Then decide on your purpose and whether to focus on causes, effects, or both. Keep the length of your essay in mind as you think about these issues. It would be unrealistic, for example, to try to discuss both the causes and the effects of child abuse in a five-page paper.

Discovering Causes and Effects

The next step is to discover causes, effects, or both. You can approach this task in a number of ways.

1. **Brainstorm.** Write your topic in the middle of a blank page, turning the page sideways to allow for extra writing space. Brainstorm all possible causes and effects, writing causes on the left and effects on the right.

2. **Visualize.** Replay the event in your mind. Focus on one or both of the following questions: Why did the event happen? What happened as a result of it? Make notes on your answers.

3. **Ask questions.** Try asking questions and writing assertions about the problem or phenomenon. Did a chain of events cause the phenomenon? What effects are not so obvious?

4. **Discuss.** Talk about your topic with a classmate or friend. Ask his or her opinion on the topic's causes, effects, or both.

5. **Research.** Look up your topic at the library or on the Internet. Make notes on possible causes and effects, or print out or photocopy relevant information you discover.

Identifying Primary Causes and Effects

Once you have a list of causes or effects (or both), the next task is to sort through them and decide which ones are *primary*, or most important. For example, if your topic is the possible effects of television violence on young viewers, two primary effects might be an increase in aggressive behavior and a willingness to accept violence as normal. Less important, or *secondary*, effects might include learning inappropriate or offensive words and spending less time viewing family-oriented shows. In essays about controversial issues, the writer's interests may determine which causes or effects are primary and which are secondary.

Use the following questions to help you decide which causes and effects are most important.

Causes

- What are the most obvious and immediate causes?
- What cause(s), if eliminated, would drastically change the event, problem, or phenomenon?

Effects

- What are the obvious effects of the event, problem, or phenomenon?
- Which effects have the most serious consequences? For whom?

After you have identified primary and secondary causes and effects, examine them to be sure you have not overlooked any *hidden* causes or effects. For example, if a child often reports to the nurse's office complaining of a stomachache, a parent may assume that the child has digestive problems. However, a closer study of the behavior may reveal that the child is worried about attending a physical-education class and that the stomachaches are the result of stress and anxiety. The physical-education class is the hidden cause. As you analyze causes and effects, do not assume that the most obvious or simplest explanation is the only one.

You should also be on the lookout for assumptions that involve errors in reasoning. For example, the fact that Event A preceded Event B does not necessarily mean that Event A caused Event B. Suppose you decide against having a cup of coffee one morning and later that day you score higher than ever before on a political science exam. Although one event followed the other in time, you cannot assume that reducing your coffee intake caused the high grade. To avoid such errors, look for evidence that one event did, indeed, cause the other.

Once you feel confident about your list of causes and effects, you need to provide a complete explanation of each primary cause or effect that will be included in the essay. To do so, you'll probably use one or more other patterns of development. For example, you may need to narrate events, present descriptive details, define important terms, explain unfamiliar processes, include examples, or make comparisons to explain unfamiliar concepts. At this point, it is a good idea to do some additional prewriting or research to gather evidence to support the causes, effects, or both. Try to come up with several types of evidence, including facts, expert opinion, personal observation, quotations, and statistics.

Developing Your Thesis

Once you are satisfied with the causes and effects and the evidence you have generated to support them, the next step is to develop a working thesis. The thesis for a causal analysis identifies the topic, makes an assertion about the topic, and tells whether the essay will focus on causes, effects, or both. Use the following tips to develop your thesis:

1. Avoid overly broad or absolute assertions. Such statements are difficult or impossible to support.

2. Use qualifying words such as *many, most, several,* and *often* (instead of *all, always,* or *never*). Unless a cause-and-effect relationship is well established and accepted, qualify your thesis statement.

3. Avoid an overly assertive or dogmatic tone. The tone of your essay, including the thesis, should be confident but not overbearing. You want readers to accept your premise based on its merits; an essay with a hostile or dismissive tone will alienate readers before they have a chance to evaluate its position.

Drafting Your Cause-and-Effect Essay

Once you have evaluated the cause-and-effect relationship and thesis, it is time to organize your ideas and draft your essay. Review Figures 17.1, 17.2, and 17.3 (pp. 501–02) to see which is closest to your essay's basic structure. Then choose a method of organization that will present your ideas effectively (see Chapter 7, pp. 126–30).

After you have decided how to organize the essay, the next step is to write a first draft. Use the following guidelines to draft your essay:

1. **Write an effective introduction.** Your introduction should identify the topic and causal relationship as well as draw readers into the essay. It should make your purpose clear and may also recognize and dispel readers' assumptions.

2. **Provide well-developed explanations.** Be sure to provide sufficient evidence that the causal relationship exists. Offer a number of reasons and choose a variety of types of evidence (examples, statistics, expert opinion, etc.). Try to develop each cause or effect into a detailed paragraph with a clear topic sentence.

3. **Use strong transitions.** Use a transition each time you move from an explanation of one cause or effect to an explanation of another. Transitional words and phrases that are useful in cause-and-effect essays include *because*, *since*, *as a result*, and *therefore*.

4. **Avoid overstating causal relationships.** When writing about causes and effects, avoid words and phrases that overstate the causal relationship, such as *it is obvious*, *without doubt*, *always*, and *never*. These words and phrases wrongly suggest that a causal relationship is absolute and without exception. Instead, use words and phrases that qualify, such as *it is possible*, *it is likely*, and *most likely*.

5. **Write a satisfying conclusion.** Your conclusion may remind readers of the thesis and draw the essay to a satisfying close. You might also summon the readers to action or provide advice, as Amy Tan does when she recommends that readers say "No ice" when ordering a drink.

Revising Your Cause-and-Effect Essay

If possible, set your draft aside for a day or two before rereading and revising it. As you review the draft, concentrate on how you organize and present your ideas, not on grammar, punctuation, or mechanics. Use the flowchart in Figure 17.5 to guide your analysis of the strengths and weaknesses of your draft.

Editing and Proofreading Your Essay

The final step is to check your revised essay for errors in grammar, spelling, punctuation, and mechanics. In addition, check for the types of errors you commonly make in any writing assignments, whether for this class or in other situations. Check the handbook (pp. 645–714) for assistance with common errors in your writing.

Figure 17.5 Revising a Cause-and-Effect Essay

QUESTIONS		REVISION STRATEGIES
1. Thesis Does it express a qualified, manageable assertion? (Can you prove your thesis?)	No	• Use a branching diagram to narrow your topic (see Chapter 4). • Revise to focus only on primary causes or effects. • Add qualifying words or phrases to your thesis.
↓ Yes		
2. Using causes and effects Does your essay clearly focus on causes, effects, or both?	No	• Reconsider whether you want to explain causes, effects, or both. Will the essay be skimpy if you focus on only one or too long or complicated if you use both?
↓ Yes		
3. Explanations of causes and effects Is each explained fully?	No	• Add anecdotes or observations from personal experience or other details and examples. • Do research to locate facts, research studies, statistics, and expert opinions.
↓ Yes		
4. Organization Did you use chronological, least-to-most, or most-to-least organization? Is it clear and effective? Do your ideas progress logically?	No	• Choose a different order if necessary. • Rearrange your causes, effects, or both.
↓ Yes		
5. Readers' assumptions Have you identified all likely pre-conceptions and challenged or addressed them?	No	• Brainstorm popular ideas readers might assume about your topic and either support or challenge them.
↓ Yes		
6. Topic sentence Is each paragraph focused on a separate cause or effect?	No	• Be sure each paragraph has a topic sentence and supporting details (see Chapter 6). • Consider combining closely related paragraphs. • Split paragraphs that cover more than one cause or effect.
↓ Yes		
7. Introduction and conclusion Are they effective?	No	• Revise your introduction and conclusion so that they meet the guidelines presented in Chapter 7.

Readings for Practice, Ideas for Writing

Why Do Violent Videos Go Viral?

Kate Wheeling has used her background in behavioral neuroscience and science journalism to write about a range of scientific topics from heliophysics to human cells. She is an associate editor for *Pacific Standard* and has also written for *Science* and *Discover Magazine*. This article appeared in the *Pacific Standard*.

Reading Tip

As you read, highlight and annotate the essay to identify the specific evidence the author provides to explain each of the causes she offers in answering the question in her title.

Previewing the Reading

Preview the reading using the guidelines on pages 28–29, and then answer the following questions.

1. What do you predict the author's attitude toward violent videos will be?
2. What reasons does the author offer to explain why people enjoy watching violent videos?

www.psmag.com

Why Do Violent Videos Go Viral?

By Kate Wheeling

School administrators in Atlanta are trying to shut down Instagram accounts documenting hundreds of brawls between Clayton County middle and high school students. Clayton was one of four suburban counties within the Atlanta metropolitan area that had Instagram pages dedicated to violence between students, the largest of which, called Clayco.fights, had tens of thousands of followers. Hoping to prevent the spread of future videos, school officials are now scrambling to update rules to restrict students' use of the Internet. Not surprisingly, students caught on video fighting on school grounds may be suspended, the *Atlanta Journal-Constitution* reports.

Violent videos often go viral, and despite the fact that Instagram itself has policies prohibiting violent content, the fight pages are hard to suppress. When the first Clayco.fights page was shut down, another similarly titled page popped up to replace it (shrewdly adding another 's' to "fights"). *The International Business Times* reports:

> The brief clips depict brawls with students punching each other and pulling hair in school parking lots, gymnasiums, and classrooms. Clayco.fights, the largest and

most notorious account with 384 posts and more than 30,000 followers, could not be accessed on Instagram Thursday morning. But a new profile immediately sprung up in its place: Clayco.fightss had 36 posts and more than 3,200 followers as of 10 a.m. [*The International Business Times*]

So why do we like violence so much? A look at athletics, which have played an integral role in society since the earliest civilizations, may hold some potential answers. While the games we enjoy have evolved over time, most of our modern-day sports share one commonality with their ancient counterparts: violence. Professional wrestling, boxing, and mixed martial arts all trace back to ancient combat sports, R. Todd Jewell, Afsheen Moti, and Dennis Coates wrote in 2012, in their book *Violence and Aggression in Sporting Contests*. Even in sports where violence is not the end goal, it often occupies a central role. The National Hockey League, for example, believes that violence is not just unavoidable, but "therapeutic and cathartic in minor forms," Jewell, Moti, and Coates wrote.

The authors lay out a few theories about why we love violent sports, but those ideas could also provide some insight into the persistence of these Instagram accounts for schoolyard fights.

Spectating is essentially living vicariously through participants

The asserting dominance theory holds that those watching the action—be it a football 5 game or a backyard brawl—may be living vicariously through the event participants. When we watch a hockey player slam an opponent into the boards, or our peers punch each other on the playground, we can sometimes feel as if we made the play (or threw the punch) ourselves. At the same time, we can take comfort in the knowledge that just watching the violence play out is harmless; we did no wrong, and are therefore safe from any consequences or retaliation.

It's cathartic to watch

Some social scientists believe that violent sports may actually curb aggressive behaviors in both athletes and spectators. The theory is that humans build up "destructive energy," which playing or watching aggressive sports can help release. "The theory also suggests that the more violent the sport is, the greater the pleasure received for both the participant and the viewer," Jewell, Moti, and Coates wrote. But, the authors caution, in some cases violence can also serve to build up destructive energy. That explains the tendency of some sports fans to commit violent and destructive acts post-game (cough, soccer hooligans, cough), and perhaps why the violent school fight videos lead to, well, more violent videos.

Continued >

Maybe we just crave violence

Research on mice has shown that, like food, sex, and drugs, violence can activate the reward pathways in our brains. *LiveScience* reported on a study from 2008 in which researchers instigated an initial skirmish by introducing an intruder mouse into the cage of another male mouse. When the resident rodent was given the opportunity to return the intruder to his own cage by poking a target, the mouse consistently chose to bring the intruder back and continue the fight. But when the scientists treated the mice with dopamine blockers to inhibit the reward pathway, the mice were less likely to bring the intruders back for another round. The study indicates that the mice found aggression itself rewarding, which has important implications for humans as well, given that the reward pathways in humans and mice are remarkably conserved[1].

The rise of social media, coupled with our predilection for gruesome entertainment, has made violent videos hard for school officials to contain. Keeping students off the Internet is one strategy, but there is perhaps a better way to prevent them from posting these videos: figuring out a more effective way to keep students from fighting in the first place.

[1] **conserved** Genetically similar.

Understanding and Reviewing the Reading

1. **Thesis** Where does Wheeling state her thesis? Express it in your own words.
2. **Examples** What are some of the specific examples Wheeling includes as supporting details?
3. **Vocabulary** Using context clues (p. 37), define each of the following words as it is used in the essay, consulting a dictionary if necessary: *suppress* (para. 2), *notorious* (2), *integral* (3), *cathartic* (3), *vicariously* (5), *instigated* (7), and *predilection* (8).
4. **Organization** Complete the graphic organizer on the next page to help you see the organization of the essay.

Analyzing the Reading

1. **Introduction and conclusion** How do the first two paragraphs relate to the final paragraph?
2. **Audience** How does the author envision her intended audience, and what does she hope to achieve with this audience? How can you tell?

Title	Why Do Violent Videos Go Viral?
Introduction	**Background:** **Thesis:** The same reasons people love violent sports may help explain the popularity of violent videos.
Body paragraphs	**Cause 1:** Spectating is living vicariously through others. **Cause 2:** **Cause 3:**
Conclusion	

3. **Assumptions** What assumptions does the author make? What details does she include that support her assumptions? (Hint: Examine the assumption the author seems to be making when she asks "So why do we like violence so much?")

4. **Purpose** Wheeling makes a comparison between most modern-day sports and their ancient counterparts. What is the purpose of this comparison?

5. **Language** Overall, how would you characterize the level of the language Wheeling uses in the essay? How does her language in general contribute to the impression you get of her? Point to some specific examples to explain your answer.

Evaluating the Reading

1. **Presentation** How well does Wheeling connect the reasons people enjoy watching violent sports to the popularity of violent videos?

2. **Organization** Does Wheeling present her list of causes in a meaningful order? Can you determine a clear method to her organization?

3. **Evidence** Wheeling uses the book *Violence and Aggression in Sporting Contests* as a primary source. Should she have used evidence from other sources to expand her ideas? What other supporting details would you add?

4. **Language** In paragraph 2, Wheeling uses the word *shrewdly* to describe how a new fight page was put on the Internet to replace the original. Why did she use this word?

5. **Content** In paragraph 7, Wheeling cites a study on aggression in mice to illustrate her third reason. Do you think this research fits in with the rest of the essay?

Discussing the Reading

1. Discuss the asserting dominance theory described in paragraph 5. Have you ever experienced the feeling that you were living vicariously through event participants?

2. In your view, what is the most important reason Wheeling offers in her essay? Which reason do you think is most typical? Which reason is most disturbing?

3. In her explanation of the asserting dominance theory, Wheeling says that observers "can take comfort in the knowledge that just watching the violence play out is harmless; we did no wrong." Do you agree that there is no harm in watching violence play out? If you disagree, why?

Writing about the Reading

1. **Paragraph** In a paragraph, describe your personal attitude toward watching violent sports. (Hint: First, draft a topic sentence that summarizes your attitude. Then develop your paragraph by explaining the reasons for your attitude.)

2. **Paragraph** Write a paragraph explaining the theory of destructive energy in your own words. Do you think playing or watching aggressive sports is more likely to build up or release destructive energy? Use examples to support your opinion.

3. **Essay** Write an essay titled "Why Do People Like _____ ?" (Fill in the blank with your subject, of course.) Start by brainstorming a number of different subjects, focusing on interests of your own that you could explain to readers. Then choose one subject for which you can come up with four or five reasons people enjoy the activity. Alternatively, you might have as your topic an activity, such as smoking, that people choose to enagage in even though it has negative outcomes. (Hint: Like Wheeling, create a heading for each section that summarizes the reason you explain in that section.)

Why We Procrastinate

Hara Estroff Marano is an award-winning writer and editor-at-large for *Psychology Today*. She also writes the magazine's advice column, Unconventional Wisdom. In addition, she writes for numerous other publications, including the *New York Times, USA Today*, and *The Smithsonian*. In 1998, she published *Why Doesn't Anybody Like Me?: A Guide to Raising Socially Confident Kids*. Her most recent book, *A Nation of Wimps: The High Cost of Invasive Parenting* (2008), speaks out about what Marano believes to be a social crisis caused by overparenting. The essay that follows first appeared in *Psychology Today* in July of 2005.

Reading Tip

Marano starts the essay by introducing two world-renowned experts on procrastination. Notice how this sets the tone for a factual and analytical look at procrastination. Also pay attention to the primary and secondary causes Marano identifies and the examples she uses to illustrate her points.

Previewing the Reading

Preview the reading using the guidelines on pages 28–29, and then answer the following questions.

1. How do procrastinators sabotage themselves?
2. How do you think this essay will be organized?

Why We Procrastinate

Hara Estroff Marano

There are many ways to avoid success in life, but the most sure-fire just might be procrastination. Procrastinators sabotage themselves. They put obstacles in their own path. They actually choose paths that hurt their performance.

Why would people do that? I talked to two of the world's leading experts on procrastination: Joseph Ferrari, Ph.D., associate professor of psychology at De Paul University in Chicago, and Timothy Pychyl, Ph.D., associate professor of psychology at Carleton University in Ottawa, Canada. Neither one is a procrastinator, and both provided answers to my question immediately.

E+/Getty Images

1. Twenty percent of people identify themselves as chronic procrastinators. For them procrastination is a lifestyle, albeit a maladaptive one. And it cuts

Continued >

across all domains of their life. They don't pay bills on time. They miss opportunities for buying tickets to concerts. They don't cash gift certificates or checks. They file income tax returns late. They leave their Christmas shopping until Christmas eve.

2. It's not trivial, although as a culture we don't take it seriously as a problem. It represents a profound problem of self-regulation. And there may be more of it in the U.S. than in other countries because we are so nice; we don't call people on their excuses ("my grandmother died last week") even when we don't believe them.

5   3. Procrastination is not a problem of time management or of planning. Procrastinators are not different in their ability to estimate time, although they are more optimistic than others. They actually think they have plenty of time to complete the task at hand. "Telling someone who procrastinates to buy a weekly planner is like telling someone with chronic depression to just cheer up," insists Dr. Ferrari.

4. Procrastinators are made not born. Procrastination is learned in the family milieu, but not directly. It is one response to an authoritarian parenting style. Having a harsh, controlling father keeps children from developing the ability to regulate themselves, from internalizing their own intentions and then learning to act on them. Procrastination can even be a form of rebellion, one of the few forms available under such circumstances. What's more, under those household conditions, procrastinators turn more to friends than to parents for support, and their friends may

reinforce procrastination because they tend to be tolerant of their excuses.

5. Procrastination predicts higher levels of consumption of alcohol among those people who drink. Procrastinators drink more than they intend to—a manifestation of generalized problems in self-regulation. That is over and above the effect of avoidant coping styles that underlie procrastination and lead to disengagement via substance abuse.

6. Procrastinators tell lies to themselves. Such as, "I'll feel more like doing this tomorrow." Or "I work best under pressure." But in fact they do not get the urge the next day or work best under pressure. In addition, they protect their sense of self by saying "this isn't important." Another big lie procrastinators indulge in is that time pressure makes them more creative. Unfortunately they do not turn out to be more creative; they only feel that way. They squander their resources avoiding.

7. Procrastinators actively look for distractions, particularly ones that don't take a lot of commitment on their part. Checking e-mail is almost perfect for this purpose. They distract themselves as a way of regulating their emotions such as fear of failure.

8. There's more than one flavor of   10 procrastination. People procrastinate for different reasons. Dr. Ferrari identifies three basic types of procrastinators:

- Arousal types, or thrill-seekers, who wait until the last minute for the euphoric rush.
- Avoiders, who may be avoiding fear of failure or even fear of

success, but in either case are very concerned with what others think of them; they would rather have others think they lack effort than ability.

- Decisional procrastinators, who cannot make a decision. Not making a decision absolves procrastinators of responsibility for the outcome of events.

There are big costs to procrastination. Health is one. Just over the course of a single academic term, procrastinating college students had such evidence of compromised immune systems as more colds and flu, more gastrointestinal problems. And they had insomnia. In addition, procrastination has a high cost to others as well as oneself; it shifts the burden of responsibilities onto others, who become resentful. Procrastination destroys teamwork in the workplace and private relationships.

Procrastinators can change their behavior—but doing so consumes a lot of psychic energy. And it doesn't necessarily mean one feels transformed internally. It can be done with highly structured cognitive behavioral therapy.

Understanding and Reviewing the Reading

1. **Audience** How does Marano envision her intended audience, and what does she hope to achieve with this audience? How can you tell?

2. **Cause** According to Marano, what is the primary cause of procrastination?

3. **Background information** What information does Marano include to add credibility to her writing?

4. **Detail** According to the author, how does being nice enable procrastinators?

Analyzing the Reading

1. **Purpose** What main point does the author make, and how does that relate to her purpose in writing?

2. **Cause and effect** Identify the causes and effects discussed in Marano's essay. Is each cause or effect explained in a detailed and understandable way? Does she provide sufficient supporting evidence to prove the existence of a causal relationship between events? Explain.

3. **Language** The author states that procrastinators have to consume "a lot of psychic energy" in order to change their behavior. What is psychic energy, and how can it affect a change in behavior?

4. **Language** Dr. Ferrari, one of the associate professors of psychology interviewed, says, "Telling someone who procrastinates to buy a weekly planner is like telling someone with chronic depression to just cheer up." Explain the meaning of this statement.

Evaluating the Reading

1. **Visual** How does the photograph on page 525 add meaning to the essay? What type of visual might you suggest to the author that would further enhance the meaning of the essay? Is the tone of the visual's message consistent with the tone of the text? Explain your answers.

2. **Patterns** What other patterns of development does the author use? How do these patterns enhance the causal analysis?

3. **Conclusion** Consider Marano's conclusion. In what ways does it reinforce her main assertion about the topic? Do you find this ending satisfying? Why, or why not?

4. **Fact and opinion** Because authors often include both facts and opinions in their writing, it is up to the reader to distinguish verifiable facts from opinions or statements of belief. Use your knowledge of fact and opinion to determine whether the following statements from the article are facts or opinions. For each, include a brief explanation of why you think it is one or the other.

Statement	Fact or Opinion?
"There are many ways to avoid success in life, but the most sure-fire way just might be procrastination." (para. 1)	
"Twenty percent of people identify themselves as chronic procrastinators." (para. 3)	
"... there may be more of it in the U.S. than in other countries...." (para. 4)	
"Checking e-mail is almost perfect for this purpose." (para. 9)	
"People procrastinate for different reasons." (para. 10)	
"Procrastination destroys teamwork...." (para. 11)	

Discussing the Reading

1. The author of "Why We Procrastinate" presents both causes and effects of procrastination, but she does not discuss *all* of the causes and effects. There could be many more. Working with a small group of your peers, make a list of at least five causes and effects that were not mentioned in the reading. Be prepared to share your list and discuss it with the class.

2. Discuss the notion of self-regulation. Do you agree or disagree with Marano's statement that procrastination "represents a profound problem of self-regulation" (para. 4)? Defend your position.

Writing about the Reading

1. **Paragraph** Procrastination can have serious effects on your success in school. In a paragraph, write about a time you procrastinated with your schoolwork and describe the effects of that procrastination. Conclude the paragraph by discussing what you learned from the experience.

2. **Essay** To some people, procrastination is simply a bad habit. Brainstorm a list of bad habits you have. Choose one and write a cause-and-effect essay for your classmates describing the habit, the causes of it, and how it affects you. Be sure to fully explain the multiple causes and effects.

3. **Internet research** In the concluding paragraph of Marano's essay, she mentions cognitive behavioral therapy as a way to help procrastinators change their behavior. Conduct Internet research on cognitive behavioral therapy. Be sure to find information on why it is used and what results it produces. Using cause-and-effect analysis, write an essay that explores the reasons a psychologist or counselor would use cognitive behavioral therapy and the results gained from its use. There is a lot of information on this topic on the Internet, so consider narrowing your topic to three reasons a psychologist or counselor would use cognitive behavioral therapy.

TV as Birth Control: Defusing the Population Bomb

Fred Pearce is a British writer and journalist. His areas of interest include the environment, popular science, and development issues around the world. He has contributed articles to numerous publications, written books, and been an international speaker on environmental issues. "TV as Birth Control" first appeared in *Conservation* (Fall 2013), a quarterly science magazine, dedicated to environmental issues of worldwide concern.

Reading Tip

As you read, highlight and annotate the essay to identify the specific evidence the author provides to indicate the causal relationship that exists between TV and birth control.

Previewing the Reading

Preview the reading (see pp. 28–29), and then answer the following questions.

1. What countries does the author use as evidence of a causal relationship between TV and birth control?
2. What qualified Martin Lewis to investigate the decline in Indian fertility, and what method did he use in his research?

TV as Birth Control: Defusing the Population Bomb

Fred Pearce

Earlier this year Stanford human geographer Martin Lewis asked his students a simple question: How did they think U.S. family sizes compared with those in India? Between Indian and American women, who had the most children? It was, they replied, a no-brainer. Of course Indian women had more—they estimated twice as many. Lewis tried the question out on his academic colleagues. They thought much the same.

But it's not true. Indian women have more kids, it is true, but only marginally so: an average of 2.5 compared to 2.1. Within a generation, Indian women have halved the number of children they bear, and the numbers keep falling.

It's not that the population problem has gone away in India—yet. India has a lot of young women of childbearing age. Even if they have only two or three children each, that will still continue to push up the population, already over a billion, for a while yet. India will probably overtake China to become the world's most populous nation before 2030.

But India is defusing its population bomb. A fertility rate of 2.5 is only a smidgen above the long-term replacement level, which—allowing for girls who don't reach adulthood and some alarming rates of aborting female fetuses—is around 2.3. The end is in sight.

A TV in the living room might have the power to transform behavior in the bedroom.

5   With most of the country still extremely poor, this is a triumph against all expectations. And it offers some intriguing clues to a question that has dogged demographers ever since Paul Ehrlich published his blockbuster book *The Population Bomb*: What can persuade poor people in developing countries to have fewer babies?

Taking time off from bemusing his students, Lewis decided to investigate. Being a geographer, he tackled the question with maps. He noted that, within the overall rapid decline in Indian fertility, there continued to be great regional variations. So he mapped fertility in each Indian state and examined those patterns against the patterns for some of the demographers' favored drivers of lowered fertility. When he compared his maps, he found that variations in female education fit pretty well. So did economic wealth and the Human Development Index, which measures education, health, and income. The extent of urbanization looked like a pretty good match, too. But he also found that TV ownership tallied well with fertility across India. Not perfectly, he concluded, but as well as or better than the more standard

indicators. A TV in the living room, in other words, might have the power to transform behavior in the bedroom.

Surprising? Maybe not. Lewis was following the lead of Robert Jensen and Emily Oster, development economists from the University of California, Los Angeles, and the University of Chicago, respectively. Four years ago, they reported compelling direct evidence from Indian villages that TV empowers women. They carried out detailed interviews in rural India as commercial cable and satellite TV were replacing the mostly dull and uninspired government programming. The pair noted that the new diet of game shows, soap operas, and reality shows instantly became the villagers' main source of information about the outside world—especially about India's emerging urban ways of life. At the top of the ratings was *Kyunki Saas Bhi K'abhi Bahu Thi* (meaning "Because a mother-in-law was once also a daughter-in-law"). Based on life in the megacity of Mumbai, it was Asia's most watched TV show between 2000 and 2008 and was an eye-opener for millions of rural Indian women. They saw their urban sisters working outside the home, running businesses,

Continued >

controlling money, and—crucially—achieving these things by having fewer children. Here was TV showing women a world of possibilities beyond bearing and raising children—a world in which small families are the key to a better life.

Soap operas give viewers time to develop strong emotional bonds with the characters, many of whom live as they do and experience the life traumas that they do. The impact of the new TV programming in rural India has been profound—and very positive, say Jensen and Oster. Their interviews revealed that when the new TV services arrived, women's autonomy increased while fertility and the acceptability of domestic violence toward women significantly decreased. Most of the changes occurred within a few months of the arrival of TV reception, when (as they put it) "interactions with the television are more intense." In fact, the researchers found that TV's influence on gender attitudes, social advancement, and fertility rates was equivalent to the impact of an extra five years of female education. This was the social revolution that delivered the geographical variation in Lewis's maps.

There is a history to using soap operas to cut fertility. It goes back to Mexico in the late 1970s, a time when the average Mexican woman had five or six babies and Mexico City was becoming the world's largest megacity. Miguel Sabido, then vice president of Televisa, the national TV network, developed a soap-opera format in which viewers were encouraged to relate to a character on the cusp of doing right or wrong—a "transitional character" whose ethical and practical dilemmas drove the plotlines.

10   His prime soap opera, or telenovela, *Acompáñame* ("Accompany Me"),

focused on the travails of a poor woman in a large family living in a run-down shack in a crime-ridden neighborhood. She wanted to break out and, after many travails and setbacks, did so by choosing contraception and limiting her family size. It was a morality tale, and nobody could mistake the message. The lessons were reinforced with an epilogue at the end of each episode, giving advice about family planning services.

Some accused Sabido of crude social engineering. But according to research by the country's National Family Planning Program, half a million women enrolled at family planning clinics while the soap was on, and contraceptive sales rose 23 percent in a year. A rash of similar soap operas with names such as *Vamos Juntos* ("We Go Together") and *Nosotros las Mujeres* ("We the Women") ran in Mexico throughout the 1980s. They were credited, at least anecdotally, with helping slash Mexican fertility rates. Thomas Donnelly, USAID's local man at the time, concluded that they "have made the single most powerful contribution to the Mexican population success story."

The "Sabido Method" caught on. American population campaigner William Ryerson later launched the Population Media Center in Shelburne, Vermont, to promote it worldwide. Among many copycat shows were Jamaica's *Naseberry Street*, which ran from 1985 through 1989, a period during which the fertility rate on the Caribbean island fell from 3.3 to 2.9; and Kenya's long-running *Tushauriane* ("Let's Talk About It"), launched in 1987. It topped the ratings and coincided with a cut in Kenyan fertility rates from 6.3 to 4.4 children.

But the precise contribution of such programs to falling fertility rates was always elusive. And more sophisticated

TV viewers reacted against the crude propaganda of some Sabido soaps, with their clunky storylines and dialogue right out of government leaflets. The next wave of soap operas became more subtle: soft soap, if you will. Their narratives offered a realism that simply associated smaller families and use of family planning services with aspirational lifestyles, perfect family lives, and female emancipation. Thus it is not overt propaganda messages that really transform, so much as the window TV offers on a world previously unknown to most women. Seeing is believing.

Television's spread throughout the world is extraordinary. There are today something like 1.4 billion TV sets worldwide, or roughly one for every five people. In Asia and Latin America, even the poorest are glued to the box. In India, states where the average daily income is below two dollars per person still have TV sets in more than half of households, say Jensen and Oster.

15   In Africa, however, the spread has been slower. Across the continent, a billion people have only around 50 million TV sets. Government television broadcasting is mostly amateurish and unattractive. Satellite dishes to access other stations remain rare outside southern Africa. Most people still listen primarily to the radio.

But growing evidence suggests that TV could be the catalyst for change. In Kenya, *Makutano Junction*, a TV soap funded by the British government's Department for International Development (DFID) together with family planning agency Marie Stopes International, is now in its 12th series. The Sunday evening prime-time staple has 7 million viewers in Kenya and many more in neighboring Tanzania and Uganda. It addresses a range of social issues, with family planning at the forefront.

Since *Makutano Junction* went on air in 2001, Kenya's fertility rate has fallen from 5.0 to 3.8. DFID makes no great claim that *Makutano Junction* caused this drop. "The extent to which *MJ* is able to contribute to actual changes in behavior is difficult to establish," it says. But audience research shows viewers appreciate and act on "very specific and practical information" that *MJ* provides—for instance, how to find Marie Stopes clinics.

Similarly, Ethiopia's Amharic-language radio show *Yeken Kignit* ("Looking Over One's Daily Life"), broadcast from 2002 to 2004, coincided with an estimated fall in fertility rates in Amharic-speaking areas from 5.4 to 4.3. That also coincided with a big increase in demand for contraceptives in those areas, says the Population Media Center's Ryerson.

We should not think the power of soaps is a purely developing world phenomenon. Many argue that soaps have played a role in triggering changes in attitudes toward homosexuality and gay marriage in Europe and North America, for instance. And even Sabido-style programs are being tried in rich nations. Witness the arrival of online soaps with overt messages, such as *East Los High* at hulu.com. Launched in June 2013, the soap— funded by the Population Media Center with help from the California Family Health Council—targets Latino teens with tales of a girl from a single-parent household who struggles against temptation.

20   Looking back, it's ironic that many of the same activists warning of the population bomb back in the 1960s were also telling people to "kill your TV." They saw TV as a socially damaging technology, bringing in its wake violence, destructive consumer desires, and social dislocation.

Continued >

But TV can also be a force for good, giving isolated and underprivileged people—especially women—a window on different worlds and a sense that they can change their lives. It empowers and increases aspirations—and even delivers lower fertility rates. Could the humble soap save the world? Stay tuned.

Understanding and Reviewing the Reading

1. **Thesis** What is Pearce's thesis, and where does he state it directly?
2. **Detail** What type of TV programming seems to be most effective in cutting fertility rates?
3. **Meaning** What is Pearce's point in the final sentence of paragraph 13?
4. **Secondary effects** What secondary effects does the author present in the essay?
5. **Introduction** What does the opening anecdote about Martin Lewis and his students illustrate?

Analyzing the Reading

1. **Audience** Pearce is a journalist who reports on environmental and development issues around the world. How do you think he defined the readers for this essay: as other environmentalists, sociology students, general readers, or some other group? What makes you think so?
2. **Cause-and-effect relationship** In your own words, explain the causal relationship Pearce details. What implications does he suggest for the world's overpopulated countries?
3. **Language** In paragraph 13, the author speaks of *soft soap*. Explain the double meaning of these words. How do these two words and their meanings affect the tone of the paragraph?
4. **Purpose** Is Pearce's purpose basically to inform, or do you think he is making a larger argument here? Explain your answer.
5. **Visuals** How does the visual that accompanies the piece contribute to the overall tone of the piece? Be sure to notice the simplicity of the TV. Why do you think the author chose to use this picture when there are hundreds of pictures of TVs from which he could have chosen?
6. **Conclusion** Consider Pearce's conclusion. In what ways does it reinforce his main assertion about the topic? Do you find the ending satisfying? Explain your answer.

Evaluating the Reading

1. **Patterns** What other patterns of development does the author use? How do these patterns enhance the causal analysis?

2. **Statistical evidence** Throughout the essay, Pearce presents statistical comparisons to demonstrate a causal effect on fertility rates. What statistical evidence do you find to be most convincing? Explain your answer.

3. **Organization** Evaluate the essay's organization. Does Pearce present his list of effects in a meaningful order? If so, what is the method?

4. **Assumptions** What assumptions does Pearce make? Do you agree with them?

Discussing the Reading

1. Pearce presents a fairly simplistic solution to the rising fertility rate in developing countries. Do you agree with his solution? Can you think of other ways to attack this problem?

2. In paragraph 11, Pearce mentions the idea of social engineering, an attempt to influence the thoughts and behaviors of a certain segment of the population in order to produce a desired result. Can you think of an example of social engineering in the United States today? Do you think social engineering is ethical?

3. Working with a small group of your peers, brainstorm a list of soap operas (or programs of a similar genre) with which you are familiar. Once you have brainstormed, make a list of issues that have been presented through these shows. As you compare the programs, do you see any common themes emerging? Be prepared to share your ideas with the class.

Writing about the Reading

1. **Essay** In some countries, a family planning policy exists to curb population growth. This policy is enacted and implemented by the government. Write an essay in which you present what you believe is the proper balance between the negative impact on personal freedom of allowing a government to limit the number of children a couple may have and the benefits to society of the ultimate outcomes.

2. **Essay** In this essay, the author writes of a large segment of the population in developing countries that has been affected by television, specifically soap operas. As an individual, you also have been affected by both external and internal influences. Write a cause-and-effect essay in which you explore how you developed into the person you are today. Think about traits likely passed down to you genetically, as well as experiences and people that you believe shaped your core identity. To begin, brainstorm words you would use to describe yourself. Then choose three or four specific personality traits and explain their possible causes in your essay.

3. **Internet research** Write an essay focusing on the positive or negative effects of television on children. To begin, spend some time researching this phenomenon, looking specifically for data that support your ideas. Be sure to clearly identify the sources you find so that you can cite them correctly in your essay (see Chapter 19, "Finding and Using Sources").

📖 **COMBINING THE PATTERNS | TEXTBOOK EXCERPT: NUTRITION**

What Factors Contribute to Hunger around the World?

Joan Salge Blake and **Kathy D. Munoz** teach nutrition at Boston University and Humboldt State University, respectively. **Stella Volpe** is a professor and Chair of the Department of Nutrition Sciences at Drexel University. All three collaborated on *Nutrition: From Science to You*, an introductory nutrition textbook. This selection is excerpted from a chapter on hunger at home and abroad.

Reading Tip

As you read, make notes about the different types of evidence the authors use to support their main point.

Previewing the Reading

Preview the reading (see pp. 28–29 for guidelines), and briefly define the causes being explained and what, in general, is being affected in this causal relationship.

What Factors Contribute to Hunger around the World?

Joan Salge Blake, Kathy D. Munoz, and Stella Volpe

Hunger in the developing world is often caused by a complex set of factors. Once again, poverty lies at the heart of the problem; however, war, political unrest, agricultural challenges, disease, or natural disasters can also cause food insecurity for large numbers of people, particularly in Asian and African nations (Figure 1).

Discrimination and Inequality Promote Poverty

In many poor countries, discrimination and inequality exist at both the national and local levels. For example, at the national level, control over land and other assets is often unequal, so that even increased crop yields do not decrease food insecurity. Very few people in these countries own their own land, and a plentiful crop will primarily benefit the landowner, not the farm laborer. Women, especially, suffer from discrimination. The Hunger Project found that while women produce 50 percent of the world's food, they own only 1 percent of the land.

Cultural practices may also compromise access to food at the local or household level. In some cultures and within some families, the amount of food available to an individual is influenced by gender, control of income, education, birth order, and age. Gender inequity is a serious problem worldwide. In many cultures women and girls are viewed as less valuable than men and boys, and they therefore receive

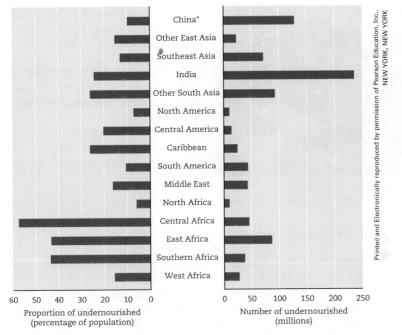

Figure 1 Number and Proportion of Undernourished People Many developing and least developed nations have high rates of food insecurity.

less food and education. In sub-Saharan Africa the ratio of boys' to girls' enrollment in primary and secondary schools is eight to one. Accordingly, two-thirds of the almost 900 million illiterate adults in the world are women. It is estimated that 70 percent of the 1.2 billion people who live in extreme poverty are female.

Political Sanctions and Armed Conflicts Disrupt the Food Supply

Political **sanctions** and agricultural embargoes create food shortages by decreasing access to agricultural supplies, fuel, or crops. Shortages of these crucial items often hurt the average citizen more than the government they are meant to target.

5   One country or group of countries may use sanctions to postpone or replace military action and force political change on another government. Other goals for sanctions include restoring democracy, condemning human rights abuses, and punishing groups that protect terrorists or international criminals. Sanctions often result in harm to innocent people and can create or intensify a cycle of chronic food shortages. Higher prices for fuel, food, and other essentials may deprive

sanctions: Boycotts or trade embargoes used by one country or international group to apply political pressure on another.

Continued >

Many hunger relief programs work to provide food aid to needy nations. However, successfully delivering the food to those who need it is often challenging.

average citizens of clean drinking water and food. Sanctions also contribute to a failing economy by decreasing household income. If the imposed sanction lowers the demand for certain products by blocking their import by other countries, businesses and workers that rely on this trade will suffer negative economic effects. All of these factors can lead to widespread food shortages that, if left unchecked, may cause a collapse in food production and distribution and, ultimately, famine.

Armed conflict is another serious problem. According to the World Food Programme, armed conflicts are a major cause of world hunger. War and civil and political unrest cause hunger because of the disruption to agriculture, food distribution, and normal community activities. During the past two decades, the world has experienced an increase in regional conflicts. Examples include ethnic warfare, terrorism, and internal struggles for resources in countries such as Colombia, Ethiopia, Rwanda, Somalia, Sierra Leone, Congo, and Sudan. During wars and regional conflicts, government money is often diverted from nutrition and food distribution programs and redirected toward weapons and military support. Conflicts have caused a rise in global hunger and overwhelmed the efforts of humanitarian agencies. Political turbulence can compromise humanitarian food distribution, making it difficult for food aid to reach the people in need. In some cases, assistance programs and aid workers may have to abandon war-torn areas and curtail their relief efforts.

Natural Disasters and Depleted Resources Limit Food Production

Natural disasters such as droughts, floods, storms, earthquakes, crop diseases, and insect plagues can create food and water shortages in any country. However, in American communities, relief programs are in place to help affected populations. In the developing world, the impact of natural disasters can completely devastate communities. Lack of communication and transportation systems, inadequate funding for relief programs, an inability to relocate populations from disaster-prone areas, and the incapacity to make homes and farms less vulnerable to destructive weather forces can all contribute to the problem.

Drought is the leading cause of severe food shortages in the developing world. When drought conditions exist or access to safe and clean drinking water is limited, **famine** and undernutrition result. This is particularly true in rural areas where people depend on agriculture for both food and income. Similarly, lack of water can force livestock owners to slaughter part of their herd or sell animals at "distress sales."

Floods and excessive rain can also destroy food crops, and are major causes of food shortage. For example, in India, more than 70 percent of the annual rainfall occurs during the three months of monsoon season. Farmers must contend with water scarcity for nine months of the year only to be faced with crop failure later if monsoon rains are overly heavy.

Shortsighted farming techniques can take a heavy toll on crops and farmland.

The depletion of natural resources also causes reduced food production. Specific agricultural practices such as the misuse of fertilizers, pesticides, and water may increase the yield in the short term, but inhibit production in the long term. When the population of a poor country expands and food is in short supply, critical decisions are often made concerning the use of water, forest resources, and land. These choices often pit the needs of the people against concerns for the environment, threatening limited resources even more. Thus, a long-term investment in preserving natural resources could help reduce poverty and hunger.

10

famine:
A severe shortage of food caused by weather-related crop destruction, poor agricultural practices, pestilence, war, or other factors.

Overpopulation Leads to Food Scarcity

The projected world population is 7.8 billion people by 2020, and 9.7 billion by 2050. Most of this growth is taking place in less developed regions, where the population in expected to rise from 5.4 billion people in 2007 to 8.3 billion people in 2050. Whenever rapid population growth occurs in areas that are strained for food production, the resulting **overpopulation** can take a toll on the local people's nutritional status.

People in the developing world tend to have more children due to poor health conditions. Because the infant and child death rate is so high, many children do not live to reach adulthood. Therefore, parents have more children to ensure that some of their offspring will survive into adolescence. Large families are needed to work on farms

overpopulation:
When a region has more people than its natural resources can support.

Continued >

to help generate income and to support older family members later in life. This tendency contributes to the cycle of poverty and hunger because the economy cannot sustain such rapid population growth. The World Bank promotes gender equality and development to break this cycle, ensuring that girls and women in particular receive a basic education.

THE TAKE-HOME MESSAGE

Factors that give rise to hunger around the world include poverty, discrimination, political sanctions and conflicts, poor agricultural practices, and overpopulation.

Understanding and Reviewing the Reading

1. **Textbook reading** What is a "political sanction" (para. 4)? According to the reading, how do political sanctions contribute to the world's hunger problem?
2. **Thesis** What is the central thesis of the selection?
3. **Causal chain** What causal chain is presented in paragraph 6? Explain it in your own words.
4. **Outline** Create an outline that would help you learn and remember the content of this reading.

Analyzing the Reading

1. **Similarities and differences** Compare this reading to another cause-and-effect reading in this chapter. What are some striking differences?
2. **Predicting exam questions** A useful way to prepare for an essay exam is to predict possible questions your instructor might ask and then to practice answering them. Compose an essay question that would likely appear on an exam covering this essay.
3. **Multiple patterns** Although the overriding pattern of organization in this reading is cause and effect, the authors also use other patterns throughout the reading. Identify the other patterns used by the authors.

Evaluating the Reading

1. **Value of information** Do you think that this selection taught you something useful? Explain your answer.
2. **Conclusion** At the end of the reading, the authors include a statement about the World Bank. Does this statement flow logically from the rest of the

reading? How well does it sum up the major focus of the reading? Explain your answer.

3. **Graphics** How helpful do you find the graph on page 537? How could you use it to study / learn the content it illustrates? What other type(s) of graphic could the authors have used to communicate their message? Explain your answer.

4. **Detail** Which three details from the reading do you find particularly strong and helpful in communicating the main message of the excerpt? Explain your answer.

Discussing the Reading

1. In paragraphs 4 and 5, the authors address the causal relationship of political sanctions to world hunger. There is some controversy surrounding the idea of forcing change in a government at the risk of hurting innocent citizens. Discuss this political tactic, where you have seen it used in today's world, and the ethical ramifications of such drastic measures.

2. The authors devote only one paragraph to overpopulation as a cause of world hunger. Discuss other possible effects of overpopulation in the world. What effects are we already suffering as a result of overpopulation?

3. The authors write in paragraph 10 about the depletion of natural resources as a cause of world hunger. How seriously do you take this issue? What efforts have you made to protect the environment and preserve natural resources? What changes can you make in your life to help preserve the natural resources of your world?

Writing about the Reading

1. **Summary** Assume you are preparing for a class discussion about this reading. Write a summary in which you answer the following question: How does gender inequality contribute to the world's hunger problem?

2. **Essay-exam answer** Write a cause-and-effect essay on the exam question you created for question 2 in Analyzing the Reading. Be sure to use a prewriting strategy (see Chapter 4) to help you plan your essay.

3. **Internet research** This textbook excerpt focuses on the causes of hunger in developing countries around the world. But in the United States, a well-developed country, there are starving people, too. Research this topic in order to write an essay on the causes of hunger in the United States.

Working with Cause and Effect as a Reader and Writer

The following table reviews the key elements of cause-and-effect essays and explains how these elements are important to both readers and writers.

Reading ⊕ Writing   Cause-and-Effect Essays

Element of a Cause-and-Effect Essay	The Reader's Perspective	The Writer's Perspective
Purpose	Examine your purpose for reading, and determine the writer's purpose for writing. Do your purposes match? Readers tend to read cause-and-effect materials when they seek a deeper understanding of a chain of events. Understanding the writer's purpose will help you determine how you can apply the information you are reading.	By stating or implying a specific purpose, you give your readers a reason to care about the causes and effects under discussion. Without a purpose, a cause-and-effect essay is just a collection of facts. Ask yourself, How will my readers *use* the information in my essay?
Causes and Effects	As you read, keep track of the causes and effects, perhaps by highlighting each cause and its effect(s) in a different color. Draw a graphic organizer to determine the essay's organization. Take notes in the margin, and clearly summarize which cause(s) lead to which effect(s).	To write a credible cause-and-effect essay, you must often conduct at least some preliminary research to ensure that you fully understand the causes and effects involved. Readers particularly appreciate writers who uncover (and then write about) hidden causes or false effects.
Recognizing and Dispelling Assumptions	As you read, identify your own assumptions and note where they agree or disagree with the author's. Determine how the author's recognition of assumptions affects your approach to reading and your willingness to accept the author's thesis.	As a writer, seek to establish common ground with your readers. Shared assumptions are a good way of "bonding" with readers early in the essay (but also in other parts of the essay).

| **Complete Explanations** | As you read, evaluate how completely and logically the writer has linked causes and effects. Be skeptical of causal essays in which effects are not traced cautiously and step by step. For example, no critical reader would accept "high taxes" as the cause of "an increase in teenage pregnancy." Several causal steps are missing between the cause and the outcome. | Providing complete explanations helps you establish your credibility as a writer. To write an effective causal essay, writers *themselves* must be convinced that the stated causes led to the stated effects. If you see gaps in your own logic or don't quite believe your own conclusions, it is time to reconsider the essay from scratch. |

In this chapter, you will learn to

- Recognize the elements of an argument.

- Identify the structure and content of argument essays.

- Understand, analyze, and evaluate argument essays.

- Write your own argument essay.

- Work with argument as a reader and a writer.

18
Argumentation: Supporting a Claim

© Buddie/Alamy

Reflect on a Visual Text

1 Ask yourself questions. Study the image at the left. It is a photograph of a demonstration. What is the issue? What is the demonstrators' position on the issue? What evidence would they likely offer in support of their position?

2 Brainstorm ideas. Brainstorm a list of other ways this issue could be depicted.

3 Write. Write a paragraph that could be used in place of this photo. Make a statement about the issue, and give several reasons to support your position on the issue.

The paragraph you just wrote makes an *argument*. It makes a claim about opposing violence toward black people. In everyday conversation, an argument can be a heated exchange of ideas between two people. For example, college roommates might argue over who should clean the sink or who left the door unlocked last night. In writing, however, an argument is a logical, well-thought-out presentation of ideas that makes a claim about an issue and supports that claim with reasons and evidence.

What Is an Argument?

An **argument** has three basic parts: an issue, a claim, and support.

- An **issue** is a problem or idea about which people disagree.
- A **claim** is a statement that tells readers the author's position on the issue.
- **Support** comes in the form of evidence that backs up the claim.

In most arguments, it is also important to argue against opposing viewpoints, which is known as **refutation**. The ability to construct and write sound arguments is an important skill in many aspects of life. For instance, political, social, and economic issues are often resolved through public and private debate.

Knowing how to construct an effective argument is also essential to success in college and on the job. For example, for a health science course you might write an argument essay claiming that the results of genetic testing, which can predict a person's likelihood of contracting serious diseases, should be kept confidential. As a lawyer representing a client whose hand was seriously injured on the job, you might have to argue to a jury that your client deserves compensation for the work-related injury.

A successful argument has all or most of the following elements:

1. It focuses on a narrowed issue.
2. It states a specific claim in a thesis.
3. It depends on careful audience analysis.
4. It presents reasons supported by convincing evidence.
5. It avoids errors in reasoning.
6. It appeals to readers' needs and values.
7. It recognizes opposing views.

Knowing how writers (and other communicators) use argument will help you understand, analyze, and evaluate this pattern when you read and help you use it in your own writing.

A Model Argument Essay

The following model argument essay will be used throughout this chapter to demonstrate strategies for reading and writing argument essays. Read it now, looking for the ways the writer uses the above argument techniques. Use the annotations in the margin to guide you.

Argument focuses on a narrowed issue: The issue here is not simply "the environment," which would be too broad. Rather, the issue is whether eating meat harms or helps the environment.

Eating Meat for the Environment

Lisa M. Hamilton

Lisa M. Hamilton is a writer and photographer who focuses on agricultural issues. She is the author of *Deeply Rooted: Unconventional Farmers in the Age of Agribusiness* (2009) and *Farming to Create Heaven on Earth* (2007). Her works have been published in *The Nation, Harper's, National Geographic Traveler, Orion,* and *Audubon,* where this essay originally appeared.

Argument depends on careful audience analysis: This article recognizes its audience's likely skepticism about the title and content. The author sets the essay up by acknowledging that readers want to help improve the environment.

In fall 2008 Rajendra Pachauri, head of the United Nations Intergovernmental Panel on Climate Change, offered a simple directive for combating global warming: Eat less meat.

Critics pointed out that the economist and environmental scientist is a vegetarian, but the numbers back up his idea. A 2006 U.N. report found that 18 percent of the world's greenhouse gas emissions come from raising livestock for food. While Pachauri's advice is good overall, I would propose a corollary: At the same time that we begin eating less meat, we should be eating more of it.

Argument states a specific claim in a thesis: The claim here is that eating more of a certain type of meat — from animals raised on organic pasture land — can be good for the environment.

More of a different kind, that is. Animals reared on organic pasture have a different climate equation from those raised in confinement on imported feed. Much of the emissions associated with livestock production come as the result of dismantling the natural farm system and replacing it with an artificial environment. For instance, in large-scale confinement systems, or CAFOs (concentrated animal feeding operations), manure has nowhere to go. Managed in human-made lagoons, it produces millions of tons of methane and nitrous oxide every year through anaerobic decomposition. On pasture, that same manure is simply assimilated back into the soil with a carbon cost close to zero.

Argument presents reasons supported by convincing evidence: The author's reasons are highlighted in green, the evidence in blue.

Some would argue that pasture-raised animals are just the lesser of two evils. Given that livestock make for some emissions no matter where they're raised — cows, for instance, like any other ruminant, produce methane as a by-product of their digestion — wouldn't it be better to have no livestock at all? Not according to

Argument recognizes opposing views:
Here the author acknowledges that her claim is likely to be controversial. The author goes on to refute the opposing view by providing evidence from Jason Mann's farm in the next paragraph.

farmer Jason Mann, who grows produce and raises chickens, hogs, and cattle on pasture outside Athens, Georgia. In the age of CAFOs, many people have come to regard livestock as a problem to be solved. But on a sustainable farm system like his, animals are an essential part of the equation.

Mann likens his farm to a bank account: Every time he harvests an ear of corn or a head of lettuce, he withdraws from the soil's fertility. If he doesn't redeposit that fertility, his account will hit zero. He could certainly truck in compost from 250 miles away or apply chemical fertilizers to make his vegetables grow. But by his own carbon calculation the best option is to return that fertility to the soil by using livestock, particularly cows. They do more than keep his soil rich. When cattle are managed properly, they can boost soil's ability to sequester carbon. Their manure adds organic matter to the soil, their grazing symbiotically encourages plant growth, and their heavy hooves help break down dead plant residue. Some proponents argue that highly managed, intensive grazing can shift cattle's carbon count so dramatically that the animals actually help reduce greenhouse gases. . . .

In addition to completing the farm's ecology, Mann's livestock also complement the farm's economy with critical revenue for the real bank account—which keeps the operation afloat in a way that lettuce alone cannot. But that happens only when animals become meat. With the exception of laying hens, if animals stand around eating all day but never produce more than manure, they are a net loss. In order for livestock to be worthwhile in a whole farm system, they must be eaten. For Mann's farm to be sustainable, his neighbors must buy and eat his meat.

The same applies on a larger scale: In order for pasture-based livestock to become a significant part of the meat industry, we need to eat more of its meat, not less. As it is, grass-fed beef accounts for less than 1 percent of U.S. beef consumption, and the numbers for chicken and pork hardly register. Even where the industry is growing, it is stunted by inadequate infrastructure. The greatest challenge is a lack of small-scale

Argument appeals to readers' needs and values:
The conclusion acknowledges readers' desire to help preserve the environment and to make decisions they feel good about.

slaughterhouses, but it also suffers from a dearth of research, outreach for new producers, and investment in breeding for pasture-based systems. And those things will change only as the market grows.

So by all means follow Rajendra Pachauri's suggestion and enjoy a meatless Monday. But on Tuesday, have a grass-fed burger—and feel good about it.

Note that one of the key aspects of argument is an omission: Argument avoids errors in reasoning. In "Eating Meat for the Environment," Lisa Hamilton's reasoning is strong and grounded in evidence. While her claim is controversial, her essay does not use faulty reasoning.

The Structure and Content of Argument Essays

In this section, you will learn about the structure of an argument essay and practice using the guidelines for understanding, analyzing, and evaluating argument essays. This key information will help you skillfully read and write essays that use argument.

Figure 18.1 shows the structure of an effective argument essay. Each part of the essay plays a role in helping to make the argument clear and compelling to readers.

1. THE INTRODUCTION OFTEN INCLUDES THE THESIS STATEMENT AND CLAIM AND IDENTIFIES THE ISSUE

The introduction, which usually includes the thesis statement and a claim, may provide background information about the issue. The issue should be narrow and specific rather than broad and general. The introduction might also make a subtle nod to (or an outright acknowledgment of) the audience's needs and values, suggesting why the issue is important and defining terms to be used in the argument.

A Narrowed Issue   Recall that a good issue is one that is a subject of controversy—a problem or an idea about which people disagree. Be sure, therefore, to choose an issue that people have different opinions about. For example, arguing that education is important in today's job market would be pointless because people generally agree on that issue. It would be worthwhile, however, to argue the merits of a liberal arts education versus technical training as preparation for after-graduation employment.

Figure 18.1   Graphic Organizer for an Argument Essay

Title		
Introduction		Issue
		Background information
		Definition of terms
		Thesis statement* (the claim)

⬇

Body paragraphs	Reasons and evidence	Reason 1
		Various types of evidence
		Reason 2
		Various types of evidence
		Reason 3
		Various types of evidence
	Emotional appeals	Need or value 1
		Need or value 2
		Need or value 3
	Opposing viewpoints	Opposing view 1
		Acknowledgment, accommodation, or refutation
		Opposing view 2
		Acknowledgment, accommodation, or refutation

⬇

Conclusion	Restatement of claim
	Final appeal to needs or values
	Request that readers take action

*The thesis statement may appear elsewhere within the argument.

The issue you choose should be narrow enough for an essay-length argument. When you narrow the issue, your thesis will be more precise and your evidence more specific. You will also be able to provide more effective arguments against an opposing viewpoint. A detailed and specific argument is a strong argument, leaving no "holes" or gaps for opponents to uncover. In "Eating Meat for the Environment," Lisa Hamilton focuses on the narrow issue specified in the title.

Background Information   Depending on the issue you choose and the intended audience, your readers may need background information. For example, in writing an argument about the need for more organ donations, you would provide information about the large numbers of people awaiting transplants. Lisa Hamilton begins her essay by providing background information about the United Nations' recommendation for combating global warming: Eat less meat.

Thesis Statement and Claim   The thesis statement in an argument essay makes a claim that reflects your position on the issue. The claim should be as narrow and as specific as possible. Here is an example of how a general claim can be narrowed to become a clear and specific thesis statement.

General	The use of animals in testing should be prohibited.
Specific	The testing of cosmetics and skin-care products on animals should be prohibited.

While all arguments make and support a claim, some also call for action. An essay opposing human cloning, for example, might argue for a ban on that practice and urge readers to take action, perhaps by voicing their opinion in letters to congressional representatives. Lisa Hamilton's essay both makes a claim — We should eat more meat, but pasture-raised meat — and calls readers to action: "Have a grass-fed burger — and feel good about it" (the last sentence of the essay).

Acknowledgment of Audience   Finally, most argument essays in their introduction acknowledge the audience in some positive way that engages readers and creates a sense of goodwill and trust toward the writer. Lisa Hamilton acknowledges her audience's desire to protect the environment by adding a "corollary" to the U.N. directive, not refuting it. This subtle technique likely opens readers' minds to her argument.

2. THE BODY PARAGRAPHS PRESENT THE REASONS AND EVIDENCE TO SUPPORT THE THESIS AND MAY INCLUDE EMOTIONAL APPEALS AND ADDRESS OPPOSING VIEWPOINTS

The body paragraphs should provide detailed reasons, supported by evidence, to back up the claim. Often one paragraph is devoted to each reason. The reason may be stated in the topic sentence, with the remainder of the paragraph consisting of evidence supporting it. Research and statistics are often cited as evidence. The body paragraphs may make emotional appeals, tied to the needs and values of the audience. They may also recognize or refute opposing viewpoints.

Reading ⊕ Writing The Introduction to an Argument Essay

The Reader's Perspective	The Writer's Perspective
When reading the introduction to an argument essay, identify the issue and the claim. Then determine what you already know about the issue. Doing so will help you decide how to read and what strategies to use to build comprehension and recall. If you already have a position on the issue, determine whether the essay agrees or disagrees with your position.	When writing an argument essay, especially if the practice is new to you, it is usually best to state your claim in a strong thesis early in the piece. Doing so will help keep your argument on track. As you gain experience with writing arguments, you can experiment with placing the thesis later in the essay.

Reasons and Evidence   A **reason** is a general statement that backs up a claim. It answers the question Why do I have this opinion about the issue? Each reason needs to be supported with evidence. Suppose, for example, you argue that high-school uniforms should be mandatory for three reasons: The uniforms (1) reduce clothing costs for parents, (2) eliminate distractions in the classroom, thus improving academic performance, and (3) reduce peer pressure. Each reason needs to be supported by **evidence** — facts, statistics, examples, personal experience, or expert testimony. Carefully linking evidence to reasons helps readers see how the evidence supports the claim.

Be sure to choose reasons and evidence that will appeal to your audience. In an argument about mandatory school uniforms, high-school students would probably not be impressed by the first reason listed above — reduced clothing costs for parents — but they might consider the second and third reasons if you cite evidence that appeals to them, such as personal anecdotes from students. For an audience of parents, however, facts and statistics about reduced clothing costs and improved academic performance would be appealing types of evidence.

The reasons offered in "Eating Meat for the Environment" clearly point to the benefits of eating more pasture-raised meat: The manure of pasture-raised animals goes back to the soil, with no carbon cost (paragraph 3); the same manure returns fertility to the soil (paragraph 5); managed properly, farm animals can reduce greenhouse gases (paragraph 5); selling animals for meat helps farmers like Jason Mann keep their farms going (paragraph 6); by buying pasture-raised meat, we can help the grass-fed meat industry expand (paragraph 7). Each reason has ample support and is likely to appeal to the audience's values and beliefs.

Avoiding Errors in Reasoning   In an argument essay, it is important to avoid introducing **fallacies**, or errors in reasoning or thinking. Table 18.1 provides a brief review of the most common fallacies.

Table 18.1   Common Logical Fallacies

Fallacy	Definition and Example
Circular reasoning (Begging the question)	Occurs when a writer simply repeats the claim in different words and uses the rewording as evidence. The statement "*Cruel* and unusual experimentation on helpless animals is *inhumane*" is an example.
Hasty generalization	Occurs when the writer draws a conclusion based on insufficient evidence. If you were to taste three pieces of chocolate cake and then conclude that all chocolate cake was overly sweet, you would be making a hasty generalization.
Sweeping generalization	Occurs when the writer claims that something applies to all situations without exception. The claim that all cameras are easy to use is a sweeping generalization.
False analogy	Results when a writer compares two situations that are not sufficiently similar. The fact that two items or events are alike in *some* ways does not mean they are alike in *all* ways. If you wrote, "Just as a human body needs rest after strenuous work, a car needs rest after a long trip," you would be falsely comparing the human body with an automobile.
Non sequitur ("It does not follow")	Occurs when no logical relationship exists between two or more connected ideas. "Because my sister is rich, she will make a good parent" is a non sequitur because no logical relationship exists between wealth and good parenting.
Red herring	Distracts readers from the main issue by raising an irrelevant point. For example, suppose you are arguing that television commercials for alcoholic beverages should be banned. Mentioning that some parents actually give sips of alcohol to their children would create a red herring, distracting readers from the issue of television commercials for alcohol.

Table 18.1   (continued)

Post hoc fallacy	Occurs when a writer assumes that Event A caused Event B simply because B followed A. The claim "Student enrollment fell dramatically this semester because of the appointment of the new college president" is likely a post hoc fallacy because other factors probably contributed to the decline in enrollment (such as changes in the economy or in the availability of financial aid).
Either-or fallacy	Occurs when a writer argues as if a multi-faceted issue had only two sides, one of which is correct. For instance, on the issue of legalizing drugs, a writer may argue that all drugs must be *either* legalized *or* banned, ignoring other positions (such as legalizing marijuana use for cancer patients undergoing chemotherapy).

Emotional Appeals   Although an effective argument relies mainly on credible evidence and logical reasoning, emotional appeals in the body of an essay can support and enhance a sound argument. **Emotional appeals** are directed toward readers' needs and values.

- **Needs** may be biological (such as the need to eat and to drink) or psychological (such as the need to belong and to have self-esteem).
- **Values** are principles or qualities that readers consider important, worthwhile, or desirable (honesty, loyalty, privacy, and patriotism, for example).

Lisa Hamilton's essay concludes with an emotional appeal: By eating meat, you'll be helping the environment. This appeal seeks to tap into readers' values — particularly their desire to engage in environmental conservation and "do the right thing."

Opposing Viewpoints   Recognizing opposing arguments within the body paragraphs forces you to think hard about your own claims — and perhaps to adjust them. In addition, readers will be more willing to consider your claim if you take their viewpoint into account. There are three methods of recognizing opposing views in an argument essay.

- When you **acknowledge** an opposing viewpoint, you admit that it exists and indicate that you have given it serious consideration.
- When you **accommodate** an opposing viewpoint, you acknowledge readers' concerns, accept some of them, and incorporate them into your own argument.
- When you **refute** an opposing viewpoint, you demonstrate its weaknesses.

These methods are not mutually exclusive. In paragraph 4 of Lisa Hamilton's essay, the author acknowledges an opposing viewpoint: that "pasture-raised animals are just the lesser of two evils." She then refutes this viewpoint by describing farmer Jason Mann's experience, describing pasture-raised animals as a worthy solution to a problem, not as the lesser of two evils.

Reading ⟲ Writing   The Body Paragraphs of an Argument Essay

The Reader's Perspective	The Writer's Perspective
When reading the body of an argument essay, consider whether you are in agreement or disagreement with the claim. Be aware that if you disagree with it, you may be inclined to quickly discount or ignore reasons or evidence, or if you agree with it, you may tend to accept the author's reasoning and evidence without analyzing it carefully.	When writing the body of an argument essay, be sure to use a tone appropriate for your audience. The tone you choose will depend on the issue, the claim, and whether your audience agrees, disagrees, or is neutral. For a weighty issue, such as use of the death penalty, a serious, even somber, tone would be appropriate. For a claim that calls for action, an energetic or enthusiastic tone would help motivate readers. For a disagreeing audience, you might use a friendly, nonthreatening tone.

3. THE CONCLUSION REINFORCES THE THESIS, MAKES A FINAL APPEAL, AND MAY URGE READERS TO ACTION

An argument may end in a number of ways, such as by restating the thesis, making a final appeal to values, projecting into the future, urging a specific action, or calling for further research. Lisa Hamilton's essay concludes by referring back to the opening with a call to action: Help the environment by eating pasture-fed meat.

Reading ⟲ Writing   The Conclusion of an Argument Essay

The Reader's Perspective	The Writer's Perspective
When reading the conclusion of an argument essay, ask yourself, Am I convinced? Why, or why not?	When writing the conclusion of an argument essay, reread your essay and ask yourself, Have I provided convincing evidence? What final statement will make my claim stick in my reader's mind or push neutral or disagreeing audiences toward agreement? Revise your conclusion as necessary.

Understanding, Analyzing, and Evaluating Argument Essays

In reading and writing argument essays, your goal is to get beyond mere competence. That is, you want to do more than merely understand the content of the essays you read or convey just your basic ideas to the audience you're writing for.

Understanding an Argument Essay

Reading arguments requires careful attention and analysis, so you should plan on reading an argument several times. Preview it to identify the issue and assess the overall level of difficulty. Read it once to get an overview. Then read it several more times to analyze and critique it. As you read and reread, use the skills you learned in Chapter 2 and look for answers to the following questions.

- **What does the title suggest about the focus and purpose of the essay?** A title such as "Voting: Why Not Make It Mandatory?" clearly suggests that the writer will advocate mandatory voting, while a title such as "Confusion in the Streets: A Call for Caring Treatment of Street People" will urge action on behalf of the homeless.

- **Who is the author, what are his or her credentials, and where was the essay published?** Some authors and publications are known for a particular (or biased) point of view, so be sure to read all headnotes, footnotes, and citations for information related to viewpoint, as well as to determine when the essay was first published and what qualifies the author to write on the subject. If the publication or author has a particular viewpoint or audience — such as liberal or conservative — you can sometimes predict the position an essay will take on a particular issue.

- **What is the issue?** Highlight the issue, and notice how the writer introduces it and any background information.

- **What do you already know about the issue?** Before reading, create two columns for pros and cons about the issue, and list as many ideas as you can in each column. If you think through the issue before reading, you will be less influenced by the writer's appeals and more likely to maintain an objective, critical viewpoint.

- **What is the claim?** Highlight the writer's claim. Notice any qualifying or limiting words.

- **What reasons and evidence does the author offer?** Study and highlight the types of evidence used to support the claim — facts, statistics, expert opinion, examples, and personal experience. Add annotations indicating your initial reactions to or questions about the reasons or evidence. Make marginal notes summarizing reasons and key supporting evidence.

- **Which terms are unfamiliar, and are they defined or left undefined?** Because an argument can depend on terms used in specific ways with specific meanings, highlight key terms and make sure to note exactly how they are defined. If any terms are undefined, seek out accurate definitions in other sources.

- **Does the writer acknowledge, accommodate, or refute opposing views?** Highlight each instance. It may help to create a graphic organizer to keep track of the author's view as well as his or her treatment of opposing positions. Figure 18.2 is a graphic organizer for "Eating Meat for the Environment."

Understanding in Action

Exercise 18.1

Following is one student's summary of the introduction of "Eating Meat for the Environment," including its thesis.

> Based on evidence that almost one-fifth of greenhouse gases are from livestock being raised for meat, the United Nations recommended that people eat less meat. The author agrees with this recommendation but says we should also eat more meat that comes from animals that are pasture raised.

Using the above summary as a model, write your own summary of the whole essay.

Analyzing an Argument Essay

Analyzing an argument essay involves examining the reasons and evidence provided to support the claim. Use the following questions to guide your analysis:

- **Is the claim narrow and specific?** The claim should be narrow enough to be fully addressed and supported in the essay.

- **What is the author's purpose?** Ask yourself, Why does the writer want to convince me of this? What, if anything, does he or she stand to gain? If a writer stands to profit personally from the acceptance of an argument, be particularly cautious and critical.

- **Is each reason supported with convincing, detailed evidence?** The evidence should be presented in a clear, understandable way.

- **Are key terms defined clearly and used consistently?** Each term should have one specific meaning that is used consistently throughout the essay.

- **Is the argument presented in a logical and organized way?** Expect authors to use paragraphing, headings, and transitional words and phrases to help readers follow the presentation of ideas.

Figure 18.2   Graphic Organizer for "Eating Meat for the Environment"

Title	Eating Meat for the Environment
Introduction	**Issue:** Eating meat and its effect on global warming
	Background: U.N. report showing 18% of greenhouse gases are from raising livestock for food, and call to eat less meat
	Claim (thesis): We should eat more meat from pasture-raised animals.
Body paragraphs	**Reason 1:** Carbon cost of manure from pasture-raised animals is close to zero.
	Opposing view: Pasture-raised animals are just the lesser of two evils.
	Refutation: From Jason Mann, who raises crops and livestock sustainably: Animals are an essential part of a sustainable system.
	Reason 2: Manure from pasture-raised animals returns fertility to the soil.
	Reason 3: Grazing and hooves of pasture-raised animals encourage plant growth, reducing greenhouse gases.
	Reason 4: Sale of meat from pasture-raised animals helps make environmentally sustainable farms economically profitable.
	Reason 5: To help this kind of farming expand, we must buy more pasture-raised meat.
	Evidence: Today less than 1% of U.S. beef, pork, and chicken comes from pasture-raised animals.
Conclusion	**Emotional appeal:** Eating (the right) meat can lead to feelings of doing the environmentally right thing, rather than of guilt.
	Returns to idea in introduction of eating less meat (a viewpoint that's been accommodated) and to opening claim, urging readers to eat pasture-raised meat

- **Does the author provide source citations where needed?** Sources, when used, should be properly and correctly documented. All paraphrases and quotations should be cited.
- **Are opposing viewpoints addressed?** The author should recognize, accommodate, or refute opposing ideas.

Analysis in Action

Exercise 18.2

Here the student who wrote the summary for Understanding in Action annotated the first two paragraphs of the essay.

Can the U.N. tell people to do this? And what's the connection?	In fall 2008 Rajendra Pachauri, head of the United Nations Intergovernmental Panel on Climate Change, offered a simple directive for combating global warming: Eat less meat.
Meaning Pachauri?	Critics pointed out that the economist and environmental scientist is a vegetarian, but the numbers
18% is a lot!	back up his idea. A 2006 U.N. report found that 18 percent of the world's greenhouse gas emissions come from raising livestock for food. While Pachauri's advice is good overall, I
What is a corollary? This doesn't seem possible!	would propose a corollary: At the same time that we begin eating less meat, we should be eating more of it.

Annotate the rest of "Eating Meat for the Environment" on your own.

📊 Evaluating an Argument Essay

Evaluating an argument essay involves judging how accurately and effectively the author presents and supports his or her claim. Use the following questions to guide your evaluation of argument essays:

- **Is the claim reasonable and logical?** The claim should be realistic, reasonable, and practical.
- **Is the evidence relevant, accurate, current, and typical?** Facts offered as evidence should be accurate, current, complete, and taken from reliable sources.
- **Is there sufficient evidence?** The author should provide a sufficient number of facts, statistics, examples, and so forth to fully support each reason. A variety of types of evidence should be offered.
- **Does the writer rely on emotional appeals?** Appeals are a legitimate part of an argument, but the writer should not attempt to manipulate your emotions to distract you from the issue and the evidence.

- **Are opposing viewpoints dealt with fairly?** The writer should not denigrate or ridicule opposing ideas. Instead, he or she should present reasoned responses to the ideas of others. When refuting opposing viewpoints, the writer should clearly show why they are wrong, misguided, or inappropriate.

- **Does the author avoid errors in reasoning?** If a writer makes errors in reasoning, you have the right to question his or her credibility. Check Table 18.1 (pp. 552–53) to make sure the essay does not include any fallacies.

Evaluation in Action

Exercise 18.3

The same student who wrote the summary and the annotations also wrote the following response to the essay's argument.

> Since I'm a vegetarian, this isn't an easy argument for me to agree with! I am impressed by the way Hamilton shows that if farmers raise animals for meat the right way, this can even reduce greenhouse gases. But if 99% of people are buying regular meat that isn't raised this way (maybe partly because they can't afford pasture-raised meat), it might be that there's no way to change things enough to make eating meat be good for the environment.

Using the above response as a springboard, write your own response to "Eating Meat for the Environment."

Writing Your Own Argument Essay

Now that you have learned about the major characteristics, structure, and purposes of an argument essay, you know everything necessary to write your own argument. In this section, you will read a student's argument essay and get advice on finding ideas, drafting your essay, and revising and editing it. You may want to use the essay prompts in "Readings for Practice, Ideas for Writing" (p. 569) or choose your own topic.

A Student Model Argument Essay

James Sturm wrote this essay when he was a student at Kalamazoo College, where he graduated with a degree in international and area studies. As you read, notice how Sturm uses comparison and contrast as well as illustration to strengthen his argument.

Pull the Plug on Explicit Lyrics

James Sturm

Title indicates position.

Introduction establishes common ground.

Many kids pass through a rebellious phase in middle school. If the teacher asks them to stop throwing pencils, they toss one more. If the sign reads "No Trespassing," they cross the line. If they hear their father listening to classical music, they tune in to rap and punk rock. This is exactly what I did, although I now look back with regret on my actions. Having matured significantly since my middle-school days, I understand the negative effect that explicit lyrics have on youth, and I believe such music should be off-limits until the age of sixteen.

Thesis statement clearly states claim.

Currently, the government takes a rather laissez-faire attitude with regard to the music industry. Thousands of albums are readily available to young people regardless of explicit content. In fact, the main control mechanism for protecting youthful consumers from harmful content comes from the recording companies themselves. Under the Parental Advisory campaign of the Recording Industry Association of America (RIAA), it is the responsibility of artists and record labels themselves to decide if their albums should receive the infamous "Parental Advisory: Explicit Content" label. Children are allowed to purchase the albums regardless ("Parental Advisory").

Background information: government regulation and record labeling
Source citation
Transition

This lack of regulation would not be a problem if the music did not produce negative effects on its listeners. Although it is difficult to prove statistically that music full of hateful content fuels similar attitudes in its listeners, it requires only common sense to understand why. That is, people are influenced by what they think about. If a child thinks, for example, that he is unimportant or unloved, then he will act out in various ways to gain attention from his peers. Problem thinking is a result of a variety of influences, including friends, parents, and the media. Negative music, if listened to frequently enough, naturally implants negative thoughts in the minds of its listeners.

Reason 1: Music influences listeners' attitudes.

Furthermore, consider the unique influence of music as opposed to other forms of media. Unlike movies, video games, and magazines, music has a way of saturating one's mind. Everyone knows the feeling of having a song "stuck" in their head, repeating itself throughout the day. Unlike a movie, which is seen once, discussed among friends, and then forgotten, a song can remain lodged in one's mind for weeks on end. And if the songs are

Reason 2: Music is more influential than other entertainment.
Evidence: We all know what getting a song stuck in our head feels like.

steeped in content such as violence against women, happiness found in harmful drugs, and hatred of the police, these themes will continue reverberating in the minds of the listeners, slowly desensitizing them to otherwise repulsive ideas. Becoming numb to such ideas is the first step toward passively agreeing with them or even personally acting upon them.

Reason 3: Children are strongly influenced by music.

Whereas adults can usually listen to such music with no behavioral ramifications, children are far more susceptible to its subtle influence. With less experience of life, a lower level of maturity, and a lack of long-term thinking, young people are prone to make impulsive decisions. Providing them with access to music that fuels negative and harmful thoughts is a dangerous decision. We live in an age where violent tragedies such as school shootings are increasingly commonplace. Although various factors contribute to such acts of violence, hatred-themed music is likely a part of the equation. Therefore, given the influential power of music and the heightened effect it can have on those still in the developmental stage of their lives, young people should have limited access to music with explicit lyrics.

Evidence:

accommodates opposing view while connecting music and violence

Offers an explanation for choosing sixteen as age cutoff

I propose sixteen years of age as a reasonable cutoff. Until children reach that age, they should not be allowed to purchase music with a Parental Advisory label. At sixteen, they are becoming young adults and making more and more of their own decisions. Before sixteen, they are weathering the turbulent transition from middle school to high school. This transition should not be accompanied by music that promotes rebellion as a means of coping with stress and difficulty. After reaching age sixteen, however, most young people will have obtained a driver's license, and the freedom that it allows eliminates the possibility of protecting youth from certain music. That is, those with a driver's license can seek out their own venues to hear explicit content, whether concerts or elsewhere.

Opposing view:
Three critiques are expressed.

The main critique of my position is not new. Many say that it's pointless to censor music's explicit content because, as the RIAA's Web site contends, "music is a reflection, not a cause; it doesn't create the problems our society faces, it forces us to confront them" ("Freedom of Speech"). It is true that music reflects our culture. But it is also true that music fuels the perpetuation of that culture, for better or for worse. Guarding youth from explicit music does not equate to ignoring the issues raised in the music. It merely delegates that task to adults rather than to children.

Another critique says that limiting youth access to explicit music would take a financial toll on the music industry. This is true, but it would also force the music industry to adapt. We can either allow the youth of our nation to adapt to the music industry, or we can force the industry to adapt to an impressionable generation of kids.

A third critique is that even if explicit music were restricted to those of a certain age, younger kids would find access to it anyway. This is a legitimate concern, especially given the explosion of music-downloading software. But if not only music outlet stores but also online companies such as Amazon.com and iTunes were included in the regulations, progress would surely come.

Conclusion quotes hip-hop artist to offer final support for claim.

Hip-hop artist Ja Rule has spoken in favor of the current Parental Advisory system, saying, "That's what we can do as musicians to try to deter the kids from getting that lyrical content." But he added, "I don't think it deters the kids—it's just another sticker on the tape right now" (Bowes). Even hip-hop artists agree that protecting the minds of our youth is a necessity. But until laws are passed to restrict access to this music, the "Parental Advisory" label will just be another logo on the CD cover.

Works Cited

Sources are documented.

Bowes, Peter. "Spotlight on Explicit Lyrics Warning." *BBC News World Edition*, 27 May 2002, news.bbc.co.uk/2/hi/entertainment /2010641.stm.

"Freedom of Speech." *RIAA*, Recording Industry Association of America, riaasalestool.shoshkey.com/aboutus.php?content _selector=History. Accessed 17 Sept. 2012.

"Parental Advisory." *RIAA*, Recording Industry Association of America, www.riaa.com/resources-learning/parental-advisory -label/. Accessed 18 Sept. 2012.

Responding to Sturm's Essay

1. Discuss Sturm's proposal to ban the sale of "explicit music" to children. How is children's access to other media — such as books, movies, magazines, and TV shows — treated similarly or differently?

2. What is the benefit, if any, of having explicit lyrics in music? Why are they needed, or why should they be allowed at all?

3. Write an essay discussing the following dilemma: A middle-school student wants to listen to explicit music, but it is not legally available to her age group and her parents do not want her to have access to it. Is there a compromise position? What advice would you offer to each side?

Finding Ideas for Your Argument Essay

Reading assignments for this class and your other college courses are good sources of ideas for argument essays. Class discussions and college lectures are other good sources. You can also discover issues by reading or listening to the national news, reading print or online magazines, reading blogs, and checking social media. If you keep a writing journal, you may find good ideas there, as well. Here are a few guidelines to use in choosing an issue.

- **Think about issues on which you've heard different positions.** These can be school or community issues or national or international ones — or they can simply be issues related to people's everyday lives.
- **Think about a topic on which you *haven't* heard different positions.** Are there nevertheless different positions that could be taken?
- **Brainstorm about *various* — not just two — different sides of an issue.** Think of reasons and evidence that support these different viewpoints.
- **Look online to see what people are saying about a topic that interests you.** Or go to an online newspaper and read people's comments on articles. (These comments can be eye-opening, even shocking.)

Selecting an Issue to Write About

The first step is to choose an issue that interests you and that you want to learn more about. Also consider how much you already know about the topic; if you choose an unfamiliar issue, you will need to conduct extensive research. To discover a workable issue, try some of the prewriting strategies discussed in Chapter 4. Regardless of the issue you choose, make sure that it is arguable and that it is narrow enough for an essay-length argument.

Considering Your Audience

Once you choose an issue, think about the audience for your essay. The reasons and the types of evidence you offer, and the needs and values to which you appeal, will all depend on the audience. Ask the following questions to analyze your intended readers:

- What do my readers already know about the issue? What do they still need to know?
- Do my readers care about the issue? Why, or why not?

Because an argument is intended to influence readers' thinking, it is important to determine not only how familiar readers are with the issue but also their likely position: Will they be likely to agree with the claim, be neutral about or waver on it, or disagree with it?

- **Agreeing audiences**   When writing for an audience that will likely agree with your claim, the focus is usually on urging readers to take action.

Instead of presenting large amounts of evidence, concentrate on reinforcing your shared viewpoint and building emotional ties with the audience. By doing so, you encourage readers to act on their beliefs.

- **Neutral or wavering audiences**   Neutral readers may be somewhat familiar with the issue, but they usually do not have strong feelings about it. Instead, they may have questions or misunderstandings about it, or they may simply be uninterested. In writing for this type of audience, be straightforward. Emphasize the importance of the issue, and offer explanations that clear up possible misunderstandings. Your goals are to establish your credibility, engender readers' trust, and present solid evidence in support of your claim.

- **Disagreeing audiences**   The most challenging type of audience is the disagreeing audience because they believe their position is correct and are not eager to accept your views. They may also distrust you because you don't share their views on something they care deeply about.

In writing for a disagreeing audience, your goal is to persuade readers to consider your views on the issue. Be sure to follow a logical line of reasoning. Rather than stating your claim early in the essay, for this type of audience it may be more effective to build slowly to your thesis. First establish **common ground** — a basis of trust and goodwill — with readers by mentioning interests, concerns, and experiences that you share. Then, when you state your claim, the audience may be more open to considering your argument.

Developing a Claim in Your Thesis

Research is often an essential part of developing an argument. Reading what others have written on the issue helps you gather crucial background information, reliable evidence, and alternative viewpoints. For many arguments, you will need to consult both library and Internet sources.

After doing research about the issue, your views on it may soften, harden, or change in some other way. For instance, research on the mandatory use of seat belts may turn up statistics, expert testimony, and firsthand accounts of lives saved by seat belts in automobile accidents, leading you to reconsider your earlier view opposing mandatory use. Therefore, before developing a thesis and making a claim, reconsider your views in light of your research.

As noted earlier, the thesis for an argument essay makes a claim about the issue. As you draft your thesis, be careful to avoid general statements that are not arguable. Instead, make your claim arguable and specific, and state it clearly. Note the difference between a vague statement and a specific claim in the following examples.

Vague	In recent years, U.S. citizens have experienced an increase in credit-card fraud.
Specific	Although the carelessness of merchants and electronic tampering contribute to the problem, U.S. consumers are largely to blame for the recent increase in credit-card fraud.

The first example merely states a fact and is not a valid thesis for an argument. The second example makes a specific arguable claim about an issue.

Considering Opposing Viewpoints

Once you are satisfied with your claim, reasons, and evidence, you are ready to consider opposing viewpoints; it is time to decide how to acknowledge, accommodate, and / or refute them. If you fail to at least acknowledge opposing viewpoints, readers may assume that you did not think the issue through or that you dismissed alternative views without seriously considering them. In some situations, you may choose merely to acknowledge opposing ideas. At other times, you may need to accommodate opposing views, refute them, or both.

Create a list of all the pros and cons on your issue, if you haven't already done so. Then make another list of all possible objections to your argument. Try to group the objections to form two or more points of opposition.

To acknowledge an opposing viewpoint without refuting it, you can mention the opposition in your claim, as shown in this claim about sexual harassment.

> Although mere insensitivity may occasionally be confused with sexual harassment, most instances of sexual harassment are clear-cut.

The opposing viewpoint mentioned here is that insensitivity may be confused with sexual harassment. By including the opposing viewpoint as part of the claim, the writer shows that he or she takes it seriously.

To accommodate an opposing viewpoint, find a portion of the opposing argument that you can build into your own argument. One common way to accommodate readers' objections is to suggest alternative causes for a particular situation. For example, suppose your argument defends the competency of most high-school teachers. You suspect, however, that some readers think the quality of most high-school instruction is poor and attribute it to teachers' laziness or lack of skill. You can accommodate this opposing view by recognizing that there are some high schools in which poor instruction is widespread. You could then suggest that the problem is often owing to a lack of instructional supplies and students' disruptive behavior rather than to teachers' incompetence.

If you choose to argue that an opposing view is not sound, you must refute it by pointing out problems or flaws in your opponent's reasoning or evidence. Check to see if your opponent uses faulty reasoning or fallacies. To refute an opponent's evidence, use one or more of the following strategies:

1. **Give a counterexample, or exception, to the opposing view.** For instance, if an opponent argues that dogs are protective, give an example of a situation in which a dog did not protect its owner.
2. **Question the opponent's facts.** If an opponent claims that few professors give essay exams, present statistics demonstrating that a significant percentage of professors do give essay exams.

3. **Demonstrate that an example is not representative.** If an opponent argues that professional athletes are overpaid and cites the salaries of two famous quarterbacks, cite statistics showing that these salaries are not representative of those of professional athletes overall.

4. **Demonstrate that the examples are insufficient.** If an opponent argues that horseback riding is a dangerous sport and offers two examples of riders who were seriously injured, point out that two examples are not sufficient proof.

5. **Question the credibility of an authority.** If an opponent quotes a television personality regarding welfare reform, point out that the TV personality is not a sociologist or a public-policy expert and therefore is not an authority on welfare reform.

6. **Question outdated examples, facts, or statistics.** If an opponent presents dated evidence to support an argument in favor of more campus parking, you can argue that the situation has changed (for example, enrollment has declined or bus service has increased).

7. **Present the full context of a quotation or statistical evidence.** If an opponent cites incomplete statistics from a research study linking sunburn and skin cancer, you can put the statistics in context to show that your opponent has "edited" the evidence to suit his or her claim.

Drafting Your Argument Essay

You are now ready to organize your ideas and draft your essay. To organize and draft your argument, you must decide on a line of reasoning, choose a method of organization, and develop the essay accordingly.

Here are four common ways to organize an argument.

Method I	Method II	Method III	Method IV
Claim/thesis	Claim/thesis	Support	Opposing viewpoints
Support	Opposing viewpoints	Opposing viewpoints	Support
Opposing viewpoints	Support	Claim/thesis	Claim/thesis

The method you choose will depend on your audience, purpose, and issue. Often, it is best to state your claim at the outset. In some cases, however, stating the claim at the end of the argument is more effective. You also need to decide whether to present reasons and supporting evidence before or after you discuss opposing viewpoints. Finally, decide the order in which you will discuss your reasons and supporting evidence: Will you arrange them from strongest to weakest? From most to least obvious? From most familiar to unfamiliar?

Once you have chosen a method of organization, it is time to write the first draft. Use the following guidelines:

1. **Write an effective introduction.** The introduction should identify the issue and offer background information based on the audience's knowledge and experience. Many introductions to argument essays also include a thesis, where the writers make their claim. To engage your readers, you might relate a personal experience, make an attention-getting remark, or recognize a counterargument.

2. **In the body paragraphs, clearly state the reasons for your claim, and provide supporting evidence.** Each reason can be used to anchor the evidence that follows it. One approach is to use each reason as a topic sentence. The rest of the paragraph and perhaps some that follow would then consist of evidence supporting that particular reason.

3. **Cite the sources of your research.** As you present the evidence, you must include a citation for each quotation, summary, or paraphrase of ideas or information you borrowed from sources.

4. **Use transitions to help readers follow your argument.** Make sure you use transitions to move clearly from reason to reason, as in "*Also relevant to the issue . . .*" and "*Furthermore*, it is important to consider . . . ." Also, be certain to distinguish your reasons and evidence from those of the opposition. Use a transitional sentence—such as "Those opposed to the death penalty claim . . ."—to indicate that you are about to introduce an opposing viewpoint. A transition can also be used to signal a refutation, such as "Contrary to what those in favor of the death penalty maintain, ..."

Revising Your Argument Essay

If possible, set your draft aside for a day or two before rereading and revising it. Then, as you review your draft, focus on discovering weak areas and strengthening the overall argument, not on grammar or mechanics. Use the flowchart in Figure 18.3 (p. 568) to guide your analysis.

Editing and Proofreading Your Essay

The last step is to check your revised essay for errors in grammar, spelling, punctuation, and mechanics. In addition, be sure to look for the types of errors you tend to make in any writing, whether for this class or in other situations. Check the handbook (pp. 645–714) for assistance with common errors in your writing.

Figure 18.3 Revising an Argument Essay

QUESTIONS		REVISION STRATEGIES

1. Issue Is the issue clearly defined? Is enough information provided? Is the issue sufficiently narrow?

> No

- Ask a friend unfamiliar with the issue to read the definition of the issue and identify missing information.
- Use a branching diagram or questions to limit your issue (see Chapter 4).

↓ Yes

2. Thesis Is your claim stated clearly in your thesis? Is it arguable? Is it sufficiently specific and limited?

> No

- Write a one-sentence summary of what the essay intends to prove.
- Try limiting the claim.
- Add a qualifying word or phrase (*may, possibly*) to your thesis.

↓ Yes

3. Intended audience Is your essay targeted to your readers—to their knowledge and attitudes? Do you appeal to their needs and values?

> No

- Add more background information.
- Add reasons and evidence based on the needs, values, and experiences you share with your readers.

↓ Yes

4. Reasons and evidence Do you have enough reasons and evidence? Will they be convincing and appealing to your audience?

> No

- Brainstorm or conduct research to discover more reasons, stronger evidence, or more appealing reasons and evidence.

↓ Yes

5. Argument progression Does each step follow a logical progression? Is your reasoning free of errors?

> No

- Check progression by creating an outline or a graphic organizer.
- Omit faulty reasoning and fallacies.

↓ Yes

6. Organization Is your method of organization clear? Is it effective?

> No

- Experiment with one or more other methods of organization (see Chapter 7).

↓ Yes

7. Opposing viewpoints Do you acknowledge, accommodate, or refute opposing viewpoints?

> No

- Acknowledge an opposing viewpoint.
- Build an opposing viewpoint into your argument.
- Refute an opponent's evidence.

↓ Yes

8. Introduction and conclusion Are they effective?

> No

- Revise your introduction and conclusion so that they meet the guidelines in Chapter 7.

Readings for Practice, Ideas for Writing

Ain't I a Woman?

Originally named Isabella Baumfree, **Sojourner Truth** was born into slavery in New York in about 1795. As a child and young adult, she was sold several times until she finally escaped to freedom in 1827. For a while, she lived with a Quaker family, but then she struck out on her own, working as a housekeeper and living in the homes of several preachers. In 1843, she changed her name to Sojourner Truth and became a traveling preacher. It was also during this time that Truth became an outspoken anti-slavery and women's rights activist. Although she never learned to read or write, she delivered powerful speeches on equality for slaves and women as she traveled throughout the northeast and midwest.

One of the most powerful and memorable speeches of Sojourner Truth was "Ain't I a Woman?" On May 29, 1851, she attended the Ohio Women's Rights Convention in Akron, Ohio. Sitting alone in a corner of the building, Truth heard several male ministers arguing from the floor that women should not have the same rights as men. Spontaneously rising from her seat, Sojourner Truth walked to the podium as some members appealed to the president of the Convention to deny her the right to speak. Instead, the president silenced the crowd and yielded the podium to Truth. Confident and impassioned, she delivered her speech. As you read the speech, note Truth's masterful use of repetition and the way she refutes the ministers' argument.

Reading Tip

Try reading the speech aloud so that your ear gets used to the sound of the words. Or listen to an authentic reading of the speech by accessing a Web site that archives historical speeches (for example, www.history.com/speeches). These strategies will help you to more easily comprehend the meaning and tone of Truth's speech.

Previewing the Reading

Preview the reading, using the guidelines on pages 28–29 to discover the issues Truth is addressing.

Ain't I a Woman?

=== SOJOURNER TRUTH ===

Well, children, where there is so much racket there must be something out of kilter. I think that 'twixt the negroes of the South and the women at the North, all talking about rights, the white men will be in a fix pretty soon. But what's all this here talking about?

Continued >

That man over there says that women need to be helped into carriages, and lifted over ditches, and to have the best place everywhere. Nobody ever helps me into carriages, or over mud-puddles, or gives me any best place! And ain't I a woman? Look at me! Look at my arm! I have ploughed and planted, and gathered into barns, and no man could head me! And ain't I a woman? I could work as much and eat as much as a man—when I could get it—and bear the lash as well! And ain't I a woman? I have borne thirteen children, and seen most all sold off to slavery, and when I cried out with my mother's grief, none but Jesus heard me! And ain't I a woman?

Then they talk about this thing in the head; what's this they call it? [member of audience whispers, "intellect"] That's it, honey. What's that got to do with women's rights or negroes' rights? If my cup won't hold but a pint, and yours holds a quart, wouldn't you be mean not to let me have my little half measure full?

Then that little man in black there, he says women can't have as much rights as men, 'cause Christ wasn't a woman! Where did your Christ come from? Where did your Christ come from? From God and a woman! Man had nothing to do with Him.

5   If the first woman God ever made was strong enough to turn the world upside down all alone, these women together ought to be able to turn it back, and get it right side up again! And now they is asking to do it, the men better let them.

Obliged to you for hearing me, and now old Sojourner ain't got nothing more to say.

Understanding and Reviewing the Reading

1. **Detail** Why did Truth invite the audience to look at her arm?

2. **Detail** What information does Truth divulge about her life as a slave?

3. **Conclusion** In a sentence or two, explain what it is that men had better let women do.

4. **Analogy** Explain the analogy Truth makes between intellect and a cup. What does she say that men should let women have?

5. **Organization** To analyze Truth's organization, complete the graphic organizer on the next page.

Analyzing the Reading

1. **Audience** Truth delivered "Ain't I a Woman?" to a diverse crowd assembled for a women's rights convention. What kind of audience was Truth addressing—agreeing, neutral or wavering, or disagreeing—and how did that affect her argument? Be sure to read the background information included before the reading.

2. **Claim** What claim does Truth make? How does she present it?

3. **Evidence** What kinds of reasons and evidence does Truth use to support her claim? Are her details persuasive? Why or why not?

4. **Opposing viewpoints** What opposing viewpoints does Truth address? Explain how she recognizes them and counters them.

Title	Ain't I a Woman?
Introduction	**Background** on the issues that Truth intends to discuss
	Claim (thesis):
Body paragraphs	**Reason 1:**
	Evidence:
	Reason 2:
	Evidence:
	Reason 3:
	Evidence:
	Opposing view 1:
	Refutation:
	Opposing view 2:
	Refutation:
	Opposing view 3:
	Refutation:
Conclusion	

5. **Needs and values** Identify the needs and values that Truth appeals to. How effectively do these emotional appeals strengthen her argument? Explain your answer.

6. **Language** In her speech, Truth addresses her audience as "children" and "honey." How do these words affect the tone of the speech?

Evaluating the Reading

1. **Structure of a speech** A well-written speech captures the audience's attention and keeps listeners interested. How does Truth capture the audience in "Ain't I a Woman?"

2. **Title** Sojourner Truth's speech to the Ohio Women's Rights Convention did not have a title. How well do you think the title assigned to the speech, "Ain't I a Woman?," predicts and summarizes the argument? What title would you suggest for this speech?

3. **Conclusion** Evaluate the conclusion of the speech. What final impression does it make? Explain how it appeals to values, projects into the future, or urges listeners to take action—or does all three.

4. **Fact versus opinion** Is Truth's essay made up primarily of fact or opinion? Explain how this balance affects the effectiveness of the argument.

Discussing the Reading

1. Discuss what you know about the women's rights movement in America. What has been accomplished since the time of Sojourner Truth?

2. Sojourner Truth is a pseudonym for Isabella Baumfree. Discuss some possible meanings of the name, why you think she chose the name, and how her life and work exemplified that name.

Writing about the Reading

1. **Essay** Sojourner Truth was an impassioned advocate for women's rights and racial equality. How far have Americans come in these two areas? Have we just traded one inequality for another (for example, income, age, gender, health, housing, education)? Choose a realm in which inequality still exists in this nation, and write an argument essay that demonstrates the existence of this inequality and suggests a remedy.

2. **Essay** Though she was an escaped and then emancipated slave with little to no voice, Sojourner Truth never missed the opportunity to boldly speak for the rights of women and slaves. By doing so, she rallied hundreds of people to join her in her quest for freedom from the chains that bound women and slaves. As citizens, it is our obligation to become involved if we want to effect change. One of the most basic levels of involvement is voting, yet voting rates have been declining since the 1960s. In an essay, argue for the importance of voting. Your audience is people in their late teens and early twenties.

3. **Internet research** Listen to some speeches from the History Channel's archive (www.history.com/speeches) or another Web site that archives historical speeches. Browse the collection and choose a speech that uses argument to call people to action, such as John F. Kennedy's inaugural address. Evaluate its effectiveness, and then write an essay in which you argue that the speech does or does not have relevance today. To better understand the context of the speech, it may be necessary to conduct further research.

Why Would Anyone Miss War?

Sebastian Junger is the best-selling author of *The Perfect Storm*, *A Death in Belmont*, *Fire*, and *War*. He also codirected the documentary *Restrepo*, which won a Grand Jury Prize at the 2010 Sundance Film Festival. This opinion piece appeared in the *New York Times* in 2011.

Reading Tip

As you read, highlight those sentences in the text that best summarize the writer's main argument.

Previewing the Reading

Preview the reading using the guidelines on pages 28–29, and then answer the following questions.

1. What war is this essay primarily concerned with?
2. What is the writer's attitude toward war?

SEBASTIAN JUNGER

Why Would Anyone Miss War?

Several years ago I spent time with a platoon of army infantry at a remote outpost in eastern Afghanistan, and after the deployment I was surprised that only one of the soldiers chose to leave the military at the end of his contract; many others re-upped and eventually went on to fight for another year in the same area. The soldier who got out, Brendan O'Byrne, remained a good friend of mine as he struggled to fit in to civilian life back home.

About a year later I invited Brendan to a dinner party, and a woman asked him if he missed anything at all about life at the outpost. It was a good question: The platoon had endured a year without Internet, running water, or hot food and had been in more combat than almost any platoon in the United States

military. By any measure it was hell, but Brendan didn't hesitate: "Ma'am," he said, "I miss almost all of it."

Civilians are often confused, if not appalled[1], by that answer. The idea that a psychologically healthy person could miss war seems an affront to the idea that war is evil. Combat is supposed to feel bad because undeniably bad things happen in it, but a fully human reaction is far more complex than that. If we civilians don't understand that complexity, we won't do a very good job of bringing these people home and making a place for them in our society.

My understanding of that truth came partly from my own time in Afghanistan and partly from my conversations with a Vietnam veteran named Karl Marlantes, who wrote about his experiences in a devastating novel called *Matterhorn*. Some time after I met Karl, a woman asked me why soldiers "compartmentalize"[2] the

[1] **appalled** Overcome with shock or horror.
[2] **compartmentalize** Separate or set aside from other experiences.

Continued >

experience of war, and I answered as I imagined Karl might have: because society does. We avoid any direct look at the reality of war. And both sides of the political spectrum indulge in this; liberals tend to be scandalized that war can be tremendously alluring to young men, and conservatives rarely acknowledge that war kills far more innocent people than guilty ones. Soldiers understand both of these things but don't know how to talk about them when met with blank stares from friends and family back home.

5   "For a while I started thinking that God hated me because I had sinned," Brendan told me after he got back from Afghanistan. "Everyone tells you that you did what you had to do, and I just hate that comment because I didn't have to do any of it. I didn't have to join the army; I didn't have to become airborne infantry. But I did. And that comment—'You did what you had to do'—just drives me insane. Because is that what God's going to say—'You did what you had to do? Welcome to heaven?' I don't think so."

If society were willing to acknowledge the very real horrors of war—even a just war, as I believe some are—then men like Brendan would not have to struggle with the gap between their worldview and ours. Every year on the anniversary of D-Day, for example, we acknowledge the heroism and sacrifice of those who stormed the beaches of Normandy. But for a full and honest understanding of that war, we must also remember the firebombing of Dresden, Frankfurt, and Hamburg that killed as many as 100,000 Germans, as well as both conventional and nuclear strikes against Japan that killed hundreds of thousands more.

Photographs taken after Allied air raids in Germany show piles of bodies 10 or 15 feet high being soaked in gasoline for burning. At first you think you're looking at images from Nazi concentration camps, but you're not—you're looking at people we killed.

Marine waits to take psychological tests at the Marine Corps Air Ground Combat Center in Twentynine Palms, CA.

I am in no way questioning the strategic necessity of those actions; frankly, few of us are qualified to do so after so much time. I am simply pointing out that if we as a nation avoid coming to terms with events like these, the airmen who drop the bombs have a much harder time coming to terms with them as individuals. And they bear almost all the psychic harm.

Change history a bit, however, and imagine those men coming back after World War II to a country that has collectively taken responsibility for the decision to firebomb German cities. (Firebombing inflicted mass civilian casualties and nearly wiped out cities.) This would be no admission of wrongdoing—many wars, like Afghanistan and World War II, were triggered by attacks against us. It would simply be a way to commemorate the loss of life, as one might after a terrible earthquake or a flood. Imagine how much better the bomber crews of World War II might have handled their confusion and grief if the entire country had been struggling with those same feelings. Imagine how much better they might have fared if there had been a monument for them to visit that commemorated all the people they were ordered to kill.

10   At first, such a monument might be controversial—but so was the Vietnam memorial on the Mall in Washington.

Eventually, however, that memorial proved to be extremely therapeutic for veterans struggling with feelings of guilt and loss after the war.

Every war kills civilians, and thankfully our military now goes to great lengths to keep those deaths to a minimum. Personally, I believe that our involvement in Afghanistan has saved far more civilian lives than it has cost. I was there in the 1990s; I know how horrific that civil war was. But that knowledge is of faint comfort to the American soldiers I know who mistakenly emptied their rifles into a truck full of civilians because they thought they were about to be blown up. A monument to the civilian dead of Iraq and Afghanistan would not only provide comfort to these young men but also signal to the world that our nation understands the cost of war.

It doesn't matter that most civilian deaths in Iraq and Afghanistan were caused by insurgent[3] attacks; if our soldiers died for freedom there—as presidents are fond of saying—then those people did as well. They, too, are among the casualties of 9/11. Nearly a decade after that terrible day, what a powerful message we would send to the world by honoring those deaths with our grief.

[3] **insurgent** A person who fights against lawful authority.

Understanding and Reviewing the Reading

1. **Thesis** What is the thesis of Junger's argument, and where does he state it most directly and completely?

2. **Reasons** What reasons for his argument does Junger offer in paragraph 3?

3. **Evidence** What is the point of Junger's inclusion of two quotations from Brendan O'Byrne in paragraphs 2 and 5? How do they support his claim in paragraph 3?

4. **Viewpoint** Why does Junger feel as he does about honoring those killed by U.S. forces? Where do his sympathies lie?

5. **Conclusion** What is Junger's underlying point in his final sentence about "what a powerful message we would send to the world"?

Analyzing the Reading

1. **Introduction** How does the opening paragraph establish Junger's relationship to the subject?

2. **Presentation** What contrast does Junger describe in paragraph 4, and how does it relate to his topic?

3. **Evidence** Why does Junger devote so much time to World War II in paragraphs 6–9?

4. **Visuals** How does the photograph that accompanies this piece relate to the author's argument? How does it help Junger present his argument and contribute to the tone of the piece?

5. **Conclusion** Why does Junger make the point in his final paragraph that "most civilian deaths in Iraq and Afghanistan were caused by insurgent attacks"?

Evaluating the Reading

1. **Title** How well do you think the title of the essay predicts and summarizes its argument?

2. **Language** In paragraph 3, Junger presents the idea that most people see war as "evil," and in paragraph 5 returning soldier O'Byrne is quoted as wondering whether he had "sinned" in combat. How appropriate is such language to the point Junger is making?

3. **Main point** Do you think Junger's thesis about creating a memorial for those killed by American soldiers in wartime has merit? Do you think erecting such a memorial would help achieve his stated goals?

Discussing the Reading

1. Why do you think Brendan O'Byrne says he misses "almost all" of his time in combat (para. 2)? Are you "appalled" by this?

2. Do you, as Junger suggests in paragraph 4, "avoid any direct look at the reality of war"? Why, or why not?

3. Junger is essentially supportive of the actions of the military, even if those actions result in civilian casualties. What's your response to this attitude?

Writing about the Reading

1. **Paragraph** In a paragraph, respond to what Brendan O'Byrne has to say about his wartime experiences in paragraphs 2 and 5. Do you think he did "what he had to do"?

2. **Internet research** Junger makes the point in his opening paragraph that returning veterans face numerous difficulties when they come home. Research this issue, and then write an essay arguing for specific policies that would ease their transition.

3. **Essay** Is there such a thing as a "just war," or do you believe that war is inherently "evil"? In an essay, argue for your own beliefs about the necessity or the futility of war.

The Racial Parenting Divide: What Adrian Peterson Reveals about Black vs. White Child-Rearing

Brittney Cooper is an assistant professor of women's and gender studies and Africana studies at Rutgers University. She writes a weekly column on race and gender politics at *Salon.com*, and she is a co-founder of the Crunk Feminist Collective, a feminist blog. The following article originally appeared on *Salon.com* in 2014.

Reading Tip

As you read, annotate and highlight language that reveals the writer's attitudes about parenting and discipline.

Previewing the Reading

Preview the reading (see pp. 28–29 for guidelines), and predict the writer's position on how parenting differs according to race.

Salon.com

The Racial Parenting Divide: What Adrian Peterson Reveals about Black vs. White Child-Rearing

By Brittney Cooper

In college, I once found myself on the D.C. metro with one of my favorite professors. As we were riding, a young white child began to climb on the seats and hang from the bars of the train. His mother never moved to restrain him. But I began to see the very familiar, strained looks of disdain and dismay on the countenances of the mostly black passengers. They exchanged eye contact with one another, dispositions tight with annoyance at the audacity of this white child, but mostly at the refusal of his mother to act as a disciplinarian. I, too, was appalled. I thought, if that were my child, I would snatch him down and tell him to sit his little behind in a seat immediately. My professor took the opportunity to teach: "Do you see how this child feels the prerogative to roam freely in this train, unhindered by rules or regulations or propriety?"

"Yes," I nodded. "What kinds of messages do you think are being communicated to him right now about how he should move through the world?" And I began to understand, quite starkly, in that moment, the freedom that white children have to see the world as a place that they can explore, a place in which they can sit, or stand, or climb at will. The world, they are learning, is theirs for the taking.

Then I thought about what it means to parent a black child, any black child, in similar circumstances. I think of the swiftness with which a black mother would have ushered her child into a seat, with firm looks and not a little scolding, the implied if unspoken threat of either a grounding or a whupping, if her request were not immediately met with compliance. So much is wrapped up in that moment: a desire to demonstrate that one's black child is well-behaved, non-threatening, well-trained. Disciplined. I think of the centuries of imminent fear that have shaped and contoured African-American working-class cultures of discipline, the sternness of our mothers' and grandmothers' looks, the firmness of the belts and switches applied to our hind parts, the rhythmic, loving, painful scoldings accompanying spankings as if the messages could be imprinted on our bodies with a sure and swift and repetitive show of force.

I think with fond memories of the big tree that grew in my grandmother's yard, with branches that were the perfect size for switches. I hear her booming and shrill voice now, commanding, "Go and pick a switch." I laugh when I remember that she cut that tree down once we were all past the age of switches.

Tom Lynn/AP Images

Adrian Peterson.

And then I turn to Adrian Peterson. Not even 5 a year ago, Peterson's 2-year-old son, whom he did not know, was murdered by his son's mother's boyfriend. More recently, Adrian Peterson has been charged with negligent injury to a child, for hitting his 4-year-old son with a switch, in a disciplinary episode that left the child with bruises and open cuts on his hands, legs, buttocks and scrotum.

In the text messages that Peterson sent to the boy's mother, he acknowledged having gone too far, letting her know that he accidentally "got him in the nuts," and that because the child didn't cry, he didn't realize the switch was hurting him. It would be easy to demonize Peterson as an abuser, but the forthrightness with which he talked about using belts and switches but not extension cords, because he "remembers how it feels to get whooped with an extension cord," as part of his modes of discipline suggests he is merely riffing on scripts handed down to him as an African-American man.

These cultures of violent punishment are ingrained within African-American communities. In fact, they are often considered marks of good parenting. In my childhood, parents who "thought their children were too good to be spanked" were looked upon with derision. I have heard everyone from preachers to comedians lament the passing of days when a child would do something wrong at a neighbor's house, get spanked by that neighbor, and then come home and get spanked again for daring to misbehave at someone else's house. For many that is a vision of a strong black community, in which children are so loved and cared for that everyone has a

Continued >

stake in making sure that those children turn out well, and "know how to act." In other words, it is clear to me that Peterson views his willingness to engage in strong discipline as a mark of being a good father.

Perhaps it is time to acknowledge that the loving intent and sincerity behind these violent modes of discipline makes them no less violent, no more acceptable. Some of our ideas about discipline are unproductive, dangerous and wrong. It's time we had the courage to say that.

I am not interested in haggling any more with black people about the difference between spankings and abuse, because when emotions and stakes are both as high as they are, lines are far too easily crossed. Stakes are high because parenting black children in a culture of white supremacy forces us to place too high a price on making sure our children are disciplined and well-behaved. I know that I personally place an extremely high value on children being respectful, well-behaved and submissive to authority figures. I'm fairly sure this isn't a good thing.

10   If black folks are honest, many of us will admit to both internally and vocally balking at the very "free" ways that we have heard white children address their parents in public. Many a black person has seen a white child yelling at his or her parents, while the parents calmly respond, gently scold, ignore, attempt to soothe, or failing all else, look embarrassed. I can never recount one time, ever seeing a black child yell at his or her mother in public. Never. It is almost unfathomable.

As a kid in the 1980s and 1990s I loved family sitcoms. "Full House," "Who's the Boss?," "Growing Pains." You name it. But even before my own racial consciousness was fully formed, I remember knowing that I was watching white families very different from my own, in part, because of how children interacted with their families. Invariably on an episode, a child would get mad, yell at a parent, and then run up the stairs (white people's sitcom houses always had stairs) and slam the door.

What I know for sure is that yelling, running away or slamming anything in the house that my single mama worked hard to pay for would be grounds for some serious disciplinary reprisal. Even now, when I think about what kind of behavior I would permit as a parent, I am clear that slamming doors in my home is unacceptable. Still, I also know that my anger was not an emotion that found a free and healthy range of expression in my household. My mother is my own personal hero, but just as she did many things differently than her own mother did when it came to raising daughters, I know I will think very intentionally about making space for my children to experience a full range of emotions—anger included—in the safety of home. They can't slam the door, but they can close it.

As for Adrian Peterson, he will have to deal with the legal consequences of his actions. It has long been time for us to forgo violence as a disciplinary strategy. But as Charles

Salon.com

Barkley notes, if we lock up Adrian Peterson, we could lock up every other black parent in the South for the same behavior. Instead, I hope Peterson is a cautionary tale, not about the state intruding on our "right" to discipline our children but rather a wakeup call about how much (fear of) state violence informs the way we discipline our children.

If the murder of Michael Brown has taught us nothing else, we should know by now that the U.S. nation-state often uses deadly violence both here and abroad as a primary mode of disciplining people with black and brown bodies. Darren Wilson used deadly force against Michael Brown as a mode of discipline (and a terroristic act) for Brown's failure to comply with the request to walk on the sidewalk.

The loving intent and sincerity of our disciplinary strategies does not preclude them   15
from being imbricated in these larger state-based ideas about how to compel black bodies to act in ways that are seen as non-menacing, unobtrusive and basically invisible. Many hope that by enacting these micro-level violences on black bodies, we can protect our children from macro and deadly forms of violence later.

Perhaps it is audacious of me to encourage black parents to focus less on producing well-behaved children in a world that clearly hates them. Black boys and girls are suspended or expelled from school more than all other demographics of boys and girls, often for similar behaviors, simply because their engagement in those behaviors is perceived as more aggressive.

White children in general are raised to be Columbus, to "discover" the world anew and then to manipulate and order the universe to their own liking. If we take away the colonizing impulse in living this way, I think it would be amazing to have the luxury of raising black children who also view the world as a space of their own making, a space to be explored, a space to build anew. A space where occasionally, simply because you live there, you can opt to walk in the middle of the street instead of being confined to the sidewalk, much as you might sling your leg across the arm of a chair in your own home, because it is home.

But for so many black children, these kinds of frivolous choices will get you killed or locked up. For black children, finding disciplinary methods that instill a healthy sense of fear in a world that is exceptionally violent toward them is a hard balance to find. The thing is, though: Beating, whupping or spanking your children will not protect them from state violence. It won't keep them out of prison. Ruling homes and children with an iron fist will not restore the dignity and respect that the outside world fails to confer on adult black people. What these actions might do is curtail creativity, inculcate a narrative about "acceptable" forms of violence enacted against black bodies, and breed fear and resentment between parents and children that far outlasts childhood.

Violence in any form is not love. Let us make sure first to learn that lesson. And then if we do nothing else, let us teach it to our children.

📊 Understanding and Reviewing the Reading

1. **Introduction** What is the purpose of Cooper's story about being on the train with her college professor?

2. **Thesis** Summarize the writer's thesis, or claim. Where does she state it most directly?

3. **Reasons and evidence** What are the main reasons presented in the selection in support of the writer's claim? What evidence is offered for each reason?

4. **Vocabulary** Using context clues (p. 37) and a dictionary if necessary, define each of the following words as it is used in the essay: *audacity* (paragraph 1), *prerogative* (1), *compliance* (3), *unfathomable* (10), *reprisal* (12), *preclude* (15), *imbricated* (15), and *inculcate* (18).

📊 Analyzing the Reading

1. **Title** According to Cooper, what does Adrian Peterson reveal about black vs. white child-rearing?

2 **Predicting quiz questions** Draft three questions that an instructor might pose on a quiz about this reading. Then briefly answer your questions.

3. **Meaning** What does Cooper mean by "micro-level violences" in paragraph 15? How does she say these may protect children from "macro and deadly" violence later?

4. **Conclusion** How do the writer's final three paragraphs lead up to her concluding sentence? What is the basic argument here?

📊 Evaluating the Reading

1. **Evidence** How effective is the evidence offered by Cooper in support of her argument? Which details in the reading do you find most convincing or compelling? Why?

2. **Emotional appeals** What emotional appeals does the author make? Does she make any generalizations in her argument?

3. **Language and tone** What can you tell about Cooper's attitude from her choice of language? How is her tone different when she describes the discipline methods of mothers and grandmothers and when she describes those of the U.S. nation-state?

4. **Opposing arguments** Does the author address any opposing arguments or acknowledge the difficulty of making a change?

5. **Audience** How sympathetic do you think the author expects her readers to be toward her argument? Describe what type of audience (agreeing, neutral/wavering, or disagreeing) she seems to be writing for.

Discussing the Reading

1. Why does Cooper say she has fond memories of her grandmother's tree? How does her memory in paragraph 4 contrast with the Adrian Peterson story in the paragraphs that follow?

2. What's your response to the writer's statement "Perhaps it is audacious of me to encourage black parents to focus less on producing well-behaved children in a world that clearly hates them"?

3. After Cooper describes valuing respectful, well-behaved, and submissive children, she goes on to say, "I'm fairly sure this isn't a good thing." Why does she say this? Do you agree with her?

Writing about the Reading

1. **Essay** In an essay, present your own viewpoint on disciplining children. What kind of behavior would you permit as a parent? What is your disciplinary strategy? Does your strategy differ from that of your parents? Explain why or why not.

2. **Essay** How might a culture of violent punishment in a particular community be changed? In what ways could Adrian Peterson's example be used to encourage change in the African-American community? Brainstorm ways to address the issue and then, before you begin to draft, develop a thesis based on what you see as the best of those ideas.

3. **Essay** Cooper describes learning about racial differences as a child watching family sitcoms and as a college student on the train with her professor. When did you become aware of racial or cultural differences? Did television shows or movies help form your ideas about other racial or cultural groups? Write an essay about how you learned about families different from your own.

ARGUMENT PAIR: DEBATING A HIGHER MINIMUM WAGE

Why We Should Raise the Minimum Wage

Robert Reich is a political economist who has served in the administrations of three presidents. He is currently the Chancellor's Professor of Public Policy at the University of California, Berkeley. Reich is a well-known regular political commentator on television and was named one of the most influential business thinkers by the *Wall Street Journal* in 2008. The following article first appeared on *CNBC.com* in 2015.

Reading Tip

As you read, highlight the main reasons the writer supports raising the minimum wage.

Previewing the Reading

Preview the reading (see pp. 28–29 for guidelines), and then answer the following questions.

1. What city does the author use to illustrate his argument?
2. What types of evidence does the author use to support his claim?

cnbc.com

Why We Should Raise the Minimum Wage

By Robert Reich

Across America, the ranks of the working poor are growing. While low-paying industries such as retail and food preparation accounted for 22 percent of the jobs lost in the Great Recession, they've generated 44 percent of the jobs added since then, according to a report from the National Employment Law Project. Last February, the Congressional Budget Office estimated that raising the national minimum wage to $10.10 an hour from $7.25 would lift 900,000 people out of poverty.

Seattle estimates that, before its historic decision, almost a fourth of its workers earned below $15 an hour. That translates into about $31,000 a year for a full-time worker. In a high-cost city like Seattle, that's barely enough to support a family. Most minimum-wage workers aren't teenagers these days. They're major breadwinners who need a higher minimum wage in order to keep their families out of poverty.

cnbc.com

The gains from a higher minimum wage extend beyond those who receive it. More money in the pockets of low-wage workers means more sales, especially in the locales they live in—which, in turn, creates faster growth and more jobs. A major reason the current economic recovery is anemic is that so many Americans lack the purchasing power to get the economy moving again.

With a higher minimum wage, moreover, we'd all end up paying less for Medicaid, food stamps and other assistance the working poor now need in order to have a minimally decent standard of living.

Some worry about job losses accompanying a higher minimum wage. I wouldn't advise any place to raise its minimum wage immediately to $15 an hour from the current federal minimum of $7.25. That would be too big a leap all at once. Employers—especially small ones—need time to adapt.   5

But this isn't what Seattle is doing. It's raising its minimum to $15 incrementally over several years from $9.32 (Washington State's current statewide minimum). Large employers (with over 500 workers) that don't offer employer-sponsored health insurance have three years to comply; those that offer health insurance have four; smaller employers, up to seven. (That may be too long a phase-in.)

My guess is Seattle's businesses will adapt without any net loss of employment. Seattle's employers will also have more employees to choose from—as the $15 an hour minimum attracts into the labor force some people who otherwise haven't been interested. That means they'll end up with workers who are highly reliable and likely to stay longer, resulting in real savings.

Research by Michael Reich (no relation) and Arindrajit Dube confirms these results. They examined employment in several hundred pairs of adjacent counties lying on opposite sides of state borders, each with different minimum wages, and found no statistically significant increase in unemployment in the higher-minimum counties, even after four years. (Other researchers who found contrary results failed to control for counties where unemployment was already growing before the minimum wage was increased.) They also found that employee turnover was lower where the minimum was higher.

Not every city or state can meet the bar Seattle has just set. But many can—and should.

Understanding and Reviewing the Reading

1. **Thesis** Summarize Reich's claim, or thesis. Where does he state it most clearly?
2. **Reasons and evidence** What main reasons does Reich offer to support raising the minimum wage? What specific evidence does he use to support his reasoning?

Title	Why We Should Raise the Minimum Wage
Introduction	**Background:**
	Claim (thesis):
Body paragraphs	**Reason 1:**
	Reason 2:
	Opposing arguments:
Conclusion	

3. **Opposing arguments** How does Reich address concerns about job losses accompanying a higher minimum wage?
4. **Organization** Complete the graphic organizer above for help in understanding the organization of the argument.

Analyzing the Reading

1. **Introduction** Why does the writer open by citing data from the National Employment Law Project and the Congressional Budget Office? What kind of appeal is being made?
2. **Methods of development** Why does Reich point to a cause-and-effect relationship in paragraphs 3–4, and how does this relate to his point in paragraph 2?
3. **Opposing arguments** Where does Reich address concerns about potential job losses related to raising the minimum wage? How does he support his view?
4. **Conclusion** What does the writer mean by "the bar Seattle has just set" in paragraph 9?

Evaluating the Reading

1. **Reasons** Which do you think is Reich's most convincing reason for raising the minimum wage? In general, do you think he makes a strong argument, or do some of his reasons fail to convince you?
2. **Evidence** Reich suggests in paragraph 4 that we would all stand to benefit from a higher minimum wage. Does he make a clear connection between this purported benefit and support for the higher minimum wage?

3. **Language** Why do you think Reich refers specifically to "major breadwin-ners" in paragraph 2? Do you think this is an accurate characterization?

4. **Purpose and audience** What is the purpose of Reich's argument, and who might his intended audience be? How effective do you find the strategy he uses in appealing to this audience?

Discussing the Reading

1. Does Reich convince you that the gains from a higher minimum wage extend beyond workers who receive it? Why, or why not?

2. How well do you understand the incremental wage increase process that Reich writes about in paragraph 6? Do you find Reich's explanation clear and complete?

3. Would you recommend that your city or state raise its current minimum wage? Why, or why not? What reasons from this reading would you cite or refute in your recommendation?

Writing about the Reading

1. **Essay** According to the Congressional Budget Office, raising the national minimum wage by $2.85 could lift 900,000 people out of poverty. What other strategies, from the local level to national policy, do you think are important for helping lift people out of poverty? Write an essay discussing various strat-egies, and include your opinion of the value of raising the minimum wage.

2. **Essay** Reich concedes that raising the minimum wage immediately to $15 an hour would be "too big a leap." Do you agree that employers need time to adapt, or do you think the needs of the working poor should prompt more rapid change? Write an essay arguing for or against an immediate increase in the minimum wage.

3. **Essay** Some have argued that the minimum wage should be set at a higher level for adults than for minors. Are you in favor of a minimum wage that varies based on age or other factors? Why, or why not? Research the topic, as needed, to locate supporting information for your viewpoint.

The Fight Against 15

Reihan Salam is a conservative political commentator and writer. He serves as executive editor of *National Review* and is a columnist for *Slate.com*. Salam is a fellow at the University of Chicago Institute of Politics. He has appeared on many radio and television programs. This article first appeared on *Slate.com* in 2015.

Reading Tip

As you read, look for and highlight the reasons the author gives for his position.

Previewing the Reading

Preview the reading (see pp. 28–29 for guidelines), and then predict the author's position on the issue.

Slate.com

The Fight Against 15

By Reihan Salam

Getty Images News/Getty Images

A McDonald's employee sweeps up in front of the restaurant on the morning when thousands took to the streets to demand a $15 minimum wage on April 15, 2015, in Brooklyn, New York.

The "Fight for 15" is just getting started. Last week, protesters gathered in cities across the country to demand a $15 hourly minimum wage, and at least some national politicians are heeding their call. Martin O'Malley, the former governor of Maryland who is positioning himself as Hillary Clinton's liberal rival for the Democratic presidential nomination, endorsed a $15 minimum wage, and it's all but certain that other Democrats will soon follow. So might a handful of Republicans looking to demonstrate that they too care about stagnant incomes for low-wage workers. Minimum wage ballot initiatives passed by substantial margins in four Republican-leaning states in November, and GOP Senate candidates Tom Cotton of Arkansas and Dan Sullivan of Alaska came out in favor of state (but not federal) minimum wage hikes.

None of this should come as a shock. Public support for a minimum wage hike is overwhelming. One recent survey, sponsored by the National Employment Law Project, found that 63 percent of Americans favor increasing the minimum wage to

$15 over the next five years, and that a more modest increase to $12.50 is backed by 75 percent of Americans, including 53 percent of Republicans. Opposing a minimum wage increase could be hazardous to your political health, and my guess is that opponents will prefer to dodge the issue than to engage it head on.

Why beat your head against the wall when you can just go with the flow and embrace a very popular idea? I can think of only one good reason: that increasing the minimum wage so dramatically will damage the economic prospects of millions of vulnerable people. My view is that the labor market is changing in ways that make huge minimum wage hikes, like the one backed by the Fight for 15 movement, very dangerous.

First, let me stipulate that there is a lively, ongoing debate among serious, thoughtful people about the wisdom of more modest increases in the federal minimum wage. For years, scholars have been drawing on variation in minimum wage levels across states to determine whether minimum wage hikes reduce employment levels. Can we discern the effects of a minimum wage hike by, say, comparing two neighboring counties, one in which the minimum wage increased and the other in which it did not? Can we screen out all of the nonrandom differences between states and cities that might influence their local minimum wage laws? I'm skeptical, but many scholars, like University of Massachusetts–Amherst economist Arindrajit Dube, have tried to do just that. Dube and his collaborators have concluded that modest minimum wage hikes don't appear to reduce employment levels. Other economists, like David Neumark and William Wascher, disagree.

But let's say that Dube is right about modest minimum wage hikes. Does that settle   5 the issue? Should we all join the Fight for 15? Not quite. There is a big difference between raising the federal minimum wage from its current $7.25 to $10.10 versus raising it to $15. (If you don't believe me, just ask Thomas Piketty.) By definition, the federal minimum wage applies across the country, despite the fact that average wages and price levels vary considerably from place to place. One scholar who has been particularly thoughtful as to why this matters is Dube himself, who has argued against a one-size-fits-all approach to the minimum wage. In a paper for the Hamilton Project, Dube observed that "states as dissimilar as Massachusetts and Mississippi have different capacities to absorb a minimum wage of, say, $11.00 per hour, and a single minimum wage has to balance the needs of states at both ends of the spectrum."

What does it mean for different states to have different capacities to absorb a higher minimum wage? Consider the contrast between Massachusetts, a high-cost, high-wage jurisdiction, and Mississippi, a low-cost, low-wage one. In Massachusetts, very few workers would be affected by an increase in the federal minimum wage to $10.10, as the Bay State already has a $9 minimum wage that is set to increase to $11 by 2017. But in Mississippi, as many as 28 percent of workers would be affected. In Massachusetts, wages are higher, and so are prices. Relatively few employers will

Continued >

Slate.com

have to spend substantially more on their workforce under a higher federal minimum wage, and relatively few will have to raise their prices to account for it. In Mississippi, by contrast, many employers will have to raise their wages, and it's a safe bet that virtually all of the cost of this minimum wage hike will be passed on to consumers in the form of higher prices. You might think that, well, this isn't a huge deal if it's rich people who are paying these higher prices. But of course it will often be poor people who pay them, particularly in a poor state like Mississippi. This makes poor consumers worse off in a direct sense, in that they can purchase less with their earnings. And if consumers are at all sensitive to prices, at least some of them will choose to spend less on labor-intensive goods and services now that they are more expensive. That could reduce the number of minimum wage jobs available.

That is why Dube recommends that state and local governments set minimum wages that take into account local wages and local price levels. Specifically, he advocates setting a minimum wage at half of the median full-time wage in a given jurisdiction, a standard that would have yielded minimum wages ranging from $12.45 in Massachusetts to $7.97 in Mississippi. Suffice it to say, there is a great deal of distance between $7.97 and $15. It could be that Dube is a right-wing agitator and friend of the plutocracy who can't be trusted. I tend to think he's a sober, cautious scholar who recognizes that raising the minimum wage involves tradeoffs.

The truth is that I go further than Dube. One reason is that I'm not sure looking at short-run employment effects is the right way to understand the impact of the minimum wage. When gas prices start to climb, consumers don't respond immediately by replacing their gas-guzzlers with more fuel-efficient vehicles. They drive a bit less, depending on how high prices have gone and how much control they have over their commutes. But it takes them a bit longer to replace the cars they drive. What actually happens is that consumers scrap their gas-guzzlers faster than they would have otherwise, and when they do replace their cars, they replace them with more fuel-efficient models. Could there be a similar lag when it comes to the minimum wage? It could take time for low-wage employers to develop business models that allow them to get away with fewer less-skilled employees, meaning that we don't see the full effect of a hike right away. The economist Isaac Sorkin has made a compelling case that to really understand the impact of minimum wage laws, we need to have a much better understanding of these long-run effects.

But even if we completely ignore the possibility that firms will learn to economize on less-skilled labor, $15 an hour is a bridge too far. My deeper concern is that people who in decades past might have had a fighting chance at making their way into the middle class are now finding it hard to get on the bottom rungs of the job ladder. This matters because low-wage employers aren't just employers. They're also institutions that invest in the human capital of their workforces. Some people learn the basics of what it takes to get and to keep a job (the ability to exercise self-control, to be

Slate.com

persistent, to show up on time, to get along with others, to speak the language of your workplace reasonably well) from their parents. Formal education also helps, but not everyone flourishes in formal education. Even the most heroic and dedicated public school teachers can only do so much to close the gap between kids from stable, supportive families and kids from fragile ones.

Low-wage employers take on the challenge of succeeding where families and schools 10 have failed. They don't do this because they're saints. They take on this challenge when they have no choice—they'd much prefer to hire workers who are already fully qualified to take on demanding jobs than to nurture talent in-house. What happens when they do have a choice? Firms are losing interest in financing the training of their employees. Peter Cappelli, director of Wharton's Center for Human Resources, notes that although "employers in the postwar era typically selected employees for general abilities at entry-level positions, then trained them over a lifetime to meet the employers' needs," things have changed. Though employers don't generally say this outright, the new expectation is that "job candidates' skills, which are either adequate or not, are supposed to arrive with the applicants." There are many theories as to why this has happened. One obvious possibility is that firms have grown less willing to train workers in-house as skilled employees have grown more footloose, and they are reluctant to spend time and resources training workers who will eventually wind up at other firms.

Where does this leave job candidates who don't arrive readymade, with all the skills they need to climb the corporate ladder thanks to Mom, Dad, and good old Selective U.? It leaves them in a really tough place. Employers will give these employees a shot only if it's not too expensive for them to do so. As the wage floor rises, why wouldn't employers hire more experienced workers or workers with fewer personal challenges, who need less hand-holding in their first months on the job? A higher minimum wage could be good news for people who are willing to work at today's minimum wage. Yet it might also draw in, say, candidates from more affluent backgrounds who will now compete for the same jobs. Then, of course, there is the possibility that employers will hire fewer, better-skilled employees and augment their pricier labor with machines.

This doesn't strike me as a good time to decide that jobs paying less than $15 an hour should literally be against the law. There are millions of people—struggling teenagers, less-skilled immigrants, people who've been unemployed for years, ex-offenders who are trying to get on their feet—who need on-the-job experience if they're ever going to be in positions to command higher wages down the road. Let's increase wage subsidies for low-wage workers. Let's expand apprenticeship programs. Let's try all kinds of things, like celebrating employers that successfully upgrade the skills of their low-wage workers and not just the Googles of the world, which hire only the high-skilled and expect to get patted on the back for it. But let's not lock millions of people out of entry-level employment by raising the minimum wage to $15 an hour.

Understanding and Reviewing the Reading

1. **Thesis** What is Salam's thesis? Where is it summarized most clearly?
2. **Reasons** What main reason does Salam give for opposing a dramatic minimum wage increase? What other reason(s) does he give?
3. **Evidence** What specific evidence does Salam offer to support his reasoning?
4. **Opposing arguments** Does Salam acknowledge or refute opposing views?
5. **Organization** Complete the graphic organizer below to help you understand the organization of the argument.

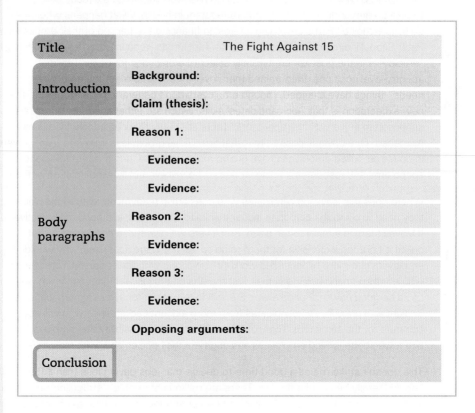

Title	The Fight Against 15
Introduction	**Background:**
	Claim (thesis):
Body paragraphs	**Reason 1:**
	Evidence:
	Evidence:
	Reason 2:
	Evidence:
	Reason 3:
	Evidence:
	Opposing arguments:
Conclusion	

Analyzing the Reading

1. **Introduction** Why does the writer open by describing politicians who support a minimum wage increase? How does he use the popularity of a wage hike to introduce his argument?
2. **Methods of development** How does Salam use comparison and contrast to explain how states have different capacities to absorb a higher minimum wage?

3. **Method of presentation** Why does Salam refer to "Mom, Dad, and good old Selective U." in paragraph 11?

4. **Conclusion** What emotional appeals does the writer make in his conclusion? Describe his call for action.

Evaluating the Reading

1. **Title** How well do you think the title of the reading predicts its argument? What do you need to know to understand the meaning of the title?

2. **Opposing arguments** In your view, does the reading present and refute opposing arguments as fully as it should? In formulating your response, you might consider the arguments made in the preceding essay by Robert Reich.

3. **Language** In paragraph 3, Salam states that wage hikes such as the one backed by the Fight for 15 movement are "very dangerous." How do you interpret this phrase, and do you find the point convincing?

4. **Analogy** The writer makes an analogy in paragraph 8 between a minimum wage hike and an increase in gas prices. Does his analogy make the concept easier for you to understand? Try to explain the analogy in your own words.

5. **Conclusion** Evaluate the argument's conclusion. Does it provide a strong enough restatement of the thesis? What does it suggest to you about the intended audience?

Discussing the Reading

1. Does Salam convince you that a minimum wage increase to $15 would be detrimental to low-wage workers? Why, or why not?

2. Do the writer's tone and language make his argument more effective? Find examples that reveal how the writer feels about the subject.

3. How clear is Salam's example in explaining how different states have different capacities to absorb a minimum wage? Could you apply his example to your own state?

Writing about the Reading

1. **Essay** In paragraph 9, Salam gives a list of "the basics of what it takes to get and to keep a job." Can you think of other "basics" for getting and keeping a job? From whom did you learn these skills? Do you agree with the author that teaching these basics is a role of employers? Write an essay detailing what you consider the "basics" and describing your experience in acquiring these skills for the workplace.

2. **Essay** In his conclusion, the author suggests several alternatives to raising the minimum wage, including wage subsidies, apprenticeship programs, and

celebrating employers that improve their workers' skills. Which of these ideas do you think has the most merit? Can you think of other alternatives that would help low-wage workers such as the ones identified in the conclusion? Choose one or two alternatives to raising the minimum wage and write an essay arguing for your choice(s).

3. **Research** Conduct research to determine the current status of an increase in the minimum wage on both state and federal levels. Write an essay summarizing your findings and commenting on the action or inaction.

Comparing the Arguments

1. Compare how Reich and Salam introduce the issue. With what context does each writer frame the issue?

2. Evaluate the evidence the authors offer in support of their claims. Which author presents more substantial evidence? Explain.

3. Which writer's argument do you find to be more convincing? Why?

4. How do you think Reich might respond to Salam's claim?

5. What did you learn about this topic from the essays? Can you reach a conclusion about raising the minimum wage on the basis of these two sources? Explain.

ARGUMENT PAIR: DEBATING MULTITASKING

How (and Why) to Stop Multitasking

Peter Bregman is a leadership consultant and CEO of Bregman Partners, Inc., a global management consulting firm. He is the author of *Point B: A Short Guide to Leading a Big Change* (2007) and *18 Minutes: Find Your Focus, Master Distraction, and Get the Right Things Done* (2011). He also blogs for *Harvard Business Review*, where this essay appeared in 2010.

Reading Tip

Bregman focuses primarily on personal experience in this argument. Pay close attention to how he uses data in his argument and consider how he balances personal experience and outside information.

Previewing the Reading

Preview the reading (see pp. 28–29 for guidelines), and list at least one reason the author opposes multitasking.

---

blogs.hbr.org

How (and Why) to Stop Multitasking

By Peter Bregman

During a conference call with the executive committee of a nonprofit board on which I sit, I decided to send an email to a client. I know, I know. You'd think I'd have learned. Last week I wrote about the dangers of using a cell phone while driving. Multitasking is dangerous. And so I proposed a way to stop. But when I sent that email, I wasn't in a car. I was safe at my desk. What could go wrong?

Well, I sent the client the message. Then I had to send him another one, this time with the attachment I had forgotten to append. Finally, my third email to him explained why that attachment wasn't what he was expecting. When I eventually refocused on the call, I realized I hadn't heard a question the chair of the board had asked me.

I swear I wasn't smoking anything. But I might as well have been. A study showed that people distracted by incoming email and phone calls saw a 10-point fall in their IQs. What's the impact of a 10-point drop? The same as losing a night of sleep. More than twice the effect of smoking marijuana.

Continued >

Doing several things at once is a trick we play on ourselves, thinking we're getting more done. In reality, our productivity goes down by as much as 40%. We don't actually multitask. We switch-task, rapidly shifting from one thing to another, interrupting ourselves unproductively, and losing time in the process.

5 You might think you're different, that you've done it so much you've become good at it. Practice makes perfect and all that. But you'd be wrong. Research shows that heavy multitaskers are *less competent* at doing several things at once than light multitaskers. In other words, in contrast to almost everything else in your life, the more you multitask, the worse you are at it. Practice, in this case, works against you.

I decided to do an experiment. For one week I would do no multitasking and see what happened. What techniques would help? Could I sustain a focus on one thing at a time for that long? For the most part, I succeeded. If I was on the phone, all I did was talk or listen on the phone. In a meeting I did nothing but focus on the meeting. Any interruptions—email, a knock on the door—I held off until I finished what I was working on.

During the week I discovered six things:

- **First, it was delightful.** I noticed this most dramatically when I was with my children. I shut my cell phone off and found myself much more deeply engaged and present with them. I never realized how significantly a short moment of checking my email disengaged me from the people and things right there in front of me. Don't laugh, but I actually—for the first time in a while—noticed the beauty of leaves blowing in the wind.
- **Second, I made significant progress on challenging projects,** the kind that—like writing or strategizing—require thought and persistence. The kind I usually try to distract myself from. I stayed with each project when it got hard, and experienced a number of breakthroughs.
- **Third, my stress dropped dramatically.** Research shows that multitasking isn't just inefficient, it's stressful. And I found that to be true. It was a relief to do only one thing at a time. I felt liberated from the strain of keeping so many balls in the air at each moment. It felt reassuring to finish one thing before going to the next.
- **Fourth, I lost all patience for things I felt were not a good use of my time.** An hour-long meeting seemed interminably long. A meandering pointless conversation was excruciating. I became laser-focused on getting things done. Since I wasn't doing anything else, I got bored much more quickly. I had no tolerance for wasted time.
- **Fifth, I had tremendous patience for things I felt were useful and enjoyable.** When I listened to my wife Eleanor, I was in no rush. When I was brainstorming about a difficult problem, I stuck with it. Nothing else was competing for my attention so I was able to settle into the one thing I was doing.
- **Sixth, there was no downside.** I lost nothing by not multitasking. No projects were left unfinished. No one became frustrated with me for not answering a call or failing to return an email the second I received it.

That's why it's so surprising that multitasking is so hard to resist. If there's no downside to stopping, why don't we all just stop? I think it's because our minds move considerably faster than the outside world. You can hear far more words a minute than someone else can speak. We have so much to do, why waste any time? So, while you're on the phone listening to someone, why not use that *extra* brain power to book a trip to Florence? What we neglect to realize is that we're already using that brain power to pick up nuance, think about what we're hearing, access our creativity, and stay connected to what's happening around us. It's not really extra brain power, and diverting it has negative consequences.

So how do we resist the temptation? First, the obvious: The best way to avoid interruptions is to turn them off. Often I write at 6 A.M. when there's nothing to distract me, I disconnect my computer from its wireless connection and turn my phone off. In my car, I leave my phone in the trunk. Drastic? Maybe. But most of us shouldn't trust ourselves. Second, the less obvious: Use your loss of patience to your advantage. Create unrealistically short deadlines. Cut all meetings in half. Give yourself a third of the time you think you need to accomplish something. There's nothing like a deadline to keep things moving. And when things are moving fast, we can't help but focus on them. How many people run a race while texting? If you really only have thirty minutes to finish a presentation you thought would take an hour, are you really going to answer an interrupting call? Interestingly, because multitasking is so stressful, single-tasking to meet a tight deadline will actually reduce your stress. In other words, giving yourself less time to do things could make you more productive and relaxed.

Finally, it's good to remember that we're not perfect. Every once in a while it might be   10 OK to allow for a little multitasking. As I was writing this, Daniel, my two-year-old son, walked into my office, climbed on my lap, and said "*Monsters, Inc.* movie please." So, here we are, I'm finishing this piece on the left side of my computer screen while Daniel is on my lap watching a movie on the right side of my computer screen. Sometimes, it is simply impossible to resist a little multitasking.

Understanding and Reviewing the Reading

1. **Claim** Why does Bregman believe we should stop most of our multitasking?
2. **Opposing view** Summarize the opposing views favoring multitasking that Bregman refutes.
3. **Evidence** What did Bregman discover after he stopped multitasking?
4. **Vocabulary** Explain the meaning of each of the following words as it is used in the reading, consulting a dictionary as necessary: *refocused* (para. 2), *competent* (5), *disengaged* (7), *persistence* (7), and *meandering* (7).
5. **Organization** Create a graphic organizer for the argument in this essay.

Analyzing the Reading

1. **Claim** What is Bregman's claim? What is his purpose in making the claim?

2. **Emotional appeals** What types of emotional appeals does Bregman make? Identify the needs and values to which he appeals.

3. **Evidence** What types of evidence does Bregman use to support his claim?

4. **Reasoning** Are there any errors in Bregman's reasoning? If so, what are they, and where in the selection do they occur?

Evaluating the Reading

1. **Tone** Describe Bregman's tone. Highlight several words or phrases that reveal this tone.

2. **Sources** Bregman mentions research but fails to cite his sources. How does that influence the effectiveness of his argument?

3. **Language** What is the connotation of *delightful* (para. 7)?

4. **Language** What is "smoking anything" (para. 3) a euphemism for?

Discussing the Reading

1. Evaluate Bregman's description of his discoveries when he stopped multitasking. Are they persuasive? Could he have added anything that would have made them more persuasive?

2. What do you think of Bregman's tips on how to stop multitasking? Are these things you could apply to your life? Why, or why not?

Writing about the Reading

1. **Essay** Keep a journal for a day, and record all the times you multitask and how doing so affects you. Then write an essay describing your experiences with multitasking. Offer examples of why it has or has not been useful for you.

2. **Essay** Pick another habit or activity that, like multitasking, has benefits and disadvantages, and try to give it up for a week. Then write an essay like Bregman's that argues for or against the habit based on your experience. Consider including in your essay a list of discoveries like Bregman's.

3. **Internet research** Bregman provides statistics about multitasking but does not cite his sources. Do some library and Internet research on recent studies on multitasking. Based on the information you find, write an essay that either supports or argues against Bregman's claims. Remember to consider opposing viewpoints in your argument.

In Defense of Multitasking

David Silverman has worked in business and taught business writing. He is the author of *Typo: The Last American Typesetter or How I Made and Lost 4 Million Dollars* (2007). He blogs for *Harvard Business Review,* where this essay appeared in 2010, three weeks after "How (and Why) to Stop Multitasking."

Reading Tip

Silverman's piece is a direct response to Peter Bregman's "How (and Why) to Stop Multitasking" (p. 595). As you read, pay careful attention to the ways he uses Bregman's structure to make his own argument.

Previewing the Reading

Preview the reading (see pp. 28–29 for guidelines), and list several reasons why the author defends multitasking.

---

blogs.hbr.org

In Defense of Multitasking

By David Silverman

HBR.org blogger Peter Bregman recently made some excellent points about the downside of multitasking. I will not deny that single-minded devotion often produces high quality. Nor will I attempt to join the misguided (and scientifically discredited) many who say, "Yeah, other people can't do it, but I'm super awesome at doing ten things at once."

But let's remember, unitasking has a downside too—namely, what works for one person slows down others. Multitasking isn't just an addiction for the short-attention-spanned among us; it's crucial to survival in today's workplace. To see why, take a look at computing, where the concept of multitasking came from.

Long ago, in the days of vacuum tubes and relays, computers worked in "batch" mode. Jobs were loaded from punched cards, and each job waited until the one before it was completed. This created serious problems. You didn't know if your job had an error until it ran, which could be hours after you submitted it. You didn't know if it would cause an infinite loop and block all the other jobs from starting. And any changes in external information that occurred during processing couldn't be accounted for.

The invention of time-sharing resolved these issues: Multiple tasks can now be done concurrently, and you can interrupt a task in an emergency. Incoming missile? Stop

Continued >

the backup tape and send an alert to HQ. So, how does all that apply to the way people work? In several ways:

1. **Multitasking helps us get and give critical information faster.** You can get responses to questions quickly, even if the person you're asking is on another task. For example: I was at an all-day off-site (no BlackBerrys allowed) when one of my direct reports received a request from an internal customer to make a slide. Since I was unreachable by phone when he started on it, my employee worked the entire afternoon on something that, after I finally read my email and called him, took us only thirty minutes to do together because I had information he didn't have.

2. **It keeps others from being held up.** If I don't allow for distractions in an attempt to be more efficient, other people may be held up waiting for me. This is the classic batch job problem. Going back to my slide example: The next day, the person who had requested the slide said he only needed a couple of bullet points. Had he been reachable earlier, and not devoted to a single task and blocking all interruptions, we wouldn't have wasted what ended up being nearly six hours of work time (my employee's and mine).

3. **It gives you something to turn to when you're stuck.** Sometimes it's good to butt your head against a task that is challenging. And sometimes it's good to walk away, do something else, and let your subconscious ponder the ponderable. When you return twenty-five minutes later, maybe you'll reach a better solution than you would have if you'd just stuck it out. And in the meantime, you've finished some other task, such as writing a blog post. (By the way, my 10.6 minute attempt to uncover how many minutes it takes to get back to a task after an interruption yielded a variety of answers—11, 25, 30—and links to a lot of dubious research, such as a University of California study of thirty-six workers and a study that tracked "eleven experienced Microsoft Windows users [three female].")

4. **The higher up you are in the organization, the more important multitasking is.** The fewer things you have to do, the more you should concentrate on them. If I'm painting my house, and I'm on a ladder, I've got to keep on that one task. But if I'm the general contractor, I need to stay on top of the house painter, the carpenter, the electrician, and the guy swinging that big ball on the end of a giant chain, lest the wrong wall or an unsuspecting worker get demolished. To take this to the logical extreme: Does Barack Obama get to unitask? Can he say, "I'm not available for the rest of the day, because I'll be working on that spreadsheet I've been trying to get done on the number of my Facebook friends who aren't updating their pages with posts about their pet cats?" Or does he have to keep doing his job while handling whatever spilled milk (or, say, zillions of gallons of oil) comes his way?

blogs.hbr.org

What do you think? Are we comfortable pretending we really can live our lives not   5
multitasking? Or are we like my father and others who say smoking is bad but can
be found on the front porch in the dead of night, a small red glow at their lips, puffing
away while texting their BFFs and playing Words with Friends?

Before you answer, think about the eight *Washington Post* reporters who tried to go
a week without the Internet and failed miserably. The truth is, we need multitasking
as much as we need air.

Understanding and Reviewing the Reading

1. **Claim** What claim does Silverman make?
2. **Reasons** Summarize Silverman's reasons for defending multitasking.
3. **Message** What message does Silverman convey by discussing his father in
   the next-to-last paragraph?
4. **Vocabulary** Explain the meaning of each of the following words as it is used
   in the reading: *discredited* (para. 1), *unitasking* (2), *concurrently* (4), *ponderable* (4), and *lest* (4).
5. **Organization** Create a graphic organizer for the argument in this essay.

Analyzing the Reading

1. **Analogy** Explain Silverman's analogy about computers. What is he trying to
   show with it?
2. **Effectiveness** Is Silverman's analogy about computers effective? Why, or
   why not?
3. **Evidence** What additional information, evidence, or explanation would
   make this essay more convincing?
4. **Evidence** The end of the essay talks about multitasking and the presidency.
   Is this an effective example? How useful is it in applying the issues in this
   essay to regular people?
5. **Audience** Who is Silverman's intended audience?

Evaluating the Reading

1. **Appeals** To what needs and values does Silverman appeal?
2. **Fallacies** What fallacies, if any, can you find in Silverman's essay?

3. **Sources** Evaluate Silverman's use of sources in this essay. What kinds of sources could he have added?

4. **Opposing viewpoints** How does Silverman present opposing viewpoints? Does he refute them? If so, how?

5. **Fact versus opinion** Discuss whether Silverman's essay is made up primarily of fact or of opinion. How does this balance affect the success of his argument?

6. **Language** What are the connotations of *addiction* in paragraph 2 and *missile* in paragraph 4?

Discussing the Reading

1. Do you agree or disagree with Silverman's assertion that multitasking is essential for survival at work? Why?

2. Imagine you were having surgery under local anesthetic and discovered your surgeon multitasking while performing the procedure. Discuss your response.

Writing about the Reading

1. **Essay** Write an essay describing how and why multitasking might have developed as a human behavior. When would it have been a valuable skill? How would it have helped early humans?

2. **Essay** Try working on only one task at a time for one day, and then, in an essay, report what you accomplished, your level of productivity, and / or what you missed.

3. **Essay** Find a professional essay that presents an argument you disagree with. (You may use one of the essays in this book or, perhaps, an opinion piece in a school, local, or national newspaper or on a Web site.) Write an essay arguing against the piece.

Comparing the Arguments

1. Which writer's argument did you find more convincing? Why?

2. Compare how each writer introduces the issue. With what context does each writer frame it?

3. In their discussions of what people try to do when they multitask, Silverman and Bregman do not seem to be talking about exactly the same kinds of activities. How do you think this difference affects their opinions of multitasking?

4. What is the primary difference in the ways that Bregman and Silverman view multitasking? Do they define it differently? If so, describe how each might define it.

5. How do you think Bregman might respond to Silverman's claims?

Working with Argument as a Reader and Writer

The following table reviews the key elements of argument essays and explains how these elements are important to both readers and writers.

Reading ◑ Writing   Argument Essays

Element of an Argument Essay	The Reader's Perspective	The Writer's Perspective
Narrowed Issue	As you read, identify both the large issue and the narrower focus. For instance, the large issue may be "First Amendment rights," but the narrowed issue may be "hate speech."	Millions of words have been written about the most controversial issues of the day. To keep your paper focused, and to do justice to your topic in the allotted space, narrow the issue to one very specific aspect of the subject.
Claim	To identify the claim in an argument, use a method similar to the one you use to identify the thesis statement: Ask yourself, What is the one key idea that the entire essay supports? Often the claim is included directly within the thesis statement.	Before making any claim, be sure to do your research; you don't want to argue in favor of anything that you don't personally believe in—your writing will suffer and your readers will detect your lack of commitment.
Audience	As you read, identify the author's approach to his or her audience. Does the author consider you to be part of an agreeing, wavering, or disagreeing audience? Identify words, phrases, and sentences that point to the author's approach.	To argue effectively, you must have a sense of your readers' expectations, values, beliefs, and attitudes. To get started, consider preparing a brief (paragraph-length) audience profile that identifies your intended audience.

Continued >

Reasons and Evidence	To identify reasons and evidence, look closely at the individual paragraphs. The reason will often be the topic sentence, and the evidence in the supporting details.	Before you begin writing, list all the reasons in favor of your argument and select only the strongest reasons, with the most convincing evidence, to support. Eliminate any weak reasons or evidence.
Errors in Reasoning	When reading an argument essay, be especially alert for the logical fallacies listed in Table 18.1. If you detect an error in reasoning, you have identified a weakness in the argument. Make note in the margin of any logical fallacies and identify exactly how the logic is flawed.	Before finalizing your essay, ask a friend or classmate to read your paper and identify any errors in reasoning. Sometimes writers get so wrapped up in the case they are building that they miss the flaws in their argument. An objective opinion can help you ensure that your logic remains crystal clear.
Needs and Values	A reader's needs and values are part of his or her core personality. As you read, explore how the claims and viewpoints affect you emotionally. Write annotations in the margin to react to the reading. If you feel personally offended or upset by something in the essay, keep an open mind and keep reading. Then, upon rereading, examine your values to determine why you reacted so strongly.	Understanding the needs and values of the audience is key to creating an effective appeal. For example, some readers react well to emotional appeals, while others look for cold, hard facts and logic. Writers should use the best examples (and other types of support) to make their case, always keeping their readers' needs and values in mind.
Opposing Views	As you read, determine whether the writer has acknowledged, accommodated, and/or refuted opposing viewpoints. Highlight each opposing viewpoint and write a summary statement in the margin. Then determine how effectively the writer has presented and debunked the opposition.	Acknowledging opposing viewpoints is an excellent way to show that your writing, while strong and passionate, is also fair and unbiased.

Part 3

Student Research Guide

19
Finding and Using Sources

Sources of information come in many forms. Among the most commonly used are materials that may be available in print or electronic format (such as books, newspapers, magazines, brochures, and scholarly journals), media sources (DVDs, television, radio), and electronic sources (blogs and podcasts, emails). Interviews, personal observations, and surveys are also sources of information.

You can use sources in a variety of ways. For instance, when you are working on a paper that you planned to base on your own experiences, you may discover that you need additional support from outside sources for aspects of the topic. Or, you may start a paper by checking several sources to narrow your topic or become more familiar with it. Finally, you may need to write a research paper, which requires the most extensive use of sources.

When you plan and develop an essay using sources, you will follow the same process described in Chapters 4 through 7. The following guidelines will help you to make your paper with sources successful.

1. **Start with your own ideas.** Your essay should be based on your own ideas. Starting with the sources themselves would result in a summary, not an essay.

2. **Use sources to support your ideas.** Once you have identified the main points of your paper, decide what information is needed to support them. Incorporate sources that will make your ideas believable and acceptable to the reader.

3. **Focus on ideas, not facts.** To maintain a focus on ideas, ask yourself, What do all these facts add up to? For example, when writing about campaign-finance reform, instead of concentrating on the amount of money corporations give to politicians, consider what impact the money has on the politicians' agendas.

4. **Avoid strings of facts and quotations.** Writing that strings together fact after fact or quotation after quotation is dull and does not convey ideas effectively. Try to refer to no more than one or two sources per paragraph.

Primary and Secondary Sources

Sources are classified as *primary* or *secondary*. **Primary sources** include historical documents (letters, diaries, speeches); literary works; autobiographies; original research reports; eyewitness accounts; and your own interviews, observations, or correspondence. For example, a report on a study of heart disease written by the researcher who conducted the study is a primary source, as is a novel by William Faulkner. **Secondary sources** report or comment on primary sources. A journal article that reviews several previously published research reports on heart disease is a secondary source. A book written about Faulkner by a literary critic or biographer is a secondary source.

How to Locate Sources

Since sources of information range from books and videos to interviews and Web sites, it's helpful to use a systematic process to locate and then evaluate and use sources (see Figure 19.1).

Figure 19.1   Locating and Using Sources: An Overview

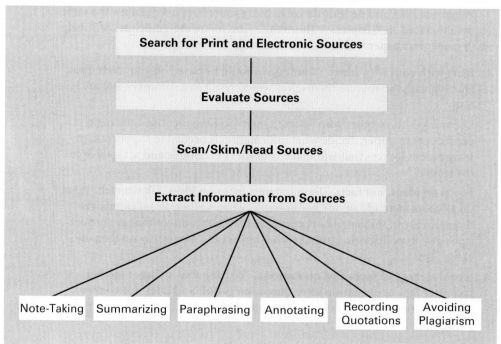

Search for Print and Electronic Sources

Evaluate Sources

Scan/Skim/Read Sources

Extract Information from Sources

Note-Taking   Summarizing   Paraphrasing   Annotating   Recording Quotations   Avoiding Plagiarism

Locating Useful Library Sources

Your college library is one of the best places to look for reference materials. Learning to use the library will help you locate sources effectively, which is imperative for college success. To get the most out of your library, you need to know which of its research tools are best for particular purposes.

USING THE LIBRARY CATALOG

A library's catalog lists books owned by the library. It may also list available magazines, newspapers, government documents, and electronic sources. Most library catalogs are online these days, and most libraries allow access to their catalogs from outside computers, at home or in a computer lab on campus. Catalog entries often indicate whether the book is on the shelf or, if it has been checked out, when it is due back. Some systems allow you to reserve a book by entering your request on the computer. Figure 19.2 shows a typical search page of an online library catalog.

Figure 19.2   Library Catalog Search Page

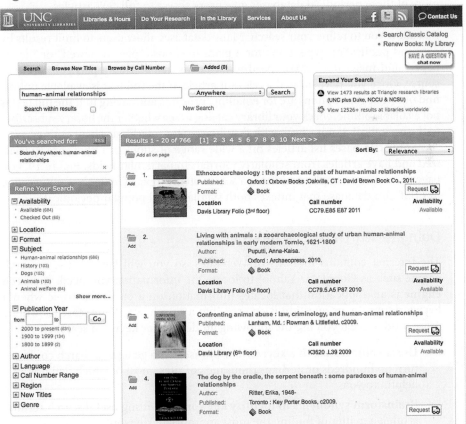

All catalogs provide call numbers, which tell you where to locate books on the library's shelves. Once you have a specific call number, use your library's floor plan and the call-number guides posted on shelves to locate the appropriate section of the library and the book you need. Be sure to scan the surrounding books, which are usually on related topics. You may discover other useful sources that you overlooked in the catalog.

LOCATING ARTICLES USING PERIODICAL DATABASES

Periodicals include newspapers, popular magazines, and scholarly journals. Because periodicals are published daily, weekly, or monthly, they often contain up-to-date information about a subject. Table 19.1 summarizes the differences between popular magazines (such as *People*) and scholarly journals (such as the *American Journal of Psychology*). For academic essays, it is best not to rely solely on information from popular magazines.

A library's catalog does not list specific articles from magazines or journals. To find such articles, you must consult a periodical database. Most electronic library catalogs provide access to a number of such databases, and more and more of these periodical databases give users access to full-text articles.

When you are searching for articles in a periodical database, look for options that allow you to refine your search. Many databases allow users to limit results by date and publication type. Look for a place to choose "peer reviewed" or "newspapers and magazines" if you need to locate an article from a particular kind of source. Once you have located a relevant article, if the full text is available online, find out what your options are for emailing, printing, and saving it. If the full text is not available online, check your library catalog to see whether the library subscribes to the periodical. If not, check with the librarian for interlibrary loan options.

Some databases list articles on a wide range of subjects. Others are specialized and have articles from scholarly journals in particular fields. Figure 19.3 on page 612 shows a sample result from a search on the topic of *animal communication* in *EBSCO*, a database that indexes both scholarly and popular periodicals.

Doing Research on the Internet

The Internet contains millions of Web sites, so you will have to use a search engine such as Google or Yahoo! to locate the information you need. A **search engine** is an application that locates information on a particular topic when a keyword, phrase, or question is entered into a search box. Your searches will be more productive if you use the following guidelines for keyword searches:

- **Use specific terms.** If a keyword or phrase is too general, a search could turn up hundreds or perhaps thousands of sites, most of which will not be helpful to you.

- **Brainstorm synonyms to identify keywords.** Getting useful search results is often a matter of finding the most appropriate keywords.

Table 19.1   A Comparison of Scholarly Journals and Popular Magazines

	Scholarly Journal	Popular Magazine
Who reads it?	Researchers, professionals, students	General public
Who writes it?	Researchers, professionals	Reporters, journalists, freelance writers
Who decides what to publish in it?	Other researchers (peer review)	Editors, publishers
What does it look like?	Mostly text, some charts and graphs, little or no advertising	Many photos, many advertisements, eye-catching layout
What kind of information does it contain?	Results of research studies and experiments, statistics and analysis, in-depth evaluations of specialized topics, overviews of all the research on a subject (literature review), bibliographies and references	Articles of general interest, easy-to-understand language, news items, interviews, opinion pieces, no bibliographies (instead, sources cited informally within the article)
Where is it available?	Sometimes by subscription only, large bookstores, large public library branches, college/university libraries, online	Newsstands, most bookstores, most public library branches, online
How often is it published?	Monthly to quarterly	Weekly to monthly
What are some examples?	*Journal of Bioethics, American Journal of Family Law, Film Quarterly*	*Popular Science, Psychology Today, Time*

Figure 19.3   Result from Search in EBSCO

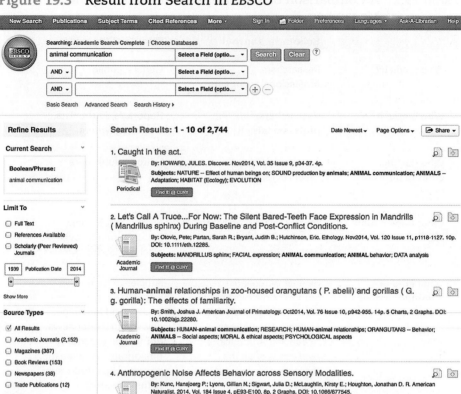

- **Use advanced search functions**. Some search engines, such as Google, allow you to search for an exact phrase and to specify words that should *not* appear in your search results. It also allows you to filter your results by language, reading level, date, region, and so forth.

- **Limit or expand search terms**. If your searches are returning too many results, combine keywords to make search terms more specific or use a specialized database. Remove search terms to broaden your search.

Evaluating Sources for Relevance and Reliability

Avoid the mistake of photocopying many articles, printing out dozens of Web pages, and lugging home numerous books only to find that the sources are not useful. Save yourself time by thinking about which sources will be most relevant and reliable.

Questions for Evaluating Sources for Relevance

A *relevant source* contains information that helps you answer one or more of your research questions. Answering the following questions will help you determine whether a source is relevant:

1. **Is the source appropriate — not too general or too specialized — for your intended audience?** Some sources may not contain the detailed information your audience requires; others may be too technical and require background knowledge that your audience does not have. For example, suppose you are writing about the environmental effects of recycling cans and bottles for an audience of science majors. An article in *Reader's Digest* might be too general. An article in *Environmental Science and Technology*, written for scientists, might be a bit too technical.

2. **Is the source recent enough for your purposes?** In rapidly changing fields of study, outdated sources are not useful unless you need to give a historical perspective. For example, a ten-year-old article on using air bags to improve car safety will not include information on recent discoveries about the dangers that air bags pose to children riding in the front passenger seat.

Questions for Evaluating Sources for Reliability

A *reliable source* is honest, accurate, and credible. Answering the questions below will help you determine whether a source is reliable. To check the reliability of an Internet source, answer the questions in Table 19.2 on page 614 as well.

1. **Is the source scholarly?** Although scholars often disagree with one another, they make a serious attempt to present accurate information. In addition, an article that appears in a scholarly journal or textbook has been reviewed by a panel of professionals in the field prior to publication. Therefore, scholarly sources tend to be trustworthy. For more on the differences between scholarly and popular sources, refer to Table 19.1 on page 611.

2. **Does the source have a solid reputation?** Some popular magazines, such as *Time* and *Newsweek*, are known for responsible reporting, whereas others have a reputation for sensationalism and should be avoided or approached skeptically. Web sites, too, may or may not be reputable.

3. **Is the author an expert in the field?** Check the author's credentials. Information about authors may be given in a headnote; at the end of an article; on a home page in a link; or in the preface, on the dust jacket, or at the beginning or end of a book.

4. **Does the author approach the topic fairly and objectively?** A writer who states a strong opinion is not necessarily biased. However, a writer who ignores opposing views, distorts facts, or ignores information that does not fit his or her opinion is presenting a biased and incomplete view of a topic. Although you can use a biased source to understand a particular viewpoint, you must also seek out other sources that present alternative views.

Table 19.2   Evaluating Internet Sources

Purpose	• Who sponsors or publishes the site — an organization, a corporation, a government agency, or an individual?
	• What are the sponsor's goals — to present information or news, to voice opinions, to sell products, or to promote fun?
Author	• Who wrote the information on the site?
	• Is the information clearly presented and well written?
Accuracy	• Are ideas supported by credible evidence? Is there a works-cited list or bibliography?
	• Is the information presented verifiable?
	• Are opinions clearly identified as such?
Timeliness	• When was the site first created? What is the date of the last revision?
	• Does the specific document you are using have a date?
	• Are the links up to date?

Working with Text: Reading Sources

Reading sources involves some special skills. Unlike textbook reading, in which your purpose is to learn and recall the material, source reading usually is carried out to extract specific information you need about a topic. Therefore, you can often read sources selectively, reading only the relevant parts and skipping over the rest. Use the following strategies for reading sources:

1. **Determine how the source is organized.** For example, is it organized chronologically or by topic?

2. **For journal articles, check the abstract or summary; for books, scan the index and table of contents.** You can quickly determine whether the source contains the information you need and, if so, approximately where to find it.

3. **Look through the source quickly to determine whether it suits your purposes.** Mark or jot down sections that might be worth returning to later for closer reading.

4. **Read worthwhile sections closely and carefully.** To be sure you do not take information out of context, also read the paragraphs before and after the material you have chosen. (For more on strategies for close reading, see Chapters 2 and 3.)

5. **Keep in mind that text on Web sites does not usually follow the traditional text pattern.** Instead of containing paragraphs, a Web page may have a list of topic sentences that you have to click on to get details. In addition, electronic pages are often designed to stand alone: They are brief and do not depend on other pages for meaning. In many instances, background information is not supplied.

Extracting Information from Sources

As you read sources, you will need to take notes to use later. Careful note-taking can help you avoid plagiarism.

Gathering Necessary Citation Information

Be sure to record information for each source. Figure 19.4 provides an example of a form showing necessary information. Recording this information will help you locate the source again, if needed, and give you the information you need for citing the source.

Systems of Note-Taking

When you take research notes, you'll probably need to copy quotes, write paraphrases, and make summary notes. There are three ways to record your research — on note cards, on your computer, or on copies of source material.

Regardless of the system you use, be sure to designate a place to record your own ideas, such as different-colored index cards, a notepad, or a computer folder.

Figure 19.4 Bibliographic Information Worksheet

Author(s) _____

Title and subtitle _____

Page/paragraph/screen numbers (first/last) _____

Title of journal/anthology/Web site _____

Volume/Issue number _____

Date of issue _____

Call number/URL/DOI (Digital Object Identifier) _____

Publisher/Web site sponsor _____

Place of publication _____

Copyright date _____

Be careful as well not to simply record (or highlight) quotations. Writing summary notes or paraphrases helps you think about the ideas in your source, how they fit with other ideas, and how they might work in your research paper.

WRITING NOTES ON NOTE CARDS

Some researchers use 4- by 6-inch or 5- by 8-inch index cards for note-taking, as shown in Figure 19.5. Put information from only one source and about only one subtopic on each card. At the top of the card, indicate the author of the source and the subtopic that the note covers. Include page numbers in case you need to go back and reread the article or passage. If you copy an author's exact words, place the information in quotation marks and include the term *direct quotation* and the page number in parentheses. If you write a summary note (see p. 617) or paraphrase (see pp. 618–19), write *paraphrase* or *summary* on the card and the page number of the source. When you use this system, you can rearrange your cards to experiment with different ways of organizing as you plan your paper.

COMPUTERIZED NOTE-TAKING

To type your notes into computer files and organize your files by subtopic, you can use a computer notebook to create small "note cards" or you can use a hypertext card program. As with note cards, keep track of sources by including the author's name and the page numbers for each source, and make a back-up copy of your notes. If you have access to a computer in the library, you can type in summaries, paraphrases, and direct quotations while you are doing the research.

Figure 19.5   Sample Note Card

Schmoke & Roques, 17-25

Medicalization

Medicalization is a system in which the government would control the release of narcotics to drug addicts.
— would work like a prescription does now — only gov't official would write prescription
— addicts would be required to get counseling and health services
— would take drug control out of hands of drug traffickers (paraphrase, 18)

ANNOTATING COPIES OF SOURCES

To annotate copies of your sources, you photocopy or print the source material, highlight useful information, and write your reactions, paraphrases, and summary notes in the margins or you can use the annotation and highlighting features available with some electronic documents. While annotating source material often saves time, this system does not allow you to sort and rearrange notes by subtopic. For advice on highlighting and annotating, see Chapter 2, pages 34–36.

Writing Summary Notes

Summary notes condense information from sources. Use them when you want to record the gist of an author's ideas but do not need the exact wording or a paraphrase. Use the guidelines below to write effective summary notes. Remember that everything you put in summary notes must be in your own words.

1. **Record only information that relates to your topic and purpose.** Do not include irrelevant information.

2. **Write notes that condense the author's ideas into your own words.** Include key terms and concepts. Do not include specific examples, quotations, or anything that is not essential to the main point. (You can include any comments in a separate note, as suggested earlier.)

3. **Record the ideas in the order in which they appear in the original source.** Reordering ideas might affect the meaning.

4. **Reread your summary to determine whether it contains sufficient information.** Would it be understandable to someone who has not read the original source? If not, revise the summary to include additional information.

5. **Jot down the publication information for the sources you summarize.** Unless you summarize an entire book or poem, you will need page references to cite your sources.

A sample summary is shown below. It summarizes the first three paragraphs of the essay "Snoopers at Work," which appears in Chapter 12 (pp. 274–76). Read the paragraphs, and then study the summary.

Sample Summary

Retail stores can legally spy on people in dressing rooms. Ellen Alderman and Caroline Kennedy wrote *The Right to Privacy* to expose the ways that businesses invade the privacy of their employees and customers. In 1983, a customer in a Michigan department store spotted a store employee spying on him through a vent while he was in a dressing room. The customer sued the department store and lost because the court said that retail business owners could legally spy on customers to help prevent shoplifting.

Writing Paraphrases

When you **paraphrase**, you restate the author's ideas in your own words. You do not condense ideas or eliminate details as you do in a summary. Instead, you use different sentence patterns and vocabulary but keep the author's meaning. In most cases, a paraphrase is approximately the same length as the original material. Compose a paraphrase when you want to record the author's ideas and details but do not want to use a direct quotation. When paraphrasing, be especially careful not to use the author's sentence patterns or vocabulary, as doing so would result in *plagiarism* (see pp. 620–21). Read the excerpt from a source below; then compare it to the paraphrase that follows.

Excerpt from Original

Learning some items may interfere with retrieving others, especially when the items are similar. If someone gives you a phone number to remember, you may be able to recall it later. But if two more people give you their numbers, each successive number will be more difficult to recall. Such proactive interference occurs when something you learned earlier disrupts recall of something you experienced later. As you collect more and more information, your mental attic never fills, but it certainly gets cluttered.

—David G. Myers, *Psychology*

Acceptable Paraphrase

When proactive interference happens, things you have already learned prevent you from remembering things you learn later. In other words, details you learn first may make it harder to recall closely related details you learn subsequently. You can think of your memory as an attic. As you add more junk to it, it will become messy and disorganized. For example, you can remember one new phone number, but if you have two or more new numbers to remember, the task becomes harder.

Unacceptable Paraphrase—Includes Plagiarism

When you learn some things, it may interfere with your ability to remember others. This happens when the things are similar. Suppose a person gives you a phone number to remember. You probably will be able to remember it later. Now, suppose two persons give you their numbers. Each successive number will be harder to remember. Proactive interference happens when something you already learned prevents you from recalling something you experience later. As you learn more and more information, your mental attic never gets full, but it will get cluttered.

Replaces terms with synonyms

Copied terms and phrases

The unacceptable paraphrase does substitute some synonyms—*remember* for *retrieving,* for example—but it is still an example of plagiarism. Not only are some words copied directly from the original, but also the structure of the sentences is nearly identical to the original structure.

Writing paraphrases can be tricky, both because there are so many ways to paraphrase a particular passage and because an author's language can easily "creep in." The following guidelines should help you write effective paraphrases:

1. **Read first; then write.** You may find it helpful to read material more than once before you try paraphrasing.

2. **If you must use any of the author's wording, enclose it in quotation marks.** If you do not use quotation marks, you may inadvertently use the same wording in your paper, which would result in plagiarism.

3. **Work sentence by sentence, restating each in your own words.** To avoid copying an author's words, read a sentence, cover it up, and then write. Be sure your version is accurate but not too similar to the original. As a rule of thumb, no more than two or three consecutive words should be the same as in the original.

4. **Choose synonyms that do not change the author's meaning or intent.** Consult a dictionary if necessary.

5. **Use your own sentence structure.** Using an author's sentence structure can be considered plagiarism. If the original uses lengthy sentences, for example, your paraphrase of it should use shorter sentences.

6. **Record the publication information.** You will need this information to document the sources in your paper.

Recording Quotations

Sometimes it is advisable, and even necessary, to use a direct quotation — a writer's words exactly as they appear in the original source. Use quotations to record wording that is unusual or striking or to report the exact words of an expert on your topic. Be sure to record a direct quotation precisely as it appears in the source. The author's spelling, punctuation, and capitalization must be copied exactly. Also write down the page number on which the material being quoted appears in the source. Be sure to indicate that you are copying directly by writing *direct quotation* in parentheses.

You may delete a word, phrase, or sentence from a quotation as long as you do not change the meaning of the quotation. Use an ellipsis mark (three spaced periods) — . . . — to indicate that you have made a deletion.

Avoiding Plagiarism

In writing a paper with sources, you must avoid **plagiarism** — using someone else's ideas, wording, organization, or sentence structure as if it were your own. Plagiarizing is intellectually dishonest and is considered a form of cheating because it involves submitting someone else's work as your own. Harsh academic penalties are applied to students found guilty of plagiarism; these include receiving a failing grade on the paper, failing the entire course, or even being dismissed from the institution. 🔖

What Counts as Plagiarism

There are two types of plagiarism — intentional (deliberate) and unintentional (accidental). Both are serious and carry the same academic penalties. Table 19.3 can help you determine if you have plagiarized.

Table 19.3   Quick Reference Guide to Plagiarism

Whether you are working with print or Internet sources, you have plagiarized if you have
• copied information word for word without appropriate quotation marks, even if you acknowledged the source
• paraphrased, summarized, or otherwise used information without acknowledging the source
• borrowed someone else's organization, sentence structure, or sequence of ideas without giving that person credit
• used someone else's visual material (graphs, tables, charts, maps, diagrams) without acknowledging the source
• used another student's work or purchased a paper online and submitted it as your own

How to Avoid Plagiarism

To avoid plagiarism, you need to be very careful both when taking notes and when composing your paper. Here are some guidelines to follow.

- **Acknowledge all information from your sources unless it is common knowledge. Common knowledge** includes well-known facts (everyday information, scientific facts, historical events, and so on).

🔖 **LaunchPad Solo**
macmillan learning   Visit **LaunchPad Solo for Readers and Writers > Working with Sources** for more practice with integrating sources and avoiding plagiarism.

- **Place anything you copy in quotation marks and record the source.**
- **Record the complete source information** for any material you paraphrase, summarize, or otherwise include in your notes.
- **Always acknowledge the ideas or opinions of others, even if you do not quote them directly and regardless of whether they are in print or another medium.** For example, movies, videos, documentaries, interviews, and computerized sources all require acknowledgment.
- **Be sure to separate your own ideas and opinions from those expressed in your sources.** Try using two different colors of ink or two different print sizes for your ideas and your sources' ideas. Alternatively, use two different sections of a notebook or two different computer files.
- **Make sure that a paraphrase does not mix the author's wording and your own.**
- **Always cut and paste information you want to save into a file for notes,** rather than directly into your paper.

See Chapter 20 for guidelines on how to document sources in your papers, an important step in avoiding plagiarism.

20
Documenting Your Sources

To avoid plagiarism, you need to acknowledge your sources by **documenting** them. Documentation also helps interested readers find those sources.

There are various systems of documentation that have become the standards for specific disciplines. This chapter covers the styles recommended by the Modern Language Association (MLA) and the American Psychological Association (APA). MLA style is commonly used in English and the humanities, whereas APA style is commonly used in the social sciences. If you are unsure about which system to use, check with your instructor.

Numerous online citation generators such as Easy Bib can help you generate needed documentation, but remember that these tools are only as accurate as the information you supply. If you fail to include a volume number, for example, the documentation the tool generates will also be incomplete. 📚

📚 **LaunchPad Solo** Visit **LaunchPad Solo for Readers and Writers > Search and Citation**
macmillan learning   **Tutorials** for more practice with documenting sources in MLA and APA style.

622

Documenting Sources in MLA Style

The first section of this chapter provides models for documenting some common types of sources. For more information, consult

> *MLA Handbook*. 8th ed., The Modern Language Association of America, 2016.

The sample student paper that appears on pp. 631–34 uses MLA style, as do student papers in Chapters 12, 14, and 16–18.

In the MLA system, documentation has two parts that work together.

1. **In-text citations** identify sources within the text of the paper.
2. **A list of works cited**, at the end of the paper, gives full information on each of the sources.

MLA-Style In-Text Citations

When you paraphrase, summarize, or quote from a source, you must credit the source by providing an in-text citation at that point in your paper. The MLA-style in-text citation is a brief reference to the source, on which there is more complete information in the list of works cited. There are two basic ways to write an in-text citation:

1. **Use an attribution with parenthetical source information.** When you use an attribution, you mention the author's name *before* presenting the borrowed material. Use the author's full name for the first mention; subsequent mentions generally include only the last name. (Upon first mention, you might also provide background context that establishes the source as relevant.) The parenthetical content, with the page number(s) and sometimes a shortened title of the source, immediately follows the borrowed material.

   Jo-Ellan Dimitius, a jury-selection consultant whose book *Reading People* discusses methods of predicting behavior, observes that big spenders often suffer from low self-esteem (35).

2. **Use an entirely parenthetical citation.** When citing a source parenthetically, include both the author's last name and the page number(s) in parentheses at the end of the sentence. Do not separate the name and page number with a comma.

   Big spenders often suffer from low self-esteem (Dimitius 35).

RULES FOR IN-TEXT CITATIONS

Many instructors prefer that you use attributions rather than parenthetical citations. For either type of citation, the following rules apply.

- Do not use the word *page* or the abbreviation *p.* or *pp.*
- Place the sentence period after the closing parenthesis, unless the citation follows a block quotation (see below).
- Insert the closing quotation mark before the opening parenthesis.

> "Countercultures reject the conventional wisdom and standards of
> the dominant culture and provide alternatives to mainstream culture"
> (Thompson and Hickey 76).

In MLA style, lengthy quotations (more than three lines of poetry or more than four typed lines of prose) are indented in *block form*, one-half inch from the left margin. Double-space a block quotation and do not put it in quotation marks. Introduce a block quotation in the sentence that precedes it; a colon is often used at the end of the introduction. The parenthetical citation appears at the end of the block quotation, *after* the final sentence's period.

Block Quotation, MLA Style

Although a business is a profit-making organization, it is also a social

organization, as Hicks and Gwynne note:

> In Western society, businesses are essentially economic organizations,
> with both the organizations themselves and the individuals in them
> dedicated to making as much money as possible in the most efficient
> way. But businesses are also social organizations, each of which has
> its unique culture. (174)

MLA-Style List of Works Cited

Follow these general guidelines for preparing the list. For an example of a student MLA-style works-cited list, see page 634.

1. **List only the sources you cite in your paper.** If you consulted a source but did not cite it in your paper, do not include it in the list of works cited.
2. **Put the list on a separate page at the end of your paper.** The heading *Works Cited* should be centered an inch below the top of the page. Do not use quotation marks, underlining, or bold type for the heading.
3. **Alphabetize the list by authors' last names.** For works with multiple authors, invert only the first author's name. If no author is listed, begin the entry with the title.

4. **Capitalize the first word and all other words in a title except** *a, an, the, to,* **coordinating conjunctions, and prepositions.**

5. **Italicize titles of books and names of periodicals.**

6. **Include the publication date.** If no publication date is available for an online source, add the word *Accessed* and the date you accessed the source at the end of the entry.

7. **Give inclusive page numbers of articles in periodicals.** Use the abbreviation *p.* or *pp.* before the page number(s).

8. **Include the URL of sources accessed online.** Do not include *http://* or *https://*.

9. **Indent the second and all subsequent lines half an inch.** This is known as the *hanging indent* style.

10. **Double-space the entire list.**

Some MLA-Style Models

The following are examples of in-text citations and accompanying works-cited entries for some common types of sources.

BOOKS

One Author

In-Text Citations

According to Witold Rybczynski, . . . (58).

. . . (Rybczynski 58).

Works-Cited Entry

Rybczynski, Witold. *Makeshift Metropolis: Ideas about Cities.* Scribner, 2010.

Two or More Authors

In-Text Citations

Postel and Richter assert . . . (74).

. . . (Postel and Richter 74).

Works-Cited Entry

Postel, Sandra, and Brian Richter. *Rivers for Life: Managing Water for People and Nature.* Island Press, 2003.

For three or more authors, use the first author's last name followed by either a phrase referring to the other authors (in an attribution) or *et al.*, Latin for "and others" (in a parenthetical citation and works-cited entry).

Figure 20.1 Where to Find Documentation Information for a Book

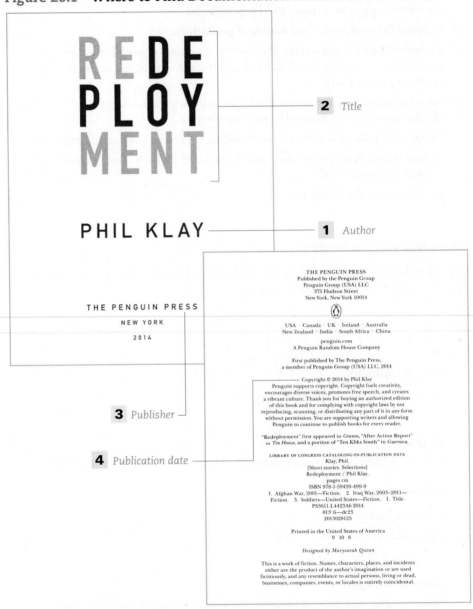

Klay, Phil. *Redeployment*. Penguin Press, 2014.

In-Text Citations

Krebs and colleagues maintain . . . (198).

. . . (Krebs et al. 198).

Works-Cited Entry

Krebs, Jocelyn, et al. *Lewin's Genes XI*. Jones & Bartlett Learning, 2014.

PERIODICALS

Article in a Magazine

In-Text Citations

Jason Killingsworth contends that . . . (50).

. . . (Killingsworth 50).

Works-Cited Entry

Killingsworth, Jason. "The Unbearable Lightness of Being Jonsi." *Paste Magazine*, May 2010, pp. 49-53.

Note: For weekly magazines, include the day of publication before the month, as shown on page 628.

Article in a Newspaper

In-Text Citations

Alex Pham reports . . . (B2).

. . . (Pham B2).

Works-Cited Entry

Pham, Alex. "Pandora Online Radio Service IPO." *Los Angeles Times*, 12 Feb. 2011, p. B2.

Article in a Scholarly Journal

In-Text Citations

As described by Francine Prose, . . . (42).

. . . (Prose 42).

Works-Cited Entry

Prose, Francine. "Genocide without Apology." *The American Scholar*, vol. 72, no. 2, Spring 2003, pp. 39-43.

Figure 20.2   **Where to Find Documentation Information for an Article**

2 Article title

1 Author

5 Page

3 **4** Date

Periodical title

1 **2** **3** **4** **5**

Gladwell, Malcolm. "Starting Over." *The New Yorker*, 24 Aug. 2015, pp. 32–37.

INTERNET SOURCES

Work from a Web Site

If an Internet source does not have page numbers, provide only the author name in an in-text citation; for works with no author, use a shortened form of the title instead. In works-cited entries for Internet sources, include the URL.

In-Text Citations

Marc Hogan theorizes . . . .

. . . (Hogan).

Works-Cited Entry

Hogan, Marc. "Live Transmission." *Pitchfork*, 6 Feb. 2011, pitchfork.com
/features/article/7919-live-transmission.

Figure 20.3 Where to Find Documentation Information for a Web Site

5 URL
3 Title of site
1 Author
2 Title of work
4 Publication date

1   **2**   **3**   **4**

Chen, Jane. "A Warm Embrace That Saves Lives." *TED*, Nov. 2009,

5

www.ted.com/talks/jane_chen_a_warm_embrace_that_saves_lives.

Article in an Online Newspaper or Magazine

In-Text Citations

Andrew Leonard discusses . . . .

. . . (Leonard).

Works-Cited Entry

Leonard, Andrew. "The Surveillance State High School." *Salon*, 27 Nov. 2012,
www.salon.com/2012/11/27/the_surveillance_state_high_school/.

Article from an Online Periodical Database

In-Text Citations

As Coles explains, . . . (902).

. . . (Coles 902).

Works-Cited Entry

Coles, Kimberly Anne. "The Matter of Belief in John Donne's Holy Sonnets."
Renaissance Quarterly, vol. 68, no. 3, Fall 2015, pp. 899-931. JSTOR,
doi:10.1086/683855.

Sample Pages from an MLA-Style Paper

The following pages are from a research paper written by Nicholas Destino for
his first-year writing course at Niagara County Community College. Destino
used MLA style for formatting his paper and documenting his sources. Notice
how he uses in-text citations and quotations to provide evidence that supports
his thesis.

First Page of MLA-Style Paper

Destino 1

Nicholas Destino

Professor Thomas

English 101

11 Mar. 2011

Identification: Double-space writer's name, instructor's name, course title, and date

Do Animals Have Emotions?

Title centered

Double-space throughout

Somewhere in the savannas of Africa a mother elephant is dying in the company of many other pachyderms. Some of them are part of her family; some are fellow members of her herd. The dying elephant tips from side to side and seems to be balancing on a thin thread in order to sustain her life. Many of the other elephants surround her as she struggles to regain her balance. They also try to help by feeding and caressing her. After many attempts by the herd to save her life, they seem to realize that there is simply nothing more that can be done. She finally collapses to the ground in the presence of her companions. Most of the other elephants move away from the scene. There are, however, two elephants who remain behind with the dead elephant-- another mother and her calf. The mother turns her back to the body and taps it with one foot. Soon the other elephants call for them to follow and eventually they do (Masson and McCarthy, *When Elephants Weep* 95). These movements, which are slow and ritualistic, suggest that elephants may be capable of interpreting and responding to the notion of death.

In-text citation of a work with two authors; short title included because another work by these authors is cited later in the essay

The topic of animal emotions is one that, until recently, has rarely been discussed or studied by scientists. However, since the now-famous comprehensive field studies of chimpanzees by the internationally renowned primatologist Jane Goodall, those who study animal behavior have begun to look more closely at the notion that animals feel emotions. As

Body Page from MLA-Style Paper

Header: student's name and page number

a result of their observations of various species of animals, a number of these researchers have come to the conclusion that animals do exhibit a wide range of emotions, such as grief, sympathy, and joy.

One of the major reasons that research into animal emotions was traditionally avoided is that scientists fear being accused of *anthropomorphism*--the act of attributing human qualities to animals. To do so is perceived as unscientific (Masson and McCarthy, "Hope and Joy" 45).

Attribution of summaries and quotations within text

Frans de Waal, of the Yerkes Regional Primate Research Center in Atlanta, believes that if people are not open to the possibility of animals having emotions, they may be overlooking important information about both animals and humans. He explains his position in his article "Are We in Anthropodenial?" The term *anthropodenial*, which he coined, refers to "a blindness to the humanlike characteristics of other animals, or the animal-like characteristics of

Page numbers follow quotations

Attributions of paraphrase and quotation

ourselves" (52). De Waal proposes that because humans and animals are so closely related, it would be impossible for one not to have some characteristics of the other. He contends, "If two closely related species act in the same manner, their underlying mental processes are probably the same, too" (53). If de Waal is correct, then humans can presume that animals do have emotions because of the many similarities between human and animal behavior.

Grief has been observed in many different species. In many instances, their behaviors (and presumably, therefore, their emotions) are uncannily similar to the behaviors of humans. Birds that mate for life have been observed showing obvious signs of grief when their mates die. In *The Human Nature of Birds*, Theodore Barber includes a report from

Body Page from MLA-Style Paper

Destino 3

one Dr. Franklin, who witnessed a male parrot caring for his mate by feeding her and trying to help her raise herself when she was dying. Franklin observed the following scene:

> Her unhappy spouse moved around her incessantly, his attention and tender cares redoubled. He even tried to open her beak to give her some nourishment. . . . At intervals, he uttered the most plaintive cries, then with his eyes fixed on her, kept a mournful silence. At length his companion breathed her last; from that moment he pined away, and died in the course of a few weeks.
> (qtd. in Barber 116)

Professor of ecology and evolutionary biology Marc Beckoff notes, "Among the different emotions that animals display clearly and unambiguously is grief. Many animals display profound grief at the loss or absence of a close friend or loved one." This observation reinforces de Waal's position that animals experience some of the same emotions as humans.

Perhaps the most extreme case of grief experienced by an animal is exemplified by the true story of Flint, a chimp, when Flo, his mother, died. In her book *Through a Window*, which elaborates on her thirty years of experience studying and living among the chimps in Gombe, Tanzania, Jane Goodall gives the following account of Flint's experience with grief.

> Flint became increasingly lethargic, refused most food and, with his immune system thus weakened, fell sick. The last time I saw him alive, he was hollow-eyed, gaunt and utterly depressed, huddled in the vegetation close to where Flo had died. . . . The last short journey he made, pausing to rest every few feet, was to the very place where Flo's body had lain. There

Quotation longer than four lines indented half an inch and not enclosed in quotation marks; period precedes citation

Citation for an indirect source

Source's **credentials** included within the text

Ellipsis marks used to indicate omitted material

The **works-cited list** appears on a new page; heading is centered; list is double-spaced throughout.

Works Cited Page from MLA-Style Paper

Works Cited

Barber, Theodore Xenophone. *The Human Nature of Birds: A Scientific Discovery with Startling Implications*. St. Martin's Press, 1993.

Online magazine

Beckoff, Marc. "Grief in Animals: It's Arrogant to Think We're the Only Animals Who Mourn." *Psychology Today,* 29 Oct. 2009, www.psychologytoday.com/blog/animal-emotions/200910/grief-in-animals-its-arrogant-think-were-the-only-animals-who-mourn.

Web site

Butler, Rhett A. "Marathon Swimmer: An Interview with the First Man to Swim the Length of the Amazon." *Mongabay.com*, 23 Jan. 2011, news.mongabay.com/2011/01/marathon-swimmer-an-interview-with-the-first-man-to-swim-the-length-of-the-amazon.

Monthly magazine

de Waal, Frans. "Are We in Anthropodenial?" *Discover*, July 1997, pp. 50-53.

Weekly magazine

"Going Ape." *The Economist*, 17 Feb. 1997, p. 78.

Book

Goodall, Jane. *Through a Window*. Houghton Mifflin, 1990.

Scholarly journal

Hemelrijk, Charlotte K. "Support for Being Groomed in Long-Tailed Macaques, Macaca Fascicularis." *Animal Behaviour*, vol. 48, no. 2, Aug. 1994, pp. 479-81.

Two authors

Masson, Jeffrey Moussaieff, and Susan McCarthy. "Hope and Joy among the Animals." *Utne Reader*, July-Aug. 1995, pp. 44-46.

Second work by same authors

—. *When Elephants Weep: The Emotional Lives of Animals*. Delacorte Press, 1995.

Entries are alphabetized by authors' last names.

Mercer, Phil. "Dolphins Prevent NZ Shark Attack." *BBC News*, 23 Nov. 2004, news.bbc.co.uk/2/hi/asia-pacific/4034383.stm.

Peterson, Dale, and Jane Goodall. *Visions of Caliban: On Chimpanzees and People*. Houghton Mifflin, 1993.

First line of each entry is flush with the left margin; subsequent lines are indented half an inch.

Walter, Elizabeth. "Tickled Pink: Why Scientists Want to Make Rats Laugh." *Greater Good*, Greater Good Science Center, 1 June 2008, greatergood.berkeley.edu/article/item/tickled_pink_why_scientists_want_make_rats_laugh.

Documenting Sources in APA Style

APA style, recommended by the American Psychological Association, is commonly used in the social sciences. Both in-text citations and a list of references are used to document sources, as the models below show. For more information on citing sources in APA style, consult the following reference work:

> American Psychological Association. (2010). *Publication manual of the American Psychological Association* (6th ed.). Washington, DC: Author.

The sample pages that appear on pages 641–43 use APA style.

APA-Style In-Text Citations

Your paper must include in-text citations for all material you summarize, paraphrase, or quote from sources. There are two basic ways to write an in-text citation:

1. **Use an attribution and a parenthetical citation.** Mention the author or authors' names in a phrase or sentence introducing the material, and include the year of publication in parentheses immediately following the names.

   Avery and Ehrlich (2008) said, "Nasal sounds are made with air passing through the nose" (p. 21).

2. **Use only a parenthetical citation.** Include the author or authors' last names, the year of publication, and the page number in parentheses (separated by commas).

   Snorts, snores, and other such sounds are created "with air passing through the nose" (Avery & Ehrlich, 2008, p. 21).

APA style requires that you include page numbers only for quotations, but your instructor may want you to include a page number for paraphrases and summaries as well, so make sure you ask.

RULES FOR IN-TEXT CITATIONS

Attributions allow you to put your sources in context, so use an attribution for most citations. For either type of citation, follow these rules.

- Place the sentence period after the closing parenthesis. When a quotation ends the sentence, insert the closing quotation mark before the opening parenthesis. Block quotations are an exception to these rules (see below).
- For direct quotations and paraphrases, include the page number after the year, separating it from the year with a comma. Use the abbreviation *p.* or *pp.* followed by a space and the page number(s).

In APA style, lengthy quotations (40 words or longer) are indented in *block form*, one half inch from the left margin. Double-space a block quotation and do not put it in quotation marks. Introduce a block quotation in the sentence that precedes it; a colon is often used at the end of the introductory sentence. The parenthetical citation appears at the end of the block quotation, *after* the final sentence's closing punctuation mark.

Block Quotation, APA Style

Although a business is a profit-making organization, it is also a social organization, as Hicks and Gwynne (2008) note:

> In Western society, businesses are essentially economic organizations, with both the organizations themselves and the individuals in them dedicated to making as much money as possible in the most efficient way. But businesses are also social organizations, each of which has its unique culture. (p. 174)

APA-Style List of References

Follow these general guidelines for preparing the list of references. For an example of a student APA-style reference list, see page 643.

1. **List only the sources you cite in your paper.** If you consulted a source but did not cite it in your paper, do not include it in the list of references.

2. **Put the list on a separate page at the end of your paper.** The heading *References* should be centered an inch below the top of the page. Do not use quotation marks, underlining, or bold type for the heading.

3. **Alphabetize the list by authors' last names.** Give the last name first, followed by a comma and an initial or initials. Do not spell out authors' first names; use a space between initials: *Myers, D. G.* For works with multiple authors (up to seven), list all authors' names in inverted order.

   Avery, P., & Ehlrich, S. (2008). *Teaching American English pronunciation.* New York, NY: Oxford University Press.

4. **Put the publication date in parentheses after the author's name.**

5. **For titles of books, articles, and Web pages, capitalize the first word, the first word following a colon, and any proper nouns. For titles of periodicals, capitalize all important words.**

6. **Include the word *A*, *An*, or *The* at the beginning of a title, but ignore it when you alphabetize.**

7. **Italicize titles of books and names of journals, newspapers, and magazines.** Do not italicize, underline, or use quotation marks with article titles.

8. **For magazine and journal articles, italicize the volume number.**

9. **For materials accessed electronically, end with the digital object identi-fier (DOI); if there is no DOI, insert the URL** of the home page for the journal or publishing company that published the source or for the source itself, preceded by the words *Retrieved from*. If necessary, break URLs before punctuation marks, such as dots (.) and question marks (?). DOIs and URLs are not followed by periods.

10. **Indent the second and all subsequent lines half an inch, hanging indent style.**

11. **Double-space the entire list.**

Some APA-Style Models

The following are some examples of in-text citations and accompanying reference entries for some common types of sources.

BOOKS

APA Format for Citing a Book

parentheses

1 *period* **2** *period* **3** *period* **4** *colon*

Author's last name, initial(s) . (Year) . Title (italics) . Place of publication :

5 *period*

Publisher .

1 **2**   **3**   **4**   **5**

Parfitt, M. (2012). *Writing in response*. Boston MA: Bedford/St. Martin's.

ONE AUTHOR

In-Text Citations

According to Witold Rybczynski (2010), ...

. . . (Rybczynski, 2010).

Reference Entry

Rybczynski, W. (2010). *Makeshift metropolis: Ideas about cities*. New York, NY: Scribner.

Two Authors

In-Text Citations

Postel and Richter (2003) assert . . . .

. . . (Postel & Richter, 2003).

Reference Entry

Postel, S., & Richter, B. (2003). *Rivers for life: Managing water for people and nature.* Washington, DC: Island Press.

Note: When a document has three to five authors, the in-text citation will include all authors' last names the first time the source is mentioned. In subsequent references to the same source, use the first author's last name followed by *et al.* (Latin for "and others").

First Reference

Lewin, Krebs, Kilpatrick, and Goldstein (2011) have found . . . .

. . . (Lewin, Krebs, Kilpatrick, & Goldstein, 2011).

Later References

Lewin et al. (2011) discovered . . . .

. . . (Lewin et al., 2011).

For six or more authors, use the first author's last name followed by *et al.* in all in-text citations.

PERIODICALS

APA Format for Citing a Periodical Article

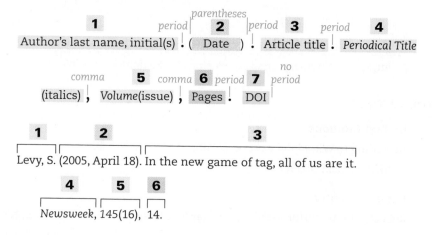

Article in a Monthly Magazine

In-Text Citations

Jason Killingsworth (2010) contends that . . . .

. . . (Killingsworth, 2010).

Reference Entry

Killingsworth, J. (2010, May).The unbearable lightness of being Jonsi. *Paste Magazine*, 49-53.

Note: For weekly magazines, include the year, followed by the month and the day—for example: (2010, May 18).

Article in a Newspaper

In-Text Citations

Alex Pham (2011) reports . . . .

. . . (Pham, 2011).

Reference Entry

Pham, A. (2011, February 12). Pandora online radio service IPO. *Los Angeles Times*, p. B2.

Article in a Scholarly Journal

Note: If issues in each volume are numbered continuously (issue 1 ends on page 159 and issue 2 begins on page 160, for example), omit the issue number.

In-Text Citations

As described by Francine Prose (2005), ...

. . . (Prose, 2005).

Reference Entry

Prose, F. (2005). Genocide without apology. *American Scholar, 72*(1), 39-43.

INTERNET SOURCES

For Internet sources, include enough information to allow readers to locate the sources online.

APA Format for Citing Internet Sources

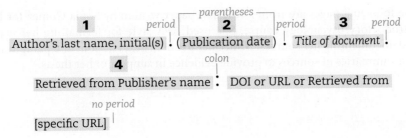

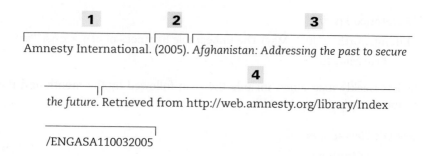

Amnesty International. (2005). *Afghanistan: Addressing the past to secure*

the future. Retrieved from http://web.amnesty.org/library/Index

/ENGASA110032005

Article in an Online Newspaper or Magazine

In-Text Citations

Sullivan (2008) reports . . . .

. . . (Sullivan, 2008).

Reference Entry

Sullivan, P. (2008, May 6). Quiet Va. wife ended interracial marriage ban. *The*
   Washington Post. Retrieved from http://www.washingtonpost.com

Article from an Online Journal

In-Text Citations

Schubert (2008) argues . . . .

. . . (Schubert, 2008).

Reference Entry

Schubert, C. (2008, May 6). The need to consider the impact of
   previous stressors on current stress parameter measurements.
   Stress: The International Journal on the Biology of Stress, 11(2), 85–87.
   doi:10.1080/10253890801895811

Sample Pages from an APA-Style Paper

The following pages are from a research paper written by Sonia Gomez for her introductory psychology course. She used APA style for formatting her paper and documenting her sources. Notice her use of in-text citations and paraphrases and summaries of sources to provide evidence in support of her thesis.

APA-Style Title Page

SCHIZOPHRENIA: DEFINITION AND TREATMENT   1

Schizophrenia: Definition and Treatment

Sonia Gomez

Psychology 101

Professor McCombs

Header: Title at top left, page number at top right

Identification: Double-space and include on title page writer's name, course title, and instructor's name.

Information on title page should be centered vertically and horizontally. (Vertical centering not shown here.)

APA-Style Abstract

SCHIZOPHRENIA: DEFINITION AND TREATMENT   2

Abstract

Schizophrenia is a mental/brain disorder that affects about 1% of the population. The five types of schizophrenia include paranoid, disorganized, catatonic, undifferentiated, and residual. There are three categories of symptoms—positive, disorganized or cognitive, and negative. The causes of schizophrenia are not well known, but there is likely a genetic component and an environmental component. The structure of the brain of schizophrenics is also unusual. Treatments include drug therapy with typical and atypical antipsychotics and psychosocial and cognitive-behavioral therapies.

Abstract: Include an abstract, a brief summary of the report; heading centered, not bold

Double-space essay, leave one-inch margins on all sides

APA-Style Body Page

SCHIZOPHRENIA: DEFINITION AND TREATMENT   3

Title: Repeat full title just before text of paper begins; title centered, not bold

Schizophrenia: Definition and Treatment

Introduction: Presentation of the topic researched by Gomez

The disorder schizophrenia comes with an ugly cultural stigma. There is a common belief that all schizophrenics are violent. In fact, they are more a danger to themselves than to others because they often commit suicide. Many of the movies, books, and TV shows in our culture do not help to diminish this stigma. The movie *A Beautiful Mind*, for example, features a paranoid schizophrenic who comes close to harming his family and others around him because of his hallucinations and delusions. He believes that the government is out to

Sources: Authors named in parenthetical citation; ampersand (&), not the word *and*, between names

get him (Grazer & Howard, 2001). Many people are afraid of schizophrenics and believe their permanent home should be in a mental hospital or psychiatric ward. This paper helps to dispel misperceptions of the disorder by providing facts about and treatments of the disorder.

Heading: First-level heading is centered, bold

What Is Schizophrenia?

Sources: No individual author named, so Web site sponsor listed as author

Schizophrenia is a mental/brain disorder that affects about 1% of the population or 2.2 million Americans (National Institutes of Mental Health, 2010). There is no cure for schizophrenia, but it can often be successfully treated (National Institutes of Mental Health, 2010). Schizophrenia does not seem to favor a specific gender or ethnic group. The disease rarely occurs in children. Hallucinations and delusions usually begin between ages 16 and 30 (National Alliance on Mental Illness, 2007).

Heading: Second-level heading at left margin, bold

Types of Schizophrenia

There are five types of schizophrenia—paranoid, disorganized, catatonic, undifferentiated, and residual.

APA-Style References Page

SCHIZOPHRENIA: DEFINITION AND TREATMENT   8

References

Barch, D. (2003). Cognition in schizophrenia: Does working memory work? *Current Directions in Psychological Science, 12*(4), 146–150. doi:10.1111/1467-8721.01251

Bower, B. (2008). Rare mutations tied to schizophrenia. *Science News, 173*(14), 222.

Conklin, H., & Iacono, W. (2002). Schizophrenia: A neurodevelopmental perspective. *Current Directions in Psychological Science, 11*(1), 33–37.

Grazer, B. (Producer), & Howard, R. (Director). (2001). *A Beautiful Mind* [Motion picture]. Los Angeles, CA: Universal Pictures.

Internet Mental Health Initiative. (2001). UCLA maps how schizophrenia engulfs teen brains. Retrieved from http://www.schizophrenia.com/research/schiz.brain.htm

National Alliance on Mental Illness. (2007). Schizophrenia. In *Mental illnesses.* Retrieved from http://www.nami.org/Template.cfm?Section=By_Illness&Template=/TaggedPage/TaggedPageDisplay.cfm&TPLID=54&ContentID=23036

National Institutes of Mental Health. (2010). Schizophrenia. In *Health topics.* Retrieved from http://www.nimh.nih.gov/health/topics/schizophrenia/index.shtml

WebMD. (2010). Schizophrenia guide. In *Mental health center.* Retrieved from http://www.webmd.com/schizophrenia/guide/default.htm

References heading is centered, not bold; list appears on a new page.

DOI: The DOI is provided when available for printed and online works.

List is double-spaced throughout.

Entries are alphabetized by author's last name or name of sponsor. Only the first word and proper nouns/adjectives are capitalized in titles of shorter works (such as articles in a periodical or Web pages on a Web site). First, last, and all key words are capitalized in titles of longer, stand-alone works (such as books, periodicals, films, Web sites).

URL: The URL is provided for Web sites and Web pages.

Part **4**

Handbook:
Writing Problems
and How to
Correct Them

Handbook Contents

Review of Basic Grammar

Writing Correct Sentences

Using Punctuation and Mechanics Correctly

Review of Basic Grammar

1 Parts of Speech

Each word in a sentence acts as one of eight parts of speech: *nouns, pronouns, verbs, adjectives, adverbs, conjunctions, prepositions,* and *interjections.* These building blocks of our language are summarized in Table H1.1. Often, to revise your writing or to correct sentence errors, you need to understand how a word or phrase functions in a particular sentence.

Table H1.1   Parts of Speech

Part of Speech	Definition/ Primary Function	Examples
Noun	Names a person, place, thing, or idea A **proper noun** refers to a specific person, place, thing, or idea and should be capitalized.	• Person: *waiter, Professor Wainwright* • Place: *classroom, Texas* • Thing: *textbook, Xbox* • Idea: *excitement, Marxism*
Pronoun	Takes the place of a noun • *I, me, my, mine* • *You, your, yours* • *He, his, she, her, hers, it, its, they, their, theirs* The noun to which a pronoun refers is called its **antecedent**.	• *I* have several questions about the job. • *You* really should try to help *your* father more. • The *managers* believe *they* are being true to *their* values, but *their* stubbornness will be *their* undoing. • Is this iPad *mine* or *yours*?
Verb	Shows action, occurrence, or a state of being Sometimes verb phrases include a **helping verb**.	• Action: *read, study, think, do, eat* • Occurrence: *become, happen* • State of being: *be, am, is, are, feel, seem* • Verb phrases (with helping verbs in italics): *can* help, *could* go, *have* seen, *had* created, *may* visit, *might have* cried, *should* plan, *will* live, *would* awaken

Continued >

LaunchPad Solo
macmillan learning

Visit **LaunchPad Solo for Readers and Writers > Overview: Parts of Speech** for tutorials, videos, and practice exercises on the parts of speech.

Table H1.1   (continued)

Part of Speech	Definition/ Primary Function	Examples
Adjective	Modifies a noun or pronoun by describing it, limiting it, or giving more information about it Answers one of these questions: • Which one? • What kind? • How many?	Which one? • The *cutest* puppy belongs to the neighbors. What kind? • Use only *academic* sources for the paper. • *Japanese* tourists are visiting by the busload. How many? • *Several* friends are visiting for the weekend. • He read *eight* books by Stephen King. *Note*: Articles (*a, an, the*) are considered adjectives.
Adverb	Modifies a verb, adjective, other adverb, or entire sentence. Adverbs often end in -*ly*. Answers one of these questions: • How? • When? • Where? • How often? • To what extent?	How? • The Rolling Stones performed *brilliantly*. When? • *Later*, they met to discuss the proposal. Where? • The taxi driver headed *downtown*. How often? • The bobcat is *rarely* seen in the wild. To what extent? • He agreed to cooperate *fully* with the investigation.
Conjunction	Connects words, **phrases** (groups of words that lack a subject, a predicate, or both — see Section 2b), or **clauses** (groups of words that contain both a subject and a predicate — see Section 2c)	• **Coordinating conjunctions** connect words, phrases, or clauses of the same kind: *and, but, for, nor, or, so, yet* • **Correlative conjunctions** are used in pairs: *either . . . or, neither . . . nor, not only . . . but also, whether . . . or* • **Subordinating conjunctions** connect ideas of unequal importance: *after, before, until, when, while, because, since, so that, if, unless, whether, even if, even though, in order to*

Table H1.1 (continued)

Part of Speech	Definition/ Primary Function	Examples
Preposition	Links and relates a noun or a pronoun to the rest of the sentence; may be a word or a phrase A **prepositional phrase** includes the preposition along with its object and modifiers.	• Prepositions: *according to, about, along, as, as well as, at, below, by, despite, for, in, in spite of, near, on, onto, out, over, past, through, to, under, until, up, with, with regard to, without* • Prepositional phrases: *in the deep blue sea, on top of the high mountain, alongside the rugged Atlantic coast*
Interjection	Expresses surprise or some other strong feeling; often followed by an exclamation point	• *Ouch!* • *No way!* • *Oh,* it wasn't important.

2 Sentence Structure ⚏

2a Sentence parts

A **sentence** is a group of words that expresses a complete thought about something or someone. Every sentence must contain two basic parts: a subject and a predicate.

Subjects

The **subject** of a sentence names a person, place, or thing and tells whom or what the sentence is about. It identifies the performer or receiver of the action expressed in the predicate.

▸ *Lady Gaga*, the flamboyant performer, has made savvy decisions about her career.
▸ The *clock* on the mantel was given to her by her grandmother.

The noun or pronoun that names what the sentence is about is called the **simple subject**.

▸ *Mozart* began composing at the age of four.
▸ The postal *worker* was bitten by a dog.

The simple subject of an imperative sentence (command) is understood as *you*, but *you* is not stated directly.

▸ Be quiet.
  The sentence is understood as *[You] be quiet.*

 **LaunchPad Solo**
macmillan learning

Visit **LaunchPad Solo for Readers and Writers > Overview: Sentences** for tutorials, videos, and practice exercises on sentence structure.

The **complete subject** is the simple subject plus its modifiers — words that describe, identify, qualify, or limit the meaning of a noun or pronoun.

```
          ┌──── complete subject ────┐
```
▶   A series of very bad *decisions* doomed the project.

```
              ┌──────── complete subject ────────┐
```
▶   There are too many *books* to fit on the shelves.

A sentence with a **compound subject** contains two or more simple subjects joined by a coordinating conjunction (*and, but, for, nor, or, so,* or *yet*).

▶   *Joel and Ethan Coen* produce and direct their films.
▶   *A doctor or a physician's assistant* will explain the results.

Predicates

The **predicate** of a sentence indicates what the subject does, what happens to the subject, or what is said about the subject. The predicate can indicate an action or a state of being.

Action	Plant respiration *produces* oxygen.
State of being	Stonehenge has *existed* for many centuries.

The **simple predicate** is the main verb along with its helping verbs.

▶   Reporters *should call* the subjects of their stories for comment.
▶   A snow bicycle for Antarctic workers *has been developed.*

The **complete predicate** consists of the simple predicate plus its modifiers and any objects or complements. (See below for more about complements. For more on verbs, see Section 6.)

```
                         ┌─────────── complete predicate ───────────┐
```
▶   The growth of Los Angeles *depended* to a large extent on finding a way to get water to the desert.

```
                         ┌─────────── complete predicate ───────────┐
```
▶   Watching fishing boats *is a relaxing and pleasant way to spend an afternoon.*

A **compound predicate** contains two or more predicates that have the same subject and that are joined by *and, but, or, nor,* or another conjunction (see Section 1 for a review of the parts of speech).

▶   AIDS drugs *can save many lives but are seldom available in poor countries that need them desperately.*

▶ President Johnson *neither* wanted to run for a second term *nor* planned to serve if elected.

Objects

A **direct object** is a noun or pronoun that receives the action of a verb. A direct object answers the question What? or Whom?

▶ The Scottish fiddler played a lively *reel*.

The noun *reel* answers the question What did he play?

▶ The crowd in the stadium jeered the *quarterback*.

The noun *quarterback* answers the question Whom did they jeer?

An **indirect object** is a noun or pronoun that names the person or thing to whom or for whom something is done.

▶ Habitat for Humanity gave *him* an award for his work.

▶ A woman on a bench tossed the *pigeons* some crumbs.

Complements

A **complement** is a word or group of words that describes a subject or object and completes the meaning of the sentence. There are two kinds of complements: subject complements and object complements.

   A **linking verb** (such as *be, become, feel, seem,* or *taste*) connects the subject of a sentence to a **subject complement**, a noun, noun phrase, or adjective that renames or describes the subject.

▶ Michael Jackson was *a much-loved performer*.

▶ She was too *disorganized to finish her science project*.

An **object complement** is a noun, noun phrase, or adjective that modifies or renames the direct object. Object complements appear with **transitive verbs** (such as *name, find, make, think, elect, appoint, choose,* and *consider*), which express action directed toward something or someone.

▶ The council appointed him *its new vice president*.

▶ The undercooked meat made several children *sick*.

2b Phrases

A **phrase** is a group of related words that lacks a subject, a predicate, or both. A phrase cannot stand alone as a sentence. There are four common types of phrases: prepositional phrases, verbal phrases, appositive phrases, and absolute phrases.

Prepositional Phrases

A **prepositional phrase** consists of a preposition (such as *in, above, with, at,* or *behind*), the object of the preposition (a noun or pronoun), and any modifiers of the object. Prepositional phrases usually function as adjectives or adverbs to tell more about people, places, objects, or actions. They can also function as nouns. A prepositional phrase generally adds information about time, place, direction, or manner.

Adjective phrase	The plants *on the edge of the field* are weeds.
	On the edge and *of the field* tell *where*.
Adverb phrase	New Orleans is very crowded *during Mardi Gras*.
	During Mardi Gras tells *when*.
Noun phrase	*Down the hill* is the shortest way to town.
	Down the hill acts as the subject of the sentence.

The following sentences have been edited to include a prepositional phrase or phrases that expand the meaning of the sentence by adding detail.

▸   He fell/ *on the icy sidewalk.*

▸   The ship suddenly appeared/ *through the mist near the shore.*

Verbal Phrases

A **verbal** is a verb form used as a noun (the *barking* of the dog), an adjective (a *barking* dog), or an adverb (continued *to bark*). It cannot be used alone as the verb of a sentence, however. The three kinds of verbals are participles, gerunds, and infinitives. A **verbal phrase** consists of a verbal and its modifiers.

Participles and participial phrases.   All verbs have two participles: present and past. The **present participle** is the *-ing* form of a verb (*being, hoping, studying*). The **past participle** of most verbs ends in *-d* or *-ed* (*hoped, consisted*). Some verbs, called *irregular verbs,* have no set pattern in their past participle form (*been, ridden*). Both the present participle and the past participle can function as adjectives modifying nouns and pronouns.

▸   The planes flew over the foggy airport in a *holding* pattern.

▸   The pot was made of *molded* clay.

A **participial phrase,** which consists of a participle and its modifiers, can also function as an adjective in a sentence.

▸   The suspect, *wanted for questioning* on robbery charges, had vanished.

Gerunds and gerund phrases.   A **gerund** is the present participle, or -*ing* form, of a verb that functions as a noun.

▶   *Driving* can be a frustrating activity.
▶   The government has not done enough to build *housing*.

A **gerund phrase** consists of a gerund and its modifiers. Like a gerund, a gerund phrase is used as a noun and can therefore function in a sentence as a subject, a direct object, an indirect object, an object of a preposition, or a subject complement.

Subject	*Catching the flu* is unpleasant.
Direct object	All the new recruits practiced *marching*.
Indirect object	One director gave *his acting* a chance.
Object of a preposition	An ambitious employee may rise by *impressing her boss*.
Subject complement	The biggest thrill was *the skydiving*.

Infinitives and infinitive phrases.   An **infinitive** is the base form of a verb preceded by *to*: *to study, to sleep*. An **infinitive phrase** consists of the infinitive plus any modifiers or objects. An infinitive phrase can function as a noun, an adjective, or an adverb.

Subject	*To become an actor* is my greatest ambition.
Adjective	She had a job *to do*.
Adverb	The weary travelers were eager *to sleep*.

Sometimes the *to* in an infinitive phrase is understood but not written.

▶   Her demonstration helped me *learn* the software.

Note: Be sure to distinguish between infinitive phrases and prepositional phrases beginning with the preposition *to*. In an infinitive phrase, *to* is followed by a verb (*to paint*); in a prepositional phrase, *to* is followed by a noun or pronoun (*to a movie*).

Appositive Phrases

An **appositive** is a word that explains, restates, or adds new information about a noun. An **appositive phrase** consists of an appositive and its modifiers.

▶   Ben Affleck, *a famous actor,* is very active in trying to improve conditions in the Congo.

The appositive phrase adds information about the noun *Ben Affleck*.

Absolute Phrases

An **absolute phrase** consists of a noun or pronoun and any modifiers, usually followed by a participle. An absolute phrase modifies an entire sentence, not any particular word or words within the sentence. It can appear anywhere in a sentence and is set off from the rest of the sentence with commas.

▶   *Their shift completed,* the night workers walked out at sunrise.
▶   *An unsuspecting insect clamped in its mandible,* the praying mantis, *its legs folded piously,* appears serenely uninvolved.

2c Clauses

A **clause** is a group of words that contains a subject and a predicate. A clause is either independent (also called *main*) or dependent (also called *subordinate*). An **independent clause** can stand alone as a grammatically complete sentence.

▶   Einstein was a clerk at the Swiss Patent Office.
▶   Ethnic disputes followed the disintegration of Yugoslavia.

A **dependent clause** has a subject and a predicate, but it cannot stand alone as a grammatically complete sentence because it does not express a complete thought. A dependent clause usually begins with either a **subordinating conjunction** (see Table H2.1) or a **relative pronoun** (see Table H2.2) that connects it to an independent clause.

Table H2.1   Subordinating Conjunctions

Subordinating conjunctions can be used to connect a less important idea (expressed in a dependent clause) to a more important idea (expressed in an independent clause).

Relationship Shown	Subordinating Conjunctions	Example
Time	*after, before, until, when, while*	*While* the sky was still dark, the army prepared for battle.
Cause or effect	*because, since, so that*	*Because* he doesn't like math, he should avoid calculus.
Condition	*even if, if, unless, whether*	We don't do volunteer work *unless* it is for a good cause.
Circumstance	*as, as far as, as if, as soon as, as though, even if, even though, in order to*	In-line skating is a popular sport, *even though* it is somewhat dangerous.

Table H2.2   Relative Pronouns

Relative pronouns introduce dependent clauses that function as adjectives. Relative pronouns refer back to a noun or pronoun that the clause modifies.

Relationship Shown	Relative Pronouns	Example
Reference to people	*who, whoever, whom, whomever, whose*	Sylvia Plath was married to Ted Hughes, *who* later became poet laureate of England.
Reference to things	*that, what, whatever, which, whose*	The research *that* caused the literacy-test controversy was outdated.

The following examples show subordinating conjunctions and relative pronouns and their use in dependent clauses.

    dependent clause beginning with a subordinating conjunction

▶   **When the puppies were born, the breeder examined them carefully.**

    dependent clause beginning with a subordinating conjunction

▶   **Van Gogh's paintings began to command high prices *after he died.***

    dependent clause beginning with a relative pronoun

▶   **Isadora Duncan, *who personified modern dance*, died in a bizarre accident.**

Writing Correct Sentences

3 Sentence Fragments

A **sentence fragment** is a group of words that cannot stand alone as a complete sentence. A fragment is often missing a subject, a complete verb, or both. 🔳

Fragment	Are hatched in sand.
	This group of words does not tell *who* or *what* are hatched in sand. It lacks a subject.
Fragment	Especially his rebounding ability.
	This group of words has a subject, *his rebounding ability,* but lacks a verb.
Fragment	To notice a friendly smile.
	This group of words lacks both a subject and a verb. *To notice* is not a complete verb. It is an infinitive.

A group of words can have both a subject and a verb but still be a fragment because it does not express a complete thought.

Recognizing Fragments

Fragment	Because the *number* of voters *has* declined.
	This group of words does not tell what happened as a result of the voter decline. Its meaning is incomplete.

Notice that the preceding fragment begins with the subordinating conjunction *because*. A clause that begins with a subordinating conjunction cannot stand alone as a complete sentence. Word groups that begin with a relative pronoun (*that, which, who*) are also not complete sentences. (For a list of common subordinating conjunctions and relative pronouns, see Tables H2.1 and H2.2.)

Fragment	Which *scientists studied* for many years.
	The group of words does not tell *what* the scientists studied.

🔳 **LaunchPad Solo**
macmillan learning

Visit **LaunchPad Solo for Readers and Writers > Fragments** for extra practice in the skills covered in this section.

Finally, when a word group begins with a transitional word or phrase (*for example, also*), make sure that it includes both a subject and a verb.

┌────── *subject* ──────┐

Fragment   For example, *the Gulf Coast of Florida.*

Use the flowchart on page 658 to help you decide whether a particular word group is a complete sentence or a sentence fragment.

Correcting Fragments

A sentence fragment can be revised in two general ways: (1) by attaching it to a nearby sentence or (2) by rewriting it as a complete sentence. The method you choose will depend on the element the fragment lacks as well as your intended meaning.

▶   *Certain turtle eggs are*
    ~~Are~~ hatched in sand.
    ^

▶   Jamal is a basketball player of many talents/, ~~E~~specially his rebounding
    ability.

▶   *Sam was too busy to*
    ~~To~~ notice a friendly smile.
    ^

▶   *The*
    ~~Because the~~ number of voters has declined.
    ^

3a Join a fragment lacking a subject to another sentence or rewrite it as a complete sentence.

Attach a fragment lacking a subject to a neighboring sentence if the two are about the same person, place, or thing.

▶   *and*
    Jessica speaks Spanish fluently/ ~~And~~ reads French well.
    ^

Alternatively, you can add a subject to turn the fragment into a complete sentence.

▶   *She also*
    Jessica speaks Spanish fluently. ~~And~~ reads French well.
    ^

3b Add a helping verb to a fragment lacking a complete verb.

Make sure that every sentence you write contains a *complete* verb. For example, verb forms ending in *-ing* need helping verbs to make them complete. Helping verbs include forms of *do, be,* and *have* as well as such words as *will, can, could, shall, should, may, might,* and *must.* When you use an *-ing* verb form in a sentence without a helping verb, you create a fragment. To correct the fragment, add the helping verb.

▶   *is*
    The college installing a furnace to heat the library.
    ^

How to Identify a Fragment

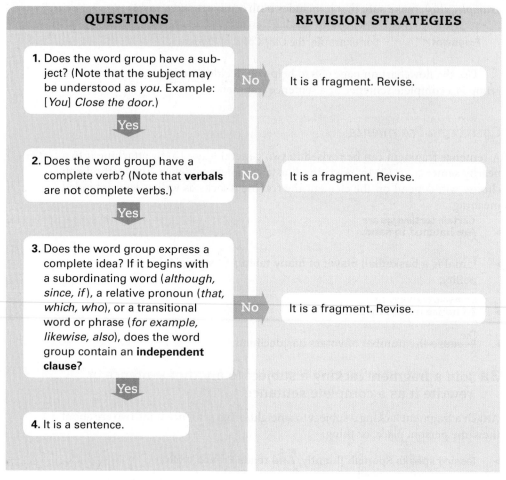

QUESTIONS	REVISION STRATEGIES
1. Does the word group have a subject? (Note that the subject may be understood as *you*. Example: [*You*] *Close the door.*) — No →	It is a fragment. Revise.
↓ Yes	
2. Does the word group have a complete verb? (Note that **verbals** are not complete verbs.) — No →	It is a fragment. Revise.
↓ Yes	
3. Does the word group express a complete idea? If it begins with a subordinating word (*although, since, if*), a relative pronoun (*that, which, who*), or a transitional word or phrase (*for example, likewise, also*), does the word group contain an **independent clause?** — No →	It is a fragment. Revise.
↓ Yes	
4. It is a sentence.	

3c Join a fragment that lacks either a subject or a verb (or both) to another sentence, or add the missing subject or verb.

Often, fragments lacking a subject and verb begin with an **infinitive** (such as *to hope, to walk,* or *to play*), which is not a complete verb, or they begin with an *-ed* or *-ing* form of a verb. Revise a fragment that begins with an infinitive or an *-ed* or *-ing* verb form by combining it with a previous sentence.

▶   I plan to transfer next semester, ~~To~~ live closer to home. *[to]*

▶   Robert E. Lee and Ulysses S. Grant met on April 9, 1865, ~~Bringing~~ an end to the Civil War. *[bringing]*

You can also revise a fragment beginning with an infinitive or an *-ed* or *-ing* verb form by adding both a subject and a verb to make it a complete sentence.

▶ Linda was reluctant to go out alone at night. ~~To~~ walk across campus from the library.
She was unwilling to

▶ Kyle was determined to do well on his math exam. ~~Studied~~ during every available hour.
He studied

Watch out for fragments that begin with a transitional word or phrase. They can usually be corrected by joining them to the previous sentence.

▶ Annie has always wanted to become an orthopedist. ~~That~~ is, a bone specialist.
—that

3d Join a fragment beginning with a subordinating word to another sentence, or drop the subordinating word.

You can correct a fragment beginning with a subordinating word by joining it to the sentence before or after it.

▶ The students stared spellbound. ~~While~~ the professor lectured.
while

▶ Until Dr. Jonas Salk invented a vaccine. ~~Polio~~ was a serious threat to public health.
polio

Alternatively, you can revise this type of fragment by dropping the subordinating word.

▶ ~~Because the~~ 800 area code for toll-free dialing is overused. New codes— 888 and 877—have been added.
The

3e Join a fragment beginning with a relative pronoun such as *who* or *whom* to another sentence, or rewrite it as a complete sentence.

Another common type of sentence fragment begins with a relative pronoun. **Relative pronouns** include *who, whom, whose, whoever, whomever, what, whatever, which,* and *that.*

▶ My contemporary fiction instructor assigned a novel by Amy Tan. ~~Whose~~ work I admire.
whose

▶ The dodo is an extinct bird. ~~That~~ disappeared in the seventeenth century.
It

Professional writers sometimes use sentence fragments intentionally to achieve a certain effect, particularly in works of fiction or articles written for popular magazines. An *intentional* fragment may be used to emphasize a point, answer a question, re-create a conversation, or make an exclamation. However, you should avoid using intentional fragments in academic writing. Instructors and other readers may find the fragments distracting or too informal, or they may assume you used a fragment in error.

Exercise H3.1

Correct any fragments in the following sentences. Some groups of sentences may be correct as written.

> More people are going to college every year. ~~Especially~~ young women.
>   *, especially*

1. In the past, higher education was accessible only to a small number of people. However, access to higher education has expanded over the last 200 years.

2. In the United States, for example. Colleges and universities provide education to Americans of all classes and backgrounds.

3. At first, state universities were publicly funded schools. That trained students in fields such as engineering, education, and agriculture.

4. During the nineteenth and early twentieth centuries. Graduates of state universities played a key role in America's development as an industrial and economic power.

5. The number of students in college. Increased greatly in the years after World War II.

4 Run-on Sentences and Comma Splices

A **run-on sentence** occurs when two or more independent clauses are joined without a punctuation mark or a coordinating conjunction. Run-on sentences are also known as **fused sentences**.

	┌────── *independent clause* ──────────────────┐ ┌─*independent*
Run-on sentence	A television addict is dependent on television I have
	clause ────────────────────────────────────┘

suffered from this addiction for years.

Visit **LaunchPad Solo for Readers and Writers > Run-ons** for extra practice in the skills covered in this section.

A **comma splice** occurs when two or more independent clauses are joined with a comma but without a coordinating conjunction (such as *and, or,* or *but*).

Comma splice   A typical magic act includes tricks and illusions, both depend on deception.

                  Notice that only a comma separates the two independent clauses, causing the comma splice.

Another type of comma splice occurs when a word other than a coordinating conjunction is used with a comma to join two or more independent clauses.

                             ——————*independent clause*——————

Comma splice   A typical magic act includes tricks and illusions,

                        ——*independent clause*——

                  however, both depend on deception.

However is not a coordinating conjunction. There are only seven coordinating conjunctions: *and, but, for, nor, or, so,* and *yet.*

Recognizing Run-on Sentences and Comma Splices

Many students have difficulty spotting run-on sentences and comma splices in their own writing. Use the flowchart on page 662 to help you identify these types of errors in your sentences.

Correcting Run-on Sentences and Comma Splices

There are four basic ways to correct a run-on sentence or comma splice. Choose the method that best fits your sentence or intended meaning.

4a Revise by creating two separate sentences.

Correct a run-on sentence or comma splice by creating two separate sentences. Make sure each independent clause has the appropriate end punctuation mark — a period, a question mark, or (on rare occasions) an exclamation mark.

                 period   *period*

    Independent clause . *Independent clause* .

Run-on sentence   A résumé should be directed to a specific audience. ~~it~~ *It*

                  should emphasize the applicant's potential value to the company.

Comma splice   To evaluate a charity, you should start by examining

                  its goals, *.* *T*hen you should investigate its management practices.

How to Identify Run-on Sentences and Comma Splices

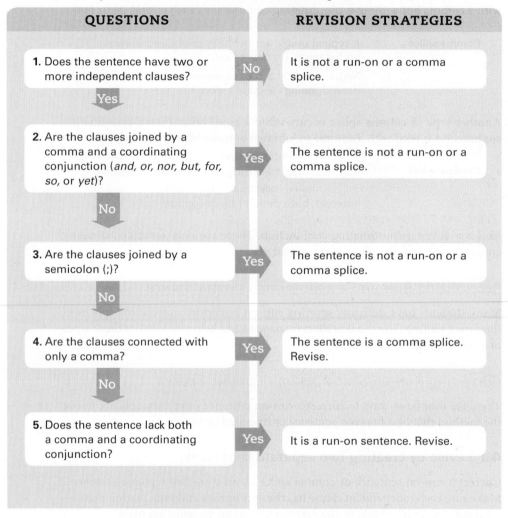

QUESTIONS		REVISION STRATEGIES
1. Does the sentence have two or more independent clauses?	No	It is not a run-on or a comma splice.
	Yes	
2. Are the clauses joined by a comma and a coordinating conjunction (*and, or, nor, but, for, so,* or *yet*)?	Yes	The sentence is not a run-on or a comma splice.
	No	
3. Are the clauses joined by a semicolon (;)?	Yes	The sentence is not a run-on or a comma splice.
	No	
4. Are the clauses connected with only a comma?	Yes	The sentence is a comma splice. Revise.
	No	
5. Does the sentence lack both a comma and a coordinating conjunction?	Yes	It is a run-on sentence. Revise.

4b Revise by joining the clauses with a semicolon (;).

When the independent clauses are closely connected in meaning, consider join-ing them with a semicolon. Note that a coordinating conjunction (such as *and, or,* or *but*) is *not* included when you revise with a semicolon (see 4c).

> *semicolon*
>
> *Independent clause* ; *independent clause* .

Run-on sentence Specialty products are unique items that consumers take time purchasing; these items include cars, parachutes, and skis.

Comma splice Studies have shown that male and female managers have different leadership styles; as a result, workers may respond differently to each.

In the second example, the semicolon joins the two clauses connected by the **conjunctive adverb** *as a result*. When two independent clauses are joined by a conjunctive adverb, a semicolon is needed.

Conjunctive adverbs link sentence parts that are of equal importance; they also serve as modifiers (see Table H4.1).

Table H4.1   Conjunctive Adverbs

Conjunctive adverbs show relationships between the elements they connect.

Relationship Shown	Conjunctive Adverbs	Example
Time	*afterward, finally, later, meanwhile, next, subsequently, then*	The candidates campaigned for months; *finally*, a primary election was held.
Example	*for example, for instance, to illustrate*	Some members of the party — *for example*, the governor — supported another candidate.
Continuation or addition	*also, furthermore, in addition, in the second place, moreover*	He is poorly organized; *in addition*, his arguments are not logical.
Cause or effect	*accordingly, as a result, consequently, hence, therefore, thus, unfortunately*	*As a result*, he may convince few voters.
Differences or contrast	*conversely, however, in contrast, nevertheless, on the contrary, on the other hand, otherwise*	*Nevertheless*, he has support from some groups.
Emphasis	*in fact, in other words, that is, undoubtedly*	*In fact*, some politicians are tired of constantly needing to raise money for campaigns.
Similarities or comparison	*likewise, similarly*	*Similarly*, their opponents have received many large donations.

4c Revise by joining the clauses with a comma and a coordinating conjunction.

Two independent clauses can be joined by using *both* a comma and a coordinating conjunction (*and, but, for, nor, or, so,* or *yet*). The coordinating conjunction indicates how the two clauses are related.

comma + coordinating conjunction

Independent clause   *, and*   *independent clause* .

Run-on sentence   Closed-minded people often refuse to recognize
                       opposing views, they reject ideas without evaluating
                       and
                       them.

Comma splice   Some educators support home schooling, others
                    but
                    oppose it vehemently.

4d Revise by making one clause dependent or by turning one clause into a phrase.

A **dependent clause** contains a subject and a verb but does not express a complete thought. It must always be linked to an independent clause. You can correct a run-on sentence or a comma splice by adding a **subordinating conjunction** (such as *because* or *although*; see 2c) to one of the independent clauses, thereby making it a dependent clause. The subordinating conjunction makes the thought incomplete and dependent on the independent clause.

subordinating conjunction

Because   *dependent clause* ,   *independent clause* .

or

subordinating conjunction

Independent clause   *because*   *dependent clause* .

Run-on sentence   Facial expressions are very revealing they are an
                       important communication tool.

Independent clause   Facial expressions are very revealing.

Dependent clause   *Because* facial expressions are very revealing

Joined to independent clause   *Because* facial expressions are very revealing, they
                                     are an important communication tool.

You can also correct a run-on sentence or a comma splice by changing one of the independent clauses to a phrase.

Phrase ,   independent clause .

or

Independent clause ,   phrase .

or

Beginning of independent clause ,   phrase ,   end of independent clause

Comma splice	Medieval peasants in Europe had a simple, hearty diet, they relied almost totally on agriculture.
Independent clause	Medieval peasants in Europe had a simple, hearty diet.
Clause reduced to phrase	relying almost totally on agriculture
Embedded in independent clause	Medieval peasants in Europe—relying almost totally on agriculture—had a simple, hearty diet.

Note: A comma or commas may or may not be needed to separate a phrase from the rest of the sentence, depending on how the phrase affects the meaning of the sentence (see Section 12e).

Exercise H4.1

Correct any run-ons or comma splices in the following sentences.

A deadly nerve poison is found on the skin of some Amazon tree frogs; native tribes use the poison on the tips of their arrows when they hunt.

1. Nearly every American child dreams of going to Disney World, it has become one of the most popular family vacation destinations.

2. Shopping through online bookstores is convenient, some people miss the atmosphere of a traditional bookstore.

3. Openness is one way to build trust in a relationship another is to demonstrate tolerance and patience.

4. In the 1960s, some Americans treated Vietnam veterans disrespectfully this situation has changed dramatically since that time.

5. William Faulkner wrote classic novels about life in the U.S. South, Eudora Welty has also written vividly about southern life.

5 Subject-Verb Agreement

Subjects and verbs must agree in person and number. **Person** refers to the forms *I* and *we* (first person), *you* (second person), and *he, she, it,* and *they* (third person). **Number** shows whether a word refers to one thing (singular) or more than one thing (plural). In a sentence, subjects and verbs need to be consistent in person and number: *I drive, you drive, she drives.* The following sections will help you look for and revise common errors in subject-verb agreement. 📖

5a Make sure the verb agrees with the subject, not with words that come between the subject and the verb.

▶ The *number* of farm workers *has* remained constant over several decades.

The subject *number* is singular and requires a singular verb, even though the words *of farm workers* appear between the subject and the verb.

5b Use a plural verb when two or more subjects are joined by *and*.

▶ A dot and a dash represents the letter A in Morse code.

▶ Basketball star Shaquille O'Neal, comedian D. L. Hughley, and actor Tom
         were
    Arnold was all born on March 6.

5c Make sure the verb agrees with the subject closest to it when two or more subjects are joined by *or, either . . . or,* or *neither . . . nor.*

When two or more singular subjects are joined by *or, either . . . or,* or *neither . . . nor,* use a singular verb.

▶ Either the *waiter* or the *customer has* misplaced the bill.

When one singular and one plural subject are joined by *or, either . . . or,* or *neither . . . nor,* the verb should agree in number with the subject nearest to it.

▶ Neither the *sailors* nor the *boat was* harmed by the storm.

▶ Neither the *boat* nor the *sailors were* harmed by the storm.

LaunchPad Solo
macmillan learning   Visit **LaunchPad Solo for Readers and Writers > Subject-Verb Agreement** for extra practice in the skills covered in this section.

5d Use a singular verb with most collective nouns, such as *family, couple,* and *class.*

A **collective noun** refers to a group as one unit acting together, such as a *jury, team,* or *class.* When the subject is a collective noun, use a singular verb. When the members of the group are acting as individuals, use a plural verb.

▶ The school *committee has* voted to increase teachers' salaries.

    The committee is acting as a unit.

▶ The family ~~are~~ ^{is} living in a cramped apartment.

▶ The *team members are* traveling by train, bus, and bike.

    The team members are acting individually.

5e Use a singular verb with most indefinite pronouns, such as *anyone, everyone, each, every, no one,* and *something.*

Indefinite pronouns do not refer to a specific person, place, or object. They refer to people, places, or things in general. Singular indefinite pronouns include the following: *each, either, neither, anyone, anybody, anything, everyone, everybody, everything, one, no one, nobody, nothing, someone, somebody, something.*

▶ *Everyone* in this room is welcome to express an opinion.

▶ Neither of the candidates ~~have~~ ^{has} run for office before.

Other indefinite pronouns, such as *several, both, many,* and *few,* take a plural verb.

▶ Every year *many succeed* in starting new small businesses.

▶ Several of you jogs at least three miles a day.

Some indefinite pronouns, such as *all, any, more, most, some,* and *none,* take either a singular or a plural verb depending on the noun they refer to. To decide which verb to use, follow this rule: Treat the indefinite pronoun as singular if it refers to something that cannot be counted and as plural if it refers to more than one of something that can be counted.

▶ Most of the water go^{es} into this kettle.

    You cannot count water.

▶ Some of the children in the study chooses immediate rather than delayed rewards.

    You can count children.

5f Make sure verbs agree with the antecedents of *who, which,* and *that.*

When a **relative pronoun** (*who, which, that*) refers to a singular noun, use a singular verb. When it refers to a plural noun, use a plural verb.

▶ Toni Morrison, *who enjoys* unique success as both a popular and a literary author, won the Nobel Prize in literature in 1993.

  Who refers to Toni Morrison, and because *Toni Morrison* is singular, the verb *enjoys* is singular.

▶ Look for *stores that display* this sign.

  That refers to *stores,* a plural noun.

Using *one of the* often leads to errors in subject-verb agreement. The phrase *one of the* plus a noun is plural.

▶ A pigeon is *one of the two birds that drink* by suction.

  That refers to *birds,* and since *birds* is plural, the verb *drink* is plural.

However, *only one of the* plus a noun is singular: *The cheetah is the only one of the big cats that has nonretractable claws.*

5g Make sure the verb agrees with a subject that follows it.

When a sentence begins with either *here* or *there* (which cannot function as a subject) or with a **prepositional phrase,** the subject often follows the verb. Look for the subject after the verb and make sure the subject and verb agree.

▶ There *is* a false *panel* somewhere in this room.

▶ Under the stairs *lurks* a solitary *spider.*

5h Make sure a linking verb agrees with its subject, not a word or phrase that renames the subject.

Linking verbs, such as forms of *be,* connect a subject with a word or phrase that renames or describes it. In sentences with linking verbs, the verb should agree with the subject.

▶ The *bluebell is* any of several plants in the lily family.

▶ The *issue* discussed at the meeting *was* the low wages earned by factory workers.

5i Use a singular verb when the subject is a title.

► Gulliver's Travels ~~are~~ ^{is} a satire by the eighteenth-century British writer
   Jonathan Swift. ^

5j Use singular verbs with singular nouns that end in -s, such
   as *physics* and *news.*

► Linguistics deals with the study of human speech.

Exercise H5.1

Correct any subject-verb agreement errors in the following sentences. Some sentences may be correct as written.

> Most of the people in the world believes that learning a second language
>
> is important.

1. Many members of the international business community communicates by
   speaking English, the international language of business.
2. A student in most non-English-speaking industrialized nations expect to
   spend six or more years studying English.
3. The United States are different.
4. Working for laws that requires all Americans to speak English is a fairly common U.S. political tactic.
5. In American schools, often neither a teaching staff nor enough money have
   been available for good foreign-language programs.

6 Verb Forms and Tense

Working with verbs requires understanding verb form and verb tense.

Verb Forms

Except for *be,* all English verbs have five forms.

Base Form	Past Tense	Past Participle	Present Participle	-s Form
move	moved	moved	moving	moves

► Many designers *visit* Milan for fashion shows each year.
► Sarah *visited* her best friend in Thailand.

▶   Students have *visited* the state capital every spring for decades.
▶   His cousin from Iowa is *visiting* this week.
▶   Maria *visits* her grandmother in Puerto Rico as often as possible.

6a Use -s or -es endings for present tense verbs that have third-person singular subjects.

The *-s* form is made up of the verb's base form plus *-s* or *-es*.

▶   Mr. King *teaches* English.

A third-person singular subject can consist of a singular noun, a singular pronoun (*he, she,* or *it*), or a singular indefinite pronoun (such as *everyone*).

Singular noun	The flower opens.
Singular pronoun	He opens the door.
Singular indefinite pronoun	Everybody knows the truth.

▶   She ~~want~~ wants to be a veterinarian.

▶   Neither of his parents ~~understand~~ understands him.

6b Use the correct form of irregular verbs such as *lay* and *lie*.

The verb pairs *lay* and *lie* and *sit* and *set* have similar forms and are often confused. Each verb has its own meaning: *lie* means to recline or rest on a surface, and *lay* means to put or place something; *sit* means to be seated, as in a chair, and *set* means to place something on a surface. If you are unsure about the correct form of a verb, check a dictionary.

▶   Our dog likes to ~~lay~~ lie on the couch all afternoon.

▶   Let me ~~set~~ sit in this chair for a while.

6c Use the active and passive voice appropriately.

When a verb is in the **active voice**, the subject performs the action. When a verb is in the **passive voice**, the subject receives the action.

Active voice	The Mississippi River flows into the Gulf of Mexico.
Passive voice	The computer file was deleted.
	Notice that the sentence in the passive voice does not tell *who* deleted the file.

LaunchPad Solo
macmillan learning
Visit **LaunchPad Solo for Readers and Writers > Active and Passive Voice** for extra practice in the skills covered in this section.

The active voice expresses ideas more vividly and emphatically than does the passive voice. Whenever possible, use the active voice in your sentences.

> *The colonists threw tea*
> ~~Tea was thrown~~ into Boston Harbor. ~~by the colonists.~~
>   ^   ^

> *The government does not allow people to sell illegal*
> ~~Illegal~~ drugs. ~~are not allowed to be sold.~~
>   ^   ^

Sentences in the passive voice may seem indirect, as if the writer were purposely withholding information. In general, use the passive voice sparingly.

Verb Tense

The **tenses** of a verb express time. They convey whether an action, a state of being, or an occurrence takes place in the present, past, or future. There are six basic tenses: present, past, future, present perfect, past perfect, and future perfect. There are also three groups of tenses: simple, perfect, and progressive. 🔲

Simple tenses indicate whether an action occurs in the present, past, or future.

> He *loves* Kabuki theater.
> I *downloaded* their new release immediately.
> Oprah's reputation *will grow*.

Perfect tenses indicate that the action was or will be finished by the time of some other action.

> By now, Rosa *has taken* the exam.
> Dave Matthews *had* already *performed* when they arrived.
> The centennial celebration *will have begun* before he completes the sculpture.

Progressive tenses indicate that the action does, did, or will continue.

> She *is going* to kindergarten.
> When the ambulance arrived, he *was sweating* profusely.
> During spring break, we *will be basking* on a sunny beach.

Table H6.1 on page 672 summarizes verb tenses.

6d Use the present tense to make a generalization, state a
        principle or fact, or indicate an action that occurs regularly
        or habitually.

> Thanksgiving *falls* on the fourth Thursday of November each year.
> Walking *is* excellent exercise.
> My sister *takes* frequent trips to Dallas.

🔲 **LaunchPad Solo**   Visit **LaunchPad Solo for Readers and Writers > Verb Tense** for extra
macmillan learning   practice in the skills covered in this section.

Table H6.1   Verb Tenses: A Summary

Tense	Example
Present Tense	
Simple present: happening now or occurring regularly	He *performs* his own stunts.
Present progressive: happening now; going on (in progress) now	The governor *is considering* a Senate campaign.
Present perfect: began in the past and was completed in the past or is continuing now	The children's benefactor *has followed* their progress closely.
Present perfect progressive: began in the past and is continuing now	She *has been singing* in nightclubs for thirty years.
Past Tense	
Simple past: began and ended in the past	The doctor *treated* him with experimental drugs.
Past progressive: began and continued in the past	They *were expecting* visitors.
Past perfect: occurred before a certain time in the past or was completed before another action was begun	The birds *had eaten* all the berries before we knew they were ripe.
Past perfect progressive: was taking place until a second action occurred	He *had been seeing* a psychiatrist before his collapse.
Future Tense	
Simple future: will take place in the future	The play *will begin* on time.
Future progressive: will begin in the future and continue for a period of time	After we get on the plane, we *will be sitting* for hours.
Future perfect: will be completed by a certain time in the future or before another action will begin	By next month, the new apprentice *will have become* an expert.
Future perfect progressive: will continue until a certain time in the future	By the time she earns her Ph.D., she *will have been studying* history for twelve years.

6e Do not omit -ed endings on verbs that require them.

For regular verbs, both the past tense and the past participle are formed by adding *-ed* or *-d* to the base form of the verb. Some speakers do not fully pronounce the *-ed* endings of verbs (*asked, fixed, supposed to, used to*). As a result, they may unintentionally omit these endings in their writing.

▶ He ~~talk~~ talked to the safety inspectors about plant security.

▶ They ~~use~~ used to order lattes every morning.

6f Use the present tense when writing about literary works, even though they were written in the past.

depicts
▶   Chaucer's *Canterbury Tales* ~~depicted~~ a tremendously varied group of travelers.
            ^

Also use the present tense to refer to authors no longer living when you are discussing their works.

▶   Borges frequently *employs* magical realism in his fiction.

6g Be sure to distinguish between the immediate past and the less immediate past.

Use the past perfect form of the verb, formed by adding *had* to the past participle, to indicate an action that was completed before another action or a specified time.

Unclear	Roberto finished three research papers when the semester ended.
	Roberto did not finish all three right at the end of the semester.
Revised	Roberto had finished three research papers when the semester ended.

Exercise H6.1

Correct the errors in verb form in the following sentences. Also revise any sentences that use the passive voice. Some sentences may be correct as written.

United States entered the
The Spanish-American War ~~was entered by the United States~~ in 1898.
        ^

1. When the nineteenth century change into the twentieth, many people in the United States became eager to expel Spain from the Americas.
2. Cuba, an island that lays ninety miles off the Florida coast, provided them with an excuse to do so.
3. Cuban rebels were trying to free themselves from Spain, and many Americans wanted to help them.
4. In addition, many people in the United States wanted to take over Spain's territories for a long time.
5. The United States won the war very quickly and assume control of Cuba, the Philippines, Guam, and Puerto Rico.

7 Pronoun Problems

Pronouns are words used in place of nouns. They provide a quick, convenient way to refer to a word that has already been named. Common problems in using pronouns include problems with pronoun reference, agreement, and case. ▨

Pronoun Reference

A pronoun should refer clearly to its **antecedent**, the noun or pronoun for which it substitutes. If an antecedent is missing or unclear, the meaning of the sentence will be unclear. Use the following guidelines to make certain your pronoun references are clear and correct.

7a Make sure each pronoun refers clearly to one antecedent.

▶   The hip-hop radio station battled the alternative rock station for the
                              the alternative rock station
   highest ratings. Eventually, ~~it~~ won.
                              ^

   The revised sentence makes it clear which station won: the alternative rock station.

7b Check for vague uses of *they, it,* and *you.*

They, it, and *you* often refer vaguely to antecedents in preceding sentences or to no antecedent at all.

Omitted antecedent	On the Internet, they claimed that an asteroid would collide with Earth.
	On the Internet does not explain what *they* refers to.
Clear	On the Internet, a blog claimed that an asteroid would collide with Earth.
	Adding the noun *a blog* clears up the mystery.

▶   When political scientists study early political cartoons, ~~it provides~~ insight
                                                            they gain
                                                                 ^
   into historical events.

▶   In Florida, ~~you often hear~~ about hurricane threats of previous years.
                 people often talk
                     ^

7c Make sure pronouns do not refer to adjectives or possessives.

Pronouns must refer to nouns or other pronouns. Adjectives and possessives cannot serve as antecedents, although they may seem to suggest a noun the pronoun *could* refer to.

▨ **LaunchPad Solo**   Visit **LaunchPad Solo for Readers and Writers > Pronouns** for extra
macmillan learning   practice in the skills covered in this section.

he was

▶ He became so depressed that ~~it made him~~ unable to get out of bed.
                                          ^

The pronoun *it* seems to refer to the adjective *depressed,* which suggests the noun *depression.* This noun is not in the sentence, however.

stocks

▶ The stock market's rapid rise made ~~it~~ appear to be an attractive investment.
                                       ^

The pronoun *it* seems to refer to *stock market's,* which is a possessive, not a noun.

7d Make sure the pronouns *who, whom, which,* and *that* clearly refer to specific nouns.

These storms make

▶ Lake-effect storms hit cities along the Great Lakes. ~~That makes~~ winter
                                                         ^
   travel treacherous.

Exercise H7.1

Correct any errors in pronoun reference in the following sentences.

are

Innovative codes are important because ~~it means that~~ they ~~will be~~ hard
                                                                ^
to break.

1. A country at war must be able to convey information to military personnel. That is always a challenge.
2. The information's importance often requires it to be transmitted secretly.
3. Military strategists use codes for these transmissions because they baffle the enemy.
4. They say that using "invisible ink," which cannot be seen until the paper is heated, was once a popular way to communicate secretly.
5. Lemon juice and vinegar are good choices for invisible ink because you can't see them unless they are burned.

Pronoun-Antecedent Agreement

A pronouns and its antecedent (the word to which the pronoun refers) must agree. If the antecedent is singular, use a singular pronoun. If the antecedent is plural, use a plural pronoun. Here are a few guidelines to follow when you are unsure of which pronoun or antecedent to use.

7e Use singular pronouns to refer to indefinite pronouns that are singular in meaning.

Singular indefinite pronouns include the following:

another	anywhere	everyone	no one	somebody
anybody	each	everything	nothing	someone
anyone	either	neither	one	something
anything	everybody	nobody	other	

▶ *Each* of the experiments produced *its* desired result.

▶ *Everyone* in America should exercise *his or her* right to vote so that *his or her* voice can be heard.

If the pronoun and antecedent do not agree, change either the pronoun or the indefinite pronoun to which it refers. If you need to use a singular pronoun, use *he or she* or *him or her* to avoid sexism.

▶ ~~Everyone~~ People should check their credit card statements monthly.

▶ Everyone should check ~~their~~ his or her credit card statement monthly.

An alternative is to eliminate the pronoun or pronouns entirely.

▶ No one should lose ~~their~~ a job because of family responsibilities.

Note: Overuse of *him or her* and *his or her* can create awkward sentences. To avoid this problem, you can revise your sentences in one of two ways: by using a plural antecedent and a plural pronoun or by omitting the pronouns altogether.

7f Use plural pronouns to refer to indefinite pronouns that are plural in meaning.

The indefinite pronouns *all, any, more, most,* and *some* can be either singular or plural, depending on how they are used in a sentence. When an indefinite pronoun refers to something that can be counted, use a plural pronoun to refer to it. When an indefinite pronoun refers to something that cannot be counted, use a singular pronoun to refer to it.

▶ Of the tropical plants studied, *some* have proven *their* usefulness in fighting disease.

Because the word *plants* is a plural, countable noun, the pronoun *some* is plural in this sentence.

▶ The water was warm, and *most* of it was murky.

Water is not countable, so *most* is singular.

7g Use a plural pronoun to refer to a compound antecedent joined by *and*.

▶   The *walrus <u>and</u> the carpenter* ate *their* oysters greedily.

Exception: When the singular antecedents joined by *and* refer to the same person, place, or thing, use a singular pronoun.

▶   As *a father and a husband,* he is a success.

Exception: When *each* or *every* comes before the antecedent, use a singular pronoun.

▶   *Every nut and bolt* was in its place for the inspection.

When a compound antecedent is joined by *or* or *nor,* the pronoun should agree with the noun closer to the verb.

▶   Either the panda or the sea otters should have ~~its~~ their new habitat soon.

7h Use a singular or a plural pronoun to refer to a collective noun, depending on the meaning.

A **collective noun** names a group of people or things acting together or individually (*herd, class, team*) and may be referred to by a singular or a plural pronoun, depending on your intended meaning. When you refer to a group acting together as a unit, use a singular pronoun.

▶   The *wolf pack* surrounds *its* quarry.

    The pack is acting as a unit.

When you refer to the members of the group as acting individually, use a plural pronoun.

▶   After the false alarm, *members* of the bomb squad returned to *their* homes.

    The members of the squad acted individually.

Exercise H7.2

Correct any errors in pronoun-antecedent agreement in the following sentences. Some sentences may be correct as written.

<u>his or her</u>
Every scientist has ~~their~~ own idea about the state of the environment.
                    ^

1. Neither the many species of dinosaurs nor the flightless dodo bird could prevent their own extinction.

2. A team of researchers might disagree on its conclusions about the disappearance of the dinosaur.

3. However, most believe that their findings indicate the dodo died out because of competition from other species.

4. In one way, animals resemble plants: Some are "weeds" because it has the ability to thrive under many conditions.

5. Any species that cannot withstand their competitors may be doomed to extinction.

Pronoun Case

A pronoun's case indicates its function in a sentence. The three cases are **subjective, objective,** and **possessive.** When a pronoun functions as a subject in a sentence, the subjective case (*I*) is used. When a pronoun functions as a **direct object,** an **indirect object,** or an **object of a preposition,** the objective case (*me*) is used. When a pronoun indicates ownership, the possessive case (*mine*) is used.

Subjective Case	*Objective Case*	*Possessive Case*
I	me	my, mine
we	us	our, ours
you	you	your, yours
he, she, it	him, her, it	his, her, hers, its
they	them	their, theirs
who	whom	whose

A **direct object** receives the action of the verb: *He drove <u>me</u> home.*

An **indirect object** indicates to or for whom an action is performed: *I gave <u>her</u> the keys.*

An **object of a preposition** is a word or phrase that follows a preposition: *with <u>him</u>, above <u>the table</u>.*

Use the following guidelines to correct errors in pronoun case.

7i To decide which pronoun to use in a compound construction (*Yolanda and I, Yolanda and me*), read the sentence aloud without the noun and the word *and.*

Incorrect	Yolanda and me graduated from high school last year.
	If you mentally delete *Yolanda and,* the sentence sounds wrong: *Me graduated from high school last year.*
Revised	Yolanda and I graduated from high school last year.
	If you mentally delete *Yolanda and,* the sentence sounds correct: *I graduated from high school last year.*
Incorrect	The mayor presented the citizenship award to Mrs. Alvarez and I.
	If you delete *Mrs. Alvarez and,* the sentence sounds wrong: *The mayor presented the citizenship award to I.*
Revised	The mayor presented the citizenship award to Mrs. Alvarez and me.
	If you delete *Mrs. Alvarez and,* the sentence sounds correct: *The mayor presented the citizenship award to me.*

7j When a pronoun follows a form of the verb *be* (*is, are, was, were*), read the sentence aloud with the pronoun as the subject.

Incorrect	The leader is him.
	If you substitute *him* for *the leader,* the sentence sounds wrong: *Him is the leader.*
Revised	The leader is he.
	If you substitute *he* for *the leader,* the sentence sounds correct: *He is the leader.*

7k To determine whether *we* or *us* should come before a noun, read the sentence aloud without the noun.

▶ If we hikers frighten them, the bears may attack.

If you mentally delete *hikers,* the sentence sounds correct: *If we frighten them, the bears may attack.*

▶ The older children never paid attention to us kindergartners.

If you mentally delete *kindergartners,* the sentence sounds correct: *The older children never paid attention to us.*

7l To choose the correct pronoun form for a comparison using *than* or *as*, mentally add the verb that is implied.

▶   Diedre is a better athlete than I [am].
▶   The coach likes her better than [he likes] me.

7m Use *who* or *whoever* when the pronoun functions as the subject of a sentence. Use *whom* or *whomever* when the pronoun functions as the object of a verb or preposition.

To decide whether to use *who* or *whom* in a question, answer the question yourself by using the word *he* or *him* or *she* or *her*. If you use *he* or *she* in the answer, use *who* in the question. If you use *him* or *her* in the answer, use *whom* in the question.

Question	(*Who, Whom*) photocopied the article?
Answer	*She* photocopied the article.
Correct pronoun	*Who* photocopied the article?

Question	To (*who, whom*) is that question addressed?
Answer	It is addressed to *him*.
Correct pronoun	To *whom* is that question addressed?

Similarly, to decide whether to use *who* or *whom* in a **dependent clause**, turn the dependent clause into a question. The pronoun you use to answer that question will tell you whether *who* or *whom* should appear in the clause.

▶   Aphra Behn's *Oronooko* dramatizes the life of a slave ~~whom~~ who came from African royalty.

   If you ask the question (*Who, whom*) *came from African royalty?*, the answer, *He came from African royalty,* indicates that the correct pronoun is *who*.

▶   The leader ~~who~~ whom we seek must unite the community.

   If you ask the question (*Who, whom*) *do we seek?*, the answer, *We seek him,* indicates that the correct pronoun is *whom*.

7n Use a possessive pronoun to modify a gerund.

▶   *His moralizing* has never been welcome.

   The possessive pronoun *his* modifies the gerund *moralizing*.

Exercise H7.3

Correct any errors in pronoun case in the following sentences. Some sentences may be correct as written.

>   *who*
> Cave explorers, ~~whom~~ are called spelunkers, sometimes find
>   ^
> underground rooms no one has seen before.

1. Whomever discovers a large cave is usually able to attract tourists.
2. Much of Kentucky's Mammoth Cave was explored in the 1830s by Stephen Bishop, a slave who worked as a cave guide.
3. Few spelunkers today are better known than he.
4. Following the success of Mammoth Cave, many Kentucky cavers hoped to make a fortune from them spelunking.
5. Floyd Collins was one Kentucky native whom searched his property for caves.

8 Shifts and Mixed Constructions

A **shift** is a sudden, unexpected change in point of view, verb tense, voice, mood, or level of diction that may confuse your readers. A **mixed construction** is a sentence containing parts that do not sensibly fit together. This section will help you identify and correct shifts and mixed constructions in your sentences.

Shifts

8a   Refer to yourself, your audience, and the people you are writing about in a consistent way.

Person shows the writer's point of view. Personal pronouns indicate whether the subject is the speaker (first person: *I, we*), the person spoken to (second person: *you*), or the person or thing spoken about (third person: *he, she, it, they, one*).

Inconsistent	I discovered that *you* could touch some of the museum exhibits.
	Notice that the writer shifts from the first-person *I* to the second-person *you*.
Consistent	I discovered that *I* could touch some of the museum exhibits.
	The writer uses the first-person *I* consistently within the sentence.

>   *they*
> ▸   When people study a foreign language, ~~you~~ also learn about another
>   culture.
>   ^

8b Maintain consistency in verb tense throughout a paragraph or an essay unless the meaning requires you to change tenses.

Inconsistent	The virus *mutated* so quickly that it *develops* a resistance to most vaccines.
	The sentence shifts from past to present.
Revised	The virus *mutates* so quickly that it *develops* a resistance to most vaccines.

8c Change verb tense when you want to indicate an actual time change.

Use the present tense for events that occur in the present; use the past tense for events that occurred in the past. When the time changes, be sure to change the tense. Notice the intentional shifts in the following passage (the verbs are in italics).

> Every spring, migratory birds *return* to cooler climates to raise their young. This year, a pair of bluejays *is occupying* a nest in my yard, and I *spy* on them. The hatchlings *are growing* larger and *developing* feathers. Last spring, robins *built* the nest that the jays now *call* home, and I *watched* them every morning until the young birds *left* home for the last time.

As the events switch from this year (present) to the previous year (past), the writer changes from the present tense (*is occupying*) to the past tense (*built*). (For more on verb tense, see Sections 6d–6g.)

8d Use a consistent voice.

Needless shifts between the **active voice** and the **passive voice** can disorient readers and create wordy sentences.

▸ *The researchers gave one* ~~One~~ group of volunteers ~~was given~~ a placebo, and ~~the researchers~~ *they* treated another group with the new drug.

▸ Drought and windstorms made farming impossible, and many families *the specter of starvation forced* ~~were forced~~ to leave Oklahoma. ~~by the specter of starvation.~~

To change a sentence from the passive voice to the active voice, make the performer of the action the subject of the sentence. The original subject of the sentence becomes the direct object. Delete the form of the verb *be*.

Passive	The restraining order was signed by the judge.
Active	The judge signed the restraining order.

For more on voice, see Section 6c.

8e Avoid sudden shifts from indirect to direct questions or quotations.

An indirect question tells what a question is or was.

| Indirect question | The defense attorney asked where I was on the evening of May 10. |
| Direct question | The defense attorney asked, "Where were you on the evening of May 10?" |

Avoid shifting from direct to indirect questions.

▶ Sal asked what could ~~I~~ do to solve the problem.
  he

8f Use a consistent mood throughout a paragraph or an essay.

Mood indicates whether the sentence states a fact or asks a question (**indicative mood**); gives a command or direction (**imperative mood**); or expresses a condition contrary to fact, a wish, or a suggestion (**subjunctive mood**). The subjunctive mood is also used for hypothetical situations or impossible or unlikely events.

Inconsistent

You shouldn't expect to learn ballroom dancing immediately, and remember that even Fred Astaire had to start somewhere. First, find a qualified instructor. Then, you should not be embarrassed even if everyone else seems more graceful than you are. Finally, keep your goal in mind, and you need to practice, practice, practice.

This paragraph contains shifts between the indicative and imperative moods.

Consistent

Don't expect to learn ballroom dancing immediately, and remember that even Fred Astaire had to start somewhere. First, find a qualified instructor. Then, don't be embarrassed even if everyone else seems more graceful than you are. Finally, keep your goal in mind, and practice, practice, practice.

This revised paragraph uses the imperative mood consistently.

8g Use a consistent level of diction.

Your level of diction can range from formal to informal. The level you choose should be appropriate for your audience, your subject matter, and your purpose for writing. As you revise your essays, look for inappropriate shifts in diction, such as from a formal to an informal tone or vice versa.

William H. Whyte's studies of human behavior in public space yielded

a number of surprises. Perhaps most unexpected was the revelation that

people seem to be drawn toward, rather than driven from, crowded spaces.

They tend to congregate near the entrances of stores or on street corners.

Plazas and shopping districts crowded with pedestrians attract more

enjoy gathering together in public spaces.

pedestrians. For some reason, people seem to ~~get a charge out of hanging out~~

^

~~where lots of other folks are hanging out, too.~~

For academic writing, including class assignments and research papers, use formal language.

Exercise H8.1

Correct the shifts in person, verb tense, voice, mood, and level of diction in the following sentences.

> **Experts continue to break new ground in child psychology,**
> *many parents have studied*
> **and their research. ~~has been studied by many parents.~~**
> ^   ^

1. A new idea about the development of children's personalities had surprised many American psychologists because it challenges widely accepted theories.
2. We wondered whether our professor knew of the new theory and did she agree with it.
3. Personality is believed by some experts to be the result of parental care, but other specialists think that biology influences personality more strongly.
4. Most parents think you have a major influence on your child's behavior.
5. The new theory suggests that children's peers are a heck of a lot more influential than parents.

Mixed Constructions

8h Make sure clauses and phrases fit together logically.

A **mixed construction** contains phrases or clauses that do not work together logically and that cause confusion in meaning. 📠

Mixed   The fact that the marathon is twenty-six miles, a length that explains why I have never finished it.

📠 **LaunchPad Solo**
macmillan learning   Visit **LaunchPad Solo for Readers and Writers > Mixed and Incomplete Constructions** for extra practice in the skills covered in this section.

The sentence starts with a subject (*The fact*) followed by a dependent clause (*that the marathon is twenty-six miles*). The sentence needs a predicate to complete the independent clause. Instead it includes a noun (*a length*) and another dependent clause (*that explains why I have never finished it*). The independent clause that begins with *The fact* is never completed.

Revised	The marathon is twenty-six miles long, which is why I have never finished it.
	In the revision, the parts of the sentence work together.

8i Make subjects and predicates consistent.

Faulty predication occurs when a subject does not work grammatically with its predicate.

Faulty	The most valued trait in an employee is a person who is loyal.
	A person is not a trait.
Revised	The most valued trait in an employee is loyalty.

▶ Rising health-care costs decrease health insurance. <u>the number of people who can afford</u> ~~for many people.~~

Costs do not decrease health insurance.

8j Avoid the constructions *is when* or *is where* or *reason . . . is because*.

Faulty	Indigestion is when you cannot digest food.
Revised	Indigestion is the inability to digest food.

▶ Gravitation is <u>the attraction of</u> ~~where~~ one body ~~is being attracted by~~ <u>to</u> another.

▶ ~~The reason~~ I enjoy jogging ~~is~~ because it provides outdoor exercise.

Exercise H8.2

Correct the mixed constructions in the following sentences.

~~The reason~~ internships are valuable ~~is~~ because they give students real-world experience.

1. Many interns earn college credit for their work, but they also gain practical experience and important contacts.

2. Surveys showing that college graduates who intern receive higher salary offers than their classmates who do not.

3. The fact that students must be careful, as all internships are not created equal.

4. The most important qualities are an intern with curiosity and a good work ethic.

5. A good internship is when the intern gains knowledge and skills in a professional environment.

9 Adjectives and Adverbs

Adjectives modify nouns or pronouns and indicate which one, what kind, or how many. **Adverbs** modify verbs, adjectives, other adverbs, clauses, or entire sentences and indicate how, when, where, how often, or to what extent. (See Section 1.) Use the following guidelines to identify and correct common errors in using adjectives and adverbs. ≋

9a Use adverbs, not adjectives, to modify verbs, adjectives, or other adverbs.

▶   Those pants are ~~awful~~ *awfully* expensive.

▶   The headlights shone ~~bright.~~ *brightly.*

9b Use adjectives, not adverbs, after linking verbs.

Linking verbs, often forms of *be* and other verbs such as *feel, look, make,* and *seem,* express a state of being. A linking verb takes a **subject complement** — a word group that completes or renames the subject of the sentence. Verbs such as *feel* and *look* can also be action verbs; when they function as action verbs in a sentence, they may be modified by an adverb.

If you are not sure whether a word should be an adjective or adverb, determine how it is used in the sentence. If the word modifies a noun, it should be an adjective.

Adjective	Our *waiter* looked *slow.*
	Slow modifies the word *waiter,* a noun. In this sentence, *looked* is a linking verb.
Adverb	Our waiter looked slowly for some menus.
	In this sentence, *looked* is expressing an action and is not a linking verb; *slowly* modifies *looked.*

⌘ LaunchPad Solo
macmillan learning   Visit **LaunchPad Solo for Readers and Writers > Adjectives and Adverbs** for extra practice in the skills covered in this section.

9c Use *good* and *bad* as adjectives; use *well* and *badly* as adverbs.

▶   Einstein was not a *good* student.

The adjective *good* modifies the noun *student*.

▶   Einstein did not *perform well* in school.

The adverb *well* modifies the verb *perform*.

▶   He did ~~bad~~ ^badly^ in the leading role.

The adverb *badly* modifies the verb *did*.

When you are describing someone's health, *well* can also function as an adjective.

▶   The disease was in remission, but the *patients* were not yet *well*.

9d Do not use adjectives such as *real* and *sure* to modify adverbs or other adjectives.

▶   The produce was crisp and ~~real~~ ^really^ fresh.

The adverb *really* modifies the adjective *fresh*.

9e Use the comparative form of adjectives and adverbs to compare two things; use the superlative form to compare three or more things.

Adjectives and adverbs can be used to compare two or more persons, objects, actions, or ideas. The **comparative** form of an adjective or adverb compares two items. The **superlative** form compares three or more items. Use the list below to check the comparative and superlative forms of most regular adjectives and adverbs in your sentences.

	Comparatives	*Superlatives*
One-syllable adjectives and adverbs	Add *-er: colder, faster*	Add *-est: coldest, fastest*
Two-syllable adjectives	Add *-er: greasier**	Add *-est: greasiest**
Adjectives with three or more syllables or adverbs ending in -ly	Add *more* in front of the word: *more beautiful, more quickly*	Add *most* in front of the word: *most beautiful, most quickly*

*To form the comparative and superlative forms of adjectives ending in -y, change the y to i and add -er or -est.

Irregular adjectives and adverbs form their comparative and superlative forms in unpredictable ways, as the following list illustrates.

	Comparative	*Superlative*
Adjectives		
good	better	best
bad	worse	worst
little	less	least
Adverbs		
well	better	best
badly	worse	worst
Words That Function as Adjectives and Adverbs		
many	more	most
some	more	most
much	more	most

9f When using comparative and superlative forms, check your comparisons to make sure they are complete.

An incomplete comparison can leave your reader confused about what is being compared.

Incomplete	The Internet works more efficiently.
Revised	For sending correspondence and documents, the Internet works more efficiently than the postal service.
Incomplete	The catcher sustained the most crippling knee injury.
Revised	The catcher sustained the most crippling knee injury of his career.

9g Do not use *more* or *most* with the *-er* or *-est* form of an adjective or adverb.

▶   The hypothesis must be ~~more~~ clearer.

Exercise H9.1

Correct any errors involving adjectives and adverbs in the following sentences.

> *the most*
> *Wikipedia* is probably ~~a more~~ popular reference source in the world.
>   ^

1. The site is an open source, online encyclopedia where anyone can contribute, even if he or she writes bad or inaccurate.
2. *Wikipedia* has many advantages that reflect good on it as a source.
3. There is not nothing more convenient for getting information real quick.
4. In a way, encyclopedias are more unique because Web sites can grow to include any subject that anyone finds interesting.
5. *Wikipedia* relies heavy on the knowledge and interests of millions of people, rather than on the choices of a small group of experts.

10 Misplaced and Dangling Modifiers

A **modifier** is a word or group of words that describes, changes, qualifies, or limits the meaning of another word or group of words in a sentence. 📖

▶   **The contestant** *smiled* **delightedly.**

The adverb *delightedly* modifies the verb *smiled*.

▶   *Pretending to be surprised,* **he greeted the guests.**

The adjective phrase *Pretending to be surprised* modifies the pronoun *he*.

     Modifiers that are carefully placed in sentences give your readers a clear picture of the details you want to convey. However, when a sentence contains a **misplaced modifier**, it is hard for the reader to tell which word or group of words the modifier is supposed to be describing.

10a Place modifiers close to the words they describe.

Misplaced	The mayor *chided* the pedestrians for jaywalking *angrily*.
	The adverb *angrily* should be closer to the verb it modifies, *chided*. Here, the adverb appears to be modifying *jaywalking*, so the sentence is confusing.
Revised	The mayor *angrily chided* the pedestrians for jaywalking.
Misplaced	The press *reacted* to the story leaked from the Pentagon *with horror*.
	The adverb phrase *with horror* should explain how the press reacted, not how the story was leaked, so the modifier should be closer to the verb *reacted*.
Revised	The press *reacted with horror* to the story leaked from the Pentagon.

 **LaunchPad Solo**
macmillan learning

Visit **LaunchPad Solo for Readers and Writers > Modifier Placement** for extra practice in the skills covered in this section.

10b Make sure each modifier clearly modifies only one word or phrase in a sentence.

Even when a modifier is placed near or next to the word or phrase it modifies, it may also be near another word it could conceivably modify. When a modifier's placement may cause ambiguity, rewrite the sentence, placing the modifier so that it clearly refers to the word or phrase it is supposed to modify.

Unclear	The film's attempt to portray war accurately depicts a survivor's anguish.
	Does the film attempt to portray war accurately, or does it accurately depict a survivor's anguish? The following revisions eliminate the uncertainty.
Revised	<u>In its</u> ~~The film's~~ attempt to portray war accurately depicts a ^ <u>, the film</u> ^ survivor's anguish.
Revised	<u>film</u> The ~~film's attempt to portray war~~ accurately depicts a ^ <u>in its attempt to portray war realistically.</u> survivor's anguish.

10c Revise a dangling modifier by rewriting the sentence.

A **dangling modifier** is a word or phrase that does not modify or refer to anything in a sentence. Instead, it seems to modify something that has been left out of the sentence. A dangling modifier can make the meaning of a sentence unclear, inaccurate, or even comical. Most dangling modifiers appear at the beginning or end of sentences.

Dangling	After singing a thrilling ballad, the crowd surged toward the stage.
	This sentence suggests that the crowd sang the ballad.
Dangling	Laying an average of ten eggs a day, the neighboring farmer is proud of his henhouse.
	This sentence suggests that the farmer lays eggs.

To revise a sentence with a dangling modifier, follow these steps.

1. Identify the word or words that the modifier is supposed to modify.
2. Revise the sentence to correct the confusion either by changing the modifier into a clause with its own subject and verb or by rewriting the sentence so that the word being modified becomes the subject.

▶   <u>Kelly sang</u>
   After ~~singing~~ a thrilling ballad, the crowd surged toward the stage.
     ^

▶   <u>his prize chickens give</u>   <u>reason to be</u>
   Laying an average of ten eggs a day, the neighboring farmer ~~is~~ proud of
                                    ^   ^

his henhouse.

Exercise H10.1

Correct any misplaced or dangling modifiers in the following sentences.

                                    scientists have built
    Hoping to get a message from outer space, a huge telescope. ~~has been built.~~

1. Solar systems exist throughout the galaxy like our own.
2. So far, no proof on other planets of the existence of life forms has been found.
3. A tremendously powerful telescope searches distant stars for signs of life in the Caribbean.
4. Astronomers monitor signals coming from other parts of the solar system carefully.
5. Wondering whether humans are alone in the universe, the telescope may provide answers.

Using Punctuation and Mechanics Correctly

11 End Punctuation

The end of a sentence can be marked with a period (.), a question mark (?), or an exclamation point (!).

11a Use a period to mark the end of a sentence that makes a statement, gives an instruction, or includes an indirect question.

Statement	Amnesty International investigates human-rights violations.
Instruction	Use as little water as possible during the drought.

Writers sometimes mistake an indirect question for a direct one, however.

▶ Most visitors want to know where the dinosaur bones were found?.

This sentence states what question was asked; it does not ask the question directly.

11b Use periods with most abbreviations.

Many abbreviations use periods (*Mass., Co., St.*). If you are not sure whether an abbreviation should include periods, check a dictionary. When an abbreviation that uses periods ends a sentence, an additional period is not needed.

▶ My brother works for Apple Computer, Inc./

Note, however, that the Modern Language Association (MLA) recommends omitting periods in abbreviations that consist of capital letters (*IBM, USA, BC*) but including periods in abbreviations that consist of lowercase letters (*a.m.*).

11c Use a question mark to end a sentence that asks a direct question.

Direct question	Why was the flight delayed?

When a question is also a quotation, the question mark is placed within the quotation marks (see also Section 15d).

▶ "What did she want?"? Marcia asked.

11d Use an exclamation point to end a sentence that expresses a strong emotion or a forceful command.

▶ Altering experimental results to make them conform to a hypothesis is never ethical!

Use exclamation points sparingly; they lose their impact when used too frequently.

▶ Government officials immediately suspected terrorism̷.
                                                    ^

Exercise H11.1

Correct any errors in the use of end punctuation marks in the following sentences. Some sentences may be correct as written.

Is it possible that hemophilia in the Russian czar's family contributed to the Russian Revolution̷?
                                                                         ^

1. When the daughters of Queen Victoria of England, who carried the gene for hemophilia, married royalty in Germany and Russia, those royal families inherited hemophilia as well?

2. The Russian czar's only son and heir to the throne suffered from hemophilia.

3. You might ask if internal bleeding can occur when a hemophiliac receives a bruise?

4. Czar Nicholas and his wife Alexandra often saw their little boy in terrible pain!

5. A phony monk named Rasputin eased the child's pain, but was he a gifted healer or just a con man.

12 Commas

A **comma** (,) is used to separate parts of a sentence from one another. When used correctly, commas make your sentences clear and help readers understand your meaning. 🖼

12a Use a comma before a coordinating word (*and, but, for, nor, or, so, yet*) that joins two independent clauses.

▶ The ball flew past the goalie, but the score did not count.
                               ^

▶ Her dog was enormous, so many people found it threatening.
                       ^

An **independent clause** contains a subject and verb and can stand alone as a sentence.

12b Use a comma to separate three or more items in a series.

A **series** is a list of three or more items — words, phrases, or clauses.

▶   Dancing, singing, and acting are just a few of her talents.
▶   Sunflowers grew on the hillsides, along the roads, and in the middle of every pasture.

A comma is not used after the last item in a series.

▶   Aphids, slugs, and beetles⁄ can severely damage a crop.

(See also Section 13c on when to use semicolons to separate items in a series.)

12c When two or more adjectives that modify the same noun are not joined by a coordinating word, use a comma to separate them.

▶   Rescue workers found the frightened, hungry child.

To be sure a comma is needed, try reversing the two adjectives. If the phrase still sounds correct when the adjectives are reversed, a comma is needed. If the phrase sounds wrong, a comma is not needed.

▶   The airy, open atrium makes visitors feel at home.
    The phrase *open, airy atrium* sounds right, so a comma is needed.

▶   Local businesses donated the bright red uniforms.
    The phrase *red, bright uniforms* sounds wrong because *bright* modifies *red uniforms* in the original sentence. A comma is not needed.

12d Use a comma to separate introductory words, phrases, and clauses from the rest of a sentence.

Introductory word	Above, the sky was a mass of clouds.
	Without the comma, this sentence would be confusing.
Introductory phrase	At the start of the project, the researchers were optimistic.
Introductory clause	When alcohol was outlawed, many solid citizens broke the law.

Exception: A comma is optional after a single word or short phrase or clause when there is no possibility of confusion.

▶   Then a rainbow appeared.

12e Use a comma to set off a nonrestrictive word group from the rest of the sentence.

A **nonrestrictive word group** describes or modifies a word or phrase in a sentence, but it does not change the meaning of the word or phrase. To decide whether a comma is needed, read the sentence without the word group. If the basic meaning is unchanged, a comma is needed.

▶ **Most people either love or hate fruitcake,** *which is a traditional holiday dessert.*

> The meaning of *fruitcake* is not changed by the relative clause *which is a traditional holiday dessert,* so the word group is nonrestrictive and a comma is needed.

▶ **The child** *wearing a tutu* **delights in ballet lessons.**

> The phrase *wearing a tutu* identifies which child delights in ballet lessons, so the word group is **restrictive** — necessary to explain what the word it modifies means — and a comma is not used.

12f Use a comma to set off parenthetical expressions.

A **parenthetical expression** provides extra information. It can also be a transitional word or phrase (*however, for example, at the beginning*) that is not essential to the meaning of the sentence.

▶ *Furthermore,* **his essay had not been proofread.**
▶ **Islamic countries were,** *in fact,* **responsible for preserving much classical scientific knowledge.**

12g Use commas with dates, addresses, titles, and numbers.

▶ **She graduated on June 8, 2014.**

When you give only a month and year, a comma is not needed.

▶ **She graduated in June 2014.**

Place a comma after a complete date when it appears before the end of the sentence.

▶ **The 2014 winter Olympics began on February 7, 2014, in Socci, Russia.**

When you give an address within a sentence, do not place a comma between the state and the ZIP code.

▶ **Send the package to PO Box 100, McPherson, Kansas 67460.**

Separate a name from a title with a comma.

▶ **The featured speaker was Kate Silverstein, Ph.D.**

Use commas in numbers that have more than four digits.

► **Estimates of the number of protesters ranged from 250,000 to 700,000.**

In a number with four digits, the comma is optional: *1500* or *1,500*.

12h Use a comma to separate a direct quotation from an identifying phrase such as *he replied* or *she said*.

► **She asked, "What's the score?"**

Place the comma before the closing quotation mark.

► **"Wait and see," he replied, infuriatingly.**

(See also Sections 15b and 15e.)

12i Use commas to set off the name of someone directly addressed, to set off an echo question, and with a "not" phrase.

Direct address	"James, answer the question concisely." "Bail has not been granted, your honor."
Echo question	More development will require a more expensive infrastructure, won't it?
"Not" phrase	Labor Day, not the autumnal equinox, marks the end of summer for most Americans.

12j Omit unnecessary commas.

As you edit and proofread your papers, watch out for common errors in comma usage.

Do not use a comma between a subject and a verb.

subject   *verb*

► **The poet Wilfred Owen, was killed a week before World War I ended.**

Do not use a comma between a verb and a complement.

A **complement** is a word or group of words that describes or renames a subject or object.

verb   *complement*

► **The school referendum is considered, very likely to pass.**

Do not use a comma between an adjective and the word it modifies.

adjective   *noun modified*

► **A growing family needs a large, house.**

Do not use a comma between two verbs in a compound predicate.

compound predicate

▶   We sat, and waited for our punishment.

Do not use a comma between two nouns or pronouns in a compound subject.

compound subject

▶   Harold Johnson, and Margaret Simpson led the expedition.

Do not use a comma before a coordinating word joining two dependent clauses.

dependent clause   *dependent clause*

▶   The band began to play before we arrived, but after the rain stopped.

Do not use a comma after *than* in a comparison.

▶   The Homestead Act made the cost of land to pioneers less than, the price the government had paid.

Do not use a comma after *like* or *such as*.

▶   Direct marketing techniques such as, mass mailings and telephone solicitations can be effective.

Do not use a comma next to a question mark, an exclamation point, or a dash or before an opening parenthesis.

▶   "Where have you been?," she would always ask.

▶   "Stop!," the guard shouted.

▶   Keep spending to a minimum,—our resources are limited—and throw nothing away.

▶   All over the world, people are eating more fast food, (which is usually high in fat).

Do not use commas around words that not only rename but also restrict another word before them.

If the words are **restrictive**—necessary to explain what the word they modify means—do not enclose them with commas.

▶   The man, who brought his car in for transmission work, is a lawyer.

Exercise H12.1

Correct any errors in the use of commas in the following sentences. Some sentences may be correct as written.

> After slavery was abolished in New York in 1827, several black settlements
> were established in what is now New York City.

1. Seneca Village a crowded shantytown on the Upper West Side was the home of many poorer black New Yorkers.
2. The city of New York, bought the land where the Seneca villagers lived.
3. The land became part of Central Park and everyone, who lived there, had to leave in the 1850s.
4. Household items from Seneca Village still turn up in Central Park today and a museum exhibit was recently devoted to life in the long-gone settlement.
5. In present-day Brooklyn, there was once a middle-class black settlement, called Weeksville.
6. James Weeks, an early resident owned much of the land.
7. Another, early, landholder, Sylvanus Smith, was a trustee of the African Free Schools of Brooklyn.
8. His daughter, Susan Smith McKinney-Steward, was born in Weeksville, and was the valedictorian of New York Medical College in 1870.
9. McKinney-Steward became the first, female, African American physician in New York, and the third in the United States.
10. Weeksville was a success story, for some of the houses survived into the twentieth century and have been preserved as historical monuments.

13 Semicolons

A **semicolon** (;) indicates a stronger pause than a comma but not as strong a pause as a period.

13a Use a semicolon to join two closely related independent clauses.

Use a semicolon to join two closely related independent clauses not connected by a coordinating word (*and, but, for, nor, or, so,* or *yet*). An **independent clause** contains a subject and a verb and can stand alone as a sentence. ⊠

⊠ **LaunchPad Solo**
macmillan learning

Visit **LaunchPad Solo for Readers and Writers > Semicolons and Colons**
for extra practice in the skills covered in this section.

▶ In January and February, sunny days are rare and very short in northern countries; winter depression is common in the north.

For advice on other ways to join two independent clauses, see Section 4.

13b Use a semicolon to join two independent clauses linked by a conjunctive adverb or transitional expression.

▶ The stunt pilot had to eject from the cockpit; nevertheless, he was not injured.

▶ Mass transit is good for the environment; for example, as many people can fit in a bus as in fifteen cars.

For more on conjunctive adverbs (words such as *also*, *however*, or *still* that link two independent clauses), see Section 4b.

13c Use semicolons to separate items in a series if commas are used within the items.

Semicolons help prevent confusion in a sentence that contains a series of items with one or more commas within the items.

▶ Fairy tales inspire children by depicting magical events, which appeal to their imaginations; clever boys and girls, who encourage young readers' problem-solving skills; evil creatures, who provide thrills; and good, heroic adults, who make the childhood world seem safer.

Also use a semicolon to separate a series of independent clauses that contain commas.

▶ He is stubborn, selfish, and conservative; she is stubborn, combative, and liberal; and no one is surprised that they do not get along.

(See also Section 12b on when to use commas to separate items in a series.)

13d Do not use a semicolon to introduce a list or to separate a phrase or dependent clause from the rest of the sentence.

▶ A growing number of companies employ prison inmates for certain jobs: selling magazines, conducting surveys, reserving airplane tickets, and taking telephone orders.

▶ On the other hand, taking risks can bring impressive results.

(For more on introducing lists, see Section 14a.)

Exercise H13.1

Correct any errors in the use of semicolons in the following sentences. Some sentences may be correct as written.

> Myths and stories about vampires have been around for centuries~~,~~;
>
> however, Bram Stoker's 1897 novel *Dracula* is probably the most famous
>
> fictional account of these monsters.

1. In the years since Stoker's novel, vampires have become a movie fixture; in America and throughout the world.

2. Silent versions of the vampire tale include *Les Vampires* (1915), a French film, *Nosferatu* (1921), a German film, and *London After Midnight* (1927), an American film.

3. Actor Bela Lugosi played Count Dracula as more of a romantic figure than a monster in the 1931 film *Dracula*; this depiction provided the standard image of the vampire as a sexy fiend.

4. The vampire tale has several standard traits; yet it remains remarkably versatile.

5. The vampire tale was adapted to the American movie western; for example, in *Billy the Kid vs. Dracula* in 1966.

14 Colons

You can use a **colon** (:) to introduce a list, an explanation, an example, or a further thought within a sentence. The information following the colon should clarify or offer specifics about the information that comes before it. 🔲

14a Use a colon to introduce a list or a series.

When you use a **colon** to introduce a list, make sure the list is preceded by a complete sentence.

▶ The archaeologists uncovered several items: pieces of pottery, seeds, animal bones, and household tools.

▶ All students must be immunized against: *common childhood illnesses* measles, mumps, and rubella.

🔲 **LaunchPad Solo**   Visit **LaunchPad Solo for Readers and Writers > Semicolons and Colons**
macmillan learning   for extra practice in the skills covered in this section.

14b Use a colon to introduce an explanation, an example, or a summary.

▶ In many ways, Hollywood is very predictable: Action movies arrive in the summer, dramas in the fall.

▶ One tree is particularly famous for its spectacular autumn colors: the sugar maple.

▶ Disaster relief efforts began all over the country: Volunteers raised forty million dollars.

Note: If the group of words following a colon is a complete sentence, the first word can begin with either a capital or a lowercase letter. Whichever option you choose, be consistent throughout your paper.

14c Use a colon to introduce a word or phrase that renames another noun.

▶ A hushed group of tourists stared at the most famous statue in Florence: Michelangelo's *David*.

14d Use a colon to introduce a lengthy or heavily punctuated quotation.

A quotation that is more than one or two lines long or that contains two or more commas may be introduced by a colon.

▶ Without pausing for breath, his campaign manager intoned the introduction: "Ladies and gentlemen, today it is my very great privilege to introduce to you the person on whose behalf you have all worked so tirelessly and with such impressive results, the man who is the reason we are all here today—the next president of the United States."

▶ The instructions were confusing: "After adjusting toggles A, B, and C, connect bracket A to post A, bracket B to post B, and bracket C to post C, securing with clamps A, B, and C, as illustrated in figure 1."

14e Use a colon to separate hours and minutes, in salutations for business letters, between titles and subtitles, and in ratios.

Hours and minutes	9:15 a.m.
Salutations	Dear Professor Sung:
Titles and subtitles	*American Sphinx: The Character of Thomas Jefferson*
Ratios	7:1

14f Make sure the words preceding a colon are an
independent clause.

The words before a colon should be an independent clause. An **independent
clause** contains a subject and a verb and can stand alone as a sentence. Do not
use a colon between a verb and its object; between a preposition and its object; or
before a list introduced by such words as *for example, including, is,* and *such as.*

▶   A medieval map is hard to read: The top of the map points to the east, not
the north.

   A medieval map is hard to read is an independent clause.

▶   Even a small garden can produce; beans, squash, tomatoes, and corn.

▶   Bird-watchers are thrilled to spy birds of prey such as; peregrine falcons,
red-tailed hawks, and owls.

Exercise H14.1

Correct any errors in the use of colons in the following sentences. Some sentences
may be correct as written.

   Young, impeccably dressed couples participated in the latest craze; swing

   dancing.
   ⌃

1. The shuttle launch is scheduled for precisely 10.00 a.m.
2. The proposed zoning change was defeated by a margin of 2 / 1.
3. On early rap records, listeners heard percussion from unusual sources such
   as: turntables, microphones, and synthesizers.
4. To find out whether a film is historically accurate, consult *Past Imperfect:
   History According to the Movies.*
5. He believes that the most American of all sports is: baseball.

---

15 Quotation Marks, Ellipses, and Brackets

Quotation Marks

Quotation marks (" ") are used to indicate direct quotations or to mark words
used as words in your sentences. A **direct quotation** gives a person's *exact* words,
either spoken or written, set off by quotation marks. Quotation marks are always
used in pairs. The opening quotation mark (") appears at the beginning of a word
or quoted passage, and the closing mark (") appears at the end.

15a Place quotation marks around direct statements from other speakers or writers.

Be careful to include the *exact* words of the speaker or writer within the quotation marks.

▶   Lincoln recalled that the United States was "dedicated to the proposition that all men are created equal."

    Because *dedicated to the proposition that all men are created equal* repeats Lincoln's exact words, quotation marks are required.

In dialogue, place quotation marks around each speaker's words. Every time a different person speaks, begin a new paragraph.

> He said, "Sit down."
> "No, thank you," I replied.

For details on quoting from original sources using MLA style, see pages 623–34; for details on quoting using APA style, see pages 635–43.

15b Place a comma or period that follows a direct quotation *within* the quotation marks.

▶   "Play it, Sam," Rick tells the piano player in *Casablanca*.

▶   Willie Sutton robbed banks because "that's where the money is."

15c Place colons and semicolons *outside* of quotation marks.

▶   The marching band played "Seventy-Six Trombones"; the drum major's favorite song.

▶   A new national anthem should replace "The Star-Spangled Banner"; no one can sing that song.

15d Place question marks and exclamation points according to the meaning of the sentence.

If the quotation is a question or exclamation, place the question mark or exclamation point *within* the closing quotation mark. If the punctuation mark comes at the end of a sentence, no other end punctuation is needed.

▶   "How does the bridge stand up?" the child wondered.

▶   Poe's insane narrator confesses, "It is the beating of his hideous heart!"

If the entire sentence, of which the quotation is part, is a question or exclamation, the question mark or exclamation point goes *outside* the closing quotation mark at the end of the sentence.

▶   Was Scarlett O'Hara serious when she said, "Tomorrow is another day"?

15e Use a comma to separate a short quotation from an introductory or identifying phrase such as *he replied* or *she said*.

▶ "Video games improve eye-hand coordination," he replied.

▶ "The homeless population," she reported, "grew steadily throughout the 1980s."

15f Use single quotation marks (' ') to indicate a quotation or title within a quotation.

▶ The mysterious caller repeatedly insists, "Play 'Misty' for me."

15g Place quotation marks around the titles of short works.

Section of a book	Chapter 1, "Ozzie and Harriet in Spanish Harlem"
Poem	"Ode on a Grecian Urn"
Short story	"The Yellow Wallpaper"
Essay or article	"Their Malcolm, My Problem"
Song	"Bad Romance"
Episode of a television program	"Larry's Last Goodbye"

15h Do not use quotation marks to call unnecessary attention to words or phrases.

▶ The manager who was originally in charge of the project ~~"~~jumped ship~~"~~ before the deadline.

Quotation marks can be used to mark words used as words (as an acceptable alternative to italics; see Section 18i).

▶ The word "receive" is often misspelled.

Exercise H15.1

Correct any errors in the use of quotation marks in the following sentences. Some sentences may be correct as written.

The hotel has an excellent restaurant specializing in ~~"~~fresh~~"~~ fish.

1. Her essay was entitled " "To Be or Not to Be": Shakespeare and Existentialism."
2. Why did the professor assign "To an Athlete Dying Young?"
3. A movie line many teenagers imitated was "Hasta la vista, baby".

4. After September 11, 2001, President Bush said he was going to "fight terror".

5. "I have a dream," Martin Luther King Jr. told the civil rights marchers.

Ellipsis Marks

An **ellipsis mark** (. . .) is written as three equally spaced periods. It is used within a direct quotation to indicate where you have left out part of the original quotation. You use an ellipsis mark to shorten a quotation so that it includes just the parts you want or need to quote.

Original quotation	"The prison, a high percentage of whose inmates are serving life sentences, looked surprisingly ordinary."
Shortened	"The prison . . . looked surprisingly ordinary."
	Notice that the two commas were also omitted when the quotation was shortened.

15i When you shorten a quotation, be careful not to change the meaning of the original passage.

Do not omit any parts that will alter or misrepresent the writer's intended meaning.

Original	"Magicians create illusions, but sometimes audience members want to believe that magic is real."
Meaning altered	"Magicians . . . want to believe that magic is real."

When you omit the last part of a quoted sentence, add a sentence period, for a total of four periods (the ellipsis mark plus a period).

Original quotation	"In the sphere of psychology, details are also the thing. God preserve us from commonplaces. Best of all is to avoid depicting the hero's state of mind; you ought to try to make it clear from the hero's actions. It is not necessary to portray many characters. The center of gravity should be in two persons: him and her." —Anton Chekhov, Letter to Alexander P. Chekhov
Shortened	"God preserve us from commonplaces. Best of all is to avoid depicting the hero's state of mind . . . . It is not necessary to portray many characters. The center of gravity should be in two persons: him and her."

An ellipsis mark is not needed to indicate that the quoted passage continues after the last sentence you quote ends.

▶ He is modest about his contributions to the abolitionist cause: "I could do but little; but what I could, I did with a joyful heart⌒" (Douglass 54).

15j Do not use an ellipsis mark at the beginning of a quotation, even though there is material in the original that comes before it.

Original quotation	"As was the case after the recent cleaning of the Sistine Chapel, the makeover of the starry ceiling in Grand Central Station has revealed surprisingly brilliant color."
Shortened	"[T]he makeover of the starry ceiling in Grand Central Station has revealed surprisingly brilliant color."

Note: The first word of a quoted sentence should be capitalized. If you change from a lowercase to a capital letter, enclose the letter in brackets (see Section 15k).

Brackets

Brackets ([   ]) are used within quotations and within parentheses.

15k Use brackets to add information or indicate changes you have made to a quotation.

▶ Whitman's preface argued, "Here [the United States] is not merely a nation but a teeming nation of nations."

The explanation tells where *here* is.

▶ "Along came a spider and sat down beside [Miss Muffett]," who apparently suffered from a phobia.

The bracketed name replaces *her* in the original.

Use brackets to enclose the word *sic* when signaling an error in original quoted material.

▶ The incumbent's letter to the editor announced, "My opponant's [sic] claims regarding my record are simply not true."

The Latin word *sic* lets your readers know that the misspelled word or other error in the quoted material is the original author's error, not yours.

15l Use brackets to enclose parenthetical material in a group of words already enclosed in parentheses.

▶ The demonstrators (including members of the National Rifle Association [NRA]) crowded around the candidate.

Exercise H15.2

Shorten each of the following quotations by omitting the underlined portion and adding an ellipsis mark and brackets where appropriate.

> "Some people who call themselves vegetarians still
>
> eat ~~less cuddly creatures such as~~ chicken and fish."

1. "The structure of DNA, <u>as Watson and Crick discovered</u>, is a double helix."
2. "<u>Although African Americans had won Academy Awards before</u>, Halle Berry was the first African American woman to win the Academy Award for Best Actress."
3. "Cole Porter cultivated a suave, sophisticated urban persona <u>even though he came from a small town in Indiana</u>."
4. "<u>Many Americans do not realize that</u> people of all classes receive financial help from the government."
5. Nathan Hale regretted that he had "but one life to give for <u>my</u> country."

16 Apostrophes

An **apostrophe** (') has three functions: to show ownership or possession, to indicate omitted letters in contractions, and to form some plurals. ⚏

16a Use an apostrophe to indicate possession or ownership.

Add -'s to make singular nouns possessive, including nouns that end with *s* or the sound of *s* and indefinite pronouns (*anyone, nobody*). An **indefinite pronoun** does not refer to a specific person, place, or object. It refers to people, places, or things in general (*anywhere, everyone, everything*).

▶ The *fox's* prey led it across the field.
▶ Whether she can win the nomination is *anybody's* guess.

Note that the possessive forms of personal pronouns do not take apostrophes: *mine, yours, his, hers, ours, theirs, its.*

▶ Each bee has it/s function in the hive.

The possessive form of *who* is *whose* (not *who's*).

▶ Marie Curie, *whose* work in chemistry made history, discovered radium.

 **LaunchPad Solo**   Visit **LaunchPad Solo for Readers and Writers > Apostrophes** for extra
macmillan learning   practice in the skills covered in this section.

Add an apostrophe to a plural noun to make it possessive, or add -'s if the plural noun does not end in *s*.

> ▶ Both *farms'* crops were lost in the flood.
> ▶ Our *children's* children will reap the benefits of our efforts to preserve the environment today.

To show individual possession by two or more people or groups, add an apostrophe or -'s to each noun.

> ▶ Sam is equipment manager for both the *boys'* and the *girls'* basketball teams.
>   Sam works for two different teams.

To show joint possession by two people or groups, add an apostrophe or -'s to the last noun.

> ▶ The *coaches and players'* dream came true at the end of the season.

Add -'s to the last word of a compound noun to show possession.

> ▶ My *father-in-law's* boat needs a new engine.
> ▶ We were ushered into the *chairman of the department's* office.

16b Use an apostrophe to indicate the omitted letter or letters in a contraction.

> ▶ *I've* [I have] seen the answers.
> ▶ Jason *didn't* [did not] arrive last night.

16c Use an apostrophe to form the plural of a number, letter, symbol, abbreviation, or word treated as a word.

> ▶ There are three 5's on the license plate.
> ▶ She spells her name with two C's.
> ▶ The ?'s stand for unknown quantities.
> ▶ Using two *etc.*'s is unnecessary.
> ▶ Replace all *can's* in the contract with *cannot's*.

In the sentences above, note that numbers, letters, and words used as themselves are in italics. The -*s* ending should not be italicized, however. (For more on italics and underlining, see Sections 18f–i.)

When referring to the years in a decade, do not use an apostrophe before the -*s* ending.

> ▶ The fashions of the 1970s returned in the 1990s.

However, an apostrophe is used to signal the omission of the numerals that indicate the century.

> the class of '03   music of the '90s

16d Do not use apostrophes to form plurals or to form possessives for personal pronouns.

▶ The trapper̶'̶s came to town to trade.
▶ She paid for my lunch as well as her̶'̶s.

Exercise H16.1

Correct the errors in the use of apostrophes in the following sentences. Some sentences may be correct as written.

> As Twitter, Facebook, and text messaging take over our lives, we should
>
> ask whether we̓re becoming more connected or less connected with other
>   ^
> people.

1. Our's is a society almost too willing to share.
2. We probably know more about the day-to-day lives of other's than ever before, as the details of our many friend's days are recorded in online status report's.
3. Its unclear, however, whether anyone is truly benefiting from all this sharing of private information, even as the various social networking sites privacy settings reveal more and more about user's.
4. Todays parents' can find out about their sons and daughters personal live's online, but they have less face-to-face contact with their children.
5. Of course, theyll have to figure out the meaning of all the *LOLs*', *BTWs*, and other shorthand slang in their kids online and text messages.

17 Dashes

Use a **dash** (—) to separate parts of a sentence. A dash suggests a stronger separation than a comma, colon, or semicolon does. To type a dash, hit the hyphen key twice (- -), with no spaces before, between, or after the hyphens. Some word-processing programs automatically convert the two hyphens to a solid dash (—).

17a Use a dash or dashes to emphasize a sudden shift or break in thought or mood.

▶ Computers have given the world instant communication—and electronic junk mail.

17b Use a dash or dashes to introduce an explanation, an example, or items in a series.

▶ The tattoo artist had completed a large body of work—Fred's!
▶ The tattoo artist had seen everything—a full-size bear claw on a back, a bleeding heart on a bicep, even an Irish cross on the tip of a nose.

When the added thought appears in the middle of a sentence, use two dashes to set it off.

▶ The tattoo artist—who would prefer to remain nameless—thinks tattoos are a waste of money.

17c Use dashes sparingly.

Dashes are emphatic. Do not overuse them, or they will lose their effectiveness. Also be careful not to use a dash as a substitute for a conjunction or transition. A **conjunction** is a word or words used to connect clauses, phrases, or individual words.

▶ Einstein's job in Switzerland was dull,~~—~~ but it offered him plenty of time to think;~~—~~ while working there he came up with the theory of relativity.

Exercise H17.1

Add a dash or pair of dashes where it might be effective, and correct any errors in the use of dashes in the following sentences.

Food—who eats what and why?—is now a subject studied by academics.

1. One issue particularly concerns scholars of food; why are certain foods acceptable in some cultures but not in others?

2. Some foods such as the cabbage palm were once popular, but today — hardly anyone has heard of them.

3. In the 1990s, people in Great Britain were alerted to a new danger, mad cow disease.

4. In the 1960s, frozen foods — icy blocks of corn, peas, and string beans — were popular — and convenient — alternatives to fresh produce.

5. Today, fresh fruits and vegetables are valued once again, unless a busy cook has no time for peeling and chopping.

18 Capitalization and Italics/Underlining

Capitalization

Capitalize the first word of a sentence, proper nouns, and the pronoun *I*. 🔲

LaunchPad Solo   Visit **LaunchPad Solo for Readers and Writers > Capitalization** for extra
macmillan learning   practice in the skills covered in this section.

18a Capitalize the first word in a sentence and in a direct quotation.

▶　　^R
　　ŗevision is important.
　　^

Capitalize the first word in a direct quotation unless it is incorporated into your own sentence or it continues a sentence started in an earlier quotation.

▶　　The union representative said, "^Tthat meeting did not take place."
　　　　　　　　　　　　　　　　　^

▶　　Sam Verdon complained that "ⁿNo one takes college athletes seriously."
　　　　　　　　　　　　　　　^

▶　　"I̱ prefer not to interpret my paintings," replied the famous watercolorist, "Ḇecause they should speak for themselves."
　　^

18b Capitalize proper nouns, including the names of specific people, places, things, and groups.

People and animals	Franklin Roosevelt, his dog Fala
Cities, states, nations	St. Paul, Minnesota, the United States
Geographic regions	the Gulf Coast, the U.S. Southwest
Government offices, departments, buildings	the Pentagon, the Supreme Court, the Puck Building
Organizations (cultural, political, etc.)	League of Women Voters, National Basketball Association
Months, days, holidays	February, Thursday, Labor Day
Chapter or section titles in books	"Why America Has Changed"
Nationalities and languages	Ethiopian, Dutch
Religions and sacred books	Judaism, the Koran
Trade names	Coca-Cola, Brillo
Historic events	the Treaty of Versailles, Reconstruction
Specific course titles	Organic Chemistry 101

18c Do not capitalize common nouns.

Family members	my uncle, his father
General areas of the country	southwestern United States
Subjects	my chemistry class
Centuries	seventeenth-century England
Geographical areas	the lake in the park

18d Capitalize the titles of literary and other works, such as books, articles, poems, plays, songs, films, and paintings.

Capitalize the first and last words of the title, the first word following a colon, and all other words except articles (*a, an,* and *the*), coordinating conjunctions (*and, but, for, nor, or, so, yet*), and prepositions (such as *before, on,* and *to*).

Book	*The Fault in Our Stars*
Article	"Making History at Madison Park"
Poem	"Aunt Jennifer's Tigers"
Play	*A Raisin in the Sun*
Song	"Heart of Glass"
Film	*Gone Girl*
Painting	*The Starry Night*

18e Capitalize a personal title only when it directly precedes a person's name.

▶   Vice President Maria Washington briefed the stockholders.
▶   Maria Washington was hired from a rival company to be the new vice president.

It is acceptable to capitalize the titles of high-level government officials regardless of whether they precede a name: *the President of the United States.*

Italics/Underlining

Italics, or *slanted type,* is used for emphasizing particular words or phrases. It is also used to set off titles of longer works, names of vehicles, non-English words, and words deserving special emphasis.

When writing by hand, use <u>underlining</u> to indicate italics. Most word-processing programs provide italic type, and most style guides used for college writing, such as the *MLA Handbook for Writers of Research Papers* and the *Publication Manual of the American Psychological Association* (APA), require it.

18f Italicize or underline titles of works published separately.

Books	*Great Expectations*
Plays and musicals	*Rent*

LaunchPad Solo — macmillan learning   Visit **LaunchPad Solo for Readers and Writers > Italics** for extra practice in the skills covered in this section.

Long poems	*The Iliad*
Magazines and journals	*Entertainment Weekly*, the *New York Review of Books*
Newspapers	the *Columbus Dispatch*
Movies and DVDs	*The Twilight Saga: Eclipse*
Long musical works, recordings	*Exile on Main St.*
Television and radio series	*Jersey Shore*
Visual works of art (paintings, sculptures)	*Birth of Venus*

The titles of shorter works, such as the titles of articles, short stories, and songs, should be enclosed in quotation marks (see Section 15g).

18g Italicize or underline the names of ships, trains, aircraft, and spacecraft.

Titanic	*Spirit of St. Louis*
Orient Express	space shuttle *Challenger*

18h Italicize or underline non-English words not in everyday use.

Words from other languages should be italicized unless they have become a part of the English language, such as "chic" or "burrito." If you are unsure, check an English dictionary. If the word is not listed, it should be italicized.

▶   Our instructor lectured on the technique of *Verstehen*.
▶   Tacos are now as much a part of American cuisine as pizza.

18i Italicize or underline numbers, letters, words, or phrases called out for special emphasis.

Use italics for numbers, letters, or words used as terms.

▶   Every bottle has *33* on the label.
▶   Hester Prynne is forced to wear a scarlet *A*.
▶   Today, *ain't* is listed in most dictionaries.

Italicize a word or phrase that is being defined or emphasized.

▶   *Alliteration*—the same sounds repeated at the beginning of each word in a group—can be an effective literary device.

Use italics for emphasis sparingly. When you italicize too many words in a sentence or paragraph, the emphasis is lost.

> ▶   (no italics)
> The U.S. National Park system is *extremely important* because it protects
> (no italics)   (no italics)
> some of the most *beautiful* and *unusual* parts of this country.

Exercise H18.1

Correct the errors in the use of italics and capital letters in the following sentences. Some sentences may be correct as written.

> Oedipus, written by Sophocles in the fifth century BC, is possibly the most
>
> famous play of the classical period.

1. During world war II, the governments of twenty-six countries, including the united states, pledged their willingness to continue fighting on behalf of the Allies.

2. His professor insisted that Soap Opera Digest was not an acceptable research source.

3. Patrick Henry said, "give me Liberty or give me Death."

4. The first European settlers at Plymouth arrived on the mayflower.

5. His book is discussed in depth in the article *Africa: The hidden history.*

Answers to Even-Numbered Exercises in Handbook

Exercise H3.1, p. 660

Possible Revisions:

2. In the United States, for example, colleges and universities provide education to Americans of all classes and backgrounds.

4. During the nineteenth and early twentieth centuries, graduates of state universities played a key role in America's development as an industrial and economic power.

Exercise H4.1, p. 665

Possible Revisions:

2. Shopping through online bookstores is convenient, but some people miss the atmosphere of a traditional bookstore.

4. In the 1960s, some Americans treated Vietnam veterans disrespectfully, a situation that has changed dramatically since that time.

Exercise H5.1, p. 669

Answers:

2. A student in most non-English-speaking industrialized nations expects to spend six or more years studying English.

4. Working for laws that require all Americans to speak English is a fairly common U.S. political tactic.

Exercise H6.1, p. 673

Answers:

2. Cuba, an island that lies ninety miles off the Florida coast, provided them with an excuse to do so.

4. In addition, many people in the United States had wanted to take over Spain's territories for a long time.

Exercise H7.1, p. 675

Possible Revisions:

2. Because of the importance of the information, it often must be transmitted secretly.

4. Using "invisible ink," which cannot be seen until the paper is heated, was once a popular way to communicate secretly.

Exercise H7.2, p. 678

Answers:

2. A team of researchers might disagree on their conclusions about the disappearance of the dinosaur.

4. In one way, animals resemble plants: Some are "weeds" because they have the ability to thrive under many conditions.

Exercise H7.3, p. 681

Answers:

2. Correct

4. Following the success of Mammoth Cave, many Kentucky cavers hoped to make a fortune from their spelunking.

Exercise H8.1, p. 684

Possible Revisions:

2. We wondered whether our professor knew of the new theory and whether she agreed with it.

4. Most parents think they have a major influence on their children's behavior.

Exercise H8.2, p. 685

Possible Revisions:

2. Surveys show that college graduates who intern receive higher salary offers than their classmates who do not.

4. The most important qualities are curiosity and a good work ethic.

Exercise H9.1, p. 689

Answers:

2. *Wikipedia* has many advantages that reflect well on it as a source.

4. In a way, encyclopedias are unique because Web sites can grow to include any subject that anyone finds interesting.

Exercise H10.1, p. 691

Possible Revisions:

2. So far, no proof of the existence of life forms on other planets has been found.

4. Astronomers carefully monitor signals coming from other parts of the solar system.

Exercise H11.1, p. 693

Answers:

2. Correct

4. Czar Nicholas and his wife Alexandra often saw their little boy in terrible pain.

Exercise H12.1, p. 698

Answers:

2. The city of New York bought the land where the Seneca villagers lived.

4. Household items from Seneca Village still turn up in Central Park today, and a museum exhibit was recently devoted to life in the long-gone settlement.

6. James Weeks, an early resident, owned much of the land.

8. His daughter, Susan Smith McKinney-Steward, was born in Weeksville and was the valedictorian of New York Medical College in 1870.

10. Correct

Exercise H13.1, p. 700

Answers:

2. Silent versions of the vampire tale include *Les Vampires* (1915), a French film; *Nosferatu* (1921), a German film; and *London After Midnight* (1927), an American film.

4. The vampire tale has several standard traits, yet it remains remarkably versatile.

Exercise H14.1, p. 702

Answers:

2. The proposed zoning change was defeated by a margin of 2:1.

4. Correct

Exercise H15.1, p. 704

Answers:

2. Why did the professor assign "To an Athlete Dying Young"?

4. After September 11, 2001, President Bush said he was going to "fight terror."

Exercise H15.2, p. 707

Answers:

2. "Halle Berry was the first African American woman to win the Academy Award for Best Actress."

4. "[P]eople of all classes receive financial help from the government."

Exercise H16.1, p. 709

Answers:

2. We probably know more about the day-to-day lives of others than ever before, as the details of our many friends' days are recorded in online status reports.

4. Today's parents can find out about their sons and daughters' personal lives online, but they have less face-to-face contact with their children.

Exercise H17.1, p. 710

Answers:

2. Some foods such as the cabbage palm were once popular, but today hardly anyone has heard of them.

4. In the 1960s, frozen foods — icy blocks of corn, peas, and string beans — were popular and convenient alternatives to fresh produce.

Exercise H18.1, p. 714

Answers:

2. His professor insisted that *Soap Opera Digest* was not an acceptable research source.

4. The first European settlers at Plymouth arrived on the *Mayflower*.

Acknowledgments

Sherry Amatenstein, "Talking a Stranger Through the Night" from *Newsweek*, Nov. 18, 2002. Copyright © 2002 by IBT Media. All rights reserved. Used by permission and protected by the Copyright Laws of the United States. The printing, copying, redistribution, or retransmission of this Content without express written permission is prohibited.

Dave Barry, "We've Got the Dirt on Guy Brains," by Dave Barry from *The Miami Herald*, Nov. 23, 2003, is reprinted by permission of the author.

George Beekman and Ben Beekman, "History of the Future," from DIGITAL PLANET: TOMORROW'S TECHNOLOGY AND YOU, 10th ed., copyright © 2012. Reprinted by permission of Pearson Education, Inc., New York, NY.

Joan Salge Blake, Kathy D. Munoz, Stella Volpe, from NUTRITION: FROM SCIENCE TO YOU, 2nd ed. Copyright © 2014. Printed and Electronically reproduced by permission of Pearson Education, Inc., New York, NY.

David Bodanis, "A Brush with Reality: Surprises in the Tube" from THE SECRET HOUSE, pp. 10–16. Copyright © 1986 by David Bodanis. Reprinted with permission of the Carol Mann Agency.

Peter Bregman, "How (and Why) to Stop Multitasking," *Harvard Business Review*, May 20, 2010. Copyright © 2010 by Harvard Business Publishing. All rights reserved. Reprinted by permission of the publisher.

Bill Bryson, excerpts from I'M A STRANGER HERE MYSELF: NOTES ON RETURNING TO AMERICA AFTER TWENTY YEARS AWAY. Copyright © 1999 by Bill Bryson. Used by permission of Broadway Books, an imprint of the Crown Publishing Group, a division of Penguin Random House LLC. All rights reserved. Any third party use of this material, outside of this publication, is prohibited. Interested parties must apply directly to Penguin Random House LLC for permission. Rights in Canada by permission of Doubleday Canada, a division of Penguin Random House Canada Limited. Excerpted from NOTES FROM A BIG COUNTRY. Copyright © 1998 by Bill Bryson.

Veronica Chambers, "The Secret Latina" from *Essence*, July 2000. Reprinted by permission of the author.

Amy Chua, excerpt from pp. 3–5, 29, 50–54, 60–63 from *The Wall Street Journal*, Jan. 8, 2011, adapted from BATTLE HYMN OF THE TIGER MOTHER. Copyright © 2011 by Amy Chua. Used by permission of Penguin Press, an imprint of Penguin Publishing Group, a division of Penguin Random House LLC.

Brittney Cooper, "The Racial Parenting Divide: What Adrian Peterson Reveals About Black vs. White Child-rearing." This article first appeared in *Salon.com*, at http://www.Salon .com. An online version remains in the Salon archives. Reprinted with permission.

Bethe Dufresne, "Gullible Travels" from *Utne Reader*, excerpted from *Commonweal* magazine, Dec. 17, 2010. Copyright © 2010 by Commonweal Foundation. Reprinted with permission of Commonweal Foundation, www.commonwealmagazine.org.

Lars Eighner, "On Dumpster Diving," an excerpt from TRAVELS WITH LIZBETH, copyright © 1993 by Lars Eighner. Reprinted by permission of St. Martin's Press. All rights reserved.

Anna Erelle, Text as serialized in *Vogue* magazine, June 2014, from IN THE SKIN OF A JIHADIST. Translated from the French by Erin Potter. Copyright © 2015 by Anna Erelle. English language translation copyright © 2015 by HarperCollins Publishers. Reprinted by permission of HarperCollins Publishers.

Patrick L. Frank, Duane Preble, Sarah Preble, "Issue-Oriented Art" and "Street Art" from PREBLES' ARTFORMS, 9th ed., copyright © 2009. Reprinted by permission of Pearson Education, Inc., New York, NY.

Joshua Fruhlinger, "Five Things to Avoid When Dating Online," from www.switched.com, August 7, 2008. Original publication copyright © 2007 by Joshua Fruhlinger. Reprinted by permission of the author.

Louis Giannetti, from UNDERSTANDING MOVIES, 12th edition. Copyright © 2011. Reprinted by permission of Pearson Education, Inc., New York, NY.

Stefany Anne Golberg, "Can You See Me Now? Deaf America" from *Utne Reader*, Sept.-Oct. 2011 is excerpted from *The Smart Set*, May 23, 2011, www.thesmartset.com. Reprinted by permission of the author.

Lisa M. Hamilton, "Eating Meat for the Environment" was originally published in *Perch*, the blog of Audubon Magazine, June 26, 2009. Reprinted by permission of the author.

Michael Hanlon, "What Happened to Innovation" was published as "The Golden Quarter" by Aeon Media, a digital magazine for ideas and culture, http://www.aeon.co. Follow them on Twitter at @aeon.mag. Reprinted by permission of the publisher.

Sebastian Junger, "Why Would Anyone Miss War?" from *The New York Times*, July 16, 2011. Copyright © 2011 by Sebastian Junger. Reprinted by permission of the Stuart Krichevsky Literary Agency, Inc.

Mindy Kaling, Excerpts from IS EVERYONE HANGING OUT WITHOUT ME? (AND OTHER CONCERNS). Copyright © 2011 by Mindy Kaling. Used by permission of Crown Archetype, an imprint of the Crown Publishing Group, a division of Penguin Random House LLC. All rights reserved. Any third party use of this material, outside of this publication, is prohibited. Interested parties must apply directly to Penguin Random House LLC for permission.

Roland Kelts, "The Satori Generation: A New Breed of Young People Who Have Outdone the Tricksters of Advertising" published May, 7, 2014, issue #133, *Adbusters.org*. Reprinted by permission of the author.

Jordan Kisner, "Rain is sizzling bacon, cars are lions roaring: the art of sound in movies" from *The Guardian*, July 22, 2015. Copyright © 2015 by Guardian News & Media Ltd. Reprinted by permission of the publisher.

Morgan Lowrie, "Comparing Online and Traditional Education" from *helium.com*, Feb. 11, 2009. Reprinted by permission of the author.

April Lynch, Barry Elmore, Jerome Kotecki, from HEALTH: MAKING CHOICES FOR LIFE, BOOKS A LA CARTE EDITION, 1st edition. Copyright © 2014. Reprinted by permission of Pearson Education, Inc., New York, NY.

Jeremy MacClancy, "Eating Chilli Peppers" from CONSUMING CULTURE: WHY YOU EAT WHAT YOU EAT. Copyright © 1992 by Jeremy MacClancy. Used by permission of Henry Holt and Company, LLC. All rights reserved.

Hara Estroff Marano, "Why We Procrastinate" from *Psychology Today*, July 1, 2005, is reprinted by permission of the author.

Scott Matteson, "How Does Google Search Really Work?" from *TechRepublic*, Dec. 11, 2013. Used with permission of TechRepublic.com. Copyright © 2016. All rights reserved.

Robinson Meyer, "To Remember a Lecture Better, Take Notes by Hand" as first published in *The Atlantic*. Copyright © 2014 by The Atlantic Media Co. All rights reserved. Distributed by Tribune Content Agency, LLC.

Austin Netzley, "8 Steps to Pay Off $81,000 of Debt in Less Than 3 Years" from "Business Insider," Dec. 3, 2014. Reprinted and edited by permission of the author. Austin Netzley is the best-selling author of MAKE MONEY, LIVE WEALTHY.

Fred Pearce, "TV as Birth Control" excerpted from *Utne Reader*, Summer 2014, originally published in *Conservation*, Fall 2013. Reprinted by permission of the author.

Roger Porter, "A Reinterpretation of Tears: Learning How to Be a Father That Won't Leave" from *Rad Dad*, Spring 2014. Reprinted by permission of the author.

Sara Rashkin, "What Kind of H2O Should You Drink? We Asked L.A.'s Only Water Sommelier" published in slightly different form in *LA Weekly*, Sept. 10, 2015. Reprinted by permission of the author.

Robert Reich, "Why We Should Raise the Minimum Wage" from *CNBC.com*, April 27, 2015. Reprinted by permission of ICM/Sagalyn and the author.

Eric Rosenberg, "How to Make Money With YouTube" from *Investopedia*, Feb. 24, 2015. Reprinted by permission of the publisher.

Cristina Rouvalis, "Hey, Mom, Dad, May I Have My Room Back?" from the *Pittsburgh Post-Gazette*, Aug. 31, 2008. Copyright © 2008 by Pittsburgh Post-Gazette. All rights reserved. Reprinted with permission of the publisher.

Index

Revision Symbols

The numbers and letters refer to chapters and sections in the Handbook. Page numbers are provided for references to sections outside of the Handbook.

ad	Misuse of adjective or adverb **1, 9**	ꞌ	Apostrophe **16**
agr	Faulty agreement **5, 7e–7h**	" "	Quotation mark **15a–15h**
appr	Inappropriate language *p. 156*	. ? !	End punctuation **11**
awk	Awkward **7, 8, 10**	—	Dash **17**
cap	Capital letter **18**	[ ]	Brackets **15k, 15l**
case	Error in pronoun case **7i–7n**	. . .	Ellipsis mark **15i, 15j**
cliché	Cliché *p. 156*	ref	Reference, pronoun **7a–7d**
coh	Coherence *pp. 120–22*	run-on	Run-on sentence **4**
cs	Comma splice **4**	sexist	Sexist language **7e**
dm	Dangling modifier **10c**	shift	Shift **8a–8g**
exact	Inexact word *p. 156*	sl	Slang *p. 156*
frag	Fragment **3**	sp	Spelling error
irreg	Error in irregular verb **6b**	sub	Subordination **2c**
ital	Italics **18f–18i**	t	Error in verb tense **6d–6g**
lc	Lowercase letter **18a–18e**	trans	Transition *pp. 120–22*
mix	Mixed construction **8h–8j**	v	Voice **6c**
mm	Misplaced modifier **10a, 10b**	var	Sentence variety *p. 155*
para, ¶	New paragraph *pp. 109–10*	vb	Verb error **5, 6**
pass	Ineffective passive *p. 155,* **6c**	wrdy	Wordiness *p. 155*
p	Punctuation **11–17**	//	Faulty parallelism *p. 156*
,	Comma **12**	⌒	Close up
no ⌄	No comma **12j**	⌃	Insert
;	Semicolon **13**	X	Obvious error
:	Colon **14**		

List of Readings

*textbook selection/**student selection

Instructor's Manual

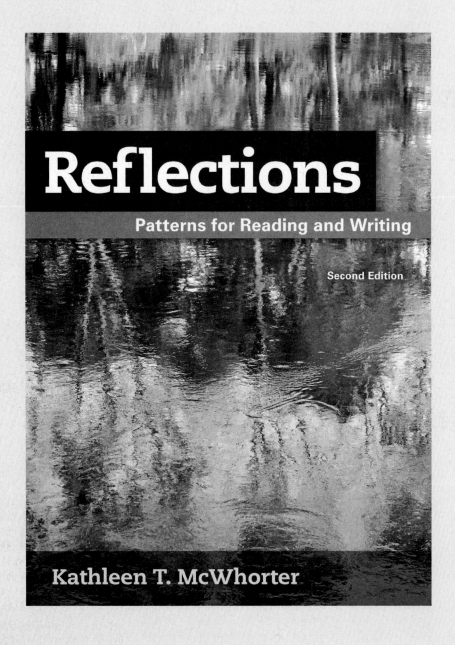

Reflections

Patterns for Reading and Writing

Second Edition

Kathleen T. McWhorter

Instructor's Manual

Reflections: Patterns for Reading and Writing

Second Edition

Kathleen T. McWhorter
Niagara County Community College

bedford/st.martin's
Macmillan Learning

Boston | New York

Manufactured in the United States of America.

1   0   9   8   7   6
f   e   d   c   b   a

For information, write: Bedford/St. Martin's, 75 Arlington Street,
Boston, MA 02116   (617-399-4000)

ISBN: 978-1-319-04438-1
Cover image: AGF/Getty Images

Preface

This manual is intended to assist both new and experienced instructors in using *Reflections* more effectively and to save them time in developing courses that use this text. Rather than suggest how to teach first-year composition, the manual offers a wide variety of tips, strategies, and approaches, allowing instructors to choose methodology that is compatible with their teaching style and philosophy.

Unit 1, "Resources for Teaching Reading and Writing with *Reflections*" (p. 1), offers practical suggestions for developing a composition course using the text. The first section, "Teaching with *Reflections*" (p. 3), introduces the textbook; includes organizational tips; discusses course goals, relationships with students, journal writing, and collaborative activities; and offers suggestions on how to use computers and software. To assist instructors further, "Developing Your Course Plan" (p. 14) presents sample course plans and a sample syllabus. Because so many students enrolled in first-year composition courses lack certain basic writing and reading skills, a section on teaching underprepared students has been included: "Helping Underprepared Students Improve Their Skills" (p. 20) describes both cognitive and affective characteristics of underprepared students and discusses instructional accommodations. It also offers suggestions for developing basic writing skills, building students' reading skills, and fostering critical reading and thinking. At the end of this section is a bibliography of books and articles for instructor reference.

Unit 2, "Teaching Tips and Suggested Answers for Individual Chapters in *Reflections*" (p. 29), is designed to help instructors new to the book as well as those who are looking for new ways of teaching familiar readings. This section includes an introduction to each chapter in the text. In addition, specific teaching suggestions are included for each reading in Chapters 10 to 18, along with suggested answers to the apparatus that accompanies each reading. These answers are not intended to be definitive; rather they are brief, sample responses designed to both aid instructors teaching a reading for the first time and stimulate discussion in the classroom while opening up a dialogue between instructors and students. Unit 2's coverage of the *Reflections* Handbook section (beginning on page 145) provides advice for correcting sentence-level errors in student papers. It also includes answers to all exercises in Part 4.

I wish to thank Mark Gallaher for contributing to this manual and for preparing teaching tips and suggested answers to the apparatus for readings in the book. At Bedford/St. Martin's, I thank Vivian Garcia, Cara Kaufman, and Lou Bruno. I am indebted to freelance development editor Michelle McSweeney, for her guidance and assistance in developing both the parent text and this resource. Without all of their contributions, this manual would not have been possible.

Kathleen T. McWhorter

Contents

Resources for Teaching Reading and Writing with *Reflections*

Teaching with *Reflections*

Reflections has been designed with instructors' needs in mind. To get the most out of this text, however, you'll need to organize in advance, keep up with your responsibilities for the course, preview chapter contents and assignments, and structure the course in a balanced way. If you make every effort to chart a plan as you begin, you will find that the end result of the course will be much more satisfying. This *Instructor's Manual* will give you practical advice for using *Reflections* and for making the best use of your time. It will also help you identify appropriate course activities to support your objectives.

Planning and Organizing Your Course

Before you even begin your semester or quarter, decide how you will meet the requirements of your department, division, or academic area. Typically, the department chair or an administrative assistant will be able to provide you with any departmental guidelines and syllabi from previous terms. This information will assist you in planning your syllabus, particularly if this is your first term using *Reflections* or your first term teaching this course. See pages 15–20 of this manual for sample course outlines and advice on writing a syllabus.

When you develop a course syllabus, it is usually a prudent strategy to make a weekly outline of assignments, with due dates for first and revised drafts of essays, as well as for other assignments or journals. (See the sample syllabus on p. 15 of this manual.) For yourself, make a more detailed outline in which you develop a fairly accurate plan of how the activities for the term will be coordinated. For instance, you will want to determine if and when you will be scheduling student conferences, a library orientation, and visits to the writing center or the learning assistance center. If you are planning to visit any of your college's services, contact the appropriate person at the start of the term to get the visit added to his or her calendar.

Finally, make sure that you connect your class activities throughout the term. For instance, as you make a detailed term plan, look at your planned essays, in-class writings, discussions, and other activities to see if you can link them. You should attempt to move from lower-level rhetorical skills to higher-level skills by using a coordinated plan throughout the term. This plan will assist you in focusing on long-term goals and objectives. And if you have an especially busy week at a certain point in the term, you will find that you already have a basic idea or outline of what should be done for the next week.

If at all possible, develop your notes for the first two weeks of the class before the term begins. The first two weeks can feel overwhelming, so you are always well advised to have a plan already prepared. In addition, your level of confidence will be much higher going into the course if you have clear objectives and activities in mind. The impression that you give to your students in those initial weeks can be lasting.

Considering Your Primary Goals for the Course

When you are planning your course syllabus — and as you progress through the term — you should consider the four or five most critical skills that students should master. Consult the departmental course syllabus or course description to determine the most critical skills. If you're uncertain, ask another faculty member.

Focusing on Expressive and Informative Writing

If your course focuses primarily on expressive writing, you will need to concentrate on writing that exhibits a clear and consistent main idea. You will typically assign a sequence of essays that exhibit logical progression, cohesiveness, and meaningful connection of ideas. The course will likely also focus on basic editing, sentence construction, and paragraph-level writing. During the course, you will help students develop a fuller awareness of the various rhetorical patterns of development as you assign progressively more difficult readings. Strive to help students develop some higher-level thinking, reading, and writing skills as the term progresses. Keep in mind that you should see improvement in students' writing and their organization of ideas. Writing involves thinking, and revision involves re-seeing, so students will usually became more reflective and focused in their writing by the end of the term.

Many instructors begin a course based on expressive writing by assigning either a narrative or a descriptive essay. Of course, if your department allows, you may choose another option. Whatever you do, try to avoid going beyond the initial limitations of your students. If you discover that your students are struggling with a particular essay, consider extending the due date for the assignment. However, not all students will master every pattern of development, so you will need to move on. And keep in mind that if you get too far off schedule, your whole term plan will start to unravel. Always strive to have your students complete the minimum number of essays or assignments established by your department.

Likewise, with informative writing, you will focus on essay formats such as comparison and contrast, classification or division, definition, and cause and effect. The focus of such essay formats is to inform the reader more fully, with or without material from sources. These types of essays can be written without consulting sources if students choose a narrowly defined topic at the start. The informative essays help students make the transition between personal writing and more complex types of research writing, such as argumentation. Writing informative essays helps students develop skill in looking beyond their own experiences as they synthesize outside information to use in their essays.

Focusing on Informative and Research Writing

If your course focuses on both informative and research-oriented writing, you will typically divide the course into two segments; be sure to allow more time for the research-oriented essays. For such a course, follow the main strategies suggested in the previous section for the first part of the term, and then start to focus on developing the use of sources in writing. An excellent starting point is a fairly straightforward research-oriented essay, such as a comparison-and-contrast or definition essay (using two or three sources). (See Chapters 14 and 16 in *Reflections*.) Some instructors ask students to write a definition paper in which they cite several dictionary definitions of a particular word (for denotations) and then uses of the word in a different book or periodical (for connotations) to show how the definitions differ. Other instructors assign an essay in which students compare and contrast two authors who write in the same genre, using two or three reference books as sources.

Keep in mind that you should introduce more complex readings (by both student and professional writers) with sources as you move through this section of the course. Try to place particular emphasis on analysis or interpretation of essays, synthesis of several essays, and evaluation of both sources and student essays. The writing in the second half of the course will help students develop a high degree of independent thought and will facilitate these levels of thinking as well. You want to help students feel comfortable in moving to a research paper and develop strong reading skills that will promote future academic success.

When students are working on papers using sources, you should allow extra time for peer review, conferences, and revisions. It can be a good strategy to require a rough draft, a revised draft, and then an edited draft. If you do this, you will discover that students will have stronger final drafts and less tendency to procrastinate. The critical aspect of a course that includes research isn't the writing but the level of students' thinking as the term progresses. You should require more detailed comments on the peer-edited essays and ask for more detailed responses to the professional essays and journal assignments.

Establishing a Good Relationship with Your Students

Developing a good relationship with your students is important. You will be learning a great deal about your students through their writing and your discussions with them, so you need to develop a level of trust and understanding from the start.

Getting to Know Your Students

At the very beginning of the term, get acquainted with students by handing out 3½- by 5-inch index cards or a form that elicits basic information such as contact information, writing courses they have taken so far, the types of reading they enjoy, and their strengths and weaknesses in writing. This activity will allow the students to see that you are personally interested in them. Also, you will get to know their names more quickly.

Clarifying Your Expectations

Many students who take a first-year writing course will be uncertain about what is expected of them. It is helpful to focus on major and minor expectations in the first week. For instance, you may want the assignments for the class to have particular headings. If you have other specific expectations, go over these while reviewing your syllabus or during the first week of class. It's always a good idea to limit class rules to several basics: be on time, work hard while in class, ask questions when something is unclear, and treat classmates and instructor with respect. Students often appreciate it when you set limits because they know what you will allow and what you will not accept.

Discuss evaluation practices and their consistent application throughout the term. Do this at the start of the term so that the students understand your system for weighting grades and averaging the components (essays, peer reviewing, journals, portfolios, homework, class participation, quizzes, and so on). Try to be as specific as possible about how you will grade the essays and the prewriting, first draft, and revised draft. If you factor peer reviewing into the class participation grade or into some other category, be sure to mention that fact early in the course so that students will learn to give specific comments from the start of the term. It is helpful to include this breakdown in the course syllabus, but you should also refer to it at several points during the term.

Most institutions have some type of attendance policy. If your institution has a specific policy, try to follow it consistently, keeping in mind, however, that specific situations may occur in which you will have to allow a student some leeway. Some institutions have no attendance policy, in which case you will have to develop some standards of your own. A very reasonable policy is to allow students to miss no more than 20% of the scheduled classes; after that, you can impose a penalty on their in-class grade. Give both scheduled and unscheduled assignments and quizzes throughout the term. Missing one or two of these won't cause problems; missing more than that will affect a student's grade. If a student has not attended class for an extended period of time, it is advisable to contact that student directly or have a faculty-initiated withdrawal form sent to that student.

Setting the Classroom Tone

When working with a new class, you should initially set the tone or atmosphere that you would like to maintain throughout the course. Don't be concerned with trying to emulate another instructor who is very successful with students. Be comfortable with your own style, because it is a big part of your personal identity. If you develop a very informal and relaxed approach early on and then switch to a demanding style, you will encounter problems with students. The best approach is to start off with a slightly more demanding style and then loosen up as you get to know the class.

Also make sure you inform your students how they should submit and organize essays and revisions. At the very least, it's a good idea to require students to put prewriting, peer reviews, and drafts of an essay into a manila folder for submission. This strategy forces students to be organized and makes it easier for you to follow the flow of their work.

Anticipating Problems and Using Services at Your Institution

During each week of the term, you will typically encounter at least one type of academic, personal, or classroom-centered problem that you must deal with to keep a student or your class focused. In such cases, you should attempt to utilize the resources of your institution. Your school likely has a writing center or an academic skills center. Don't personally try to tutor each student with writing-related problems. Refer students with writing difficulties to the writing center instead. Likewise, students who are having difficulties with study habits or organization can be referred to the academic skills center. If you have serious concerns about a particular student, you may want to take on a more personal role to ensure that he or she gets the needed help as soon as possible.

If a student approaches you to express concern about a busy work schedule that is preventing him or her from completing course assignments, you may want to recommend that this individual consult with financial aid for a student loan. This is especially critical in the first three weeks of class, because this is the time when a student may decide to withdraw from all classes rather than explore other options.

If you have a student with personal issues, especially those involving psychological concerns such as depression or a total lack of focus, you should advise the student to make an appointment with a campus counselor or psychologist. As an English instructor, you can certainly be an empathetic listener, but you should always be cautious when offering advice. A student who demonstrates clear signs of depression or has other serious problems should be referred to counseling as quickly as possible.

Finally, you have several choices in dealing with class behavior problems. Some of the most common situations are arriving consistently late to class, talking excessively while you are talking, and attempting to dominate the class discussion. The best way to resolve these situations is to address them as quickly as possible with an oral comment. However, if they can't be addressed effectively in this manner, it's advisable to discuss the problem with the student after class. Be firm and direct, but initially try asking a series of questions to determine the root of the problem. Talk about the possible consequences of continuing the behavior. After this initial meeting, give the student one more chance. Then, if the problem persists, consider taking administrative action, as indicated in the faculty handbook of your institution.

Staying Organized as the Term Progresses

At the start of the term, you need to develop some basic strategies for staying organized. You should keep one copy of the course syllabus and your detailed course outline on the wall next to your desk and tape another one to the inside cover of *Reflections*. You will likely refer to both of these as the term progresses.

Keeping Consistent Records

It is always a good strategy to organize the overall record-keeping for the class in advance. You won't be able to establish totally objective grades or criteria for all assignments because there is invariably a level of subjectivity in a writing course. However, you should track daily attendance, check off the submission of prewriting and multiple drafts, give points for major in-class assignments, and record all the grades for revised essays. Be sure to establish a clear policy on how many revisions you allow and what your essay grading policy is.

Whatever grading policies you establish, you should give students an accurate estimate of their class grade at several points during the term. This will help to reduce disagreements at the end of the term and allow you to catch any errors that you have made in recording grades. Many English instructors are now using spreadsheets and online course management systems for tracking grades. If you record grades the traditional way, you may want to photocopy your class grades at several times during the term in case you lose your grade book.

Finally, if you feel that you are struggling to keep up with the paper load, keep in mind that not all essays, journals, and assignments need to be graded with equal thoroughness. For the graded essays, you might want to focus on several criteria in your own comments and then use peer reviewing to cover other areas. For the nongraded assignments, you can give a Credit or No Credit designation and focus on one or several areas for commentary.

Meeting Individually with Students

It is beneficial to have at least two conferences with each student during the term. You can use these conferences to discuss a student's overall progress or to discuss the development of a particular essay. If you use class time for conferences, you can have the other students do peer reviews or collaborative small-group work while you are holding conferences or you can give students an out-of-class assignment.

Using *Reflections* Effectively

If you dedicate a limited amount of time early in the term — and as the term progresses — to explaining the critical sections of *Reflections*, you will find that your students will better understand key writing concepts. Be sure to inform your students that the preface at the front of the textbook includes information about the book and its features. Consider assigning this section or taking some time on the first day of class to go through the book's features, showing students what is in the book and explaining how to use it.

Using the Visual Features of *Reflections*

You will notice that an excellent feature of *Reflections* is the visual nature of the text. Illustrations and diagrams offer a visual approach to writing and engage today's more visual students. Each chapter in Parts 1 and 2 begins with a Reflect feature — an image with a writing prompt that gives students a preview of the major objectives of the chapter and the pattern of writing. These activities act as a critical starting point for writing and discussion.

The graphic organizers in each chapter are especially valuable for spatial learners, but this feature of the book should be helpful to all students. Graphic organizers are diagrams that *visually* present the relationships among ideas within a piece of text. Many students, especially underprepared students, have difficulty recognizing the organization and overall structure of what they read. They fail to recognize hierarchical and coordinate relationships and consequently have difficulty remembering what they read. Graphic organizers offer a meaningful conceptual framework that enables students to understand relationships and make connections with their existing knowledge. Creating these kinds of graphic organizers builds a bridge, or "scaffolding," that enables readers and learners to construct and reconstruct meaning within text.

Graphic organizers work effectively because they encode information in memory in two ways — verbally and spatially. Thus, they provide two different layers of cueing, or two memory paths; if one fails, the other may work. Graphic organizers in *Reflections* can be used in connection with both reading and writing strategies. For each method of development, students are shown two graphic organizers. The first demonstrates the relationship among the unique elements of the particular type of essay and also functions as a model. The second applies the model to a specific essay included in the chapter. Students are also asked to complete a graphic organizer for one of the readings in the chapter. Viewing a created graphic organizer and then creating their own graphic organizer facilitates students' comprehension and recall. You may want to experiment with having students fill out graphic organizers or make their own organizers at various phases in their reading process.

Graphic organizers can also be used for the revision of writing. When a student draws a graphic organizer of an essay he or she has written, the structure of the essay and the relationship of ideas (or lack thereof) become apparent. Lack of supporting ideas also becomes immediately obvious, as does misplaced or irrelevant information. Some students find these tools very helpful and decide to work with organizers on a regular basis. Assign at least one organizer exercise online and then make organizers optional if you find that only a few students like to use them.

Annotated professional and student essays provide excellent models for students to evaluate because key sections and points (such as the thesis statement) are clearly highlighted. Modeling is a very effective method for helping students improve their writing. At first, they may be more apt to critique a student essay than a professional one. Once they become accustomed to the process, they can move on to model professional essays. Annotated text is also visually stimulating and thus easier for students with visual learning styles to comprehend.

Throughout *Reflections*, bulleted and numbered lists make the text visually accessible and aesthetically pleasing. For example, each chapter includes a list identifying what to look for as the student reads an essay in a particular rhetorical mode. Wtihin the list, each idea is clearly and simply stated. You might recommend that students highlight or flag any lists they find themselves consulting frequently.

Using the Reading Apparatus in Part 2

The reading apparatus in Part 2 will help you to motivate students to read assigned essays more carefully so that they will be prepared to discuss or write about the essays in class. Once students become accustomed to working with these questions, either as take-home or as in-class work, they will begin to read more actively, highlighting and annotating their text and looking up vocabulary words in anticipation of doing the assignments.

Understanding and Reviewing the Reading

These questions focus on the content rather than the form of each essay. Occasionally questions will ask students to visualize the reading by creating a response in the form of a table or outline. These questions typically ask about the reading's rhetorical pattern as it pertains to the chapter's focus. If you find that students are not reading the assigned essays actively, remind them to read and reread closely, annotating and highlighting as they go along. If they are still not reading closely enough, assign the Understanding and Reviewing the Reading questions before students read an essay. You may also use Understanding and Reviewing the Reading questions as quick prediscussion quizzes. If you prefer not to give quizzes, you can ask students to read and answer these questions before class discussion, allowing them to formulate their ideas on paper before venturing into group discussion.

Analyzing the Reading

This section invites students to move beyond the content of the reading and into its rhetoric. Questions reflect the chapter's focus on a particular rhetorical pattern. For instance, questions in Chapter 10, "Narration," ask about conflict and narrative climax, while questions in Chapter 14, "Comparison and Contrast," ask students to identify an author's purpose and organization. Analyzing the Reading sections may be used in class as a way to propel small-group discussions or as a warm-up for a class discussion. Alternatively, you could assign this section for homework to accompany outside reading in order to encourage students to get in the habit of analyzing in addition to reading for content.

Evaluating the Reading

The questions in this section also respond to authors' rhetorical strategies and require students to analyze the readings. However, the questions focus more on reader response, allowing students to consider whether each text was effective and fulfilled its purpose. Students may enjoy this section, as it gives them an opportunity to voice personal reactions to pieces, but each question prompts students to provide thoughtful analysis and support for their opinions. You may choose to assign these questions as preparation for class discussion or as a prewriting exercise aimed at generating a thesis or argument based on the reading.

Discussing the Reading

Discussing the Reading sections may be assigned individually but work especially well when used by large or small groups. Questions typically ask students to respond to the themes or main ideas of a piece rather than its particular details. With prompts that encourage students to consider similar ideas, the questions help students place a reading in a larger context, perhaps as a precursor to writing a source-based argument essay. These questions can be used for brainstorming and prewriting, particularly in a thematic course structure, and their broader approach makes them useful in group discussions for connecting texts throughout *Reflections*.

Writing about the Reading

The prompts in this section are assignment-based and may be used for everything from in-class writing to fully drafted essays. The detail in each prompt guides students through the steps they need to take to complete each assignment, giving students the tools they need to answer each prompt with confidence. Some questions focus on developing research skills and ask students to visit a particular Web site or conduct a certain kind of research. You may choose to use these questions as brainstorming activities for individuals or groups, or you may use them as a guide in developing your own tailored writing assignments for each rhetorical pattern.

Assigning the Patterns of Development in Part 2

Like other parts of the text, the chapters in Part 2 are designed to be flexible. Some instructors cover fewer chapters than others, but in greater detail. This approach can be effective, helping students see the range that exists within a particular pattern of development. Other instructors cover many of the patterns of development in less detail and assign more short papers or assignments during the term.

Another excellent possibility is to pair or cluster professional and student essays that are related thematically. For instance, an instructor could develop an assignment emphasizing synthesis, using a cluster of readings or a series of related themes throughout the term. If you are interested in organizing your course this way, refer to the Thematic Contents included in *Reflections*.

When using Part 2 of the book, you may decide to focus on one or two patterns of development emphasized in conjunction with Chapters 1–8, or you may want to assign a broader selection of chapters. If you are teaching expressive writing, you may want to start off with narration or description. Many instructors like to begin with illustration or classification and division as a way of getting students to organize their thoughts from the very start. It is especially critical early in the term to help students work through the section on writing an essay using the given pattern of development. This section appears as the fourth section in each of Chapters 10–18. For the first one or two essays, you can work with students as a class or in small groups as they develop their essays. Typically, you would work on the prewriting stage in class or have students do this stage as a journal exercise. Drafting, revising, and editing can be done outside of class or in conjunction with peer review. Most instructors look at a first draft and a revised draft of an essay, but you can also have students do peer reviews of drafts in progress. During this process, you can act as a guide or adviser, but don't feel that you always have to be the authority on writing in the class. You will find that some of your best students are sharp and perceptive in their editing and in providing feedback. You can develop any additional questions or comments on the essays in progress that you like, but for consistency you may want to use the specific questions in the revision flowcharts for the chapters in Part 2.

Using Part 3 with Part 1

Part 3 of *Reflections* was designed in part as a reference for students, but you may find it helpful to assign students all or part of this section of the book. If you include research writing in your course, Chapter 19 offers a brief guide to using and evaluating sources, and Chapter 20 provides instructions for documenting sources in both MLA and APA styles.

If you are asking your students to use sources in an essay, consider scheduling a library orientation before they get started. Spend part of at least one class talking about evaluating sources for use in an academic essay. The sources that a student chooses can have a major impact on the overall quality of the finished essay, especially if only two or three sources are used.

You might want to refer students to Chapter 1, "Succeeding in College," early in the term. This chapter gives special attention to study skills, providing practical strategies for successful college work before class, in class, and while studying. It also reinforces necessary study, reading, and work habits that underprepared students need special help with.

Integrating Grammar into the Course

Part 4: Handbook

You can refer to the handbook section in Part 4 at regular intervals or as needed. Consider giving mini-lessons on some major writing errors throughout the term. You may want students to keep basic notes on these mini-lessons with an error log. One useful technique is to mark student essays with different-colored stars, based on the types of errors the essays contain, and then pair students with the same-colored stars. This technique allows students to see the same writing errors they made in another writer's paper. Sometimes the error that a student fails to see in his or her own essay will be easier to see in another student's paper.

Electronic Resource: LaunchPad Solo for Readers and Writers

With *LaunchPad Solo for Readers and Writers*, students can work at their own pace on the writing issues they need the most help with.

- **Pre-built units support a learning arc.** Each unit is composed of a pre-test check, multimedia instruction and assessment, and a post-test that assesses what students have learned about critical reading, the writing process, using sources, grammar, style, and mechanics.

- **Diagnostics help establish a baseline.** Two comprehensive tests for grammar and two for reading allow instructors to assign diagnostics in a pre/post format and serve to help students and instructors identify areas of strength and areas for improvement. Through a reports screen, instructors can preview questions and view results by skill, roster, or individual student.

- **Animated videos introduce many topics,** providing an illustrated overview of important grammatical concepts.

- **Adaptive quizzing for targeted learning.** Most units include LearningCurve, game-like adaptive quizzing that focuses on the areas in which each student needs the most help.

- **Twenty-five reading selections, with quizzes, teach critical reading.** You can assign a range of classic and contemporary essays, each of which includes a label indicating Lexile level to help you scaffold instruction in critical reading.

- **Gradebooks monitor student progress.** Use the gradebook to see which students are on track and which need additional help with specific topics.

LaunchPad Solo for Readers and Writers can be packaged at a significant discount. Order ISBN 978-1-319-10377-4 to ensure your students can take full advantage.

Visit macmillanlearning.com/catalog/readwrite for more information.

Using Journals in the Course

You can use journals in several ways in conjunction with *Reflections*. The Writing about the Reading sections in Chapters 10–18 are designed to support journal writing. These questions can help you integrate journal writing into the course in a consistent way. You can also use journal writing with the Previewing the Reading questions in Chapters 10–18. To encourage prewriting, you might consider having students use their journals to develop their ideas for writing. Consider suggesting that students use a loose-leaf binder for a journal so that pages can be added.

Keep in mind that you don't have to collect all the journal assignments and preliminary essay work. To reduce the paper load, you can take ten minutes at the end of a class to walk around the room and scan student journals. Also, use peer review for journal entries in connection with student essays. If you do collect journals, you have several options. You can give a Credit/No Credit designation when you check journals every week or two, and a letter grade at two points during the course. If you count the journal as equivalent to an essay, as many instructors do, you might want to grade the journals at two points during the course and average the grades. You should grade the journals periodically so that students will put more effort into them. When they do, they will also appreciate your emphasis on the development of ideas in preparation for writing an essay. When grading journals, you should focus more on the quantity of students' entries than on the quality of their thinking. Try to reward effort and consistency rather than detailed insights, which students will learn to develop further as your class proceeds.

Winding Up the Course

As you move into the final weeks and days of your class, you will be slowing down the pace of assignments and essays, but don't allow students to become lax. Try to maintain the structured, organized class you started with at the beginning of the term. You will need to stress to students the importance of finishing off the term in a strong manner. Just as the first two weeks are critical for overall success, the last two weeks can definitely make a difference in a student's grade.

Be sure to complete the class evaluations given by your department, division, or academic area. You may also want to ask students to complete a brief, anonymous evaluation of the class, with questions that you develop. Look for patterns or trends in students' comments, either negative or positive, to evaluate your overall performance in the class.

If time allows, collect final essays before the last week of class. Alternatively, if you collect them on the last day of class, either meet on the assigned finals day or give students a time, date, and location where you will be available to return papers with their final grades. That way, if a student questions a final grade, you will be able to deal with the issue promptly, reducing extra work for yourself during the next term. When you return papers, also give each student an overall assessment of his or her progress in the course. Try to make this final conference a positive experience for the student.

Developing Your Course Plan

When developing a course plan, you need to choose a structure that is appropriate for the level of your students' abilities and consistent with the guidelines of your department. You also need to consider the goals of the course, the length of instruction (ten weeks or fifteen weeks), and the number of terms (one or two).

Writing a Course Syllabus

The syllabus is an important document in the classroom. It is the contract between the instructor and the students with respect to the topics, policies, and procedures of the course. The syllabus should contain all relevant information pertaining to the course, so that students will know exactly what is expected of them. Likewise, information such as the instructor's office hours, email address, and phone number should be included, so that students know how and when to get in contact with the instructor. The following is a sample syllabus with a course plan for a sixteen-week semester course that includes research.

Sample Syllabus for a One-Semester Course That Includes Research

I. *General Information*

Course Title: English Composition I

Prerequisite: English 070 or placement test

Instructor: John Gillam

Email: gillam@indiana.edu

Course Number: ENG 161

Semester: Fall

Phone: (724) 555-7890

Office Hours & Location:
MWF 3–5
English Department offices,
Ryan Hall

II. *Text*

McWhorter, Kathleen T. *Reflections: Patterns for Reading and Writing.* 2nd ed., Bedford/St. Martin's, 2017.

III. *Course Description*

This course covers the fundamentals of college writing, including the paragraph, the expository essay, and the research essay. Emphasis is placed on developing a coherent thesis, writing concisely and clearly, and adapting one's writing to a particular audience. This course also emphasizes self-editing, mechanics, and grammar. (Taken from college catalog.)

IV. *General Course Objectives*

1. The student will learn to write well-organized and well-researched papers.
2. The student will learn to recognize her or his common grammatical mistakes.
3. The student will become familiar with different patterns of expository writing.
4. The student will be able to use several different writing patterns.

V. *Specific Course Objectives*

1. The student will write papers using the following strategies: illustration, process analysis, classification and division, comparison and contrast, definition, cause and effect, and argumentation.

2. The student will edit and proofread for errors in grammar, punctuation, mechanics, and spelling.

3. The student will be tested on reading comprehension.

4. The student will critically analyze readings that use specific writing strategies.

5. The student will use the Internet as a tool for research.

6. The student will write a research paper using appropriate documentation.

VI. *Classroom Procedures*

Absences: The student is responsible for attendance. Attendance affects performance, and all students are expected to take part in class discussions and peer-review editing sessions. Each student is expected to be present and is responsible for class notes and assignments. If absent, the student is responsible for arranging an appointment with the instructor to discuss the notes and assignments missed. *Format for papers:* Papers must be typed double-spaced using a 12-point font. Be sure to keep a copy of each assignment for yourself.

VII. *Disability Statement*

If you need special arrangements made to accommodate a physical or learning disability, please notify the instructor as soon as possible. (Disclosure of the type of disability is not required.)

VIII. *Grading*

All papers must be turned in on the due date. The grade on a late paper will be lowered by one letter. No papers will be accepted after the last day of class. Please save all papers in a folder to be collected periodically.

IX. *Tentative Schedule*

Week of Sept. 2:	*Course Introduction* Ch. 2 ("Active Reading," especially "Draw a Graphic Organizer")
Week of Sept. 9:	*Writing Assessments* Ch. 1 ("Succeeding in College"), Ch. 4 ("Prewriting: How to Find and Focus Ideas"), and Ch. 5 ("Developing and Supporting a Thesis")
Week of Sept. 16:	Ch. 7 ("Drafting an Essay") Draft of Essay #1 due

Week of Sept. 23: Ch. 12 ("Illustration: Explaining with Examples") and Ch. 19 ("Finding and Using Sources")
Draft of Essay #2 due

Week of Sept. 30: Ch. 13 ("Process Analysis: Explaining How Something Works or Is Done")
Peer review of Essay #1 or #2
Revision of Essay #1 or #2 due

Week of Oct. 7: Ch. 8 ("Revising Content and Organization")
Final draft of Essay #1 or #2 due

Week of Oct. 14: Ch. 14 ("Comparison and Contrast: Showing Similarities and Differences")
Draft of Essay #3 due
Peer review of Essay #3

Week of Oct. 21: Ch. 15 ("Classification and Division: Explaining Categories and Parts") and Ch. 19 (*continued*, especially "Evaluating Internet Sources")
Draft of Essay #4 due
Peer review of Essay #4
Final draft of Essay #3 due

Week of Oct. 28: Ch. 16 ("Definition: Explaining What You Mean")
Draft of Essay #5 due
Peer review of Essay #5
Final draft of Essay #4 due

Week of Nov. 4: Ch. 17 ("Cause and Effect: Using Reasons and Results to Explain")
Draft of Essay #6 due
Peer review of Essay #6
Final draft of Essay #5 due

Week of Nov. 11: Ch. 18 ("Argumentation: Supporting a Claim") and Ch. 19 (*continued*, especially "Avoiding Plagiarism")
Library Orientation
Final draft of Essay #6 due

Week of Nov. 18: Ch. 18 (*continued*) and Ch. 19 (*continued*)
Working thesis and research questions due

Week of Nov. 25: Ch. 18 (*continued*) and Ch. 20 ("Documenting Your Sources")
Summary and paraphrase due

Week of Dec. 2: Ch. 9 ("Patterns: An Introduction")
Research paper draft due

Week of Dec. 9: Ch. 9 (*continued*)
Peer review of selections from research paper drafts

Week of Dec. 16: Ch. 9 (*continued*)
Final research paper due

Single-Quarter Course Plan

This plan consists of a ten-week quarter including five written essays: one expressive, one informative, and three argumentative. Other essays or chapters can be substituted based on individual preferences.

Week 1   Ch. 2 ("Active Reading") and Ch. 3 ("Critical Reading and Thinking Strategies)

Week 2   Ch. 4 ("Prewriting: How to Find and Focus Ideas") and Ch. 5 ("Developing and Supporting a Thesis")

Week 3   Ch. 7 ("Drafting an Essay") and Ch. 1 ("Succeeding in College")

Week 4   Ch. 10 ("Narration: Recounting Events") or Ch. 11 ("Description: Portraying People, Places, and Things") and Ch. 8 ("Revising Content and Organization")

Week 5   Ch. 8 (*continued*) and Ch. 17 ("Cause and Effect: Using Reasons and Results to Explain")

Week 6   Ch. 17 (*continued*)

Week 7   Ch. 18 ("Argumentation: Supporting a Claim")

Week 8   Ch. 18 (*continued*) and Ch. 19 ("Finding and Using Sources")

Week 9   Ch. 9 ("Patterns: An Introduction") and Ch. 19 (*continued*)

Week 10   Ch. 20 ("Documenting Your Sources")

A Course Plan Based on Expressive Writing

This plan is based on a fifteen-week semester that focuses on writing from personal experience. Students begin by narrating and describing past events. They then move on to writing about current topics and finally to describing problems and solutions based on field research.

Week 1   Ch. 2 ("Active Reading") and Ch. 3 ("Critical Reading and Thinking Strategies")

Week 2   Ch. 4 ("Prewriting: How to Find and Focus Ideas") and Ch. 5 ("Developing and Supporting a Thesis")

Week 3   Ch. 6 ("Writing Effective Paragraphs") and Ch. 7 ("Drafting an Essay")

Week 4   Ch. 8 ("Revising Content and Organization") and Ch. 10 ("Narration: Recounting Events")

Week 5   Ch. 11 ("Description: Portraying People, Places, and Things")

Week 6   Ch. 12 ("Illustration: Explaining with Examples")

Week 7   Ch. 13 ("Process Analysis: Explaining How Something Works or Is Done")

Week 8   Ch. 14 ("Comparison and Contrast: Showing Similarities and Differences")

Week 9   Ch. 14 (*continued*)

Week 10   Ch. 16 ("Definition: Explaining What You Mean")

Week 11   Ch. 17 ("Cause and Effect: Using Reasons and Results to Explain")

Week 12   Ch. 18 ("Argumentation: Supporting a Claim")

Week 13   Ch. 13 (*continued*)

Week 14   Ch. 9 ("Patterns: An Introduction")

Week 15   Ch. 9 (*continued*)

A Course Plan Based on a Thematic Approach

This plan follows the various patterns of writing, from narration to argumentation. Students will learn each writing pattern while reading essays and doing guided assignments based on different writing patterns over a fifteen-week period.

Week 1   Ch. 2 ("Active Reading") and Ch. 3 ("Critical Reading and Thinking Strategies")

Week 2   Ch. 4 ("Prewriting: How to Find and Focus Ideas"), Ch. 5 ("Developing and Supporting a Thesis"), and Ch. 1 ("Succeeding in College")

Week 3   Ch. 6 ("Writing Effective Paragraphs"), Ch. 7 ("Drafting an Essay"), and Ch. 8 ("Revising Content and Organization")

Week 4   Ch. 8 (*continued*) and Ch. 2 (*continued*)

Week 5   Ch. 10 ("Narration: Recounting Events")

Week 6   Ch. 11 ("Description: Portraying People, Places, and Things")

Week 7   Ch. 12 ("Illustration: Explaining with Examples")

Week 8   Ch. 13 ("Process Analysis: Explaining How Something Works or Is Done")

Week 9   Ch. 14 ("Comparison and Contrast: Showing Similarities and Differences")

Week 10   Ch. 15 ("Classification and Division: Explaining Categories and Parts")

Week 11   Ch. 16 ("Definition: Explaining What You Mean")

Week 12   Ch. 17 ("Cause and Effect: Using Reasons and Results to Explain")
Week 13   Ch. 18 ("Argumentation: Supporting a Claim")

Week 14   Ch. 9 ("Patterns: An Introduction")

Week 15   Ch. 9 (*continued*) and Ch. 18 (*continued*)

A Course Plan Based on Research Writing

This plan concentrates on the steps involved in research writing. The students will do guided assignments based on different writing patterns while conducting research.

Week 1   Ch. 1 ("Succeeding in College"), Ch. 2 ("Active Reading"), and Ch. 3 ("Critical Reading and Thinking Strategies")

Week 2   Ch. 5 ("Developing and Supporting a Thesis") and Ch. 1 (*continued*)

Week 3	Ch. 6 ("Writing Effective Paragraphs") and Ch. 7 ("Drafting an Essay")
Week 4	Ch. 8 ("Revising Content and Organization") and Ch. 12 ("Illustration: Explaining with Examples")
Week 5	Ch. 13 ("Process Analysis: Explaining How Something Works or Is Done") and Ch. 19 ("Finding and Using Sources")
Week 6	Ch. 15 ("Classification and Division: Explaining Categories and Parts")
Week 7	Ch. 14 ("Comparison and Contrast: Showing Similarities and Differences") and Ch. 19 (*continued*)
Week 8	Ch. 16 ("Definition: Explaining What You Mean")
Week 9	Ch. 17 ("Cause and Effect: Using Reasons and Results to Explain")
Week 10	Ch. 18 ("Argumentation: Supporting a Claim") and Ch. 19 (*continued*, especially Avoiding Plagiarism)
Week 11	Ch. 18 (*continued*) and Ch. 20 ("Documenting Your Sources")
Week 12	Ch. 18 (*continued*)
Week 13	Ch. 9 ("Patterns: An Introduction")
Week 14	Ch. 9 (*continued*)
Week 15	Ch. 9 (*continued*)

Helping Underprepared Students Improve Their Skills

The first-year college classroom is continually evolving. Over the years, instructors have welcomed increasing numbers of adult students, ESL students, and minority students. Now instructors are facing growing numbers of underprepared students who lack many of the academic skills that traditional first-year college students possess. This section will describe underprepared students and offer teaching suggestions for helping these students become successful college writers. It will also discuss how to strengthen students' reading and critical-thinking skills. Although the discussion must necessarily focus on the academic deficiencies of underprepared students, it is important to point out that these students have as many positive qualities as traditional students. Underprepared students also make substantial and worthwhile contributions to a writing classroom — adding a variety of perspectives, new experiences, and diverse viewpoints.

Identifying the Characteristics of Underprepared Students

Underprepared students are challenging but rewarding. They often require special attention and may learn and think differently than other students. Instructors of underprepared students not only must determine what and how to teach but also must discover new ways to help these students learn.

The accommodations described in this section need not be limited to underprepared students. You may find that these strategies will help all kinds of students learn more easily and develop a more positive attitude toward writing instruction.

Identifying Negative Academic Self-Image

Many underprepared students regard themselves as academic failures. Some think they lack the ability to learn and, specifically, the ability to learn to write. Many students think of themselves as unable to achieve or compete in an academic environment. This attitude may be largely a result of numerous failures they have experienced in previous educational settings. Consistent, then, with their past history, they expect little of themselves and may seem negative, defeated, or disengaged even before the course begins.

Designing Instructional Accommodations. Refer students to Chapter 1, "Succeeding in College," for advice on improving academic self-image. Try to design assignments, especially initial ones in the term, that allow students to experience immediate success. For example, the first assignment in learning to use descriptive language might involve asking students to write a list of words describing but not naming an interesting object you bring to class. No matter what a student writes, it will be correct, and it will demonstrate to the student that he or she can use descriptive language.

Recognizing Lack of Self-Direction

Underprepared students often lack goals and direction in their pursuit of a college education as well as in the management of their lives. They may have few or no long-term goals; their short-term goals are often unclear and changeable. As a result, these students tend to lack the discipline and focus to attend class, complete assignments, or work independently on long-term projects.

Designing Instructional Accommodations. Refer students to Chapter 1, "Succeeding in College," for advice on becoming self-motivated. Make assignments immediate and short-term. Establish clear due dates and supply regular feedback. Distribute a written course syllabus that details all requirements, your grading system, and as many due dates of assignments as possible. Check frequently to be sure that students complete assignments, do homework, and are keeping up with the course. For graded essays, it may be helpful to require students to submit their work at various stages of the writing process so that you can approve their thesis statement and then their first draft, for example.

Identifying a Passive Approach to Learning

Partly because of their lack of experience in and success with academic environments, underprepared students often exhibit a passive approach to learning. They seldom ask questions, initiate study plans, seek help from instructors, or pursue solutions to academic problems. Instead, they follow procedures as well as they are able to understand them, wait to be told what to do, and take whatever action seems expected.

Designing Instructional Accommodations. Refer students to Chapter 1, "Succeeding in College," for advice on becoming an active learner. Initiate class discussions and construct collaborative activities that require involvement and problem solving to encourage and shape more active learning. Often a forthright discussion of active versus passive learning characteristics is effective as well. To encourage students to ask questions and to improve their ability to do so, direct students at the beginning of class to write at least two or three questions they hope the course will answer or several statements of what they want to learn.

Coping with Negative Attitudes toward Instructors

As a result of previous negative educational experiences, many underprepared students have come to associate instructors with unpleasant or uncomfortable learning environments. As a result, students are often closed, unresponsive, or evasive with their instructors.

Designing Instructional Accommodations. Refer students to Chapter 1, "Succeeding in College," for advice on communicating with instructors. Establishing a framework of trust is difficult but necessary. Try to encourage openness, directness, honesty, and patience. Give careful, detailed explanations of course requirements, and listen willingly to students. Once you have established your authority and made sure that there are no behavior problems, you may find it helpful to present yourself as a person who experiences successes and failures just as students do.

Recognizing Lack of Familiarity with College Life and Academic Procedures

Some underprepared students are confused and frustrated by the strangeness, formality, and seeming unfriendliness of the academic environment. Many underprepared students are the first in their families or among their friends to attend college; therefore, they lack the advantage of practical advice and support that many students receive from family and peers. They are unfamiliar with class schedules, college policies, and instructors' expectations.

Designing Instructional Accommodations.   As a means of establishing trust as well as building familiarity with college life, offer as many practical "how-to-get-around" tips as possible. Also, as events occur on campus, take a few minutes to explain them. For example, when drop-and-add day begins, explain what is going on; when advance registration for the next term begins, alert the class and explain the procedures involved.

Identifying Lack of Time-Management Skills

Many underprepared students lack the ability to plan and organize their time. Others are working too many hours at part-time or even full-time jobs, and they may have numerous family responsibilities as well. Some underprepared students — especially those coming directly from high school, where their time is tightly structured — have difficulty adapting to the relatively unstructured college environment. Underprepared students also tend to have high absentee rates. Their absenteeism is, of course, related not only to poor time-management skills but also to other characteristics such as lack of self-direction. In addition, many underprepared students are over-committed. They have not yet found a balance among family life, work, friends, and academic responsibilities.

Designing Instructional Accommodations. Refer students to Chapter 1, "Succeeding in College," for advice on time management. You can help students by structuring your course consistently. For example, make essays always due on Fridays and in-chapter exercises always due on Mondays. Make deadlines and due dates clear, distributing them in writing and also announcing them in class. Establish a clear, firm limit on class absences. You may have to make exceptions in obvious emergencies, but a firm absence policy is important. Do not accept late papers without imposing a penalty, and include a class participation component in your grading system.

Compensating for Lack of Experiential Background

Owing perhaps to inadequate preparation in high school or an immature approach to learning while in high school, underprepared students sometimes lack basic knowledge expected of first-year college students.

Designing Instructional Accommodations. Refer students to Chapter 1, "Succeeding in College," for advice on communicating with instructors. The immediate solution is, of course, to fill in gaps in knowledge as they arise by providing needed background information. For example, point out to the class that glosses added to the professional readings in the text supply information students may need to understand the reading.

Recognizing Avoidance of Reading

Many underprepared students choose not to read, because reading is not their primary method of obtaining information. Some find reading difficult, noninteractive, and time-consuming; consequently, a few will try to get by without reading assigned essays.

Designing Instructional Accommodations. Refer students to Chapter 1, "Succeeding in College," for advice on using a syllabus. To encourage active reading, make sure that you accompany any given reading assignment with an activity that will engage the students and produce tangible results. In the head-note for most essays in the text, for example, a reading tip directs students to identify and highlight a particular feature of the essay. Also use the prereading questions that precede each reading to help focus students on something specific to consider while reading the essay.

Identifying Lack of Perseverance with Academic Tasks

Some underprepared students have difficulty persevering with lengthy or complicated academic tasks and multistage processes. Their goal is to complete a task as quickly as possible; as a result, they tend to jump immediately to the final step. These students, then, may skip prewriting, planning, and organizing their ideas and may begin by writing what they perceive to be a nearly final draft.

Designing Instructional Accommodations.   Refer students to Chapter 1, "Succeeding in College," for advice on staying focused. Offer incentives for students to work through the writing process. Award a specific number of points for the submission of prewriting and so forth.

Developing Basic Writing Skills

Many underprepared students lack certain basic writing skills. Their writing contains errors in sentence structure (especially comma splices, fragments, and run-ons) and in grammar, punctuation, and mechanics. The reasons for these deficiencies are diverse. Some students never learned these basic skills in high school. Others have been out of school for a while and have forgotten standard conventions. Still others are unaware that correctness is important and write carelessly, ignoring conventions. Refer students with recurring grammatical issues to specific sections in Part 4, "Handbook: Writing Problems and How to Correct Them."

Valuable instructor and classroom time need not be consumed addressing basic writing problems because students can learn to correct their own problems by using the exercises and activities found in *LaunchPad Solo for Readers and Writers* (p. 13).

Strengthening Students' Reading Skills

Many underprepared students do not read at the college level. As a result, they find assigned textbooks and essays challenging and sometimes frustrating. To assist such students, *Reflections* contains numerous features to guide students through essays in the text, while providing them with skills and strategies for improving their reading ability. Numerous tables, bulleted lists, and diagrams both emphasize and condense important information.

Chapter 2, "Active Reading," provides a framework for improving students' reading skills. It dispels misconceptions students may have about reading, presents a step-by-step guide to reading actively, and offers strategies for special reading situations (such as using textbooks and understanding visual aids). Chapter 3, "Critical Reading and Thinking Strategies," teaches students basic techniques for introductory rhetorical analysis. It invites them to begin interpreting a text by identifying its message and purpose, its reliability, and its relevance. These chapters can be taught in class, assigned for students to work through independently, or assigned selectively to students who demonstrate reading problems. Chapter 19, "Finding and Using Sources," provides useful information on reading critically to evaluate sources.

Building Active Reading Strategies

Many students are passive readers; they do not interact with the ideas they read, and they fail to make connections between the ideas presented in the text and their own knowledge and experience on the topic. They accept ideas rather than questioning and evaluating them. Further, they do not monitor their comprehension or initiate strategies that will improve it. Unless directed to do so, many students do not preview before reading, identify main ideas as they read, highlight and annotate key points, or review after they read. Chapter 2 offers students a step-by-step process for approaching a reading assignment. They learn to preview before reading, activate background knowledge, read for meaning, highlight and annotate, and review after reading. These steps can be applied to all essays in the text as well as to readings and textbook assignments in other academic courses. In fact, the process is a variation of the well-known SQ3R system, developed by Francis P. Robinson in 1961 and used ever since as a means of strengthening both reading and recall of expository text. Encourage students to use these active reading strategies in all of their academic coursework.

The text contains several other features that promote active reading. Reading tips and prereading questions that accompany readings direct students to search for a particular element or apply specific skills. Each chapter includes a question directing students to draw a graphic organizer of at least one of the chapter readings, thereby encouraging the application of active reading strategies. Chapters 10 through 18 offer specific suggestions for reading essays based on each method of development, showing students how to adapt and apply the active reading strategies to specific types of reading materials. In these chapters, the questions that follow the readings help students to evaluate their reading strategies and guide them in analyzing each essay.

Using Graphic Organizers

Many underprepared students have difficulty recognizing the organization and overall structure of what they read. They fail to see how ideas within the text connect and develop. Since material that is perceived as organized is easier to recall, these students often have difficulty remembering what they read. Graphic organizers diagram these relationships *visually*, creating a meaningful conceptual framework that allows underprepared students to recognize patterns within the text. (For more on graphic organizers, see p. 9 of this manual.)

Strengthening Vocabulary Skills

Underprepared students often need to improve their vocabulary as well as their comprehension. Chapter 2, "Active Reading," offers advice on how to expand vocabulary, and the essays in *Reflections* offer ample opportunity for practice. Many of the essays contain words that may be vaguely familiar to students but that students are not likely to use either in speaking or in writing. Vocabulary questions following each reading have students analyze the use of language and require them to define words from the reading, placing a continuing emphasis on vocabulary development. Here are a few suggestions for helping students improve their vocabulary.

1. Encourage students to develop word awareness. You can do this by bringing to their attention a particularly well-chosen word, an apt phrase, or a high-impact word as you discuss professional essays in the text.

2. As you read student essays, mark a place or two where a more forceful or more descriptive word or phrase is needed.

3. Encourage students to keep a computer file or notebook of new words they want to begin to use in their own writing or speech.

4. Show students how to figure out the meanings of words from context clues. Giving a few quick examples from one of the chapter essays is often sufficient to get them started. Also direct them to the section on "Specialized Reading Strategies" in Chapter 2, "Active Reading."

5. Refer students with serious vocabulary problems to the college's academic skills center for further instruction.

Fostering Critical Reading and Thinking

Underprepared students often lack critical-reading and critical-thinking skills. They accept a writer's ideas at face value and fail to interpret, evaluate, and react to ideas. *Reflections* promotes critical thinking and critical reading in several ways. Chapter 3 provides detailed guidance on how to approach readings with a critical eye. The readings in Chapters 10–18 include questions that introduce students to important critical-thinking skills such as paying attention to tone, evaluating sources, and identifying bias. Students must then apply these skills to the essay they have just read.

You can promote critical thinking in the classroom in the following ways.

1. Establish an open environment in which students are welcome to ask serious questions freely at appropriate times.

2. Serve as a role model. Ask critical questions often and encourage students to explore them with you.

3. Correct the misguided notion that critical thinking means finding fault and that it emphasizes the negative.

4. Use a problem-solving paradigm to teach critical thinking. Use daily classroom problems, such as a fire drill that interrupts an in-class revision

workshop, to guide students through the stages of (1) gathering information, (2) defining the problem, (3) identifying possible solutions, (4) evaluating solution paths, and (5) making a decision.

5. Require generalization. Give students practice in seeing how a specific writing skill can apply to a wide range of situations. Ask the class, for example, when a narrative might be useful in workplace settings or in what college courses comparison and contrast might commonly be used.

Works Consulted

Ausubel, David P. *Educational Psychology: A Cognitive View*. Holt, Rinehart, and Winston, 1968.

Robinson, Francis P. *Effective Study*. Harper & Brothers, 1961.

Teaching Tips and Suggested Answers for Individual Chapters in *Reflections*

Part 1: Skills for Success in Reading and Writing

Part 1 is a guide to active reading and writing and provides a broad overview of the relationship between the two. Because this is a subject that students may initially consider unnecessary and simplistic, it may be challengeing to help them to recognize how important it is to relearn or refine their previous understanding of what it means to "read" an essay and to "write a good paper." Therefore, you will probably find it helpful to devote several class sessions at the start of the term to Part 1 of *Reflections* in order to dissuade students from the idea that they can simply go on reading texts and writing papers exactly as they did in high school. Although you may at first encounter resistance to the idea that they need to relearn how to read an essay and write and revise their papers, over time, as their writing improves, first-year students will begin to appreciate the writing and reading skills they develop in your introductory class.

CHAPTER 1: Succeeding in College, p. 3

Chapter 1 is designed as a guide for students, providing them with keys for academic success that can help them succeed in the composition course and beyond. Since many students today enter college or university underprepared for the demands of higher education — especially when it comes to writing — this chapter may prove extraordinarily useful to your students. The chapter opens with a reading on page 4, "To Remember a Lecture Better, Take Notes by Hand," by Robinson Meyer (Lexile level: 1060L). The reading provides a useful entry to discussing the focus of the chapter: techniques for succeeding in college. The sections in Strategies for College Success (p. 6) will help students organize their coursework, while sections in Classroom Skills (p. 12) stress proper classroom etiquette and encourage collaborative learning. Depending on the time you have allotted in your course schedule and the type of student atmosphere in your classroom, you may choose to assign sections from this chapter, including the opening reading on effective notetaking. Alternatively, you may choose to place reminders or references to the chapter in your syllabus and assignments, thereby encouraging students to take advantage of the material on their own.

CHAPTER 2: Active Reading, p. 21

CHAPTER 3: Critical Reading and Thinking Strategies, p. 50

Chapters 2 and 3 are devoted to the idea of "active reading," also called close, or critical, reading. The essay beginning on page 25, "Comparing Online and Traditional Education," by Morgan Lowrie (Lexile level: 1160L), serves as a useful example for guiding students through the various elements of active reading, which are presented throughout Chapter 2. It is important to establish the connection between reading and writing critically early in the semester. If you take the time early on to reinforce the idea that analytical reading and writing are closely related, your students' abilities to read, think, and write critically will develop more readily over the course of the semester. You may find it especially worthwhile to devote some class time to the concept of critical thinking, emphasizing that college-level writing depends on the ability to analyze readings and to support opinions with evidence from a text (or texts). The section beginning on page 30 — Reading for Meaning: The Thesis Statement and Key Elements of Paragraphs — is a good way to open up a discussion of critical thinking. This kind of discussion will help your students understand that they are being asked to engage in a new level of scholarly thinking.

Before giving the first reading assignment, you should review the Strategies for Active Reading section (pp. 22–24) with your students. This section provides a basic overview of active reading strategies that you may want to encourage your students to follow on a regular basis. You might want to follow up with more detail by reviewing the subsequent sections that elaborate on active reading before, during, and after the reading process. For example, read Table 2.2, Guidelines for Previewing (p. 29) aloud with your students to show them how to "preview" the essays you assign in class. One way to make use of this feature would be to go down the list with them, asking them what kind of information a reader can glean from each of the previewing suggestions listed. Encourage your students to go through the previewing steps for every assigned reading throughout the semester.

Many first-year students simply do not understand why they should highlight key points (pp. 34–35) and annotate their impressions (pp. 35–37) or why they need to look up and remember the meaning of unfamiliar vocabulary words (pp. 37–38). Remind them that college-level courses require a new kind of reading and that rereading or "reviewing" (pp. 42–49) will foster a more sophisticated level of thinking. You might want to ask them to show you their copy of *Reflections* at the beginning of the first few classes after you have discussed highlighting and annotating. Observe whether or not they are underscoring and writing in the margins. If you are still not seeing much annotation, remind them of what you would like to see. You might want to show them your own text, which is undoubtedly marked up, as an example of what you expect to see. Once they are highlighting and annotating their texts, ask them to share a word or idea they underscored (or questioned) with the class. Ask them to explain why they marked it and what they learned from doing so.

Another important concept that you may wish to introduce to your students is the idea that a text can be looked at visually, *before being read*, as if it were an object. Surprisingly enough, many students are completely unaware of the meaning of "key elements" such as headings and type size or font differences. Point out that the formatting of titles, headnotes, headings, and so on indicates various kinds of text or levels of headings. Let students know that you will be questioning them about or asking them to identify key elements, such as thesis statements, in every reading you assign during the semester.

Because all students will at some point encounter texts that are difficult to understand, it is a good idea to show them the table titled Troubleshooting Guide for Difficult Readings (p. 38). Explain how they can use this table to identify the problem they are having (in the left-hand column) and then find reading and comprehension strategies to address this difficulty (in the right-hand column).

You may want to go over the section Draw a Graphic Organizer (pp. 46–48) carefully, as these visual representations of an essay's content and structure are used throughout *Reflections*. Many students find graphic organizers very helpful for identifying the flow of ideas in an essay. The graphic organizer is also a useful device for slowing down a student's pace as he or she reads a text. Identifying the thesis statement and other key aspects of the essay and seeing them arranged visually into sections may help students who have difficulty understanding how a text is organized. As they fill in the boxes, students can visualize the text in a new way, organized into parts: *introduction*, with background material and thesis; *body paragraphs*, with topic sentences and key details; and *conclusion*, with restatement of the thesis. By learning to slow down, reread, and pick apart a reading in order to fill out the graphic organizer, students will eventually become able to structure and revise their own writing with greater ease.

Finally, if you plan to have your students work with the visuals included in *Reflections* or in other texts, you may want to take a little time to discuss Recognize the Importance of Visual Aids (p. 40). Students are generally comfortable with and eager to discuss visuals but may have given little thought to how to think critically about them. As an in-class exercise, you might ask students to apply the questions to ask about visuals (p. 43) to an image that appears with one of the readings in this text or elsewhere.

CHAPTER 4: Prewriting: How to Find and Focus Ideas, p. 79

CHAPTER 5: Developing and Supporting a Thesis, p. 97

Chapters 4 and 5 give an overview of different prewriting strategies and then explain how to use these techniques in order to develop and support a thesis statement. Many students consider prewriting a pointless exercise, preferring instead to write a single draft in just one sitting — something that they often did in high school. In order to prevent this tendency to skip the preliminary phases of developing an essay, you may want to assign papers in a step-by-step fashion. Ask students to hand in their papers phase by phase, over a period of weeks. For example, you might ask them to hand in their freewriting first, followed by any notes they jotted down, their narrowed topic, thesis statement, outline, first draft, and so on. Reiterating the advantages of using this technique throughout the semester will increase students' willingness to employ prewriting and will result in more carefully thought out and executed essays.

Note that the writing process steps are reinforced throughout Chapters 4 through 8 in two ways. Beginning on page 82, Essay in Progress exercises guide students through the process of working on key stages of their own drafts. And the Students Write feature at the end of each of these chapters (marked by beige-tipped pages, beginning with page 94) allows students to follow a sample essay in progress as it moves from the prewriting stage through the final draft.

Chapter 4 addresses many of the aspects of the first draft that cause students difficulty, including considering audience and tone. You may find it useful to assign Exercise 4.3 (p. 88) to help students discern often-subtle differences in tone and point of view, depending upon their audience. First-year students often have difficulty with the idea of "audience," asking what is meant by it since the only person who is going to see their writing is you, the instructor. You may need to review this topic over several class periods, explaining that it is necessary to assume that the audience needs some background even if they are familiar with the subject. It is often worthwhile to generate some discussion about this idea, experimenting with various audiences, from journal writing to freewriting that will be read aloud in class.

Narrowing down a topic is another skill that first-year students tend to have difficulty with. Exercises 4.1 (p. 84) and 4.2 (p. 85) can be used in class to give students practice in setting the parameters of paper topics. Once they've developed an understanding of how to successfully narrow and define a topic, they will be ready to move on to Chapter 5 on the thesis statement, one of the most difficult of all concepts to teach. Be prepared to show your students how to refine their thesis statements throughout the term. Tools for thesis development that you may find especially useful include the list of guidelines in Writing an Effective Thesis Statement (pp. 100–101) and Exercise 5.1 (p. 101), which will help your students work toward a better understanding of what makes an effective thesis statement. Explain, too, that although many of the professional writers whose work appears in this text use "implied" thesis statements, it is best to begin by perfecting the explicit thesis statement (pp. 101–102).

CHAPTER 6: Writing Effective Paragraphs, p. 108

CHAPTER 7: Drafting an Essay, p. 124

Chapters 6 and 7 explain how to outline and organize paragraphs and essays. As an introduction to this topic, you may want to start with Chapter 7, referring students to the graphic organizer on The Structure of an Essay: Parts and Functions (p. 125). Students may better grasp this subject if they work through a draft of their own using the Essay in Progress exercises included in this chapter. By applying the various stages of drafting an essay to writing of their own, students will better see how important an organizational plan is to the development of an essay.

By looking at the examples from the student essay discussed in Chapter 7, "The Reality of Real TV," your students can observe three different ways to develop their ideas: using an informal outline (p. 130), preparing a formal topic outline (p. 131), and creating a graphic organizer (p. 132). You may find it helpful to have the students create an outline or graphic organizer for all of the writing they do for the course. By requiring this step, you give students the opportunity to review and make changes to the organizational plan for their essay before they begin drafting it.

Once your students understand the importance of developing an organizational plan, they are ready to begin drafting their essay. Their writing will likely be strengthened if you spend some time in class working through Chapter 6 on Writing Effective Paragraphs. This chapter includes a discussion on Writing a Topic Sentence (p. 110). Point out to your students how closely the purpose of a topic sentence relates to that of a thesis statement. The list of specific functions of topic sentences on pages 111 to 114 can serve as a useful guide for students as they draft paragraphs for their essays, and the guidelines for writing effective paragraphs on pages 114 to 119 will be of use in coaxing students to develop paragraphs that are more specific and interesting. Finally, in order to show students how to link their ideas within and between paragraphs, you should spend a little time discussing the Using Transitions and Repetition sections (pp. 120–122 and 135–136). Commonly Used Transitional Expressions (p. 120) offers a handy list that will help your students to make their writing flow clearly from topic to topic.

You will probably want to review the structure of an essay throughout the term, letting students work in pairs or small groups to evaluate their own writing on a regular basis. The guidelines for writing effective introductions and conclusions (pp. 136–138 and 138–139, respectively) are especially useful tools; you will likely need to refer some students back to this material over the course of the term. Knowing that other students will be reading their writing motivates students to write well, so you may want to devote some class time every week to peer review. Remember that what seems obvious to you, such as the function of a title (to "suggest your topic" and "spark your readers' interest"; p. 139), often needs to be explicitly pointed out to first-year students. Even after you have done so, their titles may remain generic and vague (for instance, "Red States versus Blue States: A Comparison and Contrast Paper") for the first few weeks. Refer to the list of five tips for Writing a Good Title (p. 140) over and over, and have students evaluate each other's titles in pairs, until you see results.

CHAPTER 8: Revising Content and Organization, p. 143

Chapter 8 provides an overview of the revising and editing process. The revision process is one of the most difficult of all phases to explain to beginning students. Many of them simply do not understand what revision entails, no matter how many revision checklists you give them. Even if you assign first and second drafts, often they will make only whatever changes you explicitly marked on their copy. It is important, therefore, to stress early on the importance of revision. You may need to remind your students, over and over, what editing involves. Remind them that most professional writers edit their own work through countless drafts, even before submitting it to a professional editor, who then edits it yet again. In the way of example, you might explain to the class the steps that you take to revise your own writing. The process may be more real for students if they understand that all writers work through multiple drafts before finalizing a piece of writing.

Encourage students to visit you during office hours to discuss their drafts, or if time allows, set aside time in class to meet with students individually to discuss their drafts and how they might be improved. In addition, you might use peer review (p. 150). Go over the Questions for Reviewers (p. 152) so that each student understands her or his responsibility as a critic and what elements to evaluate. Engaging students in an active discussion about their writing can open up their minds to a more critical evaluation of the strengths and weaknesses of their work, leading to stronger revisions. In addition to incorporating peer reviews, consider going over the section Using Your Instructor's Comments (pp. 153–154), which helps students learn to pay attention to your comments and suggestions and to actively incorporate them into their revision process.

You will probably find it helpful to have students apply the skills in this chapter to their own writing by using the Essay in Progress activities included throughout this chapter. You may also want to have students apply the Key Questions for Revision (p. 146) to all of the writing that they do in the class. These questions will make the process of revision clearer and more enjoyable for them. Other useful tools include the revision flowcharts Evaluating Your Thesis Statement, Topic Sentences, and Evidence (p. 148) and Evaluating Your Paragraphs (p. 150). These visual features walk the students through the process of revision step by step, breaking the process down into a series of parts and helping them to see, for example, that they can add in transitional words or transitional sentences if they forgot to insert them earlier.

If particular issues need attention (for instance, confusing shifts), either on an individual level or by the entire class, you might want to assign sections of the Part 4 Handbook (p. 645) or have students work through additional online materials. One resource for supplemental activities and exercises is *LaunchPad Solo for Readers and Writers*. Gradually, as students grow accustomed to revising their work and studying lists like the Key Questions for Revisions (p. 146), they will begin to recognize their own mistakes. They will also begin to catch their errors more quickly in the revision process.

Part 2: Readings for Writers

CHAPTER 9: Patterns: An Introduction, p. 169

This chapter introduces students to rhetorical patterns of development and demonstrates the various ways of understanding and presenting ideas. Providing students with visual aids such as color-coordinated paragraphs and charts, the chapter invites students to think about how they will develop their own writing using one of the rhetorical modes, from personal narration to source-based argumentation. The Combining Patterns section (pp. 173–174) illustrates how multiple methods can be joined in a paragraph or essay for greater effect, and the Writing an Essay That Combines Patterns section (pp. 174–177) provides an outline (with references to other useful chapters in *Reflections*) to guide students toward well-organized essays that incorporate a variety of rhetorical modes. Finally, the guidelines on pages 177–178 explain to students how each of the upcoming chapters is organized so that they will know what to expect. You may choose to assign this chapter as a broad overview of the patterns, or you may choose to return to this chapter once students have learned a few of the patterns individually.

CHAPTER 10: Narration: Recounting Events, p. 179

The narrative essay is usually familiar to most first-year college students because it involves storytelling of the kind they hear every day. You might want to begin with a definition of *narration* — that is, a story that makes a point. When presented as a story, the narrative essay becomes much more accessible to students who are apprehensive about expository writing. Another way to explain a narrative is to see it as an answer to the question "What happened?" You will want to emphasize that creating a story is not just a matter of saying, "This happened, then that happened." Every narrative needs to be propelled by a strong narrative line. The narrator (or storyteller) uses language to shape the narrative or tell the story in the most effective way. Pacing and point of view are important. The writer must leave out irrelevant details and organize the narrative to best effect (chronologically, spatially, or otherwise). Stress also that while a narrative is essentially a story, it is also a story that makes a point. This point is crucial because students will need to make a point in their own narratives through the use of a clear thesis statement.

This chapter includes a wide range of narratives. The annotated essay "Right Place, Wrong Face" by Alton Fitzgerald White (p. 181) recounts events in a straightforward, chronological way — the tension mounts as readers see the author's belief in the justice system being dashed. Sherry Amatenstein's narrative "Talking a Stranger through the Night" (p. 200) sets up tension through the use of foreshadowing when she prays not to get a suicide caller as she staffs a crisis hotline in New York City. When the call comes in, she then finds herself absorbed in making sure that the caller wants to live. Although the phone call takes hours, the author selects only those lines of dialogue that are crucial to the reader's sense of the progress being made. The tension is based on the question in the reader's mind, "Will the suicide caller stay on the line or hang up and kill herself ?"

Roger Porter's "A New Interpretation of Tears" (p. 204) and Anna Erelle's "Excerpt from *In the Skin of a Jihadist . . .*" (p. 209) rely on first-person narration to relate a personal circumstance that calls attention to a life-changing experience. Porter relates a story about learning to be a real man and a father who won't leave, and Erelle uses her experience as a freelance journalist to gain information about the life of a jihadist. Ben Beekman and George Beekman also rely on description in "History of the Future" (p. 220), a hypothetical second-person narration about a "normal" day in the near future, which illustrates the artificiality of our technology-dependent modern life by placing the reader in the story. All of these readings offer models of narration that students can emulate in their own writing.

Alton Fitzgerald White, "Right Place, Wrong Face," p. 181 (Lexile level: 1060L)

Alton Fitzgerald White, a young, successful black actor who lives in Harlem, is arrested as a suspect when the police respond to a call describing "young Hispanics with guns" (para. 6). Ironically, at the time of the story White is playing the part of Coalhouse Walker Jr. — a black man who is similarly accused — in the Broadway play *Ragtime*, yet the event takes White by surprise and causes him to lose faith in the justice system. He had naively expected to be treated with "consideration" (2) by the police.

In opening up a discussion about this essay, you might ask students about their knowledge of New York City, especially Harlem and Midtown Manhattan, where White works. For background, be sure to point out that although Harlem has a reputation for being dangerous, it has many safe neighborhoods for black middle-class professionals, such as the neighborhood White lives in. You might want to initiate a discussion about situations in which black men are wrongly considered suspects by police officers. This scenario is one that is documented and well known in the black community; most black men are warned early that such a thing might happen in their lifetime. You might want to discuss the reasons that White identifies himself not as black but simply as an actor from Cincinnati, Ohio, who was raised to be a "gentleman" (1) and to have "manners" (2).

As you work through the section on What Is Narration? (p. 180), you might return again to the White essay. The annotations clearly mark the points of conflict, tension, and climax and other narrative techniques used by White. You might have students add annotations of their own to mark notable passages of dialogue and physical description as well as events that build suspense and further the narrative.

Mina Raine, "Taking Back Control," p. 193

(Student Essay)

In addition to exhibiting the features of a narration essay, Mina Raine's essay tells a story that is both gripping and thought-provoking. Readers become invested in the actions and details pertaining to Beth's dilemma, and the climax of the story holds weight as a result of effective tension-building and foreshadowing.

In discussing this essay with students, be sure to bring up the topic of emotional investment. Raine makes it clear throughout the story that Beth is an important person to her, and her feelings lend credibility to the thesis she establishes. She conveys the deep concern and surprise (1) caused by Beth's transformation, and this makes it easy to empathize with her. The emotional investment of the writer thus produces a corresponding response in readers. Encourage students to handle the subjects of their own essays in a similarly invested way.

Responding to Raine's Essay, p. 196

1. Most will agree that Raine's thesis is strong. It is an extremely clear and specific statement that captures the experience of the narrator and her reaction to Beth's eating disorder.

2. Answers will vary.

3. Raine establishes conflict and creates tension largely through her descriptions of Beth's appearance, which become increasingly unsettling as the story progresses.

4. Raine uses foreshadowing early in the story when she makes a parenthetical reference to "[l]ater" (2). It is a generally effective usage that raises the implicative significance of an outwardly minor detail.

5. Answers will vary.

Sherry Amatenstein, "Talking a Stranger through the Night," p. 200

(Lexile level: 1050L)

Amatenstein's narrative vividly establishes how the events of a single night spent staffing a crisis hotline changed her view of the world. The first two nights quickly diminish the author's idealism as she deals with problem callers, one after another. Then, on the third night, a dreaded suicide call comes in, after only a brief training session on how to handle such emergencies. Several hours later, Amatenstein has successfully calmed the caller's fears and possibly averted a suicide. After she hangs up, Amatenstein realizes how the process of helping the suicide caller made her feel more connected to the human community, a moment of true epiphany for her.

In discussing this essay, you might want to provide some background information about the issue of suicide and how it is prevented or addressed by psychologists and others. A discussion about volunteering or helping those less fortunate, and where such altruism fits into our culture, might also be useful. Ask students to share their experiences volunteering and how their expectations were met or foiled. In particular, ask if any of them want to share an experience in which helping someone else helped them as well.

Understanding and Reviewing the Reading, p. 202

1. Amatenstein was motivated to volunteer because she is the child of Holocaust survivors and has always wanted to "ease other people's pain," particularly after 9/11 (para. 1).

2. When Amatenstein received Sandy's call, she became quickly alert and remembered the questions her training had taught her to ask.

3. Amatenstein found out that Sandy had been disowned by her parents many years before, had twice been seriously injured in ways that left her unable to work, had recently lost her boyfriend to cancer, and lived in constant pain in a dark apartment with no companionship except the occasional visit from a nurse's aide. She felt she had nothing to live for.

4. Amatenstein recalled that she was not supposed to give callers advice, only to help them find their own way through their crisis.

5. Amatenstein learned that because she herself had been feeling lonely "[d]espite having people in my life" (13), the experience with Sandy meant just as much to her as it did to Sandy. Through this experience the author learned that connecting with "another troubled soul in New York City" (13) was of greater value than the material comforts of her own life.

6. *Horrific* (3): This strong, negative term describes something that causes (or has the ability to cause) terror, revulsion, or shock. Amatenstein uses it with the word "childhood," implying that the callers experienced some sort of terrible tragedy or abuse in their youth.
   Rationale (4): This term applies to a way of thinking about something, usually a particular opinion, belief, or set of logical principles. Amatenstein uses the term to refer to her notion that she could imagine the callers' circumstances and feelings.
   Signified (4): To *signify* is to mean or to imply something else: an idea, emotion, object, etc. In the essay, the phone ringing represented an unwelcome problem for Amatenstein.
   Imminent (5): Impending; likely to occur very soon. Amatenstein wonders if Sandy had a plan to kill herself in the near future — during or after the phone call.
   Botching (5): To *botch* is to bungle or to mess up, usually clumsily. Sandy was worried that she would fail in her suicide attempt.
   Dictum (7): This term refers to a noteworthy phrase or saying, usually one with authority, such as a rule. In training, Amatenstein was told to avoid giving advice.

7. The following graphic organizer shows one possible answer.

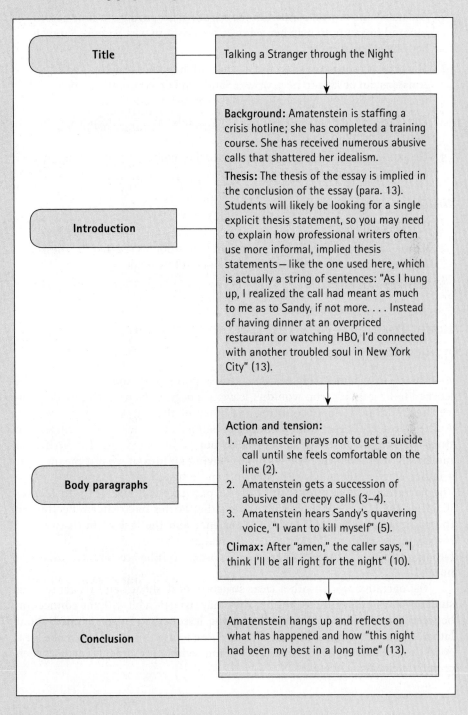

Title — Talking a Stranger through the Night

Introduction

Background: Amatenstein is staffing a crisis hotline; she has completed a training course. She has received numerous abusive calls that shattered her idealism.

Thesis: The thesis of the essay is implied in the conclusion of the essay (para. 13). Students will likely be looking for a single explicit thesis statement, so you may need to explain how professional writers often use more informal, implied thesis statements—like the one used here, which is actually a string of sentences: "As I hung up, I realized the call had meant as much to me as to Sandy, if not more. . . . Instead of having dinner at an overpriced restaurant or watching HBO, I'd connected with another troubled soul in New York City" (13).

Body paragraphs

Action and tension:
1. Amatenstein prays not to get a suicide call until she feels comfortable on the line (2).
2. Amatenstein gets a succession of abusive and creepy calls (3–4).
3. Amatenstein hears Sandy's quavering voice, "I want to kill myself" (5).

Climax: After "amen," the caller says, "I think I'll be all right for the night" (10).

Conclusion

Amatenstein hangs up and reflects on what has happened and how "this night had been my best in a long time" (13).

Analyzing the Reading, p. 202

1. Amatenstein's central conflict in the narrative is figuring out how best to respond to Sandy, to help her get over her crisis, in part because Sandy is her first suicidal caller.

2. The primary source of suspense is what will happen to Sandy — will Amatenstein be able to help, or will Sandy end up committing suicide? The tension arises directly from her initial expression of despair.

3. The climax of the narration comes when Sandy says, "I'll think I'll be all right for the night."

4. To "fan the spark" means to blow on a coal or ember to make a fire burn again rather than go out altogether.

Evaluating the Reading, p. 203

1. Answers will vary.

2. Again, answers will vary, but you might help students see that the thesis is implied because the point is intended to be subtly made.

3. Answers will vary.

Roger Porter, "A New Interpretation of Tears," p. 204
(Lexile level: 950L)

As a black man and a single father, Roger Porter tells the story of how he learned to be a father who wouldn't leave. He begins the narrative by describing his childhood and recounting the story of the day his father left him. At the age of 22, Porter got a real taste of being a father when his girlfriend of three years gave birth to a baby girl, but soon afterward, his girlfriend moved out and took the baby with her. Having no idea of what it meant to be a father, Porter struggled with how to handle his child on his weekly visits. The narrative uses flashback skillfully in paragraphs 8 and 12–15 to further illustrate the lack of positive role models that Porter had. After reflecting on the painfulness of his barbershop experience and the lack of nurturing and love from his father, Porter comes to realize what his daughter needs — a father who would "listen to her cries in order to interpret exactly what she needed" (17).

The narrative works with a clear structure of flashback and reflection that students may find helpful to outline. They may struggle a bit with the connection between the barbershop flashback and the lesson that Porter learned about fatherhood, but talking about why Porter chose to use this event will make for a good class discussion about what options and techniques students can use when crafting their own narratives.

Understanding and Reviewing the Reading, p. 207

1. Porter and his friends looked to their mothers and grandmothers for an idea of what a "real man" should look like. From hearing stories about his dad, Porter was able to infer what a real man was NOT.

2. In paragraphs 3–5 and 12–15, Porter describes various aspects of his father's behavior. He was basically an absent dad. When he was with his children, he was serious and inattentive to their needs, but to the outside world, he was meticulous about his looks, confident, and in charge. Occasionally, he would show up and take his children out to eat, but when Porter was seven years old, his dad remarried and moved to Tennessee to be a pastor. As time passed, his calls and visits became infrequent, at best.

3. Staying in his daughter's life was not what his ex-girlfriend or society expected of him. As a young black man, he was expected to be absent from his daughter's life. Porter felt as if he was not following society's script.

4. *Subversive* (1): Intended to subvert, overturn, or undermine a government or authority. Porter felt that he was committing a subversive act every time he went against society's script for a young black dad by continuing to be in his child's life after she and her mom moved out.
   Visceral (9): Coming from strong emotions and not from logic or reason. When Porter picked up his daughter each week, both he and his wife responded in "visceral silence."
   Unraveled (10): Undone. When Porter's baby screamed uncontrollably, he became totally undone.
   Abhorred (13): Regarded with disgust and hatred. Porter's father hated conversations about sports.
   Adulation (15): Excessive admiration or praise. Porter's brother basked in the praise that the barber heaped on him.

5. A "real man" is one who is in touch with his emotions and the emotions of others. He is one who listens well and communicates effectively.

Analyzing the Reading, p. 207

1. Porter creates tension at the beginning of the essay with his description of the life he lived with his mostly absent father. He then adds to the tension by briefly describing the life he lived with his girlfriend and baby and the ultimate ending of the relationship. After describing his once-a-week outings with his screaming baby daughter, he delays the story by flashing back to an experience in the barbershop with his father and brother.

2. The climax is the moment Porter finally understands how to be a father to his baby girl. He removed her from the car seat and gave her what she needed — someone who would listen to her and reassure her.

3. Porter uses flashback in paragraph 8 and paragraphs 12–15 to further explain his lack of understanding of what being a father means.

4. Porter describes his dad as the "unofficial maestro of the barbershop" because he was able to direct the conversation to exactly what he wanted to discuss.

5. The brief dialogue in paragraph 11 shows Porter's frustration at not understanding what his baby needed from him and not being able to help her.

6. Porter moves back and forth in time in order to provide background to help the reader understand both the actual story and his emotional journey. Not only does the reader come to understand the story, but he or she also comes to understand why Porter struggles as a father and how he ultimately discovers the true meaning of fatherhood. If Porter had simply told the story in chronological order, the emotional journey would have been lost in the details of the story.

Evaluating the Reading, p. 208

1. Answers will vary, though students may be curious about the details of his mother, his adolescence, and the three-year relationship with his girlfriend.

2. From the details that Porter shares, the reader can infer that his dad favored Porter's brother over him. Porter's brother had a recollection of his father, and it seems as if he had a relationship with him (3). In the barbershop scene, Porter notes that his brother always went first and the barber raved about his soft, thick hair. Porter's hair was just the opposite — unkempt and nappy. One can infer that the father preferred the older son because he was easy, attractive, and self-disciplined. He was obedient, and he made no fuss while getting his hair cut. On the other hand, Porter had difficult hair, he was tender-headed, he cried, and he was an embarrassment to his father (15).

3. The visual shows a man with an older child — not a baby. Perhaps Porter included this visual to send the message to the reader that he did not disappear out of his child's life. The visual relates to the thesis in that it depicts a tranquil scene in which the two are most likely talking and listening to each other.

4. Answers will vary.

5. Answers will vary, though students are likely to choose the barbershop flashback and the crying incident that occurs when Porter picks up his baby daughter from his ex-girlfriend's house, since they are sustained descriptions.

Anna Erelle, Excerpt from *In the Skin of a Jihadist: A Young Journalist Enters the ISIS Recruitment Network*, p. 209

(Lexile level: 810L)

Anna Erelle, a freelance journalist, offers a truly unique perspective in this story of her interview with a French jihadist conducted on Facebook by her fictional persona, Mélodie. Her initial goal was to understand what drove "European teenagers to be tempted by Islamic extremists" and ultimately move to Syria and become radicalized. Through a series of digital conversations and Skype sessions, Abu Bilel, the French jihadist, woos Mélodie and proposes to her, while Anna Erelle, the journalist, gains invaluable information about Abu Bilel and his life as a jihadist. As the essay ends, Mélodie expresses her hesitation to move to Syria, and Abu Bilel reassures her by saying, "You'll be important. And if you agree to marry me, I'll treat you like a queen."

Students will be fascinated by the fabricated story that Erelle creates and the interesting information that she is able to mine from her conversations with Abu Bilel. You might begin discussion by asking students what they know about radicalized Muslims and ISIS, what they learned from the narrative, and whether it changes their view of the reality of the ISIS recruitment network in any way.

Understanding and Reviewing the Reading, p. 216

1. As the essay begins, Erelle writes that she is frustrated because a magazine that she wrote for as a freelancer had received a letter from an attorney who forbade them to publish an article that she had written about a young female jihadist. Several years before this event, Erelle had created a fictional persona, Mélodie, and a Facebook account so that she could mine for information on current events, remain anonymous to the social media audience, and also express herself freely under the guise of Mélodie.

2. One night, as Erelle scrolled through a social network, she came upon a video of a Syrian jihadist named Abu Bilel. After intently watching the video, she shared it online, and within a matter of minutes, she received three messages in her private in-box from the person in the video — Abu Bilel.

3. When Mélodie expressed her concern for innocent children who had been killed in Toulouse, France, by Mohammed Merah, Abu Bilel ignored Mélodie's concern and told her that she was naive. He masterfully turned her question into an opportunity to talk about the ISIS sisters in Syria who take care of orphaned children. He flattered Mélodie by telling her that she had a lot in common with these remarkable ladies. He masterfully twisted her words and used her affection for children in an attempt to manipulate her and convince her that she should go to Syria to become a surrogate mother.

4. Answers will vary, but the instructor should narrow the focus and lead students to consider the ease with which ISIS (and other such groups) can gain access to people and valuable information through social media. Students may also consider the way that seemingly innocent conversations with these groups can lead to serious, life-changing decisions.

5. In paragraph 23, Erelle uses a metaphor to describe Mélodie as "the new fish swimming in his net." She wonders if Abu Bilel finds the new fish to be "appetizing." The connotation of *appetizing* suggests that Abu Bilel is checking Mélodie out to make sure she is appealing to his taste and, perhaps, even able to be consumed.

Analyzing the Reading, p. 216

1. Erelle refers to Abu Bilel as "a demon imprisoned behind a retina display" (19). In another place in the essay, she refers to Abu Bilel as being "diabolical" (35). Erelle is drawn to the computer, where an evil and diabolical terrorist awaits her behind the screen.

2. Erelle builds suspense within the narrative by alternating between conversations with Abu Bilel and narration that provides details and gives background information. She also delays the action by breaking her narrative into days. At each day's end, Erelle leaves the reader longing for more. The reader can feel the suspense as Erelle details the planning that went into the Skype session. When the planning is complete and the hour has come, Mélodie logs in to Facebook, Abu Bilel is there, and then the day ends. Leading up to the actual Skype session, Erelle again slows the action by beginning the session with one-liners followed by paragraph-length narration until, finally, the conversation takes off.

3. In paragraph 17, Erelle provides information about future events that happen after the events of the narrative. Indeed, she got herself involved in much more than she had planned. In one sentence, the reader learns that Abu Bilel talked Erelle into going to Syria, that something terrible went on in Amsterdam, and that her life today is spent in hiding and in fear that Abu Bilel will, once again, track her down. This foreshadowing causes the audience to continue reading in hopes that Erelle will reveal the rest of the story.

4. The tension builds throughout the Skype conversation between Abu Bilel and Mélodie. It begins to resolve when Abu Bilel hints at the "real" purpose of his call. In paragraph 74, it becomes clear that he already considers Mélodie his betrothed. The climax comes in paragraph 76 when Mélodie states, "I am not sure that I want to go . . . ." Every word of Abu Bilel's conversations has been for this reason — to woo Mélodie and convince her to move to Syria to be with him.

5. Answers will vary, but below is one possible answer.

Narrative Characteristic	Examples
Makes a point or thesis	Erelle makes the point that social networks contain precious information for people who know how to look for it.
Uses dialogue	Beginning with para. 10, the essay is filled with dialogue/conversation between Erelle (Mélodie) and Abu Bilel.
Includes sensory details	Para. 5 describes the back of Abu Bilel's car and Abu Bilel's eyes.
Recounts action	Para. 44 tells the story of the photographer's preparation for the Skype session.
Builds tension	Erelle recounts the details of the Skype conversation that led to Abu Bilel's invitation to move to Syria.
Presents a sequence of events	Each conversation is detailed, day by day.

Evaluating the Reading, p. 217

1. Erelle does not explain words like *jihadist, mujahideen, hijrah,* and *mujahid.* Judging from her use of Syrian words, it seems reasonable to believe that she was writing for an audience that would have some understanding of Syria and ISIS.

2. Erelle created the fictional account in order to provide anonymity for herself and to allow her to express herself more freely and gain precious information. She created Mélodie by giving her traits from all of the teens she had met who had been won over to jihadism. Islamic men seemed to be targeting women in their teens and early twenties with their propaganda, so Erelle created Mélodie as a twenty-year-old woman. Erelle's decision to make Mélodie a naive young woman made her attractive to Islamist suitors who were looking for young women who could be wooed easily and who were gullible enough to believe the propaganda that was being disseminated. Finally, Mélodie's naivete enabled her to ask questions and get information while appearing to be innocent. Students may provide varying examples of Mélodie's behavior that support the above statements.

3. Erelle uses dialogue as her primary means of telling the story because the narrative centers on social media conversations and a Skype session. The dialogue adds a sense of truthfulness and immediacy to the story. Read aloud, it seems realistic and authentic. Erelle even made Mélodie use teenage vocabulary (LOL, LMAO, ROFL) and make deliberate spelling errors. Abu Bilel spoke perfect French with a slight Algerian accent, and he peppered his conversation with authentic Islamic words and expressions.

4. Answers will vary, but students may choose to discuss the "surprise" picture of Abu Bilel in paragraph 22 or the description of him in paragraph 48.

5. Answers will vary, but Erelle certainly comes off as bold and determined.

6. Answers will vary.

Ben Beekman and George Beekman, "History of the Future," p. 220

(Lexile level: 1050L)

This brief excerpt from the opening chapter of a computer-science textbook provides an imaginative narrative exploring how evolving technology will affect people's lives in the future. The protagonist is a hypothetical "you," and the narrative focuses primarily on the "you" preparing for an overseas trip — driving to the airport, parking, checking in, and so forth — all the while demonstrating the state-of-the-art technology available at this unspecified future date.

Ask students whether they find any of the technology described surprising at all. Or do they think the technology imagined doesn't go far enough?

Understanding and Reviewing the Reading, p. 222

1. Some examples include *hacker* (para. 2), *chip implant* (3), *prosthetic* (3), *spam* (6), *ad filter* (6), *identity thief* (7), *wireless earpiece* (9), *genetic structure* (11), and *sensor* (11).

2. Students may have different responses here. The point the authors are making is that technological developments will shape not only people's lives but also how they interact with the rest of the world.

3. Answers will vary, but students may mention the chip implant and the prosthetic hand, the electric car with a computer that talks, the computer that sends messages about how to navigate traffic, the phone that can answer questions and translate words into other languages, the system that uses your handprint and retina scan to identify you, and the downloading of books to a phone.

Analyzing the Reading, p. 223

1. Basically, this excerpt communicates something of the technological innovations students are likely to encounter in the near future. One point that seems to be made almost subliminally is that technology will tend increasingly to isolate people. Note that the "you" written about has no human interaction at all over the course of the morning.

2. Answers will vary. Readers might possibly expect the rest of the textbook to view technological advances more or less positively — though to consider

the potential ramifications more broadly as well — raising "fascinating and difficult questions" (1). They might also expect the writers to reach out to readers as they do here ("you"); after all, the title of the text is *Digital Planet: Tomorrow's Technology and You*.

3. In addition to using narrative techniques, the authors use description as a pattern. In paragraph 3, the authors describe the relationship between "you" and your lab partner, Tony. Also, in paragraph 10, the authors use the pattern of process to explain how "you" check in for your flight.

Evaluating the Reading, p. 223

1. Answers will vary. Some students may even find that the level of detail doesn't begin to suggest what they expect from future technology.

2. Some students may not be familiar with the terms *far-fetched* and *exponential*. They may find the level of difficulty higher than that of other readings and the main narrative.

3. Answers will vary depending on what courses students are taking.

CHAPTER 11: Description: Portraying People, Places, and Things, p. 227

The description essay is enjoyable for most first-year college students because it involves vivid, sensory details and can be written in the first person. You might want to begin with a definition of *description* — that is, writing that appeals to the senses through the use of vivid detail. You might also want to briefly discuss how narration and description overlap, because they are most often presented together. Give students lots of examples of what you mean by "vivid" and "precise" details, using the examples in this chapter to help them recognize when a description is dull and vague. You will also want to emphasize the idea of "significant detail," the concept that not every single detail is as important as another. Explain how tiresome it would be if a writer told a story in which every single detail he saw or heard or tasted was thrown in. Remind students that they are already familiar with the use of descriptive language through the stories they hear or tell on a daily basis to their friends or families. You might ask them to think, for example, of someone they know who is a particularly good storyteller. How does this individual use details to create a vivid impression?

Just as you did when you talked about narration, you may want to explain that the storyteller shapes the narrative in a descriptive essay artfully by arranging the storyline in the most effective way possible. The author accomplishes this by choosing only those details that create a single dominant impression and point of view. A storyteller or writer must organize the story or narrative to best effect (chronologically, spatially, or from least-to-most or most-to-least importance).

The revision flowchart included in this chapter (p. 247) will help students understand what revising or editing a descriptive essay entails. As mentioned in Part 1, revision is often a difficult concept for first-year students to grasp, so using the revision flowchart throughout the semester will increase their understanding of the editing process. Because students often work harder to polish a descriptive passage when they know that they will be sharing it with the other students in the class, you might want to have them read each other's work on a regular basis. Using the flowchart to evaluate each other's work in pairs may also increase their interest in the process.

In this chapter, Jeremy MacClancy's essay "Eating Chilli Peppers" (p. 229) assembles an array of sensory details, using similes to describe the stimulating sensations hot peppers create. In "The Discus Thrower" (p. 248), Richard Selzer also uses many similes, comparing his amputee patient to a bonsai tree, a log, and a sailor on deck. Jordan Kisner uses details and narration in "Rain Is Sizzling Bacon, Cars Are Lions Roaring: The Art of Sound in Movies" (p. 253) to describe the process of creating sound for movies. Kisner limits the dialogue to short, almost-clipped sentences to underscore the difficulty of the job and the extreme concentration required. In "The Secret Latina" (p. 260), Veronica Chambers uses details of her parents' cultural heritage, specifically focusing on her mother's Panamanian culture, as a way to describe the experience of identifying as both Black and Latina. Taking an approach from pop culture in a textbook excerpt, "Costumes" (p. 265), Louis Giannetti analyzes the details of costumes in movies to show how they reveal character and may or may not be realistic.

The readings in this chapter also offer a range of perspectives from which to discuss point of view. MacClancy uses the third person to lend his informational piece about the use of hot chillies a formal but conversational tone. Chambers uses first person to explain how she connected with a distinct and mixed cultural heritage, using a specific story about a trip to Panama to illustrate the strengthening relationship with her culture and her mother. While Chambers focuses on relationships between people, Kisner and Selzer use third person to single out individual personas. Selzer focuses on a patient who affected his life as a doctor, and Kisner, in addition to describing the sound editing process, writes about master sound designer Skip Lievsay.

Jeremy MacClancy, "Eating Chilli Peppers," p. 229
(Lexile level: 1130L)

As the graphic organizer on page 231 shows, Jeremy MacClancy's essay moves from a description of hot peppers as painful and thrillingly stimulating to an argument that they are beneficial. He uses plenty of active verbs to convey the taste of the peppers and the exciting physical and psychological sensations they cause. Because he is an anthropologist and because this essay was written as an informative piece, he uses the third person to educate the reader about cross-cultural eating habits and motivations for eating chillies, comparing the pleasurable side effects to a drug high. He also outlines the more productive cross-cultural use of hot peppers in folk medicine.

MacClancy's essay can be used to illustrate how even informative or academic essays can be made more lively and compelling through the use of active verbs, varied sentences, and figurative language (p. 233). Remind students that they will be doing similar work when they begin to write comparison-and-contrast and other more analytical essays.

Madeleine Massey, "Small Town New Orleans," p. 240 (Student Essay)

Madeleine Massey uses the details of a small-town festival to engage her readers. The writer presents her information through sensory descriptions that paint a vivid picture of both the event and the experience that the attendees enjoy. She adopts a casual tone throughout the piece that allows her to convey the charm and down-home flavor of the festival. The essay's casual style is further enhanced by the activities that the writer chooses to describe.

In discussing this essay with students, it might be a good idea to focus on the precise ways in which Massey appeals to the reader's five senses. While many of the essay's sensory details are obvious (such as the "rainbow-colored, sticky pieces of sugary delight" in paragraph 2), some are more subtle. The reference to the "cold gust of wind" in paragraph 3, for instance, can cause readers to unconsciously shiver as they recall an early spring day that still had remnants left over from winter. Once the essay has been dissected, encourage students to aspire to a similar level of sensory detail within their own essays.

Responding to Massey's Essay, p. 242

1. Massey describes her hometown with words such as *quaint, unique, conservative, southern community*, and *old-fashioned*. By using these words, she creates the impression of a charming small town where people enjoy the simpler things of life.

2. In the final sentence of paragraph 1, the author indicates that she will·organize her essay by the street festival events.

3. Answers will vary, but students may choose words such as *little community celebration, subdued, narrow streets*, and *corn hole and horse shoe toss* to show the old-fashioned charm of the festival.

4. By describing the street artists as "fearless masters, in their own rights, who know no bounds," Massey is trying to convey the free spirit and creative

talents of the artists who start with a blank piece of worn concrete and some colored chalk and craft a finished product that dazzles the passersby.

5. Answers will vary, but students may focus on the community atmosphere, the small-town event, and the homey southern culture.

Richard Selzer, "The Discus Thrower," p. 248

(Lexile level: 640L)

Selzer's essay describes a few brief, fairly unproductive encounters between a doctor (the narrator) and his dying amputee patient. As his doctor, Selzer is curious about the patient but remains detached. Selzer knows that the patient is dying alone and angry — alienating the nurses by repeatedly throwing his plate at the wall — yet he doesn't communicate with him. Instead, Selzer "spies" on or observes him for clues about his background and his behavior. Sparse dialogue conveys the lack of communication between them.

Encourage students to read this piece several times, looking carefully at Selzer's tone, which may be difficult for many students to comprehend. You might want to talk briefly about the issue of patient care in the United States and what is expected or not expected of doctors and other medical professionals. You might also ask students to consider a doctor's mandate to "cure" and how that might be thwarted when he or she knows that a patient is terminal. You might have students break into small groups to discuss the role of empathy in the doctor/patient relationship — has it been shown, for example, to enhance healing? Students could share an experience of feeling cared for (or not cared for) and how it influenced their progress.

Understanding and Reviewing the Reading, p. 250

1. According to Selzer, the patient is blind and legless, and something "vile" is making his skin turn brown (para. 2). Over the course of the essay, readers never learn what caused his amputations or his blindness and, ultimately, his death.

2. The head nurse is upset because the patient won't eat, throws his plate, and, in a word, is "[n]asty" (27). She wants the doctor to do something about the situation, but Selzer only stalls her, saying, "We'll see" (30).

3. The dominant impression is that the patient in the bed is unhappy (except when he throws his plate) and waiting to die. Selzer's purpose for writing might be to describe his own sense of helplessness as a doctor when he cannot do anything to save a patient.

4. The patient exhibits delight, laughing when he throws his plate (34). Even though it is a violent action, throwing something with force and emotion is the only action the patient can take and his only opportunity to control something in his life.

5. Selzer learns of the patient's death from the head nurse, who feels that his death is a "blessing" (49). Selzer reacts to the man's death much as he has throughout the essay: unemotionally. He returns to the man's room, "a spy looking for secrets," to view his body, lying there "grave, dignified" (50) in bed.

6. *Furtive* (1): This word describes something that is characterized by stealth. Selzer does not make an effort to conceal himself while observing patients.
   Shard (19): This word describes a small piece or fragment of a brittle substance such as bone.
   Inert (20): This word describes something that is unable to move or act. Selzer fittingly applies it to his patient, who is completely immobilized in a hospital bed.
   Athwart (20): This word essentially means "across." Selzer is likening his patient to a sailor lying across a slanted deck.
   Hefts (32): To *heft* something is to lift or hoist it, often to get a sense of weight. The patient is roughly weighing the plate in his hand.

7. The following graphic organizer is one possible answer.

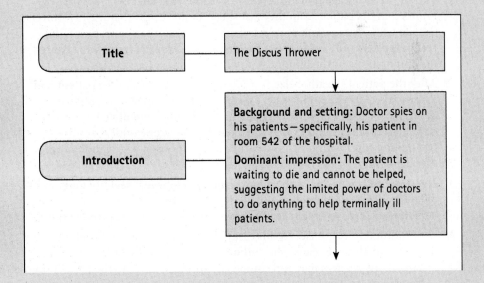

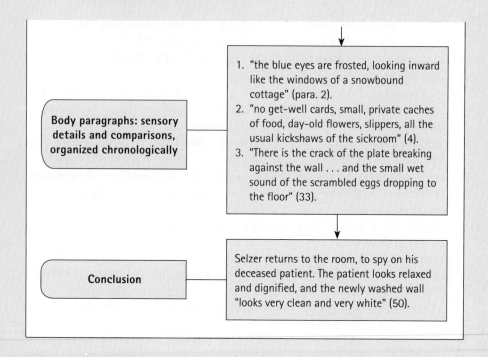

Analyzing the Reading, p. 251

1. The author's vantage point as a doctor is somewhat effective because Selzer knows that the patient is in the "last stage" of his illness (para. 2). However, despite what most people would consider an insider's vantage point, the reader receives only hints about the disease and doesn't know what caused the amputations or the blindness or why the patient has no visitors.

2. After the patient's death, Selzer notices that the wall where the patient had thrown his plate every day is very clean. Earlier, the hospital room was described as empty of personal effects (4); after the patient's death, it is described as "very white" (50). The overall sense is one of peace and tranquility, contrasting with the earlier descriptions of a very ill man who is detached and angry at his predicament.

3. The connotation of *spy* (verb) in paragraph 1 is to watch secretly in order to obtain information. In paragraph 50, the connotation of *spy* (noun) is a person who seeks to obtain secret information through close observation.

4. Expect different responses to this essay, depending on how students react to the perceived tone. Because the author's tone is generally unemotional and distant, many readers may feel somewhat unsympathetic to the patient. But some readers may feel a little curious about the patient, perhaps even slightly sympathetic to him, because he is alone, is unable to connect with the staff, and does not complain. The tone will also affect how students perceive the doctor, who remains a mysterious figure throughout. Some will

likely be offended by his somewhat "cold" actions, while others will find his behaviors and quiet contemplation to be caring and understanding in a quiet and respectful way.

Evaluating the Reading, p. 251

1. Encourage students to reread the essay, highlighter in hand, to mark all the places where Selzer uses effective sensory details. Examples include a body like a "bonsai" (para. 2) and dreaming of a time "when his body was not a rotting log" (19). Selzer also uses sound to effectively describe key events: the patient's laughter "could cure cancer" (34) and "the crack of the plate breaking against the wall" (33).

2. The dialogue, used sparingly by Selzer, is neutral; it's not very emotional or expressive, except for the nurse's and aide's remarks (27, 36, 41), which exhibit frustration, bewilderment, and anger. Students are likely to have different views on the tone of the essay. Selzer's overall tone is distanced or neutral, though some students may find it to be sad or pessimistic.

3. The "snowbound cottage" image (2) is effective because the patient's blind eyes are like windows glazed with ice and snow. The "bonsai" (2) analogy is only partially accurate because the patient's limbs are truncated, but his body is not really in miniature; it is more like a tree that has lost its limbs. The "log" (19) image works well because the patient's body is mostly trunk. The "sailor" (20) analogy may sound less effective to students because sailors would use their legs to steady themselves on deck and the patient has no legs.

Jordan Kisner, "Rain Is Sizzling Bacon, Cars Are Lions Roaring: The Art of Sound in Movies," p. 253

(Lexile level: 1210L)

Kisner's subject is, as her title suggests, "the art of sound in movies." As she shadows Skip Lievsay and his colleagues, she describes the intricacies of sound editing and the talents that are required of those who work in the industry. Within her description of sound editing, she embeds an extended description of Skip Lievsay, one of the best in the business. He comes across as a patient yet demanding man who has an amazing "ear" for sound and a keen understanding of how "hearers" perceive sound.

In discussing this essay, you might begin by asking students why they think the writer refers to making sound in movies as an art. What makes a professional in any field an artist? Is teaching an art? What distinguishes "artists" from technically proficient professionals?

Understanding and Reviewing the Reading, p. 258

1. The dominant impression is of a precise and intricate industry staffed by gifted and creative individuals. The impression is created by the author's

description of the process as she shadows two masters of sound editing in paragraphs 1–3.

2. Kisner uses Lievsay, a sound genius, as the vehicle for describing the sound industry. As she describes watching him work for several days, she also describes the industry, the role he assumes, and the supporting cast of his associates. Answers will vary as to which of the two — the industry or Skip Lievsay — the author describes more effectively.

3. Answers will vary.

4. In paragraph 15, Kisner writes that "a tiny aural cue" can have an astonishing impact on the brain's understanding of what is going on. Usually, there is more than one sound at work, and what we hear is actually affected by what we see.

5. "Sound by the pound" is just your ordinary, run-of-the mill sound editing job. There is nothing ordinary about Lievsay. He strives for perfection in every sound he creates. In paragraph 9, Jonathan Demme, one of Lievsay's former colleagues, describes him as "a genius."

Analyzing the Reading, p. 258

1. The essay is both objective and subjective. Kisner describes Lievsay subjectively. She portrays him in a way that she hopes will lead readers to find him to be gifted, one of the best, special, precise, and a genius. In her description of Lievsay, Kisner relates not only what she observes, but also her feelings about her observations. When describing the process of creating sound effects, Kisner is objective as she relates what she observes or gleans from Lievsay about the process.

2. Answers will vary, but students may include words such as *crunch, smoking, crumpled, hissing,* and *crackling.* These descriptive words suggest that the accident was a serious one with major damage to both vehicles.

3. Answers will vary.

4. The point being made is that sound editing requires extreme patience.

5. One pattern of writing that the author uses, other than description, is process. Kisner seeks to explain how sound is designed and edited for films. In paragraph 11, she writes, "At the beginning of this process . . . ." Kisner also incorporates illustration in the essay. In paragraph 12, she uses a scene from *No Country for Old Men* as an example of how Lievsay takes his team's work and turns it into a scene that contains real-world sounds. In addition, Kisner uses narration as she tells the story of how a perfect sound came into being. Throughout the essay, Kisner presents the events in chronological order and uses transitions to indicate the sequence of events. For example, in paragraph 23, she transitions with the phrase "What came next . . . ."

6. Answers will vary.

Evaluating the Reading, p. 258

1. The description is biased. Kisner wants readers to view Lievsay as a super-talented genius who is the best in the business.

2. There is very little dialogue in the essay. First of all, the process being described focuses on sound, not words. Second, Lievsay seems to be a man of few words. When he is working, he is listening, analyzing, and problem solving — all activities that require few words. The lack of dialogue contributes to the tone of the essay by highlighting the concentration and effort involved in the creation of sound.

3. Kisner wants to persuade readers of the talent required to create sound for movies and the difficulty of the task.

4. Answers will vary. Students may use adjectives such as *creative*, *talented*, *patient*, *quiet*, *demanding*, and *brilliant*. Students may find that their words reveal a conflict (*patient* and *demanding*, for example). The intricacy of the process and the time that it takes to create a twenty-second sound reveal Lievsay's patience. On the other hand, the level of excellence that he requires of his colleagues reveals his demanding nature.

Veronica Chambers, "The Secret Latina," p. 260
(Lexile level: 1040L)

This essay is unusual in that it is actually a dual description — Chambers opens by focusing on her mother, but then goes on to describe herself as well, in terms of being very much her mother's daughter. Panamanian by birth, Chambers's mother considers herself Hispanic, as Chambers considers herself also, even though their skin color and features lead people to think they are Black (growing up, Chambers was asked by friends why her mother spoke Spanish at home). Chambers writes about the bond she forged with her mother when she was finally able to speak Spanish with her, as well as how close she and her mother grew after Chambers returned from her first trip to Panama at the age of twenty-seven — she even describes details of the trip that helped create this connection. Chambers concludes with a very direct comparison of herself and her mother shaking their hips while dancing salsa.

You might begin class discussion by asking students to evaluate the appropriateness of the title. Emphasize the structure of the essay, pointing out how the comparison-and-contrast format of the descriptions contributes to the parent-child dynamic. Can students relate to this kind of experience?

Understanding and Reviewing the Reading, p. 262

1. Opinions may vary here, but one way of describing the dominant impression of the two women is "vibrant": the mother is a "plantain-frying, malta Dukesa-drinking, salsa-dancing Mamacita" and the daughter has followed in her footsteps.

2. Chambers's point in these paragraphs is that because of her skin color, she was not seen by her friends as Hispanic — hence her role as a "secret Latina."

3. The visit was important as a connection to her heritage and her extended family, and thus to her mother.

Analyzing the Reading, p. 262

1. Chambers wants readers to see her and her mother as women who embrace their Latin heritage fully — with hips shaking, so to speak.

2. In the first two paragraphs, Chambers establishes first her mother's character and then how she herself reflects that character as a daughter.

3. Chambers, as she says in her final paragraph, is obviously her mother's daughter — they are clearly similar physically and temperamentally and also share a very close emotional bond.

4. The idea of being a "fish with feathers" suggests that one is neither this nor that, not able to be clearly defined. Panamanians, Chambers writes, are indeed an odd mix drawn from all over the Caribbean.

5. Chambers's bond with her mother was strengthened when the two were able to speak Spanish together.

Evaluating the Reading, p. 263

1. Answers will vary.

2. Chambers's use of Spanish terms should not cause significant problems for non-Spanish-speaking readers.

3. Most students will find Chambers likable and the essay an enjoyable look at her life as a "secret Latina."

4. The conclusion clearly brings the essay full circle — Chambers shows herself completely as the daughter of the mother described in paragraph 1.

Louis Giannetti, "Costumes," p. 265
(Lexile level: 1130L)

This excerpt from a film studies textbook should be of immediate interest to most students. It provides a number of interesting insights into the language of costume in films, citing the contrasting Capulet/Montague color schemes in Zeffirelli's *Romeo and Juliet*, Marilyn Monroe's iconic white dress from *The Seven Year Itch* (which is discussed in detail), the costume devised by Charlie Chaplin for his Little Tramp persona, and the realistic costumes for *On the Waterfront* that were purchased in used clothing stores. The author also discusses how costumes may be designed to complement particular stars, in spite of their appropriateness in context.

As this is a textbook excerpt, begin by asking students what they learned from the reading. You might give them a few minutes to scan the reading again and then a few minutes more to list what they believe are the most important points it makes. Also of interest is the extent to which the excerpt makes them think differently about movie costumes.

Understanding and Reviewing the Reading, p. 268

1. Answers will vary. In addition to having students do highlighting, you might assign them separate paragraphs to summarize either in class or before class and then collate these summaries together either physically on the board or electronically.

2. The italicized words in the description of Monroe's dress represent the categories through which costumes can be described.

3. Juliet's family is aggressive, and the colors that represent this characteristic are "hot" colors — reds, yellows, and oranges. Romeo's family is an older, established family that is in decline. The colors associated with this family are blue, deep green, and purple. Thus, when Juliet marries Romeo, the color of her dress changes from red to blue.

4. In films and plays, costumes play an important role as a symbolic form of communication.

Analyzing the Reading, p. 268

1. There are many possibilities — for example, "How can color be used in costume design to suggest attributes of the characters?"

2. Examples include the costumes in Zeffirelli's *Romeo and Juliet*, Chaplin's Little Tramp costume, and the thrift-store costumes in *On the Waterfront*. The examples suggest the wide variety of costumes, depending on the setting and the story of the film.

3. This particular photo of Marilyn Monroe is one that is recognized by almost everyone in the world, and almost every aspect of the photo is symbolic of some aspect of either the culture, the period of time, or Marilyn Monroe herself. The white costume is sexy, with a plunging neck, a tight midriff, the skirt blown up, and strappy shoes. The amount of "skin" showing also contributes to the sexiness of the costume. The color of the dress sends an almost contradictory message of purity.

Evaluating the Reading, p. 269

1. Answers will vary.

2. Paragraph 5 considers what the writer sees as poor, or inauthentic, design prevalent during the studio era, when "glamour" and a "contemporary look" were more important than being true to a film's period and the actor's character. The point is important in a historical context and for any analysis of costumes in such films.

3. Answers will vary.

CHAPTER 12: Illustration: Explaining with Examples, p. 272

The main aspect of the illustrative essay — giving a series of examples to support an idea — should be familiar to most first-year college students because it is something that they likely do themselves in the course of everyday conversation. You might want to begin with a definition of *illustration* — that is, backing up one's thesis with examples. Illustration is an essential skill for your students because they will be required to provide examples, or evidence, whenever they write a paper in college. Good writing is characterized by generalizations that are well supported by specific examples. Explain to the class that examples are the evidence, anecdotes, facts, quotations, and statistics that back up a thesis. Just as in narration and description essays, the examples in an illustration essay must be organized in a meaningful way.

The graphic organizer on page 277 will help students visualize how to organize the examples in an illustration essay. The revision flowchart on page 291 will help them revise their drafts to make sure that the examples used are relevant, representative, and of interest to readers. Examples and details in the student essay "Waste, Away!" (p. 285) are highlighted so that students can follow the structure of the essay.

Each essay in this chapter uses a series of illustrations or examples to lend credibility to its thesis. For example, Bill Bryson's "Snoopers at Work" (p. 274) declares that Americans are being spied on and that this violation of privacy is considered legal. Bryson then delivers a series of examples of legal violations taking place everywhere from changing rooms to office cubicles, thus backing up his thesis with examples that prove his case.

In "What Happened to Innovation?" (p. 292), Michael Hanlon illustrates how innovation has stalled since 1971 by providing examples of innovation that revolutionized the modern world during the Golden Quarter — the period from 1945 to 1971. He further illustrates his thesis by pointing to more current progress that some consider to be innovative but that he considers to be nothing more than improvements in information technology. In "Hey Mom, Dad, May I Have My Room Back?" (p. 299), Cristina Rouvalis uses statistics to illustrate the rising numbers (and acceptance) of "boomerangers," college graduates who return to live in their childhood homes. Rouvalis uses quotations to humanize her subjects and support her thesis.

In "Just Walk On By: A Black Man Ponders His Power to Alter Public Space" (p. 305), Brent Staples gives a series of vivid examples to show how he and other black men experience social discomfort and discrimination because white people stereotype and fear them. Patrick Frank describes two movements in contemporary art in "Issue-Oriented and Street Art" (p. 310) and explains how they take up and respond to social issues. He profiles famous street artists like Banksy and Swoon and offers a variety of examples from photography to museum installations to illustrate the social consciousness of contemporary artists.

Bill Bryson, "Snoopers at Work," p. 274

(Lexile level: 1240L)

Bill Bryson declares that American citizens' right to privacy does not extend to changing rooms, office email, or even the local bar after work because secret surveillance has been upheld by the courts. Although his thesis is shocking, Bryson backs it up with a rich assortment of valid and striking examples that provide convincing support. Point out to your students how Bryson uses helpful transitions to keep the reader apprised of his thesis and where he is headed (for instance, "I know this because . . ." [para. 2]; "But it gets even more sinister than that . . ." [11]).

You might want to do some research on the issue of privacy and how it is defined legally so that you can preface this essay with a short talk. For discussion or debate, you might ask students to consider how much privacy they think people should be willing to forgo and under what circumstances. You might ask them to freewrite on the meaning of the phrase "innocent until proven guilty" or break into small groups to discuss "the right to privacy."

The graphic organizer for Bryson's essay (p. 282) provides students with the thesis at the heart of the essay and also identifies the examples he provides, one by one. It might be helpful to go over this graphic organizer with the class slowly and carefully. Review each of Bryson's examples to evaluate its effectiveness; this will prepare your students to analyze other essays that are less clearly outlined. You could initiate a discussion about the pattern used to present the examples — does it progressively illuminate the importance of the issue of privacy? Does the pattern gradually introduce examples that might persuade a skeptical reader that there is something seriously wrong with this erosion of American privacy?

Kaitlyn Frey, "Waste, Away!" p. 285

(Student Essay)

In this student essay, Kaitlyn Frey uses her own experiences and observations, coupled with research, to illustrate the growing problem of food waste in the United States. She organizes her essay very logically. She introduces the problem of food waste in her opening paragraph, ends the opening paragraph with a clear thesis statement, provides details for each of the main points in her body paragraphs, and concludes with a summary and a call for change. Consumers, vendors, and food producers are the three examples of contributors to the problem of food waste, and the writer provides both observational and researched details to support each of the examples. Students should notice the detail of the observations, from the "person sitting in McDonald's with a tray full of half-eaten food" (2) to the "high volume of perfectly decent and often untouched portions of meals" (4) to the shopper who "throws out perfectly good food because of a date" (6). Ask students to evaluate these details and think about how they support the author's thesis. You might want to have students suggest other details or examples that could have illustrated the point more effectively.

Responding to Frey's Essay, p. 288

1. Frey opens her essay with three questions to draw attention to the problem of food waste and also to capture the reader's attention. The questions are personal (they all contain the pronoun *you*); thus, they draw the reader in by making him or her assume some responsibility for the problem right from the start of the essay.

2. Frey indicates the three groups of people who are the main contributors to the problem of food waste: the consumer, the vendor, and the food producers. The order in the thesis corresponds to the order of Frey's discussion.

3. Frey uses research in her essay to help her discover examples outside her own experience and observations and also to give substantial and authoritative support to her main points.

4. Frey's clever title has a double meaning. In one sense, she is referring to the food that people are literally throwing away. In another sense, Frey is demanding that wasteful practices be abolished — sent away. It may be a stretch, but there could also be a third meaning. Those who do not have enough food to nourish their bodies are physically wasting away.

5. In the conclusion, Frey mentions all three of the major contributors — consumers, vendors, and food producers — and issues a call for change by each of these groups. She closes her essay by hearkening back to the title when she writes, "It's time to do away with waste and work toward more sustainable living."

Michael Hanlon, "What Happened to Innovation?" p. 292 (Lexile level: 1050L)

In this journalistic piece originally published in *Aeon* magazine, Michael Hanlon, a science writer, discusses what happened to innovation in the United States. He contends that the big breakthroughs in innovation occurred between 1945 and 1971 (The Golden Quarter), and since that time, progress has stalled. Hanlon begins the article by discussing the innovations that came about during the Golden Quarter, and then he moves on to give examples of the "banal improvements in information technology" that account for much of what people consider to be innovations. He uses a variety of examples of both innovations and improvements to support his thesis.

The organization of this writing makes it very easy for students to follow. Hanlon uses questions to signal a change in thought. After answering a question with examples and specific details, he poses another question and follows the same pattern. After students read the article, you might consider using these questions to structure a discussion.

Students will easily be able to identify the examples used in this article, largely because of its straightforward approach. You might want to make a chart or list of the examples to illustrate paragraph construction in an illustration essay. Additionally, you could begin a class discussion by asking students to brainstorm examples of additional innovations during the Golden Quarter and improvements since 1971.

Understanding and Reviewing the Reading, p. 296

1. The main topic of the essay is the lack of innovation since 1971.

2. Hanlon's main idea is that the big innovative breakthroughs came during the Golden Quarter, 1945–1971, and since that time, progress has stalled. He says that "breathless reports of progress" are mere exaggeration or even fantasy.

3. Hanlon considers many of today's examples of progress not progress at all. He cites examples such as today's airliners, which are basically updates of 1960s models, and the 5% drop in the cancer death rate between 1950 and 2005, which really is not progress. The chances of beating cancer in 2014 were not much better than they were in 1974. Also, we landed on the moon in 1969, and despite advances in technology and space travel, nobody has been to the moon since.

4. When the economic boom came to an end in the 1970s, so did the age of innovation. However, when the United States recovered from the recession of the 1970s, innovation did not pick back up. The United States and the world are much richer than they were during the Golden Quarter, but there has not been growth in innovation.

5. Some of the relatively newly created products on the market that are designed to become obsolete as quickly as possible are cell phones, televisions, computers, and cars.

6. According to Hanlon, some risks that led to innovations include risking killing several thousand people with a smallpox vaccination campaign in order to save the lives of tens of millions, risking the lives of astronauts in sending them to the moon, and risking rushing drugs like penicillin to market without the lengthy testing that is now required.

7. *Banal* (5): Commonplace or devoid of originality. In this essay, Hanlon uses the word to refer to today's commonplace improvements in information technology.
   Paradigm (6): A model or typical example of something. Today's cars are faster, sleeker, and more efficient than cars were in 1971, but there has not really been any shift in the overall model.
   Obsolescence (18): Significant decline in the usefulness or value of an article. Developers of products like TVs, cell phones, and cars plan for the products to lose their usefulness quickly so that they can sell consumers the next version.

Ingenuity (21): The quality of being clever, creative, or original. Hanlon says that the stall in ingenuity can be explained by several different factors. *Entrenched* (26): Firmly established and unlikely to change. According to Hanlon, the concept of civil rights is so firmly established in the world that people react with disgust and outrage when they encounter or hear of racist thinking and behavior.

8. The following graphic organizer is one possible answer.

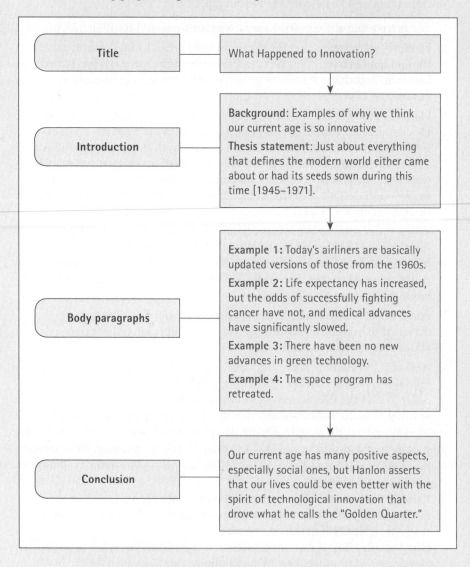

| Title | What Happened to Innovation? |

Introduction

Background: Examples of why we think our current age is so innovative

Thesis statement: Just about everything that defines the modern world either came about or had its seeds sown during this time [1945–1971].

Body paragraphs

Example 1: Today's airliners are basically updated versions of those from the 1960s.

Example 2: Life expectancy has increased, but the odds of successfully fighting cancer have not, and medical advances have significantly slowed.

Example 3: There have been no new advances in green technology.

Example 4: The space program has retreated.

Conclusion

Our current age has many positive aspects, especially social ones, but Hanlon asserts that our lives could be even better with the spirit of technological innovation that drove what he calls the "Golden Quarter."

Analyzing the Reading, p. 297

1. Because it was originally published in *Aeon*, an online magazine that contains articles about ideas and culture, the intended audience is most likely techno-savvy males and females. The subject of the article would be of interest to those who remember the Golden Quarter as well as those who know the history of that period of time. Young people would be especially interested in this article because of its discussion of developments in information technology. Because most of the innovations and improvements have had a worldwide impact, the article would be of interest to a broad cultural base.

2. Hanlon uses different categories of illustrations to show how innovation has stalled: avionics, medicine, green initiatives, technology, and space exploration. This range allows him to present examples that will be familiar to most individuals.

Evaluating the Reading, p. 297

1. Answers will vary. You may want to discuss with students what is *missing*. The writer presents many examples to support his thesis, but are there examples that he doesn't use? Are there examples that might even be more convincing than the ones he used? Are there examples that don't quite "work"? You might decide to use this question for a small-group discussion that culminates in a class discussion.

2. The tone of this piece is informative and journalistic yet biased. Although the author presents convincing evidence, the article is, after all, a piece that presents the opinion of one man.

Cristina Rouvalis, "Hey Mom, Dad, May I Have My Room Back?" p. 299

(Lexile level: 1110L)

In this article, Rouvalis explores a contemporary phenomenon referred to as the "boomerangers," a growing group of eighteen- to twenty-four-year-olds who move back home to live with their parents after they graduate from college. Rouvalis's attitude toward this group is mostly positive; she seeks to explain not only that the perception of a lazy or unambitious college graduate has changed but also that moving home might be a financially astute move. Most of the attention given to explaining this phenomenon refers to the economic downturn and its effects on changing lifestyles, including postponing marriage and having children (though she does credit other social shifts for some of this change). With a variety of examples in the narrative, Rouvalis illustrates how the boomerangers' numbers are increasing. Her hard, logical evidence comes from polls and surveys from the U.S. Census and CollegeGrad.com, which provide examples of statistical changes. She supplements this with quotes and narratives from intelligent, ambitious "boomerangers."

Students may have differing opinions on and reactions to this text, depending on their age and how near they are to graduation (as well as their relationships with their parents). This essay is useful for focusing on combining different types of examples and the different effects these examples can have on an intended audience's emotions and logical thinking. Ask students what other types of evidence might be included in the article or whether one type of evidence is more effective than another. You might also want to ask students to focus on whether counterarguments are effectively addressed in the article.

Understanding and Reviewing the Reading, p. 302

1. The difficulties that boomerangers face reflect a poor economic climate: low-paying jobs, outstanding college loans, and unaffordable rents in cities. At home, they face the lack of freedom under their parents' watchful eyes, and they may face culture shock returning to the suburbs from a busy college campus.

2. Parents sometimes like not knowing what their children are doing; when the children move back home, the parents are conscious of what hours they keep and who their friends are, potentially leading to worry. They may also worry that their children are not being independent enough.

Analyzing the Reading, p. 302

1. Rouvalis primarily addresses an older, settled audience, perhaps the parents of boomerangers. She wants to convince them that college graduates who return home are not abnormal, and she provides examples from smart, rational, driven students who moved back home to support her point that they are not "bums" and to convince her audience that this phenomenon is acceptable.

2. Rouvalis uses statistics from the U.S. Census and polls from CollegeGrad.com.

3. Rouvalis's tone is accepting and supportive.

4. Possible answers include the following.

Example	What It Contributes
Franklin (paras. 1, 10–12)	Franklin's response that "Everyone is doing it" shows how acceptable the practice of moving back home has become.
Masilunas (paras. 6–8)	Masilunas's job as a financial consultant, along with his clear plan to "put $600 toward school loans instead of rent," shows that the boomerang trend is not necessarily about being lazy. However, he shows awareness of the stigma and potential problems by acknowledging his mother's nagging.
O'Shea (paras. 8–9)	O'Shea illustrates the downside of moving back home, the culture shock of expected proper behavior in a suburban setting versus behavior on a college campus.

5. The subject, Bobby Franklin Jr., is clearly pictured in the front center of the photograph, while the background is blurry. The focus on Franklin with his computer, next to a clean, well-made bed, shows that he is not a bum but a responsible individual. It matches the author's tone and goal of humanizing her example subjects.

Evaluating the Reading, p. 303

1. The return of college graduates to their parents' homes is becoming increasingly acceptable and is an economically wise choice, though it is not without consequences. Rouvalis states her thesis in paragraph 2: "The sight of a college graduate moving into his or her childhood bedroom, filled with dusty high school trophies and curling rock-star posters, is no longer an oddity. A sour economy, big college loans, and sky-high city rents have made some new graduates defer their plans to strike out on their own."

2. This technique draws the reader in, making the "boomerangers" less of a statistic and more real by giving them names, quoting them, and even describing their personalities. In the middle, the author uses objective evidence to support her point, but ultimately she returns to personalizing the same young man, Franklin, to reiterate that he's not a lazy graduate.

3. Rouvalis uses examples of students who plan to move out eventually, some having already begun their careers. She does not provide examples of students who lack ambition or students whom Masilunas identifies as "the ones spending money like idiots" (para. 7).

4. The U.S. Census is a longstanding government procedure that is reliable, but the CollegeGrad.com site is user-reported and informal, so probably

not very reliable. However, Rouvalis's acknowledgment that it is an "unscientific" study helps establish her credibility.

5. Answers will vary.

Brent Staples, "Just Walk On By: A Black Man Ponders His Power to Alter Public Space," p. 305

(Lexile level: 1170L)

Staples eloquently illustrates the irony that he, an educated journalist and self-described "softy" (para. 2), should be often mistaken for a criminal, as many black men are. He opens his essay with the startling phrase "My first victim was . . . ," and then he proceeds to give examples of all the times he has been mistaken for a mugger or rapist since that first experience of being mislabeled as a threat at the age of twenty-two. His willingness to consider the issue of racial profiling with an open mind, to probe the possibility that his first experience might have been caused by his clothing or the late hour or something else, his eloquent writing style, and his genuine concern for women (who have real reason to fear men on the street at night) all add to the strength of his examples. From Chicago to Soho, he has experienced white people's fear and suspicion and has smothered his rage and shame to develop a series of effective personal remedies. In order to reduce the fear he creates in white people, he now employs various calming strategies, from keeping his distance to whistling classical music whenever he walks down the street at night.

Understanding and Reviewing the Reading, p. 308

1. Because Staples is a black man, other people — particularly white females — regard him as a threat. What he perceives to be a safe distance between himself and the other person is far too close for the other person's comfort, and she moves away quickly. The atmosphere of a place becomes immediately tense as other people react to Staples in fear.

2. Staples did not give in to the aggressive, dangerous lifestyle that claimed the lives of some of his relatives and friends in his hometown.

3. Just as hikers wear cowbells around their necks to clear a bear-inhabited area of danger, Staples whistles classical music to assure people that he is no threat, thereby clearing the area of (imagined) danger.

4. Other terms might include *quarry* (para. 2), *stalking* (2), and *flight* (2). These terms make the stranger who fears Staples appear like a deer in headlights, overly skittish prey.

Analyzing the Reading, p. 308

1. Staples uses description to help readers visualize the people and places in his essay. He also uses brief narrative passages to breathe life into his examples.

2. Answers may vary. One example students might notice is the "enormous red Doberman pinscher straining at the end of a leash" (9), which illustrates with great detail the measures the woman in the jewelry store was taking to intimidate someone she falsely assumed was a threat.

3. By illustrating his point before he makes it using the first example, Staples allows his readers to see from his perspective and to react to the situation with their own opinions, which may make their reaction to his thesis either more poignant or more critical. By ending with examples — a personal anecdote and an analogy — Staples leaves his readers with a lasting impression and support for his thesis.

4. Staples could use the work of other writers who have published on the topic, which would show that the problem of racial profiling isn't just Staples's problem — it's a social problem. In addition, Staples might be able to find statistics, such as data from psychological or sociological studies, that back up his thesis.

5. The opening of the essay employs irony as well as an aura of innocence as Staples recounts his reflections as a twenty-two-year-old. As the essay progresses, Staples becomes more reflective and resigned to the circumstances.

Evaluating the Reading, p. 308

1. Staples would argue that though racial profiling is wrong and a harmful practice, failing to "smother the rage" (11) will lead to either madness or an aggressive, life-threatening lifestyle.

2. An uninvolved, objective narrator wouldn't be able to effectively convey the experiences of a black man and might even come across as racist or as making assumptions. Not all black males share Staples's experiences and reflections, so his narration avoids stereotypes and harmful generalizations.

3. Answers will vary.

4. Answers will vary, largely depending on students' experiences and the communities in which students live. You may want to draw students' attention to pop culture references, such as hip-hop or movies.

5. Staples is writing for a general audience that includes well-informed adults.

Patrick Frank, "Issue-Oriented and Street Art," p. 310 (Lexile level: 1260L)

Patrick Frank introduces this textbook selection by listing famous modern artists, such as Matisse, Cézanne, Monet, Picasso, van Gogh, and Pollock, who were once considered radicals but are now widely accepted as important artists. He moves on to a discussion of contemporary art, implying that movements from the 1980s to today that have been viewed as radical are legitimate forms of art even though they may not be creating "objects of timeless beauty." He introduces two movements that are particularly socially engaged in the present moment. In the section on issue-oriented art, Frank first defines the movement as art that moves beyond purely aesthetic matters and engages with pressing problems or social commentary. He describes works from photographer Richard Misrach, magazine designer Barbara Kruger, political artist Thomas Hirschhorn, and African-American artist Fred Wilson, who created a museum installation to comment on the racism and class bias in museum displays. In the section on street art, Frank distinguishes between graffiti and street artists who (sometimes illegally) create murals or pieces on public walls. He describes works by Shepard Fairey, Swoon, and Banksy to show how these artists use common materials and common spaces to create smart, witty, and often socially conscious artwork. He ends by addressing the blurred line between legal and illegal, vandalism and art.

Frank's piece is well informed, given his art background. The piece is largely explanatory and informative, without a clear argumentative thesis. However, the description of these works, especially following a brief introduction including artists almost universally acknowledged as "great," suggests that these art movements are innovative and will be historically important. Highlighting particular artists and describing examples of their work grants them an elite status in these movements and lends legitimacy to this kind of art. Students may be divided in opinion about whether these are notable or worthy art forms. Ask them to discuss the individual examples and perhaps search the Internet for examples of this kind of art that they deem important enough to support Frank's point.

Understanding and Reviewing the Reading, p. 314

1. Answers will vary; check student books for highlighting/underlining.
2. Answers will vary but may include *modern* (1), *form* (2), *aesthetic* (3), *landscape* (4), *silkscreened* (5), *installation* (6), *busts* (6), *metalwork* (6), *gallery* (7), *abstract* (7), *Street Art* (8), *mural* (10), and *motif* (10).
3. Answers will vary; students may choose to use an outline, graphic organizer, summary, or other technique to create a study guide for an exam.

Analyzing the Reading, p. 314

1. Answers will vary.
2. Answers will vary.
3. This essay is purely expository and informative. Unlike some of the other essays, it includes no personal narrative, quotations, or statistics. Instead, it is descriptive with no bias, offering terms and definitions to explain a movement in contemporary art.
4. Answers will vary but may include statements such as the following:
   "In general, most artists of the present generation do not appear intent on perfecting form, creating beauty, or fine-tuning their sense of sight. They

mostly want to comment on life in all of its aspects. They want to create work that illuminates the relationships between what we see and how we think" (2). "[Misrach's] brand of nature photography is the opposite of the common calendars that include soothing views of pristine landscapes. He wants us to know that such scenes are fast disappearing" (4).

"Rather, the street artists made much broader statements about themselves and the world in a language that was widely understandable" (8).

Evaluating the Reading, p. 315

1. The visuals in the chapter are important to illustrate Frank's points. Particularly with art, which is so visual, it is important for the reader to actually see the art rather than simply read a description in order to get the full effect.

2. Answers will vary.

3. Answers will vary.

CHAPTER 13: Process Analysis: Explaining How Something Works or Is Done, p. 317

Process analysis is a simple, direct way of explaining how something is done, step by step. Recipes and directions are good examples of how process analysis is used in ordinary life. Students enjoy writing process analysis essays when they are presented as a challenge. You might, for example, want to ask them to explain something as routine as making a peanut butter sandwich in the simplest way possible so that even someone who has never seen or eaten one can make it. Remind students that, as in description and narration essays, it is essential to use sensory details and figures of speech to make their writing compelling, especially if the essay includes technical jargon or outlines a complicated process.

Although it can stand alone, the process analysis pattern is sometimes inserted into the midst of another kind of essay. Writers often incorporate it into essays that are principally defined by a pattern such as comparison and contrast. When a writer does this, he or she should clearly introduce the transition into process analysis and then transition back into the primary pattern of development.

To begin, you might want to go over all of the characteristics of the process analysis essay as outlined in the chapter. Note in particular that such essays usually include an explicit thesis statement. Most of the pieces in this chapter have an explicit thesis statement, so you will have ample opportunity to model for students how to develop explicit thesis statements of their own. The annotated essay "How to Make Money with YouTube" (p. 319) presents a clear example of process analysis. The graphic organizer on page 322 shows the organizational structure of the essay and presents a model for how students might outline their own process analysis essay. When they begin writing, encourage them to make use of the flowchart on p. 338; it will help them identify and number the steps in their process to make sure that their essay is clear and organized in chronological or logical order.

The process analysis essay should present clearly outlined steps, usually in chronological order. For example, in "How to Make Money with YouTube" (p. 319), Eric Rosenberg outlines the steps one can take to make YouTube a revenue source for an online business. Austin Netzley describes the steps in paying off a large debt in "8 Steps to Pay Off $81,000 of Debt in Less Than 3 Years" (p. 339). Scott Matteson in "How Does Google Search Really Work?" (p. 346) uses logical order to explain how a Google search works — for example, how Googlebot crawls the Web. The textbook excerpt "The Nature of Stress" (p. 351) provides an explanation of how stressors disrupt the body's equilibrium and how the body fights off these stressors.

Process analysis should define key terms (the way Scott Matteson defines *PageRank*) and other words that may be unfamiliar to readers. Process analysis should also provide necessary background information, the way "8 Steps to Pay Off $81,000 of Debt in Less Than 3 Years" (p. 339) provides information on how young adults can quickly amass considerable debt when first starting out on their own.

Austin Netzley supplies adequate detail, and because his is a how-to essay, he anticipates and offers help with potential problems. He instructs the reader to beware of scams by consulting with a financial advisor before agreeing to any debt-relief program.

Analogies are another important component of process analysis. In "How Does Google Search Really Work?" (p. 346), Scott Matteson uses an extended analogy between looking at the underlying structure of Google Search and pulling back a curtain.

Eric Rosenberg, "How to Make Money with YouTube," p. 319

(Lexile level: 1190L)

This is a clear and informative essay from Investopedia, an online finance and investing site that publishes new content every day. In this essay, Eric Rosenberg, a contributing author, writes about the process of making money by creating YouTube videos. The writer makes his central point in the first paragraph and again in the conclusion: making money with YouTube is hard work to start with, but it has the possibility of becoming a substantial source of revenue. After making his central point, the writer walks the reader through each of the steps involved in the process, from creating a YouTube account and an AdSense account to promoting the video and collecting a check. Along the way, he points out potential pitfalls and explains technical terms. The process appears to be a relatively simple one; the hard work comes in promoting the video and growing an audience. The payment actually comes from AdSense, and it is based on the number of hits the ads accompanying the video receive. So the creator of the video must promote his or her product in as many online platforms as possible in order to grow his or her audience. Before there can be any income, there must be a sizable and loyal audience.

This how-to process essay is an excellent model for students. It contains the three major structural parts: an introduction, body paragraphs, and a conclusion. The introduction includes a clear thesis statement, the body paragraphs are arranged chronologically, and the conclusion summarizes the value of the process. Students might like to put this process into action by signing up for their own YouTube and AdSense accounts and creating and uploading videos.

Aurora Gilbert, "The Pleasures and Particulars of Philanthropy: How to Publicize Your Fund-Raising Event," p. 331

(Student Essay)

This student essay details the steps involved in the process of planning and publicizing a charitable fund-raising event, using as an example a fund-raiser carried out by the writer and her campus service group. As the text annotations suggest, the steps are clearly outlined and explained, with the final step divided into three stages. Characteristics of the essay to point out are how genuinely the writer cares about raising funds for good causes and her efforts to establish rapport with readers, encouraging them to organize their own fund-raisers for causes they support.

Responding to Gilbert's Essay, p. 334

1. Answers may vary. Not all students will necessarily see this as a "useful and enjoyable" skill, though the writer makes a good case.
2. The example, while a bit specific to be generally applicable, does help illustrate the process for readers who are unfamiliar with it.
3. The thesis clearly identifies the steps in the process.
4. Some students may quibble here. The instructions may not be entirely adequate for a different kind of fund-raising event.
5. The final paragraphs provide an adequate conclusion — very upbeat, as is the rest of the essay.

Austin Netzley, "8 Steps to Pay Off $81,000 of Debt in Less Than 3 Years," p. 339

(Lexile level: 1160L)

Debt-management expert Austin Netzley opens his essay by appealing to a young audience just getting started in life. He notes that student loans coupled with a car payment and other bills can add up to significant debt, but he ends his introduction on a positive note by offering hope and encouragement to those who choose to follow his 8-step process for paying off $81,000 of debt in three years. Netzley then begins to walk readers through the process, step by step. As he presents the process, he describes each step in a conversational tone, defines key terms, points out potential pitfalls, directs readers to sources of professional help, offers encouragement, and presents the advantages of a debt-free life.

This is a very clear model for students: the introduction provides background information and suggests the importance of the process, the steps are clearly delineated using bold headings, and the development of each step is detailed and easy to follow. You might begin discussion by asking students to identify the most important thing they learned from the essay. Alternatively, you might divide students into small groups to come up with a list of what they believe are the most important points, which they can then share with the rest of the class.

Understanding and Reviewing the Reading, p. 342

1. In paragraph 2, Netzley presents his thesis. He writes, "In under three years, you can be debt-free and on your way to achieving financial freedom in your mid-20s."

2. Netzley's audience is most likely his peers — those people who have recently graduated from college, gotten their first "real" job, and begun living on their own with bills and college loans to pay.

3. This is a how-to essay. Netzley hopes that those who follow his plan will be free of debt and also able to invest money for the future. This idea is stated in the thesis and restated in the concluding paragraph.

4. In the title, Netzley states that this process should take three years or perhaps less. In Step 7, he also refers to the three-year time frame.

5. According to Netzley, the most exciting step in the process and also the one that requires the most work is Step 6: Make more money! After interviewing 75 wealthy men, Netzley noted that each of them had the same secret: working hard to overcome substantial debt in a short period of time. This work might involve taking on a second job, putting in longer hours, or some other sacrifice.

6. Netzley writes that the biggest challenge in Step 2 is to get out and stay out of the debt cycle. It is easy to get right back into the debt cycle.

7. Answers will vary. Debt stacking is a strategy for repaying debt. Put simply, it is determining which debt has the highest interest rate and paying off that debt first. At the same time, you should be making the minimum monthly payment on all other debts. Once you pay off the debt with the highest interest rate, you then move to the debt with the second highest interest rate and pay as much as you can on that debt while you are still paying the minimum monthly charge on the rest of the debts.

8. *Reeling* (para. 1): Knocked off one's footing or feeling unsteady. Netzley states that the initial shock of realizing exactly how much debt you are facing can cause you to feel unsteady from the sick feeling that overwhelms you.

Accrued (2): Been accumulated piece by piece or in increments. There is a way for you to recover from the debt that has added up over time.

Consolidating (11): Combining into a single more effective whole. One debt-relief option involves combining all of your loans into one more manageable loan.

Strapped (18): In financial need. Netzley said he still remembered that initial feeling of being in financial need every time he saw a Sallie Mae envelope, so he pulled money out of the stock market and paid the final $35,000 balance as a lump sum.

Surge (20): To move forward with force or sweep. When Netzley made the last payment, a feeling that he will always remember rushed through his body.

Strategic (22): Part of a plan, method, or series of maneuvers for obtaining a specific goal. Netzley paid off his debt in a methodical manner by using the eight steps he presents in this article.

9. The following graphic organizer is one possible answer.

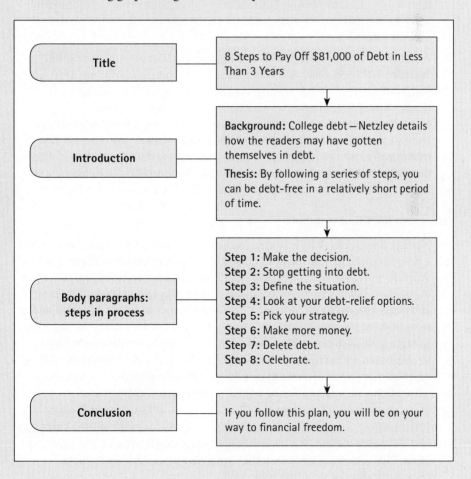

Title — 8 Steps to Pay Off $81,000 of Debt in Less Than 3 Years

Introduction — **Background:** College debt — Netzley details how the readers may have gotten themselves in debt.

Thesis: By following a series of steps, you can be debt-free in a relatively short period of time.

Body paragraphs: steps in process —
Step 1: Make the decision.
Step 2: Stop getting into debt.
Step 3: Define the situation.
Step 4: Look at your debt-relief options.
Step 5: Pick your strategy.
Step 6: Make more money.
Step 7: Delete debt.
Step 8: Celebrate.

Conclusion — If you follow this plan, you will be on your way to financial freedom.

Analyzing the Reading, p. 344

1. In the two introductory paragraphs, Netzley draws readers in by asking a question to which all readers can relate. As the introduction progresses, he lets readers know that he understands their situation. By doing this, he is able to gain the readers' trust before he walks them through the process. Finally, he communicates hope to his readers by letting them know that there is a way for them to become debt-free.

2. Answers will vary.

3. Answers will vary. Although he does present some facts, Netzley inserts his opinion in almost every step. For example, in Step 1, Netzley writes, "This sounds like a simple first step, because we all say that we really want to be debt-free, but our actions don't follow our words." This is Netzley's opinion, and he offers no support to back up his statement. In Step 4, he includes a factual statement when he says, "Debt-relief options include loan-forgiveness programs, consolidating all of your loans into something more manageable, debt settlement, or credit counseling (reducing the interest rates)."

4. Answers will vary, but students are likely to find the advice interesting, regardless of their financial situation.

5. Netzley links the introduction and conclusion together by repeating the thesis. Furthermore, in the introductory paragraphs, he begins positively, and in the conclusion, he ends positively and indicates what might be in store in the future for those who complete the process. The cycle of debt management comes full circle — the past and how the debt occurred, the present and how the debt was deleted, and the future and how being debt-free may lead to financial freedom.

Evaluating the Reading, p. 344

1. Netzley does seem to be knowledgeable and experienced. This essay is in fact a description of how he himself erased $81,000 in debt in less than three years. In the essay, when he speaks of financial freedom, he is speaking from experience. He has been out of college for almost eight years, and he now considers himself to be "retired." He is an investor, an author of books and essays on the subject of financial freedom, and a popular speaker.

2. In Step 4, Netzley warns his readers that there are many debt-relief scams. In order to help his readers be more aware of legitimate debt-relief options, he gives them a list of some to consider and advises his readers to consult with a financial advisor before committing to any of the options.

3. The point that Netzley makes is that being in debt can become a burden to you — a heavy weight on your shoulders — but paying off the debt will make you feel as if a weight had been taken off your shoulders and a burden lifted. This is a figure of speech that most people understand, and it communicates the meaning quite well.

4. Netzley uses personal experience, facts about debt-relief options and repayment strategies, and advice from experts. The support he uses is adequate, but Netzley probably needs to cite more convincing sources — bankers, debt-relief counselors, statistics, etc. The essay could use more fact and less opinion.

Scott Matteson, "How Does Google Search Really Work?" p. 346

(Lexile level: 1380L)

In this essay from *TechRepublic*, Scott Matteson takes a complicated process and, in simplified and informal language, explains how it works. Most people know something about his subject, Google Search, but have little to no understanding of how it actually works. He begins the essay with his own experience and explains what led him to search for an explanation of how Google Search works: he performed a search on Google Search. Using the metaphor of pulling back the curtain, he sets out to explain the underlying structure of Google Search and how results are found.

After presenting a brief, paragraph-long history of Google Search, Matteson begins explaining the process. In three steps and an attention-getting visual, he explains, in lay terms and almost folksy language, the basics of the process. As he comes to the end of his explanation, he puts in a plug for the next article he plans to publish, which will take the reader even further into the process.

Start by asking students what they know about Google Search. Try to ascertain how many students are interested in knowing how things work on a computer and how many students simply want to use the computer without any idea of what's behind the curtain. After students have read the essay, discuss how their attitudes affect their understanding of the essay. This discussion could also be supported by the students' answers to question 5 in Evaluating the Reading.

Understanding and Reviewing the Reading, p. 349

1. Most people just know that Google Search works and don't bother to understand how it works, but the author chooses to pull back the curtain and explain the underlying structure and how results are returned.

2. Matteson was inspired to research Google Search after he performed a search himself and then began to reflect on how particular pages ended up near the top of the search results. He became curious about how Google Search really works, so he "Googled" Google for an explanation.

3. This is a how-it-works essay. Matteson wrote this article to explain how Google Search works. Giving people a look behind the curtain and expanding their knowledge of how Google Search works may improve their ability both to evaluate their search results and to influence the results of other people's searches.

4. Googlebot is the special software that Google uses to crawl the Web and follow links from site to site. Its purpose is to look for new sites, changes to current sites, and invalid links.

5. PageRank rates Web pages based on a score. Links from higher-authority sites or high-traffic, well-established pages will appear higher on the search result list. The better the quality of the links to a site, the higher its PageRank score will be.

Analyzing the Reading, p. 349

1. This article was originally posted in *TechRepublic*, so one can assume that Matteson was writing for those who already had some understanding of computer technology. The purpose of the article is to educate the "techie" audience on the inner workings of Google Search — to let them "see what's behind the curtain." Matteson notes in paragraph 3 that people who "own or work in a business on which Google returns search results for the public" might be especially interested in the essay.

2. Matteson indicates the how-it-works process by the headings that read "Step 1: Exploring the Web," "Step 2: Organizing the data," and "Step 3: Presenting the data." He explains the process by which PageRank rates Web pages. In his discussion of PageRank, he focuses on a relationship between cause and effect as he presents examples from the *New York Times* and Evolven.

3. Student answers may vary. Matteson makes his explanation of the process interesting and understandable by inserting personal information, using nontechnical vocabulary as much as possible, including entertaining references such as the one to Minions, adding personal remarks, and breaking up the information into manageable sections with headings. Although Matteson wrote this essay for *TechRepublic*, he presented the information in such a way as to be easily understood by people who are not considered to be "techies."

4. Answers will vary. Based on the language and the style of writing, the tone of the essay seems informal and informative.

Evaluating the Reading, p. 349

1. Students may struggle with the two metaphors simply because of lack of familiarity with them. The metaphor of pulling back the curtain (from *The Wizard of Oz*) is effective in communicating Matteson's message about his purpose for writing the essay. In pulling back the curtain, Matteson explains the underlying structure of Google Search and how results are returned. The Coca-Cola recipe metaphor effectively delivers the message that some information about Google Search and the data it presents is kept confidential to keep people like "scammers and other scum and villainy" from rigging the system to benefit themselves or their businesses.

Although Coca-Cola releases some of the details of how it makes its soda, it withholds other information that would allow its competitors to re-create its product.

2. Answers will vary. Matteson does make his point well, but he may have gone to an extreme to do so. Perhaps this was an attempt at humor. Few people who would read this essay would have anything in common with Joe-Bob, but the use of this example contributes to the informality of the essay. The author has no intention of insulting anyone or any group. In fact, he offers his apology to Joe-Bob in paragraph 13.

3. Most of Matteson's Web sites are reputable sources of information. The one questionable source is Wikipedia, which is not known for its reliability.

4. Matteson does seem knowledgeable and experienced. He works in the field of technology and also has experience as a writer. Not only does he know his subject matter, but he is able to communicate his knowledge clearly and logically to others.

5. Answers will vary.

6. Answers will vary. Matteson says that his explanation of how PageRank works sounds simple, but actually there is a lot more going on behind the curtain. He includes a visual of a "simplified" algorithm that, even in its simplified form, looks very difficult. This visual is effective in illustrating Matteson's point about the limitation of his ability to simplify the explanation of how PageRank works.

Carole Wade, Carol Tavris, and Maryanne Garry, "The Nature of Stress," p. 351

(Lexile level: 1380L)

This textbook excerpt presents the process by which the body responds to stress and an explanation of the effects of external sources of stress. Although the content is technical, the authors try to simplify the process by presenting it in a series of three phases — the alarm phase, the resistance phase, and the exhaustion phase. They also personalize the technical information by using real-life examples that students can relate to. For example, the authors use taking a test that you have not studied for as an example of a threat that sets off the alarm phase. In the final paragraphs of the excerpt, the authors discuss the negative effects that stress can have on a person's body and his or her life. Less technical than the details of the process, this section contains information that students will immediately connect with and, most likely, be able to provide examples of from their own lives or the lives of people they know.

Even if the subject matter does not appeal to you or the level of difficulty concerns you, assign this reading to your students. They may find the content challenging, but a discussion of their challenges can yield an opportunity for you to review reading strategies that students can use to tackle challenging texts in other college courses.

Understanding and Reviewing the Reading, p. 355

1. Answers will vary. You might have students divide into groups to complete the brief summary of the text and then give students an opportunity to share and compare their summaries.

2. Answers will vary. Students may say that a fight-or-flight response to stress is exactly that—a response that causes someone to either take on a perceived threat or run away from it. According to the authors, "fight or flight" means that a person, when confronted with an immediate threat, will respond with intense emotion that comes from the release of adrenal hormones.

3. Elevated levels of cortisol, a hormone secreted by the adrenal glands when a body is under stress, cause animals and humans to seek out comfort foods.

4. Answers will vary. The sentence that comes the closest to being the thesis is found under the heading "Current Approaches": " . . . the very biological changes that are adaptive in the short run, because they permit the body to respond quickly to danger, can become hazardous in the long run." This section of the textbook is devoted to the physiological details of how the body responds to stress. Stress means all sorts of things to people, and although the body goes through the same process of responding to stressors through the set of physiological reactions, stress manifests itself differently in different people.

5. Answers will vary.

Analyzing the Reading, p. 355

1. Answers will vary. Have students share their proposed questions to see how easily they can be answered.

2. In explaining the general adaptation syndrome in paragraphs 3–6, the authors use process analysis. Again, in paragraph 9, the authors use process analysis as they explain how the hypothalamus sends messages to the endocrine glands. In paragraphs 10–12, the authors use cause and effect to explain the cumulative effects of external sources of stress.

3. Answers will vary. A whole-class discussion of this question will be beneficial to students. Since this is a textbook selection that is representative of the type of material students will be asked to read and comprehend in most of their college classes, a discussion of the challenges students faced with the text and the strategies they could use to help them more clearly understand the selection would yield valuable information for students and give you an idea of what reading strategies you might need to review.

Evaluating the Reading, p. 356

1. Most students should find the presentation sufficiently detailed. Some may find it too detailed and will need help organizing the information.

2. The voice is academic, technical, and matter-of-fact, although the authors do use examples that are relevant to students. It is important to note that in other sections of this textbook students might find a more informal approach, depending on the topic. Students may find this formal approach in science or business textbooks, for example, whereas in other subject area textbooks students may find a more friendly, personal voice.

3. Answers will vary.

4. Answers will vary. The diagram helps to organize the material and illustrate the process. In order to have all the information necessary to fully understand the process, students must also read the information that accompanies the visual and the information contained in paragraph 9.

CHAPTER 14: Comparison and Contrast: Showing Similarities and Differences, p. 359

This chapter should be of great interest to students because *comparison and contrast* is one of the most useful of all essay forms. Students who master this rhetorical mode will have mastered a skill that they can readily utilize in future college papers and on essay exams. You will probably want to devote several sessions to comparison and contrast, explaining that these essays must be organized carefully, point by point or subject by subject. To illustrate the organizational structure of comparison and contrast, it might be helpful to show students the graphic organizers on pages 364 and 365 for subject-by-subject and point-by-point arrangements, respectively. Careful planning and outlining are essential preliminary steps for this mode. It is very important to reiterate that the points of comparison must be significant and similar enough to warrant comparison. Analogies, although useful, must be accurate in order to be effective. You will want to emphasize that to create comparison-and-contrast essays that flow well, students must include clear transitional words and phrases (such as *similarly*, *in contrast*, and *on the one hand*) as signals or markers for the reader. Have students do revision exercises in order to perfect their ability to guide the reader through a series of points.

The essays in this chapter present a wide range of examples of the mode for students to analyze, evaluate, and model. In "We've Got the Dirt on Guy Brains" (p. 361), Dave Barry humorously argues that differences between men and women are genetically determined. In "Why Chinese Mothers Are Superior" (p. 395), Amy Chua takes on the more serious topic of parenting by contrasting strict Chinese principles with more forgiving Western parenting styles. The textbook selection "Dealing with Cultural Differences" (p. 403) compares and contrasts a variety of cultural practices, from hand-shaking to shopping.

The essays in this chapter offer examples of both subject-by-subject and point-by-point organization, the two main ways that comparison-and-contrast essays are typically presented. Focusing on organizational methods is especially important with this pattern of development. Students should be made conscious of the distinction between organizational strategies as they read and analyze the essays. Sara Rashkin uses a subject-by-subject comparison structure to evaluate the differences among tap water, purified water, and mineral and spring water in "What Kind of H2O Should You Drink? We Asked L.A.'s Only Water Sommelier" (p. 381). In "Sex, Lies, and Conversation" (p. 388), Deborah Tannen uses a point-by-point organization to argue that although there are differences in how men and women perceive communication, the differences can be modified by learning.

Dave Barry, "We've Got the Dirt on Guy Brains," p. 361

(Lexile level: 1290L)

In this essay reprinted from his well-known weekly humor column, humorist Dave Barry lays claim to a scientific breakthrough called "Male Genetic Dirt Blindness" (para. 4). Using pseudoscientific jargon to compare and contrast male and female perceptions of dirt, he playfully contends that men's reluctance to do housework or communicate with their partners at home may be genetic rather than learned. You might like to use this essay to initiate a discussion of humor and how it works in this instance. Another discussion topic could be generalizations or stereotypes, especially age-old gender stereotypes such as the one Barry treats. You might invite students to provide counterexamples from their own store of anecdotal evidence to the contrary or to explore the idea that Barry's thesis is dated, not applicable to younger generations now in college. Students might also write an in-class essay that provides a similarly humorous pseudo-theory, but one that takes the woman's point of view.

Heather Gianakos, "Border Bites," p. 374

(Student Essay)

In this student essay, Heather Gianakos skillfully compares Mexican and southwestern cuisines in a point-by-point style, focusing on key points such as uses of corn, chicken, beef, and pork. You might want to assign students to write in-class essays of their own about a particular cuisine, using this essay as a model. You might also review Gianakos's "Works Cited" list in class in order to familiarize students with the more extensive research they will do later in the term. Have them discuss which quotes most impress them and how they would evaluate the sources Gianakos cites.

Responding to Gianakos's Essay, p. 376

1. Gianakos's purpose in writing is to compare and contrast Mexican and southwestern cooking. She supports her thesis effectively by detailing the

"subtle, flavorful differences between the foods featured in Mexican and southwestern cuisine" (para. 1) through a comparison of the origins of ingredient use and the uses of corn, chicken, beef, and pork.

2. Within her point-by-point organization, Gianakos organizes her information chronologically. She explains the origins of ingredient use and then provides the historical background of each ingredient — the key points of comparison and contrast in her essay.

3. Generally, the author effectively presents details to support each point of comparison. For example, she effectively details how southwestern cooking often grew out of difficult conditions such as having to pack foods for travel and cook them over open fires on the range (2), whereas Mexican cuisine developed in an environment where there were plenty of fresh ingredients. To describe the differences in cooking styles and tastes, Gianakos relies heavily on sensory details of sight, smell, and taste: "Fried chicken rolled in flour and dunked into sizzling oil or fat" (4) and "the richly seasoned, corn- and tomato-heavy style of Mexican food" (7).

4. Gianakos's use of sources contributes to her essay by giving it more authority.

Sara Rashkin, "What Kind of H$_2$O Should You Drink? We Asked L.A.'s Only Water Sommelier," p. 381

(Lexile level: 1360L)

This reading selection is a very straightforward essay of comparison and contrast of four different types of drinking water. The writer opens by introducing a water expert: L.A.'s only water sommelier, Martin Riese. Riese inserts his humor into the introduction by poking fun at L.A. residents and their attitude toward water. Knowing that this essay was first published in *L.A. Weekly*, a local tabloid, makes it easy to determine the audience and also to understand how Riese has the right to speak sarcastically about people in L.A. After the introductory material, Rashkin uses subject-by-subject organization to discuss the similarities and differences in the types of drinking water, beginning with L.A. tap water, followed by purified water, and ending with spring water and mineral water. At the conclusion of her essay, Rashkin uses Riese's expertise to discuss the environmental impact of bottles, a point of comparison for all types of water except tap water.

Students should be able to see clearly that this is a logically organized and balanced presentation. Rashkin does not make a claim of her own about the merits of the four types of drinking water, but relies heavily on the opinions of the water "expert," Martin Riese.

Understanding and Reviewing the Reading, p. 384

1. Rashkin states her thesis in the third paragraph: " . . . it's important to educate people about the differences in water types and to bring an increased sense of value to water."

2. All four can be compared on the basis of taste, source of origin, health risks and/or benefits, and environmental implications.

3. Answers will vary. Students will complete a table that contains the following information:

Strengths of Tap Water	Strengths of Purified Water	Strengths of Spring and Mineral Water
1. improved taste	1. good for use in machines	1. taste
2. least expensive		2. minimal processing
3. most eco-friendly		3. variety

4. *Infused* (4): To *infuse* is to put in, add, or fill. Rashkin reports that many bottled water brands are actually filtered tap water with minerals added.
   Stringent (5): Strict or severe. Most municipal water departments have very strict water-quality regulations.
   Notoriously (6): Famously, typically for some bad quality. Chloramine is a chemical in L.A. tap water that is famously hard to filter out to meet water-quality standards.
   Leach (9): To drain or take away. Demineralized water is so aggressive that it can take metals away from pipes and minerals away from food.
   Imparting (13): Passing on, giving, or bestowing. When spring water is pumped up, the ground filters the water of contaminants, at the same time giving it minerals.

5. Rashkin mentions Iskilde from Denmark, Vichy Catalan from Spain, and Roi from Slovenia. Her point in mentioning these international waters is that there are various spring and mineral waters, and each variety has a different and unique taste. Riese, the water sommelier, believes that "many people no longer appreciate water varieties and their health properties."

6. The following graphic organizer is one possible answer.

Title	What Kind of H$_2$O Should You Drink? We Asked L.A.'s Only Water Sommelier

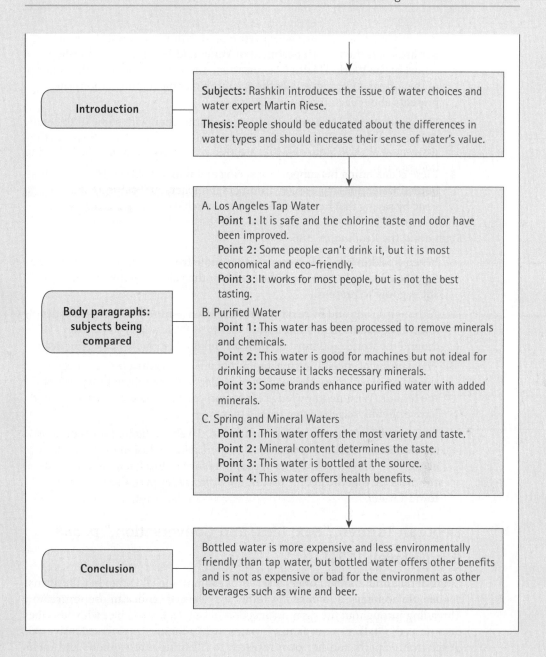

A. Los Angeles Tap Water

Introduction

Subjects: Rashkin introduces the issue of water choices and water expert Martin Riese.

Thesis: People should be educated about the differences in water types and should increase their sense of water's value.

Body paragraphs: subjects being compared

A. Los Angeles Tap Water
  Point 1: It is safe and the chlorine taste and odor have been improved.
  Point 2: Some people can't drink it, but it is most economical and eco-friendly.
  Point 3: It works for most people, but is not the best tasting.

B. Purified Water
  Point 1: This water has been processed to remove minerals and chemicals.
  Point 2: This water is good for machines but not ideal for drinking because it lacks necessary minerals.
  Point 3: Some brands enhance purified water with added minerals.

C. Spring and Mineral Waters
  Point 1: This water offers the most variety and taste.
  Point 2: Mineral content determines the taste.
  Point 3: This water is bottled at the source.
  Point 4: This water offers health benefits.

Conclusion

Bottled water is more expensive and less environmentally friendly than tap water, but bottled water offers other benefits and is not as expensive or bad for the environment as other beverages such as wine and beer.

Analyzing the Reading, p. 386

1. The purpose here is to inform. Rashkin is giving her readers the information they need to make their own decision about the type of water they will choose to drink.

2. Rashkin leans heavily on the expertise of Martin Riese, a water sommelier. She also cites the L.A. Department of Water and Power and a published report of the World Health Organization. These voices enhance the validity of the information (especially the scientific/technical information) she presents about each type of water.

3. The photo shows Martin Riese, the water sommelier, with some of the many different varieties of spring and mineral water available. This illustrates the many choices consumers are faced with.

4. Riese is defending his support for spring and mineral waters. He admits that bottled water does have an environmental impact, but he minimizes the issue by saying that beer and wine have a much worse impact than water.

Evaluating the Reading, p. 386

1. When Rashkin begins her essay with a quote from a certified water sommelier, she effectively convinces the reader of the validity of the information she is going to present.

2. Although spring and mineral waters have been around for a long time, people know little about them. Also, a wide variety of these waters come from around the world, and most of them are unknown to the average American.

3. The naming of specific spring and mineral waters contributes positively to the essay. It may spark the interest of readers and lead them to try one of the brands. With no knowledge of the names of the waters, a person would have difficulty selecting one from a menu.

4. Sara Rashkin wrote this article for the *L.A. Weekly*, a tabloid that contains articles of interest to "average" local readers. Her inclusion of the quote about " . . . only in L.A. . . ." is appropriate for her local audience. It sends the message that the people in L.A. are different, even in their attitudes toward water.

Deborah Tannen, "Sex, Lies, and Conversation," p. 388

(Lexile level: 1120L)

Linguist Deborah Tannen offers a series of examples to illustrate her thesis that gender differences in communication are learned and can be overcome. Threading throughout the essay an anecdote about a talkative man who describes his wife as the "talker in our family" (paras. 1, 22), Tanner employs extensive evidence from experts and her own research to illustrate that women's and men's expectations about communication differ. She concludes her essay optimistically, arguing that these different expectations and patterns can be transformed using the model of cross-cultural understanding.

Thematically, this essay can be linked with Barry's piece (p. 361) on gender differences revealed through evaluating dirt. You might assign students to write a comparison-and-contrast essay that utilizes the theories about learned versus innate cognition put forth by Tannen and (humorously) by Barry. Class discussion about learned versus genetic differences might also prove interesting; students could form two panels to support one or the other side of the nature-versus-nurture debate, using anecdotal or statistical evidence to reinforce their positions.

Understanding and Reviewing the Reading, p. 392

1. Tannen's thesis about gender communication is that "although American men tend to talk more than women in public situations, they often talk less at home. And this pattern is wreaking havoc with marriage" (para. 2).

2. The opening anecdote about the man at a women's group illustrates the irony that although men talk more in public, they often talk less at home (2).

3. Among the observable communication differences between young girls and boys are the following: girls use communication to "create and maintain friendships," whereas boys' friendships are based more on doing things together than on talking (9–10); when they do talk, girls face each other and look into each other's faces, whereas boys tend to sit side by side and look elsewhere, except for occasional glances at one another (12); and girls talk at length about a single subject, whereas boys change topics often (13).

4. In conversing, men tend not to face the person they are addressing, while women look into each other's faces directly. Women often perceive this difference in body language as a sign that men are not interested or are not listening.

5. Tannen uses point-by-point organization.

Analyzing the Reading, p. 392

1. Answers will vary.

2. The points of comparison that Tannen uses to support her thesis include children's development and peer interactions (7), body language (14), and conversational habits (15–20). The author focuses mostly on differences but does identify a few similarities. Students will likely agree that Tannen treats her subjects fairly and objectively.

3. Tannen's exploration of the causes of these communication differences strengthens the essay because it serves both to illustrate the differences and to illuminate her point, which is that because such differences arise through learned behavior, they can be changed.

4. The phrase "wreaking havoc" (2) brings to mind the idea of creating chaos.

5. Possible answers include the following.

Evidence	Purpose
Reference to political scientist Andrew Hacker (para. 3)	Gives legitimacy to the thesis and demonstrates that the thesis is not a new idea
Sociologist Catherine Kohler Riessman's observations from her book *Divorce Talk* (para. 3)	Illustrates the importance of the issue of communication between the sexes, and indicates that women identify "communication" as crucial to intimacy
The author's own research (para. 4)	Illustrates the different expectations about "conversation" that men and women have
American Psychologist article by Stanford University's Eleanor Maccoby (para. 7)	Identifies how children's development is shaped by differences in "peer interaction" in single-sex groups
Psychologist Bruce Dorval's videotapes (para. 12)	Show that physical alignment (face to face or at angles) is different at every age
The author's own research (paras. 13–16)	Shows how girls stay on one topic, whereas boys switch topics frequently
Linguist Lynette Hirschman's research (para. 17)	Indicates that women make more "listener noise," whereas men give silent attention
Reference to *Fighting for Life* by Walter Ong (para. 20)	Points out that men use "warlike, oppositional formats to do almost anything"

Evaluating the Reading, p. 392

1. Tannen likely chose point-by-point organization to emphasize the contrast between men and women in a clear and effective manner. Subject-by-subject organization could also be used to good effect, but the types of examples would probably need to be altered somewhat (for instance, more anecdotes) to support this type of organization.

2. Some examples of linguistic jargon used by Tannen are *peer interactions* (7), *cross-cultural communication* (8), *topical alignment* (13), *listener-noise* (17), and *participatory listenership* (18).

3. Answers will vary.

4. Answers will vary.

5. Answers will vary.

Amy Chua, "Why Chinese Mothers Are Superior," p. 395 (Lexile level: 1070L)

In this essay, Chua contrasts her own parenting techniques and those of other Chinese mothers with the parenting techniques of Westerners. From the opening paragraph, it is clear that Chua makes demands on her daughters that few Western parents would even consider, and she goes on in the rest of the essay to describe Chinese parenting in even more rigorous terms. Structurally, this is a very good model of point-by-point organization — up until the lengthy narrative section that serves to lead into the conclusion, Chua clearly focuses on a series of specific matters on which Chinese and Western parents differ in their approach to parenting. Paragraph 2 contrasts the time children are required to practice piano, paragraph 3 offers a statistical contrast, paragraphs 5–9 contrast how Chinese and Western parents talk to and encourage their children, paragraphs 11–14 focus on academic expectations, paragraphs 15–16 contrast what Chinese and Western parents believe their children owe them, paragraph 17 considers beliefs about children's autonomy, and the final two paragraphs summarize these contrasts succinctly.

This essay may seem a bit long, but it is easy to read. A good portion of it is a dramatically narrated account of a particularly intense — one might even say brutal — battle Chua waged with her younger daughter over mastering a piano piece the daughter was having trouble with. Many students will likely be appalled by this story, despite its ostensibly happy outcome, as they will be by many of the things Chua writes about herself as a parent (calling a daughter "garbage," for example). If you have many Asian students, you might ask whether this is a fair portrait of parenting in their culture — whether Chua represents the mainstream or more of an extreme. This stark contrast of parenting techniques is likely to spur some strong opinions, as it did when it was originally published. Access the essay online and click on "Comments."

Understanding and Reviewing the Reading, p. 400

1. Chua states her thesis at the beginning of paragraph 3: there are "marked and quantifiable differences between Chinese and Westerners when it comes to parenting." As her title suggests, Chua concludes that Chinese parenting is better.

2. Chua's point here is that one difference between Western and Chinese parents is that Chinese parents emphasize diligent hard work and practice, even if their children resist, an idea she illustrates in the narrative at the end of the essay about forcing her younger daughter to master a difficult piano piece.

3. Here, Chua contrasts how Chinese and Western parents criticize their children — Chinese parents are direct, even brutally blunt ("garbage," "fatty"), a tactic most Western parents avoid. Yet the example shows that the Western father's faint praise of his daughter was perceived by her as a more scathing criticism.

4. Western parents worry more about their children's self-esteem, while Chinese parents worry more about increasing their personal achievement; Western parents don't expect their children to owe them anything, while Chinese parents believe their sacrifices make their children completely indebted to them; and much more than Western parents, Chinese parents control their children's lives, allowing them little in terms of individual decision-making.

5. In addition to comparison and contrast, Chua uses illustration to give examples of child-rearing differences and narration to relay personal stories.

Analyzing the Reading, p. 401

1. Answers may vary, but Chua seems to be directing her remarks to those unfamiliar with her style of parenting. At the same time, of course, she is reinforcing the efficacy of this style of parenting to those who already practice it.

2. Chua certainly expects Western parents to be surprised by this list — and so to want to read on.

3. The statistics support Chua's opening point that there are major differences between Chinese and Western parenting techniques.

4. Chua's implicit argument is that Chinese parenting techniques result in more successful, even better-adjusted, children. Western parents are more likely to be ultimately "disappointed about how their kids turned out."

5. For one thing, it's a dramatic story. For another, it shows, at least from Chua's perspective, the benefits of "coercion" when it comes to dealing with children and so supports her implied thesis.

6. The photograph provides additional support for Chua's authority as a parent from a more objective standpoint than her own words. Chua stands front and center, arms folded in a position of power and toughness and a confident smile of accomplishment on her face. Her daughters are in the background at their respective instruments, both posed very properly and rigidly. They therefore appear as children obedient to their strict mother.

Evaluating the Reading, p. 401

1. Most students are likely to think the opening establishes an interesting context for reading the essay.

2. Answers will vary. Chua presents most Western parents as more permissive and less overtly judgmental of their children than Chinese parents.

3. It's interesting to learn so far into the essay that Chua is married to a Westerner who doesn't really share her views. Whether this strengthens her case is a matter for debate. Some students may feel that his views should be taken more into account in terms of how their daughters are raised.

4. Answers will vary.

Carole Wade and Carol Tavris, "Dealing with Cultural Differences," p. 403

(Lexile level: 1140L)

Unlike the other essays in the chapter, this excerpt from a psychology textbook doesn't compare and contrast two subjects. Rather, it uses contrast to show how cultural differences result in misunderstandings between a variety of subjects — a French salesman and his American manager (paras. 1–2), people in hand-shaking and non-hand-shaking cultures (3), Middle Eastern and Western shoppers (4), Iranians practicing *taarof* and Americans used to "straight talking" (5). The authors' point is that in an increasingly multicultural world, it is important to use critical-thinking skills in dealing with others in order not to give or take offense because of cultural differences about what is acceptable or polite behavior.

As an exercise, divide students into groups and have each group compose three multiple-choice questions that might be posed on a quiz for this selection. Then have groups trade question sets and see how well they do with the quiz. Finally, have each group evaluate the effectiveness of the quiz as a teaching and learning tool.

Understanding and Reviewing the Reading, p. 405

1. When the American manager told the French salesman to step up his sales, the French salesman quit because he believed that customer relationships took time to establish — maybe even years — and the American manager wanted instant results.

2. The writers' main point is that people shouldn't jump to conclusions about the behavior of those from other cultures because different rules may be operating.

3. In paragraph 3, the writers define *taarof*, the practice of "deliberate insincerity."

4. The authors mean that, to learn the unspoken rules of a culture, outsiders must be keen observers of how people within the culture interact with each other in both formal and informal settings. They also must listen to the tone and volume of speech being used and observe facial expressions. By thinking critically about the actions, attitudes, behaviors, etc., of people from another culture, we can more accurately interpret their behavior.

Analyzing the Reading, p. 405

1. This is a comparison focusing not just on two subjects, but on several different subjects — French and American business attitudes, for example, and Iranian and English speakers' attitudes toward "straight talking." It is made up of individual paragraphs of comparison and contrast rather than organized as an essay of comparison and contrast.

2. The opening example demonstrates specifically how corporate success in a global economy requires cultural sensitivity.

3. Narration is used to relay stories, illustration is used to give examples, description is used to provide details about people and attitudes from different cultures, and definition is used to provide information about various unfamiliar terms.

4. The title of the textbook section indicates that once people have a general understanding of psychology, they can put it into practice in their everyday interactions with others. This knowledge can equip them to better deal with others — in this particular case, people from other cultures.

Evaluating the Reading, p. 405

1. Answers will vary.

2. Again, answers will vary, but the details and examples seem sufficient for a sidebar discussion.

3. The imaginary quotations seem realistic enough to serve the intended purpose of showing how cultural differences can result in miscommunication.

CHAPTER 15: Classification and Division: Explaining Categories and Parts, p. 409

You can easily explain classification and division to students if you define *classification* as grouping things into categories and *division* (closely related to process analysis, Chapter 13) as breaking a single item into parts. Both modes describe types or parts. Each uses only one principle of classification or division, with parts that include all the members of the group. Maris Vasquez's annotated student essay, "A Profile of Facebook Users" (p. 423), will illustrate clearly to students how to craft a thesis statement that includes a "principle of classification" and use concrete examples to increase the reader's understanding of an interesting, culturally relevant topic.

In the model essay, Joshua Fruhlinger's "Online Dating — Five Things to Avoid" (p. 411), students can see a categorization of an increasingly common practice, online dating, presented as a how-to guide. Similarly examining the theme of romance, Mindy Kaling's humorous piece "Types of Women in Romantic Comedies Who Are Not Real" (p. 431) analyzes female characters in "chick flicks" by classifying them in categories ranging from "The Klutz" and "The Sassy Best Friend" to "The Woman Who Is Obsessed with Her Career and Is No Fun at All." Kaling offers contemporary examples of actors and actresses who play these roles, and she finds all of the characters as implausible as science fiction creatures. David Bodanis's "A Brush with Reality: Surprises in the Tube" (p. 438) is a division essay that breaks down an ordinary, everyday commodity — toothpaste — into its various ingredients, describing each in great detail in order to convince readers that toothpaste is not all that it is cracked up to be. The textbook excerpt in this chapter from April Lynch, Barry Elmore, and Jerome Kotecki, "Addiction" (p. 443), classifies types of addictions in order to inform students about the characteristics of common behavioral addictions.

Joshua Fruhlinger, "Online Dating—Five Things to Avoid," p. 411

(Lexile level: 1050L)

This is an excellent beginning model for classification and division. The title and introduction clearly establish interest in the subject, and the classification structure is sound and presented in a way that is easy to follow, with headings that name the five categories in quite specific terms. One especially interesting and useful aspect of the essay is that Fruhlinger doesn't just sort dishonest and/or predatory online daters and their profiles into categories; he offers specific advice for recognizing and avoiding them as well — each part ends with a section headed "How to Avoid Them." He also provides interesting statistics (para. 5), illustrative examples (6, 9, 12, and 21–22), and a good sense of why online dating is popular.

Anyone experienced with online dating—whether personally or through friends—knows that the first two categories are very common, which is likely why Fruhlinger leads off with them. Ask students what they see as his plan in sequencing the five categories he writes about. Does it seem to be an effective sequence?

Maris Vasquez, "A Profile of Facebook Users," p. 423

(Student Essay)

The subject of this very nicely developed student essay will likely appeal to students. It's a good model because the transitions between the categories — the topic sentences of the body paragraphs — are clear and name each of the categories in an interesting way, according to the writer's own observations rather than in some rote fashion. Furthermore, each category is described in sufficient detail to make the type of Facebook user come to life for readers.

Encourage students to see the originality of this essay. The writer has used her imagination to come up with categories readers would not necessarily have thought of before. Instead of stating the obvious, she provides an opportunity for readers to see Facebook users in a new light. Encourage students to engage as imaginatively with the subjects of their own essays.

Responding to Vasquez's essay, p. 426

1. Answers will vary.
2. The categories seem equally well developed.
3. The writer uses transitions, such as "the opposite of," "completely different," and "similar to," to help distinguish and delineate the categories.
4. Answers may vary, but this admission doesn't seem to pose a serious problem.

Mindy Kaling, "Types of Women in Romantic Comedies Who Are Not Real," p. 431

(Lexile level: 1100L)

This is another good model of classification and division — and quite entertaining, to boot. As in Frulinger's essay, the title and introduction spark interest in the subject, and the classification structure is clearly represented by headings that identify the categories both accurately and humorously. Admitting from the start that the world of romantic movie comedies is completely implausible — the films are "a subgenre of sci-fi" occurring in an alternative universe — and that saying one likes them suggests "mild stupidity," Kaling is nonetheless a fan and seems to have great fun here categorizing the types of women who populate these films. She describes "the Klutz" as a "drunk buffalo who has never been part of human society" though the actress who plays her has to be "perfect-looking." The "ethereal weirdo" can be seen "in movies, but nowhere else"; in real life people would "cross the street to avoid her," but she fulfills a male fantasy that even the most boring guy deserves someone to perk up his life. "The woman who is obsessed with her career and is no fun at all" must have her "hair pulled back in a severe, tight bun." The rest of the categories are presented in equally specific and amusing detail — including "the sassy best friend" who "runs a chic dildo store in the West Village" and the skinny actress, whose ribs are visible through her dress, playing a "cheesecake-loving cow."

Ask students to point out examples of their own of the kinds of descriptive language Kaling uses that appeal to their sense of humor. Kaling says in her introduction that she so enjoys watching people fall in love in movies that she can suspend her disbelief in the artificiality of the stories. Is suspending disbelief what most movies require, in students' view?

Understanding and Reviewing the Reading, p. 434

1. Kaling states her thesis in paragraph 4: The women in romantic comedies don't exist in real life, and following are some examples.

2. The principle of classification, what the categories have in common, is that they are all female characters in the same movie genre, romantic comedies; yet they can all be distinguished from one another.

3. The categories can be summarized as follows: the beautiful actress whose role is to be clumsy, the oddball romantic, the career-obsessed woman, the youngish actress playing the mother of someone nearly her own age, the sassy best friend, the skinny actress whose character eats all the time, and the gallery owner. This last one is the most specific, and Kaling also presents her male counterpart, which she doesn't do with the other categories.

4. Kaling uses details related to physical appearance, personal style, dialogue, and character actions — particularly ones that are abnormal. In some instances, she refers to details about the character's role in the movie plot, such as when the uptight career woman must "eat a hot dog in a libidinous way" (9).

5. *Sheepish* (2): Embarrassed, meek, or bashful. Kaling feels slightly embarrassed to be writing about romantic comedies since they have such a poor reputation.

    Degraded (2): Reduced in quality, reputation, estimation, etc. Romantic comedies have become so formulaic and silly that their reputation and quality have suffered.

    Contrived (3): Having an unnatural, forced, or artificial quality. The situations in romantic comedies are so unbelievable that they are clearly unrealistic.

    Heightened (3): Enhanced, intensified, augmented. The world of romantic comedies is enhanced to make the implausible situations happen; likewise, the emotion is intensified.

    Palatable (5): Acceptable or agreeable to one's taste. The female lead in a romantic comedy must still be attractive enough, devoid of any grievous flaws; therefore, the klutzy beauty is an acceptably flawed character.

    Complicit (14): Involved or participating, especially in a wrongful act. The skinny/gluttonous/disgusting character's family and friends all participate in perpetuating the lie that she is disgusting.

    Posh (16): Luxurious, fashionable, elegant. The art gallery job is very comfortable, sophisticated, and fashionable.

6. The following graphic organizer is a possible answer.

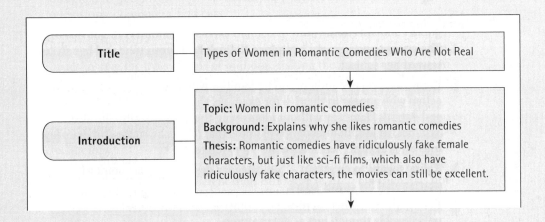

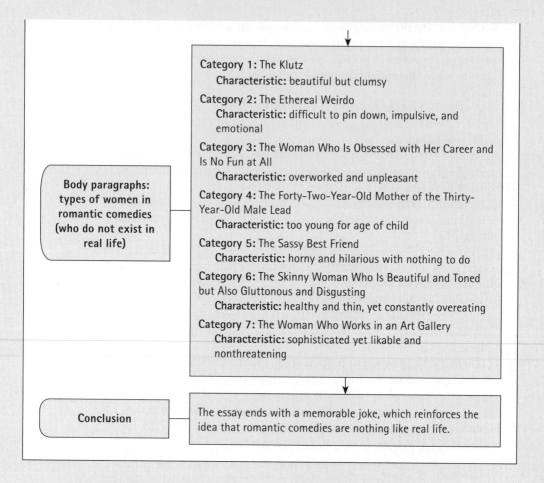

Category 1: The Klutz
  Characteristic: beautiful but clumsy

Category 2: The Ethereal Weirdo
  Characteristic: difficult to pin down, impulsive, and emotional

Category 3: The Woman Who Is Obsessed with Her Career and Is No Fun at All
  Characteristic: overworked and unpleasant

Category 4: The Forty-Two-Year-Old Mother of the Thirty-Year-Old Male Lead
  Characteristic: too young for age of child

Category 5: The Sassy Best Friend
  Characteristic: horny and hilarious with nothing to do

Category 6: The Skinny Woman Who Is Beautiful and Toned but Also Gluttonous and Disgusting
  Characteristic: healthy and thin, yet constantly overeating

Category 7: The Woman Who Works in an Art Gallery
  Characteristic: sophisticated yet likable and nonthreatening

Body paragraphs: types of women in romantic comedies (who do not exist in real life)

Conclusion

The essay ends with a memorable joke, which reinforces the idea that romantic comedies are nothing like real life.

Analyzing the Reading, p. 436

1. The opening paragraphs introduce Kaling's humorous tone and her attitude toward her subject.

2. Kaling expects her audience to be familiar with romantic comedies and the actors who appear in them — for example, she mentions Katherine Heigl and Patrick Dempsey without identifying them specifically. She also assumes, in jest, that readers will know that the really successful male love interest is always ("say it with me") an architect.

3. Kaling means to entertain — her category descriptions are somewhat exaggerated for comic effect.

4. Kaling likens women in romantic comedies to space monsters — equally unbelievable though just as entertaining.

5. The questions serve to point out how far-fetched the characters and their situations are.

Evaluating the Reading, p. 436

1. Most readers familiar with romantic comedies should find the essay entertaining.
2. The self-deprecation here makes Kaling come off as sympathetic and likable.
3. Answers will vary.
4. Answers will vary.

David Bodanis, "A Brush with Reality: Surprises in the Tube," p. 438

(Lexile level: 1270L)

David Bodanis scrutinizes the ingredients that go into toothpaste. He uses vivid details and some exaggeration to make his point that toothpaste is neither especially good for users nor worth the price. The section "Writing about the Reading" (p. 442) will be especially helpful to students because it provides writing assignments related to marketing techniques and their effect on consumers. Some discussion about an industry that does not take the health of consumers into account might prove interesting. Students might research or provide more anecdotal evidence about food products such as fast food and how they are regulated by the U.S.D.A.

Understanding and Reviewing the Reading, p. 440

1. The ingredients in toothpaste are water, chalk, titanium dioxide, glycerine glycol, seaweed, paraffin oil, detergent, peppermint oil, formaldehyde, and fluoride.
2. The author includes information about the origins of chalk ("the crushed remains of long-dead ocean creatures," para. 3) because it highlights how revolting this ingredient truly is.
3. The ingredient that inhibits the growth of bacteria is formaldehyde (11).
4. As a final thought on the subject, the author offers the idea that "plain water will often do as good a job" (12). The implication is that the author thinks that toothpaste is unnecessary.

Analyzing the Reading, p. 440

1. Students may or may not find the author's purpose clear initially, but it should be fairly obvious by the conclusion when the author says water often does as good a job as toothpaste (12).
2. The division of the ingredients in toothpaste is fairly complete. Bodanis's ingredients are clearly defined, and none overlap.

3. Answers will vary. Students will likely choose details that explain the more surprising ingredients, such as titanium dioxide, "the stuff bobbing around in white wall paint to make it come out white" (6) or glycerine glycol, "related to the most common car antifreeze ingredient" (8).

4. Bodanis's conclusion clearly expresses his negative opinion of toothpaste.

5. The phrase "reassuring white" in paragraph 6 suggests that optical whitening dye serves no other purpose than to make one's teeth extra white in order to give the appearance of cleanliness.

Evaluating the Reading, p. 441

1. The conclusion the author draws about water being the most plentiful ingredient in toothpaste is that it costs very little, allowing large profits on each tube sold. Bodanis also draws the conclusion that, because water often does just as good a job on one's teeth, people should save money and use water to brush their teeth.

2. Bodanis's conclusion about consumers of toothpaste (paras. 6, 7, 10) is that they are concerned more about appearances (for instance, the whiteness of their teeth and the look of their toothpaste) than knowing the facts behind the ingredients.

3. Based on his use of details such as that toothpaste is sold for "a neat and accountant-pleasing $2 per pound" (2) and that it contains inedible ingredients like glycerine glycol and formaldehyde, Bodanis seems to be drawing the conclusion that toothpaste is a marketing scam.

4. Answers will vary.

5. By "finicky distaste" and "host of other goodies" (7), the author suggests that manufacturers engineer an image of toothpaste contrasting with a reality that is neither appetizing nor healthy.

6. The following graphic organizer is one possible answer.

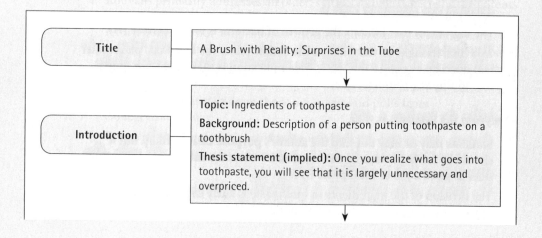

Title — A Brush with Reality: Surprises in the Tube

Introduction —
Topic: Ingredients of toothpaste

Background: Description of a person putting toothpaste on a toothbrush

Thesis statement (implied): Once you realize what goes into toothpaste, you will see that it is largely unnecessary and overpriced.

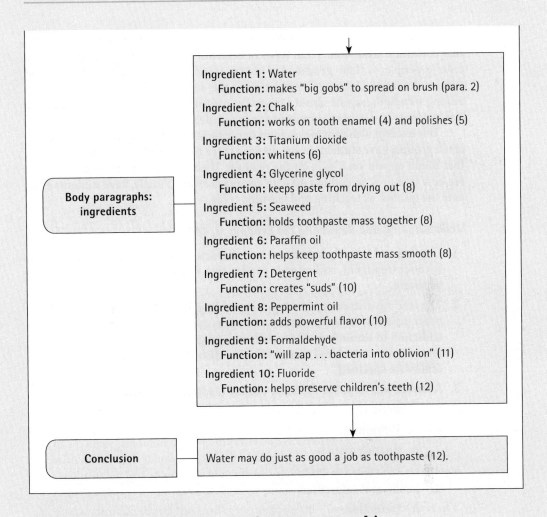

April Lynch, Barry Elmore, and Jerome Kotecki, "Addiction," p. 443

(Lexile level: 1290L)

This excerpt from a health textbook identifies the characteristics of addiction and discusses behavioral addictions, including pathological gambling, hypersexual disorder, and other potential behavioral addictions such as compulsive spending and addiction to technology. Each type of behavioral addiction is explained in detail, and the authors distinguish between true psychiatric disorders and those that are "not otherwise specified." They provide facts, statistics, and examples for each type of behavioral addiction, as well as characteristic traits (or "telltale signs"). The authors also discuss the negative consequences associated with each type of addiction and the treatment options used to address specific addictive behaviors.

Ask students to discuss the difference between normal behaviors and those that constitute addiction. What types of behavioral addictions are most common among people of their gender, age group, status, and so forth? In the section "Other Potential Behavioral Addictions," the authors acknowledge the debate among psychotherapists about assigning "disorder status" to certain behaviors. Ask students to discuss the reasons for such a debate.

This excerpt also provides a good opportunity for drafting model quizzes. In small groups, have students come up with three to five multiple-choice questions that might appear on a quiz on the reading. Then have groups swap quizzes and see how well they do coming up with correct answers. Finally, have students evaluate the quizzes as teaching and learning tools.

Understanding and Reviewing the Reading, p. 447

1. Craving and loss of pleasure are two characteristics; also, the text notes that, without treatment, addiction is progressive, becoming more frequent and/or severe.

2. The reading discusses pathological gambling, hypersexual disorder, and other potential behavior disorders such as compulsive spending and addiction to technology. Only pathological gambling and hypersexual disorder are considered true psychiatric disorders; the others are "not otherwise specified."

3. Answers will vary. See the basic outline below as an example.

    I.   Addiction

        A. Definition

        B. Characteristics

        C. Effects/consequence

    II. Behavioral Addictions

        A. Definition

        B. Types

            1. Pathological gambling

            2. Hypersexual disorder

            3. Other potential behavioral addictions

                a. Compulsive spending

                b. Addiction to technology

4. The American Society of Addiction Medicine defines *addiction* as a chronic disease of brain reward, motivation, memory, and related circuitry. *Behavioral addiction* is defined as a form of addiction involving a compulsion to engage in an activity rather than a compulsion to use a substance.

Analyzing the Reading, p. 448

1. The authors introduce the subject of addiction by first describing normal behaviors that provide short-term pleasure while potentially causing long-term trouble. They do this to differentiate these normal behaviors from the problematic behaviors that constitute addiction.

2. The authors primarily use definition in paragraphs 2–5 to define *addiction* and in pararaph 6 to define *behavioral addiction*. They use classification to cover the types of behavioral addictions in paragraphs 7–18.

3. The first photograph, of a young woman lighting a marijuana cigarette, illustrates the point that experimenting with drugs at an early age makes one more likely to become addicted later in life. The photograph of three young women looking at their phones illustrates the potential problem of addiction to technology.

4. Answers will vary. This question is addressed in various ways in paragraphs 3, 4, 5, 8, 9, 10, 11, 13, 16, 17, and 18.

5. This material seems to be intended for a broader, more general audience of students across all majors rather than those specifically in health care studies. The language is not overly specialized or technical, and the material is at a level of difficulty that suggests a non-science-oriented audience.

6. Answers will vary. A quiz might include questions on the definition and characteristics of addiction, the treatments for addiction, the types of behavioral addictions, statistics about pathological gambling and traits or signs indicating pathological gambling, the characteristics of hypersexual disorder, and facts and statistics about compulsive spending and addiction to technology.

Evaluating the Reading, p. 448

1. The authors use facts, statistics, definitions, causes/effects, examples, and expert opinions.

2. Answers will vary but may include the idea that the women do not seem to be showing an addiction; they are laughing and healthy looking and do not exhibit evidence of relationship problems or any of the other difficulties associated with addiction in the reading.

3. The authors could have included information about addiction to substances such as drugs, alcohol, tobacco, and perhaps food or sugar; they do cover drug addictions elsewhere in the chapter.

4. The headings divided the material into clear and meaningful sections; the marginal definitions emphasized/highlighted the meaning of *addiction* and *behavioral addiction* by restating and summarizing the text definitions.

5. Answers will vary, but could include connections to courses such as biology, psychology, sociology, and criminal justice.

CHAPTER 16: Definition: Explaining What You Mean, p. 451

The basic characteristic of a *definition* will be relatively easy for students to grasp. Just as a dictionary entry explains a term, a definition essay explains something, albeit in a longer, extended form. Often, in personal essays or academic papers, a standard dictionary-style definition will serve as a preliminary step or lead-in to a longer exposition on a particular topic. These kinds of expositions are called "extended definitions."

For example, in the first essay (p. 453), Roland Kelts uses definition as a rhetorical mode as he describes the "satori generation" as a new breed of young people who have outdone the "tricksters of advertising" by living an "enlightened" life free from material desires, focused on self-awareness and finding essential truths. In "Woman of Many Talents" (p. 465), student writer Sarah Frey opens her essay with a clear description and definition of *FLOTUS*, an acronym used to refer to the First Lady of the United States. By reviewing the annotations included with these two essays, you can highlight for students the key characteristics of definition essays.

The readings in this chapter will expose students to a wide variety of styles and illustrate the effectiveness of definition in writing. Lars Eighner, in "On Dumpster Diving" (p. 472), uses definition to describe what makes someone a scavenger. In "Gullible Travels" (p. 478), Bethe Dufresne describes the new practice of "reality tourism" or "poverty tourism," contrasting supporting definitions of these increasingly popular tours in poor urban areas with her own negative definition of "slum tourism."

Explain to students that an extended definition may depart from a standard, dictionary definition. It can also be used to correct popular misconceptions. For example, Stefany Anne Golberg challenges the standard, accepted definition of *deafness* as a disability by describing it as an ethnicity in her essay "Can You See Me Now? Deaf America" (p. 484). Finally, in the textbook selection "The Cult of Celebrity" (p. 490), the authors define the term *celebrity* and explain how publicists and the media work to create celebrities.

Roland Kelts, "The Satori Generation," p. 453

(Lexile level: 1050L)

Kelts opens this extended definition of the satori generation by using negation: He introduces us to satori youths by describing what they *don't* want (cars, brand-name clothes, etc.). In the second paragraph, he places the term being defined — the *satori sedai* — in the context of Japan. He provides background details and hints at why the term is worth reading about: "They're freaking their elders out." His example from a talk show colorfully illustrates the term before he goes on to address critics. In addition to providing commentary from a novelist, a social critic and researcher, and a professor, Kelts lets readers hear from members of the satori generation. These quotes from different sources help define the satori youth. Most of the details in the selection are designed to let readers decide how to answer the question (para. 5) "Is this enlightened, or resigned? Or both?"

Kelts quotes researcher Mariko Fujiwara, who explains the idea that the satori youth have "outdone the tricksters of advertising" (paras. 7–8). At this point, the definition becomes broader and more global, moving from Japan to America and Europe. Kelts expands the satori concept by applying it to a new generation around the world. Additional background information (para. 10) explores how the satori generation was shaped by and responded to historical events. Kelts concludes by leaving readers with the impression that the world can benefit from what the satori generation represents.

Students should identify and highlight distinguishing characteristics as they read. After they read the essay, ask them to define "satori generation" in their own words. What details and distinguishing characteristics do they see as most important to the definition of this term?

Sarah Frey, "Woman of Many Talents" p. 465

(Student Essay)

This student essay focuses on defining the acronym *FLOTUS*, which stands for First Lady of the United States. A new term added to the dictionary, *FLOTUS* was created as a companion to *POTUS*, the acronym for President of the United States. The writer addresses the ever-changing roles of the First Lady and focuses on three defining characteristics: hostess, politician, and volunteer. By supporting the defining characteristics with specific examples from history, the writer presents a brief overview of the evolution of the role from Martha Washington to Michelle Obama. This definition is clear and very easy to read.

Responding to Frey's Essay, p. 467

1. Answers will vary.
2. Answers will vary, but students may mention Eleanor Roosevelt's political activism, Dolly Madison's image as an average citizen and a queen, and Michelle Obama's stand on eliminating childhood obesity.
3. Answers will vary.
4. Answers will vary, but students may highlight "In addition to" (para. 3), "Perhaps the most important characteristic" (4), and "As of late" (5).
5. The concluding paragraph restates the thesis, summarizes the main points, and ends with a thought-provoking statement about the future of the title.

Lars Eighner, "On Dumpster Diving," p. 472
(Lexile level: 1100L)

Lars Eighner, a sometimes homeless fiction and essay writer, describes in exquisite detail the stages of becoming a scavenger, breaking down the process of scavenging in vivid language, as if he needed to teach his readers how to do it themselves. Using first-person narration and an informative tone, Eighner quickly makes his intelligence and radical worldview clear, but his reasons for remaining homeless are mysterious. Students may find it difficult to understand why someone so obviously talented and educated would be homeless, but they will be fascinated by the world he shows. You might like to preface the class discussion with some information about homelessness, in particular contributing factors such as the "deinstitutionalization" of the mentally ill in the United States.

Understanding and Reviewing the Reading, p. 475

1. According to the author, the stages people go through before becoming "professional" dumpster divers are feeling shame and self-loathing (para. 14), coming to the realization that people throw away "a lot of perfectly good stuff" (16), trying to acquire everything one comes across (19), and restricting oneself to acquiring only those things with immediate utility (19).

2. The principal risk associated with dumpster diving is "dysentery" (12).

3. Eighner has learned two lessons from dumpster diving: to take only what he can use and to acknowledge "the transience of material being" — that is, to remember that ideas are longer-lived than material objects.

4. The attitude the author shares with the wealthy is that there is always plenty more where something comes from, so it's unnecessary to collect "gaudy bauble[s]" (24).

5. According to Eighner, the difference between *scavenging* and *foraging* is that scavenging is picking over other people's refuse while foraging is specifically a matter of gathering things from nature like nuts and berries.

6. *Niche* (3): This term refers to a position or role in which someone fits particularly well. Eighner believes that being a scavenger is a role for which he is well suited.
   Bohemian (5): This term commonly refers to a wanderer or vagabond or a person living in a manner that is considered unconventional by society. In the essay, Eighner implies that some people who live conventional lives also brag about finding good things in the trash.
   Dilettanti (5): This term refers to people who dabble or have a superficial interest in something, usually art. The people who "dumpster dive" but don't eat the findings have only a superficial, not a real, participation in scavenging.
   Phobic (7): Having an exaggerated and often unexplainable fear. Only the most fearful people would not eat food from a can retrieved from the trash.

Pristine (16): Pure, unpolluted, perfect. The ice cream a scavenger might find that is still frozen and unspoiled is in pristine condition.

Dissipate (17): To scatter or spread thinly. "Dumpster shyness" scatters or weakens with experience.

Disparage (17): To look down upon, either in speech or in thought. Those who dismiss or look down upon the Dumpster diver are foolish.

8. The following graphic organizer is one possible answer.

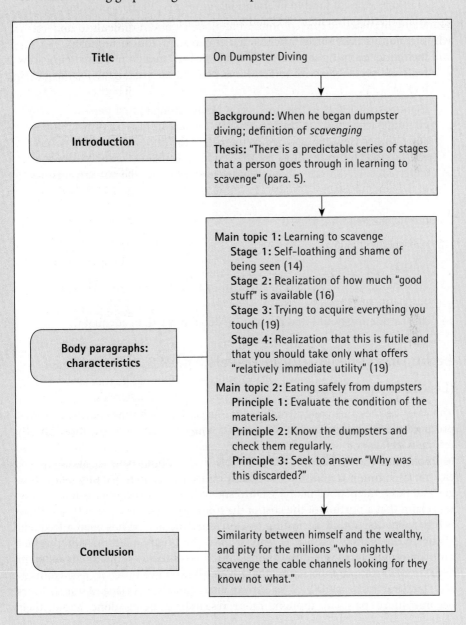

| Title | On Dumpster Diving |

| Introduction | **Background:** When he began dumpster diving; definition of *scavenging*
Thesis: "There is a predictable series of stages that a person goes through in learning to scavenge" (para. 5). |

| Body paragraphs: characteristics | **Main topic 1:** Learning to scavenge
　Stage 1: Self-loathing and shame of being seen (14)
　Stage 2: Realization of how much "good stuff" is available (16)
　Stage 3: Trying to acquire everything you touch (19)
　Stage 4: Realization that this is futile and that you should take only what offers "relatively immediate utility" (19)
Main topic 2: Eating safely from dumpsters
　Principle 1: Evaluate the condition of the materials.
　Principle 2: Know the dumpsters and check them regularly.
　Principle 3: Seek to answer "Why was this discarded?" |

| Conclusion | Similarity between himself and the wealthy, and pity for the millions "who nightly scavenge the cable channels looking for they know not what." |

Analyzing the Reading, p. 476

1. In addition to definition, other patterns used in this essay include process analysis ("a predictable series of stages" [13]), narration ("I began Dumpster diving about a year before I became homeless" [1]), comparison and contrast (scavenging vs. foraging [2–3]; relationship between the author and the wealthy [24]), description ("pristine ice cream, still frozen" [16]), division (types of food to be found in dumpsters [10–11]), and cause and effect (getting dysentery [12] and lessons learned [20–21]).

2. Eighner includes sensory details relating to sight, touch, and taste, including "running shoes that fit and look and smell brand-new" (16), "raw fruit and vegetables with intact skins" (9), and "desire to grab for the gaudy bauble" (24).

3. Eighner transitions to the conclusion by switching to first person, thereby circling back around to the introduction, where he also used the first person point of view. He also begins to explain the importance of his descriptions of the Dumpster diver by offering lessons that he learned from the experience. His shift to the present tense emphasizes the reflective nature of the conclusion.

Evaluating the Reading, p. 476

1. Answers will vary.

2. Answers will vary.

3. The one-sentence paragraphs make the point in each more striking and emphatic, but they do lack development.

4. Most students should find the level of detail more than adequate.

Bethe Dufresne, "Gullible Travels," p. 478
(Lexile level: 1250L)

This essay defines a growing attraction for tourists in developing countries — what promoters call "reality tourism" or "poverty tourism" but Dufresne more bluntly refers to as "slum tours": guided visits to massive slums in places like Nairobi, Mumbai, and Rio de Janeiro, where people live "without basic services such as electricity, running water, sanitation, and police protection." ("Come with us to gawk at desperately poor people," Dufresne writes derisively.) Slum-tour operators claim that a portion of the cost of the tours goes back to residents, but there is little evidence of this, according to Dufresne. She herself has been a frequent visitor to the Nairobi slum as a reporter, and she briefly questions whether her motives are any less tainted than those of the slum tourists. But she is different because her multiple experiences there have allowed her to see it "as a community, and not just a slum." A brief tour just skims the surface. As such tours become more popular, though, more research is being done about their economic impact, and in places like Rio the government has partnered with residents to make such tours celebrations of local arts and culture, not just quick encounters with poverty. Still, an American who heads up a nonprofit to help poor Kenyans sees them as "inherently disrespectful" because there can be "no real zone of privacy." His wife says, if you can afford to go to Africa for a slum tour, "you can afford to go and work with us."

Dufresne notes that one tour guide told her that Americans make up the bulk of his customers because they are so "kind," and students in an ethics class discussing the topic felt that most such tourists "probably want to help . . . so where is the harm?" Do students believe that charity is what motivates slum tourists in general?

Understanding and Reviewing the Reading, p. 481

1. Dufresne states her thesis in the final sentence of the third paragraph.

2. Dufresne defines "reality tourism" or "poverty tourism" — which she calls "slum tours" — as involving well-off Westerners being guided through wretched slums in developing countries either individually or in groups by a local resident.

3. The broader appeal is that part of the profit from the tours supposedly goes to the community to benefit "schools, orphanages, and other worthy projects." But Dufresne points out the lack of hard data on how much tourism money is invested in such projects.

4. Tours in Rio, encouraged by the government, promote indigenous art and culture.

5. *Infamous* (1): Notorious; having a disgraceful reputation. The Kibera slum in Nairobi is notorious for being bad.
   Debut (2): A first appearance; public opening or presentation. Dufresne covered the opening of Kibera's first free girls' school in 2009.
   Urban underbelly (8): This term refers to the hidden parts of a city, the seedy, dark, often poverty-stricken places that are usually ignored.
   Eschewing (8): Avoiding or shunning on moral principle. Reality tourists are now shunning vacations to traditionally indulgent resorts in favor of "meaningful" exposure to slums.
   Leonine (13): Catlike; feline; resembling a lion, especially its stealth, poise, and grace. Dufresne describes the young boxer as graceful and confident like a lion.
   Shrewd (18): Cunning, sharp, conniving. This term often refers to politicians' clever ways of arguing a point or passing legislation, such as the way the Brazilian government is promoting the 2016 Olympics through slum tourism.
   Demographics (19): This term refers to statistics related to a population, including age, race, nationality, and economic status. Dufresne wants to know what objectively characterizes the kind of people who participate in slum tourism.
   Inherently (21): Essentially; having as a fixed or inseparable quality. Silver argues that "disrespect" is a quality inseparably connected with the practice of slum tourism.

Analyzing the Reading, p. 482

1. Para. 1: Illustration. Para. 3: Contrast. Para. 7: Illustration. Para. 8: Cause and Effect. Paras. 9–10: Illustration. Paras. 12–15: Narration. Para. 17: Cause and Effect. Paras. 20–21: Narration.

2. Dufresne puts her term implicitly into the larger class of touring more generally, as well as, more explicitly, the class of efforts to aid the poor in developing countries.

3. Dufresne reports on the life in the Kibera slum in Nairobi. Unlike slum tourists, she has revisited the area numerous times and has come to appreciate the "resourcefulness and vitality" of its residents.

4. The quotation in paragraph 5 is made up but suggests what Dufresne sees as the real appeal of the tours. The quotes from the tourist magazine in paragraph 8 suggest how thoughtlessly such tours are treated. The quotation from a slum resident in paragraph 11 shows how demeaning such tours can be. And the quotations in the conclusion introduce the negative views of a couple who work to aid poor Kenyans.

5. Dufresne here differentiates herself from the slum tourists. Her purpose is to shed light on the conditions of the residents, not just to get a voyeuristic glimpse into their lives.

Evaluating the Reading, p. 482

1. The level of detail seems sufficient.

2. Dufresne doesn't intend to be objective. She wants her readers to view her subject skeptically.

3. The photo is a good representation of the topic.

4. Again, fairness is not the writer's purpose here.

Stefany Anne Golberg, "Can You See Me Now? Deaf America," p. 484

(Lexile level: 1220L)

Golberg's subject in this essay is deafness not as "a defect but a character trait, even a benefit" — a trait that should be viewed as "an ethnicity that, like all officially classed ethnicities, must be given its due politically and culturally." This definition reflects the fact that the deaf have their own language — in the United States, American Sign Language (ASL) — which has allowed a "rich and independent tradition of Deaf literature, theater, and journalism." While Golberg acknowledges that people may want to find a "cure" for deafness — the cochlear implant, for example, which Golberg believes is right for some "who want to better perceive sound, as well as increase their ability to communicate orally" — many deaf people find the suggestion that they have the implant "insulting, prejudiced even." In paragraphs 13–14 Golberg, who is not herself deaf, raises a series of "tough, uncomfortable questions" about cultural identity and deafness aimed at the hearing who would do all they could to persuade deaf people to assimilate into the hearing world. The final three paragraphs cite further experts on the legitimacy of deaf culture as a true ethnicity.

You might divide students into small groups to discuss some of the questions raised in paragraphs 13–14 and then report back on any consensus they have reached and any areas where disagreements persist.

Understanding and Reviewing the Reading, p. 488

1. The thesis is stated in the last sentence of paragraph 6.

2. Golberg believes that deaf people have the right to "choose" to live in the world of deaf culture, rather than assimilate into the hearing world. Her larger argument is that deaf people have this right just as any other ethnic group does.

3. She and others see deafness as an ethnicity because it has its own rich language in signing.

4. "Deafness" is a label given by the hearing. "Deafhood" is an identity within the deaf community that is continually growing and evolving.

Analyzing the Reading, p. 488

1. Words such as *ability* and *blessing* immediately suggest Golberg's presentation of deafness in a positive light.

2. Golberg's intended readers are people who live in the hearing world. She wants to introduce them to deaf culture and to change their views of the deaf.

3. The detailed discussion of ASL and its richness is important because Golberg goes on to make the point that this language constitutes an element of deaf ethnicity.

4. Golberg uses this series of questions to encourage readers to rethink their concept of the deaf world.

5. The final three paragraphs begin to answer the questions from the perspective of deaf activists.

6. The words Golberg uses here present a negative impression of the implant — which many hearing people might initially think of positively as helping the deaf.

Evaluating the Reading, p. 488

1. Answers will vary. It is a complex issue.

2. You might inquire whether any students are fluent in ASL and, if so, have them comment on this.

3. Answers will vary.

4. The language is very strong — by design, it is meant to shock.

5. Answers will vary.

Dennis Wilcox, Glen Cameron, and Bryan Reber, "The Cult of Celebrity," p. 490

(Lexile level: 1390L)

This excerpt from a public relations textbook describes the nature of *celebrity*, defining the term and explaining how publicists and the media work to create celebrities. The authors cite the observations of book reviewer Steven Cave, who makes several points about what fame is and is not ("a gold star given by the good fairy to the deserving") and how the "fame trade" has changed over the years. In addition to providing facts and statistics about different aspects of celebrity, the authors support their points using famous examples from the worlds of sports, music, film, and politics. The focus of the last four paragraphs of the reading is on the public's ongoing fascination with celebrities. The authors identify several factors behind this fascination, such as a yearning for heroes and a desire for entertainment.

Ask students to highlight words and phrases throughout the reading that could be used to expand the basic definition by Daniel Boorstin in the first sentence (for example, the word *temporary* in paragraph 2). What additional details would students include in an extended definition of *celebrity*?

Understanding and Reviewing the Reading, p. 492

1. The cult of celebrity is fueled by the public's dreams of glory, yearning for heroes, vicarious sense of belonging, and desire for entertainment. Today's mass media focus on the publicizing and glorification of celebrities in sports and entertainment.

2. A celebrity (term) is defined as a person (class) well known in one of a wide variety of fields such as science, politics, or entertainment (distinguishing characteristic). The temporary nature of celebrity status is also mentioned in paragraph 2.

3. Examples of celebrities mentioned in the reading include Barack Obama, Pope Francis, Lady Gaga, Michael Jackson, Angelina Jolie and Brad Pitt, Prince George, Nelson Mandela, Lance Armstrong, and Tiger Woods.

4. *Fueled* (2): Stimulated, strengthened.
   Exponentially (3): Increasingly fast.
   Eclipsed (4): overshadowed, made less important.
   Somber (6): Serious, sad.
   Emulate (8): To try to be like.
   Vicarious (9): Experienced indirectly by watching or hearing about.

5. Cave is emphasizing his point (and supporting the authors' use of negation in paragraph 1) that celebrity/fame is not a reward that has been earned by someone who deserves it.

6. Answers will vary. See the basic outline below as an example.

    I.   Celebrity

        A. Definition

        B. Observations about fame and celebrity (Stephen Cave)

            1. Fame is a product of certain industries.

            2. Anyone can become famous.

            3. The market for celebrity has been fueled by the media.

    II. Public fascination with celebrities

        A. Promotion by studios

        B. Public yearning for heroes

        C. Vicarious sense of belonging

        D. Desire for entertainment

Analyzing the Reading, p. 493

1. The paragraphs under the heading "The Public's Fascination with Celebrities" follow the cause/effect pattern; the authors explain the reasons/causes that lead to the public's fascination.

2. In the first several paragraphs, the authors address or acknowledge the role of publicists in perpetuating the media attention given to celebrities, especially in the entertainment and sports industries. They mention media coverage in paragraphs 4–6; they describe the publicity departments of movie studios in paragraph 7; they discuss the role of publicists in sports in paragraph 8; and they address celebrity media (fan magazines and TMZ) in paragraph 10.

3. The authors use negation to explain that, although the historical definition of *celebrity* implied special talent or achievement, today's celebrities may lack those qualities.

4. The authors end their discussion of the public's desire for entertainment by making the point that people find celebrities fun to talk about, especially in comparison to other, more serious topics.

5. Annotations should be in paragraph 3, where Stephen Cave observes that fame is a product of certain industries, not a reward for the deserving; fame itself has changed so that it is given to anyone; the fame trade has been changed by the rise of instant communications, digital media, and mass literacy.

Evaluating the Reading, p. 493

1. The authors use examples, expert opinions, facts, statistics, and reasons; answers will vary as to which are most effective.

2. Generally, this excerpt has a very accessible reading level (e.g., no difficult or technical language). Readers might find the long quote from Stephen Cave in paragraph 3 challenging, partly because he seems to be British

(reference to a "lads' magazine"). Annotating, highlighting, underlining, and outlining would be helpful.

3. The authors are mainly objective in their treatment but they do indicate that they believe becoming a celebrity does not necessarily require any outstanding achievement or accomplishment (paragraph 1). They use the terms "fixation" and "media frenzy," which have negative connotations; more positive connotations are implied in their references to the "magical gates" of Hollywood as well as "heroes" in the sports world.

4. Answers will vary.

CHAPTER 17: Cause and Effect: Using Reasons and Results to Explain, p. 497

Because *cause and effect* (also known as causal analysis) is fairly straightforward and logical to explain, you should be able to cover the material with ease. It is especially helpful to explain how cause and effect works by reviewing the graphic organizers included in this chapter. Be sure to caution students to clearly identify the difference between causes (reasons that something happens) and effects (results of the things that happen) in order to keep the chain of events clear. Note too that the cause-and-effect essay is usually informative or persuasive (rather than expressive). The three types of cause-and-effect essays are outlined in the chapter in both print and visual formats (through graphic organizers): causes and effects, a chain of causes and effects, and multiple causes and effects.

You will likely find it useful to begin discussion by analyzing the annotated essay "E. coli on the Rocks" by Amy Tan (p. 499). It outlines several causes of contamination by the E. coli virus on ice cubes as well as several effects, including convincing Tan to avoid ice almost entirely. The student essay, Nathan Nguyen's "Gambling on Our Future" (p. 511), is clearly marked and highlighted to guide readers through his argument. He speculates that a chain of events has led to an increase in problem gambling, citing statistics and providing expert opinions to support his views.

The remaining essays in this chapter reflect a wide range of types, from personal pieces to research writing. You might want to initiate a discussion of cause and effect with Kate Wheeling's "Why Do Violent Videos Go Viral?" (p. 520). Her introduction leads to the key question "So why do we like violence so much?" which she answers by turning to athletics. Wheeling offers a very clear list of causes for both participant and spectator behavior. "Why We Procrastinate" by Hara Estroff Marano (p. 525) offers an explanation of the causes of procrastination from a psychological perspective. Intended for an audience of both procrastinators and those who live, work, or socialize with them, this reading will help you better understand why procrastinators "sabotage" themselves.

Fred Pearce's "TV as Birth Control: Defusing the Population Bomb" (p. 530) reports on scientific research that shows how TV, specifically soap operas, is helping to decrease the fertility rate and empower women in developing countries. Rounding out the science theme, the textbook excerpt "What Factors Contribute to Hunger around the World?" (p. 536) examines the causes of food scarcity in developing countries, including poverty, political sanctions and conflicts, natural disasters, depleted resources, and overpopulation. Although hunger is the primary result of these causes, the authors also present secondary effects that ultimately lead to food scarcity.

Amy Tan, "E. coli on the Rocks," p. 499

(Lexile level: 930L)

In this brief essay originally posted on her blog, Tan offers the surprising observation that ice cubes, even when made with sanitary water, can carry colonies of dangerous *E. coli* bacteria, because often people use their hands to pick up ice cubes when they haven't washed their hands after using the bathroom. This appalls Tan, who has never seen anyone actually leave a public restroom without washing up but guesses that perhaps people only do so when they're not being witnessed. She remembers guests in her home using their hands to pick up ice cubes and now wonders whether what they touched might have been contaminated by someone else. From now on, she says, she's making sure her freezer is contamination-free, and she encourages readers when dining out to follow the lead of her friends in China—where water is often dirty—and say the two simple words "No ice." She says, "They can save your life."

Ask students whether they are likely to change their behavior based on Tan's warnings. Also, what do they think about Tan's observation about people washing their hands after using the bathroom? Do they think people generally do so in their own homes, for example?

Nathan Nguyen, "Gambling on Our Future," p. 511

(Student Essay)

Nathan Nguyen's research paper theorizes that a series of events has led to an increase in problem and addictive gambling in the United States. This paper on a current social problem provides an excellent model to explain not only cause and effect but also the use of research to support ideas with academic opinions and impressive statistics.

Responding to Nguyen's Essay, p. 515

1. Answers may vary.
2. Answers may vary. Alternative ways to introduce the topic might be with a question that cites a statistic about gambling's increase over the past few years or an anecdote illustrating the effects of addiction on someone of interest.

3. Answers may vary.

4. Nguyen might have ended by offering a story about a program that is helping people to stop gambling or by offering some solutions to the problem.

Kate Wheeling, "Why Do Violent Videos Go Viral?" (p. 520) (Lexile level: 1390L)

Wheeling begins this cause-and-effect essay with a description of how administrators are dealing with videos of fights between students in an Atlanta-area school system. Her introduction leads to the key question "So why do we like violence so much?" (para. 3), which she answers by turning to athletics. Wheeling connects the popularity of violent videos to the violence in sports and supports this theme with theories from the book *Violence and Aggression in Sporting Contests.* She focuses on three reasons we like violence (or why violent videos go viral) and presents them, with explanation, in a list. First, spectating is essentially living vicariously through participants. Second, it's cathartic to watch. And third, maybe we just crave violence. As part of these reasons, Wheeling explains the asserting dominance theory and the theory of destructive energy. She also cites scientific research on mice, whose behavior has significant parallels to human behavior. She concludes by returning to the initial event described in her introduction and making a recommendation about how to prevent violent videos.

Have students think about the author's purpose in writing this essay. Is it informative, persuasive, or both? How would students describe the intended audience for this essay?

Understanding and Reviewing the Reading (p. 522)

1. Wheeling first states in paragraph 3 that looking at athletics may provide some answers to why we like violence. In paragraph 3, she makes a reference to the authors of the book *Violence and Aggression in Sporting Contests* to introduce her thesis that theories about why we love violent sports may help explain why we like to watch violent videos.

2. Wheeling describes professional wrestling, boxing, and mixed martial arts as modern-day versions of ancient combat sports. She refers to the NHL's belief (as cited by the book authors) that violence is unavoidable, therapeutic, and cathartic. She supports her ideas by pointing to the violence of hockey players, soccer hooligans, and those participating in playground fights.

3. *Suppress* (2): To put down by authority or force.
   Notorious (2): Widely and unfavorably known.
   Integral (3): Essential, fundamental.
   Cathartic (3): Providing relief.
   Vicariously (5): By participating in someone else's experience through the use of imagination or sympathetic feelings.

Instigated (7): Started.
Predilection (8): Preference, liking.

4. The following graphic organizer is one possible answer.

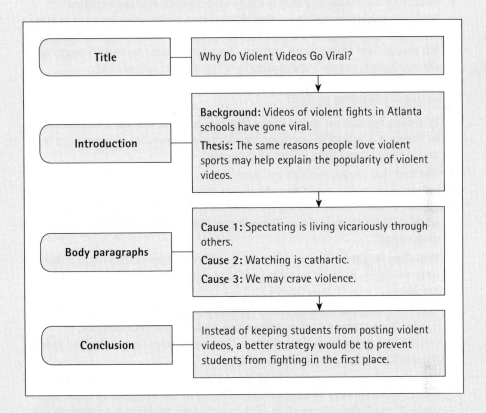

| Title | → | Why Do Violent Videos Go Viral? |

| Introduction | → | **Background:** Videos of violent fights in Atlanta schools have gone viral. **Thesis:** The same reasons people love violent sports may help explain the popularity of violent videos. |

| Body paragraphs | → | **Cause 1:** Spectating is living vicariously through others. **Cause 2:** Watching is cathartic. **Cause 3:** We may crave violence. |

| Conclusion | → | Instead of keeping students from posting violent videos, a better strategy would be to prevent students from fighting in the first place. |

Analyzing the Reading (p. 522)

1. The author cites the violent videos of fights in the Atlanta schools as examples of the popularity of violence and the difficulty of suppressing it. She refers to these videos in the final paragraph to suggest that the focus should be not on suppressing students' access to videos but on keeping students from fighting in the first place.

2. Wheeling is writing for a general audience interested in social behavior and she hopes to answer the question in the title with relevant and interesting reasons. She writes in a way that seems accessible and understandable; she uses casual, informal language that connects with the reader.

3. By using the pronoun "we" throughout, Wheeling makes the basic assumption that everyone likes to watch violence. She assumes that most people enjoy watching violent sports; her examples about hockey and a playground fight illustrate her point that "we" enjoy living vicariously through others.

4. Wheeling is pointing out what modern sports and their ancient counterparts have in common: violence. This connection supports and emphasizes her thesis that sports can help explain the appeal of violent videos.

5. Wheeling uses language that is easily understood, and she explains fairly complex theories (asserting dominance, destructive energy) in simple terms. She seems like a person who is easy to relate to partly because of her use of "we" throughout and also because of some humor ("cough, soccer hooligans, cough") and generally sympathetic, casual tone.

Evaluating the Reading (p. 523)

1. Wheeling focuses on sports in the first two reasons, but she connects sports to violence at school by mentioning playground punches in paragraph 5 and violent school fight videos in paragraph 6.

2. The first two causes/reasons are more tied to violent sports than the third reason, so it makes sense that she places the reasons in that order. The last reason, related to our craving for violence and its connection to a research study on mice, stands alone. The organization of these reasons is easy to understand.

3. Wheeling might have used other studies or resources on this topic if they were available, in order to have a wider variety of types of details to support her ideas.

4. Wheeling uses the word *shrewdly* (possibly ironically) to show how difficult it is for Instagram and other authorities, including school officials, to control and suppress violent content; the people who are posting the videos are quick to get around any restrictions.

5. The research is relevant as part of the third reason because it illustrates how the reward pathways in humans are reflected in the behavior of mice. The study is an effective illustration of the craving for violence even though it is not a sports-related example.

Hara Estroff Marano, "Why We Procrastinate," p. 525 (Lexile level: 870L)

In this essay, Hara Estroff Marano writes about procrastination — a common problem that has the potential to sabotage one's success in life. Using the work of a pair of professors who are experts on the subject as her source of information, Marano addresses the causes of this destructive behavior, identifies the types of procrastinators, and ends with the effects of procrastination. Students should find her explanation of the causes of procrastination informative, and they should be able to readily identify with the effects of this behavior since this is a central issue for college students. The essay should provoke interesting discussion and could be the basis for freewriting and personal essays about your students' own experiences with this issue, as well as other issues that are relevant to the college student population.

Understanding and Reviewing the Reading, p. 527

1. Marano is addressing both those who procrastinate and those who have a relationship with people who procrastinate. She points out in paragraph 4 that she is focusing on a U.S. audience. Her goal is to educate both groups about procrastination so that, through a better understanding of the issue, they will be able to help themselves or help others to change their behavior (para. 12).
2. According to Marano, the primary cause of procrastination is the inability to self-regulate.
3. Marano adds credibility to her writing by using the expertise of two psychologists who are leading experts on procrastination.
4. By being nice, we enable procrastinators, because we allow them to get away with their behavior. Instead, we should call them on their excuses when we don't believe them.

Analyzing the Reading, p. 527

1. Procrastination is a learned behavior. Although doing so takes hard work, procrastinators can change their behavior.
2. Causes and effects are clearly presented. The causes are (1) procrastinators are more optimistic about time than others; (2) procrastination may be a response to an authoritarian parenting style; (3) some procrastinators disengage by drinking, thus not getting their work done; (4) procrastinators tell lies to themselves; and (5) procrastinators seek distractions to avoid work. The effects are (1) one's health can suffer; (2) one can develop insomnia; (3) others become resentful of the procrastinator; and (4) procrastination destroys team work in the workplace and in personal relationships. The author provides sufficient support to explain the causal relationship between events.
3. Psychic energy pertains to transforming the way one thinks. The result is not that one "feels transformed internally," but that one thinks differently.
4. Answers will vary, but student answers should allude to the fact that it is hard for procrastinators to change without help.

Evaluating the Reading, p. 528

1. Answers will vary. The visual is a humorous one, suggesting that, rather than having a notepad that says "Things to do," procrastinators might have a notepad that says "Things to Put Off Until Next Week." The humorous tone is in keeping with the tone of the article.

2. The author also uses classification in paragraph 10 where she discusses the types of procrastinators.

3. Answers will vary. The conclusion reinforces the main assertion about procrastination by emphasizing the fact that procrastinators can change their learned and often destructive behavior.

4. Statement 1 is an opinion. Statement 2 is a fact. Statement 3 is an opinion. Statement 4 is an opinion. Statement 5 is a fact. Statement 6 is a fact.

Fred Pearce, "TV as Birth Control: Defusing the Population Bomb," p. 530

(Lexile level: 1230L)

In this essay, Pearce explores the causal relationship between TV and the fertility rate in developing countries. He begins by sharing an experience of human geographer Martin Lewis. Lewis posed two simple questions to his students: "How do you think U.S. family sizes compare with those in India? Between Indian and American women, who has the most children?" He also asked the same question of his colleagues. Students and professors alike responded that, of course, Indian families are larger and Indian women have more children. The truth is that although Indian women have more children, the difference is not significant. Intrigued by the significant drop in the fertility rate of Indian women in just one generation, Lewis investigated this phenomenon. His findings supported those of researchers Robert Jensen and Emily Oster, who reported that TV was empowering Indian women and introducing them to a world outside of their villages that offered them more than just having babies and raising children. But it wasn't just TV that was giving these women a window to the world; it was soap operas. Pearce goes on to discuss the history of using soap operas to reduce the fertility rate by providing information about a Mexican soap opera from the 1970s that targeted poor women and ended each episode with a short segment on family planning. This model expanded in various formats to other developing countries of the world, including those in Africa. Pearce ends his essay by first looking back at the 60s, when TV was often vilified, and then looking at the present, when TV offers the possibility of empowering underprivileged people.

It might be interesting and informative for students to ask their peers outside the classroom the two questions Martin Lewis posed and then report back about their findings. As an extension of this activity, students could be asked to depict their findings in a graphic of their choosing.

Understanding and Reviewing the Reading, p. 534

1. The thesis of the essay is stated at the end of paragraph 6. Pearce's thesis is that TV has the power to change people's reproductive behavior.

2. Soap operas seem to be the most effective in cutting fertility rates.

3. When viewers are able to see women in soap operas who have their own aspirations for the future and the freedom to make choices, they readily believe that they, too, can have these things.

4. Some of the secondary effects are decreased acceptance of domestic violence and changes in attitudes toward homosexuality and same-sex marriage.

5. The opening anecdote illustrates the misconception that most Americans have about India's population problem.

Analyzing the Reading, p. 534

1. This article was published in *Conservation* magazine and written by an environmentalist, so it is safe to assume that he was addressing an audience of scientists and others interested in environmental issues.

2. The cause is TV, specifically soap operas, and the effects are a reduction in the fertility rate, the empowerment of women, and an increase in women's aspirations.

3. Pearce uses the term *soft soap* to describe soap operas that did not present overt messages of propaganda. Soft soaps still delivered some of the same messages, but the messages were more subliminal. Just as the messages of soft soaps are much more easily "ingested," so is actual soft soap much easier to use.

4. Answers will vary. Pearce presents a convincing argument with research to back it up, but he does not take a firm stand on his position. He closes simply by instructing the audience to "stay tuned."

5. The simplicity of the TV alludes to the simplicity of the solution to "defusing the population bomb" in developing countries. The dial has been replaced with birth control pills, adding to the visual argument.

6. Answers will vary. Pearce reinforces his main assertion about the topic by restating the effects of television and soap operas on underprivileged women.

Evaluating the Reading, p. 534

1. Pearce uses illustration in his explanation of the "Sabido Method" in paragraphs 10–13. In paragraph 10, Pearce uses description as he writes about the subject of the telenovela *Àcompañame*. In paragraphs 14 and 15, he uses contrast to show the difference between the spread of TV in Asia and Latin America and that in Africa. These patterns of development enhance the causal analysis by enabling the author to present the information in the way that will best communicate the messages.

2. Answers will vary.

3. Answers will vary.

4. Answers will vary.

Joan Salge Blake, Kathy D. Munoz, and Stella Volpe, "What Factors Contribute to Hunger around the World?" p. 536

(Lexile level: 1300L)

This excerpt from a nutrition textbook explores some of the causes of hunger in the developing world. The writers explain that poverty is at the heart of the problem, but there are also other issues that affect the food supply around the world. Political sanctions may be placed on one country by another for a number of reasons, but the end result can be a life-threatening shortage of food and water for citizens of the sanctioned country. Also, armed conflicts in developing countries may divert money away from food programs and toward weapons and ammunition and cause those carrying out humanitarian efforts to flee the country. The authors also cite factors such as natural disasters and overpopulation that severely limit food production.

As an introduction to this reading, have students discuss the causes and effects of hunger in the United States and propose solutions to this problem.

Understanding and Reviewing the Reading, p. 540

1. Political sanctions are restrictions that one country imposes on another for political reasons. Political sanctions contribute to the world's hunger problem by making it difficult for people to access agricultural supplies, fuel, or other products because of increased prices. Furthermore, people who work in the agricultural field are often subjected to job loss and decreased income. The decline in exporting and importing caused by the sanctions also affects the income of individuals in many other occupations.

2. The authors directly state the thesis of the essay in the first sentence: "Hunger in the developing world is often caused by a complex set of factors."

3. Civil wars and conflicts lead to a disruption of agriculture. When crops are not being grown, people turn to governmental assistance. During wars and conflicts, governments often divert funds from food distribution to war supplies. This opens the door for humanitarian efforts; however, governments may intervene in humanitarian efforts by seizing food that has been air-lifted into the country. Finally, when the climate within the country becomes hostile and unsafe for humanitarian groups, they pull out. This leaves the poor with no food resources.

4. Answers will vary. Most students will be able to settle on the major causes by using the headings within the excerpt; however, the details may differ.

Analyzing the Reading, p. 540

1. Answers will vary.

2. Answers will vary.

3. Throughout the excerpt, the authors use illustration as they provide examples to support their main points. They also use description to enhance the details.

Evaluating the Reading, p. 540

1. Answers will vary.

2. The statement about the World Bank does flow logically from the rest of the reading. It sums up the major focus of the reading by striking at the very heart of the problem — the cycle of poverty and hunger. In order to break this cycle, speed up development, and manage population growth, both men and women (and girls in particular) must be given the means to exercise their right to receive a basic education.

3. Answers will vary. Most students should find the graphic helpful. The graph on page 537 illustrates that developing and least developed countries have high rates of undernourished people. The graph could be used to compare the countries' undernourished populations. It also could be used to examine the effect of population on hunger. Students' answers to the question about other types of graphics will vary. You might suggest that they look in Chapter 2, on page 41 of the text, for a review of the types of graphs the authors could have used.

4. Answers will vary.

CHAPTER 18: Argumentation: Supporting a Claim, p. 544

Many college students are eager to enter into political and social arenas, vote and debate issues, and have a voice in their broader community. Learning how to write and think critically and to formulate arguments is critical to that transition. As shown in this chapter, *argument* has three basic parts: an issue, a claim, and support. The chapter clearly defines each aspect of argumentation, and students should quickly grasp the basic stance required for it. At some point in their papers, students should also acknowledge and refute opposing viewpoints. The guidelines in "Considering Opposing Viewpoints" (pp. 565–566) will assist students in acknowledging and refuting their opposition in a step-by-step fashion. You will note that the graphic organizer for argumentation is more flexible than those for other modes; it does not designate the order in which an argument is presented, and it leaves space to begin with a claim or evidence or even opposing views. Because the form of an argument can be so variable — drawing as well on other modes of development — you will need to stress the importance of the thesis and clearly supported claims.

A number of today's controversial issues are covered in this chapter. In the annotated essay "Eating Meat for the Environment" (p. 546), Lisa M. Hamilton argues that eating meat from organically run farms will help stall — and possibly even reduce — climate change. Studying this essay in conjunction with the annotated student essay "Pull the Plug on Explicit Lyrics" by James Sturm (p. 560) will show students visually how successful arguments are structured.

Sojourner Truth adopts a very clear and impassioned plea for freedom and equal rights for all women in her speech "Ain't I a Woman?" (p. 569). Speaking in an informal manner and citing examples from her life as a poor African-American woman living in a society controlled by white men, Truth uses argument to make her case for gender equality.

Sebastian Junger writes on the psychological effect of war on soldiers in his essay "Why Would Anyone Miss War?" (p. 573). Taking on a very timely topic related to the recent wars and continued unrest in the Middle East, Junger argues that civilians need to better understand the mental complexities of soldiers' experiences in order to help them function in civilian society. Brittney Cooper explores racial differences in parenting in her article "The Racial Parenting Divide: What Adrian Peterson Reveals about Black vs. White Child-Rearing" (p. 578), arguing that a culture of violent discipline in the African-American community is wrong and must be changed.

This chapter also provides pairs of arguments for and against a higher minimum wage, with Robert Reich's "Why We Should Raise the Minimum Wage" (p. 584) in favor and Reihan Salam's "The Fight Against 15" (p. 588) against; and for and against multitasking, with Peter Bregman's "How (and Why) to Stop Multitasking" (p. 595) against the practice and David Silverman's "In Defense of Multitasking" (p. 599) in favor of it.

Lisa M. Hamilton, "Eating Meat for the Environment," p. 546

(Lexile level: 1220L)

As the title suggests, this essay argues that consumption of meat that has been raised correctly can help the environment. Hamilton wrote her article in response to a United Nations official's directive to eat *less* meat to fight global warming; thus, her argument has a very specific context and immediately begins a conversation between ideas. According to Hamilton's research, pasture-raised livestock eat and digest their food and expel waste at no cost to the environment, and their manure organically feeds the soil. She uses evidence from statistics about food consumption in the United States as well as quotations from a pasture farmer in Georgia — an expert on sustainable agriculture. Hamilton structures her argument by introducing counterarguments and refuting them with logical evidence, and she succinctly summarizes her thesis by restating it at the end of the essay.

Begin discussion by asking students whether they think the essay uses enough evidence to make its case against such an important figure as the head of the United Nations Intergovernmental Panel on Climate Change. Is this an issue they previously cared about, and does this essay help them care enough about the issue to make a change in their eating habits? Why or why not?

James Sturm, "Pull the Plug on Explicit Lyrics," p. 560

(Student Essay)

Students are likely to have strong opinions about this student essay — about its content and about the argument Sturm makes within it, in which he favors censoring music with explicit lyrics for children under the age of sixteen. Sturm's organization is very clear; he has a strong, identifiable thesis; good transitions; clear topic sentences; clear recognition of opposing arguments; and rebuttals. However, Sturm's points are often unfounded; for instance, he claims that "although various factors contribute to such acts of violence [as school shootings], hatred-themed music is likely a part of the equation" (5), but he does not offer any scholarly or scientific support for this assertion.

When discussing this essay with students, be sure to ask them to provide ample support for their arguments, whether in favor of or opposing Sturm's position in favor of a censorship policy. Since the essay builds on a cause-and-effect pattern, have them identify other causes or effects. You may also want to provide or have students provide current music that includes explicit lyrics. In groups, student might use a song or two to either support or refute Sturm's argument.

Responding to Sturm's Essay, p. 562

1. Answers may vary. Books are often categorized by intended readership: children, YA, or adult. Movies and TV shows have ratings and sometimes appear with parental advisory warnings. Magazines, especially adult magazines, are often kept out of sight or "displayed" behind a protective cover.

2. Answers will vary.

3. Answers will vary, though you may also consider having students answer this question as a class or in groups, outlining an argument visually for everyone to see.

Sojourner Truth, "Ain't I a Woman?" p. 569

(Lexile level: 750L)

Sojourner Truth gave this powerful speech in favor of women's rights at the 1851 Women's Rights Convention in Akron, Ohio. Although it contains many of the rhetorical devices commonly used in speeches, Truth did not intend it that way. She was a poor, illiterate African-American woman with slavery in her past who felt compelled to share her feelings on freedom and women's rights. Addressing an audience of sophisticated white women and disapproving white men, she spoke from her heart and made a name for herself in history. Truth's speech also holds up well as a piece of argumentative writing. You may want to provide some background on Sojourner Truth and on the anti-slavery and women's rights movements. Let students listen to a recording of someone delivering the speech, if possible, and have them examine it closely for persuasive elements.

Understanding and Reviewing the Reading, p. 570

1. Truth invited the audience to look at her arm so that they could see her muscles, which came from hard work in the fields. She did this in an attempt to show her (and other women's) strength and ability to do hard labor comparable to that done by a man.

2. As a slave, she labored in the fields, gave birth to thirteen children, saw most of her children sold off to slavery, and had no one to comfort her.

3. Truth is calling on men to let women make this world right. She is advocating for freedom and equality for both slaves and women.

4. Truth is saying that intellect has nothing to do with women's or slaves' rights. She further says that if men have so much power already — a cup that holds a quart — they can surely let white women and black women have the little bit — a cup that holds a pint — of that power that would come from having rights equal to those of men.

5. The following graphic organizer is one possible answer.

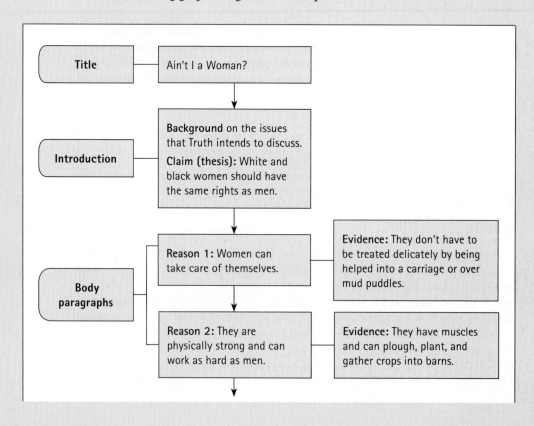

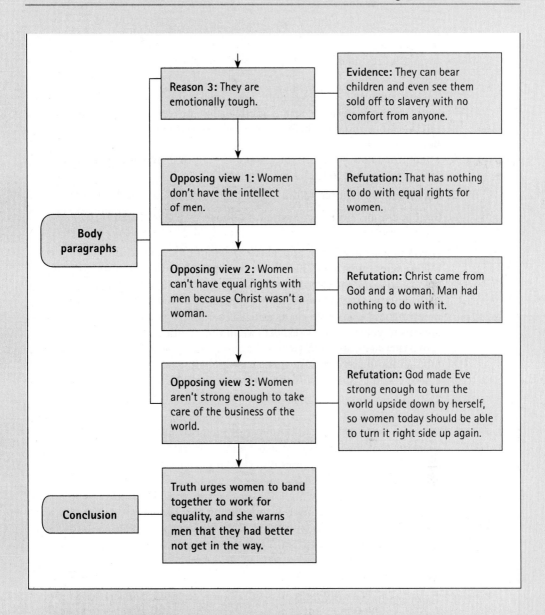

Reason 3: They are emotionally tough.

Evidence: They can bear children and even see them sold off to slavery with no comfort from anyone.

Opposing view 1: Women don't have the intellect of men.

Refutation: That has nothing to do with equal rights for women.

Body paragraphs

Opposing view 2: Women can't have equal rights with men because Christ wasn't a woman.

Refutation: Christ came from God and a woman. Man had nothing to do with it.

Opposing view 3: Women aren't strong enough to take care of the business of the world.

Refutation: God made Eve strong enough to turn the world upside down by herself, so women today should be able to turn it right side up again.

Conclusion

Truth urges women to band together to work for equality, and she warns men that they had better not get in the way.

Analyzing the Reading, p. 570

1. This speech was given at the 1851 Women's Rights Convention in Akron, Ohio. There were men in the audience who were vehemently opposed to the idea of women's rights. Although there were women in the audience, many of them did not want Truth to speak because they were afraid that men would confuse the fight for women's rights with the fight for freedom for slaves. At best, the female audience was lukewarm toward Truth's platform

until she began to speak. In her speech, Truth directly addressed the men in the audience. She played down the slavery issue and focused on equal rights for all women.

2. Truth claims that women should have equal rights with men. She says that with African Americans in the South and white women in the North all talking about equality, the white man will soon be in a fix. She then begins her argument.

3. See the graphic organizer above for reasons and evidence that Truth uses to support her claim. Student answers will vary as to how persuasive Truth's details are.

4. See the graphic organizer above for opposing viewpoints and counterarguments.

5. Answers will vary. Truth appeals to the emotional side of the audience by talking about bearing her children and seeing most of them sold off into slavery with no one to comfort her in her grief, and also citing her ability to withstand beatings like a man. She appeals to a biological need when she mentions that she could eat as much as a man. Throughout the speech, she appeals to values such as respect (when she mentions never being helped into a carriage), strength (when she shows her muscles), fairness (when she talks about the pint and the quart), and religion (when she talks about Christ coming from a woman and Eve turning the world upside down).

6. The words *children* and *honey* show Truth to be exactly what she is — a plain, uneducated, African-American woman. She makes no attempt to be someone she is not. She maintains this image by using the only way of speaking that she knows — a casual and informal tone communicated in slang, dialect, and sometimes illiterate language. By addressing the audience as children, she puts everyone there on equal footing — no white women, black women, white men, or black men — just children who are all equal in her eyes. By using this term, Truth sets herself up as the adult who is teaching a lesson to her children. Both *children* and *honey* are terms of endearment that suggest Truth's innocence and kind heart.

Evaluating the Reading, p. 571

1. Truth captures her audience by using colloquial language that most members of the audience probably had to listen to carefully in order to understand. She also repeats the rhetorical question "Ain't I a woman?" to drive home her point. In addition, she uses humor. We can imagine that she may have pointed her finger and spoken firmly but kindly. And as the roar of the audience increased, she probably raised her voice so as to be heard over the cheers and applause.

2. "Ain't I a Woman?" predicts and summarizes the argument well. Students may suggest other titles for the speech.

3. Truth's conclusion effectively calls for equal rights for women. It appeals to the value of fairness by invoking a woman's strength. She projects into the future by issuing a warning to the men in the audience. And she urges her listeners to take action by telling the women that if they get together and present a unified front, they can turn the world right side up.

4. Truth's essay is a mix of fact and opinion. She uses facts when she talks about her background and the "man's" work that she performs. She also uses facts when she mentions the opposing views. The remainder of the time, she uses opinion, which invokes strong emotion in the audience. This mix of fact and opinion shows Truth's audience that she is logical and wise — like the stereotypical man — and, at times, emotional — like the stereotypical woman.

Sebastian Junger, "Why Would Anyone Miss War?" p. 573 (Lexile level: 1170L)

Junger's argument here is that until noncombattants understand the complexity of what happens to soldiers psychologically and emotionally in combat, "we won't do a very good job of bringing these people home and making a place for them in our society." He begins by citing his own experience reporting on an infantry platoon in a remote region of Afghanistan; at the end of their contract, only one soldier chose not to stay — and, back home, he struggled to fit in, feeling, as he's quoted later, that he had "sinned." Junger then makes the point that civilians — whether liberal or conservative — don't see war for what it really is, both alluring and horrifying for soldiers, and soldiers themselves are not often able to articulate this intense dichotomy. Using the example of firebombings of German cities during World War II, Junger goes further to argue that civilians themselves have to take collective responsibility for the inevitable innocent casualties that military personnel carry with them: "Imagine how much better the bomber crews of World War II might have handled their confusion and grief if the entire country had been struggling with those same feelings. Imagine how much better they might have fared if there had been a monument for them to visit that commemorated all the people they were ordered to kill." He then argues for a similar monument to the civilian dead of Iraq and Afghanistan.

How do students respond to Junger's final point that civilians killed in Iraq and Afghanistan are "too, among the casualties of 9/11" and that we should be "honoring those deaths with our grief"?

Understanding and Reviewing the Reading, p. 575

1. Junger states his thesis at the end of paragraph 3: "If we civilians don't understand that complexity [of soldiers' reactions to combat], we won't do a very good job of bringing these people home and making a place for them in our society."

2. The evidence he offers in paragraph 3 is that noncombattants simply do not understand soldiers' responses to being in combat. What's seen as a bad thing — combat — is, in fact, much more complicated for actual participants.

3. The quotations point out the fact that a soldier's feelings about war are deeply contradictory: on the one hand, he misses "almost all of it"; on the other hand, he feels intense guilt about his participation in killing other human beings.

4. Junger is sympathetic with both U.S. troops and those they have killed, but his primary argument here is that honoring the enemy dead helps veterans come to terms with what they've been through.

5. Junger's concluding point is that innocent civilians killed in Iraq and Afghanistan deserve as much respect as American soldiers and that such honor would resonate to the benefit of the United States as a humanitarian country.

Analyzing the Reading, p. 576

1. Junger clearly has firsthand experience reporting on the soldiers he is writing about.

2. In paragraph 4, Junger contrasts liberal and conservative views of war, making the point that both are equally limited when it comes to actual combat experience and its aftermath for veterans.

3. Answers may vary, but unlike the Vietnam and Gulf Wars, World War II is widely viewed as just — despite the horrible casualties — so the example of these soldiers, Junger hopes, will create broader sympathy.

4. The visual supports Junger's argument that returning veterans are conflicted about their experience and so deserve whatever is necessary to help them deal with their experience.

5. Junger's point is that the majority of deaths in these wars were not caused by Americans, absolving U.S. troops of some of the blame.

Evaluating the Reading, p. 576

1. The title actually doesn't predict the argument very well — though it does summarize a central basis of the argument (that civilians don't understand what soldiers returning from combat feel).

2. This language contributes to Junger's point that for various reasons veterans are conflicted about their wartime experiences.

3. Answers will vary.

Brittney Cooper, "The Racial Parenting Divide: What Adrian Peterson Reveals about Black vs. White Child-Rearing," p. 578

(Lexile level: 1350L)

Cooper argues in this article that there is a deep divide between how white and black parents raise their children, one that she attributes to a culture of violent discipline ingrained in the African-American community in response to a fear of state violence. In contrast to how white parents raise their children to "see the world as a place that they can explore . . . at will," black parents employ harsh, often violent disciplinary methods intended to keep their children safe in a hostile world. Cooper uses her own experiences and the example of Adrian Peterson to illustrate the idea that violent punishment has often been considered a sign of good parenting in the black community. She goes on to explore the reasons why, expressing the hope of many black parents that "by enacting these micro-level violences on black bodies, we can protect our children from macro and deadly forms of violence later." Despite being motivated by love and sincerity, such strategies remain dangerous, unproductive, and unacceptable. Cooper asserts that violent forms of discipline do not accomplish the desired outcome and ultimately create negative and far-reaching effects.

Have students annotate the reading to point out places where Cooper reveals her unique perspective as a black woman — where she describes her own personal experiences and her observations as a member of the African-American community. What is her purpose in doing so?

Understanding and Reviewing the Reading, p. 582

1. Cooper uses the story to explain when she first realized there were differences in how white and black children view the world and in how black and white parents discipline their children. She introduces her topic (punishment/discipline) in this way.

2. The culture of violent punishment ingrained in African-American communities is unacceptable. Cooper states this thesis most directly in paragraphs 8 and 19.

3. Cooper attributes the culture of violent punishment in the African-American community to a fear of violence used by the U.S. nation-state to discipline people of color. She presents Adrian Peterson's case as an example of an African-American man following a script handed down to him, and she also gives evidence from her personal experience of discipline used by her mother and grandmother. She mentions old TV sitcoms to illustrate the difference between allowable misbehavior in white and black households. She cites Michael Brown to support her claim that the nation-state uses violence as a primary mode of disciplining people of color.

4. *Audacity* (1): Boldness, nerve.
   Prerogative (1): Privilege, right.
   Compliance (3): Obedience.
   Unfathomable (10): Impossible to comprehend or imagine.
   Reprisal (12): Retaliation, punishment, payback.
   Preclude (15): To prevent or disqualify.
   Imbricated (15): Overlapped, intertwined.
   Inculcate (18): To instill or indoctrinate.

Analyzing the Reading, p. 582

1. Cooper uses Peterson to illustrate the ingrained culture of violence in African-American communities and among African-American men, and she points out that black men may see themselves as good fathers because they are willing to engage in "strong" (i.e., violent) discipline.

2. An instructor might pose questions about what the author saw and learned on the train with her professor, the different parental responses toward misbehaving children in black and white communities, the Adrian Peterson case, differences between how white and black children are raised to see the world, or what the nation-state has done to form black disciplinary strategies.

3. Cooper is referring to violent punishments such as spankings or beatings when children are young. She claims some parents hope this type of punishment will form behavior that helps their children avoid worse treatment by authorities when they are grown up.

4. In paragraphs 17–18, Cooper asserts that white children are raised to be explorers, whereas such behavior would be too dangerous for black children. However, she maintains that violent discipline is wrong and will not have the desired effects (protection, dignity, respect). She ends with a call to action: teach children that violence is not love.

Evaluating the Reading, p. 582

1. The author supports her argument with personal experience, illustration/description (Adrian Peterson story), facts, and opinions. Answers will vary regarding how effective, convincing, or compelling her evidence is.

2. Cooper appeals to the reader's sense of fairness, tenderness toward children and family, and fear/guilt regarding state violence. She generalizes about white parents (overly permissive), white children (allowed to misbehave and disrespect their parents in public, entitled/free to explore the world), and black parents (stern, often violent disciplinarians, especially in the South).

3. Through emotional language, the author reveals her strongly held beliefs and feelings about her subject. She uses phrases such as "in a culture of white supremacy" (paragraph 9) and "in a world that clearly hates them" (16) to create a negative emotional response. She describes the discipline

methods of mothers and grandmothers fondly and sympathetically (3–4) and refers to the U.S. nation-state modes of discipline as "deadly" (14–15).

4. Cooper acknowledges the difficulty of changing a culturally acceptable behavior (8–10) and finding the right balance between discipline and freedom, especially in a hostile world (16–18). She reveals that she plans to discipline her own children differently than her mother did.

5. Cooper seems to be writing for a sympathetic audience, one that agrees with or is receptive to her ideas.

ARGUMENT PAIR: DEBATING A HIGHER MINIMUM WAGE

Robert Reich, "Why We Should Raise the Minimum Wage," p. 584

(Lexile level: 1220L)

Reich argues that raising the minimum wage would provide economic benefits to workers, employers, and others. He begins by citing information from the U.S. Congressional Budget Office showing that increasing the minimum wage from $7.25 to $10.10 an hour would lift 900,000 working poor people out of poverty. To further support his argument, he presents information about Seattle's bold move to increase the minimum wage to $15.00 an hour. The city of Seattle is phasing in an increase in the minimum wage over time, depending on several factors related to the size and type of business. But Seattle does not have as far to go as most U.S. cities. Seattle's base minimum wage is $9.32, compared to $7.25 for most U.S. cities/states. Reich recommends that states consider increasing the rate incrementally, so as to give employers time to adjust. Reich addresses the opposing view of those who believe that raising the minimum wage would deliver a severe economic blow to employers and businesses. Reich cites research from Michael Reich and Arindrajit Dube, who found no significant increase in unemployment as a result of raising the minimum wage. One benefit that was uncovered by the research was the decrease in employee turnover. His point, finally, is that this bold move is not possible for some states, but many are able to raise the minimum wage, and they should do it.

Ask students to highlight what they think is the most convincing evidence presented in the reading. Ask them how they would evaluate it in terms of previous arguments in favor of increasing the minimum wage. You might ask students to research other articles that support this point of view.

Understanding and Reviewing the Reading, p. 585

1. A higher minimum wage provides economic gains to workers, employers, and others. Reich states his thesis in paragraph 3: The gains from a higher minimum wage extend beyond those who receive it.

2. In addition to lifting workers out of poverty, more money for workers results in more sales, creating faster growth and more jobs, in turn helping the economy. A higher minimum wage also means we pay less for Medicaid, food stamps, and other assistance for the poor. Reich supports his reasons with statistics from the National Employment Law Project and the Congressional Budget office and estimates from the city of Seattle.

3. Reich acknowledges concerns in paragraph 5 and addresses them by recommending incremental increases, as in Seattle. He suggests further benefits resulting from Seattle's minimum wage increase (more employees to choose from, more reliable workers who are likely to stay longer) and supports his view by citing research in paragraph 8.

4. The following graphic organizer is one possible answer.

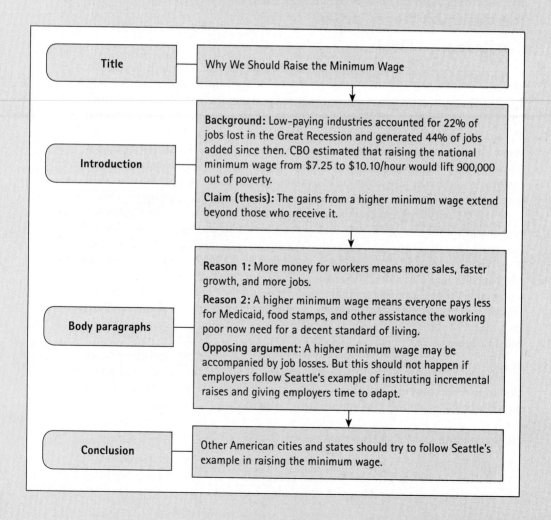

| Title | Why We Should Raise the Minimum Wage |

Introduction

Background: Low-paying industries accounted for 22% of jobs lost in the Great Recession and generated 44% of jobs added since then. CBO estimated that raising the national minimum wage from $7.25 to $10.10/hour would lift 900,000 out of poverty.

Claim (thesis): The gains from a higher minimum wage extend beyond those who receive it.

Body paragraphs

Reason 1: More money for workers means more sales, faster growth, and more jobs.

Reason 2: A higher minimum wage means everyone pays less for Medicaid, food stamps, and other assistance the working poor now need for a decent standard of living.

Opposing argument: A higher minimum wage may be accompanied by job losses. But this should not happen if employers follow Seattle's example of instituting incremental raises and giving employers time to adapt.

Conclusion

Other American cities and states should try to follow Seattle's example in raising the minimum wage.

Analyzing the Reading, p. 586

1. Reich is establishing the need for an increase in the minimum wage. He appeals to readers who value the idea of workers being able to support their families and stay out of poverty.

2. Reich is supporting his argument by pointing to the many positive effects of a raise in the minimum wage, and he ties it to his point in paragraph 2 that most workers in need of such a raise are not teenagers but family breadwinners.

3. Reich acknowledges concerns about job losses in paragraph 5 and then gives reasons he believes Seattle's strategy will prevent businesses from experiencing job losses. In paragraph 8, he supports this view by citing research conducted in adjacent counties that confirms his assertions.

4. Seattle has set a high standard in its establishment of a new minimum wage, and Reich is challenging other cities and states to aspire to the same high standard.

Evaluating the Reading, p. 586

1. Answers will vary. Reich's reasons include the fact that more money for workers would lead to more sales, faster growth, and more jobs, as well as the idea that the public would pay less for Medicaid, food stamps, and other assistance the working poor now need.

2. In paragraph 4, Reich states that the higher minimum wage would result in a lower amount that the public would have to pay to support the working poor.

3. Reich is differentiating between a minimum wage worker who supports his or her family as the head of a household (major breadwinner) and a minimum wage worker who is working simply for spending money.

4. Reich's purpose is to convince readers that raising the minimum wage is a good idea that will benefit workers as well as the tax-paying public. His intended audience could be people interested in economic and political issues such as the minimum wage.

Reihan Salam, "The Fight Against 15," p. 588

(Lexile level: 1350L)

This article, published in *Slate* magazine, argues that increasing the minimum wage drastically will hurt the economic prospects of millions of people, including those who have low-wage entry-level jobs and those who are unemployed because they lack the skills or training to land a job. Interestingly enough, Salam cites the research of Arindrajit Dube, just as Reich does in the preceding article. Dube contends that modest hikes in the minimum wage don't appear to reduce employment levels, and he also argues that a one-size-fits-all approach to raising the minimum wage could be very dangerous because some states can absorb a higher minimum wage and some states cannot. Salam goes further with his argument by citing the research of Isaac Sorkin, which concludes that we must have a better understanding of the long-term effects of an increased minimum wage in order to clearly understand the impact that it will have on states and cities. Salam admits that public and political opinion is overwhelmingly supportive of a drastic hike in the minimum wage, but he insists that now is not the time for it. He ends by recommending other ways to help low-wage and unemployed workers without the necessary skills for employment. It is this population that Salam says will be locked out of entry-level employment if the minimum wage is raised to $15.00 an hour.

In preparation for comparing and contrasting the two articles on the minimum wage hike, ask students to highlight what they see as the most convincing piece of evidence in this article. How do they evaluate it in terms of the previous argument in favor of an increase in the minimum wage? You might also ask students to research other articles that support Salam's point of view.

Understanding and Reviewing the Reading, p. 592

1. Increasing the minimum wage to $15 will damage the economic prospects of millions of vulnerable people. Salam states this thesis in paragraph 3.

2. Salam believes the labor market is changing in ways that make big minimum wage hikes dangerous. He has concerns about the long-range impact of minimum wage laws and believes that employers will not hire and train less-skilled, low-wage workers if they have other options.

3. In paragraphs 4–5 and 7, Salam cites economist Arindrajit Dube's work regarding minimum wage hikes.

4. Salam acknowledges opposing arguments (the Fight for 15) in paragraphs 1–2, and he acknowledges the debate over modest increases in the minimum wage in paragraph 4. He acknowledges Dube's recommendation of a modified wage increase and rejects it for reasons he gives in paragraphs 8–12.

5. The following graphic organizer is one possible answer.

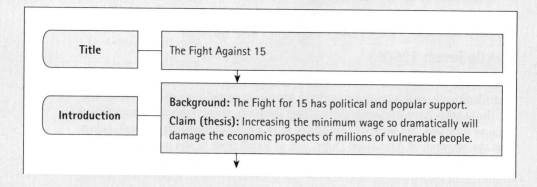

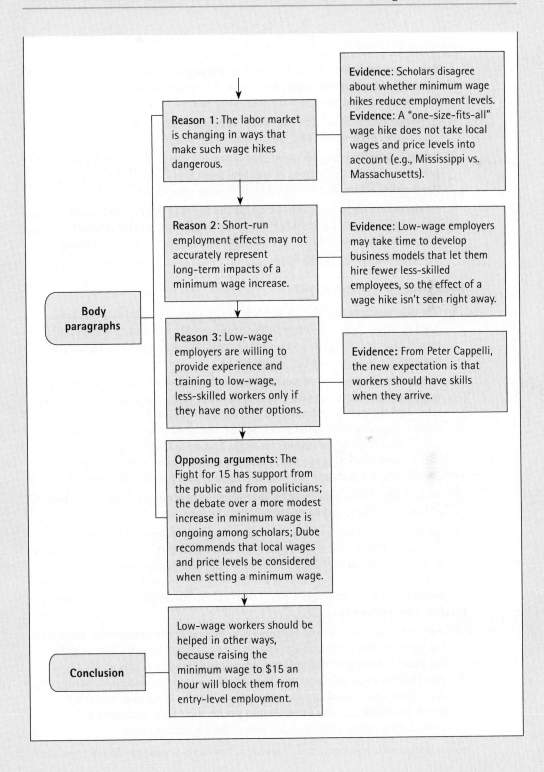

Evidence: Scholars disagree about whether minimum wage hikes reduce employment levels.
Evidence: A "one-size-fits-all" wage hike does not take local wages and price levels into account (e.g., Mississippi vs. Massachusetts).

Reason 1: The labor market is changing in ways that make such wage hikes dangerous.

Reason 2: Short-run employment effects may not accurately represent long-term impacts of a minimum wage increase.

Evidence: Low-wage employers may take time to develop business models that let them hire fewer less-skilled employees, so the effect of a wage hike isn't seen right away.

Body paragraphs

Reason 3: Low-wage employers are willing to provide experience and training to low-wage, less-skilled workers only if they have no other options.

Evidence: From Peter Cappelli, the new expectation is that workers should have skills when they arrive.

Opposing arguments: The Fight for 15 has support from the public and from politicians; the debate over a more modest increase in minimum wage is ongoing among scholars; Dube recommends that local wages and price levels be considered when setting a minimum wage.

Conclusion

Low-wage workers should be helped in other ways, because raising the minimum wage to $15 an hour will block them from entry-level employment.

Analyzing the Reading, p. 592

1. Salam is establishing the idea that this is a popular and politically appealing issue. His description of the popularity of a wage hike sets up a contrast to his argument that the Fight for 15 is a bad idea.

2. In paragraph 6, Salam illustrates the concept by contrasting Massachusetts (high-cost, high-wage) and Mississippi (low-cost, low-wage).

3. Salam is emphasizing his point that many job candidates who fill low-wage jobs do not have the benefit of training from family and school; they gain those skills when they are hired by low-wage employers.

4. Salam describes in sympathetic terms the types of people who are typical low-wage workers. He calls for action by suggesting several alternatives that he believes would be more valuable and less harmful than raising the minimum wage to $15 an hour.

Evaluating the Reading, p. 593

1. The title predicts that the author will argue against something; students need to know that "15" refers to the proposed $15 minimum wage hike. It would also be helpful to know that the movement to raise the minimum wage to $15 is known as the "Fight for 15."

2. Answers will vary. The preceding essay argues that raising the minimum wage benefits breadwinners (leading to more sales, faster growth, and more jobs) and the public (who would pay less for Medicaid, food stamps, and other forms of public assistance). Salam describes popular and political support for raising the minimum wage, and he acknowledges the debate over a more modest wage hike and an increase linked to local wages and price levels. He does not address the same issues Reich addressed.

3. Salam believes the hikes would have significantly negative effects, not all of which are understood or predictable in the long term.

4. Salam explains that when gas prices go up, people don't go out and buy a new fuel-efficient car right away. They drive less, if they can, and eventually do buy a more fuel-efficient car, after a time lag. Businesses that hire low-wage workers might take a similar time lag before they figure out how to get by with fewer (higher-paid) workers, so it's difficult to see if a wage hike eliminates jobs.

5. Answers will vary. Salam's purpose is to persuade his audience to consider his views on the issue and agree with his argument; his conclusion restates his point that people will suffer if the minimum wage is raised. He hopes that his audience will be sympathetic to the groups he describes (struggling teenagers, less-skilled immigrants, people who've been unemployed for years, ex-offenders who are trying to get on their feet) and open to considering options other than raising the minimum wage.

ARGUMENT PAIR: DEBATING MULTITASKING

Peter Bregman, "How (and Why) to Stop Multitasking," p. 595
(Lexile level: 770L)

This very relevant essay may be of particular interest to your students, many of whom have smartphones, multiple social media accounts, and a persistent need to check their electronic links to the outside world, even while writing a paper or sitting in class. Peter Bregman argues that though we often believe that we can multitask and handle all of these outlets simultaneously, multitasking actually decreases our productivity and even our IQ levels: "We don't actually multitask. We switch-task, rapidly shifting from one thing to another, interrupting ourselves unproductively, and losing time in the process" (4). Bregman presents his case against multitasking by relying heavily on personal narration and his own efforts to stop multitasking and focus on the issue or project at hand. He adopts a cause-and-effect pattern to show the positive effects of his "experiment" of a week of single-tasking; he reports that "it was delightful" and "there was no downside," and everything he needed to get accomplished was completed. Bregman refers to research and studies but provides no clear statistics or citations, which slightly damages his credibility. He concludes his essay with a few suggestions of ways to resist multitasking, including keeping the phone in the trunk while you're driving and disconnecting from the Internet.

Ask students how they feel about multitasking—do they engage in it? Do they think they're more productive when they multitask? Is it even possible to stop multitasking? Have students suggest other support for Bregman's argument, perhaps even finding studies or articles with more scientifically based conclusions.

Understanding and Reviewing the Reading, p. 597

1. According to Bregman, our IQs drop 10 points (3), and our productivity drops up to 40% (4).

2. Opposing views come from people who think they can get more work done (4) and people who think they're exceptions, that they've "done it so much [they've] become good at it" (5).

3. Bregman experienced delight and pleasure in the world around him, he made progress on challenging projects, his stress level dropped, he lost patience with meaningless tasks and conversations, he had more patience for useful and enjoyable things, and he didn't lose anything by not multitasking—everything was successfully completed and no one was upset at him for not answering a phone call or email immediately.

4. *Refocused* (2): The term means to once again concentrate on something, to redirect one's attention, say from an email to a conference call.

Competent (5): Capable; having suitable or adequate ability. Bregman argues that multitasking makes people less able to complete tasks; they are less competent.

Disengaged (7): Released from an attachment, involvement, or connection; unconnected; uninvolved. Multitasking with his technology disconnected Bregman from the people in his life.

Persistence (7): The fact or action of focused pursuit, of determination to achieve a goal. Making progress on his challenging projects required Bregman's determined focus — his *persistence*.

Meandering (7): Wandering, winding, or indirect, as a pathway. In this case, Bregman comments on conversations that meander or say a lot without getting directly to the point.

5. The following graphic organizer is one possible answer.

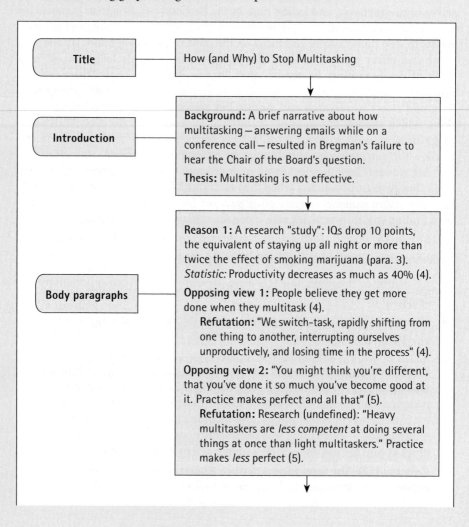

| Title | How (and Why) to Stop Multitasking |

| Introduction | **Background:** A brief narrative about how multitasking — answering emails while on a conference call — resulted in Bregman's failure to hear the Chair of the Board's question. **Thesis:** Multitasking is not effective. |

| Body paragraphs | **Reason 1:** A research "study": IQs drop 10 points, the equivalent of staying up all night or more than twice the effect of smoking marijuana (para. 3). *Statistic:* Productivity decreases as much as 40% (4). **Opposing view 1:** People believe they get more done when they multitask (4). **Refutation:** "We switch-task, rapidly shifting from one thing to another, interrupting ourselves unproductively, and losing time in the process" (4). **Opposing view 2:** "You might think you're different, that you've done it so much you've become good at it. Practice makes perfect and all that" (5). **Refutation:** Research (undefined): "Heavy multitaskers are *less competent* at doing several things at once than light multitaskers." Practice makes *less* perfect (5). |

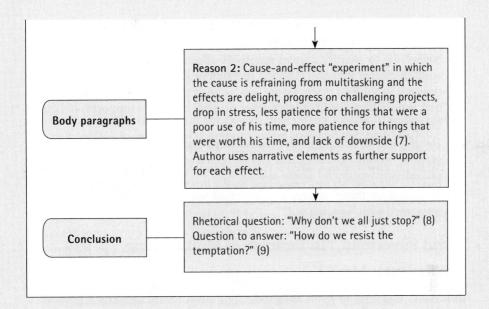

Analyzing the Reading, p. 598

1. Bregman's claim is that multitasking is an ineffective practice and we should stop trying to multitask (policy). He uses research (albeit vague) and personal experience to support the claim that multitasking is ineffective, and he includes a proposal for how the "policy" or practice should be changed.

2. Bregman appeals to family values when he talks about listening to his wife, playing with his children, and watching *Monsters, Inc.* with his son. He also appeals to readers' sense of guilt when he forces them to sympathize with his anecdote about getting caught not listening to the conference call (assuming his readers also multitask and believe they should and can do so effectively).

3. Bregman uses personal narration and unspecified research studies and undocumented statistics.

4. Answers may vary somewhat, but aside from not providing enough outside evidence, Bregman may be guilty of hasty generalization, assuming that his own problems with multitasking apply to everyone.

Evaluating the Reading, p. 598

1. Bregman's tone is informal and somewhat didactic. Clues to his informality include using conversational language such as "I know, I know" (1) and beginning sentences with "Well," (2) and "I swear" (3). Bregman's tone becomes didactic when he corrects common assumptions ("In reality"

[4] and "But you'd be wrong" [5]) and when he outlines steps to resist temptation in paragraphs 9 and 10.

2. Neglecting to identify sources negatively affects Bregman's credibility; without clearer statistics from the research or knowing who conducted the research in the first place, we are less inclined to believe that multitasking is bad, especially since Bregman's other primary source of support is personal narration.

3. *Delightful* is an exceptionally positive word that almost implies a sense of surprise; in this case, Bregman was delighted and surprised by how exceedingly wonderful single-tasking was.

4. "Smoking anything" is a reference to smoking marijuana, which is associated with "spacing out."

David Silverman, "In Defense of Multitasking," p. 599 (Lexile level: 1100L)

In a direct response to Peter Bregman's blog post, David Silverman presents a counterargument that supports multitasking and shows how important and necessary he considers the practice. Using these two essays in tandem will show students how to directly counter an opposing viewpoint and how to engage in a written conversation. Silverman begins by acknowledging Bregman and another author writing on the same topic and even concedes some of their points, then moves on to suggest that "unitasking has a downside, too" — that its effectiveness relies on solitary completion of tasks. In reality, we are dealing with multiple people who are also managing a variety of tasks, so we must multitask in order to effectively engage in today's technology-dependent workplace. Interestingly, Silverman uses a very similar argument strategy to Bregman's, outlining his supporting points in a clearly numbered list and using evidence from his personal experience. He concludes by questioning the relevance of the "unitasking" argument. Even if we agree that unitasking is ideal, we are all hypocrites who multitask, and multitasking has become a necessity in the way we live.

Ask students if they can recount any stories in which they've attempted to willfully "unplug" and focus. Do they think multitasking has become a necessity? Can they offer any additional supporting points from the life of a student?

Understanding and Reviewing the Reading, p. 601

1. Silverman makes a claim: "Multitasking isn't just an addiction for the short-attention-spanned among us; it's crucial to survival in today's workplace" (2).

2. Silverman supports his claim that multitasking is useful by asserting that we get critical information faster (4); that it prevents others from waiting (4); that it provides an alternative to being "stuck" (4); and that it is almost necessary at higher levels in an organization (4).

3. Silverman implies that we're hypocritical, saying multitasking is bad but doing it anyway, just like his father, who claims smoking is bad but smokes anyway.

4. *Discredited* (1): Proved false. In the essay, Silverman claims that science has disproven the notion that one individual might be exceptionally good at multitasking while others aren't. Because science probably wouldn't find the topic of someone's misguided arrogance worthy of research in the first place, Silverman probably is using this phrase humorously.

   Unitasking (2): This term refers to the opposite of multitasking; it means focusing and working on only one task at a time.

   Concurrently (4): Happening at the same time. Multitasking means doing multiple tasks at the same time — concurrently.

   Ponderable (4): Capable of being thought about or considered. When you can't figure out a task, Silverman suggests thinking about something else and letting your subconscious ponder the problem.

   Lest (4): Unless; or else. Silverman paints a humorous scenario in which a demolition ball will crash into the wrong thing unless a contractor multitasks.

5. The following graphic organizer is one possible answer.

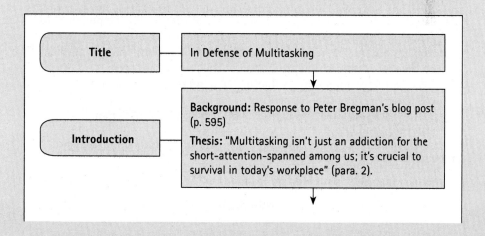

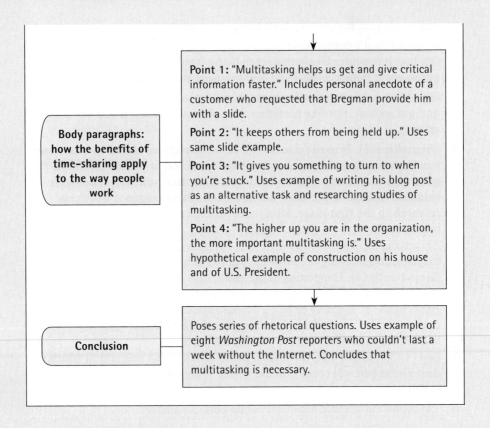

Body paragraphs: how the benefits of time-sharing apply to the way people work

Point 1: "Multitasking helps us get and give critical information faster." Includes personal anecdote of a customer who requested that Bregman provide him with a slide.

Point 2: "It keeps others from being held up." Uses same slide example.

Point 3: "It gives you something to turn to when you're stuck." Uses example of writing his blog post as an alternative task and researching studies of multitasking.

Point 4: "The higher up you are in the organization, the more important multitasking is." Uses hypothetical example of construction on his house and of U.S. President.

Conclusion

Poses series of rhetorical questions. Uses example of eight *Washington Post* reporters who couldn't last a week without the Internet. Concludes that multitasking is necessary.

Analyzing the Reading, p. 601

1. Silverman illustrates how in the early days of computers, the punch-card "batch" system was able to complete only one task at a time. If there was a problem on one job, it would stall all tasks that were in line behind that job, severely diminishing productivity. The punch cards represent our tasks, and Silverman implies that focusing on only one task in today's world has the potential for stalling other tasks. Also, as computers advance, we must keep up with changing technology and changing ways in which it can be used.

2. While some students may find the analogy difficult to understand, the analogy is an apt one, particularly because it involves the very technology that enables us to multitask so much and so effectively.

3. Answers will vary, though (as with the Bregman essay) more scientific research and use of others' experiences would be helpful.

4. The presidency example is effective both because it is easily recognizable and because it is almost impossible to disagree with the idea that the president must multitask. However, making the sarcastic suggestion that President Obama looks at cat videos on Facebook (which may be what

many ordinary people do when they "multitask") may lessen the impact of the example for regular people.

5. Silverman's intended audience is people in the workforce, particularly those who use computers and technology to communicate with others in their business.

Evaluating the Reading, p. 601

1. Silverman appeals to the values of hard work and responsibility, indicating that he needs to get his job done effectively and other people are relying on him to do so. He also appeals to our sense of practicality, since he wants readers to recognize the implausibility of only unitasking.

2. Like Bregman, Silverman may be guilty of hasty generalization, relying too heavily on his own experience to represent everyone's experience. Students may also suggest that the computer example is a false analogy since computers are machines, not people.

3. Silverman's main source is himself. More statistics, perhaps presented in the form of a graph, would be make the reading more effective.

4. Silverman presents opposing viewpoints in the first paragraph, naming Peter Bregman and saying that he "will not deny" that single-minded focus on something yields good quality. He concedes this point but also calls our attention to what Bregman neglected to mention: the downsides of unitasking (2). That is, there is no direct refutation but an introduction to other points Bregman should have considered that undermine his claims.

5. Since his essay's points are largely supported by personal experience, Silverman's essay seems to be primarily made up of opinion, which might make his essay seem biased or unfounded. Citing more scientific research could help prove the effectiveness of multitasking.

6. *Addiction* (2) suggests that multitasking is a deep need that we cannot easily rid ourselves of. *Missile* (4) is used humorously to suggest an urgent emergency.

Part 3: Student Research Guide

CHAPTER 19: Finding and Using Sources, p. 607

CHAPTER 20: Documenting Your Sources, p. 622

Chapters 19 and 20 offer students a thorough guide to research. Chapter 19, Finding and Using Sources, introduces them to types of sources, both primary and secondary, and helps them understand why and when sources are used in papers, particularly argument essays. The chapter offers guides for locating sources, particularly online, since online research has become the dominant, most convenient, and sometimes only means of research available to students. Students will glean valuable tips on how to use the library catalog, periodical databases, and the Internet. Whether you assign sections of this chapter to students as mandatory reading or simply point students to the chapter as a useful reference, the information in these pages can be a helpful guide to first-time researchers.

You might adapt the material to suit your own purposes and your school's resources. For example, involve students in a library scavenger hunt, at the physical location of the library or online (or both), that will lead them through the research process before their own papers (and grades) are at stake. Or, assign topics to groups and have each member research the same subject, reporting the process he or she used and the findings of the research, to reveal how many options research can uncover.

Once students have located sources, Chapter 19 offers information and graphic aids to help them evaluate their research, both for reliability and for usefulness to their research projects. As students move from locating sources to incorporating them into their essays as evidence and support for their arguments, sections in this chapter show them how to appropriately summarize, paraphrase, or quote information from their sources without plagiarizing. Chapter 20 provides a useful overview and reference for using MLA and APA citation styles properly.

The visual aids and graphic organizers in Part 3 will help students with different learning styles comprehend the material and incorporate the principles of effective, organized research into a source-based argument paper. Samples of course outlines that include Chapters 19 and 20 are available in this Instructor's Manual beginning on page 18.

Part 4: Handbook: Writing Problems and How to Correct Them

Review of Basic Grammar, p. 647
Writing Correct Sentences, p. 656
Using Punctuation and Mechanics Correctly, p. 692

Marking Sentence-Level Errors

Many times, students whose papers include significant sentence-level errors will also have problems with paragraph development or organization, but this is not always the case. Taking points off for sentence-level errors means that poor grammar and punctuation will likely lower the grade for a paper that is otherwise well developed and well organized. Grading such a student essay requires a great deal of judgment on the instructor's part. You will have to determine how severe the sentence-level errors are; how much they disrupt the content of the essay; and, hence, how significant a role they should play in determining the essay's total grade.

Most important, you will need to consider how to recognize sentence-level problems without making so many corrections on a student's paper that it becomes more your writing than the student's. Getting back a paper with too many comments on it can overwhelm students and hurt their morale in ways that could interfere with their future writing. It is possible to address students' patterns of error without marking every instance, however, and this strategy may be more useful to the student and more manageable for you. For example, you could signal several examples of one type of error and ask the student to try to identify the rest. The student could do this independently, with the help of a writing center tutor, or in a conference with you. Begin by focusing on the types of errors that are most serious before moving on to minor problems.

As a general practice, you shouldn't correct the sentence-level errors that you spot because it won't help the student learn to correct errors independently. Some instructors use a minimal marking method, indicating an error by a mark in the margin next to the sentence. For this type of marking, you may want to use the categories from Table 8.5, Common Errors (page 157 in the text), or symbols from the list of revision symbols near the end of *Reflections*. This list includes references to the handbook in Part 4. This can be a positive strategy, because it encourages students to look at the handbook and learn to correct their errors. Another method you might try is to identify errors and supply the appropriate handbook page numbers. This strategy puts students in control of referring to the handbook and applying the information to their work. This method also helps students develop their error logs over the course of the term as they focus on sentence-level errors. Again, marking students' errors in this way reinforces their use of the handbook and encourages them to become independent writers by identifying particular trouble spots and correcting them. You can also refer students to the appropriate online exercises available through *LaunchPad Solo for Readers and Writers.*

As you note sentence-level errors, also consider the level of insight. You will find that some of your students' papers, especially those written by ESL students, contain interesting ideas yet have major problems with style, grammar, punctuation, and word choice. Other papers may contain beautifully written sentences but say little. When a student has excellent insights in an essay, he or she is using higher-level thinking—and writing—skills. Most teachers have read papers on major moments in a student's life, such as high school graduation or a championship season, that describe what occurred but don't reveal much beyond a sequence of events. On the other hand, sometimes essays on a very simple topic, such as problems a student encountered while getting stitches in the emergency room, offer surprising insights. Students should be rewarded for effective presentation of unique and insightful ideas.

Most often, however, students who write papers with a significant number of problems with grammar, punctuation, and mechanics have trouble writing effectively in other ways as well. Students often think of language choice and grammar as being separate from the content of their writing. Students should be reminded that *how* they write can be as important as *what* they write. Writers often need to use complex sentences to communicate complex ideas effectively. Serious errors in grammar and punctuation inevitably prevent a reader from becoming absorbed and focused on what the essay is saying. An interestingly constructed and error-free essay about a walk across campus may offer more complex and thought-provoking ideas than a disorganized and confusing essay about a hiking trip in Tibet.

Answers to Exercises

Exercise H3.1, p. 660

Possible Revisions:

1. Correct
2. In the United States, for example, colleges and universities provide education to Americans of all classes and backgrounds.
3. At first, state universities were publicly funded schools that trained students in fields such as engineering, education, and agriculture.
4. During the nineteenth and early twentieth centuries, graduates of state universities played a key role in America's development as an industrial and economic power.
5. The number of students in college increased greatly in the years after World War II.

Exercise H4.1, p. 665

Possible Revisions:

1. Because nearly every American child dreams of going to Disney World, it has become one of the most popular family vacation destinations.
2. Shopping through online bookstores is convenient, but some people miss the atmosphere of a traditional bookstore.
3. Openness is one way to build trust in a relationship; another is to demonstrate tolerance and patience.
4. In the 1960s, some Americans treated Vietnam veterans disrespectfully, a situation that has changed dramatically since that time.
5. William Faulkner wrote classic novels about life in the U.S. South; Eudora Welty has also written vividly about southern life.

Exercise H5.1, p. 669

Answers:

1. Many members of the international business community communicate by speaking English, the international language of business.
2. A student in most non-English-speaking industrialized nations expects to spend six or more years studying English.
3. The United States is different.
4. Working for laws that require all Americans to speak English is a fairly common U.S. political tactic.
5. In American schools, often neither a teaching staff nor enough money has been available for good foreign-language programs.

Exercise H6.1, p. 673

Answers:

1. When the nineteenth century changed into the twentieth, many people in the United States became eager to expel Spain from the Americas.
2. Cuba, an island that lies ninety miles off the Florida coast, provided them with an excuse to do so.
3. Correct
4. In addition, many people in the United States had wanted to take over Spain's territories for a long time.
5. The United States won the war very quickly and assumed control of Cuba, the Philippines, Guam, and Puerto Rico.

Exercise H7.1, p. 675

Possible Revisions:

1. A country at war must be able to convey information to military personnel. That need for communication is always a challenge.
2. Because of the importance of the information, it often must be transmitted secretly.
3. Military strategists use codes for these transmissions because encoded messages baffle the enemy.
4. Using "invisible ink," which cannot be seen until the paper is heated, was once a popular way to communicate secretly.
5. Lemon juice and vinegar are good choices for invisible ink because they are invisible unless burned.

Exercise H7.2, p. 678

Answers:

1. Neither the many species of dinosaurs nor the flightless dodo bird could prevent its own extinction.
2. A team of researchers might disagree on their conclusions about the disappearance of the dinosaur.
3. Correct
4. In one way, animals resemble plants: Some are "weeds" because they have the ability to thrive under many conditions.
5. Any species that cannot withstand its competitors may be doomed to extinction.

Exercise H7.3, p. 681

Answers:

1. Whoever discovers a large cave is usually able to attract tourists.
2. Correct
3. Correct
4. Following the success of Mammoth Cave, many Kentucky cavers hoped to make a fortune from their spelunking.
5. Floyd Collins was one Kentucky native who searched his property for caves.

Exercise H8.1, p. 684

Possible Revisions:

1. A new idea about the development of children's personalities has surprised many American psychologists because it challenges widely accepted theories.

2. We wondered whether our professor knew of the new theory and whether she agreed with it.

3. Some experts believe that personality is the result of parental care, but other specialists think that biology influences personality more strongly.

4. Most parents think they have a major influence on their children's behavior.

5. The new theory suggests that children's peers are much more influential than parents.

Exercise H8.2, p. 685

Possible Revisions:

1. Correct

2. Surveys show that college graduates who intern receive higher salary offers than their classmates who do not.

3. Students must be careful, as all internships are not created equal.

4. The most important qualities are curiosity and a good work ethic.

5. A good internship provides knowledge and skills in a professional environment.

Exercise H9.1, p. 689

Answers:

1. The site is an open source, online encyclopedia where anyone can contribute, even if he or she writes badly or inaccurately.

2. *Wikipedia* has many advantages that reflect well on it as a source.

3. There is nothing more convenient for getting information really quickly.

4. In a way, encyclopedias are unique because Web sites can grow to include any subject that anyone finds interesting.

5. *Wikipedia* relies heavily on the knowledge and interests of millions of people, rather than on the choices of a small group of experts.

Exercise H10.1, p. 691

Possible Revisions:

1. Solar systems like our own exist throughout the galaxy.

2. So far, no proof of the existence of life forms on other planets has been found.

3. A tremendously powerful telescope in the Caribbean searches distant stars for signs of life.

4. Astronomers carefully monitor signals coming from other parts of the solar system.

5. Wondering whether humans are alone in the universe, scientists hope the telescope may provide answers.

Exercise H11.1, p. 693

Answers:

1. When the daughters of Queen Victoria of England, who carried the gene for hemophilia, married royalty in Germany and Russia, those royal families inherited hemophilia as well.

2. Correct

3. You might ask if internal bleeding can occur when a hemophiliac receives a bruise.

4. Czar Nicholas and his wife Alexandra often saw their little boy in terrible pain.

5. A phony monk named Rasputin eased the child's pain, but was he a gifted healer or just a con man?

Exercise H12.1, p. 698

Answers:

1. Seneca Village, a crowded shantytown on the Upper West Side, was the home of many poorer black New Yorkers.

2. The city of New York bought the land where the Seneca villagers lived.

3. The land became part of Central Park, and everyone who lived there had to leave in the 1850s.

4. Household items from Seneca Village still turn up in Central Park today, and a museum exhibit was recently devoted to life in the long-gone settlement.

5. In present-day Brooklyn, there was once a middle-class black settlement called Weeksville.

6. James Weeks, an early resident, owned much of the land.

7. Another early landholder, Sylvanus Smith, was a trustee of the African Free Schools of Brooklyn.

8. His daughter, Susan Smith McKinney-Steward, was born in Weeksville and was the valedictorian of New York Medical College in 1870.

9. McKinney-Steward became the first female African American physician in New York and the third in the United States.

10. Correct

Exercise H13.1, p. 700

Answers:

1. In the years since Stoker's novel, vampires have become a movie fixture in America and throughout the world.

2. Silent versions of the vampire tale include *Les Vampires* (1915), a French film; *Nosferatu* (1921), a German film; and *London After Midnight* (1927), an American film.

3. Correct

4. The vampire tale has several standard traits, yet it remains remarkably versatile.

5. The vampire tale was adapted to the American movie western, for example, in *Billy the Kid vs. Dracula* in 1966.

Exercise H14.1, p. 702

Answers:

1. The shuttle launch is scheduled for precisely 10:00 a.m.

2. The proposed zoning change was defeated by a margin of 2:1.

3. On early rap records, listeners heard percussion from unusual sources such as turntables, microphones, and synthesizers.

4. Correct

5. He believes that the most American of all sports is baseball.

Exercise H15.1, p. 704

Answers:

1. Her essay was entitled " 'To Be or Not to Be': Shakespeare and Existentialism."

2. Why did the professor assign "To an Athlete Dying Young"?

3. A movie line many teenagers imitated was "Hasta la vista, baby."

4. After September 11, 2001, President Bush said he was going to "fight terror."

5. Correct

Exercise H15.2, p. 707

Answers:

1. "The structure of DNA . . . is a double helix."

2. "Halle Berry was the first African American woman to win the Academy Award for Best Actress."

3. "Cole Porter cultivated a suave, sophisticated urban persona."

4. "[P]eople of all classes receive financial help from the government."

5. Nathan Hale regretted that he had "but one life to give for [his] country."

Exercise H16.1, p. 709

Answers:

1. Ours is a society almost too willing to share.

2. We probably know more about the day-to-day lives of others than ever before, as the details of our many friends' days are recorded in online status reports.

3. It's unclear, however, whether anyone is truly benefiting from all this sharing of private information, even as the various social networking sites' privacy settings reveal more and more about users.

4. Today's parents can find out about their sons and daughters' personal lives online, but they have less face-to-face contact with their children.

5. Of course, they'll have to figure out the meaning of all the *LOL*'s, *BTW*'s, and other shorthand slang in their kids' online and text messages.

Exercise H17.1, p. 710

Answers:

1. One issue particularly concerns scholars of food—why are certain foods acceptable in some cultures but not in others? [A colon is also acceptable.]

2. Some foods such as the cabbage palm were once popular, but today hardly anyone has heard of them.

3. Correct. [*Alternative:* In the 1990s, people in Great Britain were alerted to a new danger—mad cow disease.]

4. In the 1960s, frozen foods — icy blocks of corn, peas, and string beans — were popular and convenient alternatives to fresh produce.

5. Correct. [*Alternative:* Today, fresh fruits and vegetables are valued once again—unless a busy cook has no time for peeling and chopping.]

Exercise H18.1, p. 714

Answers:

1. During World War II, the governments of twenty-six countries, including the United States, pledged their willingness to continue fighting on behalf of the Allies.

2. His professor insisted that *Soap Opera Digest* was not an acceptable research source.

3. Patrick Henry said, "Give me liberty or give me death."

4. The first European settlers at Plymouth arrived on the *Mayflower*.

5. His book is discussed in depth in the article "Africa: The Hidden History."